Anna of Saxony

The Scarlet Woman of Orange

By
Ingrun Mann

Winged Hussar Publishing, LLC

Cover image of Anna of Saxony
by Ingrun Mann
Winged Hussar Publishing, LLC, 1525 Hulse Road, Unit 1, Point Pleasant, NJ 08742

This edition published in 2016 Copyright ©Ingrun Mann
ISBN 978-09963657-2-7
LCN 2016949222
Bibliographical references and index
1.Anna of Saxony (1544 - 1577) 2. Biography. 3. 16th Century Europe. 4. European Political

For more information on Winged Hussar Publishing, LLC, visit us at:
https://www.WingedHussarPublishing.com

For Brigitte and Horst
In tiefster Dankbarkeit

Acknowledgements

While putting Anna of Saxony's incredible biography on paper took me but a short six months, research and editing spanned several years. Along the way, a great many people helped me complete this sometimes daunting project, encouraging me when I got discouraged, and providing me with a great deal of good advice, constructive criticism, and research assistance. I would like to single out a number of these individuals for my particular thanks. On the top of my list are historians and professors emeriti, Gail L. Bernstein and Alan E. Bernstein (not related) of the University of Arizona, who not only taught me history as an undergraduate, but provided me with meticulous and invaluable suggestions during the lengthy editing process and probably saved me from countless blunders. I am very much indebted to them both.

Friends Stephen Peters, Margaret Benner, Mary-Anne Lovato, Gisela Koslowsky, Carol Lumsden, Christa Tettenborn, Dagmar Wiesmann, Darrell Bruning, Franceen Kakavoulis-Perera, Loretta Sowers, Joanna Kilroy, Terri Rubiella, Stephanie Hillyard, and Shelli Pierson read my manuscript in its entirety, offering substantive ideas on content and style. Another particular thanks goes to archivist and historian Christian Brachthäuser of the Siegen City Archives, who welcomed me to the German city of Siegen with dozens of articles and research notes on Anna, fastidiously culled from local sources. Fellow "Siegener" and long-time friend Hans-Hartwig "Hardy" Jochum graciously escorted me around town, thus giving me an important feel for Anna's "old stomping grounds." Special mention and gratitude must also go to Edward "Pat" Lowinger, without whose help and prodding the story of Anna would probably still lie buried in a drawer. My parents, Horst and Brigitte Mann, took many trips to various German libraries and then sent dozens of articles across the Atlantic, along with their unfailing support and reassurance. I am also intensely grateful to Vincent W. Rospond at Winged Hussar Publishing, who has handled all the intricacies of publication and editing, and answered a myriad of my often anxious emails within mere minutes!

Finally, I would like to acknowledge the unstinting support, patience, and love of my husband, William Kilroy, who endured innumerable hours at various playgrounds with our young son, so that "Mom" could write and read in peace. For this, and so much more: Is breá liom tú.

Ingrun Mann

Contents

Timeline of Significant Events

Late 10th century - First mention of the Saxon Wettin dynasty
Late 10th century - Founding of the noble House of Nassau
1292-1298 - Adolph of Nassau (before 1250-1298) rules as King of Germany
1423 - Emperor Sigismund awards the Saxon electorship to Margrave Frederick the Belligerent
1453 - Constantinople, Christianity's eastern outpost, falls to the Ottomans
1485 - Leipzig Partition: Frederick II of Saxony divides his lands between his two sons, Ernest and Albrecht. Ernest receives the Electorate of Ernestine Saxony in the west, Duke Albrecht becomes the founder of the Albertine Duchy of Saxony to the east
1492 - Christopher Columbus discovers the Americas
1517 - Martin Luther, an Augustine monk and professor of theology, challenges the Catholic Church with his Ninety-Five Theses of Reform
1521 – Emperor Charles V declares Luther an outlaw for his heretical religious views. The reformer is given refuge at Wartburg Castle by Frederick III, Elector of Saxony
1521-1541 – Saxon rulers introduce the Protestant faith to Ernestine and Albertine Saxony
24 April 1533 - *Birth of William of Nassau-Dillenburg, Prince of Orange*
January 1541 - Maurice of Saxony marries Agnes of Hessen
23 December 1544 – *Birth of Anna of Saxony*
1546-7 – Anna's father, Maurice of Saxony, refuses to join the Protestant Schmalkaldic League and allies himself with the Catholic Emperor, Charles V. His cousin, John Frederick I of Saxony, and father-in-law, Philip of Hessen, fight for the opposing side and spend years in captivity after the disastrous Battle of Mühlberg
February 1548 – Emperor Charles V publicly bestows the Saxon electorship on Anna's father Maurice in Augsburg
1552 – Maurice of Saxony plots against Emperor Charles V in the so-called "Princes' Rebellion." Charles reluctantly retreats from Germany, appointing Maurice the steward of German lands
July 1553 – Maurice of Saxony dies unexpectedly at the Battle of Sievershausen, near Hanover
May 1555 – Anna's mother Agnes marries the son of Maurice's erstwhile rival, John Frederick II of Saxony
October 1555 – Charles V abdicates, bequeathing the Habsburg possessions of Spain, the Americas, and the Netherlands to his son and heir, Philip II. Charles' brother Ferdinand I is subsequently declared ruler of Germany, Bohemia, and Hungary
November 1555 – Agnes of Hessen dies under mysterious circumstances leaving Anna an orphan
Late 1555 until August 1561 – Anna is raised by her paternal uncle, August of Saxony, and his wife, Anne of Denmark and Norway
1558 – Mary, Queen of Scots marries Francis, Dauphin of France. Elizabeth Tudor becomes Queen of England
1559 – Philip II appoints William of Orange governor of the provinces of Holland, Zeeland, and Utrecht
August 1561 – William of Orange marries Anna of Saxony in a lavish ceremony in Leipzig
1566 – Religious strife destabilizes the Netherlands
April 1567 – William and Anna flee the Low Countries for the safety of Dillenburg, Germany
August 1567 – The Duke of Alba arrives in the Netherlands and establishes the notorious "Council of Troubles"
5 June 1568 – The Counts Egmont and Horn are beheaded on Brussels' Grand Place
October 1568 – Anna leaves Dillenburg for Cologne
Spring 1571 – Anna and Jan Rubens are arrested for adultery

August 1571 - Anna gives birth to an illegitimate daughter named Christine
Fall 1572 - Anna is moved to remote Castle Beilstein
May 1573 - Jan Rubens released from prison
December 1576 - Anna is incarcerated in Dresden
18 December 1577 - *Death of Anna of Saxony*
10 July 1584 - Balthasar Gerard assassinates William of Orange
1588 - England under Elizabeth I repulses the Spanish Armada
5 June 1648 - Formal independence of the United Provinces of the Dutch Republic

House of Nassau

John V of Nassau-Vianden-Diez (1455-1516) married to Elizabeth of Hessen (1466-1523)

Henry III of Nassau-Breda married to Claudia of Chalon   William I (the Rich) of Nassau-Dillenburg   married to Juliana zu Stolberg

René of Chalon (died heirless in 1544)

William of Orange (1533-1584)   John   Louis   Maria   Adolph   Catherine   Magdalena   Henry

married to (1) Anne van Egmont, Countess Buren

married to (2) Anna of Saxony (1544-77) —— Jan Rubens (1530-1587)

Christine of Diez (1571-1638)

Anna   Maurice   Emilia (surviving issue)

married to (3) Charlotte of Bourbon (1546/47-1582): 6 daughters

married to (4) Louise de Coligny (1555-1620): one son, Frederick Henry, Prince of Orange (1584-1647)

married to Elizabeth of Leuchtenberg

Maria of Nassau (1556-1616)

Philip William, Prince of Orange (1554-1618)

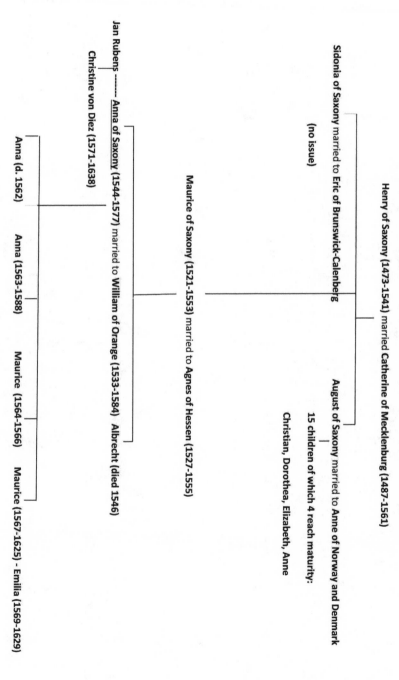

House of Wettin (Albertine Branch): Duchy/Electorate of Saxony

Henry of Saxony (1473-1541) married Catherine of Mecklenburg (1487-1561)

Sidonia of Saxony married to Eric of Brunswick-Calenberg

(no issue)

August of Saxony married to Anne of Norway and Denmark

15 children of which 4 reach maturity:

Christian, Dorothea, Elizabeth, Anne

Maurice of Saxony (1521-1553) married to Agnes of Hessen (1527-1555)

Jan Rubens ------ Anna of Saxony (1544-1577) married to William of Orange (1533-1584)   Albrecht (died 1546)

Christine von Diez (1571-1638)

Anna (d. 1562)   Anna (1563-1588)   Maurice (1564-1566)   Maurice (1567-1625) - Emilia (1569-1629)

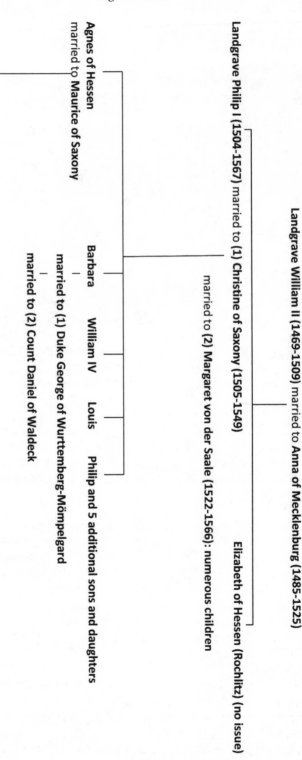

The Landgraves of Hessen

Landgrave William II (1469-1509) married to **Anna of Mecklenburg (1485-1525)**

Landgrave Philip I (1504-1567) married to (1) **Christine of Saxony (1505-1549)**

married to (2) **Margaret von der Saale (1522-1566): numerous children**

Elizabeth of Hessen (Rochlitz) (no issue)

Agnes of Hessen
married to **Maurice of Saxony**

Barbara
—
married to (1) **Duke George of Wurttemberg-Mömpelgard**
—
married to (2) **Count Daniel of Waldeck**

William IV

Louis

Philip and 5 additional sons and daughters

Anna of Saxony (1544-77)

Principal Characters

House of Wettin
Anna of Saxony, Princess of Orange
Agnes of Hessen, Duchess/Electress of Saxony, Anna's mother
Maurice, Duke/Elector of Saxony, Anna's father
Henry of Saxony, Anna's paternal grandfather
Anna of Mecklenburg, Duchess of Saxony, Anna's paternal grandmother
Sidonia of Saxony, Duchess of Brunswick-Calenberg, Anna's aunt
August, Elector of Saxony, Anna's uncle and guardian
Anne of Denmark and Norway, Electress of Saxony, August's wife
John Frederick II of (Ernestine) Saxony, Agnes of Hessen's second husband, Anna's stepfather

House of Nassau
William of Nassau-Dillenburg-Breda, Prince of Orange
William I of Nassau (the Rich), William's father
Juliana of Stolberg, William's mother
Henry III of Nassau-Breda, William's uncle
John VI of Nassau-Dillenburg, William's brother and head of the German Nassaus
Elizabeth of Leuchtenberg, Countess of Nassau-Dillenburg, wife of John
Louis of Nassau-Dillenburg, William's favorite brother
Maria of Nassau-Dillenburg, Countess Berg, William's sister
Magdalena of Nassau-Dillenburg, Countess Hohenlohe, William's sister
Godfrey of Nassau, illegitimate son of William the Rich
Philip William, Prince of Orange, William's eldest son with Anne van Buren
Emilia of Nassau, Titular Queen Consort of Portugal, Anna's daughter
Maurice of Nassau, Prince of Orange, Anna and William's son and heir
Frederick Henry, Prince of Orange, William's son with Louise de Coligny

House of Hessen
Philip, Landgrave of Hessen, Anna's maternal grandfather
Christine of Saxony, Landgravine of Hessen, Anna's maternal grandmother
Margaret von der Saale, morganatic second wife of Philip of Hessen
Agnes of Hessen, daughter of Philip and Christine of Hessen, Anna's mother
Elizabeth of Hessen, Duchess of Saxony (known as Duchess of Rochlitz), sister of Philip of Hessen, Anna's great-aunt
William IV, Landgrave of Hessen-Kassel, Anna's uncle
Barbara of Hessen, Duchess of Wurttemberg-Mömpelgard, Countess of Waldeck

House of Habsburg
Charles V, Holy Roman Emperor, ruler of the Burgundian Netherlands, and the Spanish Empire
Philip II of Spain, Charles' son, whose wives included Mary I of England, Elizabeth of Valois, and Anna of Austria
Mary of Hungary, sister of Charles V, Governor General of the Spanish Netherlands, William of Orange's mentor in the Netherlands

Margaret, Duchess of Parma, illegitimate daughter of Charles V, Governor General of the

Spanish Netherlands
Ferdinand I of Austria, Holy Roman Emperor, brother of Charles V
Maximilian II of Austria, Holy Roman Emperor, son of Ferdinand I, friend of August of Saxony

House of Navarre
Jeanne, Queen of Navarre, Protestant ally of the Nassau brothers and Charlotte of Bourbon

House of Valois
Henri II of France
Catherine de Medici, Henri's wife
Marguerite of Valois, daughter of Catherine de Medici and Henri II, wife of Henri of Navarre, son of Queen Jeanne

Other
Anne van Egmont, William of Orange's first wife
Charlotte of Bourbon, William of Orange's third wife
Louise de Coligny, William of Orange's fourth wife
Fernando Alvarez de Toledo, 3rd Duke of Alba, Governor General of the Netherlands and William's archenemy
Antoine Perrenot de Granvelle, Cardinal, leading minister of the Spanish Habsburgs and William's nemesis
Jan Rubens, Anna's lover
Maria Pypelinckx, wife of Jan Rubens
Peter Paul Rubens, son of Jan and Maria Rubens
Christine von Diez, Jan and Anna's illegitimate daughter
Eric II of Brunswick-Calenberg -Göttingen, husband of Sidonia of Saxony

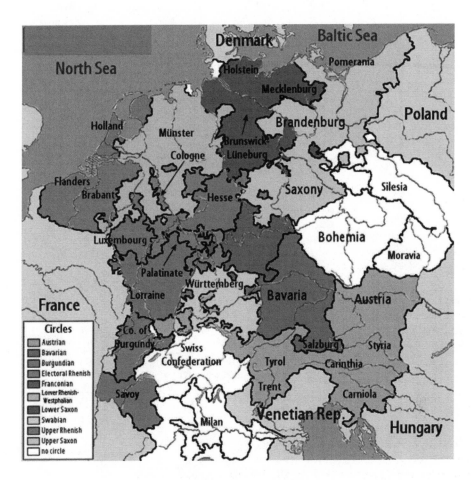

The Holy Roman Empire in 1540

Anna of Saxony (1544 - 1577)

Introduction - A Woman Like No Other

"Show me a character whose life arouses my curiosity and my flesh begins crawl-ing with suspense," wrote Fawn McKay Brodie, biographer of Thomas Jefferson, Sir Richard Burton, and Richard Nixon. My own flesh certainly began to crawl five years ago when I came across an out-of-print copy of *Prinzessinnen* by Wal-ter Fellmann, a collection of mini-biographies that promised to shed light on the lives and times of various Saxon princesses. While the life stories of most of these characters appeared to fall into generic patterns of female royalty - the pious, neglected wife regularly alternated with the charitable, storybook good moth-er — there was one chapter that immediately captivated my interest. Titled *"Anna von Sachsen, die Gefallene"* ("Anna of Saxony, the Fallen Woman"), this particular section described the scandalous exploits of a Renaissance princess who flouted the marital conventions of her time by leaving home and family behind to live on her own. Even more intriguing was her subsequent love affair with a married commoner.

I have long been fascinated by the handful of European queens and prin-cesses who, like the ill-fated Catherine Howard, wife of Henry VIII of England, did the unthinkable and committed adultery. But while Catherine's story has been amply documented in print and on screen, Anna of Saxony's was a hid-den historical treasure waiting to be fully uncovered. There was the short, six-teen-page discourse by Walter Fellmann on Anna, as well as a monograph by Maike Vogt-Lüerssen. Hans-Joachim Böttcher's 2013 biography of the princess, which, while admirably researched, draws very different conclusions about An-na's affair as well as her husband's character. I also found a thorough, if dated, article by Hans Kruse in a German 1930s periodical that cited numerous letters, diplomatic observations, and suppositions on the subject of the Saxon princess. While Kruse was a meticulous researcher, much of his essay focuses on why a lady of standing would disgrace her family in this manner.[1]

Earlier historians were even more scathing in their condemnation of the rebel princess, their short studies on Anna bursted with outrage: a disobedient ward, shrewish wife, and adulterous whore whose sins were better left unwrit-ten.[2] Viewing her conduct through their current morals, they generally shied away from delving too deeply into Anna's *chronique scandaleuse* (scandalous his-tory). The German professor Felix Rachfahl (1867-1925) maintained that her de-formed body housed an equally deformed soul; one that was petty, vicious, and lacking any trace of nobility. At the beginning of the twentieth century, European society still regarded adultery as the gravest of female crimes save murder, and the aristocracy regularly disposed of morally wayward women by shutting them away in mental institutions. *"When princesses forget themselves, [and] make a mockery out of everything … they forfeit the right to exist."* This was the contemporary opin-ion of another Saxon princess who set Dresden's fin-de-siècle aristocracy ablaze by eloping with her children's language teacher.[3] Aside from Anna's compelling

[1]Hans Kruse. Although I disagree with some of Dr. Kruse's judgments and conclusions, I am greatly indebted to his meticulous research which spanned several decades. Dedicated to bringing Anna's story back to life, Dr. Kruse travelled to countless archives in both Ger-many and the Netherlands, thus sparing me much archival "legwork."
[2]Steven Ozment. *The Bürgermeister's Daughter: Scandal in a Sixteenth-Century German Town.* (New York: St Martin's Press: 1996)., p. 189.
[3]Bestenreiner, *Luise von Toscana* (Munich: Serie Piper, 2000), p. 127. In December 1902, Archduchess Louise of Austria, Crown Princess of Saxony, and wife of Frederick August III of Saxony, eloped to Switzerland with her children's language tutor, André Giron. Her father-in-law, George of Saxony, had threatened to have her interned at a mental asylum for life.

character, it was this lack of empathy and understanding that prompted me to examine the experiences of the troublesome princess from a current perspective.

Not long after I started my research, I began to understand why Anna antagonized historians even centuries after her death; I found myself as annoyed and confounded by her quixotic personality as others had been before me. After various trips to German archives, I learned that she was a princess who alienated those around her, and made a thorough mess of her marriage to the affable William of Orange, a wealthy Dutch grand seigneur and prince of the highest standing. I caught myself wondering whether historians had been right after all in dismissing Anna as a quarrelsome, egotistical shrew with little to offer.

Some biographers fall in love with their subjects, a form of literary Stockholm Syndrome, after spending countless hours in private communion with the past voices of beguiling characters.[4] I realized my "relationship" with Anna would certainly be different. Reading about her antics filled me with a mixture of admiration and repulsion; sometimes the latter was more prevalent than the former, especially when I discovered the princess mistreated servants and lower-ranking family members. On the other hand, there was no denying that Anna enthralled me. The more articles that piled on my desk, the more engrossed I became with this deeply flawed, but flamboyant character whose bizarre actions transfixed me. Anna was not only frustrating and baffling, she also sparkled with guts and gumption like few of her peers.

Unwilling to be constricted by traditional female morals, Anna openly condemned the pervasive sexual double standard. Although she should not be categorized as a conscious "poster-child" for early women's rights, her courageous spirit deserves our attention. Anna made history through defiance and in doing so provides a rare lens through which we can view the life and times of a pariah princess, a veritable anti-heroine who possessed none of the disarming beauty of a Diana or the majestic chic of Marie Antoinette. Indeed, Anna stands as a curio in the female character cabinet of gilded aristocrats.

The sixteenth century provides an interesting backdrop to Anna's experiences. Religious wars and barbaric brutality of the Reformation had a direct bearing on her tumultuous life. As Western Europe struggled to retain order within chaos, Anna flailed against conflicting currents of faith, love, and gender.

Although history is a matter of interpretation, and a certain amount of conjecture, I have tried to retell Anna of Saxony's story as much as the fog of four hundred years have allowed me. I scrutinized primary sources that were not burned by Anna's relations, but slumbered in German and Dutch archives for many decades to reconstruct her life as it is possible to know. What I hope emerges is the biography of a lady whose fate is one of the most moving of any German princess, a fascinating "womanly aberration" whose character continues to entice the reader and historian.

---

[4] Amanda Foreman. *Georgiana Duchess of Devonshire* (New York: Modern Library, 2001), p. XIII

"Every Vein in My Body Heartily Loves Him"

In December 1560, while much of the city of Dresden hibernated in the bone-chilling grip of the Saxon winter, Anna of Saxony dreamt of becoming a wife. The prospect put her into the best of spirits, which was unusual for her. The princess was known to suffer from dark moods during the winter months, sending her servants scurrying.

She sometimes struggled with her feelings, because she felt "it was ungodly, even indecent for a young woman of her station to experience such joy". Her aunt and guardian, Electress Anne of Saxony, had already scolded her for not showing the proper reserve. The electress was the proud leader of Dresden's tightly-run, sober Protestant court, and counseled piety and restraint to her ladies every day of the week.[1]

The source of her happiness was obvious to all around her: Anna had landed a husband. This was no small feat for the princess; at sixteen, she possessed some unattractive traits that had already gained her an unfavorable reputation in certain quarters. She was slightly hunchbacked, plain girl with a "hard head," Anna was known to be argumentative.[2] Nonetheless, marriage negotiations proceeded rapidly, and Anna was impatient to tie herself to a man who was neither a toothless widower nor a penniless younger son, but the head of the House of Orange. Wedlock promised to confer the title "Her Highness, Princess of Orange" on her - an honor surpassing her current "Duchess of Saxony."

This was a triumph for a young woman who had been labeled "unmarriageable" by a number of courtiers in the Saxon capital of Dresden. Even Anna's uncle and guardian, Elector August, had questioned her fitness as a wife in previous years and rejected a number of German suitors.[3]

These embarrassments now laid in the past. William, Prince of Orange and Count of Nassau-Breda, had first approached the elector for her hand in 1559 and was showing himself as a determined suitor. At first the match had not looked auspicious; not because of Anna's controversial personality, but because that year had been considered cursed and unlucky throughout Europe. The famous Nostradamus, one of Catherine de Medici's personal soothsayers, predicted "divers calamities, weepings, and mournings" for all of 1559 , which had proven frighteningly accurate.[4] Henri II, King of France, had sustained a gruesome injury during a tournament celebrating the wedding of his daughter Elizabeth to Philip of Spain. The lance of the king's opponent had pierced his right eye and temple, and even Henri's most experienced surgeons had been unable to save him.

Disasters had also befallen Saxony. In Freiberg, south-west of Dresden, the sky had abruptly darkened at two o'clock during an August afternoon as if night was about to fall. Hail shot down in alarming shapes of crosses and roses, hurting scores of people. In fact, the tempest destroyed so many roofs that local kilns could not fire enough shingles for the rest of the year and residents had to improvise with make-shift coverings.[5] Many blamed witchcraft for the horrific

[1] Sabine Ulbricht. *Fürstinnen in der sächsischen Geschichte, 1382-1622*, (Sax Verlag Beucha: 2010), p. 176.
[2] Katrin Keller. *Kurfürstin Anna von Sachsen (1532-1585)*. (Regensburg: Verlag Friedrich Pustet, 2010), p. 211.
[3] Anne-Simone Knöfel. *Dynastie und Prestige: Die Heiratspolitik der Wettiner*. (Köln: Böhlau Verlag, 2009), pp. 134-5.
[4] Jane Dunn. *Elizabeth and Mary: Cousins, Rivals, Queens*. (New York: Alfred A. Knopf, 2004), p. 27.
[5] Stefan Militzer. "Umwelt-Klima-Mensch," in *Studien und Quellen zur Bedeutungvon Klima und Witterung in der vorindustriellen Gesellschaft*. (Abschlussbericht zum DFG Projekt MI-493, Leipzig, 1998). See also, Thomas Sävert. *Tornadoliste Deutschland*, in http://www.tornadoliste.de/tornadoliste1600.htm (accessed 10 March 2010).

destruction, and the elector was already considering the increased prosecution of sorceresses.[6]

More practical obstacles also complicated William's marriage efforts. His master and overlord, Philip II of Spain, opposed the union, and Anna's grandfather, Landgrave Philip of Hessen, roundly condemned the match. He claimed that his granddaughter's immortal soul was in danger when she disregarded his counsel. The Protestant princess would be led astray at William's Catholic court in Breda where popery and licentiousness reigned supreme.[7]

Anna closed out these concerns, however; her heart and mind were overpowered by emotion. When the Prince of Orange had visited Dresden a month earlier, in November 1560, Anna refused to leave her suitor in the dark about the intensity of her affections. "What was the point of fashionable reticence?," she appears to have queried. Her fiancé risked his standing with the Spanish King to marry her, and she wanted to reassure him of her devotion to him. Observers took note with increasing alarm that Anna threatened to overstep the bounds of both decency and noble decorum in her desire for the prince. She announced that although William was "a black traitor [a Catholic], there is not a vein in my body that does not heartily love him."[8]

Escape from personal pain certainly contributed to Anna's rapidly growing attachment. An orphan since the age of ten, the princess had become the unhappy and defiant dependent of her quick-tempered uncle and his unyielding wife, Anne of Denmark and Norway. She calculated, that after William departed Dresden for the Low Countries, her own days in the Saxon capital were finally numbered. Better days among new friends awaited her in the Netherlands as she readied herself to become Anna, Princess of Orange, wife of William.[9]

The prospect of Anna's impending departure also delighted her Saxon relations. After the death of her mother in late 1555, the Elector August, together with his stern wife, Electress Anne, had raised the young princess as befit her parentage and station. Of course, their own offspring - heirs to Saxony's ever growing wealth—came first in the electoral couple's attention and care, but they had done their best to keep Anna in style.

To August's astonishment, however, his niece showed little gratitude for all the expense and trouble lavished on her. Instead of carrying herself modestly and obediently like a good Christian woman (according to their thinking), she had developed an unusual, rebellious streak that regular blows with the rod could not break. Even more worrisome, she was raising eyebrows among Germany's nobility and threatened Saxony's reputation in the Empire.[10]

Anna also showed a pronounced lack of interest in the traditional female pursuits of housekeeping, cooking, and embroidery - skills that her uncle's wife vigorously promoted at Dresden's *Residenz* (central palace). While the electress had made a name for herself as an acclaimed household manager and expert in medicines, whose complex potions were popular even at the imperial court,

[6] Manfred Wilde. "Kursachsen – Hexenverfolgungen," in *Lexikon zur Geschichte der Hexenverfolgung*. Eds: Gudrun Gersmann, Katrin Moeller, and Jürgen-Michael Schmidt, in: historicum.net, URL: http://www.historicum.net/no_cache/persistent/artikel/1639/ (29.6.2011)

[7] Knöfel, p. 135.

[8] Hans-Jürgen Pletz-Krehahn. "Die bislang unbekannte Krankheit der Anna von Sachsen," in *Heimatjahrbuch für das Land an der Dill*, No. 24 (1981), p.208.

[9] Hans Kruse. "Wilhelm von Oranien und Anna von Sachsen," in *Nassauische Annalen*, Band 54 (1934), pp. 11-12.

[10] Kruse, p. 13

Anna exhibited a disconcerting penchant for idleness and troublemaking.[11]

Lastly, Anna's physical appearance gave the electoral couple much cause for concern. Besides being misshapen in body, she sported a set of eyes that protruded in an odd manner, highlighting her truculent features. Before Martin Luther's reforms of faith, women with similar "defects" vanished in nunneries, never to be heard of again. Now even Anna was able to enter holy wedlock. It was thus with relief that August looked forward to her marrying William and being taken off his hands for good.[12]

Before Anna's departure, however, the elector was planning to give her a rousing send-off that rivaled royal wedding celebrations anywhere in Europe. August intended to use the occasion to showcase Saxon power, while acting the part of the magnanimous, loving uncle. The Habsburgs and sundry German princelings would marvel at the economic might of his dominions, while he promoted his new familial connections with the wealthy Low Countries.[13]

Afterwards, he hoped to irrevocably send his niece on her way. Custom at the time forbade married women of rank to return to their parents' home, except in dishonorable, highly problematic circumstances, so any good-bye would be final.[14] As neither Anna, nor her uncle wanted to see any more of the other, it was a "win-win" for both parties.

[11] Alisha Rankin. "Becoming an Expert Practitioner: Court Experimentalism and the Medical Skills of Anna of Saxony (1532-1585)," in Isis, 98:23-53. *The History of Science Society (2007), p. 28.*.
[12] Kruse, "Wilhelm von Oranien," p. 14
[13] Günther Wartenberg. "Eine Ehe im Dienste kursächsischer Aussenpolitik–zur unglücklichen Ehe der Anna von Sachsen mit Wilhelm von Oranien," pages 79-86, in *Die Wettiner: Chancen und Realitäten.* Ed. Reiner Groß. (Dresden: Kulturakademie, 1990), p. 83.
[14] Antonia Fraser. *Love and Louis XIV* (New York: Anchor Books, 2006), p. 59.

Beginnings

"I am the daughter of the great elector, the savior of Protestantism," Anna of Saxony announced countless times during self-defining moments of triumph, defiance, and desperation. Over time, her heritage became the only unassailable badge of honor for the princess, especially towards the end of her provocative life, when she had become completely mired in scandal. Anna would look back wistfully at having once been "the daughter of the greatest lord that was in Germany," although at that time, she no longer felt worthy of her illustrious legacy. During the first half of her life, however, pride in her father's glory and a matching pedigree marked her personality, along with an insatiable hunger for acceptance.

Anna was the eldest child of Maurice, Elector of Saxony and his wife, Agnes of Hessen. She was born on 23 December 1544 at the family residence in Dresden, the capital of the Duchy of Saxony, one of the leading and most prosperous principalities in the Holy Roman Empire. Wedged between the Kingdom of Bohemia to the east and the Landgraviate of Hessen to the west, her father's lands were positioned in the central part of the Empire, or, on a twenty-first century map, on Germany's eastern fringe.

Not much is known of Anna's early years, except that her arrival had been eagerly awaited. Her birth drowned out those nagging voices at court that had started to question Agnes's fertility after almost four years of marriage. And although the little duchess's sex may have been a disappointment, she soon occupied the center of her mother's affections and grew into a spoiled little girl, cossetted and indulged by female relations and ladies-in-waiting. Maurice was often absent from home, allowing Agnes to devote much of her time to her daughter, perhaps more so than was common in noble households at the time. The duchess's few existing letters proudly proclaim news of her child's robust health and testify to the special mother-daughter bond that lasted until Anna reached her early teens.[1]

If her mother appeared as a concerned, even doting caregiver, Anna's father was intimidating. Hot-tempered and volatile, Maurice's explosive outbursts cut enemies as well as family members to the quick. As one of Germany's most powerful lords and leading member of the Saxon House of Wettin, the prince could be ruthless when challenged. The Wettins were one of Germany's most ancient dynasties, and Maurice was determined to affirm, if not enhance, his family's authority at all cost. His commanding personality and fabulous wealth bolstered those perceptions. Silver mines in southern Saxony had endowed the princely house with fabulous riches and by the mid-sixteenth century, the Wettins were virtually awash in money - the envy of Germany's nobility.[2]

Influence usually followed a money trail, and Maurice's standing among fellow potentates in Germany's Electoral College was accordingly prominent. Unlike England or France, the crown in the empire did not automatically pass from father to son - although this was at times the case. The Imperial crown was decid-

---

[1]Kruse, "Wilhelm von Oranien," p. 10

[2]Blaschke Karlheinz."Die Markgrafen von Meissen im 12. und 13. Jahrhundert 1089-1291," pages 13-24, in *Die Herrscher Sachsens: Markgrafen, Kurfürsten, Könige. 1089-1918*. Ed. Frank-Lothar Kroll (Munich: Becksche Reihe, 2007), p. 13, p. 18.

ed by "electors", an exclusive group of the leading houses of the German states whose votes decided the Empire's succession. The electors were royal princes in all but name and cast their ballot whenever the imperial authority fell vacant. During Anna's lifetime, the Electoral College consisted of the Protestant magnates of the Palatinate, Brandenburg, and Saxony, the Catholic prince bishops of Mainz, Cologne, and Treves as well as the King of Bohemia.[3] Among these influential rulers, Maurice had unarguably the loudest voice, and when his glittering entourage arrived at an Imperial Diet (the representative assembly of German princes) one took careful notice.

For all of Saxony's clout in Germans lands, the principality was often beset by internal strife, particularly during Anna's childhood. In the late fifteenth century, the electorate had been split into two by the brothers Ernest and Albrecht in what became known as the Leipzig Partition. The older, Ernest, received the electorship and commanded the western portion of what became known as Ernestine Saxony, while his younger sibling ruled over so-called Albertine Saxony in the east as a duke.[4] Over time, bitter conflicts developed between the main and cadet branch of the House of Wettin, and Anna's father Maurice, an Albertine, was one of the primary aggressors. He regularly sparred with his most hated opponent, John Frederick, Elector of Ernestine Saxony, whom he disparagingly called "the fat arrogance."[5] Rival cousins, the two princes engaged in a vicious war of words and the occasional hostile skirmish.

For much of her youth, Anna was unaware of these simmering tensions. Dresden was a cocoon of luxury that shielded her from most of life's unpleasantries, and, like many females of her class, this left her largely oblivious to hardships of the world at large. At Dresden's city palace, Anna had her own staff at her beck and call. Nurse maids and governesses took her on walks and outings; a group of chamber maids cared for her every personal need. She probably received her own little household at the customary age of six, next to her devoted mother's.

Unlike other royal residences at the time, the straitjacket of etiquette was not as constricting in Dresden, allowing children like Anna to engage in age-appropriate play. Saxon princesses busied themselves in replicate kitchens equipped with toy stoves, tiny bowls, jars, and pans.[6] Anna might have fried and baked with a group of little companions on a mockup stove while pretending to be a middle-class housewife. Tournaments, ring races, travelling theatrical companies, and most of all, the splendid carnival season, provided additional entertainment, all set within sumptuous surroundings.

Anna was almost four years old when she left home for the magnificent Hartenfels palace in Torgau, about seventy miles north-west of Dresden. Her father wanted to express his growing status among European royalty by having the rather old-fashioned Dresden headquarters remodeled and updated. During its refurbishment, the court moved to Hartenfels, Maurice's latest and grandest acquisition among a growing number of stately homes. Sitting on porphyry rock and surrounded by a swamp, Maurice's secondary residence was worthy of a king. While ascending the famous "snail staircase," a visitor commented admir-

[3]Maria Kroll. *Sophie Electress of Hanover*. (London: Victor Gollancz, 1973), p. 21.
[4]Bünz, "Die Kurfürsten von Sachsen bis zur Leipziger Teilung 1423-1485," *Die Herrscher Sachsens* (Munich: Beck'sche Reihe), p. 49.
[5]Maria Ulbricht. *Sophie Electress of Hanover*. (London: Victor Gollancz, 1973). p. 131.
[6]Keller, *Kurfürstin*, pp. 38-9, p. 70.

ingly, "Noble Lord, one should gladly wage war in order to win such a palace." In September 1550 Anna and her mother returned to Dresden to live in theretofore unknown comfort and opulence.[7]

Modeled on the majestic Renaissance estates of Italy and France, the Dresden *Residenz* now boasted exquisitely detailed architecture and workmanship that displayed Saxony's prosperity as well as Maurice's rising significance. Italian architects had virtually doubled the existing floor plan of the former medieval fortress, and contemporary drawings show turreted buildings and a grand courtyard embellished with intricate layers of tinted plaster called *sgraffito*.[8]

The residence's interior had received a face-lift as well. Inspired by the Duke of Mantua's Palazzo del Te, twelve larger than life frescoes sported colossal warriors in the enormous "Hall of Giants." Festooned along the windows, they appeared poised to do battle on behalf of the elector. *"Even if you be giant or dwarf,"* an inscription read, *"all those who oppose me will be crushed to a pulp."* The personification of the archetypical Machiavellian Renaissance prince, Maurice brashly advertised his preeminence among Germany's rulers.[9]

The most valuable and breathtaking works of art, however, were Maurice's tapestries. Invaluable objets d'art, they were woven in silk and embroidered with gold and silver thread in thousands of hours of painstaking work. Some hung in the palace chapel and formed part of a series of the Passion of Christ; others showed scenes from the prince's campaigns against the Ottoman Turks. Generally, these priceless possessions were not on permanent display, but mounted only for special occasions. Otherwise, these items were stored in the tapestry vault. A single wall hanging was worth as much as the most precious item in the silver chamber of treasures, but Maurice had the means to establish a superb collection. During his reign, he increased their number from fifteen to two-hundred thirty eight.[10]

Such stylish living had its provenance in the Burgundian courts of the Netherlands, near mythical places of refinement that had set the benchmark for fashionable culture since the late Middle Ages. Intricate court etiquette—elaborate, complicated, and silly to the point of absurdity - had since become the behavioral yardstick for Germany's nobility as well, and everyone, including the lordlings of the smallest principalities, attempted to mimic Burgundian airs.

In addition to eye-catching decorations and fine manners, Maurice also provided select musical entertainment for his family and visiting dignitaries. A generous patron of the arts - if only to secure bragging rights - he had hired the well-known composer and trombone player Antonio Scandello to bring musical sophistication to Saxony. The Italian court-bandmaster established an orchestra of cornettists and sackbut players who performed on festive occasions. The musicians from the south complemented the newly founded *Churfürstliche Cantorey* (Elector's Choir), a men's ensemble and one of Europe's oldest orchestras that exists to this day.[11] In February 1553, Maurice staged a number of glamorous cele-

---

[7]Ulbricht, p. 140.

[8]Helen Watanabe-O'Kelly. *Court Culture in Dresden* (New York: Palgrave, 2002), p. 37.

[9]Margitta Coban-Hensel. 'Kurfürst Moritz von Sachsen und seine Schloßausstattungen,' pages 113-136, in *Hof und Hofkultur unter Moritz von Sachsen (1521-1553)*. Eds. Andre Thieme and Jochen Vötsch (Dresden: Sax-Verlag, 2004.) p. 123, p. 135.

[10]Coban-Hensel, pp. 126-36.

[11]Watanabe, pp. 22-3, p. 40. Ulbricht, p. 142.

brations during the joyous Mardi Gras period, which his daughter surely attended.[12]

Whenever they sought a reprieve from Dresden's hustle and bustle, Anna and her parents took up residence at the Wettin's well-appointed lodge in the nearby countryside. Named *Moritzburg* (Maurice's Castle), it was the elector's private indulgence, a folly in the woods with terrific hunting grounds that offered peace and relaxation. A room named the "silver chamber" boasted a large painting depicting Henry VIII of England with his oldest daughter Mary. It rendered homage to Catherine of Aragon, the emperor's aunt and represented, by extension, the Wettins' connection to European royalty.[13] The Holy Roman Emperor Ferdinand (1503-1564) also visited Saxony in 1549 to go hunting with Maurice.[14]

Because of her father's ambitions, Anna grew up in an atmosphere of ever increasing extravagance and rarefied distractions enjoyed by a select few. Surrounded by fawning servants and lesser ranking nobles, Anna's lofty position became gradually imprinted in her mind. Life was utterly splendid for the young girl who matured in the belief that she too belonged to the sublime sphere of demi-Gods that graced the walls of the palace.[15] It was an unhealthy, but dogged conviction that would stick with Anna through most of her life - even during her lowest moments, when humility would have been advisable.

Besides being blessed with material wealth and a faultless lineage, the Wettins' personal relations were quite satisfactory - as long as one applies the nobility's notoriously low yardstick for personal happiness in matters of matrimony. Agnes of Hessen had first met Maurice at a family function when she was only seven years old, and over the years a genuine affection developed between the Saxon prince and the daughter of Landgrave Philip of Hessen. At the time of their marriage in January 1541, observers even talked of a love match.[16] The union itself, however, had caused something of a scandal. Maurice's mother, the redoubtable Catherine of Mecklenburg, had violently opposed the joining of the two houses, and when her eldest wed Agnes without parental approval, she resorted to threats and intimidation. The duchess had her son shadowed, and ranted that God's punishment awaited those who failed to honor the fourth commandment of filial piety. Full of rage, she even accused Maurice of putting his father Henry "into an early grave."[17]

But the prince, mature beyond his years at nineteen, already knew his own mind and simply ignored his mother's noisy objections - traits his daughter would also display. The issue at heart, he realized, was not with his bride, but rather a personal disagreement between Catherine and Agnes's father, Philip of Hessen.[18] "The young lion in the making," as a suspicious Martin Luther called Maurice, had no qualms about shirking parental dictates, and married his thirteen-year-old fiancée in a clandestine ceremony at her father's residence in the Hessian city of Kassel. Such self-determination came at a price. The Saxon court stood aghast at the prince's "immeasurable levity" and both of his parents re-

[12] Hans-Joachim Böttcher. *Anna Prinzessin von Sachsen.*(Dresden: Dresdner Buchverlag, 2013), p. 36
[13] Coban-Hensel, pp.115-122.
[14] Böttcher, p. 31.
[15] Janine Garrison. *Königin Margot: Das bewegte Leben der Marguerite de Valois* (Düsseldorf: Benziger, 1995), p. 23, p. 73.
[16] Karlheinz Blaschke. *Moritz von Sachsen* (Göttingen: Muster-Schmidt, 1983), p.22.
[17] Blaschke, p. 23. Knöfl, pp. 117-8, Ulbricht, p. 116.
[18] Catherine of Mecklenburg and Philip of Hessen were at odds over a disputed inheritance as well as the landgrave's scandalous second marriage which will be discussed at length in a later chapter.

fused to receive their son for several months.[19] Maurice's father, Duke Henry, coldly informed the young husband that he had better find a way to feed his wife, since support from home would not be forthcoming. He only relented when Maurice fell seriously ill, and the prodigal son duly returned to Dresden.[20]

The duke's anger was hardly surprising, since matrimony without parental consent was almost unheard of at the time, especially for a person of Maurice's stature. In the Renaissance, no greater sin of childhood and youth existed than the public humiliation of one's family, a maxim drummed into the young at school, church, and home. An act of individual selfishness like the prince's not only revealed ingratitude for the many things parents gave a child, from life and sustenance to education and inheritance; still worse, it invited gossip and ridicule upon the "offender's" family.[21] In addition, marriage between dynasties also had political and diplomatic implications which were never left to "decisions of the heart". For a while Catherine's fury was so great that relatives warned Maurice to have his food checked for poison. It was not until the late fall of 1541 - ten months after the furtive nuptials - that the prince was able to introduce Agnes to his kin. By that time, Catherine's anger had at last blown over.[22]

When adolescent Agnes joined her spouse in Saxony, she was forced to adjust to her new surroundings rather quickly. Maurice's father had passed away in the summer, forcing his son to take the helm of government and his wife to step up to the office of Duchess of Saxony. It appears that the teenager was not quite as prepared for the momentous tasks that lay ahead of her as some Saxon courtiers wished. At fourteen, Agnes was graceful and small in stature, with a thin nose and lips and an overall pious demeanor. A painting by Lucas Cranach the Younger shows a shy young woman who had already adopted the demure look of a matron, somberly clad in black. Neither pretty nor unattractive, Anna's mother gives an impression of reserved coolness that borders on frigid. Perhaps it was her way of masking certain insecurities, because the debut of her Dresden tenure was not without hurdles.

As a husband, Maurice could be a strict, even forbidding taskmaster who saw no reason to indulge his consort.[23] Even so, he had twenty-five individuals assigned to Agnes's personal household, including nine ladies-in-waiting. The young duchess, however, still felt forlorn and anxious, and her fretfulness only increased when a feud with Maurice's cousin John Frederick and an imperial campaign against the Ottomans in Hungary called the prince away for much of the first year of their marriage. One of the duke's privy counselors informed him worriedly that he had meat purchased for His Grace's young wife who was looking pale and only poked at her food.[24]

Agnes's loss of appetite was aggravated by conflict in the women's wing. Although Maurice's termagant of a mother had vacated her Dresden chambers and reluctantly retired to her widow's estate near Saxony's Ore Mountains, there was another female relation that riled the fledgling duchess. Agnes's paternal aunt, Elizabeth of Rochlitz, was a woman of great confidence who talked, med-

[19]Ozment, *Fathers*, p. 29.
[20]Knöfel, *Dynastie*, p. 118.
[21]Ozment, *Daughter*, p. 106.
[22]Ulbricht, pp. 117-8, p. 129
[23]Blaschke, *Moritz*, p. 23.
[24]Ulbricht, p. 130, p. 132.

dled, and commanded like a man. The widow of another Saxon duke, Elizabeth freewheeled on an imposing estate outside of Leipzig, unencumbered by children or a domineering consort. Whenever she sojourned in Dresden, which was apparently quite often, the forty-year-old princess intimidated her adolescent niece with her overbearing personality. In the fall of 1542 the two women had a falling out with mutual accusations of unspecified "dishonorable behavior" fueling their arguments. "Agnes better take care," Elizabeth later wrote menacingly, "or she would incur a curse".[25] Over time, the duchess developed a fear of her aunt that bordered on the pathological. It was a fear that she would pass on to her daughter Anna.[26]

Life in Dresden, however, was not all hardship. Agnes found trusted companions in her maid-of-honor, Sophia von Miltitz, and her sister-in-law Sidonia. Madame Miltitz was of ancient Saxon gentry stock and would stay at Agnes's side until her early death; she then transferred her services to young Anna, albeit with less success. While Madame Miltitz served her mistress with steady devotion, the plucky Sidonia assisted Agnes in finding her place at court. Like most women in her family, Maurice's sister was headstrong and somewhat rough around the edges, but the two women forged a lasting, if unequal friendship that was viewed with suspicion by Elizabeth.[27] Her aunt's complaints notwithstanding, Agnes enjoyed the assertive company of her sister-in-law who in time also became a confidante of Anna's.

During Maurice's irregular stays in Dresden, Agnes indulged her husband whom a contemporary described as a "longish, gaunt person, with piercing, flashing eyes,"and a forked russet beard.[28] A portrait of the time shows the couple in the expected poses of noble detachment, although Maurice appears to almost glower at the artist, his legendary temper barely in check. Over the years Agnes learned to assert herself against her formidable spouse, while the prince took her occasional grumblings in stride. In the fall of 1548, after his consort had upbraided him for leaving on a hunting expedition without her, Maurice replied sheepishly, "Most beloved wife, your anger against me and your charge that I'd rather be with the wild sows and that I prefer them to you is strange to hear."[29]

Agnes knew her husband could be kind-hearted and gentle, if not always reliable and faithful. Although a caring family man, Maurice certainly had a different side to him. During an Imperial Diet in Bavarian Augsburg in the fall of 1547, the prince engaged in a raunchy, widely publicized sexual escapade in a bath house. Contemporary chroniclers dished with relish about a piquant ménage a trois and other indiscretions during a state visit to the south. "The duke made the acquaintance of many local women and led quite an amusing life in his apartment, which belonged to a doctor," one account revealed. "The doctor had an adult daughter with the name of Jacobine. He [Maurice] bathed and played with her daily, and Margrave Albrecht of Brandenburg-Kulmbach was usually the

---

[25]Ulbricht, p. 134.

[26]Kruse, "Wilhelm von Oranien," p. 151. Agnes's fractious relationship with Elizabeth created plenty of conflict in Dresden. Elizabeth was a frequent visitor and close confidante of Maurice's with whom she laughed, joked and discussed politics. The young electress often snubbed her aunt, telling her not to call again. She even begged her mother not to invite her to Kassel when Elizabeth was present, claiming that the older woman was always "up to something." On another occasion, she told her father, Philip, "It is a shame for all of us that we have such an evil woman amongst our family." Unfortunately, she transferred her aversion onto her daughter Anna.

[27]Lilienthal, p. 186, p. 211. See also Kruse, "Wilhelm von Oranien," p. 151. On 14 July 1544, Elizabeth wrote to her brother Philip of Hessen, *"Your daughter does whatever she wants. It doesn't really help that Sidonia is with her; she [Sidonia] rules her completely. You cannot entrust her [Agnes] with anything, because she does not keep quiet [and] tells her everything ..."*

[28]Blaschke, *Moritz*, p. 68.

[29]Ulbricht, p. 143

third in the party. Some crude jokes took place between the threesome [and] the devil rejoiced at their behavior. Talk filled the entire town."[30]

Agnes reacted to the news of her husband's debauches with the patient forbearance expected of women of her class. Renaissance society permitted noble males to practice sexual license within few parameters, and like many of her peers, Anna's mother overlooked Maurice's bedroom peccadilloes with predictable poise. While she appears to have suppressed any feelings of hurt betrayal, Agnes brooded over her inability to present Maurice with a living son. Roughly a year after Anna's arrival, she had given birth to a baby boy named Albrecht, but the longed-for heir had died in April 1546 of an unknown childhood disease. Since then, the Wettins' pleasant routine was marred by worries of infertility. At the beginning of May 1548 Maurice wrote from Augsburg, "Highborn Princess, friendly dear wife ... I will be with you in fourteen days' time ... and [will stay] for a while, may God give me joy ... and tell me about our daughter and her mind, [and also of] your body's condition, as I entrust you to the Almighty."[31] Anna's parents were keenly aware that their only daughter would hardly leave an imprint on Saxony and that a son was needed to continue Maurice's legacy. Unlike England, where two sisters - Elizabeth and Mary Tudor - ruled as sovereigns in the sixteenth century, women in Germany were barred from the succession. Anna could only bring glory to the electorate by marrying well.

The problem of infertility attracts considerable attention in the Western world today, but no pressure on would-be mothers in this day and age can match the peculiar strain on a Renaissance princess. Her essential function was to bear sons; otherwise she was a failure. Duchess Agnes might be pious, intelligent, and caring, a wonderful wife who pleased her husband and treated her servants with consideration, but in the end she had to accept that her accomplishments as an individual were unimportant against her biological successes or failures.[32] Furthermore, because of Agnes's public role as consort to a ruling magnate, her inability to bear sons was not a private pain to be born with her spouse, but a shameful public issue.

In time, Agnes so longed for another child that she asked her father, Landgrave Philip, to send her baby brother George to Dresden, since the boy's mother's had died in April 1549. Philip replied in rather bad grace that Agnes and Maurice should produce an heir themselves, but eventually sent the toddler to Saxony. Anna's mother also shared her worries with her friend Sidonia, who then inquired about the name of a cleric who "knew the art of getting the Electress Agnes pregnant." Initially, the preacher's ministrations showed promise, but later that year Agnes informed one of her brothers that she was recuperating from the possible aftereffects of a miscarriage.[33]

Anna's parents certainly never gave up hope. In July 1553, while Maurice was preparing to move into battle against a renegade peer of the realm, the prince wrote a heartfelt letter to his wife, asking her to join him near his encampment as soon as possible. He was looking forward to spending time with Agnes in the spa town of Pyrmont, while trying for another child. "If you travel close to where I am, I will do my best [to meet you] at the blessed bath. I enjoin you to God's

[30] Klaus Vetter. *Am Hofe Wilhelm von Oraniens* (Stuttgart: Deutsche Verlags-Anstalt, 1991), p. 47.
[31] Ulbricht, p. 142.
[32] Eric Ives. *The Life and Death of Anne Boleyn* (Oxford: Blackwell, 2005), p. 189.
[33] Ulbricht, p. 146

protection that he may help bring us together and bless us so that we may live long, long, long lives together from hereon, and make that happen that we have desired for so long, amen."[34] Sadly enough, the Almighty failed to grant any of those earnest wishes.

---

[34]Ulbricht, p. 150

The redoubtable Elizabeth of Hessen (von Rochlitz) (1502-1557): She frightened both Agnes and her daughter Anna (Lucas Cranach the Elder, 1534)

Anna's parents, Maurice of Saxony and Agnes of Hessen, by Lucas Cranach the Younger. Over time, Agnes became a trusted confidante of her volatile husband

Power Plays

In the early summer of 1553 Maurice bade his wife and eight-year-old daughter Anna good-bye in Dresden. A former friend and ally, Margrave Albrecht of Brandenburg-Kulmbach, had gone rogue and was plundering lands belonging to the Catholic Church in northern Bavaria. Intervention was urgently necessary. The margrave's actions not only violated all laws of the empire, but jeopardized the fragile religious peace between Catholics and Protestants that Anna's father had helped broker a year earlier. Anxious to neutralize the despoiler, Maurice readied a response force that was to save the affected areas from Albrecht's reign of terror.[1] The prince - a seasoned warrior - was not overly concerned. He had faced greater opponents in the past and was confident that this particular adversary would be vanquished as well.

While Maurice's generals prepared an army of about 15,000 soldiers for combat, central Europe was only just recovering from a century of religious, social, and political upheavals. Constantinople, Christianity's eastern flagship, had fallen to the Grand Turk in 1453, a Genoese sea captain named Columbus discovered a new continent, and a horrifying disease which is now called syphilis tormented thousands of Europeans. There was also a new mechanical contraption called the printing press which made books more accessible for the common man and forever changed the dissemination of news.

Adding to these issues, the Catholic Church - an institution that had held a virtual monopoly over European religion for almost a thousand years - found herself embroiled in a crisis of faith. According to common lore, a monk named Dr. Martin Luther posted ninety-five theses on the doors of the Castle Church in the Saxon city of Wittenberg in 1517, calling for drastic reforms within the church and its clergy. Although the actual pinning of demands on church portals can no longer be verified, reaction to Luther's arguments was almost immediate. Friends of the theologian printed and circulated his writings in Germany and abroad, galvanizing large audiences. Mass conversions followed in many towns and villages in what became known as the Protestant Reformation. It was a historical milestone of such seismic proportions that some have called Luther's challenge to established religion the most profound revolution in European history.

As an outspoken critic of papal authority, Luther was quickly excommunicated and found himself the most wanted man in Europe. He survived, thanks to a forebear of Anna's, the broad-minded Frederick the Wise of Saxony, who defied Rome's request to hand him over to a clerical tribunal. For several months, the spirited Frederick sheltered Luther at one of his castles, an act of bravery and kindness that allowed the reformation to flourish in Saxony and expand into much of Germany.[2]

After Frederick's death in 1525, the reformation had gained such traction in Saxon domains that most of the aristocracy proudly proclaimed themselves *Martinisch* (followers of Martin). In fact, Luther's movement had become something of a Saxon "family enterprise," so much so that the electorate was hailed as the "motherland of the Reformation."[3]

[1] Blaschke, *Moritz*, pp. 23-4, p. 82, p. 84.
[2] Uwe Schirmer. "Die ernestinischen Kurfürsten bis zum Verlust der Kurwürde 1485-1547," *Die Herrscher Sachsens* (Munich: Becksche Reihe, 2007), p. 64.
[3] Blaschke, *Moritz*, p. 12

Anna's family converted as well; her maternal grandfather, Landgrave Philip of Hessen, was such an enthusiastic proponent of the new creed that together with Maurice's Ernestine rival, John Frederick, he headed the so-called Schmalkaldic League, a defensive association of Protestant princes in the empire.

But not everyone abjured their old faith which resulted in an uneasy co-existence between Catholics and Luther's followers in Germany. For the first time since the fall of the Roman Empire, individuals faced religious diversity and the questioning of moral absolutes - a shocking, disconcerting change that stunned and unsettled believers. Toleration, religious or otherwise, was not a regular feature of Renaissance society, despite tremendous progress in the fields of art and science. Lutheran converts despised the religiously orthodox and vice versa, and cooperation between the confessional camps was unusual. Residents of a state were obliged to stay with the religion of their respective overlords and noblemen stuck with their peers in faith, sneering at the other side. Except for Anna's father, a notable exception among Germany's pious princes.

Despite Saxony's reputation as the cradle of Protestantism, Maurice was a religiously indifferent man; devoid of sacred zeal - at least at the beginning of his reign. Unlike many Lutherans, who had fought and died for "the cause," Anna's father regarded issues of faith with a sense of cool detachment. One of the first princes in the empire to put political pragmatism before religious conviction, he collaborated with a range of political factions, including the inner circle of the Catholic Habsburg emperor, Charles V. It was a clever, if controversial stance that furthered his own goals, but alienated many of his Protestants followers. They viewed the prince's coldblooded expedience as an unacceptable betrayal of the new faith.[4]

Unscrupulous opportunism certainly played a part in many of Maurice's political machinations, especially when it involved his cousin and archrival to the west, Elector John Frederick. Born a duke, Anna's father had always coveted the Saxon electorship, and John Frederick's bumbling personality further inflamed Maurice's hatred for his burly kinsman. Over the years, mutual resentments continued to grow and fester, prompting Maurice to eschew a membership in the Protestant Schmalkaldic League. The league was partly led by John Frederick, and Anna's father had no intention of playing second fiddle to its chief. Regardless of his Lutheran affinities, he aligned himself with Emperor Charles, Protestantism's declared enemy and the empire's most powerful leader. He demonstrated his commitment to his imperial overlord by proving his mettle against the Turks in 1542 and a year later, against the French.

In the summer of 1546 the emperor moved to checkmate the Schmalkaldic League. A devout Catholic, Charles was eager to wipe out the "Protestant heresy" once and for all. After a truce with the Ottomans and a peace treaty with France quieted the empire's eastern and western fronts, he seized the opportunity. Duke Maurice pledged his support to Charles in exchange for guarantees of religious freedom in his own territories and, most importantly, a promise that victory would mean the demise of his hated Ernestine cousin and a transfer of the electoral dignity to himself.

His gamble paid off in April 1547, when Emperor Charles rode to war with 35,000 soldiers to challenge the Protestant alliance. The outcome was near-

[4]Blaschke, *Moritz*, p. 25, p. 27.

ly a foregone conclusion. With additional support from Pope Paul III, who had added 12,500 men-at-arms and 200,000 ducats to imperial coffers, Charles' forces routed the poorly organized Protestants at the Battle of Mühlberg.[5] John Frederick was taken prisoner and stripped of most of his possessions, which the emperor then conferred on Maurice, Saxony's newly appointed elector. In February of the following year, Anna's father accepted his new title during a solemn ceremony held in a public square in Augsburg. Observers commented on the twenty-six-year-old's indifferent mien during this memorable occasion - behavior that was in line with his steely character.[6]

Perhaps the prince's sang-froid also concealed feelings of disappointment and rage. On his return home Maurice's Saxon subjects had given the champion of Mühlberg a cold reception. Many resented their lord's intriguing against a fellow Lutheran and family member, and at least one observer claimed to know that, "In all of Saxony, I have not heard a single person wish the new elector well. Instead [everyone] feels sorry for the old, deposed one, John Frederick." In the aftermath of the battle, popular pamphlets branded Anna's father the "Judas of Meissen," a stinging soubriquet that would cling to Maurice for years to come.[7] Regrettably, it was Agnes who bore the brunt of the public's ill will towards their new elector. While Maurice quickly departed his domains for various inspection trips, his wife and Anna stayed behind at Hartenfels Palace - a possession just wrested away from the unhappy John Frederick. There, townsfolk confronted the novice electress and her ladies in a hostile manner. Agnes apparently stood helpless as a mob screamed insults, and eventually fled with her daughter for the temporary safety of Castle Weissenfels near Leipzig.[8]

There was criticism from neighboring Hessen as well. Maurice's father-in-law, Philip, had fought for the Schmalkaldic League and was also taken prisoner - a development that did not sit well with Agnes's relations, especially her mother Christine. Besieged by his wife's kin, Maurice shot off numerous pleas to Charles to have the landgrave released. At first the emperor appeared amenable to his request, and even promised Philip a "return home without damage to his person and without being detained," as long as the landgrave agreed to a public surrender. On 19 June 1547 and with Maurice's urging, Philip submitted to Charles at Moritzburg Castle in the city of Halle. He did not know that mercenaries were lying in wait to arrest him during dinner and that the emperor had no intention of ever issuing a pardon.

The emperor's duplicity left Maurice aghast. He had taken Charles for a man of honor and saw his own reputation impugned by such a blatant breach of promise. Philip spent several years in captivity, while imperial soldiers razed his Kassel fortress. Stunned Saxon officials reported in October 1548 that "Kassel has almost been turned into a village; its fortress razed, torn, and destroyed to such an extent that, in our opinion, the heart of the structure has been broken."[9] Soon after, the House of Hessen severed all diplomatic relations with electoral Saxony.[10]

---

[5] Florian Welle. "Ein Sieg der Toleranz," *GEO Epoche: Martin Luther und die Reformation*, Nr. 39 (Hamburg: Gruner + Jahr, 2009), p. 124
[6] Blaschke, *Moritz*, p. 68.
[7] Blaschke, *Moritz*, pp. 69-70.
[8] Ulbricht, p. 140, p. 146.
[9] Sascha Winter. "Die Residenz und Festung Kassel um 1547," *Landgraf Philipp der Großmütige von Hessen und seine Residenz Kassel* (Marburg: N. G. Elwert Verlag, 2004), pp. 120-2.
[10] Ulbricht, pp. 137-8.

Maurice never forgave Charles this particular act of treachery which, together with the emperor's failure to award him the entirety of the promised Ernestine lands, eventually turned into burning resentment.[11] When Charles ignored Maurice's pleas to grant his father-in-law clemency time and again, the new elector hatched a conspiracy against his sovereign with a select group of German princes. The emperor was showing himself too inflexible in matters of religion, Maurice convinced leading Protestants, and had taken his demands for universal Habsburg rule a step too far. His arguments found a receptive audience.

Some historians have looked down on the petty German potentates, but many were powerful lords who raised their own armies and played important roles in the game of European politics.[12] In addition, they were independent-minded and not afraid to protest the curtailment of their traditional rights and privileges by Charles, who was attempting to consolidate and streamline his administration into a more centralized government. The nobility also demurred at the emperor's attempts to re-write the terms of worship in Germany. His officials had ordered Lutherans to venerate saints, honor Catholic holy days, and celebrate mass according to Roman rites.[13] Soon a plot was under way to foil these offensive dictates.

Distracted by ill health, a succession battle within Habsburg ranks, and over-confidence after his victory at Mühlberg, Charles was completely taken off-guard by the plotters. For one, he never expected his most trusted vassals to deceive him. And yet Maurice, on whose friendship the emperor had depended for many years, engineered an anti-Habsburg alliance that included Charles's principal enemy, France.[14] Twenty-four-year old Agnes was a trusted co-conspirator in the whole affair. Maurice regularly sent her classified messages which she carefully stashed away in a wooden chest.

In the spring of 1552, French soldiers poured into a disputed region of Lorraine; German princes massed another army in Franconia (northern Bavaria). The emperor, meanwhile, was stuck in the Austrian city of Innsbruck without sufficient troops, virtually deserted by his former allies. As he was closing in on his beleaguered master, Maurice gave Charles the opportunity to take flight, allegedly saying "I don't have a cage for such a big bird."[15] In late May the world's mightiest ruler, whose empire spanned large swaths of Europe and the Americas, fled over the Brenner Pass into Italy in the midst of a raging snowstorm.[16] In Germany, grateful Lutherans declared Anna's father the empire's new hero.

Upon his triumphant return to Saxony, an exultant Maurice delivered good news to Agnes. After years of fruitless negotiations, Charles had finally released the electress's father Philip and turned his back on Germany, never to return. The Saxon elector, on the other hand, who not too long ago had been derided as the "Judas of Meissen," now basked in the adulation of his countrymen. They hailed the victor of the so-called "Princes' Rebellion" as the "Defender of Protestantism" and "Guarantor of German Freedoms," whose serpentine stratagems had sprung from the mind of a political genius.[17]

---

[11]Ulbricht, p. 137.

[12]Mansel, p. 13.

[13]Philip Welle. *Prince of Europe* (London: Phoenix, 2005), p. 13.

[14]Welle, p. 124.

[15]Ulbricht, pp. 148-9.

[16]Henry Kamen. *Philip of Spain* (New Haven, CT: Yale University, 1997), p.51.

[17]Manfred Rudersdorf. "Moritz 1541/47-1553,"*Die Herrscher Sachsens* (Munich: Beck'sche Reihe, 2007), p. 106.

With the landgrave safely returned to Kassel and Charles sulking abroad, Maurice reached the apex of his political career. The future never looked brighter for the undisputed leader of the German Lutherans, and there was already talk that a man of his caliber might soar to an even loftier position one day. The Habsburgs grudgingly called him the "little king," and had charged Maurice with keeping the peace in Germany, something that Charles had never managed himself.[18] It was almost too good to be true.

A year later Maurice rode off to face the Margrave of Brandenburg-Kulmbach in an armed encounter, hoping to meet Agnes afterwards to try for another baby. In early July 1553, the electoral army massed near the small hamlet of Sievershausen east of Hanover and defeated the rebel militia after four hours of "dreadful carnage." Maurice - in typical daredevil fashion - had thrown himself headlong into the melee. Witnesses reported that the prince received a back wound which was not considered life threatening, and was carried by loyal retainers to his tent where his doctor prescribed rest. Soon after, the elector's condition deteriorated dramatically. As he lay dying, Maurice quickly had his testament drawn up with a final message to his wife. It read, "In time, with God's help, we will see each other again."[19] He also asked to have his wedding band delivered to Agnes as a last greeting. Maurice, savior of the Lutheran faith and Germany's most powerful prince, succumbed to his injuries on 9 July. "Oh, dear Lord, won't you come to me?" were his final words.[20]

[18]Blaschke, *Moritz*, p. 79, p. 81.
[19]Ulbricht, p. 150.
[20]Blaschke, *Moritz*, pp. 23-4, p. 82, p. 84.

Anna's father, Maurice of Saxony, in full battle gear. Posthumous portrait by L. Cranach the Younger, 1578

Fall from Grace

Maurice's dying hours in a small field camp rivaled the drama and controversy that had followed him throughout much of his adult life as his passing gave immediate rise to sensational conspiracy theories. The truth can no longer be ascertained, but historical research from the 1980s unearthed the testimony of two doctors who implied that Maurice had fallen victim to a murder plot. The elector's battle injuries were superficial, they noted, and he had retired to his tent in high spirits. As a result, tales of assassination have never dried up.[1]

One account claimed that two Saxon noblemen affiliated with the deposed John Frederick had shot the Saxon elector in the back. Anna always kept a small lead bullet - most likely the projectile that caused her father's fatal injury - among her most treasured possessions.[2] Another claim asserted that the prince's death had been brought about by unidentified "Spanish methods," instigated by a disgruntled Charles.[3]

Several weeks after the fatal battle, Maurice's blood-stained harness arrived in Dresden, sporting a clearly visible bullet hole near the hip.[4] Chroniclers were silent on Agnes' reaction to the terrible sight, but she soon fell ill with grief. On 28 October she wrote to her brother-in-law, August, "I have not been well at all, since my dearest husband has departed from this vale of tears, and I have been feeling somewhat weak. I'm worried that I may become bedridden!"[5]

As Monsieur Scandello composed a memorial mass for his departed employer, Agnes pondered the catastrophic effects of Maurice's death on her own and Anna's life. First, there was the personal, human aspect of the tragedy. The electress had lost her daughter's father and a spouse with whom she had enjoyed an affectionate, even loving rapport. Repercussions on a more practical level were just as grave. Maurice had died without a male heir and his younger brother August stood to inherit his position and rank. In other words, without the elector at her side, Agnes's title of electress was nothing but an empty title as she was soon to find out. Anna's mother had never been the shining doyenne of the Dresden court, but personal enemies had not dared attack her during Maurice's tenure. Now they felt emboldened to vent their frustrations. "The highborn widow [is] a raging devil," Chancellor Erasmus von Minckwitz remarked disapprovingly. "During her husband's lifetime, [she] usurped all kinds of governing."[6] As a dowager princess, twenty-six-year-old Agnes would either have to remarry or withdraw to her widow's estate.

And then there was Anna, now a fatherless child of eight, whose position had also plummeted on that fateful July day. August's children would inherit Saxony's riches, while Maurice's daughter had precipitously slid in rank. If only little Albrecht had survived or the electress had given birth to another boy; Maurice's widow and her daughter could have remained in Dresden, with Agnes acting as her son's regent. But this was not to be. As the court went into full mourning, the electress contemplated her shocking fall from grace.

---

[1] Ulbricht, p. 150.
[2] Pletz-Krehahn, *Krankheit,* p. 209.
[3] Blaschke, *Moritz,* pp. 82-3.
[4] The harness can still be admired at Freiberg Cathedral today.
[5] Ulbricht, p. 153.
[6] Ulbricht, pp.152-3.

In the summer of 1553, while Agnes and Anna waited for male relatives to determine their fates, August assumed governance of Saxony. Although his brother's death had taken him by surprise, the twenty-seven-year-old prince had no trouble filling his sibling's sizeable shoes, and kicked off his reign with a diplomatic pro-Habsburg offensive. He glossed over Maurice's "differences" with the emperor by promising that the Wettins would continue to serve their imperial masters as they had done for centuries. As for his Ernestine cousins who were lying in wait to retrieve the electorship, Maurice's successor appeased them with generous gifts of land.[7]

Sometime in the late summer of 1553, Agnes and Anna made room for Saxony's new electress, Anne of Denmark and Norway. The Danish princess arrived with two small children, and Agnes must have watched with a heavy heart as her replacement took over the Dresden *Residenz*'s women's wing. The dowager electress and her daughter then travelled by carriage to her widow's estate Castle Weissenfels (today New-Augustusburg). Sitting atop a bluff overlooking the Saale River, the old fortress southwest of Leipzig offered dignified comforts in familiar surroundings. Initially, August had demanded that Anna remain in Dresden, but Landgrave Philip intervened on his daughter's behalf, and the girl was allowed to remain with her mother.[8] How the almost nine year old adapted to her new, reduced circumstances has gone unrecorded.

*****

Common wisdom dictated that widows were to remarry as quickly as possible, because their sexual appetites were said to be voracious.[9] Unbound from the yoke of marriage, they no longer belonged to any man and were disturbingly experienced in the bedroom. Moralists warned about the ever-present dangers of temptation as these unfettered females were wont to open themselves up to any charming fellow who came along.[10] In Agnes's case, her relatives were quick at work to bind her to a new husband, although she hardly played the "merry widow." Together with her father Philip, August arranged a match that promised to further family interests.

Agnes's reaction to her relations' choice of partner has not survived, but their pick must have stunned her. The erstwhile first lady of Albertine Saxony found herself engaged to John Frederick II, rival Duke of Ernestine Saxony. The groom was the son of Maurice's cousin and foiled opponent, John Frederick I, the man who had been dispossessed of most of his lands and titles, and spent several years in captivity on account of the late elector's ruthless politicking. Apparently Agnes's father had forged a close friendship with John Frederick the Elder during their time in detention, and this bond was now reinforced by the planned nuptials of their children.

As for August, he was anxious to mend fences with the Ernestines and decided to pawn off his sister-in-law to cement tenuous family relations. On 26 May 1555 Agnes was married to her portly groom in the town of Weimar in western Saxony. Celebrations were reportedly sumptuous and a number of high-rank-

[7]Jens Bruning. "August 1553 1556," *Die Herrscher Sachsens* (Munich: Becksche Reihe, 2007), pp. 112-9.
[8]Ulbricht, pp. 152-3.
[9]David Cressy. *Birth, Marriage and Death* (Oxford: Oxford University Press, 1999), p. 278.
[10]Laura Gowing. *Common Bodies* (New Haven, CT: Yale University Press, 2003), p. 60.

ing guests, including Dresden's electoral couple, attended.[11]

It is uncertain if John Frederick inspired any passion or affection in his bride. He was her junior by two years, bearded, and as corpulent as his late father. In turn, one wonders if the prince could feel any attraction for the widow of the man who had demeaned his own family for many years. Nonetheless, the duke kindly allowed Agnes to bring her daughter Anna along to Weimar, an altruistic and unusual gesture.[12] Noble widows generally had to leave their offspring from previous matches with their maternal families, since husbands wanted no visible reminders of their consorts' previous attachments. The widowed mother of Mary Stuart, for example, was forced to leave her three-year-old son from a first marriage behind in France when she married James V of Scotland. In comparison, John Frederick showed himself surprisingly open-minded and generous since he would be feeding the daughter of his arch foe.

After the nuptials Anna and Agnes bid farewell to friends and family as well as a certain way of life. In a prolonged period of relatively good luck the former Duchess of Saxony had risen to the rank of electress in 1547, only to be "demoted" to duchess in 1555. The move to Weimar forced the pair to give up a number of privileges, among them the luxury and conveniences Agnes had enjoyed for almost fifteen years. Compared to the Dresden and Hartenfels palaces, John Frederick's residence was a pale replica of princely living.

Weimar today is Germany's equivalent to Georgian Britain's Bath, a charming mid-size city frequented by thousands of visitors each month for its classicist buildings and spacious gardens. In the sixteenth century, it was a provincial backwater. Founded in 1250, the small town off the Saxon trade routes gained a little more prominence when John Frederick I built up a small court there after losing most of his lands to Maurice. But overwhelming change does not come quickly to small places, and Weimar's oldest map of 1590 shows a paltry 575 houses set among narrowly winding streets.[13]

While Anna adjusted to her downgraded position of step-daughter to a duke, she may have found a kindly friend in her ersatz father. Details of her relationship with John Frederick have not survived, but it is telling that he voluntarily presented Anna with a handsome dowry gift six years later.[14] Meanwhile, her mother continued to suffer from precarious health. Agnes was in constant contact with her former Dresden physicians, the doctors Roth, Grunewaldt, and Neefe, and the latter still sent her medicines via courier. But the twenty-eight-year old's condition - perhaps tuberculosis - deteriorated even further when she reportedly suffered a miscarriage in October.[15] There is no definite proof of this pregnancy, but together with "lung disease," it is frequently cited as the reason for Agnes's sudden death at the beginning of November 1555, a mere six months after her wedding to John Frederick.

For Anna, her mother's passing was the most grievous blow in a life of mounting tragedies. The last beloved remainder of her immediate family was gone now, leaving the young girl marooned in remote western Saxony. In the span of two and a half years, the young duchess had lost her parents, her home,

---

[11]Ulbricht, p. 154.
[12]Maike Vogt-Lüerssen. *Anna von Sachsen* (Norderstedt: Books on Demand, 2003), p. 14.
[13]Henrich Pleticha. *Das klassische Weimar-Texte und Zeugnisse* (Munich: Komet, 1983), p. 9.
[14]Keller, *Kurfürstin*, p. 199
[15]Ulbricht, pp. 153-4.

and her place in the world. Whispers of foul play also surrounded her mother's death, for like her husband, gossip of the period suggests Agnes might have fallen victim to a murderous plot. While the elector's assassination could have been cloaked as a battle injury, the diagnosis of a miscarriage possibly served as a front to cover up sinister events in the ducal palace.[16] A marble plaque below Agnes's funeral effigy in the City Church of St Peter and Paul in downtown Weimar has silently proclaimed her tragic end for over four centuries.

Crafted by Sebastian Grohmann, sculptor son of the eminent Ernestine court architect NikolausGrohmann (~1500-1566), the Latin inscription reads, "And so I have lived until today, progeny of Hessian blood, married to two Saxon dukes. As the widow of my first husband, Duke Maurice, I came into your marital bed, John Frederick. While you survived me by twenty-seven years, I went to my grave, redeemed by death - a death that is not devoid of suspicion of having been brought about by poison. In the end, all things hidden will be set right by God." The commissioner of this eerily cryptic epitaph remains in the shadows. The sculptor's family had always been loyal to their Ernestine masters and received handsome remuneration for their work in return.[17] For Sebastian Grohmann to craft a memorial accusing his employer of a heinous crime and displaying it in perpetuity is perplexing and may have been carried out under the threat.

There is an error in the inscription, however, which incorrectly claims that John Frederick survived his first wife by twenty-seven years. In actuality, the duke outlived the Hessian princess for another four decades. The question why his descendants would allow such a serious accusation to be displayed in a public place of worship is easier to answer. John Frederick II, who had never quite gotten over his father's humiliation by the Albertines, became entangled in a number of political plots in the early 1560s. Accused of intriguing against Anna's uncle August, he was first incarcerated in Dresden and then spent the rest of his life in imperial custody in Vienna, where he died in 1595 after tumbling down a flight of stairs. None of his sons spent much time in Weimar during their maturity, and it is feasible that someone who had held Agnes very dear had the commemorative tablet affixed in the church.

Even if true, the motives for John Frederick's hard-to-prove crime remain uncertain. Perhaps mental instability or persistent grudges born towards anything connected with Maurice and his family played a part. The scholarly duke had a penchant for brooding and, according to some observers, became increasingly removed from reality right before his nuptials. He entertained visions of a restored electorate and imperial honors - flights of fancy that naturally went nowhere.[18] Perhaps marriage to his rival's widow ultimately proved too much for him, and he took matters into his own hands. And yet his later kindness to Agnes's daughter Anna belies this theory.

Historians have also offered another hypothesis. There is the distinct possibility that the Albertines, namely Anna's uncle August, were somehow involved in the duchess's death. As later events would show, Saxony's new elector knew no bounds if he imagined his rule challenged.[19] After Agnes had married "the

---

[16]Karl Braun. "Wurde die Kurfürstin ermordet?" *Thüringische Landeszeitung* (28 April 2009), p. 2.

[17]Matthias Donath. "Grohmann (Gromann), Nikolaus (Nickel)," *Sächsische Biografie*, Online Edition: http://www.isgv.de/saebi/ (accessed 22.5.2011).

[18]Thomas Klein. "Johann Friedrich," *Neue Deutsche Biographie, Band 10* (Berlin: Duncker & Humblot, 1974), p. 530.

[19]Kruse, p. 142. August did not shy away from misappropriating funds from the disgraced family after the death of John William of Saxon-Weimar, John Frederick's second son, in 1573. Apparently, he even resorted to document forgery.

enemy," the former electress was in a position to divulge family secrets. Anna's mother possessed a store of intelligence about Dresden's inner workings - sensitive information that the desperate John Frederick might have sought to regain his father's lost title.[20] A few days before the Battle of Sievershausen, Maurice forwarded a package of confidential documents to his wife per trusted courier and asked her to hide them in an undisclosed location. Even after his death, Agnes supposedly kept these classified letters well-concealed and showed them to no one.[21]

Perhaps August placed an agent in Weimar to prevent her from disclosing private matters. This handler, possibly posing as a servant, subsequently poisoned the dowager electress. As for John Frederick, August effectively frustrated his political ambitions in the mid-1560s when the duke backed an opponent of the Albertines. With the emperor's assistance, the elector had Agnes's second husband incarcerated for life.[22] And again, it could have been Anna's uncle who had the puzzling inscription hewn into Agnes's tomb, its message casting everlasting blame and shame on a conveniently silenced adversary. Unfortunately, all "these things hidden" remain just so, leaving us with mere conjecture.

*****

If her mother had truly been the victim of treachery, Anna had to make sense of the fact that one parent, if not both, had succumbed to a violent end. In an age when psychological assistance was unheard of and grief counselors non-existent, children like Anna were forced to face personal woes and nightmares on their own. The girl that had arrived in Weimar six months earlier had been shaken up, but the same girl that was now clambering into a carriage bound for Dresden was unhinged. She was a damaged little soul, brimming with fear and anguish. Her Uncle August and his wife Anne had graciously agreed to care for the orphan, but Anna already knew that a tough journey lay ahead of her.

---

[20]Braun, p. 2.
[21]Ulbricht, p. 152.
[22]Bruning, p. 120.

Agnes of Hessen's tomb in the Church of St. Peter and Paul in Weimar with its peculiar commemorative plaque. The commissioner of the costly sepulcher remains unknown

The Danish Aunt

In early December 1555 a horse-drawn cart rumbled into the courtyard of the Dresden residence, carrying Anna and her late mother's lady-in-waiting, Sophia von Miltitz and a number of Saxon officials. It was a wrenching homecoming as the princess returned to familiar, but transformed surroundings. Only three years ago, the little duchess had been the flattered daughter of the reigning elector; now she was the orphaned niece of another prince, her Uncle August. Anna was soon to find out that she was no longer the center of attention.

Apparently, she was also frightened. Her mother had often talked of the terrifying Elizabeth, Duchess of Rochlitz, and the girl trembled at the prospect of an encounter with the older woman for however short a time. Her foster parents, however, were no strangers to her; the electoral couple had been frequent guests at the *Residenz* during her father's lifetime, and yet the idea of becoming their ward only increased Anna's unease.[1] The elector's temper was well known as was his wife's unbending strictness.

Her father's testament stipulated that Anna was to live with his brother, although Agnes had wished otherwise.[2] On her deathbed, she had pleaded for her daughter to be raised by her family in Hessen, a request that her father, Landgrave Philip, had ultimately denied.[3] "The child will be in the best of hands in Dresden," Philip determined, and informed his granddaughter that the elector would welcome her into the Wettin household "with fatherly care." "Conduct yourself in a friendly, obedient, and Christian manner towards your new guardian and his wife," he admonished with words that were not merely penned as polite phrases.

Perhaps there were certain character traits of Anna's that worried Philip. She might have been excessively spoiled by her mother or had started to misbehave after her parents' death. Perhaps it was the electress's reputed severity that caused the landgrave some alarm. Whatever the reason, Philip was sufficiently concerned to send one of his envoys to the Saxon capital to check on his granddaughter only weeks after her arrival in Dresden. In mid-February 1556 the emissary returned to Kassel with censored information. The girl had only been allowed to speak in the presence of her maid-of-honor, he reported, but was in good health and professed to be kept in "princely and honest fashion."[4] If she was happy and content with her new situation he was unable to say.

Despite these possibly empty claims, rumors quickly spread that relations between Anna and her aunt, the Electress Anne of Saxony, were less than satisfactory. August's wife had agreed to care for her husband's ward, but had been arrogantly unwelcoming when Anna first arrived in Dresden, still raw with grief. The young duchess's dress was too shabby, and the Danish princess was not willing to let such an oversight pass without immediate correction. Such clothes would not pass muster at her court, she bluntly told the bewildered orphan, because a certain level of neatness was required for all members of Saxony's ruling family and every good Christian. Filled with righteous indignation, Anne even shot off a letter to one of her secretaries, Hans von Ponickau, detailing the inci-

[1]Kruse, "Wilhelm von Oranien," p. 151.
[2]Keller, *Kurfürstin*, p. 199.
[3]Knöfel, *Dynastie*, p. 135.
[4]Kruse, "Wilhelm von Oranien," pp. 11-2.

dent. "After you saw how badly dressed Mademoiselle Anna was, Our Grace kindly ordered to have her fitted for several fine skirts so that she will not bring shame upon Him and us." She was expecting visitors from abroad and the girl had to appear in appropriate fashions, although they were to be less sumptuously tailored as the rest of the family's, of course.[5]

According to common opinion at the time - and the electress paid a good deal of attention to public opinion - a person's true spirit could be discerned by his or her clothes. Tidiness in dress was a sign of good character, disorderly attire signaled the opposite.[6] Nonetheless, the brusque manner with which she addressed the issue reveals the stern side of Anne's character, a character that could be rigid to the point of cruelty.[7] Bluntly outspoken in matters of comportment and etiquette, the electress was known for her pronounced lack of benevolence, especially when dealing with inferiors. Regrettably, this put her on an immediate "war path" with Anna who, though insecure, had the tendency to hide behind a wall of petulance when confronted. Exposed and embarrassed by the tart-tongued older woman, the girl countered her aunt's criticisms with exactly the sort of disobedience that her grandfather had warned against.[8] Over time Anna acquiesced to her elders, but she did so with bad grace. "I am the daughter of the great Elector Maurice," she reminded everyone most hours of the day.

While Anna sulked, the elector and his spouse quickly returned to their many tasks and obligations. August was busy directing government affairs; his wife's hours were filled with the raising of two small children and running the residence's enormous household which housed up to 500 souls, leaving little time to deal with the immature antics of a peevish, ungrateful niece.[9] Besides, as the undisputed mistress of Dresden's godly court, Anne had a reputation to defend: she was a daughter of the first Lutheran monarch in Christendom, King Christian III of Denmark, who had turned Scandinavia into a bastion of Protestantism.[10]

Marital ties between the royal house of Denmark and the Saxon Wettins harked back to the Middles Ages - Christian's own wife, Dorothea, was a Saxon princess - and the Danish king quickly agreed that a match between his daughter and August of Saxony would further Luther's glorious cause. For the groom's family, to be sure, the union was an enormous public relations coup: the fact that a younger son of the Albertines was to be married to a king's daughter was no small feat.[11]

In the spring of 1548 twenty-two-year-old August traveled to the Danish town of Flensborg to meet his bride and announce his engagement.[12] Observers spoke of an immediate affection between the Saxon duke and teenage Anne whose looks corresponded closely to the beauty ideal of the age. A painting by Lucas Cranach the Younger commissioned shortly after her marriage depicts a cool northern beauty: an elegant young woman with a fashionably high forehead, a narrow, slightly bent nose, thin lips, and searching blue eyes that were framed

[5] Karl von Weber. *Anna Churfürstin zu Sachsen* (Leipzig: Bernhard Tauchnitz, 1865), p. 43.
[6] Ozment, *Fathers*, p. 138.
[7] Ulbricht, p. 160.
[8] Kruse, "Wilhelm von Oranien," p. 144.
[9] Lorenz Friedrich Beck. "Residenzbildung und Ausbau des frühzeitlichen Territorialstaates im albertinischen Kursachsen," *Hof und Hofkultur unter Moritz von Sachsen* (Dresden: Sax-Verlag, 2004), pp. 50-2.; Keller, *Kurfürstin*, p. 200.
[10] Ulrike Rückert. "Erstes Reich der Reformation," *GEO Epoche: Martin Luther und die Reformation*, Nr. 39 (Hamburg: Gruner + Jahr, 2009), pp. 88-9.
[11] Jutta Kappel and Claudia Brink. *Mit Fortuna übers Meer* (Munich: Deutscher Kunstverlag, 2009), p. 91. See also Keller, *Kurfürstin*, p. 17, p. 19.
[12] Andrea Lilienthal. *Die Fürstin und die Macht* (Hannover: Verlag Hahnsche Buchhandlung, 2007), p.188.

by just a hint of eyebrows. Despite her youth, the seventeen-year-old exuded some of her famously forbidding reserve, appearing comfortably in control. Observers also commented favorably on Anne's abundance of energy which had already made an impression on August.[13]

Wedding bells rang out in October of that same year, and Maurice organized fabulous revelries for his younger brother at Hartenfels palace. Princess Anne, her mother Queen Dorothea, and an impressive retinue of Danish knights had arrived with 652 horses. Celebrations lasted six days and were attended by a number of illustrious guests, including Margrave Albrecht of Brandenburg-Kulmbach, Maurice's unwitting harbinger of death.[14]

The sophisticated, somewhat haughty bride had brought along a dowry worthy of a king's daughter. Many "skirts of gold brocade, taffeta, and damask" filled her trousseau, along with several barrettes adorned with plumed feathers.[15] Costly belts completed the collection of invaluable, jewel-studded garments which underscored Anne's love of precious stones and luxurious fabrics - a proclivity that would remain her particular passion until death. Extravagant clothing of the kind demanded matching jewelry, and the piece de resistance was a thick neckband containing six gem stones and an abundance of diamonds and pearls.[16] As for the groom, he did not disappoint his fashion-conscious bride. At the nuptial ceremony, August appeared in a silver frock beset with golden flowers.[17]

After the conclusion of the festivities, the no-nonsense princess from Denmark quickly adjusted to her new surroundings. She had been thoroughly coached by her practical mother in wifely duties, and never gave her new husband reason for concern, keeping possible feelings of homesickness well in check. Anne wore traditional German clothes and only kept her "Danish hat" - a lavishly embroidered and bejeweled cap that can be seen in most of her portraits - as a reminder of her Scandinavian heritage.[18] Due to the friendly relations between Denmark and the Wettins, she was able to see her parents and siblings rather frequently. The newlyweds travelled north in February 1550, and repeated such visits about every two years.[19]

During the first years of their marriage, August and Anne lived at Weissenfels palace and later Wolkenstein, where August's officious mother Catherine resided as a dowager.[20] It appears that Anne humbly submitted to the older woman's cantankerous rule. Perhaps Catherine showed some deference to her illustrious young daughter-in-law, or their personalities simply meshed agreeably for the two ladies frequently exchanged letters and gifts. On one occasion, Anne presented her mother-in-law with a monkey.[21]

Her decided knack for managing difficult personalities stood the young duchess in good stead, for August, like his mother, was well known for his violent outbursts of temper. Servants and officials feared the duke, and even friends took care not to offend him as he was known to nurse lifelong grudges. Over time, Anne developed the wherewithal to manage her irascible spouse. A friend of the

---

[13]Fellmann, Walter. *Prinzessinnen* (Leipzig: LKG, 1996), p. 11.
[14]Keller, *Kurfürstin*, pp. 22-3.
[15]Keller, *Kurfürstin*, p. 49.
[16]Fellmann, p. 19.
[17]Kappel and Brink, pp. 91-2.
[18]Fellmann, p. 18.
[19]Keller, *Kurfürstin*, p. 27.
[20]Keller, *Kurfürstin*, pp. 27-8.
[21]Ulbricht, p. 123.

couple noted after her death that "when he was angry, she knew how to calm him, when he was sulking, she knew how to handle him, and during tough times, she knew how to cheer him up."[22] "Woman has to please man" was Anne's motto for a felicitous conjugal life, and throughout her thirty-seven-year marriage, she labored tirelessly as her husband's devoted companion and helpmate.[23]

Her efforts were mostly repaid in kind. August was grateful and proud of his dutiful consort who always put him first in her affections. In one instance, she nursed him back to health after a bad attack of gout, although she had just given birth. Anne also put up with the elector's countless hunting expeditions, and personally supervised the washing of his underwear.[24] Unwilling to spend any time apart from him, she even insisted on shared sleeping quarters during their travels.[25] "They had truly been one heart and one soul," court preacher Dr. Martin Mirus commented during Anne's funeral oration.[26]

In addition to their successful private lives, August and his consort easily adapted to the glare of the public limelight as Saxony's first couple. Life on the world stage suited them well and was in any case nothing new for Anne, a king's daughter. Unlike his reckless brother Maurice, the new elector stayed out of foolhardy foreign adventures and limited his ambitions to the ancestral Wettin lands. Throughout his reign, he remained politically risk averse and, as a thorough pragmatist, devoted most of his time to keeping the Habsburgs content.[27] This sensible course of action would stand him in good stead and assured his primacy among Germany's princes.

Electress Anne, on the other hand, opted to keep out of the male preserve of politics as custom and religion demanded. Those issues were "above her," she claimed, thereby following Luther's injunction on female participation in men's affairs. "The wives of the greatest lords, such as kings and princes, take no part in governance, but alone the husbands," the famous reformer had once proclaimed.[28] Instead, the electress found indirect methods to assist her spouse: she dispensed advice to allies and friends, and, as a member of the Danish royal family, signed her letters "of Royal Danish Blood."[29] This imbued her missives with an extra bit of clout when addressing foreign potentates. On an ornate wooden desk embellished with precious inlay work that can still be admired in Dresden today, the princess transacted her copious correspondence. She penned some 25,000 letters during her lifetime - many to her father and brother requesting support for Saxony. [30]

While the electress never grew any political wings, she received the elector's full backing for her slightly atypical, semi-private pursuits. A practical woman who thought nothing of getting her hands dirty, Anne invited stares of disbelief when she busied herself in kitchen and garden. She preserved cherries and other fruit, made a sugary red currant wine, and came up with a new broiling method for meat which the emperor patented for her.[31] While experimenting, she dis-

[22]Fellmann, p. 14.
[23]Fellmann, p. 14.
[24]Katrin Keller. "Kurfürstin Anna von Sachsen (1532-1585): Von Möglichkeiten und Grenzen einer 'Landesmutter,'" *Das Frauenzimmer* (Stuttgart: Jan Thorbecke, 2000), pp. 265-6.
[25]Rankin, p. 16, p. 30.
[26]Fellmann, p. 14.
[27]Bruning, pp.118-21.
[28]Susan C. Karant-Nunn and Merry E. Wiesner-Hanks. *Luther on Women* (Cambridge: Cambridge University Press, 2003), p. 31.
[29]Keller, *Landesmutter*, p.278, p. 280.
[30]Kappel and Brink, p. 91.
[31]Fellmann, p. 20.

covered novel procedures for dairy production and cattle cultivation. Her "common," hands-on manner elicited negative commentary at times. A woman from Sangerhausen near Leipzig had to appear in court for saying that "The electress was running around in barns, made butter and cheese for sale, and was therefore called the 'Danish cheese mother'." And the Duke of Liegnitz snidely claimed that Anne traded in apples and pears. The elector would not stand for such gossip and had the duke placed under house arrest until he apologized.[32] Over time, the uproar over the electress's "low-born" hobbies died down. Neighboring courts sent their cooks to Dresden for training, and fellow aristocrats asked for her recipes.

Her culinary proficiency, however, was nothing to the renown Anne gained in the field of healing. Noblewomen were expected to know enough of medicine to provide basic medical care for their subjects, and the electress was at the forefront of these developments. She assisted courtiers, servants, and the poor with their ailments, and only called on learned physicians when serious illness arose. Her rapidly developing expertise soon earned her a European reputation as a knowledgeable health practitioner. To this day, thousands of letters have survived from both noble and common supplicants, asking for advice and remedies. In the 1560s, Empress Maria was Anne's highest ranking client. The imperial patient requested an antidote for poison on one occasion, a tonic for her bouts of dizziness on another. The electress was only too happy to oblige. She knew that she could curry favor with the Habsburgs by means of her own, "medical diplomacy."[33]

The trademark "cure" of this "excellent [female] doctor" was Anne's yellow and white aqua vitae, an alcoholic strengthening tonic that required a mind-boggling 387 ingredients and two years of labor.[34] Concocted from heavy white wine, eggs, sugar, and brandy, and further refined with a multitude of herbs, the tincture had the consistency of a liqueur.[35] Contemporaries praised it as a veritable panacea, and Saxon messengers delivered hundreds of jars of these herbal-infused, distilled waters to friendly families and acquaintances, especially as New Year's gifts.[36]

While his wife fermented heady draughts and tinctures, founded an apothecary, and raised a steadily growing number of children, August had just as many interests to fill his leisure time. He shared his wife's predilection for gardening and even published a small manual on growing fruit trees in 1571. But his real passion was the sciences. An expert mathematician and amateur land surveyor, he was fascinated with technical equipment such as clocks, pedometers, and odometers.[37]

And like all great Renaissance princes, the elector dabbled in alchemy. This ancient tradition centered on the quest for the so-called arcanum, a search that was almost as old as civilization itself. Its goal was to unlock the secret formula for the "philosopher's stone," a mysterious substance believed to possess

---

[32]Keller, *Landesmutter*, p. 270.
[33]Rankin, p. 39.
[34]Rankin, pp. 28-9.
[35]Ulbricht, p. 176.
[36]Rankin, pp. 34-5. As her reputation grew, Anne's husband had one of his hunting lodges torn down and replaced by a new, expanded palace aptly called *Annaburg* (Anne's Castle). The grounds contained a large distillery for her medical experiments as well as an extensive herbal garden. Here the electress could tinker to her heart's content, surrounded by a myriad of philters and mixtures, while overseeing the aqua vitae's brewing process. An elaborately staged, extremely time-consuming production, the recipe for white aqua vitae stretched over fifteen pages. Whether the concoction had any real health benefits is uncertain.
[37]Rankin, p. 32

the power to turn base metal into gold and make men immortal. For that, one had to decode the baffling writings of ancient philosophers who, it was believed, had once held the key to these mysteries. Alchemists therefore involved themselves not only with the mixing of chemical compounds, but also attempted to decipher and understand the teachings of the ancients. Their spidery scripts and mysterious diagrams spoke of ruby lions, black ravens, lily virgins, and golden mantles. Their ingredients - amalgamations of horse dung, children's urine, sulfur, mercury, and arsenic - were given deliberately obscure symbolic names, written in equally esoteric language for reasons of secrecy.[38]

A court like August's always had an alchemist in its employ as greedy princes hoped to increase their already abundant wealth by a thousand fold. Naturally, these credulous potentates often became victims of their own voracity, easy game for the numerous charlatans and tricksters who toured Europe's palaces, trying to dupe rich men into parting with real gold by means of little more than a promise that they could repay such investment. The costs of those found guilty of such sharp practices were consequently high: the penalty was likely to involve rough interrogation, torture, and ignominious death, usually on a gallows decorated with gold tinsel.[39]

Lured by the prospect of never-ending riches, Saxony's electoral couple financed their own wizard - one Daniel Bachmann, who passed himself off as a "gold maker and alchemist from London." Like the miller's daughter in Rumpelstilskin, this "gold maker" promised to "spin straw into precious metal," and upon failing, promptly landed in prison. His patron, a man not exactly known for his endless reservoir of bonhomie, subsequently received a number of pleading letters from Bachmann and his wife.[40] It is probably safe to say that those pleas went unheard.

But it was not only gold that failed to sprout in Dresden. August and Anne's seemingly charmed life with its many professional successes was continually haunted by death. Most of their children died young, and out of a proud brood of fifteen, the elector and his Danish princess saw only four children - three daughters and the longed for heir, Christian - reach maturity. Outwardly unemotional, the electress bore every funeral with well-practiced Christian stoicism. The ways of the Almighty were unfathomable and death was a puzzling, random, and inscrutable cross that high and low bore alike and in equal measure, she probably thought. Anne had no illusions about her own mortality and carefully set out her burial shrouds before each confinement in the expectation of leaving August a widower.[41] In private, of course, even the electress went through moments of profound desperation. After her favorite, little three-year-old Marie, died shortly after her much mourned brother Alexander (1554-1565), Anne wrote to her mother Dorothea, hopeful that God would dry the "tears on my heart."[42]

Regrettably, Anne displayed little empathy with the household's newest arrival, the orphaned, grief-stricken Anna who labored greatly under the loss of her parents. Perhaps her soul was constricted by her own private sorrows - the electress had already buried two children by 1555 - and was therefore unable to

---

[38]Janet Gleeson. *The Arcanum* (New York: Bantam Books, 1999), p. 7.
[39]Gleeson, p. ix, pp. 7-8.
[40]Watanabe-O'Kelly, p.115.
[41]Kruse, "Wilhelm von Oranien," p. 144.
[42]Keller, *Kurfürstin*, pp. 36-7.

comfort her husband's niece. By and large, her unresponsiveness to Anna's needs was not uncommon. At the time, even the most well-meaning parents stood help-less when children asked those unanswerable questions about death. Mothers and fathers usually replied with standard phrases that often brought more harm than solace. When a five-year-old from Cologne sought a reason for losing his two sisters to the plague, his parents told him that God "sometimes tempt[s] his friends whom he really love[s]" by letting them suffer. The confused youngster replied, "There is no love in this for me; this is pure torment."[43]

Anna might have voiced comparable protests about the unfairness of her parents' death, complaints the busy Electress had neither the time nor the incli-nation to confront. By nature, she was rather unflappable, and personal feelings rarely got the better of her. Few of her letters betray any sentiment, except when she found herself on the cusp of a medical discovery such as a treatment for "fall-ing sickness" (epilepsy).[44]

By comparison, young Anna was the polar opposite. Believing herself unfairly abandoned and neglected, she lashed out with displays of petulance and recurring temper tantrums. This in turn was behavior that the resolute electress would not excuse under any circumstances.[45] Anna better carry on calmly as befit a Christian princess, she warned, because life for bad-tempered members of the Dresden court was neither easy nor pleasant.

Tensions between aunt and niece did not slacken off in the following years, and with their contrasting, but equally hard-headed personalities, the two Anns clashed with tragic regularity. The younger resented the older woman's controlled formality while the Danish princess despised her ward's utter lack of self-control. Because of the electress's position and age, it was an unequal battle of wills, a protracted domestic combat during which Anna never gained the upper hand. On more than one occasion the electoral couple reacted to Anna's outbursts with harshness, sometimes even cruelty.[46]

Per instructions of her elders, Anna was to be taught obedience by a maid-of-honor and lady-in-waiting who were permitted to issue reprimands and phys-ical punishments if their charge demurred in any way, as was common practice in the sixteenth century.[47] Society always expected a high degree of conformity from its youth, but the first wave of Protestantism reinforced a severity towards children that had not been advocated since antiquity. A newfound sense of piety emphasized filial obedience, and Martin Luther once famously said that he would sooner have his son dead than ill-bred.[48]

According to the electress and her many of her contemporaries, a child was not a real human by birthright, but a creature that had to be pressed and formed into an upstanding Christian by whatever means available. She viewed Anna as the best example of how inherent selfishness and savagery always threat-

---

[43]Ozment, *Fathers*, p. 128.
[44]Rankin, p. 23, p. 39. Anne's "cure" gives us a revealing glimpse into Renaissance medicine which was suffused with superstition. In a letter to a friend, the Abbess Margaret of Watzdorf, the electress gave detailed instructions regarding a new remedy for "falling sickness" or epilepsy. "We have just been informed of a certain and necessary art," she wrote, "for which one requires the caul that is on the foal of a horse or donkey when it comes out of its mother, which one must gather immediately, before the mother gobbles it up." Cauls, part of the amniotic membrane occasionally found on the heads of humans and animals at birth, were said to possess certain magical and medicinal properties.
[45]Keller, *Kurfürstin*, p. 200.
[46]Ulbricht, p. 160
[47]Kruse, "Wilhelm von Oranien," p. 12.
[48]Ozment, *Fathers*, p. 167.

ens to gain the upper hand.[49] Chroniclers at the Dresden court failed to record any episodes detailing specific wrongdoings of Anna's towards her caregivers, but the pair's comments regarding "stubbornness" among their own children allow certain conclusions.

As typical upper-class parents of their time, August and Anne were strict disciplinarians. The electress modeled the raising of her sons and daughters after the teachings of the biblical scribe Jesus Sirach who had advocated the breaking of a child's will at the earliest possible opportunity, possibly by means of the rod. Youngsters should be willing to submit to their elders in every situation for it was only through strictness that children would behave "honorably." On one occasion, Anne left instructions for her daughters' ladies while she and August travelled to a royal election in Regensburg. The rod should not to be spared if little Anna misbehaved, she wrote, or Lady Dorothea fell into her "harsh, quick speech again." In her absence, the girls should busy themselves with Christian thoughts and sewing.

Directives like these did not cease upon marriage. After Anne's eldest daughter Elizabeth wed a younger son of the Elector Palatine, the electress continued to intervene in the young woman's personal life upon receiving word of obstinate behavior. "You may threaten Her Grace [Elizabeth], if she does not listen to you," she wrote to the young woman's maid-of-honor,"… and you may let us know, because undoubtedly we would not take pleasure in this and we [would not] allow her to exercise her own will." Such parenting was considered successful. In 1575 Empress Maria praised Anne for her well-mannered daughters, and members of the aristocracy frequently sent their offspring to Dresden for proper training.[50]

Filial subservience to parental dictates was custom in other parts of Europe as well. In England, even as adults, children remained kneeling or standing in the presence of their elders. "Gentlemen of thirty and forty years old," recalled the Englishman John Aubrey, "were to stand like mutes and fools bareheaded before their parents; and the daughters - grown women - were to stand at the cupboard side during the whole time of their proud mother's visit, unless, as a fashion was, leave was desired, forsooth, that a cushion should be given to them to kneel upon … after they had done sufficient penance in standing."[51]

Although caregivers usually meant well, children clearly suffered from "severe correction" such as regular beatings. As a grown man, the English aristocrat Thomas Raymond reflected with sadness on his father's "choler" of which he bore the brunt as a boy. "[It] was a great mischief unto me, being of a soft and timorous complexion,"[52] he wrote many years later. Voices of dissent were also heard from Dresden where a noble boarder, John of Mecklenburg-Schwerin, bemoaned the rigorous, joyless routine at the electoral residence. He griped in 1578 that he might as well have been put in a monastery.[53]

In the unlikely event of someone questioning the electress' strictness, she would have curtly replied that grave responsibilities rested upon her own as well as her husband's shoulders. Hers was no dissipated Renaissance court where de-

[49]Ozment, *Fathers*, pp. 137-8.
[50]Keller, *Kurfürstin*, p. 41.
[51] Lawrence Stone. *The Family, Sex and Marriage in England 1500-1800* (New York: Harper Torchbooks, 1977), p. 122.
[52]Stone, pp. 120-1.
[53]Keller, *Kurfürstin*, pp. 39-41.

praved rakes seduced precocious chamber maids and impregnated flirtatious ladies-in-waiting, but an abode where sin had no place. As the living embodiment
of Luther's vision of princely Christian rule, the couple considered themselves
not only the guardians of Reformation morals, but role models for their subjects.[54]
The uncompromising Anne once fired a female cook for diverse "offensiveness"
and then alerted the mayoralty of Freiberg to refuse the miscreant entry into the
city for a full two years. In addition, the woman's sister, who was in the local hospital, was also removed.[55]

As Anne swept through palace corridors in her extravagant outfits, she
barked orders, reprimanded, and directed. A tireless worker and overly demanding employer, the electress exhausted those around her with her boundless energy. If the help groaned under her merciless glare, her ladies-in-waiting did not
fare much better. At the time, many daughters of Saxony's nobility came to Dresden in the hope of acquiring a certain courtly polish. Although lacking the ele-
gance of the Vienna, Prague, and Munich residences, the elector's court was one
of the most glamorous in the Holy Roman Empire.[56] Young women, who looked
forward to conversations with genteel courtiers, formal dances, and other frothy
diversions, were quickly disabused of such notions by their severe taskmistress.
Anne made it abundantly clear that idlers and loafers had no place in her household, and exquisite ritual certainly took a backseat to domestic practicality.[57] If
anyone thought such activities beneath her, the electress had a ready reply. Her
own mother Dorothea had taught her spinning and housework, and if such work
befitted the reigning queen of Denmark, it was obviously right and proper for the
Saxon gentry.

Anna chafed greatly under this tightly controlled regime of her aunt's.
She was fragile, socially awkward, and filled with a pronounced independent
streak, yet forced to spend long, unhappy days in the women's quarters on the
third floor and remotest part of the palace. Notes by her uncle point to iron-fisted
household ordinances regulating every detail of daily life. Frivolousness, suggestive behavior or any lighthearted activities common at other courts had no place
in Dresden, where ladies busied themselves with "honest" female activities such
as spinning, lace making and thrice daily "praying hours."[58]

The thinking went that women, specifically unformed creatures like
Anna, were always susceptible to sexual temptation and had to be isolated from
the roués and cavaliers abundant at princely residences.[59] The electress thus kept
careful watch over "our little nation," "our young pile" by requesting daily reports about behavioral misconduct.[60] In the hunting lodge Augustusburg, her
daunting likeness stood vigil in the form of a painting below the ceiling "as if she
was looking down to see if everyone was behaving in her chambers."[61]

Unlike the Middle Ages, a time when the sexes had mingled quite freely,
young ladies rarely talked to gentlemen during Anna's time. A hundred years
prior, the main meals of the day were still taken together in the banqueting hall,
but by the turn of the century, new dictates on suitable conduct put a halt to these

---

[54]Watanabe, p. 238. Keller, *Landesmutter*, pp. 268-9.
[55]Keller, *Kurfürstin*, p. 114.
[56]Keller, *Kurfürstin*, pp. 68-9.
[57]Fellmann, p. 20.
[58]Keller, *Kurfürstin*, p. 16.
[59]Paul-Joachim Heinig. "'Umb merer zucht und ordnung willen,'" *Das Frauenzimmer* (Stuttgart: Jan Thorbecke, 2000), p. 314.
[60]Ulbricht, p. 160.
[61]Keller, *Kurfürstin*, p. 55

often lively gatherings. Separate dining rooms and tables had become the norm, and young noblemen were rarely permitted to sup with women, except on special occasions.

Herded together, Anna and her ladies spent their days segregated from the rest of the bustling residence. Once the electress entered the chambers, the women were no longer allowed to change their seating or standing position without express permission, nor could they walk freely about the room.[62] If an occasion arose to leave the women's floor, Anna's aunt admonished her charges to never venture through palace corridors unchaperoned, especially up and down the long, winding stairs lest they be intercepted by a brazen gentleman. But such "outings" should in any case be avoided, for it was preferable to send pages to run one's errands.[63] The same strict rules applied for excursions, such as drives to church, hunts, or a visit to the gardens. Ladies-in-waiting were never to be separated from each other, but seated according to rank, always watched by the electress or her maid-of-honor. And lastly, there was no running, for "He that hasteth with his feet sinneth" (Proverbs 19:2).[64]

At least once a day the electress sallied into Anna's chambers to collect her ladies for chapel.[65] The women were usually clad in demure black bonnets and somber robes with some yellow decoration, the old Wettin colors.[66] In addition to these church visits, Anna also received a thorough grounding in the Bible during private lessons. Since Saxony was the birthplace of the Reformation, the Electress liked to remind her court of their pious forbears' illustrious heritage. In later life, Anna's letters teemed with religious quotations, an indication of her thorough knowledge of Holy Scripture which she probably acquired through her aunt's prodding.[67] Much like her father Maurice, the princess practiced her faith purely in the conventional sense. If she cited Bible verses, it was to make a point rather than express religious sentiment. Besides, Anna found no appeal in the electress' joyless version of the Lutheran faith which curtailed any budding levity and pleasure.[68] Danish Anne, in turn, despaired of her niece. The girl's nonconformity was confounding, she bristled, wondering how a husband would deal with such baseness of character.

If Anna resented her aunt's religiously driven austerity, there was another put-down that grated and festered. As the only child of the late Elector Maurice, the princess still occupied a certain status at court which she insisted on being openly acknowledged. As was tradition, she had been accorded her own little household with serving personnel and a maid-of-honor. However, the electress had not assigned her an aristocratic household manager, but a woman of common extraction, the widow Barbara Spet.[69] This was a blatant affront, a figurative slap in the face that expressed Anna's inferiority of rank in her aunt's estimation.[70]

A maid-of-honor - usually a widow of a certain age - was responsible for the health and well-being of her charge, managed her public schedule as well as

[62]Stephan Heinig. "Bauliche Gestalt und Lage von Frauenwohnräumen in deutschen Residenzschlössern des späten 15. und 16. Jahrhunderts," *Das Frauenzimmer* (Stuttgart: Jan Thorbecke, 2000), p. 166, p. 168. See also Kircher-Kannemann, Anja. "Organisation der Frauenzimmer im Vergleich zu männlichen Höfen," *Das Frauenzimmer* (Stuttgart: Jan Thorbecke, 2000), pp. 241-3.
[63]Hoppe, p. 166, p. 168. Kircher-Kannemann, pp. 241-3.
[64]Heinig, p. 317.
[65]Kircher-Kannemann, p. 244
[66]Keller, *Kurfürstin*, pp. 43-4.
[67]Kruse, "Wilhelm von Oranien," p. 11.
[68]Wartenberg, p. 83.
[69]Böttcher, p. 42.
[70]Wartenberg, p. 80.

her belongings. An authority on etiquette and ceremony, she was also expected to be a model of Christian virtue.[71] Even more important, the qualifier "of honor" in her title signified her function at the palace. It was understood that this companion had been engaged to bring Anna honor which required that she be of "honorable," meaning, noble blood.[72]

Despite such frustrations, life at the prosperous Dresden court certainly had its highlights, even for Anna. Since the Reformation, exchange of presents on December 25 had become common in Lutheran lands and the electoral couple gave generously to their children, and probably their niece as well. For example, on Christmas 1565 the electress' daughters Marie and Dorothea received English puppies. A few years later, Anne had dolls dressed in traditional Meissen costume and in 1573 the Princesses Dorothea and Anne rejoiced over a mock kitchen. Some gifts, however, were of a more serious, edifying nature. In addition to their toys, the elector's offspring found prayer books and rods among their presents.[73] The latter served as a reminder that punishment awaited the pig-headed like Anna, even on holy days.

In addition to splendid holiday celebrations, members of Dresden's *Residenz* also enjoyed a variety of regular afternoon and evening entertainments. Jesters lightened the mood during meals, but also diverted the ladies in their quarters. Like many princesses of her time, the electress had a passion for keeping female dwarves about her. These women often served as fools, but were usually proficient in other arts such as singing, dancing, or acting. Wandering theatrical companies frequently performed at August's palaces, since court theaters had not yet come into existence. Around 1580 English actors arrived in Saxony for the first time. The elector's household officials also organized balls and splendid carnival celebrations with revelers clad in costly disguises.[74]

No recorded information indicates whether Anna enjoyed any of these events with a companion of her age. Instead it seems that she never grew close to anyone in Dresden as her difficult character was unfortunately not conducive to making friends, or keeping them. No mention was ever made of a trusted confidante among her aunt's younger ladies, nor was there a maid-of-honor who acted as a motherly adviser and consulted with Anna after one of her frequent arguments with the electress.

The ordeal of her parents' death might have contributed to Anna's inability to form any viable relationships, a failure that would haunt her throughout her life and was perhaps aggravated by her stepparents' harsh tutelage. The cold, bigoted environment in Dresden left little room for tenderness for a teenager who obviously struggled with a multitude of issues. In the privacy of her bedchamber, Anna raged and seethed, while courtiers smirked about her antics.

As the years dragged along with the seasons, the princess gained a reputation as the resident oddball, an unquiet soul unable to find her niche, and equally unable to adapt to her patron's regime. At times, Anna turned aggressive

---

[71]Kircher-Kannemann, p. 240.
[72] Anna-Maris Münster. "Funktionen der dames et damoiselles d'honneur im Gefolge französischer Königinnen und Herzoginnen (14.-15. Jahrhundert)," *Das Frauenzimmer* (Stuttgart: Jan Thorbecke, 2000), p. 343. By selecting a commoner for her niece's chambers, the Electress preempted any of the young woman's fanciful notions regarding her standing at court. Anna's father Maurice was dead and despite his great deeds, her choice implied, Elector August and his progeny were the new rulers of Saxony. The elector was already showing Anna great kindness, but as far as the orphan's position was concerned, it was clearly below that of his children.
[73]Keller, *Kurfürstin*, pp. 38-40.
[74]Keller, *Kurfürstin*, p. 44, pp. 59-60.

and confrontational, only to have her small acts of rebellion quickly snuffed out by the towering Electress, her equally terrifying husband, and the rod.

If the elector was indifferent to Anna's emotional well-being, her relations did not neglect their ward's education. Although contemporary sources keep silent about the girl's curriculum and teachers, adult letters written in Anna's own hand show a certain flourish and skill in penmanship as well as verbal expression. Information regarding her schooling can also be gleaned from sources describing the elector's daughters' studies. Their primary subject was of course religion, but the princesses also learned to read and write, along with adding, subtracting, and sewing. Newfangled subjects such as languages, literature, music and dance - mainstays at worldlier courts - are not mentioned.[75] Anna, for example, did not know how to dance the gaillard, the most popular dance of the time.

While Anna learned French after her marriage, her writing proficiency was a product of the Dresden schoolroom. The elector and his wife could not be described as intellectual innovators, but they were an extremely cultured pair. August had no qualms about educated females under his roof, and encouraged his spouse in her time-consuming laboratory experiments. It therefore stands to reason that even their somewhat neglected charge received a smattering of scholarly training.

Luckily for Anna, her upbringing fell into that very brief period lasting from about 1520 to roughly 1560 when humanists like Juan Luis de Vives, Erasmus of Rotterdam, and Sir Thomas More actively championed a classical education for women. As a result of this influence, for a short time there was a small group of well-read ladies who could hold their own among male academics. Lady Jane Grey and Queen Elizabeth in England, Marguerite of Valois and Marguerite of Navarre in France, are well known examples of this brief flowering that sadly reached its swan song by the end of the century.[76]

Although the "two Saxon Anns" could not hold a candle to a true scholar and bibliophile like Queen Elizabeth, they enjoyed the freedom to study and learn within accepted parameters. As her aunt dabbled in hands-on research, Anna developed a passion for reading. August was a keen collector of books, pricey luxury items that he had carefully bound in calf leather and which he purchased at a rate of about one hundred copies per year. If allowed, Anna had the choice of a variety of topics ranging from theology and history to works on warfare, horsemanship, and medicine. The electress had her own athenaeum, which was of course heavy on medicinal and pharmaceutical tracts as well as Lutheran devotional works.

Judging from Anna's taste in later years, we can assume that the young girl would have tended more toward August's sets of early prose fiction. Novels of knightly exploits complemented a long list of romances such as *Magelona, Lewfried,* and *Melusina* as well as a translation of the hugely popular *Amadis de Gaul,* a bestseller that would later play a role in Anna's turbulent married life.[77] In her youth, these forbidden tales might have been one of the few sources of cheer for Anna. Or in the words of another unhappy princess, they were her "dead counselors and comforters."[78]

---

[75]Keller, *Kurfürstin*, p. 40.
[76]Stone, pp. 142-3.
[77]Watanabe, pp. 85-88.
[78]Gristwood, Sarah. *Arbella: England's Lost Queen* (New York: Houghton Mifflin, 2003), p. 49.

Electress Anne of Saxony (1532-1585), a king's daughter and Anna's "bitterest enemy" by Lucas Cranach the Younger, around 1549

"Better Looking than in Real Life"

Sometime in 1558, after years of debilitating quarrels between the Electress and her orphaned charge, a collective sigh of relief swept through the halls of the Dresden palace: a suitor had expressed interest in Anna. A pre-existing agreement between the girl's grandfather, Philip of Hessen, and the elector stipulated that Maurice's daughter must not be given in marriage before her fifteenth birthday and that both parties had to concur on either's choice of partner for the young duchess, but the Elector decided to ignore the contract. The faster she was off his hands the better, he hoped, and warmly welcomed an envoy sent by the Swedish King, Gustav I Vasa. The diplomat was to evaluate the princess as a possible bridal candidate for the king's son, crown prince Eric.[1]

This would not be the first union between the House of Saxony and the Vasas as Gustav had been unhappily married to the electress' aunt, Catherine of Saxe-Lauenburg. Now the indebted Swedish monarch proposed another Wettin match to replenish his chronically depleted treasury. News of Saxony's wealth had spread to Scandinavia and Anna's dowry was said to be enormous. The Swedish emissary duly observed the young duchess and departed soon after for Stockholm, portrait in hand. His master, the crown prince, had demanded a likeness and was known to be fastidious.

Anna's image failed to ignite a romantic spark, but Eric was aware of her "market value" and remained open to further discussions. If she could travel to Stockholm with a relative and agree to a personal inspection, he condescendingly declared, the princess could still warrant consideration for future Queen of Sweden. Indeed, Anna was only one of many candidates vying for the position. It was said that Landgrave Philip's daughter Christine was already travelling north, prompting Anna's grandmother Catherine to declare that she would undertake the trip with her granddaughter. But August declined, infuriated by the Swedes' presumption.[2] A proposal of the sort was clearly "beneath the dignity of [any member of] the House of Wettin," he blustered, especially since the Vasa were such a recent, upstart dynasty.[3]

The Swedish prince's request, although unusual, was not completely unheard of, since putting one's trust in portrait art entailed a certain risk. German painters had a reputation for mediocrity, while the French corrected many of nature's injustices with a fine stroke of the paintbrush.[4] Ultimately, of course, neither the flattery of the canvas nor unreliable diplomatic accounts could serve as an adequate replacement for a personal encounter, establishing the possibility of affection or loathing within minutes. When Henry VIII of England received the names and descriptions of five prospective marital candidates from the King of France, he replied nervously, "By God, I trust no one but myself. The thing touches me too near. I wish to see them and know them some time before deciding." To which the French king primly replied, "It is not the custom in France to send damsels of that rank and of such noble and princely families to be passed in review as if they were hackneys [whores] for sale."[5]

---

[1] Kruse, "Wilhelm von Oranien," p. 13.
[2] Knöfel, *Dynastie*, pp. 133-4.
[3] Kruse, "Wilhelm von Oranien,"p. 14.
[4] Dirk van der Cruysse. *Madame sein ist ein ellendes Handwerck* (Munich: Serie Piper, 1995), p. 110.
[5] Eleanor Herman. *Sex with Kings* (New York: Harper Collins, 2004), p. 14.

In Anna's case, the Scandinavian match did not falter because of Eric's clumsy courting efforts or the unfortunate rendering of Anna's features, but rather the simmering tensions between Sweden and Denmark, the electress' native country. King Gustav and his son subsequently transferred their bridal search to British shores where Eric failed to impress the gamophobic Elizabeth of England. He was forced to switch his "great love" to Mary, Queen of Scots, and after another vain attempt at securing a foreign consort, eventually found conjugal felicity in his homeland. There, in an act signaling true regard, Eric married his long-time mistress, Karin Mansdotter, the low-born daughter of a soldier, whom he had officially crowned as queen. His controversial choice eventually cost him the throne and led to his removal from power by the Swedish nobles in 1569.[6] By that time, Anna was long married and had forgotten about the capricious prince. Yet in the immediate aftermath of his rebuff, the sting of rejection must have smarted. In the months that followed, the landgrave suggested several other candidates for his granddaughter, among them a son of the Elector Palatine, but August refused every potential suitor.[7] Perhaps he was loath to marry Anna to any of his German allies, already fearing marital disaster.

When a cavalier to her uncle's liking finally arrived, Anna had become acutely aware of her deficiencies in both personality and looks. She was old enough to understand that her plainness and headstrong character repelled potential husbands, and that she was the heiress to her father's willfulness, arrogance, and extreme volatility.[8] In a society that heavily emphasized female gentleness and docility, this was an unfortunate legacy indeed.

*****

At almost sixteen, Anna was a wide-eyed teenager of "awkward build" with light, curly hair.[9] Witnesses were vague about the nature of Anna's "deformity," and speculations have ranged from uneven shoulders to curvature of the spine to a limp.[10] In the early modern era only a relatively small percentage of the adult population was both healthy and attractive at any given time, quite apart from the normal features of body odor and dirt. Both sexes suffered long periods of crippling illness, which incapacitated them for months, even years. Bad breath from rotting teeth was a minor complaint compared to the disfiguring specters of suppurating ulcers, eczema, scabs, running sores, and other nauseating skin diseases that were extremely common at the time, and often chronic.[11]

Among the nobility, the absence of proper medical care coupled with constant inbreeding produced a horror chamber of congenital defects and infectious disease. Powders, padding, and brocade were artificial remedies for nature's neglect, but even they could not hide the pervasive physical decrepitude among Europe's elite. Princes, like Anna's maternal great-grandfather William II

---

[6]Dunn, p. 26. See also Ulrich Schuppener. "Das Hochzeitslied zur Trauung Wilhelms von Oranien mit Anna von Sachsen und seine Vorgeschichte," *Nassauische Annalen,* Band 188, (2007), pp. 219-21.
[7]Knöfel, *Dynastie,* pp. 133-4.
[8]Keller, *Kurfürstin,* p. 200.
[9]Kruse, "Wilhelm von Oranien," p. 13.
[10]Weber, p. 427. Weber mentions, without giving a date, that the electress had sought help for her daughter Anna's back problems. As a toddler, Anna's back had been "shifted" by a nanny, resulting in a crooked spine that could not be mended. The nanny concealed the incident from the princess's parents and nobody noticed the injury until Anna reached her third year. Unfortunately, Weber does not specify whether he is referring to the daughter of Electress Agnes or Electress Anne, both named Anna. It might have been the former, since Anna's grandfather, Landgrave Philip, wrote of her "awkward built" which could not be straightened despite strenuous efforts.
[11]Stone, p. 306.

of Hessen, often died young, their insides rotting from syphilis and over-eating. At the court of Louis XIV of France - more than a century after Anna's time - the acid-tongued Duke de Saint-Simon (1675 - 1755) drew a ghoulish list of Versailles' malformed players. According to Saint-Simon, the king's heir, Louis of Burgundy, had a spine shaped like a pretzel and an abnormally protruding upper jaw. Henri-Jules, Prince de Condé "was a hunchback with pungent armpits whose trail could be picked up from a distance," while his father was a tiny man with an unusually large head and a "livid yellow complexion." There was also the Duke de Vendome, who lost his nose after submitting to the hazardous mercury cure for syphilis, and the young Duchess of Burgundy, who only had a few teeth left, "all of them rotten." She also sported a long neck with a goiter "which rather suited her." To be beautiful in the early modern age, it was enough not to be misshapen.[12]

The extent of Anna's physical complaints is not known due to lack of information, but it is telling that chroniclers failed to include even the standard phrases of "possessing fine hands," "fresh-faced" or "beautiful eyes" when alluding to the Saxon princess. Traditionally, such platitudes were accorded to even the plainest of ladies as a measure of politeness.

Yet the Renaissance was also a time when a pleasing female countenance mattered to the wealthy; perhaps even more so than in today's beauty obsessed age. Few people were willing to look beyond a woman's physical exterior for potentially delightful qualities of the mind, and among the elite, parents considered a beautiful face the most important requisite for their daughters. The potentially disfiguring disease of smallpox greatly alarmed mothers with girls whose chances in marriage so depended on their looks.[13]

If the premier task of a princess was the bearing of sons, her second duty was decorative. As a handsome ornament adorning her husband's court, a comely wife brought renown to king and country as well as honor and fame to her own family with her face and figure. Monarchs and princes asked for attractive women at their side, not only for personal gratification, but to demonstrate to their subjects that in addition to the most glittering palaces, fastest horses, and most powerful armies, they also possessed the finest-looking consorts.[14] Even Anna's austere but attractive aunt, Electress Anne, was not averse to applying make-up to please her husband and created her own lotions to keep her delicate hands smooth and supple.[15] Her niece, however, knew that even in youth, she would never be able to play this particular female trump card.

In their search for the perfect princess - rich, beautiful, and obedient - the nobility dispatched "marital scouts" like the Swedish envoy to view and evaluate prospective brides. These emissaries examined young girls like cattle during a market fair and subjected them to degrading "inspections." Diplomats reported back to their masters on the clearness of skin, the color of hair and eyebrows, condition of teeth, size of arms and breasts as well as, of course, income.[16] In the

---

[12]Gramont, *The Age of Magnificence: The Memoirs of the Duc de Saint-Simon.* (New York: Capricorn Books, 1963), pp. 69-70, p. 80, p. 105, p. 107, pp.111-2.
[13] Lita-Rose Betcherman. *Court Lady and Country Wife* (New York: Harper Collins, 2005), p. 54. Empress Maria Theresa of Austria's most beautiful daughter Maria Elizabeth (1743-1808) was considered a wife for the widowed Louis XV of France. After smallpox disfigured her, she was no longer deemed marriageable and eventually became an abbess in a nunnery.
[14]Cruysse, p. 107.
[15]Keller, *Kurfürstin*, p. 48.
[16] Maria Perry. *The Sisters of Henry VIII* (New York: St. Martin's Press, 1998), p. 39.

sixteenth century, a high forehead and blond hair was considered a sign of great beauty. One unlucky German princess was dispatched to a nunnery simply because her hair was black.[17]

But the biggest cosmetic fixation of the age was skin tone, which often turned into a dangerous obsession. The preferred coloring for a gentlewoman was a hard-to-achieve, transparent, lily white, "a thousand times fairer than the whitest of white satin."[18] To attain this much vaunted alabaster appearance, women not only wore masks outdoors to avoid sun damage, but also applied unsafe elixirs and toxic crèmes to their faces. Some of these deadly skin whiteners contained near lethal amounts of lead which turned one's complexion into the desired shade, but also caused rashes and other serious health problems. For many, such risks were preferable to running the courtly fashion gauntlet. It was said that at Versailles, the skin of a new arrival was measured against a fine white lawn chemise that was deliberately allowed to peep through the lacings at the back of her dress.[19]

Another deadly beauty product was gold. The French believed that the metal harnessed the power of the sun which would then be transferred to the drinker, bestowing eternal youth and health. Alchemists often acted as apothecaries and prescribed potable solutions of gold chloride and diethyl ether to an eager customer base of highborn ladies. The mistress of Henri II (1519-1559) and one of the most striking beauties of the age, Diane de Poitiers, might have been a victim of this fatal trend. Scientists found high levels of gold in recently excavated remains of her hair, permanent residue of a poisonous beauty routine. Towards the end of her life, Madame de Poitiers suffered from hair loss and fragile bones, common symptoms of the chronic gold intoxication which eventually killed her.[20]

While the comely risked their lives to retain their celebrated looks, those with less appealing features like Anna found themselves weighed down by crushing feelings of guilt and shame. The early modern era was not a charitable age in many respects, and those who could not contribute to family glory in the expected manner were often treated with barely concealed disdain.[21] Louis XII (1462-1515), King of France, had no misgivings about letting his wife, Jeanne of Valois, and everyone else know how much her "malformed" appearance repulsed him. Married to "Jeanne the Lame" at age fourteen, Louis reportedly so hated the sight of his "hideous" wife that her tutor regularly hid her in his robe for safety. The disgusted husband eventually applied for a papal dispensation which resulted in a degrading inquiry for the luckless Jeanne. With the right amount of monetary prodding, a clerical tribunal ruled that someone with such grave physical faults was obviously not fit for marriage, a notion that was seconded by the princess's own father who commented, "I did not know she was so ugly."

Although the proceedings were described as "one of the seamiest ... of the age," Jeanne weathered the ordeal at least outwardly unfazed.[22] As to the charge that she could not bear children due to her alleged defects, she spiritedly

[17] Peter Moraw. "Der Harem des Kurfürsten Albrecht Achilles von Brandenburg-Ansbach (d. 1486)," *Das Frauenzimmer* (Stuttgart: Jan Thorbecke, 2000), p. 444.
[18] Mossiker, p. 24.
[19] Frances Mossiker. *Madame de Sevigny* (New York: Knopf, 1983), p. 24. Also see Fraser, Antonia. *Marie Antoinette* (New York: Anchor Books, 2002), p. 73.
[20] Claire Bates. "Dying to Look Good," *Daily Mail*, Online Version (accessed 22 December 2009).
[21] Mansel, p. 5.
[22] J. R. Hale. *Renaissance Europe* (New York: Harper & Row, 1972), pp. 15-6.

argued, "I do not think that is so. I think I am as fit to be married as the wife of my groom George, who is quite deformed, and yet has given him beautiful children." Naturally, she eventually gave in to family pressure, and even made Louis cry with her deferential sweetness before agreeing to an annulment of her marriage and retiring to a nunnery.[23] In comparison with Jeanne of Valois, Anna's disability must have been relatively minor. Witnesses described her as "fraielle," but made no references to physical restrictions that impeded travel or, God forbid, childbirth.[24]

"Much is lacking in a woman who lacks beauty," Baldassare Castiglione (1478 - 1529), one of the most influential courtiers and authors of the age once stated emphatically.[25] A lady should be respected not only for her virtue and wit, but also for her attractiveness, he asserted, since "good looks are more important in females."[26] Anna's already low self-esteem probably took a further beating after another incident at Dresden's court. Three years after the Swedish disappointment, a new suitor was making inquiries, and the elector ordered his niece to sit for a portrait. It was destined for a certain William of Orange who had been unable to send an envoy to Saxony. Once more, the results proved unsatisfactory. Upon inspection August reprimanded the artist - probably Lucas Cranach the Younger - for painting a "counterfeit" likeness. The face in the picture was "too pretty," he argued, its object "better looking than in real life." The portraitist started anew and now drew Anna's profile instead of a frontal perspective. August was dissatisfied again. This time he deemed the sitter more appealing than the canvas replica.[27] No more portraits, he finally ruled. If William or anyone else desired Anna as a wife, they would have to come and view her in person.

[23] M. Beresford Riley. *Queens of the Renaissance* (Williamstown, MA: Comer House, 1982), p. 106, p. 123. In 1514 fifty-two-year old, twice widowed Louis, gout-ridden and decrepit, married Mary, the beautiful teenage sister of Henry VIII of England. The bride was probably just as repulsed with her new husband as he had once been with Jeanne. There was no show trial this time around, and Mary was lucky; Louis died only a few months after the wedding.
[24] Ruth Putnam. *The Life of William the Silent* (London: Lulu Enterprises, 2008 [1911]), p. 58. Hufton, Olwen. *The Prospect Before Her* (New York: Alfred A. Knopf, 1996), p. 183, p. 258. A misshapen woman's ability to bear children was normally called into question and society regarded these females as "natural nuns," useless women too weak or "defective" to do anything else but pray.
[25] Baldesar Castiglione. *The Book of the Courtier* (New York: Penguin, 1987), p. 211.
[26] David Loades. *Mary Tudor* (Oxford: Basil Blackwell, 1989), p. 7.
[27] Kruse, "Wilhelm von Oranien," p. 14. See also Martin Spies. "Die Bildnisse Annas von Sachsen," *Nassauische Annalen*, Band 116 (2205), p. 238.

Courtship

By the end of the 1550s, tensions between the electress and her ward had become so antagonistic that Anna had taken to calling the older woman "my main enemy."[1] In turn, her guardians continued to bemoan the princess's "hard head," while threatening her with the rod.[2] An arranged encounter with the Prince of Orange spelled possible change for all parties involved. In fact, much of Anna's inner circle pinned their hopes on the prince from the Netherlands. With a bit of luck, he would continue to press his suit for the troubled duchess despite her well-publicized unattractiveness. Together with her ladies and the Electress, Anna donned one of her colorful dresses, expressly reserved for such occasions.[3]

Luck was on her side, prayers were answered. When Orange made his appearance at Dresden's *Residenz* in November 1560, he not only allayed fears, but encouraged and sparked a romantic flame. Twenty-seven-year old, blue-eyed William was a man unlike any other male Anna had ever met and within days she considered him the most charming, sophisticated, and kind-hearted person of her admittedly limited acquaintance. Her ardor was fueled by his near perfect looks. A contemporary description of William in his mid-twenties termed him "well developed, his figure distinguished. He is strong and manly, skilled in military science, a great favorite of all the people whose affection he gains by openhanded generosity. He is a prince of the greatest promise."[4] He quickly made it clear that he paid little mind to Anna's plainness, and unlike Eric of Sweden, was not engaging in simultaneous courtships. In fact, William intended to marry her as soon as the legalities had been put in order.

The elector and his wife gave the pair the opportunity to talk in private, an unusual concession for an unmarried couple.[5] They were hopeful that this one - William - would finally take their troublesome ward off their hands. Clearly, they did not have to worry about Anna. The young woman was already making it abundantly clear that she was taken with the personable nobleman from the Low Countries. A skilled raconteur, he was seducing her with stories of undreamed-of riches and luxurious living in the Netherlands, tales that captured her imagination and consumed Anna with an improper eagerness for the prince and a new life.

Unlike the staid Lutheran court of her uncle's, William promised, his palace in Breda was a place of much merrymaking. It was the center of almost daily galas, banquets, and balls and she would preside over it all as his wife, the Princess of Orange. Anna, of course, eagerly drank up these enticements. How could she not? If the prince's pursuit ended in a wedding it promised to be the fulfillment of a dream.

*****

By the time Orange met the smitten Anna, he was already known as a wily politician, experienced in duplicity and doubletalk. In contrast to the sheltered

---

[1] Kruse, "Wilhelm von Oranien," p. 13.
[2] Keller, *Kurfürstin, p. 211.*
[3] Keller, *Kurfürstin,* p. p. 43.
[4] Putnam, *The Life of William the Silent,* p. 52.
[5] Vogt-Lüerssen, p. 36.

girl who had spent her teenage years locked away in the women's wing memorizing bible verses, the prince was firmly set in the ways of the world. He had seen war, negotiated the Byzantine maze of court intrigue, and had a marriage behind him. A career official of the most exalted station, he was the Netherlands' richest grand seigneur; a hardened tactician and opportunist, who impressed even his political enemies with his personal magnetism. Now he was setting his sights on Germany's wealthiest heiress whom he methodically planned to conquer.

Seasoned in the elegant rituals of Burgundian courtoisie, the prince was the consummate seducer; the gauche princess easy game. His manners and regal bearing vastly differed from her aunt's homey economy and her uncle's bumbling airs. As to his appearance, there is no doubt that William was one the most handsome noblemen of his time. A portrait by Anthonis Mor van Dashorst (1516-1575) completed in 1555, shows the prince accoutered in a stunning black suit of armor with elaborate copper colored trim. Even by twenty-first century standards, he would be considered an extremely fine-looking man with his even features, wavy auburn hair, and fashionable goatee. His mien contains a trace of melancholy, coupled with determination and purpose.

William of Orange first made the acquaintance of the Wettins when he traveled to Frankfurt in February 1558 on a highly honorific mission. He had been chosen to proclaim the formal abdication of Emperor Charles V in front of the German electors, and was tasked to oversee the transfer of the imperial crown to Charles's brother and successor, Ferdinand I. The Frankfurt trip was a pivotal stepping stone in William's career as it gave him the opportunity to make the acquaintance of Germany's most powerful princes. One of these influential magnates was Anna's uncle August. The charisma that would later captivate Anna also caught the attention of the elector who quickly considered Orange a potential ally in the wealthy, but tension-fraught Netherlands.[6]

At the time of the Frankfurt meeting, William was still married to Anne van Egmont, Countess Buren, a rich heiress who had been selected for him by his overlord, Charles V, seven years prior. Although the marriage to "Antje" was considered happy, the prince carelessly declared in August's presence that matrimony was an institution solely designed for the production of legitimate heirs. [7] It was no sin to keep concubines, he prattled, what else was a man to do if he felt an amorous attraction? His partners in conversation - devout Lutherans - cringed at such forward assertions. For all his faults, the Saxon elector took his wedding vows very seriously, and there is no indication that he ever strayed from the marriage bed during his lengthy union to Anne.[8] But the Dutch nobleman failed to grasp the reason for his pique. After all, he had only voiced what was common behavior among the aristocracy, not only in the Netherlands.

Perhaps alcohol influenced that evening's animated conversation, since William was usually known for his circumspection and tact. In fact, he would later be called "the Silent," a somewhat ill-fitting sobriquet that was meant to remark on his guarded watchfulness. As for Anna's uncle, his priggishness was genuine indignation paired with affection. The Dutch had a certain reputation for lax morals, but German princes were by no means inferior when it came to

---

[6]Wartenberg, p. 82.
[7]Schuppener, "Hochzeitslied," p. 212.
[8]Keller, *Kurfürstin*, p. 29.

fast living. August's own brother Maurice had been a notorious Lothario whose capers in the bathhouses of Augsburg had once set tongues wagging. There was also the elector's brother-in-law, Duke Eric of Brunswick-Calenberg, who was shaming his older sister Sidonia with his public whoring.[9] The elector had quietly turned a blind eye to both.

One evening, while the merry party of princes was drinking the night away, a messenger arrived from the Low Countries bearing bad news. William's wife Anne had fallen very ill and doctors despaired of her life. The prince immediately hastened home, only to find that his "Petite Tanneque" was dying.[10] Despite his braggadocio in Frankfurt, William loved his consort, and his replies to letters of condolence speak of heartfelt grief. He wrote to King Philip of Spain, "I am the unhappiest man in the world."[11]

After passing the spring in deep mourning, the prince had tired of the single life by summer. Being a widower did not suit him well, William confessed to his brother John of Nassau, as he spent his time with a number of women. "In those years," Orange later admitted, "I had nothing so much in my head as the play of arms, the chase, and other exercises suitable to young lords." To his mother's distress, those "other exercises" centered on a Flemish girl named Eva Elincx, a burgomaster's daughter from the city of Emmerich on the Rhine. To judge by her later conduct, William's paramour was no professional courtesan, but a pretty patrician's daughter. Eva hailed from a respectable family who chose to look the other way in view of her admirer's station in life. After giving birth to a son who was acknowledged and educated by his father under the name of Justin of Nassau, Eva gradually passed out of her lover's life, and out of history, as the respectable wife of a respectable burgher, the secretary Abraham Arondeaux.[12] As for Justin, "le petit Monseigneur," he reappears among the list of pages at his father's Dutch country estate and later gained fame as an admiral and governor of the city of Breda, his career unhampered by his illegitimacy.

In addition to the Elincx affair, there are hints of other exploits. William was allegedly involved with a certain Barbara of Lier and a Mademoiselle de Maudrimont.[13] In a letter, the prince also mentioned his excitement over upcoming adventures with a blonde after enjoying the favors of a brunette sometime in the middle of 1560.[14] At the same time, Orange was engaged in deep talks with the Saxon court about marrying Anna.

Athough William was less concerned about the affairs' effects on his eternal soul, he worried about his responsibilities as a father. His late wife had born him two living children: a boy named Philip William, five years old, and a girl named Maria, born in 1556. They should not grow up motherless, he decided, and selected the names of several eligible princesses that his relations had put forward. His first choice fell on Renate (1544-1602), daughter of Duke Francis I of Lorraine and his wife, Christina of Denmark. It was an ambitious suit that promised to lift William's family into the imperial sphere: Renate's maternal grandfather, Christian II of Denmark, had been married to the emperor's sister, Isabella of Burgundy. In the end, the mother of William's intended reportedly halted ne-

[9]Vetter, pp. 46-7
[10]Schuppener,"Hochzeitslied," p. 211.
[11]C. V. Wedgwood. *William the Silent* (New York: Jonathan Cape, 1967), p. 25.
[12]Wedgwood, p. 27.
[13]Putnam, *The Life of William the Silent*, p. 52.
[14]Vetter, pp. 51-2.

gotiations. The spirited Danish princess cited unsettled inheritance questions as an obstacle.[15]

Since no feelings or money had been invested during these preliminary phases of courtship, the Prince of Orange speedily shifted his attentions to the next matrimonial object of interest. During a stay in France in the summer of 1559, his eyes fell on seventeen-year-old Marie de Bourbon, a daughter of the Count of Saint Pol and widow of the Duke of Enghien, who was both rich and attractive. Unfortunately, Henri II of France had no intention of letting the lands of one of France's richest heiresses fall into the hands of a Habsburg vassal, and again William's suit came to nothing.[16]

After Orange's misadventures in Lorraine and France, the Nassaus directed their searchlights eastward. In the fall of 1559 the prince asked his sister's fiancé, Günther of Schwarzburg, to travel to Dresden to sound out the elector's stance on a possible marriage to his niece Anna. The young Schwarzburg - dependable, efficient, and pleasing - was the ideal envoy for such delicate dealings. The Schwarzburgs had been proven and loyal retainers of the House of Wettin since the 1340s.[17]

As expected, the electoral couple reacted positively to the envoy's initial overtures. Other foreign suitors might be long in coming, they determined, hoping to be rid of their difficult charge as soon as possible. Besides, there was much to be said for a union between Anna and William. The Prince of Orange was the premier Habsburg liegeman in the Low Countries, and August was eager to demonstrate to his imperial Catholic friends that despite their divergent religious beliefs, the Wettins' loyalty to the dynasty was as firm as ever. In 1543, his brother Maurice had spent a month at Charles V's court in Brussels, and returned to Dresden with some marvelous "Dutch paintings"- souvenirs that still hung on the upper floor of the Dresden palace.[18]

After further negotiations, August happily gave his assent to the proposed union, especially after the prince offered to pay a sizeable portion of the wedding expenses.[19] Even so, William still faced opposition from Anna's other guardian, her formidable grandfather, Philip of Hessen. The landgrave opposed the marriage for a number of reasons and said so quite bluntly. Firstly, his granddaughter clearly outranked the Prince of Orange, despite his ownership of the minute principality of Orange in southern France. Furthermore, William was pri-

---

[15]Kruse, "Wilhelm von Oranien," p. 14. Vetter, p. 52. Christina of Denmark was a one-time love interest of King Henry VIII of England and had repelled the uxorious king's diplomatic advances by naughtily telling the English ambassador, "If I had two heads, one should be at the King of England's disposal." There might have been other reasons for the failure of the match. According to a confidante, the widowed princess considered herself better suited to become William's wife than her daughter—a possible deal breaker for Orange.

[16]Schuppener, "Hochzeitslied," p. 215. See also, Ruth Putnam. *William the Silent, Prince of Orange: The Moderate Man of the Sixteenth Century* (New York: G. P. Putnam's Sons, 1895), p. 122. The beautiful Marie de Bourbon, Madame de Touteville, had an income of one hundred thousand francs.

[17]Schuppener,"Hochzeitslied," p. 215.

[18]Coban-Hensel, p. 115. Bünz, Enno and Christoph Volkmar. "Die albertinischen Herzöge bis zur Übernahme der Kurwürde," *Die Herrscher Sachsens* (Munich: Becksche Reihe, 2007), pp. 77-9. Alliances—marital or otherwise—between Saxony and the Low Countries harked back to the first part of the fifteenth century when the Wettin Duke William III married the Habsburg princess Anna in 1439, and subsequently laid claim to parts of Flanders. A few decades later, the legendary Charles the Bold (1433-1477), Duke of Burgundy, was to marry one of the daughters of Saxony's Elector Frederick II. The whole affair ended in disaster when the high ranking Burgundian delegation was kidnapped by enemies of the elector while travelling through central Germany. At the turn of the century, Emperor Maximilian I appointed Maurice and August's grandfather Albrecht—a most diligent servant of the imperial family—"eternal governor" of the Dutch province of Friesland. As the emperor's most powerful liege, "Cousin Albrecht, Duc de Saxe" also held the most prestigious position at court in Brussels. The Saxon duke bequeathed the governorship of Friesland to his son Henry, August's father, in the summer of 1499. But the duke soon bungled affairs in his new patrimony, forcing his older brother George to take charge of the restless province. In 1515 even the more competent George had to admit defeat and sold the unquiet lands to Charles of Burgundy, later Emperor Charles V, for 100,000 guilders.

[19]Knöfel, *Dynastie,* p. 134.

marily a servant of the Dutch government, and therefore not good enough for the daughter of an independent elector. In fact, Philip reminded August, William was the son of a mere count, William the Rich of Nassau.

Such objections were not unusual. Aristocratic houses could be extremely touchy when families of lesser stature presumed to aspire to lofty marital alliances. In wedlock, the rule of thumb dictated, one selected partners by "comparing among the highest nobility, and no one below." Although the House of Nassau was as ancient as the Hessians, they could not match the pedigree of the Saxons. In other words, Orange's forced social climb could not compensate for the spiritual and moral deficiencies inherent in less important families who, it was said, could never quite leave their more modest origins behind.[20]

William had risen from count to prince when a cousin, René of Chalon, Prince of Orange, died childless in 1544. As the oldest son of the Count of Nassau-Dillenburg, William stood first in line to inherit the tiny princedom of Orange, situated in the lower Rhône Valley in southern France. The patrimony traditionally belonged to the Holy Roman Empire despite being embedded within the kingdom of France. Since the House of Chalon exercised full sovereignty over Orange, its princes could rightfully hold their own among European royalty, and despite its Lilliputian size, the political importance of this miniature state was not entirely insignificant. As its reigning prince, William was technically not subject to another monarch's commands, but a self-governing ruler in his own right.[21]

On a more practical level, the statelet was too far removed from William's power bases in western Germany and the Low Countries to be of any tangible consequence, and was essentially a fancy title without requisite authority. In fact, the prince's Provencal legacy thirteen miles north of Avignon hardly compared to his extensive holdings in the Netherlands and was so unimportant that he never visited during his lifetime.[22]

William's true wealth and influence rested in his estates in the Low Countries and Luxemburg, particularly the rich barony of Breda in the Duchy of Brabant, which he had also inherited from his cousin René. The prince's marriage to the well-heeled Anne van Buren further extended his tremendous possessions. At the end of the 1550s William's net worth was appraised at about four million florins, an almost imaginary sum at the time.[23] In the Low Countries, only Philip of Spain, sovereign of the Habsburg-ruled Spanish Netherlands and his regent, Margaret of Parma, could trump such a fantastical fortune.

In view of Orange's glorious circumstances, the reason for the landgrave's aversion to the union can only be explained as personal. Until 1557, Philip had been in litigation with William's father about an interminable land dispute. The area of contention was the county of Katzenelnbogen, a small fiefdom about sixty miles north-west of Frankfurt. After the last Count of Katzenelnbogen had died without male heirs in 1479, the Landgrave of Hessen and the Count of Nassau both laid claim to the vacant domain. Lawsuits were filed and William's father spent almost the entirety of his forty-two-year reign to recoup the swath which he considered rightfully his. The Protestant revolt came and passed through various

---

[20] Beatrice Bastl. *Tugend, Liebe, Ehre* (Vienna: Böhlau Verlag, 2000), p. 159, p. 525.

[21] Vetter, p. 11.

[22] Vogt-Lüerssen, p. 24. The princedom of Orange was subsumed by the French in 1713, although the Dutch royal family retains the title "Princes of Orange."

[23] Vetter, pp. 11-2.

stages, but the lawsuit dragged on, preventing both plaintiffs from dealing with other matters and costing each several tons of gold. In fact, Count William spent 200,000 guilders on lawyer's fees, despite an annual income of only 14,000.[24]

The tiresome grievance was only laid to rest in June 1557, at a meeting between the two foes and young William in Frankfurt. Apparently, Orange threw his weight around during the occasion. It was a question of prestige, he had written to his father a year earlier, and the House of Nassau needed to retain the title and escutcheon of the disputed county at all cost. Philip in turn railed against his neighbors and called the old count his "most ... vicious enemy," "a servant of papists" who was lying in wait to "rob him of the ... best part of his inherited princedom together with land and people."[25] Ultimately, Hessen retained Katzenelnbogen, but had to pay 600,000 florins in compensation to the Nassaus who continued to carry the contested county's coat of arms.[26] And yet, bad blood between the two families may not have been the sole reason for Philip's opposition to the match. Another rumor claimed that the landgrave was thinking about giving one of his own daughters to William in marriage.

Whatever his motivations, Philip vehemently argued against a Wettin-Orange connection, perhaps out of genuine grandfatherly concern. Not only were the Nassaus of lower station, he wrote to the elector, but William's financial situation was precarious, and his love life dubious.[27] Most importantly, he continued, the status of his grandchild's future offspring was by no means assured. William already had an heir, and he doubted that the prince had made suitable arrangements for his "secondary" children by Anna. Moreover, William had not been a good husband to his first wife, and openly flaunted his numerous love affairs. "Concerning the virtues of the prince, we let him be a righteous man of the world," he wrote, "but if he were to carry on with our daughter [granddaughter] in marriage as [he did] with his late [wife], she will have a difficult time of it." Anna was too fragile to stomach such behavior.[28]

*****

In April 1560 William dispatched Count Schwarzburg on another trip to Dresden to address Philip's concerns. During a meeting with August, the count laid all financial worries to rest by announcing on Orange's behalf that the children resulting from the union would attain the titles of margraves and each receive an annual pension of 70,000 florins. The elector and his wife were more than satisfied with these generous provisions and immediately dispatched an emissary to Kassel with some rather underhanded instructions.

The diplomat was to underpin the merits of the match by listing Anna's personal and physical shortcomings, among them perhaps scoliosis, in the starkest of terms. "William of Orange is considered young, handsome, and rich, but this is not to be expected from Princess Anna," her impatient uncle had written to the landgrave. "It is unlikely that her figure will straighten and that the propor-

[24] *Karl* Wolf. "Ein Urteil des Grafen Johann des Älteren von Nassau-Dillenburg über die Regierungszeit seines Vaters," *Nassauische Annalen*, Band 67 (1956), p. 260.
[25] Emil Becker. "Beiträge zur Geschichte Graf Wilhelms des Reichen von Nassau-Dillenburg (1487-1559)," *Nassauische Annalen*, Band 66 (1955), p. 154, p. 159.
[26] Vetter, p. 39.
[27] Wartenberg, p. 83.
[28] Vogt-Lüerssen, p. 35.

tions of her body will even out."[29] It would not be easy to find her a husband, and a suitor like Orange was heaven sent. Besides, the elector added, the landgrave should be less judgmental, if only for political reasons: William was a man of great importance in Brussels, who could further their relations with the Dutch Habsburgs.[30]

*****

While August cajoled and coaxed in Germany, William tackled courtship impediments that could not be glossed over by glib epistles. The prime source of contention was faith, an issue that was never of small consequence in the Renaissance and riled tempers like no other subject. Unlike Lutheran Anna, William was a convert to Catholicism. He had been a born and bred Protestant, but was forced to adopt the old faith to come into his magnificent inheritance in the Low Countries, where Catholicism was the only officially sanctioned religion. Like Anna's father Maurice, William was of a religiously tepid temperament and tried to stand clear of confessional debates whenever possible. As a public figure, however, he was forced to feign devotion to the Roman faith, if only for show.

Although peace still held fast in the empire and the Netherlands, the powder keg of confessional tension was about to explode in restive France with the first of many "Wars of Religion." The atrocities that would be committed in the name of the Almighty were as outrageous as they were cruel, and plunged the Gallic kingdom into decades of harrowing conflict. People readily slaughtered their neighbors, goaded on by monks who called for the annihilation of heretics; lynch mobs attacked hapless Catholics after rabble-rousing Protestant clerics called for the complete eradication of the old faith.[31] One Huguenot captain wore a necklace of priests' ears, while the infamous Baron des Adrets made Catholic prisoners leap to their death from a high tower. A century later the philosopher Blaise Pascal (1623-1662) commented resignedly, "Men never do evil so completely and cheerfully as when they do it from religious conviction."[32]

In this climate of frenzied paranoia and bigotry, "intermarriage" between partners of different creeds bordered on blasphemous. The landgrave for one immediately exploited the controversy to the fullest. How could the daughter of the defender of Protestantism marry a papist, he wanted to know. The impropriety of "sacrificing an innocent young girl" by mating her with "an irreligious courtier at a popish court" was too much to stomach.[33] Other German princes, the landgrave chided, fully agreed with his condemnation of the union. Count Wolfgang of Palatine-Zweibrücken and Duke Christian of Wurttemberg had announced they'd rather give their daughters to farm helps or swine herders than papists.[34]

Besides, Philip doubted that William—a subject of the House of Burgundy and the Spanish crown—would be able to guarantee Anna the free practice of her Lutheran faith in Breda. For that she would have to travel to neighboring Neuenahr or Geldern, the landgrave told delegates from Saxony and the Nether-

[29]Schuppener, "Hochzeitslied," p. 222.
[30]Kruse, "Wilhelm von Oranien," pp. 16-7.
[31]Janine Garrison. *Königin Margot* (Düsseldorf: Benziger, 1995), p. 7.
[32]Desmond Seward. *The First Bourbon* (Boston: Gambit, 1971), p. 18.
[33]Putnam, *The Life of William the Silent*, p. 56.
[34]Schuppener, "Hochzeitslied," p. 222.

lands.[35]   Indeed, she will be harassed by the fanatical courtiers of Philip of Spain, the ruler of the Low Countries, he forecasted glumly, and might even be forced into exile![36]

The landgrave's unremitting opposition together with objections from the Dutch Habsburgs forced William into a mad, bilateral concession scramble. To alleviate anxieties in both camps, the prince made contradictory promises which blurred the lines between lying and careful prevarication. For example, he assured August of Saxony and Philip of Hessen that, in his heart, he had always remained a Lutheran.[37] Anna would certainly be allowed to privately attend Protestant services in the Low Countries. For August, such promises were more than sufficient. He was eager to relinquish all responsibility for his niece, regardless of the state of her eternal soul. The landgrave, on the other hand, continued on his course of dogged hostility.

With the battle in Germany only half won, a wary William shifted his focus to the Netherlands. He still had to inform his liege lord, King Philip of Spain, of his planned union, and hoped to persuade the dour monarch of the viability of the match. On 7 February 1560, William formally requested permission to marry Anna in a finely honed entreaty. Slyly omitting her parentage, he merely described his would-be bride as August of Saxony's niece. Concerning religion, he fawned, nothing was closer to his heart than to remain in the bosom of the Roman church. His future wife would certainly convert to Catholicism in due time. Indeed, he would not dream of taking a spouse who declared herself unwilling to live "a Catholic life."[38]   These statements were, of course, in complete contradiction to the promises made to August.

For obvious reasons, the reply from Toledo about a fortnight later was tentative. Which niece of the elector's was William referring to, the king inquired suspiciously, obviously recalling Maurice's duplicity towards his father, Emperor Charles V. The late elector's betrayal had been shamefully disloyal, but even worse, it buttressed the heretical cause of Protestantism in Germany, resulting in Charles's eventual abdication. Nevertheless, Philip decided not to forbid the marriage outright. Overtaxed with Spanish affairs, he forwarded the matter to his premier advisor in the Low Countries, Cardinal Antoine Perrenot de Granvelle, and his half-sister, Margaret of Parma, Regent of the Netherlands.[39]

An astute, quick-thinking politician, Granvelle immediately raised all warning flags. A future alliance between the religiously indifferent Orange and the Protestant princes of Germany could only spell trouble for the Catholic Netherlands, he worried, and informed William of his objections. Together with Duchess Margaret, he also recommended a thorough investigation before consenting to the projected union. Both realized that by marrying Anna, William was bound to gain valuable allies in the religious battle currently simmering in the Netherlands. As in the rest of Europe, the "Protestant heresy" was spreading in the Low

[35]Böttcher, pp. 68-9.

[36]Kruse, "Wilhelm von Oranien," p. 17.

[37]Vetter, p. 62.

[38]Algemeen Rijksarchief van Belgïe. William claimed that his parents,"Ne m'ont laisse jamais en paix" ("don't ever leave me in peace"), but were urging him to find a wife. He went so far as to claim that his parents — although his father was already dead — were "importuning" him to such an extent that he did not dare refuse their wishes ("m'ont plus pressé et importuné de ne la point refuser"). The prestigious match, Orange claims, would bring him much credit among the lords of Germany, while still allowing him to maintain prefect devotion to His Majesty. The religion of the lady, he added reassuringly, would pose no problem — in other words, she would convert to Catholicism.

[39]M. Gachard, *Correspondance de Guillaume Le Taciturne* (Brussels: C. Muquardt, 1850), pp.435-6. "Jay tousjours voluntiers résolu avec la participation de ma seur, la duchesse de Parma, oultre ce que vos letter ne spécifient quelle ny epce c'est, ny comme elle a été nourye ..."

Countries, and Orange was not deemed altogether trustworthy. If he forged a coalition with Germany's Lutheran rulers, they agreed, the prince could ignite a conflagration between Dutch Catholics and the growing number of reform-minded believers whose ramifications were too terrifying to contemplate.

During an audience, Margaret challenged William on this particular issue, causing tempers to flare on both sides. William had not kept his word in regards to previous agreements, she argued. For instance, she had allowed one of the prince's sisters to marry a Dutch nobleman after William had assured her of the lady's imminent conversion to the Catholicism. That promise had not been kept. Would it be the same with his Saxon bride? Margaret asked not unreasonably. Unlike his sister, William responded quickly, Anna would unquestionably conform.[40]

On the other hand, Orange added defiantly, he was by no means obligated to obtain the king's permission in marriage, despite his landholder status in the Low Countries. As a member of the German aristocracy and sovereign of a princedom, he was his own master and merely informed the Habsburgs of his marital plans out of courtesy. In truth, even Philip's Dutch vassals acted independently in regards to their matrimonial decisions. Out-argued by such admittedly solid reasoning, Margaret of Parma unhappily relented. And even her brother, King Philip, though still wary, reluctantly gave his blessing to the contentious union of his premier liegeman.[41]

With the Dutch battle won, William threw himself headlong into the most crucial round of the wooing process. He had received an invitation to meet his prospective bride, which been unexpectedly issued by Philip of Hessen. Negotiations had already been delayed by a whole year due to the landgrave's fits of temper and Orange was impatient to bring the matter to a close.[42]

It was somewhat unusual for a princely suitor to travel to his intended before the wedding ceremony. The conventional method of picking a noble consort did not involve the groom travelling to meet her, but entailed a rather lengthy, serendipitous process of sending envoys and artists round to have a good look at what was on offer. Once negotiations had proceeded to the final stage, royal women often married before they left home by means of a proxy ceremony. It would have simply been beneath the dignity of many a princess to leave her native lands indecently unattached.[43]

In Anna's case, however, special circumstances applied. Because of her physical flaws and problematic personality, the princess's grandfather did not want William to espouse her sight unseen. Orange should evaluate her in person before he promised before God to spend the rest of his days with her, the landgrave wrote, and ordered a meeting between the prospective pair.[44]

---

[40]Wedgwood, p. 49. See also Gachard, p, 437. The prince even appealed to the Archbishop of Arras to intervene with the Habsburgs on his behalf. Letter dated 9 April 1560, written in Den Haag.

[41]Schuppener, "Hochzeitslied," p. 226, p. 228. See also Putnam, *Moderate Man*, pp. 131-2. Philip wrote to Granvelle, expressing his disappointment that the marriage had not fallen through. He then told his sister Margaret, "I do not really understand how the prince can mate himself with the daughter of one who acted towards his Majesty, now in glory, as Elector Maurice did."

[42]Kruse, "Wilhelm von Oranien," p. 17.

[43]Kleinman, p. 20. Frieda, pp. 2-3. Thirteen-year-old Elizabeth of Valois, eldest daughter of Henri II of France and Catherine de Medici, was the center of a magnificent proxy ceremony in the Cathedral of Notre Dame in the summer of 1559. The service was also attended by William of Orange. Because her groom, Philip of Spain, was unable to attend, his right hand man, the severe Duke of Alba, stood in for him. After the bridal mass, a primitive ritual took place. Elizabeth and Alba climbed into the huge state bed, each with one leg naked. As their bare limbs touched and they wrapped their feet together, the marriage was declared "consummated."

[44]Schuppener, "Hochzeitslied," p. 222.

On 18 November 1560 William's sister Catherine married Günther von Schwarzburg in western Saxony, prompting the prince to take a detour to Dresden after the conclusion of the festivities. He wanted to see for himself if Anna was indeed the handful her relations claimed her to be, and obey the landgrave's instructions to inspect her in the flesh. He also resolved to accomplish what he did best: win over a possible adversary by making full use of his considerable charm.

William had already charged the barriers of faith, rank, and wealth, and the only remaining obstacle was to convince the difficult Saxon girl that he would make her a worthy husband. Usually, the prince's pleasant manners and straightforward affability beguiled everyone from stable boy to ruling monarch, while his ease with the other sex rarely failed to make an impression, unintentionally or not. One of William's opponents had reluctantly charged that "Every time the prince lifts his hat he wins a friend."[45]

William naturally calculated that his labors would be well worth the effort, considering the prospect of the "return." Although she did not look it, Anna was a glittering prize. Her uncle had set her dowry at 100,000 thalers - one the largest portions ever given to a German heiress - and the young woman's dowry was sure to fill William's chronically depleted coffers.[46] Besides, no other German ladies of rank were as well connected as Anna through her uncle, August of Saxony.[47] Even if Anna "possessed few talents of body and mind, she was the bearer of the glorious Lutheran legacy, and as such, an important princess."[48] With the optimism of youth, William concluded that his intended's wealth and the prestige of the union would compensate for her lack of looks as well as any other deficiencies.

Carefree and ebullient, William made his courting expedition to Dresden a jolly affair. After his sister's wedding, the prince and a coterie of friends embarked on a boisterous "road trip" that concluded each night with plenty of beer, wine, and probably women. Apparently the party caused *desordre* wherever they went, but Orange enjoyed himself to the fullest. "[I] cannot forget the excellent cheer we have had together," he reminisced in a letter to his brother Louis several months later.[49]

William eventually arrived at the Saxon court plumed in the sort of splendor that left chambermaids and ladies-in-waiting gaping in wonder. Anna quickly followed suit — overwhelmed, awed. The prince had counted on such a reaction. A lover should look the part and Orange had probably invested thousands of florins in fashionable apparel.[50] Bedecked in Burgundian finery, he charmed the naive princess, lavishing her with attention unknown to her since her parents' death. William might have also noticed the pool of ill-concealed insecurity that lurked beneath a façade of put-on sassiness.

In the evenings, he impressed her with exquisite dance steps. Familiarity with the newest dances was a must for any self-respecting man of means as it belonged to the essential forms of aristocratic entertainment and was often taken to a competitive level. A French source gives direct information regarding the prince's talent in this sport. In the early 1550s, during a conference of German

[45]Putnam, *The Life of William the Silent*, p. 49.
[46]Vetter, p. 52.
[47]Putnam, *The Life of William the Silent*, p. 55.
[48]Schuppener, "Hochzeitslied," p. 221.
[49]Putnam, *The Life of William the Silent*, p. 58.
[50]Cressy, p. 239.

princes at the French palace of Fontainebleau, the Marquis de Vieilleville noted with surprise that among the foreign guests one visitor executed the difficult
sequences with near precision: William of Orange. "In the figures that followed
none of the strangers particularly [excelled] except the Prince of Orange, who ac-
quitted himself very dexterously and would have won the prize for the galliard,
if, with his postures, capers, turns, and evolutions, his countless flourishes, agile
bounds, and springs, he had only kept time to the music!"[51] Health permitting,
Anna might have joined her suitor in the more stately pavane, palms sweaty with
excitement. Or she might have watched breathlessly from the sidelines as the object of her affection gamboled about. Soon it was obvious to all that William's
wooing efforts - an intricate sequence of inquiries and approaches - were rapidly
paying dividends.

Given his string of courting failures in France and Lorraine, it was not
surprising that gentlemen sometimes likened courtship to siege warfare.[52] "The
motions of love are like the motions of war, very slow and uncertain," opined an
Englishman about his recent marriage with arrogant braggadocio. Writing to his
brother he described his engagement in terms of obstructions and repulses that,
eventually, led to victory. "In a word, after the discharge of some sighs, after I had
made many assaults upon a white hand, and stormed the blushing bulwarks of
her lips, the fortress surrendered, and at night I entered triumphantly at my new
possession."[53]

While William was clearly scaling Anna's figurative defenses, there was
nothing humorous or light-hearted about seeking her hand. In the Renaissance,
courtship was no titillating game, no idle dalliance, despite the princess's swoon-
ing in a cloud of romantic exhilaration. Serious courtship among Anna's peers
knew but one goal: holy matrimony. Toying with affections or sending fickle sig-
nals could be ruinous to all concerned, a source of pain and dishonor as well as a
peril to diplomatic relations with friendly allies.

Although Anna did not realize it yet, these scintillating days of sweet
nothings and whispered confidences also heralded the end of her innocent days
of youth. Her time in Dresden had never been particularly carefree and blithe,
but matrimony was destined to be even less so. Marriage was the staid business
of mature adults who were expected to shoulder the responsibilities of family,
children, and work. Enveloped in the giddy haze of first love, Anna gave little
consideration to the duties that awaited her, nor the obligations she now owed to
her Saxon relations for assisting her in becoming the Princess of Orange. While
she and her suitor sighed in corners, the elector and his wife carefully tallied their
outlays and efforts to get their niece married.[54]

William, on the other hand, was acutely aware of these dynamics. While
he pretended to feign interest in the starry-eyed reveries of his prospective bride,
he also found time to smooth out Electress Anne's concerns about his "heretical"
beliefs. The "closet Lutheran" diligently attended Protestant services in Dresden
and, to the Danish princess's great relief, behaved in an altogether appropriate
manner.[55]

[51]Putnam, *The Life of William the Silent*, p. 26.
[52]Cressy, p. 235
[53]Cressy, p. 235.
[54]Cressy, pp. 233-5
[55]Vetter, p. 63.

*****

To Anna's delight, William stayed for a full fortnight—a time during which she delighted in his attentions. As everyone knew, that was the nature of courtship: it was a woman's season of supremacy, the time when men got on their knees, instead of the other way round, and played obsequious lovers. Except for her wedding, it was, as a rule, the only period in a woman's life when she was the star and protagonist of a thrilling "adventure" of love. [56]

Not surprisingly, Anna was inconsolable when the time came for darling William to depart. Perhaps she ran up the many steps of the tall Hausmannstower, where the wind howls even during sunny days, and scanned the horizon as the last of the procession of riders disappeared from view in the hilly villages outside the Saxon capital. By this time, Anna fancied herself deeply in love. She was thirsting to be desired by her suitor who had not left her unkissed.

[56]Amanda Vickery. *The Gentleman's Daughter* (New Haven, CT: Yale University Press, 1998), pp. 58-9, p. 82.

William of Orange by Antonis Mor van Dashorst, 1555: worldly, handsome, and charming, he quickly garnered Anna's affections

The Blushing Bride

As William made his way back to the Low Countries, Anna mooned her private moments away, touching and caressing the gifts the prince had brought for her. Whether inspired by love or scripted by social convention, courtship involved the giving and acceptance of presents and tokens. Coins, ribbons, gloves, girdles, and similar knickknacks did the trick for common folk, whereas women of Anna's station could expect a superb piece of jewelry.[1] When Philip of Spain paid court to Mary, daughter of Henry VIII of England, he had the Marquis of Las Navas present her with the traditional gift of a splendid jewel.[2] Once a lady was contracted, betrothed, or "made sure," she could expect the additional present of a ring, a gesture that signaled the new strength of the couple's bond.[3]

In England, the exchange of miniatures was the latest rage among fashionable lovers. Aristocrats had themselves painted "lonely and languishing" in the depths of a forest, signaling to their betrothed that they were pining away in pastoral solitude while counting down the days to the wedding ceremony. Unlike grand official portraits, most of these tiny likenesses bore no name, proof that the people who commissioned them did so to capture and exchange intimate feelings. Literature of the time described the trading of love souvenirs in a style that was of an almost religious nature.[4] Given Anna's fervent regard for William, she must have cherished his keepsakes with profound veneration.

Although noble ladies were the sole recipients of costly gemstones, they were allowed to present their suitors with small mementos signaling affection. The image of a lady bestowing a gift was a common theme at the time, but she had to stay within certain parameters. Custom dictated that "A woman must be careful, no matter how much she claims a man as her lover, not to give him a gift that is worth very much. She may indeed give him a pillow, a towel, a kerchief, or a purse as long as they're not too expensive." Throughout the Middle Ages queens and their ladies gave elaborately embroidered purses to their wooers. Created by specially trained craftswomen, the bags sported complex romantic scenes on a few inches of fabric. One surviving example was spun in gold and silver thread and depicts a romantic garden scene with the lady grabbing a youth by his hood, drawing him closer toward her.[5] We do not know if Anna sent William on his way with such a remembrance, but she certainly labored to stay in his thoughts. Upon reaching Leipzig, a three days' ride west of Dresden, several express letters from an anxious, besotted Anna were already awaiting the prince.

William, unfortunately, hardly reciprocated her feelings, and was reluctant to reply with an equally ardent answer. He wrote letters to the Bishop of Arras and Margaret of Parma on November 30, but had his brother Louis draw up a note for his intended - a comparatively sedate, but gallant reply to her messages - which he then copied in his own handwriting.[6] If Anna did not warrant much of his personal time, the prince continued to flatter the electress - a crucial party in

[1]Cressy, p. 263.
[2]Kamen, p. 56.
[3]Cressy, p. 263.
[4]Orest Ranum. "The Refuges of Intimacy," *A History of Private Life III: Passions of the Renaissance* (Cambridge, MA: Belknap Press, 1989), p. 246, pp. 248-9.
[5]Michael Camille. *The Medieval Art of Love* (New York: Harry N. Abrams, 1998), p. 64.
[6]Gachard, pp. 465-70. The letter to Margaret of Parma spans several pages. It mentions German politics and Protestant beliefs, but contains only a passing reference concerning William's planned nuptials.

this conjugal venture who could still put a stop to the promising proceedings. In a cloying missive, Orange implored the princess to further his suit so that he could be cured from a doubtful case of lovesickness.[7] "If Your Grace could only know, how that little worm [of lovesickness] eats away at my heart," he twittered, "you would have no doubts, but sympathize with me."[8]

Orange was of course hardly pining away. His return trip home was as rowdy as his journey to Dresden, and he celebrated the prospect of coming into Anna's enormous dowry with plenty of carousing. August of Saxony received a lightheaded note from the prince in December, stating that "I drank so often to your health with the other lords that I became weak from it." And upon his arrival in the Netherlands, William admitted to a friend that his consumption of food and alcohol had been excessive.[9]

Ignorant of her beau's relative indifference, Anna considered herself the luckiest of women. She was one of only a handful of princesses marrying for love, and was filled with a giddy euphoria that manifested itself in frank broadcasts to anyone who cared to listen (or was forced to do so).

During her courtship a girl was to be quiet, chaste, and passive. Aristocratic society considered it highly inappropriate for a woman to profess her sentiments directly, because it called her virtue into question.[10] This was not simply an issue of virginity, but rather a judgment of her overall qualities: dress and language mattered as did resistance to male overtures, tact in distributing tokens of love, and constancy of choice.[11] In the eyes of her peers, Anna had "given rise to talk," a serious faux pas that endangered her honor, if not that of her family. Renaissance courts thrived on gossip, lurid stories, and innuendo, and even the most innocent tale could quickly gather a momentum of its own. Unfortunately, these were realities that Anna never quite grasped.

A century later, the Duchess of Newcastle (1623-1673) - a groundbreaking writer, poet, and philosopher - could have taught the Saxon princess a lesson in proper comportment. Although she would later be called "mad, conceited, and ridiculous" because of her allegedly unfeminine pursuits, Margaret Cavendish had been a much-admired model of womanly modesty when she accepted the attentions of William, 1st Duke of Newcastle, in her early twenties. Wishing to "be careful in things that may arise to the scandal of my reputation," Margaret felt that she could respond only infrequently to the duke's letters and poems while he publicly pursued her. "For know, my Lord," she explained while he spent time away in Paris, "it is as uncomely to see a woman too kind as to see a man too negligent." The bashful Margaret so feared for her good name that she risked appearing standoffish, even to friends. When William questioned her aloofness, his fiancée replied, "[It is] the custom I observe that I never speak to any man before they address themselves to me, nor to look so much in their face as to invite their discourse."[12]

Clearly, Anna did not subscribe to the Cavendish school of elegant female reserve; she was rather cut from her father's cloth. The mercurial, sensual

[7]Vetter, p. 63.
[8]Kruse, "Wilhelm von Oranien," p. 18.
[9]Wedgwood, pp. 96-7.
[10]Anthony Fletcher. *Gender, Sex & Subordination in England 1500-1800* (New Haven, CT: Yale University Press, 1995), p. 392.
[11]Daniel Fabre. "Families: Privacy versus Custom," *A History of Private Life III: Passions of the Renaissance* (Cambridge, MA: Belknap Press, 1989), p. 533.
[12]Katie Whitaker. *Mad Madge: The Extraordinary Life of Margaret Cavendish, Duchess of Newcastle* (New York: Basic Books, 2002), pp. 75-7.

Maurice had thrown convention to the wind in the pursuit of personal happiness, despite severe disapproval from his parents. When challenged, he cockily argued that he had simply been compelled to marry Agnes. Otherwise, he would have "fallen into sin."[13] Anna, it appears, was just as smitten with William as her father had once been with his bride. And although her affection for Orange had been officially sanctioned by the elector and his wife, the princess' ardent attachment was viewed as indecorous, love-struck madness.

In the eyes of her contemporaries, Anna was confusing notions of romantic love with married life, although wedlock was nothing like the charming make-believe stories of Camelot and the *Amadis de Gaule*. Tales about the delirious power of love were meant to entertain and divert, parents and moralists preached, but could not be taken as a yardstick for matrimony. It was true, a minority of young nobles made romance a way of life, but even then, they did not necessarily regard it as a solid foundation for a working marriage.[14] When searching for a partner, the electress had once told her own mother, sober circumspection was required. "One should not pay too much attention to a beautiful figure, but rather to honest descent of princely houses and families, piousness of the parents, sincerity of mind, godliness, and other noble Christian virtues."[15] The kind of impractical love that Anna dreamed about since Orange's departure was a fleeting illusion lacking permanence.

*****

At barely sixteen, Anna of Saxony was an alert, intelligent girl, who, like many females of her class, was entirely ill-educated in matters of the world. Beneath a facade of beautiful clothes and genteel manners hid an emotionally unsophisticated and forlorn soul, who grasped at her idealized pipe dream of marriage like a lifeline. While her mother was still alive, Anna had been overprotected and spoiled; after Agnes's death, the electoral couple corseted the adolescent princess with reprimands and restrictions. At the time of William's visit, Anna was still an unformed teenager - immature, impulsive, and hopelessly naïve.[16]

She had never handled money and only shown scant interest in the workings of a large household. Due to the tragic deaths in her family, Anna might have also developed a sense of entitlement. The calamities of her childhood made her deserve love in marriage, she imagined. This combination of entitlement and distorted notions of wedded bliss sucked Anna into a delusional vortex, a dangerous fantasy world of her own making. Over the years, these dream constructs would lead to a perpetually futile search for perfection. Preferring flights of fancy to forthright, inward reflection, Anna engaged in a never-ending chase for the ideal life. As the days grew longer and spring was nearing, she was certain that marriage to handsome William would remedy all ailments of her heart and mind.

If there was some truth to the voices of caution - her grandfather and a few unidentified Dresden courtiers - Anna chose to drown them out. This small group of individuals knew of the princess's emotional problems, and realized that the glitzy Orange was not well suited for the "fraille," challenging Anna. Irrespec-

---

[13]Blaschke, *Moritz*, p. 23.
[14]Stone, p. 128.
[15]Keller, *Kurfürstin*, p. 21.
[16]Angela Lambert. *1939: The Last Season of Peace* (New York: Weidenfeld & Nicholson, 1989), pp. 42-4.

tive of his monetary situation or religion, a grand seigneur like William required something of a paradox of a wife. She needed to be self-assured, yet patiently subservient; a devoted and dutiful helpmeet who could manage the prince's estates during his long absences, yet also act as the glamorous representative of her illustrious rank. Lastly, Orange's consort was to look sideways when her husband disported himself with other women.[17] It was clear that Anna possessed none of these prerequisites.

Her mother's sister, Elizabeth of Hessen, had spent several years at the Dresden *Residenz* and immediately expressed her misgivings when informed of the Dutch match. Sufficiently acquainted with her niece's refractory nature, she addressed an anxious letter to one of Anna's ladies-in waiting. Although this particular missive has not survived, the reply sheds sufficient light on her apprehensions. "Your Grace would like to know if Madame likes or doesn't like to get married. You can surely believe that no one talked her into it, in fact much less pressured her into it. But you know Madame's head and sense, and you know that she will never be talked into something or pressured into something, but that she always insists on things ... regardless of all counsels. I've heard her say quite often that none of her relations can talk her into taking a husband she doesn't like." This was certainly true. In December Anna wrote to her Grandfather Philip that it was Prince William and no other whom God had chosen as her husband.[18]

Anna's assertions were certainly confident, if not brazen for the time. Instead of the gratification of individual whims and longings, noble marriage was a contract that aimed to unite and please two families.[19] Anna's astounding talk of personal choice and refusal was therefore all the more daring and extraordinary. August and his wife expected Anna to gratefully return their "kindnesses" by accepting whatever partner they selected for her, a time-honored social obligation that was rarely challenged. Of course, the princess's bravado may have boiled down to nothing more than chatter confined to the woman's wing, out of earshot from the electress, who would have hardly countenanced such broadcasts to her face.

*****

There were a small number of people in this era that defied convention and followed their personal inclinations. Maurice was one of them, as was Anna's Grandfather Philip, from whom she might have drawn inspiration. It is also possible that the princess felt emboldened by a female example of partner refusal. Shortly before Anna's birth, a young girl, who would later become an ally of William of Orange, had rocked the French court with an episode of outright rebellion against an unwanted suitor. Jeanne of Navarre (1528-1572), niece of Francis I of France, had refused a match with the king's ally, William, Duke of Cleves after firmly declaring that she was not going to exchange vows with anyone not to her liking.[20] She had even told one of her uncle's advisors, "Tell the king that I will kill myself rather than consent."[21] At his wit's end, Francis had the obstinate bride

[17]Fletcher, p. 174.
[18]Kruse, "Wilhelm von Oranien," p. 18.
[19]Ozment, *Fathers*, p. 27.
[20]Nancy Lyman Roelker. *Queen of Navarre Jeanne d'Albret 1528-1572* (Cambridge, MA: Belknap Press, 1968), p. 36.
[21]Roelker, p. 50.

eventually lugged to the altar by her collar. Fortunately for Jeanne, the marriage was annulled a few years later and before it could be consummated due to a French alliance shift.

In many ways, Jeanne's character closely resembled Anna's. Her aggressiveness and headstrong resolve, the determination to be free of any authority outside herself, alienated and isolated her from others. A lonely child, Jeanne was just as solitary as a woman. Even in old age, she found it impossible to back down once she had taken a stand and considered her self-esteem at stake. As Queen of Navarre, she repeatedly risked abandonment and even annihilation by superior force in support of her own opinions.[22] Anna would act upon similar lines, but unlike the Navarrese queen, she would lose all her battles.

*****

In March 1561 William of Orange received a polite, but ponderous epistle from Anna's grandfather, Landgrave Philip. It was absolutely impossible for his granddaughter to marry him, Philip explained. In view of the aforementioned issue of religion as well as other concerns, he simply could not give his consent in good conscience.[23]

At fifty-six, Philip was increasingly incapacitated by ill health and had gained the reputation of a curmudgeon. He suffered from gout, and the long term effects of a riding accident sent shooting pains through one of his knees. He had already declined to attend the wedding of his youngest daughter Elizabeth to the son of Frederick, Elector Palatine.[24] Now he felt greatly inconvenienced by Orange's pursuit of his granddaughter. "What does Anna know of life?" he inquired cantankerously. She was blinded by emotion, unaware that free expression of faith did not exist in the Netherlands. He told others glumly, "I would rather be strangled than agree to the match."[25]

Determined not to let the landgrave derail his carefully laid out wedding plans, William decided that Anna's resolution to stand by him had to be bolstered at all cost. Since he was unable to revisit Dresden, the prince dispatched his favorite brother, Count Louis of Nassau, as his postilion d'amour. According to Orange's instructions, Louis was to squeeze Anna's hand on his behalf and tell her "How I envy your good fortune in being able to see what I cannot. Thank her for the warm affection toward me … and say further that I implore her, as our wedding day is fixed and the arrangements so advanced, to continue in the same attitude of mind and not to let her be persuaded into indefinite postponements. If anyone tries to convince her of the existence of obstacles regarding religion or anything else, tell her to rest assured that for my part I will try my best to live with her so that she may be content."

"If they attempt to put any notion in her head to increase the difficulties," he added, "I think the answer best calculated to silence everybody would be, "if God has willed this, we will agree together," which ought to stop idle talk. I beg you to make this plain to her, for you know very well the result of incessant chat-

[22]Roelker, p. 59, p. 105.
[23]Putnam, *The Life of William the Silent*, p. 58.
[24]Gerhard Aumüller and Esther Krähwinkel. "Landgraf Philipp der Großmütige von Hessen und seine Krankheiten," *Landgraf Philipp der Großmütige von Hessen und seine Residenz Kassel* (Marburg: N. G. Elwert Verlag, 2004), pp. 38-9.
[25]Kruse, "Wilhelm von Oranien," p. 18.

ter."[26]

Apparently, Louis's hand squeezing produced the desired effect. The tender gesture transported Anna to new levels of amorous bliss, and she replied to Orange's greetings by whispering such raunchy words in his brother's ear that he did not dare put them down on paper for reasons of decency. She also sent the count on his way with a love note brimming with pledges of eternal love, fidelity, and steadfastness.[27] As for the prince's suggestion that their union was God's will, Anna assured him most earnestly, "My feelings towards Your Highness are the same as when I last wrote and I mean to abide by them, for I firmly believe that what God has decreed the devil himself cannot hinder."[28] Indeed, her courtship was evolving along the lines of a storybook romance. Liaisons of the kind always went through countless trials and tribulations, heroic deeds of valor, and sacrifice on part of the suitor in order to possess his faithful lady love.[29]

Although Anna continued in her amatory dreamland, William still required the elector's final consent for the marriage and was alarmed to hear the Saxon prince wavering about "such a young woman, our own flesh and blood, being subjected to such idolatrous heresies [as Catholicism in the Low Countries]."[30] In reality, Anna's uncle was merely girding himself against any future trouble regarding his niece's exercise of the Protestant religion in the Netherlands. If she were to suffer persecution by the papists, he assured himself, he had issued plenty of warnings beforehand. The only obstacle that actually prevented August from setting a firm wedding date was a previous agreement with the landgrave which specified that Anna could only be married if both parties approved of the match.

In the spring of 1561 August banished all pangs of guilt and conscience and agreed to the union. He wanted to be rid of his unruly ward within the year, regardless of the landgrave's protests. Incensed, Anna's grandfather countered with one final gambit. He asked the elector to arrange a meeting between himself and the princess, promising Anna an additional 50,000 florins from his own private purse if she agreed to renounce Orange.

He also reminded August that the great Luther had ruled against princesses acting independent of family interest. "It is strange to hear that such a young child of sixteen should have the power to get engaged without the knowledge of her parents; that would be a fine innovation in high and lower circles." Word had reached him that Anna was already in love with the Dutch lord, but this was nothing but "puppy love," a silly crush that was being wrongly encouraged by the girl's ladies.[31] If this marriage came to pass, he would relinquish all responsibility for Anna as her guardian. Philip warned, "The elector and other persons will have to justify themselves to their Lord and Creator when the time comes."[32] Even Elizabeth I of England, who followed the controversial match with interest, commented that the intended union was like a yoke pulled by two oxen of unequal speed.[33]

[26]Putnam, *The Life of William the Silent*, p. 60. See also Putnam, *Moderate Man*, for quote of full letter, written in Brussels on 23 March 1561, pp. 134-5.
[27]Kruse, "Wilhelm von Oranien," p. 20
[28]Putnam, *The Life of William the Silent*, p. 61
[29] Barbara, Tuchman. *A Distant Mirror* (New York: Ballantine, 1978), p. 67.
[30]Kruse, "Wilhelm von Oranien," p. 18.
[31]Knöfel, *Dynastie*, p. 135.
[32]Kruse, "Wilhelm von Oranien," p. 18.
[33]Böttcher, p. 80.

The landgrave's dire warnings certainly put August in an uncomfortable position. Embarrassed, he instructed his niece to send off a letter of explanation to her grandfather. She would never veer from the path of the true religion, Anna swore, but since she had already given the prince her word, she was obliged to keep her promise as an honest girl should.[34] She also quoted Saint Paul that a pagan husband could be converted by a Christian wife.[35] As for her visiting him in Kassel, this would unfortunately not be possible, since the elector was taking her to a gathering of princes in the Saxon city of Naumburg.

Defeated by such stratagems, the hard-pressed old lord eventually submitted with some grace, "Since it must and will be, may God the Almighty grant that it goes well with the Fräulein in soul and honor as well as in weal of body and of estate."[36] But, as a matter of self-respect, it was impossible for him or any of his sons to attend the nuptials. Anna, William, and the elector breathed easier now — all for entirely different reasons, and unaware that not a single one of the old man's wishes for his grandchild would ultimately come true.

---

[34]Kruse, "Wilhelm von Oranien," p. 19.
[35]Böttcher, p. 75.
[36]Schuppener, "Hochzeitslied," p. 225.

Margaret von der Saale, seventeenth-century copy of an earlier portrait. Philip risked his reputation and political standing to have her

"An Accomplished Fornicator"

Saxon officials immediately launched extensive wedding preparations. The date had been set for August 24, St Bartholomew's Day, and there was no time to lose. Further west, a victorious William excitedly informed his mother Juliana that the Princess of Saxony would be his wife come late summer. After several months of intense negotiations, the "battle" was finally won. Objections from Brussels had quieted down, the elector had given his full approval, and even Philip of Hessen had acquiesced. Juliana, thankful that her son's sinful bachelor existence would finally be checked by matrimony, was genuinely satisfied with his choice. At the end of June she expressed the hope that "henceforth the Almighty God will have the couple in his keeping."[1]

As for Anna, she was beside herself with anticipation. William's brother-in-law, Günther of Schwarzburg, had called on her in Naumburg and presented her with the customary engagement ring from her fiancé, an expensive token of love that could not have found a more grateful recipient. "Tell William that I wish him 100,000 times goodnight," she excitedly told Günther, "and remind him not to forget me since I never could."[2] She was impatient to put the stupefying torpor of her aunt's residence behind her and counted down the days to her wedding.

While Anna envisioned herself as William's treasured ladylove, her grandfather Philip continued to fret. The young woman was his oldest grandchild, and a special bond had existed between them since her toddler days. The late Agnes once mentioned proudly that her daughter had insisted on forwarding greetings to her dear Grandfather Philip when she was merely two years old.[3] Much of the landgrave's concern for Anna's happiness probably sprung from sincere apprehension about her preparedness for wedlock. He was aware that the immature, thoughtless girl was entrusting herself to a man she hardly knew, someone who had courted her with big promises during a few stolen moments, but given little proof of his earnestness. During that early summer of 1561 Anna was indeed certain that William would keep her well in "soul, honor, body, and estate" as Philip hoped. Yet from personal experience, the landgrave agonized, the match may very well turn out otherwise. After all, his own matrimonial escapades were still on everyone's lips.

*****

Behind the stolid façade of many a pious sixteenth-century prince - Catholic or Protestant - often lurked an entirely different personality. Like today, great magnates enjoyed being seen in public at carefully staged charity events, wallowing in pious displays of godliness, despite their private behavior leaving much to be desired. Renaissance society somehow managed to reconcile these contradictions which we would condemn as blatant hypocrisy. There are plenty of examples of devout gentlemen wearing uncomfortable hair shirts throughout their lives as a sign of piety, while siring a bevy of illegitimate children. According to the undeniable axiom of the modern era, aristocrats needed the company of

---

[1] Putnam, *The Life of William the Silent*, p. 61.
[2] Kruse, "Wilhelm von Oranien," p. 18.
[3] Kruse, "Wilhelm von Oranien," p. 10.

women and could not deny themselves such pleasures. August personages of the day such as Emperor Maximilian II (1527-1576) gained notoriety with debauches that did not preclude rape, while the religious establishment turned a blind eye.[4] Martin Luther, for example, made special allowances in regards to sex for the male nobility, a group he considered exempt from certain moral precepts.

In fact, the reformer went so far as to hint that a mistress could be considered part of courtly decorum, and whoever did without such a woman was a fool, given the extremely low success rate of arranged royal marriages.[5] By extension, no one thought Landgrave Philip's behavior insincere when this shining defender of the Lutheran faith engaged in a variety of sexual indiscretions, even after assuming a leadership role in the Schmalkaldic League. The religious establishment chose to look the other way, while his fellow Protestant princes—equally questionable paradigms of virtue—remained quiet.

Born in Marburg, north of Frankfurt, in November 1504, Landgrave Philip of Hessen was the only surviving son of William II of Hessen (1469-1509) and his wife, Anna of Mecklenburg (1485-1525), a sister of Maurice's mother Catherine. Chroniclers remarked on the permissive lifestyles of both parents. Philip's father William died when the boy was only five years old, a victim of the "French disease" (syphilis) which had only recently reached European shores from the Americas.[6] For much of his youth, Philip imitated his father, relentlessly pursuing women. Tall for his time at 5'8," the young landgrave sported a slender, athletic build with an expressive face and intelligent, grey eyes.[7] His reputation as an inveterate ladies' man did by no means taper off after his marriage to Maurice's cousin, the beautiful and elegant Christine of Saxony, in 1523.[8]

For many years, Christine ignored her husband's philandering without demurring, her busy life filled with numerous pregnancies and occasional episodes of bad health. By the mid-1530s, however, the landgravine's fortunes began to decline, because Philip embarked on an amorous escapade that sullied his wife's name and reputation, along with his own, in the most upsetting manner.[9]

At first, Christine was confronted with a serious health issue. In 1539 doctors diagnosed Philip with the "French disease," and thirty-four-year-old Christine, drained and careworn after six pregnancies, was greatly distressed by the news. The landgrave still visited her bed on a regular basis, and she was understandably terrified of catching syphilis, a painfully drawn-out affliction that disfigured and could ultimately kill. Side effects of this scourge included suppurating ulcers, evil smelling pustules, diseased bones and teeth as well as fits of dementia.[10]

Although a fast and effective cure for syphilis was only found in the twentieth century, physicians in the 1530s employed a variety of more or less successful remedies to help their patients. One of the most common involved a mercurial ointment in conjunction with sweating baths known as "salivation of mercury."

---

[4] Sigrid-Maria Größing. *Karl V* (Vienna: Amalthea, 1999), pp. 303-6.
[5] Stephan Buchholz. "Rechtsgeschichte und Literatur: Die Doppelehe Philipps des Großmütigen," *Landgraf Philip der Großmütige von Hessen und seine Residenz Kassel* (Marburg: N. G. Elwert Verlag, 2004), p. 66.
[6] Aumüller and Krähwinkel, p. 27.
[7] Aumüller and Krähwinkel, p. 33
[8] Margret Lemberg. "Alltag und Feste in den Residenzen Kassel und Marburg," *Landgraf Philipp der Großmütige von Hessen und seine Residenz Kassel* (Marburg: N. G. Elwert Verlag, 2004). pp. 96-8.
[9] Cordula Nolte. "Christine von Sachsen," *Landgraf Philip der Großmütige von Hessen und seine Residenz Kassel* (Marburg: N. G. Elwert Verlag, 2004), pp. 80-2.
[10] Nolte, p. 81.

Invented by the Swiss alchemist and physician Paracelsus (1493-1541), mercury remained the standard method of treatment for more than three hundred years.[11] The regimen could last from six to eight weeks and was highly uncomfortable.

In April Philip underwent the unpleasant "sauna experience," which involved the imbibing of a brew of guajacum wood and quicksilver. Doctors administered doses of the draught until the gums ached, teeth rattled loose, and saliva flowed copiously. The patient's breath began to stink as the gum tissue died from the mercury's toxicity. Not surprisingly, the enormous concentrations of the metal could cause permanent damage to the kidneys, bones, teeth, and blood vessels, and some of Philip's health problems in old age might be attributed to this near fatal regimen. Despite, or perhaps because of these tortures, treatment could be successful.[12] Philip, for one, recovered in record time, and neither his children nor Christine ever showed signs of congenital syphilitic infection.[13]

But even after Philip's "cure," Christine remained unsettled. She had long become used to her husband's roving eye, but as of late Philip was spending an inordinate amount of time with a young woman from Saxony named Margaret von der Saale. Her worries were not unfounded. Philip, at the age of thirty-five, had fallen in love. In fact, he was so besotted with seventeen-year-old Margaret that he considered risking his reputation and standing as a prince, the respect of his peers, and even his honor, to possess her. His marriage to Christine had long run its course, the landgrave convinced himself, craving radical change in his personal life.

Philip had first espied Margaret in his sister Elizabeth's entourage during a visit to Kassel.[14] At some point during her sojourn, something stirred in Philip as he found himself utterly captivated by the young gentlewoman. A portrait of Mademoiselle von der Saale - a somewhat crude copy of a missing 1539 depiction - shows a thin, plain-looking young female with a high forehead, wide cheeks, and a thin mouth. Yet something enthralled the landgrave for his interest soon turned obsessive. In the manner of Henry VIII during his courtship of Anne Boleyn, Philip was willing to leave all reason behind in order to follow "the calling of his heart."

Margaret was certainly flattered by the landgravial attentions, but clear-headed enough to reject his advances. As a woman of virtue, she informed him, she had no intention of joining the long line of Philip's past love interests. There was no need for concern, her princely suitor assured her, because a loftier fate lay in store for her: marriage. This was easier said than done. Divorce belongs to the secular world of the twenty-first century, not to the tight order of the Renaissance, and Philip could not simply hire legal counsel to rid himself of his long-suffering wife. True, Luther's writings had disproved the theological foundation of the indissolubility of marriage, but decades, if not centuries, passed before clerical and secular courts freed unhappy spouses from the *vinculum matrimonii*(the chains of matrimony).[15]

Sixteenth-century Protestant courts granted few divorces, usually on the grounds of adultery. Since Christine had never strayed from the marriage bed,

---

[11]Ozment, *Daughter*, p. 95.
[12]John Guy. *Queen of Scots: The True Life of Mary Stuart* (New York: Houghton Mifflin, 2004), p. 278.
[13]Aumüller and Krähwinkel, p. 34. Because of his speedy recovery, it is possible that Philip was misdiagnosed and never suffered from syphilis at all.
[14]Lydia Laucht. "Margarethe von der Saale (1522-1566)," *Blickkontakt* (02/2008), p. 13.
[15]Buchholz, p. 68.

and did not desire a separation, Philip found himself in a bind. He was also assailed by moral scruples after studying certain Bible passages. St. Paul's letter to the Hebrews warned that no adulterer would see the kingdom of heaven, which, the landgrave deduced, might be permanently closed off to him after years of conscientious debauchery. As the fires of hell beckoned, Philip stopped taking the sacrament, beset by a confounding mixture of remorse, sexual dissatisfaction with Christine, and a burning desire to become intimate with Margaret.

In the fall of 1539, after months of soul-searching, the landgrave found a solution to his conjugal dilemma: he would take Margaret as his *second* wife. After assiduously scanning the Bible, Philip had come upon a number of Old Testament passages sanctioning polygamy. "God permitted even the pious cousins Lamech, Abraham, Jacob, David, and Solomon to have more than one wife," he wrote excitedly to Martin Bucer, a close friend and confidant of Martin Luther's. Indeed, there were no express prohibitions on bigamy in the New Testament: neither Christ nor the disciples had proscribed such marriages. If he took another wife, Philip argued slyly, he could rest easy in the knowledge that he was following the Almighty's commandments. And if Martin Luther were to sanction his marriage to Margaret, he would at last be able to find "love and sexual fulfillment," and put an end to his "whoredom and other evil doings with women."[16]

Besotted with his teenage paramour, the landgrave hoped to further strengthen his appeal to Luther with heart-wrenching emotional pleas. A peculiar physical anomaly contributed to his inordinate libido and urgent need for another wife: triorchidism. Unlike other men he possessed three testicles which heightened his sex drive.[17] Furthermore, after lengthy hours of introspection, the landgrave was convinced that he had been the ill-treated party in his disastrous sixteen-year marriage. Christine "might be pious, but she had been truly unfriendly to him, was ugly, and smelled bad."[18] He had been talked into the union as a young, ignorant person, although he never found her attractive. On the contrary, the landgrave wrote, he thought her downright repugnant.[19]

When Philip divulged his bigamous intentions to Christine, an exchange of bitter reproaches followed. Indeed, marital relations between the landgravial couple became so acrimonious that fictitious rumors accused Philip of having his wife immured behind thick walls.[20] In the end, the landgravine accepted the inevitable with her usual grace, obeying her husband's commands as tradition and religion dictated, while girding herself for the inevitable blackening of her name, the ridiculing of her appearance, and a firestorm of negative publicity - all through no discernible fault of her own.

Meanwhile, Martin Luther discussed the Hessian prince's bizarre petition with fellow reformers and then furnished Philip with a writ of dispensation, the so-called *Beichtrat* (Secret Advice of a Confessor). The reformers' positive ruling had ultimately been based on sober political calculation. Philip of Hessen was one of the most powerful Protestant princes in the empire and the Wittenberg visionaries did not dare lose him to "the cause" by refusing his irregular demand. Furthermore, despite the strangeness of his request, Luther agreed that Philip

---

[16]Buchholz, pp. 60-1.
[17]Knöfel, *Dynastie*, p. 113. Medical historians have long refuted Philip's claim, which, in any case, does not lead to an increase in sexual urges.
[18]Buchholz, p. 60.
[19]Nolte, p. 81.
[20]Knöfel, *Dynastie*, p. 113.

had done his "biblical homework." Lastly, the landgrave had poignantly jogged Luther's memory about another past judgment: the reformist had once argued in favor of bigamy when England's Henry VIII was seeking a divorce from Catherine of Aragon.[21]

Naturally, the learned doctor was acutely aware of the larger implications of his decision. The contentious pronouncement went far beyond religious debate as it threatened to unravel the nature of marriage in all of Christendom, thus requiring some protective measures. Due to the incendiary content of the *Beichtrat*, its specifics were not to be made public, Luther told Philip emphatically. Monogamy was still the sole accepted form of Christian matrimony and permission for a second marriage could only be granted "in an urgently pressing matter," like the landgrave's, albeit under a cloak of total secrecy. Philip's case was an exceptional one, he concluded not altogether sincere, and the sole reason for the dispensation in this "internal affair" was to prevent His Grace from falling into sin again.[22]

At the beginning of March 1540, Philip led young Margaret to the altar. It was a quiet affair and few notable guests attended. Carefully removed from larger audiences at the landgravial court in Kassel, the ceremony was held in one of Philip's country manors in the town of Rothenburg on the Fulda River. The groom's beloved sister Elizabeth had noticeably stayed away, livid about Philip's mistreatment of his first wife, while Luther had excused himself, citing illness. As to the actual proceedings, they were in full accordance with canon law. Margaret, the Protestant theologian assured her, could consider herself legitimately married.

The sole irregularity of the union was the abrogation of the bride's claims to inheritance, which also applied to her future offspring. Philip already had documents notarized stating that Christine's rights and privileges as well as those of her children would not in the least be infringed upon after his second nuptials. In fact, he excluded Margaret's issue from any claims to the landgraviate, but promised to provide for them by other means. He kept his pledges. In later years, Margaret's seven sons received the titles "born in the House of Hessen, Counts of Diez and Lißberg,"[23] but failed to play any decisive role in Hessian politics.

On Easter Sunday, a radiant Philip took the sacrament in church, for in his loved-addled mind he had rightfully returned to the Christian fold. The "accomplished fornicator" - as the landgrave has been called by American historian Lewis W. Spitz - was now a happily, *twice* married man.[24] He even managed to placate Christine. "We consider you our first and foremost wife whom we will always honor," he wrote reassuringly to the landgravine who in turn discovered that her husband treated her with greater respect after he had his selfish way. Infused with a newfound sense of lordship as the head and master of not one, but two legitimate spouses, Philip took both marriages very seriously. He even overcame his alleged "lack of attraction" and fathered three more children with Christine, who gave birth in 1541, 1543, and for a last time in 1547, at age forty-one.[25]

The Saxon princess was and remained the undisputed official consort at his side, and ironically it was Margaret, who felt the brunt of the atypical union.

[21]Buchholz, p. 62, p. 68.
[22]Buchholz, p. 63.
[23]Rene Sommerfeldt. *Der großmütige Hesse: Philip von Hessen (1504-1567)* (Marburg: Tectum Verlag, 2007), p.27.
[24]Nolte, p. 82; Buchholz, p. 58, p. 61, pp. 63-4.
[25]Nolte, p. 82; Buchholz, p. 64.

Martin Luther's insistence on continued secrecy reduced Margaret's status to that of a "lesser spouse," or concubine, regardless of her marriage. Even worse, she was all but excluded from public life and spent most of her days shut away at remote Castle Wolkersdorf in the Burgwald forest, about fifty miles south-west of Kassel. Neither her husband nor anyone else ever addressed her by her full name. She was either called "M" or "the person." And while she occasionally accompanied Philip on trips, like a visit to the Imperial Diet in Regensburg, her carriage was always completely covered.[26]

The notorious couple had nine children together, and although they appear to have found connubial happiness, notes of melancholy, disappointment, even anger crept into Margaret's correspondence during the later years of her marriage. Dissatisfied with Philip's provisions for their sons and daughters, she had bitter words for the landgrave and complained in April 1558, "Your Grace has obviously turned my children into the children of a whore."[27]

Considering this burden, it may not have been entirely accidental that none of Margaret's male progeny ended up well. All seven sons either died in captivity or suffered early deaths. And over the years Margaret herself grew tired of her imposed isolation and position of disadvantage. On one occasion she wrote, "Now I see with the rest of the world that Your Grace does not keep me like a proper wife."[28]

*****

While family life at the landgrave's court slowly recovered after months of heated debates, the public fallout following Philip's bigamous union was only just beginning. A secret of such magnitude could naturally not remain hidden, and the desired confidentiality was soon breached. Interestingly, it was Maurice's father, Henry of Saxony, who exposed the landgrave's clandestine second marriage. Upon hearing rumors of a Hessian scandal, the duke had Margaret's mother, Anna von Miltitz, intercepted by a group of knights as she was returning to her Saxon manors. They conducted her to Dresden, where she was questioned under duress, and eventually divulged the details of her daughter's marriage. Neither Henry nor his wife Catherine chose to keep quiet. They exploited the extracted intelligence to pressure their son Maurice into giving up his designs on the landgrave's daughter Agnes.[29]

Moreover, the uncovering of Philip's double marriage exploded into a cause célèbre that riveted contemporary imagination for years to come. The most fantastic tales soon circulated throughout the empire, with Philip and his women the main topic of conversation. Germany's Catholic princes could hardly believe

---

[26]Laucht, p. 13.; Buchholz, p. 64

[27]Lemberg, p. 89. Indeed, despite a remarkable amount of personal attention lavished on them in private, Philip made it hurtfully clear in society that Margaret's children were the offspring of a "minor wife." In the spring of 1553, during a visit of Philip's son-in-law Wolfgang, Count Palatine, two of Margaret's sons asked to join their father and the count for dinner. Philip brusquely refused and ordered the boys to take their seats among his privy councilors. When they found a table of their own, and asked other guests to join them, Philip intervened again. It became clear over time that Margaret's children were caught in a peculiar legal and societal limbo: they were neither illegitimate nor legitimate. Their coat of arms did not sport the bar sinister (the sign of bastardy), but neither were they recognized as the landgrave's full-fledged heirs. Philip's oldest son William protested vehemently when his father eventually elevated his "second batch" to the rank of *Reichsgrafen* (imperial counts), and condescendingly called them "Ishmaelites" in reference to the biblical half-brother of Isaac whose mother Hagar was a second wife or slave to Abraham.

[28]Buchholz, p. 63. Knöfel, *Dynasty*, p. 113. Margaret found herself equally neglected in death. After Christine of Saxony died, her children built her a magnificent tomb with a grand epitaph at St. Martin's in Kassel. In contrast, Margaret was buried in a nondescript, almost random grave from which the Hessian heraldic lion was later removed.

[29]Buchholz, p. 65.

their luck that a leading Protestant would self-engineer his own downfall because of a female. Such idiocy was an unexpected, but welcome blessing for the old faith, they cheered.

They were right. The ramifications for the House of Hessen and Philip's political standing in Germany were predictably devastating. The issue at hand was no longer a genuinely theological or dynastic problem, but a critical incident that ballooned into a colossal scandal for German Lutherans. Thousands of ink quills unleashed a tidal wave of venom, accusing Philip of sexual deviancy and perverseness. Christine's Saxon relatives joined the opprobrium, and Maurice's plans to marry Philip's daughter Agnes were not unexpectedly called into question.[30]

The political repercussions were even graver. Within days of the double marriage's publication, Philip saw his influence as the leader of the Protestant Estates and the Schmalkaldic League dwindle away. The public outcry was reminiscent of the blaze of protest engendered by Henry VIII's controversial divorce from Catherine of Aragon, but unlike Henry, the landgrave never quite recovered. For the rest of the year, he received a flood of unsolicited, negative comments from friends, allies, and even his own children. Strangely enough, their reactions came as something of a shock to a flummoxed Philip. In July 1540 he complained that the current persecutions were far worse than any of the criticism leveled at him during his younger years, when he was still whoring around.[31]

Besides losing his standing as the golden knight of Lutheranism, the landgrave's ill-conceived match also resulted in inconvenient legal challenges. In 1535 Philip had adopted the emperor's "Imperial Law of 1532" known as the *Constitutio Criminalis Carolina*. Its criminal code contained an interesting section about bigamy and its punishment of decapitation. The landgrave was lucky that local laws superseded imperial statutes, and that he had failed to adopt this particular segment of the *Constitutio* into the Hessian's penal code. Also, as supreme head of the landgraviate's legislative branch, there was no substitute authority that could have held him accountable for his offense.[32]

Philip thus kept his head on his shoulders, but his reputation took such a beating that he was forced to accommodate the Catholic emperor in some very crucial political matters. In June 1541 the cornered landgrave had to assure Charles V - the primary enemy of the Schmalkaldic League - of his loyalty. In turn, the emperor overlooked Philip's felonies against imperial law and allowed him to keep Margaret as a consort. Such graciousness came at a price. From now on, Charles dictated, Philip was to lead the Schmalkaldic League according to imperial directives. The browbeaten landgrave complied, but the results were disastrous for the union of Protestant allies. The League, once a powerful defensive alliance and rival power to the Habsburgs, was weakened to the point of relative insignificance on the European stage.[33] Moreover, Charles exploited the lull among Lutherans by planning his final assault against them.[34] Such was the price of love.

[30]Nolte, p. 81.
[31]Buchholz, p. 58, p. 65, p. 72.
[32]Buchholz, p. 71.
[33]Lilienthal, p. 232.
[34]Sommerfeldt, p. 25.

Philip I, Landgrave of Hesse (13 November 1504 – 31 March 1567), as a young man

William

"The Prince is a rare man, of great authority, universally beloved, very wise in resolution in all things, and void of pretenses, and that which is worthy of special praise in hymn, he is not dismayed with any loss, or adversity". Dr. Wilson to Lord Burghleigh, December 1576

In many respects Anna was a fortunate bride. Her aunt, the Danish princess Anne, had never laid eyes on August before he arrived for their betrothal ceremony, while her mother's sister, Barbara, had been pledged to a man thirty-eight years her senior. In comparison, William's addresses to Anna had been unusually intimate.

While William had not bared his soul during those two short weeks in Dresden, it is likely that he told Anna about his childhood and youth. The couple might then have discovered surprising parallels in their respective upbringings as well as glaring differences. For one, Philip of Hessen's assertions that the prince ranked below Anna in pedigree were not entirely true. Although the House of Nassau was not among the most distinguished in the empire, and certainly not among the wealthiest, William's family tree of ancient forbears was just as long as that of the Hessians. One of Orange's distant ancestors, Adolph of Nassau, had even been elected king of the Holy Roman Empire at the end of the thirteenth century and ruled in German lands for about six years—a little known fact that the Nassaus liked to advertise whenever possible.[1]

While their influence declined in the following centuries, the Counts of Nassau still dabbled in imperial politics. At the beginning of the fifteenth century, William's forbear Engelbert married the daughter of a Flemish lord, the wealthy heiress Johanna of Polanen. Johanna's dowry included vast tracts of land in southern Holland, the Duchy of Brabant, and Utrecht, but the grand prize was the barony of Breda. Situated on busy travel routes between the trading centers of Bruges and Cologne, the lordship included not only the city, but also its outlying towns and fields. With one stroke of marital luck, the Nassaus had become grand seigneurs of the highest importance in the Low Countries. The immense addition of Dutch lands to the family's ancestral seat in Dillenburg (sixty miles north-west of Frankfurt) enabled Engelbert to style himself as one of the great European power players. It was a position that had eluded the family since those bygone halcyon days of King Adolph.

Over time, the Netherlands became the Nassaus' western base, while the German town of Dillenburg retained its position as the family headquarters. In 1509, William's grandfather, Count John V of Nassau (1455-1516), decided to divide his patrimony among his two surviving sons, Henry and William. The governing of two disparate and geographically detached estates had simply become too cumbersome to manage.

The older one, Henry III, received the Dutch lands; William I succeeded to the hereditary holdings around Dillenburg. Although the family was now split into a Breda and Dillenburg branch, the two brothers—William's father and uncle—remained close and consulted each other regularly in matters of governance. Henry, however, was clearly in charge. He liked to boast about the opulent Burgundian pageants he attended, and his eminent role as host to royal visitors

---

[1] Olaf Mörke. *Wilhelm von Oranien* (Stuttgart: W. Kohlhammer, 2007), p. 83.

in Breda.[2] His opinions, he surmised, could only be of value to the less august Dillenburgers, especially since he enjoyed imperial favor. As a valued advisor of Emperor Charles V, the Habsburg ruler of the Spanish Netherlands, Count Henry was part of His Majesty's select inner circle as a tutor and valet of the bedchamber.[3]

In comparison to Henry's exalted existence in the Low Countries, life "back home" was somewhat rustic and staid. Even to this day, Dillenburg and its surrounding villages appear like apparitions right out of Grimm's fairy tales. Beautifully situated in wooded country on the little river Dill, the town rests in a valley among undulating hills and is framed by vineyards and sloped orchards. The visitor's immediate focal point is the "William's Tower," a majestic edifice with conical turrets, perched high above the valley.[4] The French unfortunately destroyed the Nassaus' former residence, Dillenburg Castle, in 1760, but the stately home was well known in the Renaissance. A local chronicler enthused about its pleasure gardens full of fruit trees that "have come from a foreign land," as well as grapevines, a maze, and a "jolly fountain."[5]

Like Anna's family, the Nassaus amassed a fortune through mining which earned Count William the much-envied byname "the Rich." During his reign the number of ironworks increased rapidly in the earldom's mountains to the north, near the city of Siegen. Unfortunately, the economic boom was considerably dampened by the aforementioned Katzenelnbogen dispute with the Nassaus' powerful neighbors to the east, the Landgraves of Hessen.[6]

Apart from the dogged lawsuit, Count William's chief concern was the welfare of his patrimony. A sensible and pragmatic lord, he ruled his modest lands with paternal care. Rather than intriguing at Europe's grand courts, the count focused his energies on the improvement of agriculture and the foundation of schools in his domains.[7] He also proved himself as one of the emperor's most loyal retainers. Fissures in the Nassaus' arrangement with the Catholic Charles V only began to appear with the advent of the Reformation. As a young man, Count William happened to hear Martin Luther's defense of religious reform at the Diet of Worms and was immediately taken with the theologian's novel way of reasoning.[8]

And yet he was also a cautious politician, who realized that straddling the ever more volatile divide between Catholics and Lutherans would be a difficult, if not impossible task. While wishing to please the emperor who frowned upon the Nassaus becoming *Martinisch* (followers of Martin Luther), William's father was equally loath to alienate his Lutheran neighbors. Temperamentally averse to any rash, impulsive actions, the judicious count chose to placate both sides. Whenever he was asked to take a stand, William I dithered, and this tricky, if not cowardly balancing act alienated both Catholics and Protestants who condemned him as spineless. His oldest son would later be accused of similar tendencies.[9]

[2] Ulrich Schuppener. "Die Nassau-Oranische Residenzstadt Breda," *Nassauische Annalen*, Band 120, (2009), p. 120. See also Putnam, *The Life of William the Silent*, p. 11.
[3] Mörke, pp. 16-8.
[4] Wedgwood, p. 9
[5] Ulrich Schuppener. *"Der Dillenburger Rentmeister Gottfried Hatzfeld, Chronist der Grafen Wilhelm und Johann IV von Nassau,"* *Nassauische Annalen*, Band 103 (1992), *p. 134.*
[6] *Kleine Geschichte des Oberen Schlosses in Siegen* (Siegen: Druckerei Vorländer, 2005), p 15.
[7] Wedgwood, p. 9.
[8] Putnam, *The Life of William the Silent*, p. 12.
[9] Mörke, p. 19. See also Putnam, *The Life of William the Silent*, p. 12. On the urgings of the Lutheran Elector of Saxony, Count William half-heartedly joined the Protestant Schmalkaldic League in the 1535, but when a confrontation with his imperial overlord loomed

If the heady mix of politics and religion troubled the elder William from time to time, he certainly found comfort and solace at home. By all accounts, family life in Dillenburg was mostly harmonious. After a first marriage ended in 1529 with the death of Walpurga of Egmont and no male heirs, the count quickly proposed marriage to his cousin Juliana of Stolberg, a widow and mother of five. Almost twenty years his junior, twenty-five-year-old Juliana was a woman of exceptional character. Reliable, levelheaded, and devout, she took her responsibilities as wife and manager of Dillenburg castle very seriously.[10] The kind-hearted countess was a true caregiver to all children, including those from the couple's previous unions, and was held in high esteem by all who knew her, especially her own family.

Unlike William's first wife, who had suffered ill-health for many years, Juliana proved to be "of admirable fecundity."[11] At the age of forty-six, the Count of Nassau proudly presented his first son and heir, "whose name shall be called William," to his retainers.[12] In his excitement, he persuaded Luther's friend Philip Melanchthon to cast the baby's horoscope, a customary practice that persisted well into the eighteenth century. Its results seemed rather absurd at the time: according to Melanchthon, young William was to achieve great wealth and power, but suffer extraordinary reverses of fortune in middle life and die a violent death. Since the worldly prospects of a future Count of Nassau-Dillenburg were expected to yield neither wealth nor power, the boy's father dismissed the prophesy as ridiculous, especially since his family would not stop growing.[13] Towards the end of his life, Count William was the father and step-father of seventeen children from two marriages, little counts and countesses who all needed livelihoods that cut into his first-born's ever shrinking legacy.

In addition to clothing and feeding his litter, William had to pay for the upkeep and running of Dillenburg Castle. Before his wedding to Juliana in 1531, he had parts of the medieval residence renovated and turned it into a fairly luxurious home. Marble statues and foreign plants graced the palace grounds, while the all-important tapestries hung from the residence's interior walls. The Nassaus also employed a small number of artisans and included a portrait painter and silk embroideress as well as a *Lackenwerker* (linen master) who wove beautiful patterns into bedclothes. Another craftsperson was in charge of colorful banners and flags, often adorned with silk and pearl embroidered coats of arms, which were used during tournaments.[14] Representation was paramount, and although Dillenburg could not keep pace with Breda, the count did his best to receive important visitors in style. The Duke of Brunswick arrived one year with 150 retainers; other guests with large trains paused in Dillenburg on their way to various German diets or Italy.[15]

Apart from these grand occasions, daily life was pious, regulated, and fairly simple. William and Juliana's marriage seems to have been reasonably hap-

nine years later, he buckled under pressure. Although he did not renounce his Lutheran faith, William I, much like Maurice of Saxony, withdrew from the Protestant defensive union to join Charles V's forces. His older brother Henry was delighted. He had long pleaded with William to remain with the old religion for fear of antagonizing his liege lord and repeatedly admonished his younger sibling to reject all "novelties" of faith.

[10]Putnam, *The Life of William the Silent*, pp. 14-5.
[11]Wedgwood, p. 9.
[12]Putnam, *The Life of William the Silent*, p. 17.
[13]Wedgwood, p. 11.
[14]Becker, "Die Malerei am Nassau-Dillenburger Grafenhofe im 15. bis 18. Jahrhundert," *Nassauische Annalen*, Band 69 (1958), pp. 96-8.
[15]Putnam, *The Life of William the Silent*, p. 15, p. 25.

py and no reports of scandalous liaisons made the rounds during the count's reign. He fathered at least one child out-of-wedlock; a son named Gottfried (Godfrey) who would eventually play a part in Anna's life. But William I was discreet about this extramarital affair which might have taken place during or right after the end of his first marriage.

As for Juliana, she invested her considerable energies in the establishment of a palace school for her ever growing brood. She must have been a gifted teacher, because neighboring nobles sent their children to attend as well. The countess's curriculum was heavy on religious instruction, a reflection of her own moral code of proper Protestant living.[16] Unlike pious Dresden, however, where the rod always threatened, there was no shortage of genuine warmth and affection in the Dillenburg school room. Juliana's kindness and benevolence made for self-assured, contented children who developed strong bonds with their parents and amongst each other. Years later, when political and financial turmoil shook the house to its core, the Nassaus drew on these lasting childhood ties.[17]

When William was five years old, the count hired a private tutor for the family's heir and his little brothers. Magister Jost Hoen taught the boys Latin and other languages "that are in use now," most likely Italian and French. He also instructed them in "godliness and the arts as well as good customs and virtues."[18] Count William was widely known as a consummate diplomat who easily moved in German and Dutch noble circles because of his linguistic aptitude in both Latin and French.[19] Naturally, he wanted his sons to possess similar skillsets.

In the summer of 1544 a letter arrived in Dillenburg that seemed to lend credence to Melanchthon's vision of might and wealth for young William. The boy's cousin René, son of his late uncle Henry, had been shot to death at St. Dizier while fighting the French. With no legitimate heirs, René's vast estates in the Low Countries reverted to his nearest living relative: eleven-year-old William of Nassau-Dillenburg. The fatal bullet had cut short the life of one man, but given a new life to another. The count's son was now a prince, independent of the paternal purse, and one of the wealthiest men in Europe. From this point on, William outranked his own relations.

Although the news was certainly not unwelcome, the sudden windfall of lands and money posed a mixed blessing. Young William could now call himself a lord with pretensions - he had inherited the sovereign principality of Orange, about a quarter of Brabant, large stretches of Luxembourg, Flanders, the Franche-Comte, and the Dauphiné as well as the county of Charolais - but there were certain conditions attached to the bequest that dampened his parents' pleasure in their son's good fortune. For one, young William would have to permanently leave home to accept his inheritance and become a ward of Emperor Charles V. As the Netherlands' greatest landholder next to the Habsburgs, he was to be brought up as a courtier, diplomat, and grand seigneur at the imperial court in Brussels.[20]

That was not all. In August 1544, when Count William traveled to Brussels for the reading of the will, he was informed that Charles also insisted on his

[16] Wedgwood, pp. 10-1.
[17] Wedgwood, p. 14.
[18] Heiler,"Von der Frühzeit der Reformation am Hofe und in der Grafschaft Wilhelms des Reichen Grafen von Nassau-Dillenburg," *Nassauische Annalen*, Band 58 (1938), p. 78.
[19] Becker, "Beiträge zur Geschichte," p. 137.
[20] Robert van Roosbroeck . *Wilhelm von Oranien: Der Rebell* (Göttingen: Musterschmidt Verlag, 1959), p. 15.

son's conversion to Catholicism.[21] As His Imperial Majesty's premier vassal, the legacy stipulated, it would be impossible for the new Prince of Orange to remain a Protestant. Lastly, the country boy would have to say farewell to the carefree lifestyle that he had known until now, and adapt to the particular court rituals specific to the Low Countries. In other words, informal manners, lack of etiquette, and open expression would be replaced by the complicated loneliness and court intrigue inherent in any great Renaissance court.[22] After being told that there was not the slightest chance of amending René's bequest, Count William sighed and signed. Everything in this world has its price, he knew, and personal feelings had to make way for expediency at times.[23]

The following year, twelve-year-old William left Germany for Flanders, accompanied by his father and two friends, the Counts Wolfgang of Isenburg and George of Westerburg. While his departure was probably fraught with some tears, the boyish trio must have been excited to embark on their journey. At the time, the legendary splendors of the Low Countries - or what had once been known as Burgundy - fueled the imagination of many Europeans. Since the end of the fourteenth century, the newest trends in the arts, fashion, and gracious living all originated from the Netherlands and were eagerly copied by European royal houses, even the French court.[24] Together with his companions, the emperor's newest protégé could look forward to a life of heretofore unknown opulence and material comfort. They were not disappointed.

Upon his arrival in Breda, Habsburg officials introduced William to his new household. The newly minted prince now had a tutor, teachers, a gentilhomme, a valet, a footman, and a bevy of servants at his disposal. Their main objective was to transform the country rustic into a gentleman of the finest quality who would easily fit in with his peers. It was a steep, if pleasurable learning curve.

While clothes in Dillenburg were made to last, garments in the Netherlands were made to dazzle. The master of the Breda bedchamber presented his young charge with a wardrobe of brocades, velvets slashed with gold cloth, and fine lawn shirts inset with Maline lace. Fascinated, curious, and not a little bewildered, the prince must have gaped at the marbled floors, coffered gilt ceilings, and abundantly tapestried walls of his new home. Instead of reading Luther's religious tracts, the newcomers perused illuminated books of hours whose pages glowed with colorful miniatures. The royal library kept volumes by Ovid, Petrarch, and Olivier de la Marche - the emperor's favorite reading - as well as fashionable novels in Spanish, French, and Italian. Some were pastoral or even lightly erotic, and William became an immediate devotee of the bestseller of the time, the knightly romance of *Amadis de Gaule*.[25]

*****

William's life had been interrupted by a sudden reversal of fate, but unlike Anna, who experienced momentous changes at a similar age, his fortunes rose. Orange's income was valued at an incredible 170,000 livres a year, and he enjoyed the em-

---

[21]Mörke, p. 27.
[22]Ives, p. 7.
[23]Putnam, *The Life of William the Silent*, p. 17. Wedgwood, p. 11.
[24]Otto Cartellieri. *The Court of Burgundy* (London: Kegan Paul, Trench, Trubner, 1929), p. 17.
[25]Wedgwood, pp. 12-3.

peror's particular condescension from the first. In contrast to Anna's upbringing, William suffered neither from neglect nor stultifying severity, but found surrogate parents in Charles V and his sister, the Regent Mary. A widow with no children of her own, Mary of Hungary became William's devoted caregiver and made him part of her private entourage.[26]

Under the regent's auspices, William was not only exposed to courtly refinements, but also learned culture. The emperor's erudite sister was a humanist, who read Machiavelli and Erasmus and corresponded with the latter. Intellectually open-minded, unlike her dogmatically rigid brother, she paid careful attention to William's schooling in statecraft and languages. In time, the prince honed his French - the lingua franca of the imperial court - to perfection.

Orange was less disposed towards heavy academia. Although he was generally appreciative of books and learning and quite well versed in the affairs of the day, he took no pleasure in mulling intricate theological or philosophical issues. We can tell from his letters, which he wrote in several languages with varying degrees of fluency, that his spelling was not standardized and that his style was more forceful than graceful. Nonetheless, his level of knowledge exceeded that of most of his peers.[27]

Naturally, Mary's curriculum also devoted many hours to the knightly arts of horsemanship, fencing, jousting, and dance - essential social graces for any self-respecting member of the Burgundian elite.[28] The emperor took pride in the ornate and stylized civility that ruled Flemish palaces, and was an ardent admirer of Baldassare Castiglione, the Italian diplomat and poet who had penned the ground-breaking *Book of the Courtier* in the late 1520s. This pioneering, how-to manual for gentlemen envisioned a synthesis of the warrior and the scholar, the Christian believer and the classical hero. Essential reading for the nobility, Charles expected his retainers to aspire to the author's imagined sophistication and politesse[29]. Discretion and decorum, nonchalance and gracefulness were propounded as great virtues. These were light-minded, but crucial qualities which the Prince of Orange would come to personify in time.

According to Castiglione, the ideal gentleman was ever mindful of his dress, speech, and gestures, since appearances had to be kept at any occasion. For example, when taking part in sports and common folk were watching, he was to retain a certain distance. One did not want to give the impression that one was performing for the plebs, the author cautioned. Even more questionable, if not downright contradictory, were his suggestions regarding women. In love, Castiglione wrote, the prince must conquer wherever and whenever he can; whereas the women he most admires are those who regard dishonor as a fate worse than death.[30]

In constant pursuit of seduction and preferment, Castiglione's well-trained adherents learned to mask their true feelings behind an affable front of falsity and pretense.[31] William was no exception. By the time he met Anna, Or-

[26]Putnam, *The Life of William the Silent,* p. 22.
[27]Putnam,*The Life of William the Silent,* pp. 19-20, p. 49.
[28]Mörke, pp. 40-1, p. 46.
[29]Bull, p. 14. In reality, Castiglione's conduct manual was hardly original, but largely a series of echoes: medieval ideals of chivalry and classical antiquity met new notions of Renaissance manners and style.
[30]Bull, pp. 9-17.
[31]Paul Hyams. "What Did Henry III of England Think in Bed and in French about Kingship and Anger,?" *Anger's Past* (Ithaca, NY: Cornell Univesrity Press, 1998), p. 106.

ange had become a full-fledged member of this artificial world of dissembling and subterfuge where shameless opportunism lurked under a veneer of tiresome refinement.[32] His carefully groomed attractiveness and buttery slickness, painstakingly rehearsed but casually delivered, naturally swept the awkward Saxon girl off her feet. By 1560 William was the quintessential courtier, fully adept at the game of deceit and intrigue. It was a game his intended would never master.

The courtly world of pretense and artfulness naturally led to certain character changes in William's personality. At the end of the 1540s the prince was still known for his pleasing disposition, but also for his unusual level of self-control and circumspection. More anxious to please than tell the truth, Orange had learned that it was dangerous to give anything away and carefully kept his counsel during political and diplomatic gatherings. Apparently, his exalted position had also gone to his head. Observers remarked on a proud, vain individual who was easily hurt, but demanded his own way with stubborn tenacity.[33]

Nonetheless, the prince's most effective "weapon" - his easy temper and charm - continued to leave many of his contemporaries defenseless. Mary of Hungary, a woman who did not suffer fools gladly, was her charge's biggest champion and regularly sang his praises to her brother Charles. In time, the pair of siblings came to regard William as their personal pet *in loco parentis*. In fact, the emperor's affection for the young man was so great that he permitted him to remain in imperial council chambers during private diplomatic sessions, an unprecedented concession.[34]

Despite this show of favor, Charles made it clear that imperial patronage required the fulfillment of certain expectations. His protégé's residence in Breda was not an independent entity, whatever the terms of William's inheritance might have stipulated, but a mere department or *chambre* of the Habsburg court. It was Mary, he reminded Orange, who paid for the palace's yearly expenses of more than 3,500 guilders.[35] In other words, the Habsburgs' new favorite had become deeply beholden to his patrons, and was expected to repay these "debts of preferment" with unswerving loyalty. Neither Mary nor Charles could have known at the time that they were raising a cuckoo in their sumptuous nest.

While regent and monarch doted on William, others were less agog about the prince. Philip, the emperor's son, arrived in the Low Countries in March 1549, and immediately developed a distinct dislike for his father's German minion. Raised almost exclusively in Spain, the twenty-one-year old infante visited Brussels while completing his Grand Tour and to be officially installed as Charles' successor in the Netherlands. Until then the prince had rarely been exposed to cosmopolitan company and only spoke Castilian Spanish. Known for his stiff reserve, Italian officials had already commented on his air of *austerita e severita* during the crown prince's visit of the northern city states.[36] Although he was able to relax on informal occasions, when he danced and chased after women, the infante's linguistic weakness contributed to his reputation of moody aloofness. Unlike Orange, Philip was not a natural charmer.

---

[32]Bull, George. "Introduction," *The Book of the Courtier* by Baldesar Castiglione (New York: Penguin, 1987), p. 17.
[33]Wedgwood, p. 16.
[34]Roosbroeck, *Wilhelm*, p. 16.
[35]Mörke, p. 39-40.
[36]Kamen, p. 37.

The extended journey outside his birthplace unquestionably proved an eye-opener for the untraveled prince. Spain was a cultural hinterland despite her fabulous overseas possessions, and Charles' continued absence had deprived the kingdom of a regular court. Its location at the Western fringes of Europe further contributed to the region's isolation from the outside world. Diplomats like the envoys of the Republic of Venice seldom failed to present the country in an unfavorable, backward light. Although Spaniards were at the forefront of explorations across the globe, they journeyed to Bologna and Rome to be educated, and to Venice to buy books.[37]

Before his arrival in Brussels, Philip had spent several weeks in German lands, where he met and interacted with Lutheran "heretics" like Maurice of Saxony for the very first time. The crown prince was more used to seeing people of that sort tied to a stake to be burned, but for the time being the stalwartly Catholic Philip quietly accepted his father's policy of religious coexistence in German lands and did not dare protest. He was, however, quite revolted by the level of "religious error" around him.[38]

Socially, the Spanish infante felt out of place as well. In comparison to the urbane sophisticates of northern Italy and the polished, self-assured courtiers of the Low Countries, Philip failed to shine while his father was of little help. Charles had not seen his son in six years, and to many observers, the emperor appeared closer to the Prince of Orange than to his own, introverted heir.[39] It was a slight that Philip could not help but notice.

Despite this ferment of tensions, the Habsburg prince and Orange kept up a show of good will and mutual concord during Philip's Dutch sojourn. On 1 April 1549 William was present during the infante's glamorous entrance into Brussels, and in the weeks that followed, the crown prince jousted shoulder to shoulder with the count's son on many afternoons. The two gentlemen also passed several evenings at raucous banquets where scantily clad servant girls dressed as nymphs and huntresses served delectables.[40] All along and despite his son's misgivings, the emperor made no secret of his fondness for Orange. In September of that same year, at only sixteen, William was given the honor to host the crown prince by organizing splendid entertainments for his guest in Breda, which ended with a show of fireworks.[41]

Besides carousing, whoring, and the curing of hangovers, Philip also attended to the serious business of statecraft. His father, tortured by gout and crushing political duties, was eager to prepare the prince for his future responsibilities as ruler of the Low Countries. The management of the independent-minded Netherlands required a certain amount of tact and political finesse, Charles argued, traits that Philip did not possess in ample supply.

Like Spain and Germany, the Low Countries were not a unified state in the sixteenth century, but an association of regional entities loosely held together by one ruler. Each of the seventeen Dutch provinces insisted on individual autonomy and warily eyed any moves by the Habsburgs to infringe on their hallowed

---

[37]Kamen, pp. 22-5, p. 34.
[38]Kamen, p. 39.
[39]Kamen, p. 40.
[40]Kamen, p. 42.
[41]Vetter, p. 20. See also Kamen p. 41.

privileges.[42] Local town councils had to be courted; worries carefully appeased with poise and flair. At the close of the infante's visit, Charles concluded anxiously that his son had not made as favorable an impression on the self-assured Flemish as he had wished. Several months after his departure, he asked his heir to return to Flanders as quickly as possible. "I have presented to you many times how you need to win the confidence and affection of these states," he wrote, "giving them through your presence and contact more satisfaction than they had during your last stay here. They were not able to get to know you as well enough as was required to keep them happy and gain their goodwill."[43]

Philip had neither won the hearts and minds of the Dutch nor gotten on well with his father's favorite, the Prince of Orange. His antipathy towards the latter did not come as a great surprise, since the two princes were polar opposites in many ways. Debonair, multi-lingual William easily showed up awkward, tongue-tied Philip who resented the younger man's disarming manners and hold on his parent's affections. In turn, Orange wondered how his famous charm could have failed with the future sovereign of the Netherlands. He was mystified at the infante's antipathy towards him and remarked to a French marquis in 1551, "The Prince of Spain, without any apparent cause, cannot endure me and it is impossible for me to please him. I'm unable to discover the reason for his animosity, being unconscious of having offended him."[44] For now, Philip's dislike was merely a minor aggravation. Orange's bête noire had returned to Spain while William continued to shine in Brussels. In fact, for much of the early 1550s, he could not set a foot wrong.

William's courtly triumphs were matched by his good fortune with women. While details of his personal life before his first marriage are scant, there are indications that the young prince took advantage of all the pleasures that aristocratic life afforded. [45]And even marriage, that noble game of chance with notoriously low odds of winning, was another success for William when he married a noblewoman of the Egmont family in 1551. Anne, Countess of Buren, was an heiress with extensive holdings in the Dutch provinces of Holland and Gelders.[46]

Emperor Charles and his sister Mary could congratulate themselves as William's metamorphosis from a German Lutheran princeling into a Catholic, French-speaking Burgundian grand seigneur had been completed with amazing smoothness. After the emperor's eventual passing, his son Philip could depend on the Prince of Orange's unshakeable loyalty.[47] Everything was going according to plan, or so they thought.

*****

[42]Mörke, p. 29.
[43]Kamen, p. 42, p. 52.
[44]Putnam, *The Life of William the Silent*, pp. 25-6.
[45]Vetter, p. 48.
[46]Mörke, p. 50. His father's first wife had been Walpurga of Egmont, a kinswoman of Anne's, and the Dillenburg Nassaus gave their en- thusiastic approval to a union that guaranteed material and personal gains. In addition to their fabulous wealth, the Egmonts also shared common spiritual ground with William's kin. Although outwardly Catholic, the countess's late father Maximilian had espoused some rather unorthodox religious views. He had absented himself from Mass and fasts on many occasions which calmed Orange's devoutly Lutheran mother Juliana. It was reassuring to know that her eldest would after all be espousing the daughter of a closet Protestant. Anne was the only child of Maximilian of Egmont and Françoise de Lannoy, and therefore *suo jure* Countess of Buren and Lady of Egmont. She was also Countess of Lingen (she sold this particular county to Charles V for 120,000 guilders upon her marriage to William) and Leerdam, as well as Lady of IJsselstein, Borssele, Grave, Cranendonck, Jaarsveld, Kortgene, Sint Maartensdijk, and Odijk.
[47]Mörke, p. 51.

In the ensuing years, life in the Orange household was marked by conjugal happiness and the arrival of children. After giving birth to a girl named Maria, who died as an infant, Anne presented William with a son in 1554. The proud parents called the boy Philip William after the Spanish infante and Orange's father. Another girl, again named Maria - after Mary of Hungary - was born in 1556. Anne's health deteriorated after this third and final pregnancy, and in his correspondence William worried about his wife taking medicine that made her thin and weak (possibly an emetic for purging). The rigors of childbirth might have contributed to the princess's physical ailments, but specifics of her condition have not survived.

By 1558 the Orange marriage seems to have grown a little stale. During the imperial election in Frankfurt William made those oft-repeated, blasé remarks about the procreative function of wedlock and the acceptability of mistresses - remarks that were to haunt him in the future. There was some dissatisfaction on Anne's part as well. To be sure, the prince was always the consummate gentleman, but he rarely confided in her. A year earlier the princess had told a friend that she knew William no better after six years of matrimony than on the day they had met.[48] Still, the Orange union was generally regarded as successful, and when his "Petite Tanneque" eventually caught a cold which turned into a fatal bout of pneumonia, William was genuinely grief-stricken. In fact, he was so overcome with "perplexity and unspeakable sorrow" that he "fell into a fever with convulsions," and was inconsolable for much of the spring of 1558.[49]

William was open in mourning, but like his late wife, others noticed his increasing inscrutability. The carefree, untroubled youngster from Dillenburg had turned into a cautious observer of courtly trickeries. His detachment, which was offensive and hurtful to some, served most likely as a precautionary measure. Loose talk, a careless gesture, remarks taken the wrong way could spell societal, perhaps even actual death at court. Even the bedroom - usually a consecrated area of privacy today - was not safe from prying eyes and ears that hovered between walls and curtains. Servants always lurked, hoping to gather information that could be sold to interested third parties for profit. William, despite and because of his lofty position, was keeping up his guard.

*****

The sixteenth-century court was an unforgiving environment, a slippery place of "glittering misery" where allegiances could evaporate at a moment's notice and favorites found themselves the victims of vendettas and intrigues. In this combustible atmosphere of factionalism and deceit, murder was routine and life for fast climbers fraught with considerable risks. In view of his meteoric rise to favor, this was particularly true for Orange and he adjusted accordingly. He turned into a man who prudently hedged his bets, mingled, smiled, and chatted, but ultimately revealed nothing to anyone, even his wife. At court, and apparently at home, William displayed a combination of unfaltering courtesy, seriousness, and personal restraint. This, and his pronounced distaste for taking sides, earned him the reputation of a sly, even shady opportunist; it also advanced his career.

---

[48]Wedgwood, p. 18.
[49]Putnam, *The Life of William the Silent*, p. 36

Sphinx-like and steady, Orange avoided any course of action that might set him on a collision course, particularly with Philip of Spain. Eventually he was dubbed *le taciturne* (the tight-lipped) by friends and foes, a sobriquet earned for his infuriating reluctance to take a stand. The byname is actually a misnomer, for William was a man renowned for his eloquence, and has further been worsened by its translation into English as "the Silent."[50] The prince was not quiet and retiring by any means. He simply did not wear his heart on his sleeve.

*****

    In 1556, an ailing Charles V decided to abdicate and retire to a monastery in Spain. His vast dominions were to be divided between his younger brother Ferdinand, who would become Holy Roman Emperor and rule over Germany and Austria, and his son Philip, who was to govern the Western empire of Spain, the Netherlands, some Italian possessions, as well as the Americas. Courtiers arranged for a grand ceremonial to mark the occasion in Brussels. William, who had already been appointed to the imperial State Council and Order of the Golden Fleece - a highly exclusive fellowship of knights - was to be honored with one final distinction surpassing all others.[51]

    Upon entering the Great Hall in Brussels, in front of the assembled estates and highest dignitaries of the land, the gout-ridden monarch supported himself by putting his hand on William's shoulder. This was by no means a trivial or spontaneous gesture by a man of impaired physical ability, but a staged act of the highest political symbolism. Charles's leaning on Orange had been carefully contrived, signaling to all that the prince stood above his peers in the sovereign's estimation. He could retire to his favorite abbey in peace now, Charles insinuated. The Low Countries and his heir Philip rested in good hands, because of William's unswerving loyalty and dedication to their well-being.[52]

    At first, Charles's calculations appeared to tally quite nicely. William was able to retain his position of eminence in Brussels and King Philip even flattered him with advantageous military and diplomatic appointments. For example, in 1559 the prince spent a heady summer in France, negotiating Philip's impending marriage to Elizabeth, daughter of Henri II. As expected, Orange had no trouble fitting in with the new crowd. In fact, King Henri immediately took to the visitor from Flanders and invited him to join his inner circle.[53]

    During a private chat in the forest, a jovial monarch felt sufficiently comfortable with William to share some rather sensitive intelligence. As an ardent champion of Catholicism, the king explained, he was planning to eradicate all forms of the Protestant heresy in his kingdom. Orange's overlord, Philip of Spain, had already given his enthusiastic approval. Habsburg authorities had long been arresting members of certain Protestant groups in the Netherlands (i.e. Baptists), but Henri and Philip's novel "arrangement" took religious persecution to a new and more radical level.

    Apparently, the king was unaware of William's Lutheran background as he was talking away about rooting out the Huguenots, the French followers of the

---

[50] Lisa Jardine. *The Awful End of Prince William the Silent* (New York: Harper Collins, 2005), p. 29.
[51] Rosine de Dijn. *Liebe, Last, und Leidenschaft* (Stuttgart: Deutsche Verlags-Anstalt, 2002), p. 20.
[52] Mörke, p. 57.
[53] Herman de la Fontaine Verwey. "The Bookbindings of William of Orange," *Quaerendo*, Vol XIV, Number 2 (1984), p. 92.

reformer John Calvin. Many years later, Orange commented on the incident, disclosing that he was "filled with pity and empathy concerning the fate of so many excellent people, who were to be given over to their doom."[54] Another concern of William's was his sworn allegiance to King Philip, his master in the Netherlands. He wondered how he could remain loyal to a sovereign who was preparing the wholesale destruction of his friends and allies.

Temperamentally and intellectually, the prince was repulsed by any act of senseless violence carried out in the name of "doctrinal bickering." Perhaps his forced conversion to Catholicism had led him to adopt such liberal views which were certainly unusual at the time. Then, as later in life, William remained untouched by religious fervor, admitting that faith as a whole held little interest for him. During a formal dinner, he once declared that it was not important how one honored God, only how one served him.[55] But the clearest expression of his innermost convictions was probably expressed in a letter in which he argued that Catholics and Protestants believe in the same truths, although they formulate their beliefs in different ways.[56] For that reason, he argued, princes should never attempt to rule the consciences of their subjects.[57]

*****

After Emperor Charles's abdication, the Dutch nobility had woken up to see their time-honored concessions and privileges threatened by the claims of young Philip II, a notorious micro-manager and adversary of Flemish autonomy. Lucrative appointments of civil servants and other officials would be a thing of the past, the king decreed, as he intended to centralize and streamline the Dutch bureaucracy.[58] And he cared little about the public outcry that followed these announcements. In the late summer of 1559 Philip sailed for Spain, determined to keep the Netherlands firmly in his grip.

And yet the Dutch aristocracy had no intention of standing by quietly as their imperious sovereign curtailed their ancient rights. With William at the forefront, the Low Countries' wealthy landowners banded together in an unofficial, elite protest group. Although Orange still shied away from direct confrontation, he put his palaces at the disposal of the dissenters in the early summer of 1561.[59] Philip's half-sister Margaret, the newly selected governor general of the Netherlands, watched the goings-on nervously, unsure how to appease both sides. [60]William was caught in a similar quandary. Despite their differences, Philip had just appointed him *stadholder* (governor) of the richest provinces in Flanders: Hol-

---

[54]Vetter, p. 108.
[55]Vetter, p. 110-1.
[56]Verwey, p. 106.
[57]Wedgwood, p. 63.
[58]Vetter, p. 34.
[59]Vetter, pp. 117-8.
[60]Mörke, p. 66. See also, Etienne Piret. *Marie de Hongrie* (Paris: Jourdan Editeur, 2005). Mary of Hungary had resigned as Regent of the Netherlands in 1555, when Charles decided to abdicate as emperor and left the government of the Netherlands to his son Philip, despite his brother Ferdinand's objections. When Mary learned of Charles's decision, she informed him that she too would resign. Both Charles and Philip urged her to remain in the post, but she refused. She chronicled the difficulties she had faced due to her gender, the fact that she could not act as she thought she should have because of disagreements with Charles, and her age. Furthermore, she did not wish to accommodate to the ways of her nephew after years getting used to Charles's demands. The actual reason for Mary's resignation were her numerous disagreements with Philip. She asked for Charles's permission to leave the Netherlands upon her resignation, fearing that she would be drawn into politics again if she remained. Charles finally allowed his sister to resign. She formally announced her decision on 24 September 1555 and dismissed her household on 1 October. On 25 October, her authority was transferred to Philip, who, despite his personal dislike of his aunt, tried to convince her to resume the post. After another quarrel with Philip, Mary retired to Turnhout. She remained in the Netherlands for one more year and then moved to Castile where she died in October 1558.

land, Zeeland, and Utrecht. Naturally, these honors came with obligations. The king expected Orange to faithfully represent Habsburg interests while maintaining royal "rights, highness, and lordship."[61]

Political rumblings were aggravated by growing religious discord. Unlike the rigid Spanish, the Dutch had a well-deserved reputation as liberals in matters of faith and proudly claimed the theologian Erasmus, the guiding light of European humanism, as one of their own. Until the early 1560s governmental repression had been limited to small pockets of Baptist communities in northern Flanders, but with French Huguenot refugees pouring in from the south, the Habsburg tightened legislation regarding non-Catholics. Tolerant Dutch bureaucrats were caught between royal policy which mandated arrest and punishment of these "heretics" and their own sympathies for the Protestant movement. Philip, of course, would not hear of toleration. He had been shocked to find that heresy in his Flemish lands was generally overlooked and ordered an end to these blasphemous activities.[62]

The king's personality further inflamed already jumpy tempers. Unlike his popular father, Philip was generally disliked by the Dutch who feared the introduction of the Spanish Inquisition to the Low Countries. Furthermore, despite his best efforts, Philip could not warm to his northern lands which remained foreign and strange to him and whose languages (Dutch and French) he never mastered. In fact, the king often felt offended by the free manners of his father's vivacious countrymen and, paradoxically, breathed much easier in stifling Spain.[63]

Under the surface of relative peace, a dangerous cocktail of religious dissent, political ill will, and rejection of things Spanish simmered in the Netherlands. There was talk on the streets that Philip and his soldiers were nothing but unlawful, foreign occupiers, which filled William with uncomfortable foreboding.[64] He knew that his days as the Habsburgs' cherished bon vivant were coming to a close and that serious trouble was lying ahead.

*****

In the fall of 1559 William was shouldered with additional responsibilities. His father, Count William, had died, elevating the prince to the headship of the House of Nassau for both the Breda and Dillenburg branches. The prince took his additional duties very seriously. Rarely was Orange's household in Breda without a visitor from Dillenburg, and when money was needed for his siblings' education, William made the necessary arrangements.[65] Of his many brothers, William was closest to Louis, an intelligent and spirited man five years his junior. Louis had practically moved to Breda in 1556 to be of service to Orange, and soon gained a reputation as an excellent diplomat and military commander.

Apart from Louis, the prince also doted on his twice-widowed mother, Countess Juliana. Although the two spent long months apart and Juliana did not shy away from issuing the occasional reprimand, the tight mother-son bond continued over the years. The virtuous countess had been disconcerted about reports

[61]Jardine, p. 28.
[62]Kamen, p. 41.
[63]Kamen, p. 76.
[64]Mörke, p. 77.
[65]Putnam, *The Life of William the Silent*, p. 37.

of un-Christian forms of dissipation after Anne's death, and regularly admonished her eldest to pay better heed to God's commandments. William eventually complied. He was young and, as the chief of the house, in need of a wife.

After his courting failures in France and Lorraine, a bold plan that required all of his diplomatic panache took hold in Orange's mind: with political and religious troubles on the rise, the time had come to look eastward for allies.[66] He had heard that Anna, the daughter of the late Elector of Saxony, was in search of a husband and in possession of an immense fortune. Her uncle and guardian was a Protestant, but also a friend of King Philip's cousin, the Habsburg prince Maximilian. If he were to win Anna's hand in marriage, the prince calculated, he stood to gain priceless political support among Germany's powerful Lutherans. And this could give him leverage against Philip, in case he incurred the king's displeasure.

---

[66]Verwey, p. 92.

The Leipzig Wedding

On the day of her wedding to Francis, dauphin of France, on 24 April 1558, Mary, Queen of Scots, excitedly wrote to her mother, "All I can tell you is that I count myself one of the happiest women in the world."[1] Two and a half years later, Anna of Saxony would have seconded Mary's notion as she eagerly awaited her own wedding day.

At the time, suitors often presented their intended with small medallions bearing their likenesses. The bride was then to sigh and heave in regular intervals and in public, affecting longing for her beloved. In Anna's case, such pretense was unnecessary as the princess genuinely pined for her prince. Since June, after her uncle had finalized her marriage contract with an envoy of William's at Hartenfels Palace, she was spending her days in a romantic haze.

Perhaps Anna fretted in private about moving to a foreign country after the nuptials, but at least her wedding would take place in Saxony. Unlike most princesses she did not have to travel into terra incognita for the ceremony or undergo a proxy ritual, but celebrate with her relatives and Dresden courtiers. None of her family was willing to accompany her to faraway Breda, but this she could gladly bear as long as there were no further delays. There had been a last minute hurdle that threatened to derail the festivities. Anna's stern grandmother, Catherine of Mecklenburg, had died at the beginning of June, and initially there was talk that the revelries would have to be curbed or even postponed as mourning tradition dictated. Luckily, the elector had decided against such change of plans. His Habsburg friends in Vienna had already nodded their approval for the union, and all parties agreed that an opportunity like this should not be wasted for reasons of etiquette.[2]

The date remained set for August 24, St. Bartholomew's Day, a popular day for dances and other merriments that marked the beginning of the fishing season. By custom, German housewives served meals of smoked prawns and small river fish together with farmer's bread, newly ripened tomatoes, cucumbers, and radishes on the occasion. In coastal towns, fishermen guilds hosted elaborate religious processions, and many communities elected a fisher king. Shepherds' dances were also common on St. Bartholomew's, together with the Shepherds' Run, a carefree form of amusement for unmarried folk. Young men and girls ran barefoot across a long stubble field in order to win the prize of a new dress or silver jewelry.

The popular saint's day also marked the beginning of the harvest of oats and fruit. The so-called "lucky sheaf" consisted of a bundle of the most beautiful stalks, bound together like a bouquet with wild flowers and ears of corn, and was given to the local ruling family with a blessing.[3] Fish and new crops were ancient symbols of fertility, and therefore regarded as auspicious for a wedding. In 1561, this specific date was considered particularly lucky as it fell on a Sunday, a popular day to wed in the Christian tradition.

By the end of July Saxon courtiers scrambled with the completion of the extravagant wedding preparations. Rules and guidelines for princely nuptials

[1] Guy, p. 84
[2] Schuppener, "Hochzeitslied," p. 223, p. 228.
[3] Sybil Gräfin Schönfeldt. *Das große Ravensburger Buch der Feste und Bräuche* (Ravensburg: Otto Maier, 1987), pp. 213-5.

were vague, but here was a chance for August's commissioners to create something new in both scale and content. The city of Leipzig, about seventy miles west of Dresden, was to be the setting of the festivities. Dresden had only recently become the capital of Albertine Saxony and still lagged behind Leipzig in size and importance. Not only did the Saxon estates regularly convoke there, the metropolis was a pivotal place of trade where merchants from Eastern and Western Europe converged to do business. The Leipzig fair was the most famous in German lands, and two decades earlier Hessian officials had purchased treasures for Anna's mother's dowry there.[4]

As for the flow of events, elite weddings usually consisted of an entrée or procession of the bridal couple and their entourages into the city, the church ceremonial, and a bevy of entertainments. Tournaments, banquets, and balls often lasted an entire week and took place in different venues. During the entrée, the bridal couple and a cavalcade of family and guests traversed the city from one end to the other as awed onlookers gawked and pointed. The objective was to show off the might and splendor of the respective noble houses to as many spectators as possible since large audiences were otherwise elusive in the sixteenth century. In the absence of modern media and rapid means of transport, one could not take the event to the people; instead the people had to take themselves to the event.[5]

For a party as fabled as Anna's, organizers did not have to worry about a lack of visitors. Everyone, from the very old to toddlers, pregnant women to the lame, would travel long distances by a variety of means to catch a glimpse of the glittering bride and her dazzling groom. The elector had informed his officials that the union between Saxony and Orange should furnish his subjects with topics of conversation for years to come. And it did - in more ways than one.

Leipzig's mayor Jerome Roscher probably winced when August put him in charge of the lavish occasion. Affairs of this kind always led to additional expenditures and problems with security, Roscher protested weakly, while multiplying numbers in his head. The groom had to be presented with a costly gift, and the mayoralty would have to hire extra police to handle the riffraff that always flocked to town during grand celebrations. According to Roscher's calculations, the wedding party would be sufficiently large to strain city resources to its breaking point, while the elector - the severest of taskmasters - would mete out punishments if the festivities failed to meet his expectations. The mayor immediately ordered a replacement of the old cobblestones in the market square and had Leipzig's fire protection updated.[6]

Despite the enormous expense, the Orange wedding could only heighten Leipzig's reputation in Germany and beyond, Roscher eventually reasoned. With a population of about 13,000 - seven thousand more than Dresden - Leipzig stood at the apex of its power, and the vast outlays for the installment of a race track that required over 50,000 newly cobbled bricks could be quickly recouped by trade and investments in silver mining.[7] Roscher breathed even easier when August offered to shoulder the bulk of the expenditures. The elector had sent out invita-

[4]Lemberg, pp. 103-4.
[5]David Starkey. *Six Wives: The Queens of Henry VIII* (New York: Harper Collins, 2003), pp. 49-50.
[6]Kruse, "Wilhelm von Oranien," p. 21.
[7]Fellmann, pp. 32-3.

tions, enjoining each guest to bring his or her own cooks, tableware, and kitchen utensils. He would pay for the lavish entertainments, Anna's uncle announced, but even his largesse had limits.[8]

While Roscher and his administrators organized in Leipzig, the Electress of Saxony probably busied herself with the completion of Anna's trousseau. Exact purchase orders have unfortunately not survived, but we can deduce the contents of Anna's hope chest from her mother and grandmother's still existing inventories. Agnes and Christine had arrived at their respective new homes with stunning collections of multi-colored silks, velvet, and damask dresses, all richly embroidered with sections of drawn gold and silver, gilded borders, and a myriad of pearls. Household officials had procured the fabric from Leipzig cloth traders who stood in direct contact with the Torisany of Florence, a famous family of textile dealers. Christine's luxurious wardrobe consisted of seventeen skirts of gold and red silk, embellished with gold thread. Also included in her trunk were meticulously ornamented corsets and tops as well as thirteen pairs of sleeves made of Dutch linen. Some apparel was lined with sable fur, particularly the long velvet winter coats. Belts, golden necklaces, cases of jewelry as well as fourteen bonnets, all embroidered with pearl and gold filaments, completed the accessory trunk.

In a Renaissance bride's trousseau gold and silver plate accounted for the highest expenditure as it marked the pretensions of a noble family. Anna's mother Agnes had received her plate from Augsburg in Bavaria, home to some of Germany's most renowned silver smiths.[9] Her grandmother was also given gifts of a personal nature out of "parental love": a wreath and bonnet of pearls handmade by her mother and two large pieces of gold as well as a pound of pearls from her father. Such a fantastic assortment of valuables was meant to last beyond a lifetime, and in her testament, Christine bequeathed much of her wardrobe and jewels to her children.[10]

Anna's dowry could have been no different and was, if anything, even more costly. As Germany's wealthiest heiress and future Princess of Orange, her marital bounty needed to resemble the riches of a queen, all proudly emblazoned with the Saxon coat of arms. In addition to lavishly embellished gowns, a proper noble bride also left home with finely woven Dutch bed linen, nightcaps, shifts, handkerchiefs, and ruffs made of fine batiste trimmed with Flemish lace and embroidery.[11] Some princesses even took bulky furniture with them. When Mary Tudor, sister of Henry VIII, prepared to marry Charles of Castile (later Emperor Charles V) - a match that was eventually called off - her eleven page roster listed an entire bridal bed complete with a canopy of gold cloth and matching curtains.[12] We do not know if Anna's train was encumbered by commodes and chairs, but it is certain that she brought along something that was even more valuable: a substantial amount of money.

Saxon duchesses traditionally received 10,000 florins on the eve of their wedding; Anna's was a staggering 100,000, tenfold the usual sum. Most of this fabulous treasure stemmed from her father's legacy and was boosted by an additional 35,000 from August as well as a bequest from her mother's estate. The

[8]Putnam, *The Life of William the Silent*, p. 63.
[9]Lemberg, pp. 103-4.
[10]Lemberg, pp. 101-2.
[11]Kleinman, p. 20.
[12]Perry, p. 101.

elector's generosity did, as always, come with a price as he expected his niece to relinquish all claims to Saxon lands and titles. The immense endowment was meant as a final settlement, a form of insurance policy against all future demands that the sole surviving child of Maurice might levy against the Wettins.[13]

Hundreds of miles further west, William of Orange busied himself with his own "event planning." The prince, who thrived on besting others when it came to showy display, wanted to turn his second nuptials into a glamorous spectacle, an imposing public event that marked the connection between two of the most powerful houses in Christendom. After two years of seemingly endless marriage negotiations, Orange intended to make an entrée into Leipzig befitting a monarch. That meant that nothing could be left to chance, even the more mundane details.

"Now that the wedding day is appointed," he wrote to his brother Louis, "please inquire particularly of Count Schwarzburg about the arrangements that will be necessary for my journey to Dresden: whether I should take a large escort from here, what presents I ought to give the bride and the bridesmaids, whether a wedding journey be needful or not, what Germans should be invited. Pray find out how the bride will be dressed and what colors the princess considers hers."[14] As the former son of a count, he needed to prove himself worthy of the pretensions of Anna's relations. "Send out invitations to the entire aristocratic elite of the Netherlands," he ordered tersely, "especially the provincial *stadholders*."

King Philip quickly put an end to these high-flying plans. It was bad enough that heretics spread their blasphemous teachings throughout Flanders, but to permit his most powerful vassals to leave the country for the Lutheran wedding of a Saxon princess - specifically, the daughter of the arch traitor Maurice - was insufferable. Who knew what sacrileges his Dutch barons might see, hear, and become infected with during their travels? The king decreed that William would have to content himself with a much smaller group of friends and colleagues as initially desired. The Welshman Richard Clough subsequently commented to the Antwerp-based English financier, Sir Thomas Gresham, "The Prince of Orange is departed for Germany to be married to the daughter of Duke Maurice with a small company, for whereas he thought to have divers noblemen of this country with him, there was a commandment given by the king that no man in all this low country bearing any office shall go with him on pain of losing his office and the king's displeasure besides." His ambitious plans foiled, William crossed into Germany with some lesser Dutch nobles who had been deemed unimportant enough by the Habsburgs to follow their own devices. Altogether, his cavalcade consisted of 117 horses.[15]

On the way, the prince's younger brothers John, Louis, and Adolph joined him from Dillenburg. Two sisters also begged to attend, but William's mother worried that they did not have suitably elegant attire for the festivities. Ever the generous older brother, William had them dressed in finery from Brussels. Countess Juliana, fifty-five years old, decided to forgo the long journey, but sent her heartfelt congratulations instead. "May you soon have your Fräulein Anna happily in your arms," she wrote, "and may you have every happiness and content-

---

[13]Wartenberg, p. 81.
[14]Putnam, *The Life of William the Silent*, p. 61.
[15]Putnam, *The Life of William the Silent*, pp. 62-3.

ment."[16]

Together with his companions from Dillenburg and the Netherlands, William rode northeastwards via Fulda, continued south of the Harz Mountains, and eventually entered the *Goldene Aue* (Golden Flood Plain), an undulating stretch of land spanning the borders of Thuringia and Saxony. He picked up another group of riders on August 20 at Nordhausen who escorted the prince with about one thousand horses on the final leg of his journey. In the ancient city of Merseburg just west of Leipzig, the elector awaited with as many as four thousand retainers to greet him. Four days later and amid the sound of trumpets, William of Orange, Anna's uncle, and the Elector of Brandenburg passed through one of Leipzig's gates, bedecked in cloth of gold and silver. They were followed by long trains of liveried servants, glittering pages, and gentlemen-at-arms, not to mention pack horses and wagons brimming with gifts for Anna and her family.[17]   They were ready to awe Leipzig.

*****

For days, the city had been teeming with visitors from foreign kingdoms and principalities. Large crowds clogged the streets, ready to take in the novelty and grandeur that such a spectacle offered while marveling at the prolific entourages of the Archbishop of Cologne, the Dukes of Cleves, Brunswick, and Mecklenburg as well as the Elector of Brandenburg. August had passed through town amid the applause and cheers of star-struck onlookers, surrounded by forty musicians and two hundred *Trabanten*, his personal guard armed with spears and clad in uniforms of Saxon yellow and black. To guarantee security and order, the city of Leipzig had augmented its own troops with two hundred harquebusiers (soldiers bearing pistols and lances) who were also appareled in the electoral colors. Fifty of them stood detail around the town hall, while six hundred members of the city guard patrolled the streets.[18] Mayor Roscher had left nothing to chance.

According to the elector's agents, visiting dignitaries were impressed with Roscher's preparations, the imposing Patrician residences and new Renaissance town hall as well as August's munificence. An observer commented admiringly that "Leipzig surpasses all other cities in Germany with its splendid houses."[19] The elector's guest list was equally astounding and mentioned a staggering 5500 persons who would all be entertained at his expense. Stable boys and equerries struggled with the feeding and care of roughly the same number of horses despite 13,000 bushels of specially ordered oats.[20]

Farmers crammed the already overflowing thoroughfares by steering oxen and pigs about. Cooks yelled as errand boys delivered last minute food

---

[16]Wedgwood, p. 51

[17]Wedgwood, p. 50; Putnam, *The Life of William the Silent*, p. 63.

[18]Schuppener, "Hochzeitslied," p. 233.

[19]Fellmann, p. 33.

[20]Of course, the ostentatious festivities were not designed to gratify Anna's romantic whims, far from it. The electoral couple invested themselves so eagerly in the affair to raise Saxony's image in the world and to rivet the common man who expected to be captivated by the mystique of the occasion. Ravaged by famine, war, and other disasters, the people clamored for a fairytale confection that would divert them from their miserable lives of poverty, disease, and repression. Indeed, one was simply expected to put up a spectacular show of luxury and flamboyance. Also, see Ralph Dutton. *English Court Life* (New York: Alfred A. Knopf, 2004), p. 12-13 on this particular topic. About one hundred years earlier, during his entry into London in 1471, King Henry VI (1421-1471) of England had earned the universal contempt of his countrymen by treating his subjects to a sorry display of royal glory. His personal appearance and choice of clothes vastly disappointed. People bemoaned the king's outfit, "a long blue gown of velvet" that he apparently wore on more than one occasion "as though he had not much to change with." Henry's heirs, Edward IV and Henry VII, made certain to avoid their frugal predecessor's mistakes: both understood that the illusion of affluence, power, and status was as important as the real thing and dazzled their audiences with stunning demonstrations of wealth and splendor.

supplies to nervous kitchen personnel eager to arrange menus for the dozens of scheduled banquets. Amidst this hubbub, William and his train proceeded slowly to the center of Leipzig where the mayor and his sword bearer, the city recorder, high officials, and privy counselors awaited him in ornate robes. They presented him with a golden cup worth 112 florins.[21] And then the time had come to greet Anna. At the steps of the recently completed town hall, William met a breathless bride who welcomed him with barely concealed emotion.

Unfortunately, no description of the princess on her wedding day has survived. We do not know if she was a vision in choice silks and brocades; if her dress caused her guests to gasp in wonder. But then as now, a noblewoman's wedding dress captured the imagination of an adoring public. The gown of Mary Tudor was practically handled as a state secret, with Henry VIII's most confidential secretary Dr. William Knight sworn not to divulge any details.[22] Women of the aristocracy favored silk, velvet, and damask for their dresses, only the ornamentation of skirts and sleeves had changed since Agnes's day. In the early 1560s, braids and borders were still fashioned out of gold and silver, but there was something new: now skirts were trimmed with golden necklaces and other pieces of jewelry. Anna's Aunt Elizabeth had worn a dress embellished with "six dozen golden roses and eighty-two golden pins" for her recent nuptials to Louis, Elector Palatine.[23]

Colors also varied. Although Catherine of Aragon had donned a white dress for her wedding, Renaissance brides usually married in colorful gowns as white did not become custom until the nineteenth century. For the first part of the 1500s, the Germans had outdone everyone else in their copious use of flashy feathers, slashes, and puffs. Women, like Anna's late grandmother Catherine, had sported large brimmed hats with golden plumes and red and gold-colored robes on official portraits.[24] By 1560, gowns had become more muted, even in central Europe. Still, Anna's dress could have hardly been a simple affair. Like everything else in Leipzig, it was a triumphal reflection of Saxon might and splendor.

In addition to sumptuous gowns, most brides also wore headdresses, usually crafted out of gold for those who could afford it. Veils, however, were rare before the 1800s and bridal accoutrements had little in common with the showy confections of the twenty-first century "classic" white wedding.[25] Catherine of Aragon had been swathed in a mantilla or veil of white silk that reached to her waist, much to the stupefaction of a royal herald who had never seen anything like it.[26] Royal brides usually wore their hair flowing loosely over the shoulder, a symbol of virginity.

Among the lower classes, the bridal couple was tricked out in nuptial knots, ribbons, and other small trinkets that had been exchanged during courtship, and which bride and groom distributed to friends and kinsfolk as tokens of affection or mementos of the occasion. Fresh flowers served as popular and affordable wedding ornaments. According to early modern lore, the myrtle was "dedicated by the poets to Venus, and consecrated to wedlock." The rose, as a symbol of secrecy and silence, was thought to be especially suitable for brides.

---

[21]Schuppener, "Hochzeitslied," pp. 229-30, p. 233.
[22]Perry, p. 81.
[23]Lemberg, p. 104.
[24]Tom Tierney. *Renaissance Fashions* (Mineola, NY: Dover Publications, 2000), p. 23.
[25]Cressy, p. 356.
[26]Starkey, p. 59.

Some wedding bouquets were made up of primroses, maiden's blush, violets, and rosemary to recommend obedience, patience, and faithfulness to the wife, and wisdom, love, and loyalty to the husband.[27]

We do not know if anyone paid any attention to these touching personal extras for the orphaned Anna, who, despite her high rank was not particularly well liked. Relatives and ladies-in-waiting may just have gone through the motions in preparing for the most important day of Anna's teenage life, untouched by the young princess's wedding fever.

Grand nuptials were not complete without a festive procession that escorted the couple to and from church. A throng of dancers, prancers, and musicians usually underscored the importance of the occasion by loudly extolling the virtues, good looks, and accomplishments of the happy couple. Sometimes the wife-to-be was led to church "between two sweet boys, with bride laces and rosemary tied around their silken sleeves. A fair bride cup of silver and gilt [was] carried before her, wherein was a goodly branch of rosemary gilded very fair, hung about with silken ribbons of all colors." "All the chiefest maiden of the country, some bearing bride cakes, and some garlands of wheat finely gilded," then followed the bride into the church.[28]

Naturally, such pageants also served as prime opportunities for the attending guests to show off their ruinously expensive costumes. New shoes and clothes were considered a must for a ceremony of new beginnings, even at less lavish weddings. For festivities like Anna's Leipzig nuptials, courtiers sold acres of land to pay for their extravagant outfits. Ensembles made of Genoese satin lined with Florentine silver weaving, collars set solid with pearls, and shirts boasting huge silver buttons had often been bought with the proceeds of pawned family heirlooms, all for the sake of grandiose display. After all, personal honor was directly invested in one's shiny, new finery.[29]

Of course, the era's equivalent of cars, one's pure-bred steed, had to be decked out in equally impressive regalia. Grooms dyed the manes and tails of white horses black, while saddle makers sewed silver trimmings and sequins on velvet saddle cloths to which they attached fringes of silver yarn. It goes without saying that one's servants, pages, and lackeys also took part in this perfectly staged production. It was unthinkable to send them out in last year's already passé colors.[30]

*****

After bidding William welcome to Saxony, Anna quickly retired to her rooms to don yet another dress for the official ceremony scheduled for five o'clock in the afternoon. Shortly before the appointed hour, she and William proceeded to the great banquet room of the new town hall amid much cheer and fanfare. They were greeted by the elector and his wife, William's younger brother John of Nassau, Anna's maid-of-honor Sophia von Miltitz, and the Saxon privy counselors, von Ponickau and Woltersdorff. Leipzig's superintendent, Dr. John Pfeffinger, presided over the ceremonies. As was customary, Anna waived all hereditary rights to Saxon lands or property in the so-called "act of renunciation." These

---

[27]Cressy, pp. 362-5.
[28]Cressy, p. 355, p. 367.
[29]Cressy, p. 361.
[30]Garrison, p. 79, p. 82.

legal issues had already been settled beforehand, but for the elector - who was widely known as a miser - the renunciation was of particular import. After the conclusion of the formalities, no future demands could ever be made on Anna's part, or so he thought.[31]

There was more paperwork which was not uncommon in the case of such a controversial union. In the presence of the assembled witnesses and a public notary, Dr. Woltersdorff loudly recited the contents of an unsigned document drawn up by the elector in April. Its clauses commanded the bridegroom to honor Anna's Lutheran faith: the princess would be allowed to read evangelical books in her new home, and receive communion in her chambers in case of imminent death. It even enjoined William to have any future offspring raised "in the true faith."[32] "Gracious Elector," the prince concluded, "I remember this document and all the items listed by Dr. Woltersdorff. I assure Your Grace herewith that I will keep all promises as becomes a prince." The pledge was sealed with a handshake which pleased everyone, especially Orange. By officially refusing to sign the contract, he had placated the Spanish king. At the same time, William had mollified the Saxons with his verbal guarantees. Ultimately, he could not be pinned down by anyone.[33]

The proceedings concluded with the notary drawing up a formal record of William's statements which were to be preserved in strictest secrecy. There is little doubt, however, that the elector mentioned the transaction to Anna's grandfather Philip, just in case the Hessian was to censure him for sending his ward into a papist household.[34] William, on the other hand, cared little what Anna believed. As long as she kept up appearances in the Low Countries, all would be well.[35] Dr. Pfeffinger then intoned the actual marriage ceremony among gathered friends and family in the great chamber.

After the exchange of vows and the traditional torch dance, comfits and spiced drinks were served to the newly wedded pair.[36] Afterwards, following ancient tradition, the bride and groom laid down on a magnificent "wedding bed" that had been placed in the banquet hall while the assembled company drank to their health. After the couple was covered with a blanket, the marriage was considered consummated.[37] This public demonstration of married life, which probably took place amid much laughter, was to symbolize marital unity and remind the couple of their duty of procreation. Margrave John of Brandenburg-Küstrin, speaking for the elector, solemnly committed Anna to her husband's charge, and exhorted the prince to allow her to practice her Protestant faith. Shortly thereafter, the newly wedded Prince and Princess of Orange retired to their respective apartments to dress for the evening's banquet.[38]

To many a guest's relief, the "business of the ring" now gave way to "the business of the kitchen" as the pace of the nuptials was starting to accelerate.

---

[31]Wartenberg, p. 81.

[32]Kruse, "Wilhelm von Oranien," p. 170. "Dessgleichen wollen wir auch, so viel uns immer muglich, befurdern, und darob seinn, das die Kinder, so wir nach dem willen Gottes mit I. L. erzeugen mochten, auch in der wahren Religion der Augsburgischen Confession treulich mochten unterwiesen werden."

[33]Vetter, p. 64.

[34]Putnam, *The Life of William the Silent*, pp. 63-4.

[35]Kruse, "Wilhelm von Oranien," p. 23.

[36]One of the high points of any noble wedding in Germany was the traditional dance of princes, the so-called "torch dance." A time-honored German custom, the dance was a form of polonaise dating back to Greek and Roman antiquity, and performed by twelve noblemen carrying torches. While it was also known in France, England and Denmark, the torch dance was performed at German royal nuptials up to the First World War.

[37]Keller, *Dynastie*, p. 23.

[38]Schuppener,"Hochzeitslied," p. 230. See also Putnam, *The Life of William the Silent*, p. 64.

Gluttonous eating, drinking, and dancing, together with music and sexual innu-endo were the spice of every wedding and thus eagerly awaited. Even the strictest religious moralists conceded that the occasion warranted at least some rejoicing. After all, Christ himself had graced the wedding at Cana and contributed to the revels by turning water into wine. Theologians were of course concerned that wantonness, excess, and other "unmannerly and forward customs" might sneak into the festivities, together with the devil who liked to insidiously mix in with the crowd.[39]

According to convention, an opulent banquet kicked off the merrymak-ing. It would not do to start married life hungry, or to fail to offer hospitality to the guests, and the elector made sure that nobody left the town hall's banquet chamber on an empty stomach.[40] The highest-ranked attendees took their places on one of five large tables covered in black velvet and were served by a select group of trained staff.[41]

Leaving nothing to chance, August's master of the household had or-dered dozens of gentlemen and noble pages to report to Leipzig two days prior. They were to ensure a smooth dinner service and serve the guests with the utmost courtesy. Court officials had warned the younger staff that neither drinking nor riotous conduct would be tolerated. A special injunction stated that "It would be a shameful impropriety if the foreign quality found themselves unable to hear their own voices on account of the screaming of the waiters while dining."[42]

Perhaps it was during these early hours of feasting that the elector de-cided to share Anna's matrimonial horoscope with her guests. A learned doctor from the city of Nuremberg, Dr. Erasmus Flok, had created an astrological chart for Anna on the elector's behalf. Somewhat predictably, it foretold a long life full of fun and friends, harmony, and marital bliss as well as a beautiful body that was smooth, pure, and without blemishes.[43] After these rather unlikely prophecies, especially in regards to the bride's figure, some might have thought it advisable to quickly move on to the food. Then as now, the wedding cake was a major crowd pleaser. Perhaps the electoral kitchen served "bride cake" as was practice in En-gland and usually consisted of several cakes being stacked on top of the other, much like today. Everyone looked on eagerly, as bride and groom exchanged a kiss while standing over the sweet pastry.[44]

As for the rest of the Leipzig wedding menu, it allegedly broke all cur-rent records for consumption and overindulgence. With the electoral kitchens working round the clock, steaming platters of choice delicacies arrived without pause while tables groaned under heavy loads of gilded plates, bowls, tureens, and wine goblets. Chroniclers listed perhaps somewhat exaggerated expense re-ports of four thousand bushels of wheat and eight thousand bushels of corn used for baking as well as three hundred oxen, two hundred stags, three hundred deer, over a thousand rabbits, two hundred pigs, twelve hundred calves, three thou-sand geese, over fifteen thousand hens, and 132,000 eggs in addition to rivers full of carp, trout, and other fish for general consumption.[45]

---

[39]Cressy, p. 350.
[40]Cressy, p. 369.
[41]Fellmann, p. 33.
[42]Putnam, *The Life of William the Silent*, p. 63.
[43]Schuppener, "Hochzeitslied," p. 238.
[44]Cressy, pp. 369-70.
[45]Schuppener, "Hochzeitslied," pp. 233-4

Some of the fare on offer would turn stomachs today. Food was another way to casually display one's affluence and royal cooks were known to sheathe boars' heads, fish, suckling pigs, quails, and partridges in gold. Other popular dishes included pickled ox tongue, herons with carp, eel pies as well as peacock stuffed with cabbage.[46] Of course, alcohol flowed in abundance as well. Over seven days of uninhibited feasting, William and Anna's guests gulped down almost four thousand buckets of wine and sixteen hundred barrels of beer.[47]

A sensational wedding like the Oranges' was also an occasion for grandiose gift giving. Next to expensive clothing, attendees reached deep into their pockets to present the newlyweds with presents appropriately reflective of their status. If one's honor was tied to pricey clothes, it was certainly tied to the size of one's gift. From the electoral couple, Anna had already received her astonishing dowry; other relations surprised with money pouches, finely wrought silverware, gold plate, and jewelry. King Philip's envoy Florin, Baron Montigny, presented Anna with a precious jewel worth three thousand thalers, along with "His Majesty's sincerest congratulations."[48]

Less wealthy guests might have contributed with edibles such as partridges, puddings, cheese, and wine to keep the party going.[49] Gifts of a religious or supernatural nature, such as protective charms and amulets, were also displayed on specially arranged viewing tables. The sixteenth century was still steeped in superstition and people widely acknowledged the curative or magical powers of certain objects like "unicorn horns." An obsession among the nobility and higher clergy, the horns were said to sweat in the presence of poisoned liquid or food; it was also believed that they could detect heresy. The French king Francis I received such a horn, "two cubits long, the length of two forearms, mounted on a solid gold pedestal" from the pope at the wedding of his son Henri to Catherine de Medici in 1533. The gift was actually a narwhal tusk, and intended to remind the monarch of his duty to expel the poison of the "Protestant heresy" from his kingdom.[50]

As the night wore on and gift giving and feasting were slowing down, the time had come for music and dance. Orchestras played "the merriest, most ingenious music," tables were removed, and couples got out of their seats to frolic about.[51] At this hour the effects of immoderate alcohol consumption were setting in and some of the company became rowdy. Anna might have been led to the dance floor by William amid some crude cheers and licentious comments. The elector and his wife perhaps managed to keep some control, but at this point the typical Renaissance wedding degenerated into a bacchanal of drunken debauchery. "Then there is such a running, leaping, and flinging among [the guests], then there is such a lifting up and discovering of the damsels' clothes and of other women's apparel," the English bible translator Miles Coverdale (1488-1569) wrote sourly in 1552, "that a man might think all these dancers had cast all shame behind them, and were become stark mad and out of their wits, and that they were sworn to the devil's dance."[52]

---

[46]Tuchman, pp. 242-3.
[47]H. C. Eric Midelfort. *Mad Princes of Renaissance Germany* (Charlottesville, VA: University Press of Virginia, 1994), p. 57.
[48]Schuppener, "Hochzeitslied," p. 229.
[49]Cressy, p. 365.
[50]Michael Princess of Kent. *The Serpent and the Moon* (New York: Touchstone, 2004), p. 8.
[51]Putnam, *The Life of William the Silent*, p. 64.
[52]Cressy, p. 352.

At this late hour, however, even pious participants were known to for-go all moral lecturing in order to let lose. Bawdy jests and devilish ditties were hurled at the assembled womenfolk, including the blushing bride, leading to shrieks, laughter, and mock outrage. Sometimes, the carousing got out of hand: imagined insults fueled by wine and beer led to violent brawls with bloody faces, broken bones, and head-splitting hangovers the next morning.[53]

In addition to dancing and teasing, wedding parties also liked to engage in somewhat risqué games. Frisky pranks involved garter stockings and other intimate items of clothing which heightened the sexual frisson in the already charged air. Men and women, stupefied by liquor, started pulling at buttons and laces, loosening each other's clothes. Of fifty maids in attendance, one ballad suggests, scarce five were still maids at the evening's end — an exaggeration, of course, but one gets the idea.[54]

Nuptial escapades were by no means confined to boisterous country bashes. At the wedding of Henri II and Catherine de Medici in Marseilles, the bridal ball descended into an orgy after the newlyweds had left the premises. A courtesan had been brought into the banquet hall and as the night wore on her clothes slipped off. She then dipped her breasts into goblets of wine and offered them to a number of gentlemen crowding around her. Not to be outdone, some of the ladies of the court followed suit and one observer remarked that their "honor was wounded."[55] The Leipzig revelries certainly did not descend to that level. The straitlaced electress had no patience for even the smallest hint of impropri-ety, as the groom was to find out.

With the festivities generally progressing smoothly, Anna's aunt called on William for a quick tête-à-tête. Although her niece would be out of her sight and purview in less than a week, she was still concerned about the girl's future conduct. Anna's capriciousness and impertinent behavior could bring disgrace upon the House of Wettin even after her move to Breda, unless she was carefully kept in check. Because of her youth, the electress recommended constant super-vision. Those Christian virtues that she had painstakingly spoon-fed the young woman in Dresden must be continued in Flanders, she concluded, otherwise there was no telling what trouble the princess might instigate.

To the electress's profound consternation, the prince gave a rather flip-pant reply to her request. "[I do] not want to bother her with such melancholy things," he shrugged. Instead of Scripture, he would rather have her become fa-miliar with the *Amadis de Gaulle* and similarly entertaining books about love. And instead of knitting and sewing, he blathered on, possibly inebriated, she should learn to dance the galliard and similar courtoisie. After all, these were time-hon-ored diversions in the Low Countries and "most certainly decent and befitting her rank."[56]

Orange never lived down that answer. He later excused himself by say-ing that it had all been in jest, but in view of William's character and hedonistic lifestyle at the time, we can deduce that he was no dour patriarch. A lively man with the world still at his feet, William saw no reason for his fun-starved wife

[53]Cressy, pp. 352-4.
[54]Cressy, pp. 356-8.
[55]Frieda, p. 46.
[56]Schuppener, "Hochzeitslied," p. 223.

to quietly retire to her boudoir while he amused himself. Of course, he expected Anna to bring credit to the House of Orange by comporting herself in a chaste and dutiful manner like any other princely consort, but Orange was open-minded enough to allow his new bride certain freedoms. In that he clashed most violently with the electress's unbending principles and beliefs.

In fact, William's blasé reply made the Danish princess wonder if such a pairing of imprudence - the impetuous, frivolous Anna with self-indulgent William - could possibly come to a good end. The following day, either after or before a banquet, she had Anna and several noble ladies stand by a table with their hands held up in prayer for a good amount of time.[57] The girl had to be reminded of her Christian upbringing.

The electress's stunned reaction surprised William who might have interpreted her indignation as bigoted petulance. In his mind there was nothing wrong with the enjoyment of innocent pastimes such as dancing or the reading of fashionable books. Dance was a required skill at the courts of France and Flanders, and as for the *Amadis*, all young noblemen eagerly devoured its popular stories. A mainstay among chivalric novels, the knight-errand tale graced the libraries of most European courts, including that of Elector August.

Authored by the Spanish nobleman Rodriguez de Montalvo at the beginning of the sixteenth century, its epics of passion and valor had first taken Spain and then the rest of the continent by storm, enchanting tens of thousands of readers with a "dream of heroism and love." In a string of incredible exploits and fantastic love stories, the hero Amadis and his companions traversed England and Greece in a bizarre world of giants, wizards, and dwarfs. The adventures of the sensitive, but courageous champion lent wings to the chivalric imaginations of the aristocracy, leading King Francis I of France (1494-1547) to pronounce the lengthy saga the "Bible of the King." His son Henri II was equally enthralled by the fables of knightly derring-do and even coined a new, refined way of speaking, termed *amadiser*, at his Paris court. Incidentally, the theme of the fatal tournament that cost him his life in the summer of 1559 had also been the *Amadis*.[58]

Across the border to the east, the Habsburgs were just as taken with the novel. To celebrate the birth of his son Philip in 1527, Emperor Charles V laid on "tourneys and ventures like those described in the *Amadis*." And when the grown-up infante travelled through the Low Countries in 1549, his aunt Mary of Hungary staged a superb chivalric feast based on the book in his honor.[59]

But the novel also had its detractors. One of the greatest French Huguenot captains, the pious Francis de la Noue (1531-1591), claimed that readers of the book risked to be overcome by "a sense of dizziness" after entering its imaginary worlds. In his opinion, as in the electress's, the *Amadis* posed a danger to the minds of the young who were imitating the novel in dealings with the opposite sex. Women stood in particular peril of being corrupted by Montalvo's outlandish yarn, claimed the chronicler Brantome, a contemporary of de la Noue's.[60] It was a known fact that "loose books," "impure songs," and "offensive plays" could entice females into sensory abandon.

[57]Kruse, "Wilhelm von Oranien," p. 11.
[58]Verwey, p. 93, p. 95.
[59]Kamen, p. 1, p. 42, p. 196.
[60]Verwey, p. 95.

The surest and only safeguard against such hazards was to "marry prudently" which, according to the electress, was obviously not the case with Anna and William.[61] In a letter to the princess's uncle, William IV of Hessen, she apprised him of her concerns. The landgrave's son agreed. Orange's levity portended no good and he remarked perceptively, "When the abbot carries dice with him, gambling is allowed in the monastery."[62]

*****

The following day, a colorful but bleary-eyed gaggle of nobles lurched towards St. Nicolai's to attend Anna and William's first Protestant church service as a married couple. The procession of luminaries was led by twelve torch-bearing counts, barons, and other members of the nobility who were acting as escorts for the newly minted Princess of Orange and her handsome husband. A sermon was given once again by Dr. Pfeffinger who emphasized the indissolubility and sacred nature of marriage. A choir, accompanied by brass instruments and an organ, provided the musical backdrop.[63]

After church, the newly consecrated couple passed through cheering crowds amid cries of "largesse" with William and his retainers throwing coins to the poor. The new bride might have given "ball money" to her old playfellows to symbolize her separation from the world of unmarried maids.[64] While trumpeters and trombone players sounded off, the wedding party strolled back to the town hall for another evening of guzzling, gorging, and late night debauchery.

Whoever could keep up with the dizzying pace spent the next five days embroiled in a flurry of games and entertainments. Tournaments, hunting scenes, and lance contests alternated with masquerades, formal dances, and balls. Expensive, spectacularly staged jousting competitions were the highlights of daytime distractions. Perennial audience favorites, they were nostalgic reenactments of a vanished past. Renaissance society was no longer dominated by the knight, and the once vital battle practice was now a part of festive, yet frivolous court culture. At the time, princely residences were starting to disseminate printed reports about these spectaculars, each trying to outdo their neighbors in event planning and execution. Over time a veritable "ceremonial science" developed amid much popular acclaim and copiously recounted in print.

Jousting and festive processions alternated with masquerades and acrobatic diversions.[65] More hardened souls moved on to the tiltyard where real danger lurked at breakneck speed. Henri II's gruesome accident was still on everyone's mind and although there were no fatalities in Leipzig, the elector - a heavy faller - broke an arm in the lists. Under Anna's admiring gaze in the stands, William also proved his jousting mettle, but tactfully permitted the Saxons to win at the end of the day.[66]

[61]Verwey, p. 95.
[62]Schuppener, "Hochzeitslied," p. 235.
[63]Schuppener, "Hochzeitslied," p. 232. See also Putnam, *The Life of William the Silent*, p. 64. Both ceremony and benediction followed Lutheran usages. This was strictly in accordance with the law of the empire. Martin Luther's famous Latin phrase "Cuius regio, eius religio," meaning "whose realm, his religion," stipulated that the religion of the ruler determined that of his subjects. It was therefore only right and proper that August, Saxony's sovereign, should send off his niece with a Lutheran blessing, just as it was accepted that she would consent to live "Catholically" (at least outwardly) in the Netherlands, where Philip of Spain reigned supreme.
[64]Cressy, p. 367.
[65]Lemberg, p. 100, p. 107.
[66]Wedgwood, p. 50.

Festivities continued with an elaborate procession of "colliers," in honor of Saxony's century old mining tradition. Anna's maid-of-honor, Sophia von Miltitz, and her attendants strode through town accompanied by a miners' choir with burning lamps and matching costumes.[67] At night, high-ranking guests attended a fancy masked ball organized by the Prince of Orange. August had personally requested William's help in the staging of the so-called "Dutch masquerade," the likes of which had never been performed in Saxony. Successfully executed, it gained the prince high praise, particularly from his young wife.[68] Revelers dressed as monks, knights, farmers, and cardinals, and according to one poem, there was "no room for sorrow."[69]

After all, it was a marriage made in heaven. William took home an unencumbered heiress whose dowry would silence the majority of his creditors and whose political connections would serve useful in a conflict with King Philip. Anna, on the other hand, had just married the shining prince of her teenage dreams.

---

[67]Watanabe, p. 121.
[68]Vetter, p. 65.
[69]Putnam, *The Life of William the Silent*, p. 64.

Sex

For some of the guests, if not the newly wedded couple, the actual bedding of the bride was the climax, so to speak, of the entire wedding celebration. More than any other social occasion, the sexually charged atmosphere infused the festivities with prickling piquancy. Kissing among merrymakers began right after church with the crescendo of sensual exhilaration rising by the hour. After the alcohol had begun to flow, the female partygoers, including the bride, became the objects of crude jokes and innuendoes. Miles Coverdale lamented, "Then must she oft hear and see much wickedness and many an uncomely word."[1]

To the embarrassment of many a shy spouse, throngs of people congregated in the couple's quarters as was custom, pushing and shoving their way to the nuptial chamber. Intoxicated and obnoxious, their slurred obscenities and earthy verbal eruptions often left already anxious young brides completely flustered. A considerable percentage of lower class women were no longer virgins on their wedding day (about twenty percent were already pregnant), but sheltered ladies like Anna usually entertained only hazy notions of what was in store for them. Given the double standard, it seems reasonable to assume that most aristocratic bridegrooms were already sexually initiated, though not necessarily competent or experienced.[2]

To strengthen the bride's resolve and the groom's "performance," the couple imbibed a specially prepared strengthening caudle of wine and spices similar to the brew traditionally given to mothers who had recently given birth. According to the English diarist Samuel Pepys (1633-1703), this so-called "sack posset" consisted of milk, wine, egg yolks, sugar, cinnamon, and nutmeg and supposedly made the man lusty, but also kind. Oftentimes, the couple gulped down the concoction in order to rid themselves of the wearisome company who was always loath to depart. The groom then swore, prayed, and begged the stubborn spectators to finally take their leave while his wife remained quiet, sometimes shaking like a leaf with fear.[3] Wedding parties, however, were habitually in the mood for rowdy games with the newlyweds' hose and stockings, a prelude to the sight of four bare legs in bed. Unlike modern practice, which involves the bride throwing her bridal bouquet to her unmarried friends, stockings were thrown at, not by, the married couple.

To calm the nervous bride, female relatives sometimes festooned the bed with scented violets and colorful ribbons and sprinkled the sheets with essence of jasmine. In addition to pleasing the senses, sweet herbs signified the exclusion of all conjugal strife and discord. In their place, pleasantness, cheerfulness, mildness, and love assumed the upper hand.[4]

For the upper classes, the actual making of the bridal bed was a ritual in itself and carefully described in books of royal etiquette all over Europe. In England, the princely bed was made up of several layers and required a large party of household servants to assemble. With straw as its base, a valet jumped into the litter, rolling up and down to smoothen out the straw, and to check for any concealed weapons or other devices meant to injure the bridal couple. Next,

---

[1]Cressy, p. 352, p. 374.
[2]Cressy, p. 374.
[3]Cressy, pp. 374-5.
[4]Cressy, p. 364, pp. 374-5.

attendants spread a protective canvas over the straw, followed by a feather duvet, another blanket, two sheets, an additional coverlet as well as a couple of fur rugs, one made out of ermine. Chambermaids vigorously beat and plumped the pillows and bedding, and stretched the sheets and blankets to get rid of any wrinkles.[5] Inviting and plush, the infamous noble bedstead bore witness to ecstatic happiness, tears, and abject sorrows. More often than not, it was the latter.

During Anna and William's first night together, the electress probably had her officials reign in disorderly guests. A stickler for decorum, she was known to interfere in far less bawdy activities. At the nuptials of her son Christian, she prohibited Italian fashions among her staff. Their smooth kirtles and unpleated skirts, she argued, were particularly "strange [and] naughty."[6] While Anna and William prepared for bed, a choir of young boys and girls chanted a bridal poem, the epithalamium, in front of the bedroom. Composed by an unknown author, the 179 verse-long ode recounted the magnificence of the event with descriptions of the bridal procession, the illustrious guests as well as the distinctions and copious virtues of the newlyweds in an overall theme of "honor." The host of the celebrations, Elector August, also found special mention.

Unfortunately, the dedication is annoyingly nondescript, its characters barely outlined. The bride is a stereotypical paragon of female compliance, her virtues those of a future Stepford wife (modest, chaste, pure, noble etc.) without a hint of personality. Platitudes ran along the lines of, "The tender lady welcomed the groom with fine words, and walked up to him in a modest and reverent fashion" or "The bride followed the groom, virtuously and honorably, as was deemed right at this time."

As for William, he is not even referred to by first name, but only as the Prince of Orange. It was the host of the lavish event, Elector August, who took center stage in this self-praising tribute, and his role as a sagacious father figure to his niece was frequently expounded upon. The rhyme ended in a prayer that invoked God's protection for the bride, a benediction for the couple, and an assurance of heavenly salvation.

If Anna thought that the time had finally come to retire to the privacy of her chambers with William, she was mistaken. The first poetic performance was followed by a second, even lengthier song of praise. Contrived by a certain Blasius Brun, possibly a retainer of William's, it spanned 282 endless verses, but was considered of lower quality than the first. Brun listed the heroic deeds of the couple's relations and ancestors, especially Anna's late father Maurice and her grandfather, Philip of Hessen. In closing, Brun wished "the tender lady" joy, happiness, peace, and calm as well as the Almighty's eternal blessing.[7]

With the drawn-out recitals finally at an end, the Oranges impatiently, and perhaps unsuccessfully, waited for their bedroom to clear of family members and well-wishers. But more rituals, known as the "Hymen's Revels" most likely followed, prolonging Anna's edgy suspense of what was to come. In neighboring Hessen, the married couple slipped under the sheets under the auspices of the guests during the so-called "bed beating."[8] In Saxony, it was common practice for the bride to be conducted to bed by a relative or confidante. Martin Luther had

---

[5]Starkey, p. 61.
[6]Keller, *Kurfürstin*, p. 51.
[7]Schuppener, "Hochzeitslied," pp. 239-45, p. 254.
[8]Lemberg, p. 100

done so at the wedding of the daughter of Hans Lufft, a close friend of the reformer's and printer of the first Lutheran bible. The theologian had admonished the
groom to always act the master of the house, and as a sign of husbandly supremacy, put one of the young man's shoes on top of the bed's canopy, symbolizing
male dominance in marriage.[9]

In England, the groomsmen took off the bride's garters which she had
previously untied so that they hung down and prevented "a curious hand coming
too near her knee." The bridesmaids and female family members then helped her
disrobe. As for the husband, he undressed in another room with the assistance of
friends, and afterwards entered the bedchamber in his nightgown, accompanied
by a large group of nobles, gentlemen, and clergy.

In 1478 Anna's great-grandfather Albrecht of Saxony recounted similar
proceedings at the wedding night of his seventeen-year-old niece Christina in
Copenhagen. After the banquet, the princess was led to the bedchamber where
the old queen, Dorothea of Brandenburg, took off her most precious jewels and
ordered her ladies to tuck her in. Albrecht remembered that "Our niece sat in that
bed for a good while until the king came and brought candy and drink." Shortly
afterwards, the groom - crown prince John - snuck into the chamber, clad in his
night shirt and hose and quickly jumped into bed to embrace his spouse. "Then
we pulled the blanket over both their heads," he reminisced. "And after a few
minutes of shared snacks and drinks, everyone left, except for the queen, her ladies, and some chambermaids."[10]

Now was also the time for the newlyweds to reveal more of their natural
physiques to each other as they were dressed in simple nightclothes. For some,
such disclosures came as a shock. William IV, Prince of Orange (1711-1751) and
a descendant of Anna's husband, had always concealed his "defects" by carefully cut coats and long periwigs. Unfortunately, there could be no disguise at the
public bedding ceremony where the sight of him in a thin gown and nightcap so
horrified the bride's mother, Queen Caroline of England, that she burst into tears
and had to be led from the room. One of her advisors, Lord Hervey, tried to calm
the anxious mother with the following sober assessment, "Madame, in half a year
all persons are alike. The figure of the body one is married to grows so familiar to
one's eye that one looks at it mechanically without regarding either the beauties
or deformities."[11]

In Catholic countries, such observations along with the customary jokes
and banter now gave way to solemnity as a high ranking clergyman, usually a
bishop, blessed the bed and sprinkled it with holy water to ensure fertility. Bene-
dictions usually included prayers for children, long life, and God's protection. After such sober incantations, even the most stubborn of bystanders would betake
himself elsewhere, one hoped. In many cases, however, revelers chose to linger,
spurred on by the thrill of peeking at the imminent "duty to the state" that was
about to take place in the form of sexual intercourse.

In some regions of Italy it was a courtier's robust privilege not only to
usher the bridal pair to the nuptial couch, but to remain in the room and witness the consummation of their union. At the court of the Gonzaga of Mantua a
chronicler described one such "scene": a priest was called upon to insert his hand

[9]Karant-Nunn and Wiesner-Hanks, p. 129.
[10]Michail A Bojcov. "'Das Frauenzimmer' oder 'die Frau bei Hofe'?", *Das Frauenzimmer* (Stuttgart: Jan Thorbecke, 2000), pp. 330-1.
[11]Veronica P. M. Baker-Smith. *A Life of Anne of Hanover* (New York: E. J. Brill, 1995), p. 48.

between the couple to verify full intromission and therewith the legitimacy of the future heir.[12]

In neighboring France, discomforting lack of privacy among the nobility was just as common. Years after the event, the Marquise de Sévigné still shuddered with revulsion while recollecting a wedding night filled with unwelcome intruders, ribald remarks, and leering visages.[13] Many of her peers took a more sober view of what we today consider an intensely personal act. For the elite, the matrimonial bed was a site of public spectacle in which one had to prove to observing relations and clergy that the union was legally consummated by male penetration. This had nothing to do with love, romance, or propriety. On the contrary, it was, if nothing else, a legal fulfillment.[14] In case of "performance failure," an annulment or divorce could easily be obtained, and the marriage declared null and void.

Naturally, there were cases when the groom finally had enough. He leapt up in his shirt and shouted, frightening the fleeing ladies. But even after the communal departure of the merrymakers, when the newly minted couple finally enjoyed some privacy, drums, fiddles, and grating noises from the many drunkards interrupted their pleasures.[15] Puddles collected at the door as pranksters poured water through the key hole.

*****

From a sixteenth-century perspective, there was no virtue in a bride, particularly a royal bride, who held back on her wedding night. Lawyers, statesmen, and diplomats had labored unceasingly to produce this merger of noble families, and expectations were high on all sides.[16] The young wife, regardless if she was nervous, scared out of her wits, or apathetic, was expected to perform, or at least submit with good grace.

There is no information on Anna and William's first night together. Diaries were still relatively uncommon in the early modern era and despite rather matter-of-fact attitudes about sex among the aristocracy, only very few individuals chose to commit their most intimate thoughts to paper. In the English speaking world, only six contemporary sexual records have survived, none by women.[17] Instead, it was the palace spies who typically provided posterity with reports on a couple's love life. Rival princes hired these special agents to find out if wedlock got off to a good start or if a marital catastrophe was already in the making.

To the mortification of many a bride, news of sexual problems rarely remained confined to a small circle of tactful diplomats, but spread like wildfire round court. Household personnel snitched about their employers' bedroom habits as long as the price was right, and even family members tattled. Tales of Francis I of France's unhappy second marriage to Eleanor, sister of Emperor Charles V, did not remain secret for long. The English ambassador, Sir Francis Bryan, trumpeted, "They lie not together once in four nights," and the French king continues to fondle his mistress in public. The king's sister, Marguerite, was equally

---

[12]Stanley Loomis. *The Fatal Friendship* (New York: Doubleday, 1972), p. 27.
[13]Mossiker, p. 472.
[14]Camille, p. 140.
[15]Cressy, pp. 375-6.
[16]Perry, p. 36.
[17]Stone, p. 340.

frank. She had heard that her brother found Eleanor physically repellent and told the Duchess of Norfolk, "She's very hot in bed and desireth to be too much embraced." Poor Francis could not get a wink of sleep.[18] Eleanor's reaction to such unkind gossip can easily be imagined.

Anna and William's first or any subsequent nights together hardly elicited such high levels of political interest. The future of Europe would not precariously hang in the balance if Orange's statelet in southern France fell vacant because of the lack of an heir. Besides, William already had a son, Philip William, from his first marriage to Anne van Buren. If anyone peeped through a hole in the wall while the new Princess of Orange was disporting herself, it was in all probability a drunken voyeur or curious servants snooping on their betters.

*****

Whatever transpired between Anna and William during that August night remains forever unknown, but we can safely assume that the marriage was fully consummated and that the prince found his wife a virgin. Among the nobility, an "intact" bride was imperative, a requirement rooted in practical concerns, tradition, and religion. Since antiquity, society regarded chastity as the quintessential female virtue. While men gained renown through daring deeds and liberality, sexual continence was the overriding measure of a woman's character. Apart from religious scruples, men's objective was of course to make certain that their wives' offspring was also their own. An unblemished princess guaranteed that she did not enter matrimony carrying another man's child. Virginity was therefore highly prized, celebrated, and extolled in song and verse. Princes, often thoroughly debauched and addled by syphilis, fantasized about the virginal state of ethereally pure maidens. When Henry VII of England (1457-1509) married Elizabeth of York, he raved that his bride's chasteness rivaled that of Diana and Lucretia, two unassailable role models of self-restraint.[19]

Generally, sexual liberties were acceptable only among the lower classes, particularly in the country, where segregation of the sexes was virtually non-existent. There, one played together as children, walked out together in adolescence, and fondly exchanged tokens. Teenagers teased and touched each other or engaged in games of fondling such as "barley break" and "codpiece kissing." Communities went so far as to turn a blind eye to full sexual intercourse as long as the couple had been "made sure." Religious reformers naturally deplored the practice of couples going to bed before they had gone to church, but parish registers have shown that about a quarter to nearly a third of all brides bore children within the first eight months of marriage.[20]

In Anna's circles, few unmarried princesses dared to take innocent flirtations a step further. Marguerite of Valois (1553-1615), daughter of the late Henri of France, exchanged love notes and letters with Duke Henry of Guise that subsequently fell into the wrong hands. The Spanish ambassador reported with relish that one morning at five o'clock the princess's brother Charles appeared in his mother Catherine's chambers in his nightshirt, raging about the shameful romance of a daughter of France, his own sister. Catherine de Medici immedi-

[18] Starkey, pp. 457-8.
[19] J. L Laynesmith. *The Last Medieval Queens* (Oxford: Oxford University Press, 2004), p. 59.
[20] Cressy, p. 234, p. 277.

ately summoned Marguerite to her quarters and in unison, mother and son fell upon her in unchecked fury, pulling out handfuls of her dark hair and tearing her nightdress to shreds. The princess emerged so badly mangled from the domestic scuffle that the dowager queen spent about an hour smoothing her over for fear that the servants would notice. The king meanwhile sent out an order to have her lover killed, a command that was ultimately rescinded.

Despite her family's violent reaction, it is unlikely that the Duke of Guise and Marguerite had ever gone farther than a few stolen kisses, since "despoliation" of the king's virgin sister was considered high treason.[21] It was the hint of scandal, however, that had sufficed for Marguerite to be manhandled. Honor and reputation of royal houses rested in the sexually blameless conduct of their female members, and the princess had given needless cause for talk. Three years later she was bargained off to Henry of Navarre, a man for whom she never felt the slightest physical attraction.

There was no such drama during or after Anna's wedding night. William's easygoing personality differed markedly from the Valois' in France or the vengeful Henry VIII of England. Furthermore, the Saxon princess was a *Virgo intacta*. If their first night together was mutually satisfactory is an open question. Judging from Anna's suggestive love letters during her courtship and allusions made by contemporaries, we can deduce that she was not lacking in passion. In fact, she might have approached her wedding night with gusto. Her enjoyment of erotic texts as bedtime reading later in her marriage also corroborates these assertions. The question of course remains how Anna acquired the "knowledge" so frankly expressed in her billet-doux to William, especially under the ever watchful eyes of the electress.

Romance novels, overheard conversations, and surreptitious observations probably all contributed to her "understanding" of intimate matters, but like the majority of her contemporaries, Anna's knowledge of the human body must have been woefully incomplete. For starters, there was no term in Latin, Greek, or any other European vernacular language for the female sexual organs like the ovaries or the vagina. The clitoris, first mentioned in early seventeenth-century medical textbooks, was simply called "the woman's yard."[22]

In general, any written information about things sexual was almost impossible to come by. The Middle Ages produced very little explicitly sex-oriented literature, probably because reading was almost always done aloud before the end of the 1200s. Silent reading, which became more common in the fourteenth and fifteenth centuries, gradually encouraged the writing and copying of erotic tales and stories, sometimes accompanied by explicit illustrations for the first time since late antiquity.[23]

Nonetheless, actual sex manuals were rare, and most were distressingly imprecise and vague. Unlike Chinese erotic guides, few European reference works listed any advice whatsoever about methods and varieties of sexual foreplay, intercourse, or techniques to prolong and maximize pleasures; these matters were left in decent obscurity. Seekers of purely technical information on the subject could consult the writings of Pietro Aretino (1492-1556), an Italian poet and playwright credited with inventing modern pornographic literature. Naturally,

[21]Frieda, p. 221.

[22]Fletcher, p. 35, p. 37.

[23]James A. Law Brundage. *Sex, and Christian Society in Medieval Europe* (Chicago: University of Chicago Press, 1987), pp. 549-50.

such incendiary works were kept away in inaccessible poison cabinets, out of reach for the average man, and especially the average upper class woman. In fact, there was no easy access to precise information on sex before the mid-twentieth century.[24] Unless enlightened by relatives or female confidantes, some brides approached their wedding night in complete ignorance.

Such primness notwithstanding, medical advice books did promote the argument that a good sex life and habitual orgasms were not only needed for the well-being of adult men and women, but also required to conceive children. Indeed, regular sex was vitally important for females, for marriages without it, wrote one physician, "shall see the house turned upside down." Maidens were known to fall ill with so-called "green-sickness" or "virgin's disease," a form of anemia that could only be cured by sexual activity, according to early modern medical lore. During Anna's lifetime, husbands and wives were advised to "mutually delight in each other," and it was not until the eighteenth and nineteenth centuries that women were told that sexual desire was not their business.[25]

Whether inexperienced and naïve, or lusty and expectant, certain protocol guided women's behavior even in the bedchamber. Royal handbooks enjoined princesses to act "chaste, loyal, and obedient" in all situations, including intercourse, as etiquette required the husband to initiate all sexual advances. For despite the idea of female pleasure advocated in medical literature and popular culture, women were not supposed to initiate sex. That prerogative belonged strictly to men. In fact, those females who instigated intimate relations were whores, witches or grave sinners, at least according to theologians and moralists.[26] Anna, who never put much stock in decorum, might have flouted such conventions.

*****

The morning after the wedding could find the new wife glowing with joy or looking pale and drawn. Even as late as the second half of the nineteenth century, this particular part of the day made newlyweds feel as if they were running the gauntlet through a storm of pestering inquiries, boisterous morning serenades, and more lewd jokes. As a rule, menservants and maids had already spread the word about the previous night's activities, and swarms of relatives could not wait to pry private details from the exhausted couple. Nosy parents set nerves on edge by inquiring "Are you my son-in-law? Are you my daughter-in-law?" during the wedding breakfast.[27]

The groom usually had an easier time during this very personal inquisition. After all, he had not been led like a lamb to slaughter, but bedded a pliable, inexperienced young woman. Many new husbands actually enjoyed bragging about their sexual prowess to friends and family who enthusiastically imparted the news over town. Catherine of Aragon's first husband Arthur, Prince of Wales, proudly told a friend, "Willoughby, bring me a cup of ale, for I have been this night in the midst of Spain."[28]

[24]Stone, p. 310.
[25]Gowing, p. 82-3.
[26]Gowing, p. 85.
[27]Mossiker, p. 472.
[28]Starkey, pp. 62-3.

To help shake off any lingering late night distress, it was custom to present one's new wife with a piece of precious jewelry, the so-called morning gift.[29] Anna probably accepted William's offering - a priceless bejeweled choker - with blissful gratitude. She had married the man of her choice; an attractive prince who was sexually experienced and of pleasant character. As for those mischievous rogues that tried to extract details about her first night of love, we can hope that she replied with a fittingly witty riposte.

---

[29]Lemberg, pp. 100-1.

Departures

With the festivities winding down, footmen, valets, and masters of the household shouted and sweated during the loading of the princess's immense baggage train. The newlyweds' departure was scheduled for the first of September, and the couple was busy taking their leave from hundreds of friends and family. August and his wife wished their foster child God's speed with well-concealed relief. They hoped that after she had passed through Leipzig's western *Ranstädter Tor* (Ranstädt Gate), they had seen the last of their ward. The Low Countries were more than three weeks of travel away, and there were no plans for ever paying a visit. Similar thoughts presumably crossed the princess's mind. Although one of the wedding poems claimed that she cried bitterly when the carriage finally drew away, heartily distressed at having to leave her caring "good uncle" for an unknown land, those tears might have been expressions of joy.[1]

Still, Anna's departure from Saxony was a somewhat sad affair. Because of her unpopularity, few individuals among the well-wishers truly cared enough to give the difficult girl an earnest send-off. Her grandmother Christine had received a hand-made, pearl-studded bonnet from her mother during a final heart-to-heart. Fathers usually bestowed a last blessing and vow of protection on their daughters, something that the princess also had to do without. Nor was a cluster of teary-eyed siblings clinging to her skirts as she climbed into the carriage. Perhaps Anna was still brimming with joyful emotion as the Leipzig skyline receded in the distance. The frenzied delirium of the past few days had not worn off yet as impressions, images, and memories of the wedding crowded Anna's mind. It was already said that no other German marriage was ever contracted with more hope and celebrated with greater pageantry and splendor than her own.[2]

*****

Unlike Anna's, bridal partings could be occasions of mixed feelings and dramatic scenes. For one, good byes were usually forever. Princesses rarely revisited the lands of their birth, since custom dictated the complete severance of ties to one's former home. A return to Saxony would only take place in exceptional, highly problematic circumstances such as divorce or annulment of marriage.[3] Aristocratic parents stressed this harsh reality by dispatching their terrified daughters with a Bible verse that was not comforting, but to the point: 45 Psalm 10: "Hearken, O daughter, and consider, and incline thine ear; forget also thine own people and thy father's house."[4]

After the Oranges had said their good-byes, the long snake of carriages and riders slowly heaved out of Leipzig. Splendid coaches, dozens of horse carts filled with trunks, portable writing desks, toilet stools, and other precious cargo, men-at-arms, knights, cooks, couriers, liveried servants, apothecaries, and ladies escorted the gorgeously appareled princely couple on their voyage west. Entertainment was provided by capering minstrels who had been hired to relieve

---

[1]Schuppener, "Hochzeitslied,"p. 271.
[2]Hans Kruse. "Um Peter Paul Rubens Geburt," *Siegerland, Blätter des Vereins für Heimatkunde und Heimatschutz im Siegerlande und Nachbargebieten,* Band 22 (1940), p. 7.
[3]Fraser, *Louis,* p. 59.
[4]Cruysse, p. 136.

the tedium of travel proceeding at snail's pace. Several hundred of the elector's *Trabanten* in their black and yellow uniforms accompanied the procession until Ranstädt, seven miles outside of town, before they waved Anna farewell.

Since none of her relatives had volunteered to conduct her to Breda, the princess had to make do with three Dresden ladies and several Saxon nobles, who were entering her services rather grudgingly, perhaps afraid of Anna's garrulous temper and reluctant to leave home and family behind. In addition to her current maid-of-honor, the middle-aged Sophia von Miltitz, two young women accompanied the Princess of Orange. One of them was Margaret von Ponickau, the daughter of a Saxon privy counselor, the other a Mademoiselle von Carlowitz. Margaret had departed Leipzig under the condition of being allowed to return home after one year of service.[5]

After the baggage convoy had meandered through the last Thuringian villages, the Orange party crossed into the landgraviate of Hessen at Vacha on 10 September and was greeted by two envoys dispatched by Anna's grandfather. Philip had remained intransigent about Anna's marriage to the last and had neither sent a wedding gift nor invited the newlyweds to receive his blessing in Kassel. He merely granted them safe conduct through his lands. The enormity of the situation suddenly hit the princess who broke down crying, beseeching Philip's emissaries to relay greetings to the landgrave with the request that he should not forsake her.

After a day of rest in the ancient episcopal city of Fulda, the princely cavalcade wound its way past Hanau, Frankfurt, and Mainz. There the travelers switched to a ship and sailed on to Koblenz on the Rhine and from where they rode towards Dillenburg; William's family were already expecting the head of the house and his highborn wife.[6] Countess Juliana had organized a small celebration in Anna's honor and took the opportunity to take a good look at her new daughter-in-law. Apparently, the princess exhibited certain worrisome airs, because Juliana promised to join the pair at William's home in Breda in a few weeks' time.

Barely two weeks after her grand Leipzig wedding Anna was experiencing post-nuptial jitters. The celebratory high had worn off and life as she had known it for the past six years, however unhappy, had come to a sudden end. Very possibly, she was also afraid of the challenges lying ahead. Talk amongst staff members about the princess's upcoming responsibilities as mistress of Breda might have been particularly intimidating.

Somewhere on the road to the Low Countries the princess was overtaken by such dreadful panic that either she or Orange requested the assistance of one of her grandfather's secretaries. This particular message has not survived, but on 24 September Anna sent off a letter of thanks to the landgrave's son William, expressing gratitude for his support and the dispatching of one of his officials who had most likely calmed her with words of comfort. She also enjoined her uncle to "remember your poor, deserted cousin."[7]

One has to bear in mind that Anna was only sixteen years old at the time, and had rarely, if ever travelled outside of Saxony. Within a matter of days, she was expected to blithely morph from sheltered ward into the Princess of Orange,

[5]Kruse, "Wilhelm von Oranien," p. 36.
[6]Böttcher, pp. 92-3.
[7]Böttcher, pp. 92-3.

with all the awesome responsibilities the position implied. In that light, her feelings of derailment were by no means uncommon and in fact shared by many of her peers. One of her distant descendants, Liselotte of the Palatine (1652 - 1722), experienced similar growing pains during her bumpy transition from girlhood to married life in a foreign country. When Liselotte left Heidelberg to marry the brother of Louis XIV of France in 1671, she recalled in a letter to an aunt, "I screamed from Strasbourg all the way to Chalons, because I could not deal with the farewell that I had taken." A worried observer noted that "For days on end [Liselotte] neither ate, spoke nor slept, but was shaken with constant fits of crying."[8] In comparison, Anna was doing reasonably well.

By marrying William, Anna had suddenly been flung into the ranks of adults, a "solemn change" fraught with profound consequences. While society accorded unmarried teenagers some leeway in matters of conduct, the married state called for a good amount of probity and sobriety befitting those heading their "little commonwealth" of a family. Married women were held to higher standards of respectability and became responsible for the own behavior as well as their dependents.[9] The electress had surely given Anna at least some idea of the duties that awaited her - irksome advice that the princess had perhaps brushed aside. As her carriage approached the first Dutch towns, Anna's heart sank. She realized that her aunt's many tasks would soon be her own.

As for her marriage to the prince, there was no turning back. Perhaps Anna apprehended during the long journey west that she was joined to a man for life now, a virtual stranger about whom she knew very little. Unlike today, matrimony in the sixteenth century was final, and the "until death" and "for better or worse" parts of the vows did not contain any loopholes. The English Book of Prayer cautioned with good reason that marriage was not to be entered "unadvisedly, lightly, or wantonly," as had happened in Anna's case to at least some extent.[10] After some weeks of reflection while travelling with William, Anna was beginning to comprehend that her honeymoon was already drawing to a close.

At least some bright spot awaited the princess towards the end of her trip. Anna's Grandfather Philip had at last decided to reconcile with William and sent a letter, addressing the prince as "his dearly beloved cousin and son." In lieu of a wedding gift, he had his grateful granddaughter presented with a golden necklace. Perhaps to ease Anna's transition into married life, he had also dispatched the Hessian counselor H. Krug to Breda to greet his granddaughter.[11] In return, the Prince of Orange declared himself the landgrave's loyal friend in word and deed. Perhaps Philip's kind, parental gestures dispelled some of the princess's worries as the couple made their triumphant entry into Breda at the beginning of October 1561. They were met by the magistrate, the local nobility, the city's patricians, and several thousand well-wishers with a lavish welcome ceremony.[12] Anna, the new Princess of Orange and mistress of Breda, had officially arrived.

[8]Cruysse, pp. 137-8.
[9]Cressy, p. 287.
[10]Cressy, p. 289.
[11]Böttcher, p. 94.
[12]Schuppener, "Hochzeitslied," pp. 236-7.

Burgundy

Although Anna's ladies had not been eager to travel to the Low Countries, others would have welcomed the opportunity to spend time in this fabled region of Europe. Since the late Middle Ages, the Netherlands conjured up visions of a "Promised Land." Except for the northern Italian city states, the Low Countries were second to none in progressive industry, standard of living, and overall wealth in Europe. Contemporary paintings depict proud city halls, magnificent churches with towering belfries, and streets lined with neat shops. If Anna sought to get away from the straitjacket of the Saxon court, her husband's adopted home beckoned with ample diversions.

The mighty cities on the North Sea - Ghent, Ypres, Bruges, and Antwerp - had long developed into sprawling trading metropolises. In the ports of the Zwin, the galleons of the Genoese lay anchored together with the galleys of the Venetians and the Florentines, the cogs from Hamburg, Lübeck, and Danzig, and the cutters of local herring fishers. Vessels burst with exotic cargo as dock workers unloaded heavy shipments of Russian pelts, sailcloth from Navarre, and gold brocade from Tartary. Merchants oversaw the re-stocking of giant trading crafts with the region's most famous export, the *vestes dominis gestandae*, finely woven Dutch linen. The material was of such superb quality that well-paying customers from Königsberg in East Prussia to London and the ports of the Levant eagerly awaited incoming deliveries.[1]

In the late fourteenth century, the region had fallen under the control of the celebrated Dukes of Burgundy, relations of the King of France, who claimed nominal control over their subjects. The duchy comprised swaths of territory belonging to today's Belgium, the Netherlands, Luxemburg, and France. A century later, the dukedom was absorbed into the Habsburg realm by marriage, and in 1548 Emperor Charles V formally designated the Seventeen Provinces a self-contained part within the Holy Roman Empire. He usually referred to the Netherlands as the "Burgundian Circle," his son Philip simply called the entire region Flanders.[2]

The sixteenth-century Netherlands defy modern political terminology. Neither state nor nation, they were an amorphous land mass, a tangle of duchies, counties, and seigneuries which had been amassed over generations into the hands of a single ruler. Each of the provinces had its separate privileges, its greater and lesser nobility, and courts of justice, while in their midst the cities exercised independent rights of their own, with autonomous law courts, municipal councils, and time-honored constitutional charters.[3]

Differences between the provinces were aggravated by cultural divisions: the northern areas, including Brussels, spoke Dutch; in the richer and more densely populated south, the principal language was French. In sum, the Low Countries had no political unity beyond their allegiance to a common ruler, which, at the time, was Philip of Spain.[4]

---

[1]Cartellieri, pp. 4-5

[2]Wim Blockmans and Walter Prevenier. *The Promised Lands: The Low Countries under Burgundian Rule, 1369-1530* (Philadelphia: University of Pennsylvania Press, 1999), pp. 3-4, p. 232.

[3]Wedgwood, p. 33.

[4]Kamen, pp. 40-1.

Whatever the designation, the lands perched between France and Germany prospered and thrived as evidenced in their fabulous stately homes and residences. Antwerp's new town hall was considered the most beautiful Renaissance building north of the Alps, while expensive lemon, herb, and laurel trees graced the immaculately swept inner courtyards of Patrician houses. Even grander were the palaces of the nobility which evoked mirages of otherworldly splendor.[5]

William's castle in Breda easily compared to many European royal palaces and eclipsed most princely courts in Germany, including Dresden.[6] Emperor Charles V and his son Philip were frequent guests as were the most of the Dutch elite, drawn in by Orange's famous kitchen and a seemingly inexhaustible cellar packed with heady Beaune wine. Expensive tapestries and silver ewers cluttered the hallways in an exhibition of riches that was further augmented by Anna's enormous dowry.[7]

Perhaps Anna felt overwhelmed as a deferential chamberlain explained the workings of the household to herself and her maid-of-honor. Two hundred fifty-six individuals were employed at the Breda residence whose annual kitchen expenditures were a baffling 44,000 florins - three times as much as at the elector's in Dresden.[8] Such decadence was a far cry from the electress's thrifty budget management and household economizing, but Anna had never much cared for frugality. As the new Princess of Orange wandered through her opulent chambers and soaked up the atmosphere of decadent bombast, her aunt's lessons in self-denial and duty quickly started to fade.

And then there was the food. Unlike Anna's aunt, no Dutch princess of stature would have descended to the palace kitchens to make her own cheeses and jams. One simply hired the best cooks. William's chef de cuisine was so renowned that Philip of Spain asked him to train his own kitchen personnel.[9] At the time of Anna's arrival, her husband had long been known as a spoiled gourmand who liked to surprise his guests with novel culinary delights from the palace kitchens. By the sixteenth century, heavy medieval dishes drowning in ginger, nutmeg, and garlic were considered déclassé and had long been replaced by repasts prepared with fresh herbs such as parsley and basil.

During their first weeks in Breda, Anna and her Saxon ladies may have marveled at strange looking produce that was unknown in Saxony, but readily available in Flanders. Anchovies, lemons, and bitter oranges were brought in regularly from Mediterranean markets, along with the latest arrival in noble dining rooms: Turkish cauliflower.[10] Spices were just as exclusive; their availability limited to a select few. Imported from unreachable, faraway locales with mythical names like Cathay or Persia, they evoked the exotic Orient and helped the rich in creating a fantasy world of blissful abundance amidst evergreen trees, phoenixes, and unicorns.[11]

Exquisite food demanded equally exquisite table manners, and courtiers in the Low Countries took part in elaborately staged, balletic dining productions, involving intricate rules and procedures. Codified in the fifteenth century by the

[5]de Dijn, p. 12, p. 127.
[6]Mörke, pp. 70-1.
[7]Wedgwood, p. 19.
[8]Fellmann, p. 35.
[9]Putnam, *Moderate Man*, 164. Monsieur Coels, William's steward, claimed that the reputation of Orange's cuisine was so excellent that numerous German princes sent their cooks to his Breda residence to be perfected in its art.
[10]de Dijn, pp. 127-8, pp. 156-7.
[11]Bastl, p. 234.

undisputed doyens of style and fine living, Philip, Duke of Burgundy (1396-1467) and his son Charles (1433-1477), they turned banqueting into a ritualistic pageant of courses.

Serving duties were shared by the first *panetier* (baker), the first *échanson* (cupbearer), and the first *écuyer* (squire), each of whom was attended by dozens of esquires of their own.[12] Additional nobles, pages, and servants were also lying in wait for special instructions, taking care to recall the myriad of rules that made up this complicated system. Although inane, these practices made a tremendous impression on contemporary observers and travelers from such far flung places as Spain and Bohemia eagerly sought to imitate Burgundian table culture.[13]

We do not know how much of this order of service had been adopted in Saxony, but William certainly made every effort to copy Philip the Good's gastronomic fantasies. An ordinary dinner involved twenty-four nobles with no less than eighteen pages at their heels, who served still-feathered eagles, peacocks, and swans at Breda's banquet tables, their insides filled with meat, spices, and camphor-soaked wool.[14] The wool was then set alight, giving the impression that the dead bird was spewing fire. The Prince of Orange also impressed friends and visitors with miniature artworks made of marzipan, dough, and spun sugar.[15] Tales of such Epicurean wonders quickly made the rounds abroad. Anna's grandfather Philip commented somewhat disapprovingly to the elector, "That he (William) keeps a magnificent court, we can well believe, because we have heard about a great banquet where tablecloths, plates, and everything else was made out of sugar."[16]

After-dinner entertainments were equally grandiose. William was not only a skilled dancer, but also one of the most sought-after organizers of balls and masques. Most of the time, the theme was courtly love, the dreamland of the renewed chivalric fashions of the late Middle Ages: imprisoned maidens, noble knights, exotic foreigners, wild men, vices personified, mythical beasts, mountains that moved, ships in full sail, and castles making music were mainstays of these expensive, gregarious entertainments where gentlemen let loose and wine flowed freely until the early morning hours.[17]

In addition to feasting in Breda - the official family headquarters - William also hosted grand to-dos in the center of Brussels where he owned a splendid chateau, the *Palais de Nassau*. About sixty-five miles to the south, Brussels was a crawling trader's metropolis and the political center of the Netherlands. The favored residence of the Dukes of Burgundy in the previous century and the seat of the Habsburg regent since the early 1530s, the city teemed with foreign envoys and diplomats. Because of his wealth and position in government, the Prince of Orange was a court regular.

William's *Palais de Nassau* was a, majestic mansion with steep-pitched roofs and fantastically pinnacled towers that also boasted vast gardens with tennis courts and fountains. In the opinion of some, William's Brussels residence surpassed even that of the adjacent Habsburg's in beauty. The palais' interiors

[12]Cartellieri, pp. 67-8.
[13] Edward A. Tabri. *Political Culture in the Early Northern Renaissance* (New York: Edwin Mellen Press, 2004), p. 36, p. 47.
[14]Putnam, *Moderate Man*, pp. 163-4.
[15] Jessica Kerwin Jenkins. *Encyclopedia of the Exquisite* (New York: Nan A. Talese/Doubleday, 2010), pp. 201-2.
[16]Wedgwood, p. 20.
[17]Ives, p. 20.

were full of rich carvings, along with paintings by the latest artists. One of them was Hieronymus Bosch's "Garden of Earthly Delights" triptych which eventually came to be owned by King Philip in adverse circumstances, and can be admired at the Prado in Madrid today.[18]

Philip of Hessen was not the only one who wondered just how long William would be able to finance this kind of overindulgence. Orange's manors produced high yields, but the prince already complained in 1552 that Antwerp bankers refused him credit. As a measure of goodwill, he dismissed twenty-eight of his kitchen personnel two years later, an indication of the incredible original size of the staff.

By 1558, however, the prince's expenses had almost doubled as he continued to wallow in debt-ridden luxury. In that, he was by no means an overspending, aristocratic aberration. Monarchs, princes, and gentry were forever strapped for cash. At a time when banking was still in its infancy and savings accounts virtually unknown, few people deposited their earning. Besides, "hoarding" was seen as both miserly and pointless. A little nest egg of gold coins tucked away in a closet or secret compartment in the parlor was positively déclassé. In fact, cutting back meant immediate social discredit, and those with money felt obligated to spread their wealth around.[19]

William certainly belonged to this particular mindset and he carelessly frittered his profits away. As his hill of debt grew ever larger, the prince refused to lose sleep over such trite affairs. In 1564, he wrote optimistically to his brother Louis, "It seems that we are of a kind that is unable to manage well during youth, but when we are old, we will do it better than our father."[20] His new wife Anna, an equally enthusiastic spender, put up no objections.

*****

Sometime during the fall of 1561, after weeks of self-indulgence, William probably found time to show Anna the actual town of Breda, his seat of government. The lordship, also known as the barony of Breda, encompassed the city and a number of surrounding villages, all located within the Duchy of Brabant. With a population of just under five thousand, the city on the rivers Mark and Aa was only slightly smaller than Dresden, and popular as a market town and place of transshipment. To Anna's delight, she had not landed in a backward, rural hamlet, but a sizeable town with noble families who paid regular court at the Oranges.' On 28 October, the princess also accompanied her husband to Brussels in order to meet the Regent Margaret. The latter had decided to throw a ball for Anna, now the second highest ranked lady in the Netherlands.[21] And yet neither the beautiful town nor the splendors of William's palaces could soothe Anna's growing disquiet as she tried to settle into her new surroundings.

[18]Vetter, p. 17, p. 20, pp. 91-2.
[19]Ann Rosalind Jones and Peter Stallybrass. *Renaissance Clothing and the Materials of Memory* (Cambridge: Cambridge University Press, 2000), p. 28.
[20]Vetter, p. 30.
[21]Böttcher, p. 95.

Dislocation

As fall turned into winter and the days grew shorter, nauseating waves of unease washed over the newly minted Princess of Orange. Her new home's riches and diversions did little to dispel Anna's growing disquiet and she felt lost and displaced, especially when William was not at her side. Such were the growing pains that every princess experienced as a newlywed, she was probably told, and she had better keep her composure. Etiquette dictated that no complaints of boredom, tiredness or raging epidemics, let alone her sense of forlornness, were ever to be voiced openly.[1]

Anna's Saxon attendants felt equally deserted, but had no qualms about articulating their displeasure. It had taken plenty of prodding on the electress's part to have them follow their mistress abroad; now it was obvious that they would not stay long. By the end of October, only a few weeks after their arrival in Breda, Madame Miltitz and company filled the women's quarters with their bickering.

The sheltered ladies from Dresden were taken aback by the unaccustomed, sizzling pace of living in the Netherlands. The salacious swagger of the courtly roués unsettled them, and, untied from Mother Anne's apron strings, they stood by astonished as suave gentlemen and their haughty companions volleyed clever repartees at each other. Moreover, the timid Dresden girls were frequently pestered by these perennially bored rakes, who were always baying for the fresh blood of newcomers. Anna's maid-of-honor, Sophia von Miltitz, reported indignantly that "the poor children" could not acquaint themselves with the lewd customs and practices of the Low Countries. They especially balked at the rampant sexual harassment, and "did not want to be kissed."

Scared and homesick, the bedraggled Misses Ponickau and Karlowitz eventually took their leave. We are not informed how Anna reacted to this breach in service, but Lady Miltitz offered no objections. On the contrary, she encouraged the young women to break their promises to the princess and return to Dresden prematurely. "The good girls had behaved as virtuous and honest virgins," the maid-of-honor commented after they had taken flight. And as for herself, she intended to leave the Netherlands in six months' time.[2]

Gripes and complaints of the sort reach back to time immemorial. Nostalgia for home invariably set in for new arrivals on foreign shores, while hosts carped about the objectionable morals and customs of alien folk. The world had become a smaller place in the Renaissance, but extensive voyages were still limited to a select few. Ordinary burghers rarely ventured beyond their villages or walled city confines, except for pilgrimage or trade. Adventure travel and appreciation of cultural differences were literally "foreign concepts," while prejudice and bias abounded. The influx of outsiders dressed in bizarre clothes speaking in unknown tongues taxed the already modest tolerance levels of most Renaissance courtiers quite considerably.

At least in hindsight, some grievances make for entertaining reading. When Catherine of Braganza (1638-1705) and her entourage descended on Hampton Court in May of 1662, Charles II's chancellor Edward Hyde dismissed the

---

[1]Garrison, p. 30
[2]Kruse, "Wilhelm von Oranien," pp. 36-7.

Portuguese contingent of ladies as "six frights, for the most part old, ugly, and proud." The six frights shot back with their own scathing evaluations of the British Isles. The meat in England was too fatty; the water poisonous. But the worst was their hosts' habit of urinating in public. One of Catherine's ladies snapped that "[One] cannot steer abroad without seeing in every corner great, beastly English pricks battering against every wall."[3]

Culture clashes also took place in the Low Countries. Decades before Anna's Saxon ladies voiced concerns about the ungodly Dutch, Spanish morals collided with the ostentatious, pleasure-seeking atmosphere in Flanders. The followers of Juana of Castile, Catherine of Aragon's sister, were in uproar about their hosts' way of eating, dressing, and especially, loving. Castilian observers spoke of deep moral corruption, while the hedonistic Burgundians poked fun at the Spaniards' sober simplicity. And just like in Anna's household, a Spanish exodus was taking place within a matter of months, leaving a lonely Juana bereft of comfort from trusted friends.[4]

While William might have rejoiced at the rapid departure of his wife's awkward ladies, their leaving was certainly a setback for his wife. Anna was virtually friendless now with only a small number of German servants remaining. Unease about her Lutheran faith might have compounded her disquiet. Anna had been hastily "painted over" as a Catholic in order to please William's master, King Philip, but the transition was not without hurdles. Although she was free to exercise her Protestant faith in the privacy of her quarters, Anna had been asked to refrain from reading any Lutheran literature in the presence of her Catholic servants — a request that was rather difficult to fulfill since her own women had gone and been replaced by locals.

Anna was not much bothered by these strictures; it was rather the hostile stance of certain courtiers towards her that smarted. Like William, the princess largely paid lip service to the conventions of faith and was never emotionally vested in Lutheranism like her relatives in Dresden. An indifferent worshipper, she only occasionally invoked divine assistance which, in any case, never reduced her fears nor seemed to provide her with much comfort. Her pretend conversion to Catholicism was therefore an act largely taken in stride, a basic and essential requirement for any Princess of Orange. Her personal nonchalance notwithstanding, there were others who were very much disturbed by the presence of a Protestant princess in their midst.

Philip of Spain for one could never reconcile himself to the fact that his premier liegeman in Flanders had married a heretic, and not just any heretic. Anna was the daughter of his father's nemesis Maurice, the man who had shamefully betrayed Charles in a stunning act of duplicity in 1552.[5] With William possibly straying from the Habsburg fold, Philip had to make doubly sure that nothing untoward was going on in the Oranges' private chambers. The Regent Margaret tried to allay her half-brother's concerns in a letter dated 18 October 1561, writing, "Everyone assures me that the princess will obey the will of the prince and the teachings of the Catholic religion. After all he has always been an ardent devo-

---

[3] Anne Somerset. *Ladies in Waiting* (London: Phoenix Press, 2002), pp. 137-8.
[4] Bethany Aram. *Juana the Mad* (Baltimore: Johns Hopkins University Press, 2005), pp. 35-6, p. 42. Juana's retainers were repelled by Dutch drinking binges; the sophisticated Netherlanders sneered at the modesty of Iberian dress, frugal spending, and somber dining practices.
[5] Wartenberg, p. 84.

tee of the Catholic Church, and already the lady is hearing Mass every day ..."[6] Nevertheless, every fortnight, a courier left Brussels for the Escorial in Madrid, his bag full of classified reports about the strengthening of Protestant elements in the Netherlands and the doings of the Saxon princess.[7]

Anna might have been unaware of these surreptitious machinations, and exposed to the disdain, snide barbs, but underhanded insults of the king's Spanish assistants, especially during her husband's frequent absences. In the courtly Petri dish of vicious stratagems and pet hatreds, Philip's minions had their own way of making life miserable for a woman of dubious religious affiliation and traitorous stock. Despite these hurdles, Anna made an effort to fit in. A diplomat sent by her worried grandfather reported back to Kassel that the princess remained true to her faith and had only visited one convent, allegedly "for fun."[8]

As those first winter months in the Netherlands passed, disillusion slowly took hold of Anna. It crept through her mind and blackened her waking hours after she had discerned quite clearly that she was stuck in the familiar position of outsider yet again. Despite her lofty title, Anna was the vulnerable new arrival, and except for William and perhaps her grandfather, there was no one to step in the breach for her. Once daughters had left home, they were generally expected to fend for themselves, even in relatively close knit royal families. "As much forgotten after three weeks as if she had been buried three years" went the thinking. When another friendless Anna, Princess of Orange (1709-1759) and the daughter of George II of England, wrote home desperately homesick, her unsympathetic mother replied, "You are now William's wife, God has given you skill and judgment, and you are no longer a child."[9]

To be sure, there was regular contact between the Houses of Wettin and Nassau. William forwarded political news and confidential messages about unrest in France, and answered requests for small personal favors. After August supplied the prince with Italian seeds for his garden, Orange reciprocated by sending special powders, some of which were ruined when one of the pack mules fell into a river.[10] But there were few affectionate messages for Anna. Inquiries about her health and other pious greetings lacked genuine interest in her well-being, while one "sharp letter" from August warned her to stick to Saxon morals in the decadent Low Countries.[11] Only her late mother's friend, Aunt Sidonia, provided Anna with an occasional, more personal lifeline from home.[12]

For any young bride, these new beginnings were trying times. Separated from her familiar surroundings, she was forced to meet the physical and emotional demands of a husband while facing the expectations of court officials and servants.[13] A chalk drawing of Anna, commissioned a few months after the Oranges' arrival in the Netherlands, appears to reflect her gloomy state of mind. Sketched

[6]Böttcher, p. 95.
[7]de Dijn, p. 30.
[8]Kruse, "Wilhelm von Oranien," p. 36. See also Derek Wilson. *All the King's Women* (London: Pimlico, 2004), p. 311. Although specific details have not survived, we can assume that Anna was harassed like other princesses in similar situations. Catherine of Braganza (1638-1705), Charles II's Catholic wife and a reigning queen, was booed and hissed by militant Protestants whenever she left the confines of London's Whitehall Palace in her carriage. Eventually she had to remain home. At the height of anti-Catholic frenzy, soldiers raided one of Catherine's warehouses in search of popish books while the House of Commons called on the king to repudiate her. The queen bore her trials with considerable fortitude, her main source of comfort being the unfailing support of her husband.
[9]Baker-Smith, p. ix, p. 59.
[10]Kruse, "Wilhelm von Oranien," pp. 27-8.
[11]Knöfel. *Dynastie*, p. 135
[12]Kruse, "Wilhelm von Oranien," p. 152. See also Böttcher, p. 33
[13] Adrian Tinniswood. *The Verneys* (New York: Riverhead Books, 2007), pp. 355-6.

by Jacques Le Bouq (died 1573), a popular portraitist from the Valenciennes region of the Spanish Netherlands, it is the oldest surviving likeness of the Saxon princess. The drawing was probably Anna's first sitting as Orange's wife and may have served as a template for subsequent oil paintings.

Smallish in size, it depicts a face that is characterized by wide set eyes, curly hair, and a high forehead. The princess had already adopted local dress as her gown bears the popular Spanish and French influences on Dutch fashions: narrowly tapered in the waist with puff sleeves and a standing collar opening to the front as well as an ornate *escoffion* (bonnet). Unlike later portraits, Anna's jewelry is simple: a pair of pearl earrings and a thin necklace that reappears in later depictions.[14] As for her facial expression, she seems to be staring into a void; a dislocated exile with apathetic eyes, lacking spark.

[14]Spies, p. 238, p. 240.

Earliest surviving portrait of Anna of Saxony, Princess of Orange, by Jacques Le Bouq, late 1561

Chatelaine of Breda

During blustery winter days the wind howled through the open gallery of Breda palace, and cold moisture rose up from the moats into the princely chambers - a design flaw by Thomas Vincidor, Henry III's late architect. Despite his artistic accomplishments, there was no denying that the building style of Italian palazzos was utterly unsuitable for this northern climate.[1] While courtiers bundled up in layers of clothing, Anna attempted to transform herself into a capable housewife, obedient spouse, and loyal subject of the Habsburgs.

As could be expected, the learning curve was formidably steep. The princess had to learn French and Dutch, and despite possessing linguistic talent, understood only half of what was going on around her. As for household management, Anna had never taken her domestic training in Dresden seriously, but now felt "pitchforked" into her new, ill-prepared "career" as the castle's administrator. Even if there was no stern-eyed mother-in-law to disapprove of her, others noticed her blunders.

The organization of the household belonged to the traditional tasks of a princess and was, like no other, responsible for the making or breaking of a lady's name as the "good mother" of the court. In the sixteenth century, many women of rank strove to be known as expert domestic managers as they took care of guests and children; overseeing everything from personal hygiene to laundry and menus. According to her letters, the electress concerned herself with such mundane matters as bed sheets, the ordering of clothes, and foodstuff. Well-organized and efficient, nothing went past her within her numerous palaces.[2] Anna, in comparison, possessed no managerial talents or interests of the kind which probably wreaked havoc with her already low self-esteem.

William tried to help, but he was often away on business. Margaret of Parma relied on him in a variety of matters, leaving the prince little time to care for his anxious young wife.[3] At least letters from Hessen provided some solace. Although Anna's aunt and uncle kept their distance, Landgrave Philip was making regular inquiries about his granddaughter's comfort and welfare. At the beginning of January 1652, he wrote: "Dear daughter, we cannot refrain from asking how your health is and whether you are steadfast in the religion in which you have been educated." The princess answered breezily, "Dear Lord Father, I am grateful to Your Excellency for your friendly greetings sent by your counselor. If I can serve Your Grace in any way, I gladly will do so and so would my dear master. In regards to religion, I will bear myself so that I can defend myself to the Almighty and the world. Your Grace need not doubt that." She closed another missive with the good news that her husband was "keeping her well" and treated her "like a queen."[4] Indeed, the first six months of the Orange's marriage seems to have passed quite harmoniously, despite the princess's adjustment difficulties.

*****

[1]Schuppener, "Breda", p. 118.
[2]Keller, *Kurfürstin*, pp. 111-4.
[3]Putnam, *Moderate Man*, p. 145.
[4]Putnam, *The Life of William the Silent*, pp. 73-5.

In many ways, Anna enjoyed more freedoms than most young brides. For one, there were no in-laws who expected to be flattered, cajoled, and waited on, since Countess Juliana visited Breda only occasionally, along with her son Louis, who lived in the Netherlands several months out of the year. As for William, he bore the patriarchal role as Anna's lord and master quite lightly, and included his wife in many courtly entertainments.

Harking back to his conversation with the electress in Leipzig, we already know that the prince wanted Anna to partake in various activities around the palace and acquire some worldly polish. Her exceptionally strict upbringing had made her shy, withdrawn, and prone to attacks of melancholy, he determined. Now she was to enjoy a little bit of the dolce vita that he had experienced so fully in Paris and Brussels. Books like the *Amadis* and a few lessons in galliard dancing would introduce her to a happier world and chase away those cares that often clouded her face.[5] Anna gladly responded. She was thirsting for a life of light-hearted pleasure and eagerly drank up William's suggestions.

And yet despite Orange's kindly-meant "educational" intentions, news of marital discord - long forecast by Anna's many detractors - already made the rounds in the spring of 1562, less than a year after the wedding. Saxon diplomats had kept their ears pricked for months and informed the elector that trouble was brewing. In April, August told Orange of rumors about his niece being mistreated in the Netherlands by unidentified persons. He hoped that she was doing better than "evil people wished."

William hastened to dispel these tales, attributing them to fictitious slander by envious officials. He and his wife were of one mind, he wrote, and both trusted the Almighty to quiet such vicious gossip. They were both in good health and hoping for the arrival of children in the near future. Anna backed her husband's assertions by penning some explanatory letters of her own. In a May message composed in Brussels, she thanked her uncle for his concern, but declared that she was not only free to practice her religion, but "could not thank God often enough that her dearest Lord and husband was so favorably disposed towards her." In fact, she "could not do any better." Two Saxon privy counselors, Wolf Keller and Abraham Bock, confirmed her claims. They travelled to Breda in September of that same year to take stock of her widow's estate and reported that the princess's situation in the Low Countries was indeed quite satisfactory. This, however, was not the whole story.[6]

Worried about their marriage turning into a self-fulfilling prophecy, Anna put on a brave show to prove her relations wrong, while William did the same to stay in August's good graces. There was, however, no denying that the princess's moodiness had returned, born out of the glaring insecurities that she was unable to control and the difficulties confronting her as the daughter of a traitorous Protestant. A more confident character would have turned the not inconsiderable powers of her title to her advantage. For example, Anna could have reveled in her role as savior of the Nassau finances and mother-to-be of the next generation of Oranges.[7] But such strategic self-assurance eluded the princess, who did not possess the wherewithal to manage her own life as well as a large household. She was lacking and everyone, including the princess herself, knew it.

[5]Verwey, p. 93, p. 123.
[6]Kruse, "Wilhelm von Oranien," pp. 28-9.
[7]Tinniswood, p. 356.

*****

At the end of November 1562 William met the Saxon elector in Frankfurt. King Philip's cousin Maximilian stood to become the next Holy Roman Emperor and Orange wanted to attend the election and subsequent coronation. The trip had not received the full support of the King of Spain. Maximilian was a young man with startlingly modern ideas and reputed Protestant sympathies, and Philip was distrustful enough to suspect William of hatching seditious plans while fraternizing in Germany.[8] "I'm neither Catholic nor Protestant, but a Christian!" Maximilian had once exclaimed to Philip's extreme consternation[9]. He need not have feared. Instead of plotting, William spent most of his time in August's company. Relations between the two men were quite congenial and after he had returned to Breda, Orange sent a toadying letter to Dresden, alleging that he greatly regretted to be parted from his friend's good company.[10]

In Frankfurt, William had also discussed some sad news with his Saxon in-law: he had just received word from Breda about the birth and almost immediate death of the Oranges' first child. In late spring, shortly after William had written to August that he and his wife were hoping for offspring, Anna found herself pregnant. She gave birth to a girl at the end of October, but little Anna survived for barely a month.[11]

With her strong predilection for despondency, Anna soon spiraled into a deep depression. Matters were not helped by the steady influx of congratulatory letters that lasted well into January 1563 due to the slowness of the mail during the long winter months. William tried to comfort his wife, perhaps half-heartedly, since he already had two children, including a son, from his first marriage. But Anna couldn't rally.

While her daughter's days had been cut short, life continued blithely for the rest of the court. William was arranging drinking contests and receptions for a steady throng of visitors, particularly the Counts Egmont and Horn.[12] While heads were still clear, the trio discussed the escalating political situation. For several years now, riots had plagued a number of Flemish cities and villages after the public executions of Protestants. Upset onlookers sometimes yelled out their support for the condemned, together with anti-Spanish slogans. Some brave souls even tried to storm the scaffold to stall the killings. The already tense atmosphere heated up further when rumors about the imminent introduction of the Spanish Inquisition began to circulate yet again.

William and his friends also nursed grievances of their own. As the country's premier statesmen, the troika was deeply resentful of King Philip's reorganization of the political landscape. The autocratic sovereign was fully resolved on curbing the powers of the Dutch magnates who, in his opinion, were mere vassals of the Spanish empire. For example, in an effort to streamline the administration of the Seventeen Provinces, the king decreed the diverting of funds from governors like William into crown coffers. This was an unacceptable affront to the

[8]Putnam, *The Life of William the Silent*, p. 56.
[9]Ulbricht, p. 155.
[10]Kruse, "Wilhelm von Oranien," pp. 28-9.
[11]Putnam, *The Life of William the Silent*, p. 75.
[12]Putnam, *The Life of William the Silent*, p. 79.

prince and his companions who saw their grotesque wealth shrink rapidly before their eyes.

In opposition to these policies, the Dutch peers banded together in a loose alliance with Orange in the lead. They were backed by the general populace who bitterly resented the foreign occupation of three thousand elite Spanish infantry-men and their distant king who had never bothered to learn even the basics of French or Dutch. While the father had treated the Netherlands as an autonomous part of the empire, they argued, his son merely exploited the region as his person-al "military base" and "financial cash cow."

Despite these rumblings, public criticism at the time was still relative-ly muted as the risk-averse Orange and his compatriots shied away from direct confrontation with the Habsburgs. Instead, they merely denounced Philip's "bad advisors," in particular the king's premier in the Low Countries, Cardinal Gran-velle.[13] It was during these tension-filled months that William began to be called 'the Silent' by his enemies, perhaps even Granvelle himself, because he dithered and refused to openly state his opinions about Spanish policies.[14]

In 1562, the disaffected, but still wavering Flemish peers sent one of their own, Baron Montigny, to Spain to discuss their grievances with their king. Philip listened politely, but remained intransigent. In March of the following year the triumvirate of Orange, Egmont, and Horn upped the ante. They had grown more determined in the intervening months, and feared that the king was conspiring to rob the nobility and the Netherlands as a whole of their long-standing self-rule. Their written ultimatum informed Philip that unless Granvelle resigned, they were leaving the Council of State.[15] Flanders was not to be turned into the north-ernmost province of the Spanish monarchy.[16]

The declaration was an important "game changer." The Dutch elite were uniting under a league of lords, and William had finally decided to take a stance. In the ensuing months, his Breda and Brussels palaces became meeting points for the country's disaffected magnates where days and nights were spent with political discussions, strategizing, and parties. In fact, Orange was so busy with political ploys and other pastimes that he thought little of his German allies. His brother Louis informed him that Philip of Hessen was waiting to have his letters answered. "Methinks I put in that post for nothing," the landgrave groused, "they are slow to write to me." He was not the only one feeling ignored.

For a while now, Anna had been awakening to new, and somewhat un-pleasant marital realities. The thrilling days of courtship had passed, never to return. Indeed, her "season of supremacy" had been replaced by the quotidian boredom of daily life and benign neglect. William was still the gallant with beau-tiful manners and polite phrases, but he had certainly "gotten off his knees." It was a general rule that wedlock turned the fawning lover into an imperious hus-band, and although that was not quite the case with the prince, Anna was com-ing to realize that the ardent lover of her Dresden days had vanished for good.[17] William was either busy with friends, the falcon hunt, or visiting family mem-bers. And like Anne van Buren, the princess might have felt excluded from the

---

[13]Vetter, pp. 115-7, p. 120.
[14]Mörke, p. 82.
[15]Kamen, pp. 93-4.
[16]Vetter, p. 117.
[17]Vickery, pp. 58-9.

Nassaus' inner circle, resentful of the attention William lavished on his siblings. Alone for much of the year with the prince away, Anna complained that her life was now devoid of glamour and that life in Saxony had been a thousand times more pleasant.[18]

Gossip about her husband cavorting with beautiful women rankled even more. After less than two years of marriage, there was talk of extramarital dalliances and that Orange had taken a mistress or had failed to discard a former paramour. In December 1561, the prince's brother-in-law, Count Schwarzburg, hoped that "the prince was enjoying the married state and no longer visited Barbara of Live (Lier) and others," but would soon become the father of a baby boy.[19] Anna might have reflected bitterly that William's courtship pledges had been nothing but empty flattery, and that his reasons for marrying her had been political and financial instead of personal.[20]

Since the Princess of Orange was not a popular mistress, her sorrows gained her few sympathies among her peers and staff. If she couldn't cope with her husband's philandering, contemporary wisdom dictated, the fault was hers. Lord Halifax put the matter in a nutshell in his "advice to his daughter": "Next to the danger of committing the fault [of adultery] yourself, the greatest is that of seeing it in your husband. Do not seem to look or hear that way: if he is a man of sense, he will reclaim himself; the folly of it is of its self-sufficiency to cure him. If he is not so, he will be provoked, but not reformed." Dignified silence was the proper reaction to a husband's infidelity, since this would "naturally make him more yielding in other things: and whether it be to cover or redeem his offense, you may have the good effect of it whilst it lasteth." Even the medical establishment offered nothing but censure for the resentful, angry wife. A seventeenth-century physician diagnosed the jealous rants of a desperate gentry spouse as "Zelotipia [a morbid jealousy] [which] is got into her pericranium."[21]

Unfortunately, such opinions were more than just a piece of male wish fulfillment, although it certainly was that; it was a clear statement of how the majority of men and women in Anna's social milieu expected a wronged wife to behave. Righteous anger and a confrontational attitude had no place among the female aristocracy as far as husbandly unfaithfulness was concerned. When Dr. Pfeffinger asked William during the wedding service in Leipzig if he would be "forsaking all others [and] keep thee only unto her," the groom, along with the wedding party, quite clearly thought that this was not to be taken literally. Anna's mistake was to think that it was.[22]

In her heart, Anna probably knew that she had been relegated to that grating limbo reserved for wives whose husbands did not much care for them one way or another.[23] Some of her female peers, isolated and ignored in their separate living quarters, retreated into religion and learning. Others devoted their time to children or charitable causes. Anna realized that it was entirely normal in such marriages that neither spouse had direct knowledge of what went on in the other's world, except by hearsay or formal inquiry.[24] Unlike these forbearing wives,

[18]Böttcher, p. 106
[19]Quoted in Böttcher, p. 100.
[20]Vetter, p. 70.
[21]Tinniswood, pp. 358-9.
[22]Tinniswood, pp. 358-9.
[23]Starkey, p. 160.
[24]Kleinman, p. 35.

however, the Princess of Orange had no intention of accepting behavior that she deemed unfair and degrading to her person.

From twenty-first-century perspectives as well as her own, Anna's grievances were certainly justified. The electress had taught her by example that adultery had no place in a Christian marriage, and August - an anomaly among princes - apparently never strayed from the marriage bed during almost four decades of holy wedlock.[25] William, on the other hand, paid little heed to his vows, which set off the princess's legendary temper. In April 1563, reports of such disturbing outbursts of anger reached Dresden that the electress addressed an urgent letter of warning to her niece. Her "unmerciful splutterings" of curse words would not only alienate her husband, Anne admonished, but prove detrimental to the princess's position as a role model to her inferiors. "Your Grace lived under Our command and in Our women's wing for a while, and these [incidents] might prove harmful to Our reputation and the ladies' quarters here with foreign, unknown folk. Your Grace knows only too well that, verily, it is not custom in these lands that female persons engage and are overcome by rage. Impatience, bad manners or curses have not been noted here," she scolded, "much less are they accepted in our women's section as was the case when Your Grace was here."[26]

Self-conscious and ashamed after this epistolary browbeating, Anna only plucked up the courage of a response in June. She thanked her aunt for her motherly advice regarding anger and curses, but, as in previous replies to inquiries from Germany, refuted any reports of a marital crisis. Instead, she meekly appealed to the elder Anne to continue her counsels. "As soon as Your Grace hears that I am not behaving correctly, [let me know] since I have no one here who sets me right," she wrote airily. "My dearest young husband loves me too much to tell me anything."[27] It is anyone's guess if William, much distracted by politics and feasting, casually overlooked his wife's conduct or if Anna simply made excuses to calm her relations. For all was certainly not well in the Orange household, despite Anna's protestations of being well-loved.

In fact, in a sad kind of déjà vu, the princess was starting to antagonize even those individuals who had once been favorably or at least neutrally disposed towards her. Anna's personal exchanges with her staff were awkward at best, and there is not a single mention of a female confidante or friend in historical records. After her Saxon ladies had departed, William replaced them with local, Catholic women. This turned into another point of contention between the couple, although Orange had not acted out of order.

By tradition, the female members of the women's chamber belonged as much to the court of the prince as to his wife's, and husbands unyieldingly retained the license to choose their consorts' staff, often to the chagrin of their spouses. Princesses preferred staid widows or the plain looking wives of knights as their companions; princes favored attractive young maidens who could be employed as potential bedmates or "image enhancers." Beautiful, highborn damsels played a visible role during diplomatic and ceremonial occasions as fixtures of courtly magnificence, and contributed to the atmosphere of friendship and goodwill that facilitated tough negotiations. Draped in dazzling costumes for royal

---

[25]Keller, *Kurfürstin*, p. 29.
[26]Keller, *Kurfürstin*, pp. 202-3.
[27]Kruse, "Wilhelm von Oranien," p. 29.

christenings, banquets, and tournaments, they were essential "eye candy" for any royal residence. Awestruck visitors were to leave with otherworldly images of paradisiacal feasting among ethereal, yet sexually open-minded nymphs imprinted on their minds.[28] The Princess of Orange, who had a propensity for jealousy and spite, felt threatened by such females. Reports had been circulating that William was cavorting with "a maiden in a white skirt during a banquet" which hurt Anna deeply.[29]

As her outlook on life darkened, worrying reports from home did little to lift Anna's sagging spirits. The princess had probably received the news that her aunt Sidonia - her late mother's friend and elder sister of Elector August - was being mistreated by her husband, since the two engaged letters at the time. Much like her own, Sidonia's union had once been a well-known love match.

In 1545, at the "advanced" age of twenty-six, Sidonia had married Duke Eric of Brunswick-Calenberg-Göttingen. The Saxon princess had a limp and uneven shoulder, but sixteen-year-old Eric had declared himself smitten with a fiancée who was not only homely, but ten years his senior.[30] His bride was equally enamored, and much like the Princess of Orange sixteen years later, not afraid to broadcast her feelings openly. According to Landgrave Philip, a torrent of emotion made Sidonia declare that if she could not have Eric, she would not want any other man as long as she lived. Indeed, rumors claimed that the Saxon princess had gone so far as to approach her betrothed in an indecent manner.[31]

Such forwardness could not end well, and the landgrave for one, issued dire warnings. The bride's age would weigh like a "heavy mortgage" on the marriage, he forecasted. "We think that she and Duke Eric are of disparate ages, and she is even 10 years older than he is, meaning that at the end of the kissing month (the honeymoon), there will be all sorts of problems." As in Anna's case, his predictions would unfortunately prove correct.[32]

Only a few years after their wedding, Eric not only converted to Catholicism, which his wife greatly resented, but also embarked on a life of adventure and indiscriminate whoring. Instead of managing his estates in the rural Calenberg region of Brunswick, Eric spent his time as a mercenary commander in imperial employ, fighting the Habsburgs' enemies in Spain, Italy, and the Netherlands. Sidonia saw her husband only sporadically, and during his rare visits he usually helped himself to her precious jewels to finance his glittering lifestyle abroad.[33] As the years wore on, Eric came to regard his older consort as a burdensome, unattractive nag who would not stop haranguing him about her sold treasures, his religious conversion, and extramarital affairs. In 1554 Sidonia informed her younger brother, Elector August of Saxony, that Eric was trying to poison her.[34] The couple's relations had deteriorated into that dreadful realm of conjugal hell where barely concealed hatred contaminated every comment and gesture.

Six years later, while Anna wallowed in rosy dreams of wedlock, Sidonia visited Dresden to give her relations an earful about her spouse's continued ne-

---

[28]Barbara J. Harris. *English Aristocratic Women 1450-1550* (Oxford: Oxford University Press, 2002), p. 232.
[29]Kruse, p. 87.
[30]Lilienthal, p. 184, p. 186, p. 189.
[31]Lilienthal, p. 189, p. 191.
[32]Lilienthal, p. 10. On 17 May 1545 Eric led his "mature" bride to the altar. If not fueled by love, relief surely propelled Sidonia to accept Eric's hand in matrimony. Except for August, all her siblings were already married, and the specter of single life was a daunting one for any Protestant woman for lack of better alternatives
[33]Lilienthal, pp. 194-5.
[34]Lilienthal, pp. 204-7.

glect and mistreatment. Eric had permanently settled on a costly estate in the Low Countries with his long-term mistress, Catherine von Weldam, and was financing his lifestyle with the sale of her jewels. Elector August, never unduly touched by female complaints, reluctantly decided to lecture Eric on proper connubial etiquette. It was his sister's right to be properly cared for and kept according to her station, he admonished the duke. Also, the House of Wettin categorically declined to ease the burden of the prince's enormous expenditures in Burgundy after he had already run through a vast fortune of Saxon dowry treasures.[35] He had better reform, the elector protested feebly.

Regrettably, Eric was not at all cowed by his brother-in-law's chastising, but rather devised novel ways of tormenting his wife. He had the furniture removed from her apartments and paraded his mistress among the locals during his rare stays in Brunswick. In June 1563 Sidonia fired off another letter to her brother with the latest outrage: she had been turned away at her own doorstep. "That my Lord and husband has a loose whore ... with him whom he accords the honors of a princess, I have realized ... Also, that the loose brat is everywhere, especially on my widow's estate [which] has greatly angered me. For that reason I betook myself to Calenberg, because I wanted to see what kind of woman has been there. And then came my husband's order that I was not to be received." Beside herself with rage she told a confidante, "When I manage to get to the house, I will cut the whore's nose off and gouge out one eye."[36]

And yet, after the first surge of hot anger had subsided, Sidonia came to realize that the time had come to count her losses. Lonely and increasingly isolated, she begged the elector "not to forsake me, but to take me in." Unfortunately, August had no intention of catering to unhappily married females, including his sister. The "other woman" was certainly an irritant and Eric's lack of discretion indelicate, he wrote, but he was not in the position to influence his brother-in-law in any way. A return of Sidonia's to Dresden was therefore out of the question, because she would be penniless and was too young to live alone. Furthermore, leaving her husband would set a bad example and denigrate the standing of the nobility, the dynasty, and gentlemen of rank.[37]

"Take comfort in your faith," he waxed unctuously, "exercise patience, entreat the Almighty from the bottom of your heart to show up His Grace's indecent actions, and induce him towards Christian improvement." To drive his point home, August closed with a rather smug postscript. Sidonia herself had once given similar advice to one of her younger, unhappily married sisters, he reminded her. As to her fears of being the continued target of a murder plot, these figments of her imagination did not even deserve an answer.[38]

*****

Sidonia's troubles must have disquieted Anna. She too had few, if any friends and no home to return to if she was forsaken like her aunt. The elector had refused to take in his own sister; he would surely balk at sheltering his unloved niece. William was not a villain like the Brunswick duke, but he too was straying from the marriage bed. Barely two years after her pretentious nuptials, Anna's

---

[35]Lilienthal, p. 213.
[36]Lilienthal, pp. 214-5.
[37]Lilienthal, pp. 216-7.
[38]Lilienthal, p. 217.

future looked not nearly as rosy as she had once envisioned it.

If the Princess of Orange had been ruthlessly self-assertive or a clever tactician, she might have manipulated the courtly machinery in her favor. Some of her peers were extremely adept at behind-the-scenes intrigue, a useful female weapon of self-defense which could empower a bold consort. Sidonia's mother-in-law Elizabeth was such an example of hardnosed cold-bloodedness, backbone, and guts. At age fifteen, Elizabeth of Brandenburg (1510-1558) had chased her husband's longtime paramour away by accusing her of a poison plot brought about by witchcraft. And, as a warning to all would-be lovers of the duke's, she had several of the concubine's companions burned as witches.[39]

Elizabeth's is a case of abhorrent callousness, but it shows that wives, even very young ones like Anna, could be mistresses of their fate with the right amount of gumption. It is certainly to Anna's credit that she never turned into a devious schemer like the princess from Brandenburg, but her lack of such instincts also left her unequipped to handle critical court battles. Devoid of cunning, the Princess of Orange was fighting with blunt weapons and rarely, if ever, got her way.

*****

Physical limitations further discomfited the already unstable young woman. With her misshapen figure, Anna was excluded from the livelier of formal dances, another vital form of social intercourse in Renaissance society. Every well-rounded gentleman and woman knew how to dance well, a necessary competence for anyone striving for prominence. One hired well-known, expensive dance instructors to improve dexterity and outdo others in carefully staged recitals, because like everything else at court, dance was not a pleasurable hobby but part of etiquette.

Highly stylized, the meticulous rules of performing prohibited individual improvisation and freedom of movement. The aim of every noble dancer was to gain the approval of the audience who scrutinized every step with hawk eyes, sharply critical of those who failed to keep up with the group's rapid footwork, or, even worse, breathlessly stumbled to the ground.

Dance competitions were serious affairs, but also enjoyed immense popularity, especially in France and Flanders. They were less popular at Protestant courts such as Dresden, and Calvinist communities even forbade them. The handicapped Anna certainly did not arrive in Breda an accomplished danseuse. William, on the other hand, could hold his own among the best European performers. In 1565, he played the premier part in a so called "combat ballet." Together with fifteen amazons, Orange "battled" the "dark forces" of Count d'Aigremont and his fifteen wild men.[40] His wife, whose bodily limitations forbade such exertions, probably watched her dazzling husband from the sidelines.

Ill at ease and full of untrammeled, dark moods, Anna dulled her insecurities with feasting and carousing. Except for reading she had few other hobbies

[39] Brigitte Streich. "Anna of Nassau und ihre 'Schwestern,'" *Witwenschaft in der Frühen Neuzeit* (Leipzig: Leipziger Universitätsverlag, 2003), pp. 182-3.
[40] Margaret M McGowan. *Dance in the Renaissance* (New Haven, CT: Yale University Press, 2008), pp. 18-22, p. 106, p. 168. The French King Henri III (1551-1589) once kept the ambassador of Savoy waiting, because he had danced the night away and spent the rest of the day sleeping.

and lacked the determination and concentration required for learned pursuits. A passion like the electress's medicine brewing or the elector's alchemical dabbling eluded her. Unlike Anne van Buren who had rarely steered away from Breda, and if so, only at her lord's behest, Anna of Saxony was drawn to the limelight. After being patronized for much of her youth, the princess thirsted to get drunk on life. Unfortunately, she was utterly graceless in her bearing and quickly created the wrong kind of buzz.

During her first official audience with the Regent Margaret, Anna complained about being slighted and then boldly outstared the king's astounded half-sister. Margaret was the illegitimate daughter of Emperor Charles and a Flemish serving maid, and the elector's daughter perhaps considered her equal, if not inferior in pedigree. There were other disturbing incidents. Anna had frequent tiffs with Sabine, Countess Egmont, the wife of one of her husband's oldest friends. Sabine also held the title of Princess of Gavre and two ladies were known to squeeze through narrow doorways side-by-side, neither of them willing to yield to the other. A compromise was finally reached when the quarrelsome princesses agreed to enter a room arm-in-arm at the same time.[41] And then there was the Catholic priest who received a tactless telling-off after pushing himself in front of William during a court function.[42]

Anna's embarrassing gaffes could not have come at a worse time for William. In the spring of 1563, he was nearing a direct confrontation with Cardinal Granvelle after advocating religious freedoms. The Low Countries bordered states where Protestantism was tolerated, Orange asserted. Therefore the Dutch provinces should not submit to a policy of drastic repression. "However strongly I am myself a Catholic," he announced, "I cannot approve of princes attempting to rule the consciences of their subjects."[43] Together with his friends Egmont and Horn, William criticized Granvelle's persecution of Protestants and also accused the prelate of mismanagement. No one, they argued, was more capable of governing the Seventeen Provinces than the Dutch aristocracy. If the cardinal did not resign or amend his course, they would leave the Council of State until further notice. But the cardinal was equally resolute. He had no intention of permitting even a semblance of religious openness, Granvelle retorted defiantly, let alone the curtailment of his powers.[44]

The crisis sweltered through the summer. In faraway Spain, King Philip consulted his leading general, the ferocious Duke of Alba, for a solution. "Every time I see letters from those three gentlemen in Flanders," the soldier-statesman bellowed, "I get so enraged that if I did not try to control myself, Your Majesty would take me for a madman.[45] On no account," he advised, "should Granvelle be removed." But Philip, his mind preoccupied by an imminent war against the Ottomans, decided to reluctantly beat a retreat. Although he had generally supported Granvelle's policies, especially the firm application of the heresy laws, he

[41]Böttcher, p. 106.
[42]Putnam, *The Life of William the Silent*, p. 73. See also Wedgwood, p. 64
[43]Wedgwood, p. 63.
[44]Mörke, p. 85. Orange's motives were not entirely selfless. In order to retain the continued support of the Protestant German princes like Anna's uncle and grandfather, he had to overcome their suspicions about his religious affiliation. See also Putnam, *Moderate Man*, 156. Granvelle was so distrustful of William that he asked Philip to invite him to Spain. "The Prince of Orange is a dangerous man, sly, full of ruses ...appearing sometimes Catholic, sometimes Calvinist, sometimes Lutheran. He is capable of any underhanded deed that might be inspired by an unlimited ambition." William, on the other hand, still hoped in a letter to Louis that the troubles "between the cardinal and us others" will soon end
[45]Putnam, *Moderate Man*, p. 155. "Cada vez que veo los despachos de aquell ostres señores Flamencos, me mueven la colera, de maneraque, si no procurasse mucho temparla, creo pareceria à V. M. mi opinion de hombre frenetico."

gave in to this particular demand of the Flemish troika.

In January 1564 the Spanish monarch addressed a letter to Granvelle, advising him to leave the country under the pretense of visiting his ailing mother in France. The cardinal obeyed and went into a short retirement.[46] He spent his time growing his beard, purchased new pieces for his tremendous art collection, and fantasized about the day when the Prince of Orange would receive his deserved comeuppance. Meanwhile, William and company celebrated the departure of the hated cleric with a raucous banquet.[47] The prince then wrote triumphantly to Anna's uncle, Landgrave William, "Everyone is very pleased that the good cardinal has moved on."[48]

*****

Despite the cardinal's "French vacation," religious tensions in the Netherlands did not subside. Philip's agents continued to arrest Protestant "troublemakers" and shadowed William's residences. For the Spanish, the almost constant presence of the prince's Calvinist brother Louis was a particular irritant. Unlike the cautious William, Louis sent a steady stream of secret reports to Anna's grandfather.[49] Besides the count, other Lutheran family members also regularly visited from Germany, inadvertently turning the prince's chateaux into gathering places for the religiously disaffected. Anna's Lutheran pastor resided openly at Breda and secretly in Brussels, and at both residences Protestant hymns reverberated on Sundays. The King of Spain, highly annoyed that his father's onetime ward was undermining official royal policy, angrily commanded Orange to keep his irksome relations in check.[50]

In addition to his political woes, William was plagued by continued financial pressures. On top of his own liabilities, the Dillenburg branch of the family had sunk into a morass of debt that amounted to 300,000 florins. Some employees of the ruling Count of Nassau-Dillenburg - William's younger brother John - had asked permission to seek work elsewhere after going for months without wages. Louis wrote dejectedly, "What words these were for me to hear, you can imagine."

The prince tried to take it all in stride. He casually informed Louis at the beginning of 1564 that in matters of economy "We are still about where you left us. I'm continually hampered in fulfilling my estate. My greatest difficulty is the falconers, although I have reduced them so that they only cost me twelve hundred florins. There's good company assembled to take a hand at tennis and falconry to which last I am going now in this fine weather."[51] Besides the joys of sports, there was another happy event to report. Anna had given birth to a daughter in November 1563, and this time the child seemed strong enough to survive.

Unfortunately, the birth of little Anna did nothing to lift her mother out of her ever tightening web of depressive angst. Tales of conjugal strife would not quiet down, and by now the princess had acquired the reputation of a shrew. She

[46]Kamen, pp. 94-6. See also Putnam, *Moderate Man*, pp. 160-1. A retainer of the Nassau family named Lorich described the cardinal's unwilling departure. "When he received the king's order, he growled like a bear, [and] shut himself up in one room at a time."
[47]Putnam, *Moderate Man*, p. 160. On 5 March 1564 an exuberant William wrote to his brother Louis, "It is a sure thing that our man is going. I hope he will go so far that he can never return."
[48]Quoted in Böttcher, p. 108.
[49]Putnam, *The Life of William the Silent*, p. 78.
[50]Wedgwood, p. 59.
[51]Putnam, *The Life of William the Silent*, p. 79.

had proven fertile, but her skills as a mother and stepmother were called into question. The diplomatic corps tittered about Anna's uncontrollable rages, her outbursts, her disobedience. There had been another contretemps with the Regent Margaret, it was reported, and she was unkind to her stepchildren, Philip William and Maria. In sum, Orange's wife was overly haughty and distinctly odd.[52]

William - amply occupied with his duties as provincial governor and leisure pursuits - withdrew from his wife. In contrast to his first marriage, he wrote few letters to Anna during his absences and rarely mentioned her in missives to others.

In May 1564 the prince informed Margaret of Parma that his consort was leading a "peculiar" existence, while a Monsieur Bordey kept Cardinal Granvelle abreast of the latest talk. "On Monday, Her Highness went to Mass at Sainte Gudule's, accompanied by a group of nobles ... although they were all drunk. The prince [then] dined alone with her Highness [and said to the princess that she] led a life that would be the death of him."[53]

Such phases of frenzied living alternated with periods of complete withdrawal. That same month, William informed the regent that his wife was disheartened and unsociable, and "sometimes doesn't leave her room for a fortnight."[54] Pregnant for a third time, Anna was still in the doldrums that same summer. Her sister-in-law Catherine of Schwarzburg wrote to William's younger brother Adolph, "It's getting worse and worse with this person [Anna], and even more, which I'm not allowed to write." In France, Granvelle rejoiced over his enemy's domestic troubles and gleefully circulated each damning report. He sneered that the Princess of Orange was a veritable Xantippe (the legendary harridan of the Greek philosopher Socrates).[55]

Anna, meanwhile, was still pretending that nothing was amiss chez Orange. In April 1564 she thanked the electress for her "friendly reproaches," and offered to purchase any item Anne desired from the Netherlands. In another, especially heartfelt note to Dresden, the princess expressed her gratitude for the just arrived millet seeds to ease her upcoming delivery. She also promised to remain August's "loyal daughter at all times" and "not to forget herself."[56]

Despite these repeated assurances, the princess was "forgetting herself" rather frequently; so much so that her self-conscious relations started to despair. Her volatile behavior and unchecked anger besmirched the reputation of the Houses of Hessen and Wettin and embarrassed her husband, they agonized. Honorable women kept quiet and spent their time in private and silent contemplation with "their tongues locked in their mouths."[57] In contrast, Anna's unguarded verbal eruptions were not only improper, but downright sinister. Openly displayed female arrogance, vulgarity, and fury were associated with witches, the thinking went, and not with honorable ladies. Wherever she was found, a witch had an abundance of what Scottish witch hunters called "smeddum"—a quarrelsome refusal to be put down.[58] Such anger was purely a man's preserve. The only oc-

[52]Midelfort, p. 57.
[53]Putnam, *Moderate Man*, p. 167.
[54]Vetter, p. 67.
[55]Kruse, "Wilhelm von Oranien," p. 30.
[56]Kruse, "Wilhelm von Oranien," pp. 29-30.
[57]S. P. Cerasano and Marion Wynne-Davies. "'From Myself, My Other Self I Turned:' An Introduction,"*Gloriana's Face* (Detroit: Wayne State University Press, 1992), p. 6.
[58]Ozment, *Daughter*, p. 155.

casion when women could allow themselves a moment of wrath was when their religious faith was in some way threatened.[59]

Rather than spiritual, Anna's robust outbursts were caused by a combination of unfulfilled expectations and personal frustrations that few Renaissance princes would have been willing to redress or satisfy. As mentioned before, rebuking one's husband for infidelities was considered inappropriate and inelegant. And while we sympathize and applaud Anna's courage to address such wrongs, her inability "to just make the best of it" caused a good amount of incomprehension among her peers.

She had married a young, handsome prince of her choosing whose wealth enabled her to live in luxury as the chatelaine of Breda, they argued. Indeed, Orange was a man of admirable restraint who bore her tantrums with equanimity. A gentlewoman's honor lay in the public recognition of her virtue, which Anna imperiled with her willful behavior.[60] About ten years later, the electress dispensed the following words of advice to her daughter Elizabeth, whose life paralleled Anna's in certain respects. "Even if it will be hard and hurts you to obey your husband, you should always remain patient when you cannot get your way by friendly pleading."[61]

His wife's profound unhappiness spelled just as much trouble for William. Unlike today, conjugal difficulties among noble Renaissance families were not an internal affair, but a public concern with potentially far-reaching ramifications. For one, the princess's unchecked histrionics put Orange's managerial abilities in doubt, both at home and in society. The successful male was the undisputed master of his family who firmly guided his spouse and children towards righteous obedience and moral probity. If Anna refused to mend her ways, William had to correct her behavior or risk becoming a laughing stock. Cardinal Granvelle, for one, was already spreading tales about Orange's alleged cowardice from abroad.

This was an unfortunate development, since nothing except adultery was more embarrassing to a man's ego than being suspected of allowing a *Weiberregiment* (Regiment of Women) to take over the home. The newly invented printing presses spewed forth thousands of pamphlets ridiculing males wearing fool's hats, defeated by womanly wiles and tempers. Objects of merciless mockery and scorn, they were seen as lions without claws, pansies, and "nappy washers" who had surrendered the right to wear trousers.[62]

In William's case, the situation was complicated by his political ties to Anna's relatives. If he reined her in harshly, his wife might accuse him of mistreatment which in turn could lead to the loss of crucial Protestant connections in the empire — connections that he carefully cultivated with civil war looming. On the other hand, the prince could not let Anna's disrespectfulness towards him and others go unhindered for much longer, lest he suffer a serious loss of reputation. After weeks of careful deliberation, William decided to appeal to the Elector of Saxony and to set his wife straight.

---

[59] Catherine Peyroux. "Gertrude's furor: Reading Anger in an Early Medieval Saint's Life," *Anger's Past* (Ithaca, NY: Cornell University Press, 1998), p. 36.
[60] Vickery, p. 54.
[61] Keller, *Landesmutter*, pp. 265-6.
[62] Hufton, p. 39, p. 48.

Not surprisingly, Anna became even more intransigent when confronted. She had given up her fortune, her liberty, and her person into her husband's keeping, become a slave to his humor, and even his pleasure, only to be chastised in the most humiliating fashion. Unlike other princesses, "doing right" in the face of extreme provocation did not offer Anna the near mystical satisfaction of matrimonial martyrdom. Her conception of happiness was not only to please her master, but - not unreasonably - to derive some pleasure out of life as well.[63]

The latest news from Sidonia might have reinforced Anna's darkening view of marriage. After years of maltreatment, flagrant infidelity, and another murder plot (this time directed at Eric), Anna's aunt was at her wits end. In the summer of 1563 the duke had only narrowly escaped death after a fire had broken out under his bed, and his estranged wife was the main suspect. Even before this mysterious incident, the ducal couple's dealings had hit a new low. Sidonia had requested an inventory of her silver plate from Dresden after noticing that Eric was still pawning her valuables. The elector responded by admonishing his sister to exercise patience.

Sidonia, however, was no longer willing to accept any further humiliation. After another tumultuous year was coming to a close, she asked Eric for a divorce and demanded Calenberg as her widow's estate. His adultery, she argued, had effectually rendered their union meaningless. This was technically correct. Both Catholic and Protestant theologians agreed that the biblical reasons for divorce were adultery and "malicious desertion," and Eric was certainly guilty on all counts. His affair with Catherine von Weldam was common knowledge and he had long ago relocated to the Netherlands, out of his wife's reach.

Nevertheless, a divorce initiated by a woman defied contemporary imagination. The pervasive double standard regarded a husband's infidelities with an unmarried woman as a pardonable indulgence that rarely warranted an adultery trial. Sidonia's brother August was clearly of that mindset when he characterized Eric's extra-marital liaison as a mere irritant that by no means impaired his sister's rights and privileges as a princess. Even if a court had granted Sidonia her wish of divorce, she would have most likely faced a lifetime of poverty. Property laws of that time did not make provisions for the ex-wives of noblemen, only for their widows. Eric could not be forced to grant the duchess the income of her widow's estate.[64]

While the duchess was weighing options, a shocking report from the Low Countries threatened to derail her bold plans. In 1564, after months of marital implosions, Eric had suddenly fallen very ill. He was losing his hair by the bushels, the nails of his hands and feet had fallen out, and his body was abnormally bloated. The duke's personal physician, Dr. Cornelius Mertens, diagnosed poisoning in the presence of notarized witnesses. Fortunately, Sidonia was informed, the toxin was not fatal, but only temporarily debilitating.

After a lengthy convalescence, Eric returned to Calenberg ridden by furies. The previous year's suspicious fire had still not been adequately explained and the latest attempt on his life pointed to a plot that he intended to extinguish with the most frightening means at his disposal: a witch hunt. Upon his arrival he had four women arrested, all acquaintances of his wife's. The ladies Hart, Timme,

[63]Vickery, p. 59, p. 83.
[64]Lilienthal, pp. 218-23.

and Bardelen all admitted under torture that they had put explosive fuses under the duke's bed, and then fermented a harmful substance with a fourth woman, Godela Kuckes, to do away with His Serene Highness and the duchess.

Interestingly, Mrs. Kuckes admitted without painful prompting that she had intended to poison Sidonia five years earlier. She only survived that admission by a few days, after which she was found dead by prison guards, her neck broken. It was said that the devil had killed Godela, but it was probably Duke Eric or one of his henchmen. Only an extremely influential person would have been allowed access to her cell, and the prince certainly had the motive to get rid of a dangerous witness who could reveal inconvenient truths. Although Mrs. Kuckes claimed that the poison was meant for both husband and wife, it is likely that the toxin was intended for Sidonia alone.

Godela Kuckes did not remain Eric's sole victim. Afraid of gossip, he made an example of anyone connected with the sordid affairs by the most grisly means. Forty-one individuals were burned at the stake or done away with by other methods, among them the Madams Hart, Timme, and Bardelen.

As for his wife, whom the duke also suspected of involvement in the poisoning and fire plots, she was put under immediate house arrest, watched over by armed guards, and prevented from receiving Saxon envoys or relatives. At the close of 1564, as Anna readied herself to give birth to her third child, Sidonia bemoaned her lack of proper food and clothing.[65] And while she trembled at becoming the next target of Eric's witch hunt, her niece Anna continued in her own little universe of discontent and angst.

*****

For all of Sidonia's troubles and her own sorrows, the Princess of Orange was able to close 1564 on at least one positive note. In December Anna gave birth to a boy whom she named Maurice after her father. Her proud husband, never one to miss out on an occasion to celebrate, organized a lavish christening ceremony.[66] Together with the Dutch haut monde, William and Anna treated their guests to a four-course dinner of ninety-three different dishes that included Westphalian bacon, pastries from Arles as well as chicken pâté and sausage from Bologna. There was plenty of dancing and fireworks, and little Maurice was carried to chapel past a cordon of torch bearing Breda guild members.

In gratitude, the prince accorded special honors to Anna. Priceless tapestries adorned the walls of her chambers; tables buckled under the weight of gold and silver plates. Regrettably, the princess could not share her joy with her own family. Neither the elector nor Landgrave Philip attended the festivities despite William's express invitation. The electress was about to give birth to her eleventh child and Anna's grandfather was laid low with gout, they wrote apologetically.[67] In his stead, August sent his privy counselor Abraham Bock to Breda. This was not merely a polite gesture. The elector wanted Bock to get to the bottom of his niece's continued wretchedness.

---

[65]Lilienthal, pp. 225-7.
[66]Putnam, *Moderate Man*, p. 168. Margaret of Parma wrote to the king that the child was baptized according to Catholic rites, but she was grieved that the occasion was somewhat tainted by the fact that the godparents were Lutheran princes, namely August of Saxony and Philip of Hessen.
[67]Kruse, "Wilhelm von Oranien," p. 30.

A desperate Anna immediately confided in her uncle's emissary. "I have not as much as one person that I can trust," the princess lamented in a long-winded letter addressed to her uncle. And except for one German maid, none of her servants or ladies-in-waiting hailed from her homeland.[68] Those who had gained her confidence had been removed from her service, and "evil people" were continually trying to sow discord between herself and her lord.

Her hot-tempered brother-in-law Louis was a particular troublemaker and the cause of some of her rows with William. He continually maligned her, Anna groaned, and her husband's chamberlain, Henry von Wildberg, was rude and insolent. Although she had tried to hold her tongue, she was suffering greatly from all the criticism leveled at her "as God knows."

Drowning in a bottomless pool of desperation and perhaps self-pity, she continued, "I will keep quiet about the aspersions and insults that I have to hear on a daily basis and suffer on account of them; [but] this cuts me to the quick. My master [William of Orange] is also not on my side. He does not hold me dear and does not protect me from others. I don't have anyone in this country that I can confide in, except for my master who is hard to please. Therefore, I must appeal to Your Grace and I beg Your Grace most humbly to seek means [to improve my situation]; otherwise it will not be possible for me to continue any longer. I have been patient for three years, [but] things are getting worse by the day."

Anna penned a similar entreaty to another uncle, Landgrave William of Hessen, who replied with a half-hearted promise for a visit. He was as welcome "as God from heaven," Anna rejoiced. She could not wait to discuss the many "offensive matters" that she had to endure. The Prince of Orange, meanwhile, dispatched his side of the story to Dresden. Anna was turning his life into a living hell, he wrote, because of her moodiness, constant irritability, and lack of self-control. He was desperately seeking advice. Hundreds of years after these angry dispatches left Breda, it is impossible to ascertain who was in the right, or wrong.

In the end, no one came to Anna's, or William's aid. The landgrave was detained in Kassel citing "dangerous times," and despite assurances to the contrary, the Saxons had no desire to ever see the Oranges again. An inconsolable Anna told her Uncle William that the canceled visit had meant more to her "than I can ever tell you."[69]

[68]Kruse, "Wilhelm von Oranien," p. 36..
[69]Vetter, p. 67; Kruse, pp. 30-2; Vogt-Lüerssen, p. 50.

"The Domestic Curse"

As the Orange marriage disintegrated, both partners suffered. A portrait of the time shows William still handsome, but it was clear to all, including the prince himself, that the charmed life he had known since youth was slowly starting to unravel. The mounting political troubles with Philip of Spain and his unhappy wife robbed Orange of his peace of mind. Overburdened, he left the running of his great houses in Breda and Brussels to Louis, aware that this would lead to further clashes with the unstable princess. One of the king's agents reported that the prince was looking worn and had trouble sleeping.[1]

Anna, regrettably, sank into even deeper despair. Her relatives' lack of support had been a heavy blow, and in the spring of 1565 she withdrew from genteel activities again, brimming with self-loathing. Courtiers spread tales upsetting the hypersensitive princess who, like many insecure individuals, did not possess the self-confidence to rise above the chatter. William's archenemy Granvelle crowed in April that "She never leaves her room, neither to sup nor dine. Her chamber is illuminated only by candlelight, since she keeps the curtains closed all day."[2]

As the perpetual outsider and without meaningful relationships in either Breda or Brussels, Anna was seeking refuge in solitude. She held little hope for improvement of her situation, and recoiled at any human contact for stretches of time. At her most miserable, the princess even forbade her servants to disturb her self-imposed isolation. Her closet, the innermost and most secluded space of her apartment beyond the bedchamber, served as a peaceful sanctuary.

And it was peace that Anna needed after she was apprised of the nest of spies that the King of Spain had implanted in every Orange residence. After the birth of her (second) daughter Anna, the Spanish monarch had told William that he was opposed to any Lutheran guests from Germany, even the Elector August. He also demanded a detailed report of the girl's baptism from his half-sister Margaret. "The king has learned with great joy that the daughter of Orange has been baptized and that her mother has gone to confession," one of Philip's ministers commented smugly. "Now he wants to know if she was also given absolution."[3]

When she emerged from her sepulchral quarters, Anna insulted those around her. She had never been a charming hostess, but continued to offend with her ill-mannered blunders. On at least one occasion she startled Count Horn and several other dinner guests by hurling insults at William across the table. He could not hold a candle to her in pedigree and continually failed to stand up for her rights of precedence, she wailed. "He lets everyone ride over him."[4]

*****

By this time, it must have been clear to those around her that Anna was severely depressed. Far from being twenty-first century problems, melancholy in the Renaissance - along with anger - were believed to be the two most life-threatening emotions that could attack the human body and therefore taken very seri-

[1]Putnam, *Moderate Man*, p. 169.
[2]Schuppener, *Breda*, p. 123.
[3]de Dijn, p. 30.
[4]Putnam, *The Life of William the Silent*, p. 114.

ously. They upset the so-called "humors" governing the body and made a person vulnerable to illness and disease.[5] Satan might also be involved. He was known to inflict all kinds of troubles and diseases on humans, but had a predilection for melancholy, feeling most at home in the body of a disheartened individual.[6] Courtiers and family members thus stood by helpless as the princess receded into an impenetrable fog of angst and despair. Effective treatments for her mental issues were nonexistent; tangible help for the emotionally downtrodden still hundreds of years away.

To make matters worse, instead of offering the princess emotional support, it appears that nobody, including William, took the time to delve too deeply into Anna's emotional black hole. Rather, it was a virtual "no go area" of anxiety and unhappiness, carefully cordoned off from thorough examination.[7] Whatever troubled Anna, whether it was so-called "melancholy" or a more serious mental disorder, her family chose to regard her misconduct as a major moral lapse rather than a sickness of the mind.[8] Her husband's reluctance in confronting her personal problems probably aggravated the situation even further. Not speaking his mind posed a problem for the princess who very much liked to speak hers.

Perhaps Anna's condition would have improved had she only found that "one person I can trust." Unfortunately, true friendship rarely got in the way of advantage at royal courts. In the sealed environment of elite relations, even less sensitive souls often floundered. Liselotte of the Palatine, great-great-granddaughter of William of Orange and sister-in-law of Louis XIV, was a hoydenish, fresh-faced teenager before she wilted into a frustrated, caustic woman in France. Stuck in a tragically unhappy marriage, Liselotte found relief in her monumental correspondence (about 60,000 letters) with German relations in which she unburdened sorrows not dissimilar to Anna's.

"I live quite a lonely life in the big world, deal with few people and am alone for five hours in the summer and seven in the winter. There is no conversation anymore at court, one always gambles, and when one has a conversation once a week, it is ordinary, about tracaseries and arguments. If you'd like to know how things are here, you'd not be surprised to find out that I am no longer happy. Another person in my place, who was not happy by nature, would have perhaps died of sorrow long ago; I only get fat and heavy." Liselotte's sturdy disposition allowed her to manage her blues. She passed the long hours of boredom reading, writing, playing on the guitar or walking her dogs.[9] The Princess of Orange, unfortunately, had no such outlets. Except for her romance novels, Anna possessed few other interests that could have reduced her gloomy thoughts and sated her personal needs.

Since human companionship proved elusive, the princess eventually latched on to a different kind of "friend" that held some of her demons at bay and eased the loneliness: wine. This, of course, led to additional embarrassments for William. Afraid of gossip, he no longer took his oft inebriated wife to official functions, excusing her absence to the regent by claiming illness. After another public slip-up, he wrote to a friend, "What happens secretly can well be born, but

---

[5]Steven Ozment. *Magdalena and Balthasar* (New York: Simon and Schuster, 1986), p. 12.
[6]Pieter Spierenburg. *The Broken Spell* (New Brunswick, NJ: Rutgers University Press, 1991), p. 176.
[7]Tillyard, *Aristocrats* (New York: Noonday Press, 1994), p. 131.
[8]Midelfort, p. 60, p. 154.
[9]Midelfort, p. 60, p. 154.

verily I found it hard enough to hear her speak such things in front of everyone."[10]

Voluntary seclusion alternated with fits of madcap high jinx. After weeks of withdrawal, Anna traveled to the famous watering hole of Spa with a shady clique of acquaintances, but without William. The trip in itself was highly irregular. German princesses, like her Uncle William's wife in Kassel, did not dare venture into their walled palace gardens without husbandly permission, but the Princess of Orange wassailed with questionable companions away from home and children.[11] Naturally, such independence also stood in direct contravention to all moral teachings of the time. The good wife stayed indoors, "guarding her chastity" in silent and private contemplation.[12]

Even worse was Anna's indiscreet conduct. At the famed hot springs, which had been attracting visitors since the fourteenth century, the Princess of Orange made a thorough fool of herself by "letting loose," apparently operating under the naïve assumption that word would somehow not reach Breda. She openly maligned the House of Nassau and announced, probably drunk, that her husband was planning to poison her.[13] Such scandalous behavior had inevitable consequences. Although a personal visit was still out of the questions, August of Saxony dispatched his marshal, Hans Loeser, to the Low Countries to investigate. A close friend of her late father, Loeser knew the princess personally.

Upon his arrival in Brussels, where the Oranges spent part of late spring, the Saxon envoy pulled William aside for a talk. After reminding the prince to always be heedful of the reputation of the House of Wettin, Loeser carefully listened to the prince's marital woes and came away convinced that Orange was not in the least to blame. He merely asked him to remain patient with his wife, who had been known for her quick temper and hotheaded nature since childhood.

Then he cross-examined Anna. "Your Grace had once been so happy with the Prince," he reminded her. "Although I am not married to a king, I could not live in more marvelous circumstances and could not be taken care of any better," she had written to the electress in the first days of her marriage. If "evil people" had destroyed that close conjugal bond, the emissary argued, then Anna was well advised to choose her company more carefully. As to the claim that all her trusted servants had been taken from her, he would broach the matter with William. One wonders if Loeser ever considered the fact that all of Anna's hand-picked help owed their allegiance and financial well-being to the prince, and would therefore be hard-pressed to take his wife's side.

The conversation ended with Loeser handing Anna a stern letter of warning from her uncle. She had better respect William "as the head [of the home] in all matters Christian," and refrain from provoking him with "self-opinionated and passionate words." Her parents would turn in their graves if they heard about their only daughter's bad behavior. "You will incur my and the landgrave's severest displeasure if you choose to ignore our well-meaning, Christian advice," August threatened in closing, "and you will no longer be able to count on any comfort, help or guidance from home unless you mend your ways."[14] These were certainly not the words of support Anna had hoped for. Rather, the elector's in-

---

[10]Wedgwood, pp. 64-6.
[11]Kruse, "Wilhelm von Oranien," p. 86
[12]Cerasano, p. 7.
[13]Wedgwood, p. 64.
[14]Kruse, "Wilhelm von Oranien," pp. 32-4.

junctions were like sharp projectiles that re-opened painful memories of her unfortunate Dresden days.

At first Anna denied all complaints against her, but changed tack after Loeser methodically interviewed various servants and courtiers. In a spectacularly staged repentance, the cornered princess promised reform and vowed submissively, "I'd rather die than be a source of shame for my family." At the end of June 1565 she also addressed a groveling letter to her aunt, the electress, begging "her kindest, dearest mother" to keep her in her "motherly care."[15] William, much occupied with politics, was doubtful of his wife's reformist pledges and asked her relations to consider a "contingency plan" in case of renewed marital conflict.

"As I was prevented from speaking to the Elector of Saxony's gentleman both this morning and after dinner," William told his brother Louis, "I think it would be well for you to inform him that although my wife has promised to behave better, she is active in exactly the same manner again. So that my statements may not seem like fabrications, I should like him to get testimony about her behavior from the steward, van der Eike, and from the other servants, especially from her own maid, the little German girl. After hearing all sides, the elector will perhaps be able to make some suggestions. What my wife has promised him, she has told me and others hundreds of times. So I fear it will be the same old story as soon as the envoy [Loeser] is gone. In case [Loeser] cannot find any solution, let this report reach the ears of the elector, so that he may think of something and write to my wife."[16]

William was correct. After a few weeks of relative calm, Anna relapsed, firmly set on her trajectory of self-destructive loathing. She was especially harsh with her two stepchildren, and Orange eventually had no choice but to send them away, although they were only ten and nine years old at the time. He enrolled his son prematurely at the University of Louvain, while Maria joined the Regent Margaret as a junior lady-in-waiting in Brussels.[17] The prince held his tongue, but Louis challenged his sister-in-law. Anna was ruining the life of his much-loved older brother, he berated her. As the mother of two children of her own and a pair of stepchildren, one could expect her to curtail her love of idle gossip. At the age of twenty-one, she should concentrate on being a good wife and caregiver.[18]

Much occupied with representational and managerial duties, aristocratic women were generally known to be distant mothers, who rarely broke through the cordon of etiquette which kept them apart from their children. But Anna, at least in Louis's opinion, seemed to have taken this accepted level of detachment a step further by making little or no effort to spend time with her son and daughters. Perhaps her personal problems prevented the princess from developing meaningful bonds with her progeny; or she was of the same mindset as Mary Adelaide of Savoy (1685-1712), a French princess, who once commented to a friend, "I only go and see my son very rarely in order not to be too attached to him."[19]

*****

[15]Kruse, "Wilhelm von Oranien," p. 157.
[16]Putnam, *The Life of William the Silent*, p. 114.
[17]Wedgwood, p. 66.
[18]Kruse,"Wilhelm von Oranien," p. 35
[19]Fraser, *Louis*, p. 277.

Much like Louis and William, Anna's Hessian relations despaired over the princess's continued bad conduct. In August 1565 Anna's maternal uncle, William of Hessen, wrote that he was embarrassed to hear people prattling about his niece while he was touring Wurttemberg and Alsace. At the moment, he had to deal with affairs concerning his immediate family and could only send Anna guidance via post. His sister Barbara also suffered from severe depression which forced him to take action.

Only eight years older than Anna, Barbara's life eerily paralleled her niece's in certain ways. In 1555, the daughter of Philip of Hessen had married the elderly Count George of Wurttemberg-Mömpelgard and given birth to two living children during their three year marriage. When her beloved husband unexpectedly passed away, Barbara was at a complete loss. Mömpelgard (Montbeliard today) had never become a second home for a woman who always pined for her birth family in Kassel, and when her guardians insisted that she move to the desolate widow's estate of Reichenweiher (Riquewihr) in Alsace, Barbara plunged into panicked despair. Like Anna, she complained of low spirits and felt generally unable to cope with her new living arrangements. She developed a temper that led courtiers to accuse her of "treating her children badly and beating them."

In April 1562 Barbara carped to her father about uppity servants and requested a replacement for her current, disrespectful master of the household. Three years later, a new steward forwarded novel claims of Barbara being "completely alone and forsaken by the whole world, without knowing where to seek help or comfort" to her family. Shortly afterwards, Landgrave Philip and his son William travelled south to check on the unhappy dowager countess.[20]

While they were dealing with the allegedly capricious Barbara in Wurttemberg, Anna in Breda was left to cope on her own. In the years that followed, support from Kassel was limited to a slew of sanctimonious letters and envoys, with sermons on St. Paul's teachings on wifely subservience a perennial favorite. Constructive advice, on the other hand, never materialized.[21]

While the Germans lulled their consciences in collective self-deception, William tried to keep his wits about him amidst the political and private storms raging around him. The prince and his friends had continued their appeals to King Philip in favor of a more tolerant attitude towards non-Catholics and administrative reform, issues that had not been solved after Granvelle's departure. In late 1565, William's friend Lamoral, Count Egmont, travelled to Spain to present the nobles' complaints to Philip yet again.

Forty-three-year-old Egmont, the acclaimed victor of the battle of St. Quentin and the Netherlands' most distinguished soldier, was charming, cultured, and fluent in several languages including Spanish.[22] It was hoped that he could at last effect some change for the Low Countries. The king sat and listened to the count's briefs and suggestions, but ultimately refused to make any concessions, particularly in matters of faith. Instead, he declared rather fiercely, "I should count it as nothing to lose a hundred thousand lives if I had them, rather than allow it [religious toleration]." The notion was strongly seconded by the

[20]Löwenstein, Uta. "Mera Melancholia und übermäßig großer Zorn," *Witwenschaft in der Frühen Neuzeit* (Leipzig: Leipziger Universitätsverlag, 2003), pp. 407-17.
[21]Kruse, "Wilhelm von Oranien," p. 32.
[22]Lamoral, Count Egmont was a relation of William's first wife, Anne of Egmont, Countess Buren. He was a son of her namesake and aunt, Anna of Egmont († 1574).

Duke of Alba. The crown's foremost general had recently opined that the solution for Protestant uprisings in France was to "cut off some heads."

Despite a warning from his half-sister Margaret, Philip's hardline policies continued to contest the rights of the Dutch nobility, while renewed talk about the arrival of the Spanish Inquisition along with thousands of foreign troops further inflamed anxious mind. As the provinces rose up in protest, Orange and the Counts Egmont and Horn withdrew from the Council of State. At the end of the year, Louis of Nassau and his friend Henry van Brederode called on the lesser nobility to convene in Spa to ratify a secret pact. The rebels swore to defy the King of Spain and to oppose the reviled heresy laws. In Madrid, Philip was coming to realize that Flanders had become his most pressing problem in the Old World.[23]

In February 1566, while he grappled with the deteriorating political situation, a worn-out William composed another complaint to August of Saxony. He was no longer able to live with Anna, he wrote. Her trip to Spa, which had taken place against his express wishes, as well as her slanderous talk, had been the final straw. In addition to her insufferable behavior, she had also taken to excessive spending lately and was pawning some of her jewels. He would not repudiate her, but only because he valued his friendship with the elector. In a quiet moment, Orange let his wife read the letter. Anna was immediately chastened and quickly promised improvement; the prince, in turn, decided to keep the missive unsent in his desk.

Shortly afterwards, her fervent promises notwithstanding, the princess fired off a secret note to Hessen. It vilified her husband, and for the first time also hinted at suicide.[24] This was a startling development that no one pretended to notice but of course did. At the same time, Anna was plunging into one of her reclusive phases again, and spent her days listless and withdrawn in a darkened chamber, rocking herself to and fro while crying by candlelight.[25] Distress over her failed marriage and lack of friends were certainly at the heart of her profound despair.

Landgrave William replied to his niece's wailings with the customary lectures that did not sit well with the princess. Anna was to dispel her despondency by reading Scripture and psalms, and rejoice in the fact that she was living in magnificent surroundings "like no other princess in the realm."[26] The princess replied wearily, "So far, I did not lack in showing honor and reverence to my Lord and his family, but did not get any results; everything that I have done to demonstrate good friendship was misinterpreted and falsely read." As to his accusation that she wanted to pick her own serving personnel, the princess bristled, "I was satisfied with those servants that my Lord gave to me, although I often felt I had cause to do otherwise."[27]

With Anna refusing to shoulder any blame and William too busy or indifferent to care, the Orange marriage was reaching a total impasse. Four years after their spectacular Leipzig wedding, Anna had become William's "domestic curse."

[23]Kamen, pp. 97-99.; Mörke, p. 94.
[24]Spierenburg, pp. 176-7. It was often said at the time that demonic interference contributed to a person's suicide, since the devil loved to persuade those whose bodies he took possession of to kill themselves. In Christian thought a successful suicide was the ultimate sin, since by definition repentance was impossible.
[25]Wedgwood, p. 64.
[26]Kruse, "Wilhelm von Oranien," pp. 38-9.
[27]Kruse, "Wilhelm von Oranien," p. 158.

Crisis

As winter was slowly edged out by spring and Anna and William continued to wrestle in marital gridlock, Louis of Nassau and Henry van Brederode headed to Brussels. Together with an armed force of three hundred confederates, they presented Margaret of Parma with a "request" demanding religious toleration. Although an attending minister sneeringly dismissed the men as *gueux* (beggars), the regent felt unable to brush off all rebel demands and agreed to a modification of the reviled heresy laws.

To the west in Spain, King Philip churned after hearing of his half-sister's concessions to the Dutch nobles. Neighboring France was near collapse because Protestants were rebelling against the crown, and the same turmoil would soon beckon in Flanders, he predicted. In a letter to the pope the king made his position abundantly clear, "Rather than suffer the least injury to religion in the service of God, I would [rather] lose all my states ... for I do not intend to rule over heretics."

Soon enough Philip's fears appeared to become reality. In September 1566 Margaret sent an urgent message to Madrid, reporting widespread religious riots and destruction of sacred images in the Netherlands. Rabble-rousing Calvinist preachers had incited their congregations to destroy the "idols" of Catholicism, resulting in lawless mobs ransacking churches and monasteries across the Seventeen Provinces. Religious fanatics beheaded gilded statues, smashed in windows, destroyed altars, and cut up sumptuously embroidered vestments. In August, the vandals had blown through the great port city of Antwerp, a place that, according to the regent, had recently become a collecting point for "heretics and vagabonds." The subsequent destruction was cataclysmic. "Defilements, abominations, sacrilege," she wrote glumly to Philip. "Matters are worse than you could possibly imagine."[1] Many foreign merchants, skilled artisans, and intellectuals who had proudly called worldly Antwerp their second home hastily departed the Low Countries.

Throughout this period of unrest, William tried to maintain a balance between his obligations to the Spanish Habsburgs and the beliefs of the Dutch which he represented through his position as *stadholder* and as the country's greatest property owner. Although still very much beholden to Philip whose father had raised him with such love and care, the prince also sympathized with the aspirations of the Netherlanders and their desire for self-governance.[2]

Margaret, meanwhile, hoped to exploit Orange's well-known "commitment shyness" to pry him away from the opposition. By playing on his ambition and vanity, she hoped to firmly pull the prince into the Habsburgs' inner circle. When William rebuffed her overtures, the regent hatched an intrigue to break up the close alliance between Orange and Count Egmont. Anna was to serve as the catalyst.

During a dinner party at the *Palais de Nassau* in Brussels, Margaret deliberately snubbed the princess, while paying particular attention to Egmont's wife, the lower ranking Sabine. Anna immediately fell for the ruse. "The Countess of Egmont sits with Madame while the Princess of Orange is kept standing," Gran-

---

[1] Kamen, p. 113-7.
[2] Jardine, p. 30-2.

velle nattered in his correspondence, "The princess is dying of rage." William apparently saw through the regent's ploy or disregarded the women's quarrels, because the incident did not lead to the desired breach between the two allies.[3] As for Anna, she added yet another affront to her endless list of grievances.

*****

For all her sufferings, real or imagined, Anna still enjoyed a lifestyle that was positively regal. A copper engraving by Abraham de Bruyn and a recently discovered oil painting of the princess by an anonymous artist give pictorial evidence of her luxurious existence. Both works have been dated to 1566. Unlike the simple chalk drawing four years earlier, the later works are ¾ representations that focus on details of costume, especially Anna's invaluable jewelry and dress design.

Fashion had undergone a considerable change since the days of Anna's grandmother, Catherine of Mecklenburg. Gone were the bold-patterned robes, tight bodices, and wide skirts. Waists were only slightly tapered now and often vanished under long, dark colored Spanish coats or marlottes. These somber styles had swept much of the continent, with black predominating over the bright reds and golds of the first half of the century. Looking well-nourished and a bit homely on the canvas portrait, Anna is clad in a costly white silk dress with a standing collar and silver-embroidered long sleeves.

Instead of focusing on her face, the artist intentionally directed the spectator's view towards the princess's eye-catching necklace with its enormous pendant. Gold filigree work was interlaced with diamonds, large rubies, and an oversized pearl. Anna's head is covered with an escoffion also studded with precious stones and another large pearl at its center. A heavily bejeweled belt sits around her midsection. As in all other likenesses, the princess wears a thin gold chain around her neck, perhaps a personal memento from her late mother. The painting probably had a twin, most likely a portrait of William that has since vanished, and may have been a gift to Orange's Protestant sympathizers in England.[4]

De Bruyn's engraving is in many ways identical to the oil portrait. A big-eyed, serious, but elegant looking Anna leans against a chair, holding a leather glove in her left hand. Her coat and dress sport intricate embroidery, but de Bruyn made certain to showcase the princess's necklace in exaggerated size.[5] There are no sign of physical abnormalities, such as uneven shoulders. It was not until the middle of the next century that artists started to depict their sitters in a less flattering light, "warts and all."

Unfortunately, the rather nondescript likeness does not give us a glimpse into Anna's personality. In the display culture of the sixteenth century, exquisite finery was the measure of a man, or woman, while the face was treated as a secondary feature. Anna's portraits are no exception. Her priceless jewels and expensive apparel - the embodiment of nobility and greatness - took center stage. In fact, the sitter's clothes were of such importance to commissioners that artists took great care to sketch their colors and materials in the minutest detail. In some cases, they were even sent to the studio where they had their "portrait" sketched

---

[3]Wedgwood, p. 70.
[4]Spies, pp. 244-6. The said painting is now in possession of the London Dulwich gallery.
[5]Spies, pp. 242-4.

at the painter's leisure. As an English proverb succinctly expressed it: *"We are all Adam's sons, silk only distinguishes us."*[6] And yet like so many things at court, official portrayals were often nothing but carefully crafted mirages. While they conveyed the impression of unassailable wealth and power, in many cases, like Anna's, the sitter was neither influential nor happy.

Besides the showcasing of status and wealth, clothes also served as a form of investment, since unlike today, they were never discarded after a season or two. Every single piece of attire, from button to a braid, was laboriously crafted by hand and therefore outrageously expensive. Noble costumes were extraordinarily intricate and complex, further adding to the cost of an outfit. There were over-garments and undergarments, connected by laces through a myriad of eyelet holes. Maidservants pinned, unpinned, set and unset squares, scarves, borders, puffs, and ruffes, pickadils, and lace cuffs in a process that could take hours.[7]

The gown itself came like a self-assembly kit; the lavish unwashable fabric was to be used and reused, and preserved very carefully. From the skin up, Anna would have worn a chemise or "smock" of cambric silk finely embroidered and perhaps perfumed. Over that came a corset made of wood or whale bone, followed by several petticoats which were held out by the bell-shaped farthingale. Over this went the marlotte, the sleeveless coat-like garment that hooked onto the stiff front panel. Huge padded sleeves were attached separately. With that many components, an outfit could be worth more than an estate. The Stuart princess Arbella (1575-1615) once ordered four hundred pounds worth of pearls for a single gown, imagining herself "new and richly worth more than any lady in this land."[8]

In of view of their high value and before the introduction of modern banking, men and women of every class often stored their wealth in clothes. Pawnbrokers readily accepted hand me downs as securities while friends and servants gratefully received second or even third hand apparel. In 1559, Elizabeth of England gave "valuable clothes, which had belonged to King Edward, her brother," to one of her retainers, and outfits originally belonging to Edward VI and Queen Mary are recorded in an inventory of 1600.[9]

Clothes could also be a channel for women's imagination and creativity. For Anna, who was not known to shine in dance or any other courtly pastimes, fashion may have been one of the few outlets of female self-expression. Many high ranking ladies designed their own gowns and proudly displayed such creations to the court, decked out with ornamented buttons, knots of ribbon, elaborate embroidery, and skillfully arranged "pinked" or "paned" material that was cut in a decorative arrangement of holes, or slashed to show a different fabric underneath.[10]

If Anna's personality did not have a spellbinding effect on others, she could turn heads while traversing the wide halls of the *Palais de Nassau*, festooned in gorgeous robes and inestimable jewels. Judging from the rapid drain on her expense accounts, the princess spent fortunes on choice materials, decorations, and other exotic items of dress that regularly arrived at the port of Antwerp. Brightly colored silks and satins were complemented by a huge variety of accessories such

[6]Jones and Stallybrass, p. 34, p. 38.
[7]Jones and Stallybrass, p. 23.
[8]Gristwood, pp. 60-1.
[9]Jones and Stallybrass, p. 26.
[10]Gristwood, p. 60.

DIE EDEL DOORLVCHTIGHE HOOCHGHEBOREN VROVWE
Anna, Van saßen grauinne tot naßou princeße van oraengien de Wittighe
Dochter van hertoch mauricius de ..... huysrouwe van Wilhelmus
Van snaßou den hooch edel gheboren prince van oraengien.

Anna of Saxony's portrait by de Bruyn

as ribbons, ostrich feathers, and gloves on her dressing table.[11]

Unfortunately, these glittering material possessions were but a temporary anesthetic for Anna's deep-seated emotional pain. William's absences had multiplied in recent years, and when he managed to spend a few days with her in Breda, the couple argued. Although she knew little of politics, Anna advised Orange not to oppose the Spanish, an opinion which the prince did not care to hear. She was also growing tired of life in the Netherlands, Anna wrote in a letter to her Uncle William in Hessen, and was feeling unwell. Perhaps he could visit to cheer her up.[12]

*****

Although the landgrave's son sent a reply to his niece's pleas in the spring of 1566, he had neither the time nor the inclination to humor Anna with a trip to Flanders. Alarming reports about his sister Barbara's "dissolute and wanton behavior" had just reached Kassel, forcing him to travel to Alsace. The countess's guardians had written of "swearing, cursing, beating" and other untoward activities. Yet these misdemeanors were topped by an even more shocking story about her ladyship: according to her pastor, Barbara had given birth to two children out of wedlock.

Apparently, the duchess had entered into an illicit relationship with one of her employees, the seneschal Jacob of Rheinfelden, with customary "female imbecility." Although of ancient gentry stock, the squires of Rheinfelden were vastly outranked by the royally connected Hessians. Even worse, it appears that Barbara's lover was a married man, the husband of Lady Salome of Andlau. The pair had successfully kept their four-year mesalliance under wraps until a servant divulged Barbara's plan to elope and move to Basel. Jacob had already relocated to Switzerland and bought property there which was required for citizenship. Archival records list his purchase of a small manor for 6,500 guilders from the Squire Bernhard Stehelin in September 1565.[13] Apparently, the lovers were planning to escape imperial jurisdiction and the legal reach of Barbara's minders in Wurttemberg. Most importantly, some Swiss cities such as Zürich and Basel allowed divorce under certain conditions.[14]

In response to this shocking news, a hastily convened Hessian family council debated several options of "damage control." Anna's uncle William argued for a lenient approach: Barbara should be speedily married off to Count Daniel of Waldeck. The count was a *simplex homo* (a simpleton), but was unlikely to stir up any trouble. Others suggested that "We should say and pretend her to be mad and keep her locked away in a house." Eventually, Barbara's relations agreed to put the unhappy princess under temporary house arrest somewhere in Wurttemberg. As for her paramour, the landgrave intended to send out thugs to catch him.

Regrettably for the Hessians, Barbara's guardians in Wurttemberg refused any responsibility for their fallen mistress. "Since the widow has an inclination for melancholy and excessively great anger," they wrote, she would be taken

[11]Whitaker, p. 1.
[12]Kruse,"Wilhelm von Oranien," p. 40.
[13]Staatsarchiv Basel.
[14]Ozment, *Fathers*, p. 94.

better care of back home in Kassel. Such news did not sit well with her father Philip. Although he was no stranger to domestic scandal, the landgrave saw no reason to accord his daughter the same gracious self-indulgence that he had once granted himself. Barbara implored him to take pity on her, proclaiming that she was an unworthy daughter "who no longer deserved to be borne by this earth," but Landgrave Philip disowned her. The scandal had to be kept to a minimum, he ruled, and she had gravely displeased him.

In the end, the landgravial family decided against shutting the countess away, and married her to the hapless Daniel. It is doubtful that Barbara found conjugal bliss in this second union, but she gradually salvaged her reputation and became known as a prudent administrator in the little county of Waldeck.[15] As for her erstwhile sweetheart Jacob, he remained in Basel unharmed. The two never saw each other again.

*****

It is unclear if the opprobrium of her aunt's missteps reached Breda, but Anna was surely aware of her grandfather Philip's failing health. While the first half of his life had been marked by sexual debauchery, the second half was spent in chronic pain. Starting in the early 1560s, the landgrave complained about severe aches in his toes and knees as well as a suppurating thigh wound that would not heal. By the time the scandal broke in Alsace, Philip was so wracked by his numerous afflictions that he could barely stand.

The sufferings in his dotage were compounded by the death of his beloved, second wife Margaret in July 1566. His oldest son, William, wrote to his sister Christine in northern Germany, "His Grace is acting stranger and is looking more worn out with each day, to such an extent that it is most pitiful." Tormented by grief, illness, and anger, Philip turned into a misanthrope and alienated his children with his offensive speeches and miserliness. He died of either a stroke or heart attack on Easter Monday 1567.[16]

It was a merciful release, not only for the old warrior, but also for those around him. For Anna, however, it meant the loss of the one powerful relation who had always promoted her interests and with whom she had established at least a semblance of a personal connection. Worried about the Dutch situation, the landgrave had even pleaded with the emperor to mediate in the Netherlands the year prior.[17] His passing therefore spelled the beginning of a certain disconnectedness between Anna and her German relatives. The Elector of Saxony and his wife, as well as her uncle, Landgrave William IV, sent messages and envoys when they feared for their reputations, but hardly despaired over Anna's well-being. And with her marriage disintegrating, the pool of persons who could offer consolation or refuge dwindled to a tiny number. To whom could she appeal in times of trouble? Anna probably wondered, as she aimlessly prowled about her exquisite chambers.

[15]Löwenstein, pp. 421-5.
[16]Aumüller and Krähwinkel, pp. 38-40.; Putnam, *Moderate Man*, p. 274. Philip's last advice to Orange was to refuse all compromise with the Spanish king or Alba.
[17]Knöfel, *Dynasty*, p. 136. Philip of Hessen had something of an early modern "domino theory" in mind: if Orange failed to halt Catholic domination, then German Protestantism was endangered and a religious war looming. His successor, William IV, was more careful, and steered his policies into more shallow waters, along Saxon lines.

Family solidarity was soon enough put to the test. In December 1566 the Oranges' son Maurice died suddenly, barely two years old. Anna had lost two of her three children by now, and this latest tragedy left her terribly distressed. Moreover, none of her Protestant relations deigned it necessary to attend the funeral, and William was absent as well.[18] He was caught in the unenviable role of mediator between opposition and government forces, and could rarely relax in Breda. Trouble was brewing again in Antwerp and the prince, as the city's magistrate, had ultimately been forced to take sides. He frequently consulted with the town's lay judges, especially the commissioner of the general estates, Antoon van Stralen, and a young talented lawyer named Jan Rubens, who pleaded for peace between the competing faiths. The three men worried about the slowing of the Dutch economy as well as a looming battle between Catholics and Protestants, which threatened to spell the end of the provinces' fabled wealth.[19]

For the moment, however, William's allegiance to the Habsburgs still outweighed his sympathies for the rebels. When Antwerp Calvinists gathered three thousand troops outside the metropolis, Orange refused to come to their defense and merely stood by as government troops crushed them in a surprise attack. Afterwards, the outraged Protestant community labeled the prince a traitor and threats were made on his life. He eventually negotiated a shaky truce, but the situation remained so volatile that he was unable to successfully "square the circle," his preferred habit of dealing with unpleasantness.[20]

In Spain, King Philip decided to "square the Dutch circle" by means of additional troops. In November 1566 he set plans in motion to deploy a Spanish invasion force led by the Duke of Alba - his "best and most unrestrained" soldier - to subdue the rebellious Flemish. Nobles like Egmont immediately stood up in protest, suggesting that the Dutch crisis could still be solved by the country's aristocracy. "What can an army do?" he asked the Regent Margaret, "kill 200,000 Netherlanders?"[21] And indeed, during that winter and early spring of 1567, the triumvirate of Orange, Egmont, and Horn eliminated the centers of Calvinist sedition as a sign of their continued loyalty to Madrid. A relieved Margaret promptly dispatched a courier to Spain, informing her half-brother that armed intervention was no longer necessary. But it was too late. The very day the Flemish messenger delivered the memorandum, Alba set sail from Cartagena to crush the insolent demands of "that beast, the people" once and for all.[22]

Fernando Alvarez de Toledo y Pimentel, 3rd Duke of Alba, was a tall, small-headed career warrior with sharp, piercing eyes. Widely acknowledged as the leading soldier of his day, he had distinguished himself in numerous battles in France, Germany, and Italy. In April 1547 Alba had squashed the forces of the Protestant Schmalkaldic League at Mühlberg, together with Anna's father Maurice. Hailing from one of the oldest and most powerful families in Spain, he was also in charge of the king's palaces and often summoned to mediate in a diplomatic capacity. As Philip's most loyal servant, he was now tasked with tidying up the Low Countries, although the appointment was considered controversial. The sixty-year-old suffered from gout and was generally in poor health. Still, Philip

[18]Schuppener, "Breda", p. 123; Keller, *Kurfürstin*, p. 204.
[19]de Dijn, p.34, p. 37.
[20]Mörke, p. 129.
[21]Kamen, p. 117.
[22]Putnam, *Moderate Man*, p. 277.

considered the duke sprightly enough for an army command as well as fully capable of restoring order in his restive Northern provinces.[23]

With the general's forces ominously closing in on the Low Countries, the spring of 1567 was a period of anguished hesitation for William. His friends Egmont and Horn argued that the time had come to "unite their counsels rather than to sell their lives cheaply" and urged the prince to renounce his allegiance to Philip. "Every means in our power, our money, and blood [should be employed] to prevent Alba and the Spanish from getting a foothold in the land." But rather than defying the son of his former benefactor, Orange decided on a third option. When the king forced the entire Dutch nobility and state officials to swear a new oath of allegiance or be declared traitors, William reluctantly made a stand. In a letter to the regent, he declared his intention of laying down all offices so that he would not have to carry out "orders that I could not conscientiously execute."[24]

A bewildered Margaret refused to accept his resignation, but William had made up his mind. The country was on the brink of civil war and his future uncertain. Given his leniency towards "heretics" and vocal criticism of the king's policies, it was only a matter of time until he would run afoul of the Duke of Alba. Since the French Huguenots and British Protestants were embroiled in conflicts of their own, only the German Lutherans - specifically Anna's relatives - could offer the Oranges help. After lengthy deliberations with like-minded followers, William requested assistance from Saxony. Surprised observers noted that the relationship between Anna and William began to improve as well.[25]

The prince also decided to relocate his family to the safety of his childhood home in German Dillenburg. There he could regroup, consult with Lutheran princes, and wait out the storm. Orange's supporters, particularly his Calvinist sympathizers, were aghast. The manner in which the prince was removing himself from the conflict was cowardly and irresponsible, they charged. There was further outrage when William ended one of his farewell speeches with "God save the King." Caricatures showed the prince with two faces, his hands stretched in two directions - an accusation that Orange had taken money from both sides. But the prince remained deaf to all entreaties. Those small, disorganized bands of Protestant volunteers did not stand a chance against Alba's experienced soldiers, he argued. The time had come to count one's losses.[26]

---

[23]Kamen, p. 56, p. 74, p. 26, p. 117.
[24]Putnam, *The Life of William the Silent*, p. 104.
[25]Vogt-Lüerssen, p. 55.
[26]Putnam, *The Life of William the Silent*, p. 104, pp. 108-9.

Dillenburg

In April 1567 groups of men gathered near the moat of Breda palace. The Prince of Orange was expected to arrive from Antwerp and they hoped to intercept him to change his mind about departing the Low Countries. They had come in vain. William had already ordered his household staff to pack up most of the family's belongings. Servants heaved several barrels of books into waiting carts - the traditional method of transporting reading material at the time. According to still extant shipping lists, the Oranges had chosen forty-eight volumes from the princely library. These were luxury items bound in either black velvet or calf leather which bore the prince's coat of arms in color laid on with wax. Most dealt with subjects associated with the "perfect courtier," topics that William would have little need of in the coming years.

Anna watched with mixed feelings as footmen lowered priceless Nassau tapestries and her Saxon silver plate into wooden crates. William had given directions to leave bulky furniture, paintings, and some manuscripts behind. For example, the French erotic texts - favorites of Anna's - were to remain at the castle. Perhaps he considered that kind of French sensuousness ill-suited to the sober world of his pious mother. During the family's absence, Orange's teenage son Philip William was to oversee the running of the residence and its reduced court, and represent the House of Nassau in his father's stead. Breda's sheriff van Haestrecht, had also promised assistance.[1] In any case, William soothed his dejected retainers, his move to Germany was only temporary. He and Anna were bound to return to Flanders with their daughters as soon as the King of Spain had untangled the current political disorder.

Officially, of course, Orange had another explanation at hand. His mother in Dillenburg was ailing and wished to see her granddaughter Maria - William's daughter with Anne van Buren - for a final time. For that reason, the girl had to be excused from her duties at the regent's court in Brussels for a few weeks or so. In a deliberate, leisurely fashion, Orange also wrote optimistic farewell letters to his friends Egmont and Horn.

In private, William was far less sanguine. Two hours before the heavy baggage train lumbered out of Breda, the prince had an open discussion with Elbert de Leeuw, a Dutch jurist and confidant of Margaret of Parma's. The prince was acutely aware that a return to the Low Countries would not be as easy as he liked to pretend.[2]

There was another heartrending farewell before the major domo signaled the coachmen to ready the horses. The prince's heir, Philip William, bid his father good-bye. In order to uphold the charade that Orange was not fleeing the Low Countries, but merely traveled on personal business, he had to leave his lands with a family member - in this case his son. Philip William, a student at the University of Louvain, was effectively staying behind as a pawn in order to avoid the confiscation of Nassau lands. With such "human collateral" as security, Orange hoped to hang on to his profitable Dutch holdings, especially since Philip William had promised to swear fealty to King Philip. This was of paramount significance, William impressed on his anxious heir, a duty of the highest importance. Other-

[1]Verwey, p. 85, p. 96, p. 123.
[2]Putnam, *The Life of William the Silent*, p. 110.

wise they would be reduced from princes to paupers.

The decision to have his eldest remain in the Low Countries had not come easy to Orange. In the preceding weeks, William had sought the advice of several German potentates concerning Philip William's safety and received contradictory answers. August of Saxony had assured him that his son was best left in Louvain, while the landgrave thought him safer in the Duchy of Cleves, and Günther of Schwarzburg recommended a transfer to Dillenburg. William ultimately followed the elector's advice.[3]

While the prince agonized about the well-being of his eldest child, Anna fretted about leaving Breda. Although she had recently announced that Flanders was filled with "such unchristian, godless, and untrustworthy people" that she could not wait to depart for Germany, the princess quickly changed her mind when the carters arrived. True to form, she was all of a sudden opposed to the move.[4] In the end, few tears were shed when Anna said her final adieus. As in Leipzig six years prior, the "godless people" of Breda gladly took their leave of their "overly snappy and truculent" mistress.[5]

Accompanied by an impressive number of knights and Dutch officials, the Orange caravan slogged at snail's pace via Grave towards the Duchy of Cleves, eighty miles to the east. Along the way, the train swelled with mounting numbers of refugees who joined the prince and his entourage on his exodus up the Rhine valley. After resting in Cleves, the exiles continued south past Xanten and Mörs towards the imperial city of Cologne, where they turned east on the old Cologne-Siegen trail by way of Bernberg and the Bergisches Land into the County of Nassau. On May 7, after long days of onerous travel, an exhausted Anna and her children were welcomed by William's brother, the affable Count John.[6]

John near despaired by the size of the prince's enormous entourage, but quickly arranged for temporary quarters at the fortress of Freudenberg near Siegen. It would take him until the end of the month, he apologized, to adequately prepare Dillenburg Castle - the ancestral seat of the House of Nassau - for Orange, his highborn wife, and their many followers.[7] He had been busy fortifying the castle's defenses to prepare for possible incursions by Alba's soldiers. Armed sentinels were patrolling local roads now and additional artillery pieces had just arrived in Dillenburg.[8]

As Anna took stock of Nassau County, her spirits plummeted. Except for some brief months in the backwater of Weimar, she had always lived in sizeable towns that afforded ample diversions. Life in the countryside, however, was entirely foreign to her, and after years in the highly developed Netherlands, her husband's patrimony seemed appallingly backward. The city of Dillenburg was a settlement of merely one hundred fifty houses, but even worse were the outlying villages.[9] Primitive dwellings huddled closely together, a far cry from the proud patricians' manors in Antwerp with their swept courtyards and decorative lemon trees. Dung and rubbish heaps piled up in front of windows, while inside, man

---

[3] Helmut Cellarius. "Die Propagandatätigkeit Wilhelms von Oranien in Dillenburg 1568 im Dienste des niederländischen Aufstandes," *Nassauische Annalen*, Band 96 (1985), p. 127.
[4] Putnam, *The Life of William the Silent*, p. 114.
[5] de Dijn, p. 53.
[6] Cellarius, "Die Propagandatätigkeit," p. 122.
[7] Kruse, *Rubens*, p. 2.
[8] Cellarius, "Die Propagandatätigkeit," pp. 123-4.
[9] Cellarius, p. 124.

and his animals shared rooms in the most unhygienic conditions. Chicken and other livestock wandered through family kitchens, leaving trails of droppings.[10]

In the 1560s, the County of Nassau encompassed about 620 square miles of territory with fifteen cities, about 550 villages, and a population of less than 38,000 souls.[11] In its largest town, Siegen, city fathers made every effort to greet William and Anna with all the pomp and celebration they could muster. Digging deep into city coffers, they fetched at least one hundred liters of wine for their lordships' pleasure and even donned new cloaks made out of red Brabant cloth. If Anna noticed the exertions of her anxious hosts has gone unrecorded, but she surely tried the wine.[12]

After six years of opulent living, the new realties were not easy to accept, and Anna labored heavily under the drastic reduction of her circumstances. Even the more even-keeled prince had to adapt. The brilliant careerist and coddled pleasure-seeker was his younger brother's supplicant now and suddenly had to make do with a fraction of his former earnings. But at thirty-four, William was also a mature pragmatist. He took the latest reversals of fate in relatively good stride and quickly rallied. After all, he was returning to the familiarity of his childhood home.[13]

Immediately after his arrival, William sent out express posts to various Protestant princes, indicating his willingness to "reconvert" to Lutheranism. One of the letters was an ingratiating note to Anna's uncle, Landgrave William, asking him to "loan out" one of his Protestant pastors. "We are heartily desirous of using the time we are to stay here out of the Netherlands for strengthening our character," William wheedled, "and for studying the Holy Scriptures."[14] Orange also approached the Elector of Saxony - his most powerful and wealthy contact - and informed him by courier that he and his family had left the Low Countries and were in need of his sage advice. [15]

While William "networked," the princess tried to find her bearings in the women's quarters. Unlike the elegant chaos that had reigned in Breda and Brussels, life in Dillenburg was carefully ordered. Countess Juliana and her son John needed rules and regulations to keep seventeen children, a flock of grandchildren, and rising expenditures in check. In addition, there were leftover debts incurred by the old count who had nearly bankrupted the house by employing dishonest administrators.[16] Anna, on the other hand, had never much bothered with the logistics of a functioning household, either for lack of interest or because of a budget that allowed the hiring of domestic managers.

Although Count John undoubtedly maintained a certain standard of living, there was no denying that life in Dillenburg was soberly Lutheran. Juliana would have scoffed at dainty dance competitions, wasteful squandering of food for aesthetic purposes, and ruinous purchases of fabrics to secure bragging rights. Some family members actually worked the estate in order to reduce the crushing

---

[10] Helmut Groos. "Über die Wohnverhältnisse im südlichen Dillkreis um 1830," *Heimatjahrbuch für das Land an der Dill*, No. 24 (1981), pp. 152-4.
[11] Cellarius, "Die Propagandatätigkeit," p. 122.
[12] *Kleine Geschichte*, p. 11.
[13] Putnam, *Moderate Man*, pp. 273-4. Orange took refuge with his brother, but in 1567 other options were still open to him. In July, Electress Anne's brother—Frederick II of Denmark—offered William asylum. The prince replied that he would gladly accept the Danish king's offer if his situation worsened.
[14] Putnam, *The Life of William the Silent*, p. 115.
[15] Kruse, "Wilhelm von Oranien," p. 42.
[16] Wolf, *Graf Johann*, p. 259.

bills that encumbered their domains. Louis had once written, "I am hastening to come [to Breda] as soon as possible. We have little enough past time here. We rise before six o'clock to work before and after dinner."[17]

It did not take long for Anna, who had never engaged in manual labor except embroidery, to feel that she had fallen from grace and landed in the bowels of hell. Thus far, her life in Dresden had been privileged, her position in Breda exalted, as befit someone of her unique and remarkable station. Now she was to stoop to a level so low as to defy description. Count John, a stout little man who bore little resemblance to his striking older brother, tried his best to prove himself an agreeable host—unfortunately, to little avail. A still existing Dillenburg menu gives an idea of the kind of fare served to the princess, offerings that were not to be scorned, but evidently inferior in Anna's estimation.

Lunch consisted of wine soup, roasted young hens, beef, veal's head, and rice. For official dinners, the castle kitchens served up chicken soup, poultry, salad, bacon, barbel fish, roasted veal, apple sauce, pastries, vegetables in wine, sage cake, porridge, and crawfish. Most entrees were accompanied by egg dishes.[18] A varied selection by our standards, Anna turned up her nose at these basic staples that came from local suppliers instead of being shipped in from abroad. To be sure, there was no expensive cauliflower, marzipan, oranges, or any other of the exotic fare that she had grown to love in Burgundy. A more considerate person would have accepted such economies. After all, the castle kitchen served almost 1800 weekly meals to the ever growing number of new arrivals from the Netherlands, who all clamored for more bread, bacon, and beer.[19]

Beside the food, the princess found the spartan accommodations repellant. Gothic, cold, and overcrowded, the castle possessed seventy-seven rooms that housed about two hundred persons and offered few of the amenities that Anna had enjoyed in her Flemish chateaux.[20] "Too little and too despicable" she disdainfully told her in-laws, although the residence was by no means barebones yet. A colossal depiction of the epic battle of Pavia covered the entire "vaulted hall," and a good number of tapestries still adorned the walls. The most famous of these hangings was the so-called *Piscaria* (fishery). Consisting of ten parts and 642 ells in length, it showcased Dutch towns and their respective fish. [21] And yet this particular objet d'art hardly impressed Anna who resented being stuck in a draughty medieval castle on a hilltop, far removed from other courts and even the great highways of travel. As had been her custom in Breda, she soon withdrew to her chambers and refused to see anyone except William, her only consolation.

It probably did not help matters that the Nassau's primary residences of Siegen and Dillenburg are affected by a rather unfortunate microclimate that results in fewer sunny days and more rain than in other parts of Germany. The hilly countryside around Dillenburg with its dull, grey skies might have had a suffocating effect on Anna, who was prone to depression and had long become accustomed to the open plains surrounding Breda.

As in the past, Anna also found her servants lacking. Only a few weeks earlier she had been exquisitely waited on by the wives of the Dutch nobility;

[17]Putnam, *The Life of William the Silent*, p. 75. See also Kleine *Geschichte*, p. 15.
[18]*Kleine Geschichte*, p. 15.
[19]Cellarius, "Propagandatätigkeit," p. 124.
[20]Wedgwood, p. 101.
[21]Becker, "Malerei," p. 117, p. 120. Together with the emperor's, Nassau banners had proudly flown at this epic battle against the French in 1525.

now she had to make do with sullen country girls. Perhaps the princess was not entirely to blame in this particular situation. Manners in Nassau differed quite markedly from those in Flanders, and newcomers to the earldom not only found it difficult to establish contact with locals, but had an even harder time gaining their confidence. Enclosed by constricting hills and narrow valleys, the populace in the adjacent uplands was known for their suspicion of strangers.

If Anna ever travelled through the nearby countryside, she would have heard the hammering of smiths and seen smoke columns rise up from dense forests which housed a great number of charcoal makers. In remote hamlets, desperately poor miners tried to eke out a living by spending twelve hours and more below ground, extracting iron ore from the mountains. These were unglamorous occupations that encouraged brooding and taciturnity in a people bound to the soil. In fact, except for the nobility and iron traders, few people ever left the area. Miners and smiths were officially forbidden to depart the county under pain of death, lest they divulge their professional secrets.[22]

Countess Juliana surely schooled her homegrown staff in decorum, but polite conversation might have eluded them. Words were used sparingly and to the point, lacking verbal flourishes.[23] Anna, who loved to palaver, was perhaps taken aback by this brusque bluntness, and nobody was greatly surprised when the ungracious princess started to beat the monosyllabic help.[24]

If her serving personnel and accommodations were an annoyance, Anna's loss of authority was devastating. The social standing of the former mistress of Breda had already declined as the wife of an émigré, but having to submit to William's mother was unbearable. Burgundian etiquette required Countess Juliana to assume a position of deference towards a princess of quasi royal rank like Anna. However, in matter-of-fact Dillenburg, nobody had the time or patience for such highbrow artificiality. Juliana was a straightforward, busy woman, who, though kind and affectionate, rejected any kind of starchy fussiness. And perhaps, as William's mother and premier domestic manager, she could and did "pull rank" on her daughter-in-law.

Anna, unfortunately, missed no opportunity to stand on her dignity, and alienated most of her female in-laws within a matter of weeks. She had not been loved in Breda, but household members there had done her bidding without question. In Dillenburg, she was a wife among many, her splendid heritage carelessly overlooked. Anna's frustrations culminated in particularly vicious rows with Count John's wife, Elizabeth of Leuchtenberg, as well as her mother-in-law. Juliana and her ladies were cold towards her, the Princess of Orange carped, "They let me sit by myself [in my chambers] for several days without visiting," and often deny me "a little drink of wine or beer."[25] Everyone in that tight knit clan was against her, she determined, conveniently overlooking the fact that none of the other spouses labored under similar prejudices.

*****

[22] Lothar Irle. "Der Siegerländer Mensch," *Siegerland zwischen gestern und morgen* (Landkreis Siegen: Siegen Kreisverwaltung, 1965), p. 249, p. 251.
[23] Irle, pp. 251-2, p. 254.
[24] Vetter, p. 71.
[25] W. Goebel. "Jehan Ruebens in Köln und in Siegen," *Siegerland*, 2. Band, 1. Heft (1913), p. 17. See also Kruse, "Wilhelm von Oranien," p. 49.

During their first months in Dillenburg, William refrained from reproaching his disagreeable wife. He could not afford to imperil the ties with her powerful uncles, especially in his current, reduced condition. Besides, confrontation of any kind went against his nature. Throughout his life, Orange had preferred the path of least resistance to the unpleasantries of conflict; hence his decision to leave the Low Countries. The same kind of evasiveness determined his dealings with Anna. Tussles in the women's chambers would hopefully square themselves away, he seems to have thought with wary detachment. At least his own relations with the princess had improved of late.

At the beginning of the year, while still in the Netherlands, courtiers had noticed an unexpected thaw in the Oranges' icy marriage. Anna had been temporarily buoyed by William's plans to relocate to Germany, and snapped out of her depression for short periods of time. Although she ultimately rejected the move, the couple was spending more time with each other in Dillenburg than they had in years. The prince was neither called away on business nor could he pursue clandestine liaisons with various women; the castle was simply too small and remote for such dalliances. Removal from the morass of court intrigue also contributed to this rapprochement. Although their marriage was still far from happy and healthy, the Oranges' "expulsion from the paradise" had drawn them closer together.

Whatever the reasons, and despite the princess's quarrels with family and servants, witnesses reported that the pair's dealings were quite satisfactory during those initial months in Nassau county. Anna had never lost her passion for William, and it was during that fateful spring that she became pregnant again.[26]

Unfortunately, no additional details about the couple's conjugal defrosting have survived. Until the late twentieth century, sex in marriage was a taboo topic, and while ballads, epics, and novels waxed on endlessly about the amorous trials of the likes of Guinevere and Lancelot, they were generally mum on the sensual side of wedlock. In fact, it was considered positively indecent to feel the kind of carnal affection for a wife that one expressed for a mistress, and highly offensive to remark on such "inappropriate" enthusiasm. Married couples were not to succumb to dissolute, unbridled ecstasy, but spend their days discreetly in mutual respect and restrained harmony.[27]

Still, brave exhibits of marital concord and a newfound fondness between the partners could not gloss over the fact that all was not well in Dillenburg. As in Breda, Anna continued to cling to the bottle, her companion of choice during her less frequent, but still recurring bouts of melancholy and angst. In June chronicles reported that William consumed two liters of wine during dinner, while a pregnant Anna drank three.[28]

*****

By late summer it was sadly apparent that Anna's matrimonial bright spot was invariably clouding over. Her dealings with everyone except William were toxic, and she had started to pester the prince about relocating to the Netherlands on her own. Orange was at a loss and decided to inform her uncles in

---

[26]Kruse, "Wilhelm von Oranien," p. 46.
[27]Bastl, pp. 358-60.
[28]Kruse, "Wilhelm von Oranien," p. 46.

Dresden and Kassel. Only recently Anna had railed against the unhealthy air in the Low Countries, he wrote, now she insisted on returning. Given her pregnant state he could simply not allow this; after all, she might give birth in a village or along a road. Besides, her mental condition was fragile. Anna had hinted at suicide once again and he feared that she might harm herself and the newborn in a fit of "great anger." He also did not possess the funds to pay for two households in such difficult times. Lastly, the political situation in Breda was too perilous for an unprotected woman, let alone someone as unguarded as Anna, who had recently begun to belittle God's word quite openly.

The frightful threat of scandal jolted the princess's uncles into action. The landgrave dispatched his younger brother Philip and the envoy Dr. Nordecken to Dillenburg; August of Saxony instructed his trusted advisor Eric Volkmar von Berlepsch to investigate. Berlepsch arrived in Dillenburg at the end of September and found Anna so agreeable that he decided not to deliver the elector's reproof on sinful obstinacy.[29] The seasoned Saxon diplomat had either met with Anna during one of her increasingly rare emotional highs or she was trying very hard to disprove tales of wifely waywardness.

Together with the Hessian envoys, Berlepsch eventually convinced Anna to remain in Dillenburg. Things had taken a turn for the worse in the unstable Netherlands, they informed her. In May, the Regent Margaret had confidently rebuffed a delegation of Protestant princes, among them the Elector of Saxony and Landgrave William, who had pleaded for religious toleration. Only recently, on 22 August, the Duke of Alba had triumphantly entered Brussels with 10,000 Castilian troops, despite Margaret's pleas to abstain from such overt provocation. But the duke, never doubtful of his ability to settle a problem that baffled the female mind, had rejected her suggestion and asked, "I have tamed men of iron, and shall I now not be able to tame these men of butter?"[30] A disheartened Margaret retired to Italy soon after.[31]

Upon his sister's departure, King Philip appointed Alba the new Governor General of the Spanish Netherlands, prompting the latter to issue an immediate slew of stringent directives. Among them was the establishment of a special court, the so-called "Council of Troubles," which was to "pacify" the restive Seventeen Provinces by forcing "perfect obedience."[32] It was quickly renamed the "Council of Blood" by a frightened and horrified populace who watched in shock as thousands of Dutchmen were arrested and executed after being tried by the king's novel tribunals. Among the detained were William's friends, the Counts Egmont and Horn, as well as a number of Flemish notables. Orange, who still held out hope for an arrangement with his master, penned a letter of welcome to Alba and even offered his services.[33] It was a wasted effort. The new regent had no intention of accommodating anyone, least of all the Prince of Orange.

Alba's refusal had the full backing of Philip of Spain. A Mexican insurrection by a group of Spanish aristocrats had just been averted in the Americas, and the king wanted all other protest movements dismantled forthwith. Dis-

[29]Kruse, "Wilhelm von Oranien," pp. 42-3.
[30]Putnam, *The Life of William the Silent*, p. 115.
[31]Mörke, p. 135.
[32]Putnam, *The Life of William the Silent*, p. 116. See also Putnam, *Moderate Man*, pp. 285-6. A Spanish member of Alba's privy council, Juan de Vargas, reveled in the merciless decrees promulgated by the "Council of Troubles," and exclaimed in bad Latin, "Heretici fraxerunt templa, boni nihili faxerunt contra, ergo debent omnes patibulari" ("The heretics ruined the temples, the innocent people did nothing, ergo they all deserve to be hanged.").
[33]Mörke, p. 137.

turbing messages from his cousin, Emperor Maximilian II, further strengthened his resolve. Dutch exiles were banding together in another Protestant military league, and his late father's onetime protégé was plotting against him, Maximilian had written in a letter that brought tears to Philip's eyes and relieved him of all doubts. He had been fully justified in sending the army, the king concluded, and wrote to Alba in November, "You have a free hand." By the end of the year, the Netherlands lay supine under the heavy hand of the Spanish.[34]

While the Dutch smarted under foreign rule, Anna gave birth to a son, another Maurice, on 14 November. William took advantage of the occasion to show the world that he was still a force to be reckoned with, and organized a splendid feast to celebrate the baby's baptism with the help of Count John. The brothers sent out invitations to a number of high ranking relatives, and for once the landgrave visited from Kassel. He later informed the elector that he did not want to be accused of forsaking a friend in need, and had also taken the opportunity to rebuke Anna for her garrulous temper.

Festivities lasted eight days, with grooms feeding over seven hundred horses in the castle's stables and the town below. And yet it was a labored show of grandiosity that failed to conceal the Nassau's creeping poverty. Silver plate that John had recently pawned in Frankfurt to pay for his brother's still outrageous living expenses had arrived in Dillenburg in three carts, but only because Siegen's city council was generously acting as collateral. Orange had sent word to the landgrave that he would have to make do with "minor *Westerwald* fare" and berry wine, while Anne of Cleve's brother, Duke William, graciously agreed to provide the party with game.[35]

Perhaps he had sensed his imminent misfortune, because the occasion certainly turned into William's last hurrah as a prince of means. In the midst of feasting, a courier delivered the shattering news that on December 20, the Spanish crown had seized all of Orange's lands, manors, and palaces in Flanders. With the majority of his holdings out of reach now, the prince was no longer a wealthy grand seigneur. The family's Nassau estates were of course untouched, but William had ceded all German claims to Count John when he came into his fabulous Dutch inheritance in the 1540s.[36]

Landgrave William felt sufficiently sorry for the Oranges that he pleaded with August of Saxony to put in a good word for them with the emperor. Maximilian II was the elector's former boon companion, and despite their religious differences, the two were close friends. August, afraid to cause offense in imperial circles, stalled in customary fashion, but offered financial support to William as well as some unsolicited advice on Christian reconciliation.[37]

*****

On 24 January 1568, at eleven o'clock in the morning, the imperial herald, Francois de Knibbere, stood in the courtyard of the regent's palace in Brussels,

[34]Kamen, pp. 117-8.

[35]Cellarius, "Propagandatätigkeit," p. 124.

[36]Putnam, *Moderate Man*, p. 272, p. 332. In spite of promises made by Charles IX of France, William's principality of Orange was also confiscated.

[37]Kruse, "Wilhelm von Oranien," pp. 44-5. Overall, relations between Saxony and Nassau were still quite friendly in late 1567 and early 1568, despite August's hesitation. The elector helped the stranded Oranges financially, and provided refuge for Dutch Lutherans. See Kruse, "Wilhelm von Oranien," Endnotes, p. 171. Nevertheless, he advised William to avoid a complete rupture with King Philip. Also see Putnam, *Moderate Man*, p. 284.

flanked by six trumpeters. Before a curious crowd, Knibbere raised his voice and issued a summons requiring William of Nassau, Prince of Orange, to appear before the "Council of Troubles" within three fortnights to respond to the charges of being the "chief leader, promoter, and favorer of rebels." He also called upon the prince's brother Louis to present himself as a "disturber of the public peace."[38] Afterwards, the edict was affixed to doors and walls of the country's palaces and major churches, so that William "might not excuse himself citing ignorance."[39] If the Nassau's failed to heed this command, the Governor General of the Netherlands threatened, William and Louis stood to forfeit their Flemish domains in perpetuity.[40]

William, of course, ignored the duke's subpoena, preferring the safety of Germany. Alba's arbitrary tribunal had already branded him the "real instigator of the confederates, the responsible party for every action hostile to the king," accusations which essentially nullified his chances of leaving any Spanish courtroom a free man. In revenge, the duke inflicted a final, very personal injury on the "rebel prince." In the middle of February 1568, Orange's oldest son, thirteen-year-old Philip William, was accosted by Alba's henchmen and arrested. An unidentified friend notified the stunned prince that, "The old Countess Horn wrote to me yesterday that her mounted messenger saw Your Grace's son in a pony wagon with his chamberlain, von Wildberg, riding from Louvain towards Antwerp, and the plan was that he should proceed to Zealand and be sent to Spain with the first wind. Those of the University of Louvain protested, but nothing helped." Shortly afterwards, four hundred Spanish soldiers ransacked Breda Palace.

The artless young man had apparently walked into the trap quite willingly. His exceedingly polite captors had first lured him to Antwerp where the boy enjoyed himself during a gala given in his honor, and then spirited him to Flushing where he embarked on a ship bound for Spain. Even then, the young prince appeared unconcerned. The king's officials had almost certainly assured him that the voyage was taking place with his father's blessing, and that his stay in Madrid would, in any case, be short. Sadly enough, Philip William would not see Dutch shores again until 1596.[41] By then he had become a loyal puppet of the Spanish crown and his father was dead.

Despite, or perhaps because of these mounting personal and political setbacks, William developed as a person, acquiring a theretofore unknown steeliness of character. The seizure of his livelihood in Flanders forced the spoiled aristocrat to take a stance as he reached the limits of accommodation and prevarication. Assisted by trusted Dutch confidants and a French scholar, the prince hatched a plan for an armed invasion of the Netherlands, his only option to regain the confiscated Flemish estates. Count John subsequently announced that his older brother was "God's instrument and in communion with our Lord and brother, Jesus Christ."[42]

In the months that followed, Dillenburg Castle turned into a center of frenzied activity as the Nassaus made their home into a center of military mobilization, propaganda, and recruitment. The courtyard was filling with "select

---

[38]Putnam, *The Life of William the Silent*, p.117.
[39]Cellarius,"Propagandatätigkeit," p. 126.
[40]Mörke, p. 137.
[41]Putnam,*The Life of William the Silent*, pp. 116-7.
[42]Hulmut Cellarius. "Wilhelm von Oranien im Urteil seiner Zeit und der Nachwelt," *Nassauische Annalen*, Band 79 (1968), p. 79.

German men of arms," while William appealed to Protestant princes for additional troops. He also requested financial assistance, dispatched bundles of appeals,
and received foreign envoys and diplomats. Breathless couriers arrived with
confidential messages from Venice, Rome, Brussels, and Paris, and for a while,
the level of plotting in little Dillenburg was on par with any royal residence. In
mid-April 1568, the prince welcomed a delegation of Dutch petitioners led by the
Antwerp financier Markus Perez who christened Orange the official leader of the
resistance against Alba's regime of terror.[43]

Help from other, so-called friends and allies was unfortunately not forthcoming. Glib promises made during little Maurice's baptism had long been forgotten, forcing William to pay for his planned offensive by selling or pawning his
and Anna's silver, exquisite Dutch furniture, and precious jewels. In desperation,
Orange not only appealed to Queen Elizabeth of England and the French Huguenot leader, Gaspard de Coligny, but also contacted Joseph Naci, a powerful
Jewish banker in faraway Istanbul.[44] With John mortgaging his lands and Louis
selling most of his possessions, the brothers eventually raised ten thousand florins.

The Nassau's constant talk of military schemes and expenditures did not
sit well with Anna who worried about her family's future. All of their funds were
slowly eaten up by expensive weaponry and personnel costs for Orange's newly
christened "war of liberation," she bristled, and he was hawking most of their
prized valuables. It was foolhardy to take on the Spanish empire with its endless
resources of men and New World gold from a tiny base such as Dillenburg. In
her opinion, William was being talked into a misadventure that could only end in
catastrophe and financial ruination. She also resented his growing absences and
the secret meetings she was not allowed to attend.

When William closed his ears to her objections, Anna bombarded her relatives with a flood of entreaties. Since she was a Saxon princess and daughter
of the great elector, she wrote, they could not possibly stand by and watch her
family's collapse. At the end of March she beseeched August: "Now we are in the
middle of this calamity, having lost all our lands, and now all the slander that is
done to my Lord and husband that we hear on a daily basis ... We still hope that
God the Almighty will think of us with mercy. I plead with Your Grace that my
Lord husband and our children can always commend themselves to you as your
humble servants and poor friends. Your Grace's obedient daughter, as long as I
live."[45] The elector, in no mood to deal with his niece's adversities or Orange's
anti-Habsburg schemes, chose not to reply.

In addition to worries about the planned invasion, Anna was losing
sleep over her Dutch widow's estates that had been annexed by Alba's loyalists.
If something were to happen to William — a distinct possibility with hostilities
looming — she and her children needed a regular income. The prince agreed. He
could not jeopardize his vital connections with the elector by not adequately providing for his wife and offspring, and began inquiring about estates for Anna near
Mansfeld in western Saxony.[46]

---

[43]Cellarius, "Propagandatätigkeit," pp. 120-1, p. 124. See also Cellarius, "Wilhelm," p. 79.
[44]Cellarius, "Wilhelm," p. 85.
[45]Kruse, "Wilhelm von Oranien," pp. 159-60.
[46]Kruse, "Wilhelm von Oranien," p. 44.

*****

Historians have long condemned Anna's single-mindedness in acquiring new properties at a time when William struggled to raise money for troops. Although a certain amount of criticism is certainly justified, it is also true that noble widows often found themselves in the direst monetary straits. Unless assisted by well-meaning relatives, a number of highborn dowagers faced miserable existences that included begging for leftovers. The Margravine Agnes of Baden found herself destitute after her spouse's death and signed a letter to her brother "from poor miserable me."[47]

Such hardship could easily befall someone like Anna, who had no parents or siblings to offer her a livelihood, nor in-laws with properties or funds at their disposal. Except for William, the princess's only other "lifelines" were those aunts and uncles who rarely bothered with letters of support. The elector had made it abundantly clear at her Leipzig wedding that Anna's enormous dowry was a final settlement and that no additional disbursements should ever be expected. Perhaps Anna also thought of Sidonia. Her paternal aunt was still married to a man who had taken and squandered much of her wedding portion in the Low Countries.

While the princess agonized about life after William, the prince was concerned with the here and now. Sometime in late March 1568, as the winter skies were finally clearing, he enlisted his male relations for his first campaign against Alba's forces. Except for Anna, there were no objections. The conflict was regarded as a "family enterprise" and all agreed that the irrevocable loss of the Nassau's Dutch possessions would be intolerable to the house. Along with William's younger brothers, his sisters' husbands - the Counts Solms-Braunfels, Nassau-Saarbrucken, Schwarzburg, and Berg - also joined the Orange cause.

Planning and scheming reached a feverish pitch as Count John tightened security around Dillenburg. He prohibited the spreading of any oral or written information regarding the castle's defenses, and barred regular soldiers from entering the palace's upper levels. William discussed military strategy with only a handful of individuals, and locations for recruitment often changed to confuse foreign agents. The prince was just as circumspect in his correspondence and used ciphers or code names for certain individuals and places: Gdansk was Dillenburg, Martin Willemzoon his own designation.

Others were equally cautious. The Hessian Landgrave eventually loaned the prince 30,000 guilders, but under a fake name. Spies discreetly handed off confidential notes dressed as peasants or merchants, while meetings with sympathetic factions were conducted with extreme watchfulness. More often than not they were canceled, and most took place under the cover of darkness. The Hessian envoy George von Scholley and an official in the Elector Palatine's employ were not allowed to discuss tactics in Dillenburg, where privacy could not be guaranteed. They met with Orange further north, at remote Friedelhausen Castle on the Lahn River.[48]

Unfortunately, despite these precautions and meticulous planning, Anna's gloomy predictions mostly proved correct. In May, the Nassau's three-

[47] Karl-Heinz Spiess. "Witwenversorgung im Hochadel," *Witwenschaft in der Frühen Neuzeit* (Leipzig: Leipziger Universitätsverlag, 2003), p. 92

[48] Cellarius, "Propagandatätigkeit," pp. 143-4.

pronged surprise attack on the Low Countries failed as one of William's armies was instantly routed. Three thousand men perished, while a small Huguenot contingent from the west quickly retreated into France, only to be crushed by regular French forces. Even worse, not a single Dutch town joined the rebels, and captured prisoners gave away details regarding Orange's Protestant links in allied countries.[49]

Louis of Nassau's minor victory at the Battle of Heiligerlee in Friesland was offset by a tragic death.[50] Twenty-seven-year-old Adolph of Nassau, the fourth son of the family and an experienced battle commander, was shot to death by a former friend of the Oranges, Jean de Ligne, Duke of Arenberg.[51] The rebellion had only just commenced and the Nassaus were already paying a heavy blood tax: William's oldest son was held incommunicado in faraway Spain and Adolph, who had once accompanied Orange on his wedding journey to Leipzig, lay dead. Nonetheless, William decided grimly, there was no turning back now.

Alba concurred. He was eager to teach the prince a lesson after the prince's armed incursions into his sovereign's territory. After the battle, the duke had William stripped of all of his noble rights and privileges and officially sentenced to eternal exile. Soldiers raided Orange's Brussels palace, despoiling it of its exquisite possessions. King Philip, who was in the process of expanding his book and art collection at the Escorial in Madrid, welcomed a number of priceless Breda manuscripts as well as Hieronymus Bosch's "The Garden of Earthly Delights" triptych with open arms.[52]

At least William was still a free man. As he beat a retreat to Dillenburg, Alba solemnly proclaimed Egmont and Horn accomplices of the "arch traitor" Orange and renegades of the true religion. In Spain, King Philip signed their death sentences. Egmont's wife Sabine allegedly fell on her knees, begging the duke to spare her husband's life for the sake of their eleven children, but Alba remained unmoved.[53] On 5 June 1568, on the great market square in Brussels, Egmont - the hero of St Quentin - and Horn - the onetime commander of Philip's stately fleet - were publicly beheaded for high treason.

The execution sent shock waves through Europe. Both men had been members of the exclusive Order of the Golden Fleece and thus were only to be judged by their peers. But the King of Spain, the order's Grand Master, had issued a special patent for the execution. And yet even Alba, a man who rarely erred on the side of leniency, had second thoughts about the legality of the verdict and allegedly shed tears "as big as peas."[54] He later claimed to have always regretted the loss of two men whom "I have always loved and esteemed as my own brothers." And strangely enough, the two martyrs (who became potent symbols of the Dutch liberation movement) continued to be held in great honor at the Spanish court. A book of Flemish events, published in Castile a few years later, referred to them as "outstanding princes well-loved and of the highest and finest character."[55]

---

[49]Kamen, p. 123.
[50]Mörke, pp. 143-4.
[51]Putnam, *Moderate Man*, pp. 297-9. The Duke of Arenberg had distanced himself from his good friend, William of Orange, at the onset of the rebellion. One source claims that Adolph inflicted a mortal wound on the duke before both expired.
[52]Verwey, p. 85.
[53]Hamburger Literarische und Kritische Blätter," Ed. F. Riebour, 31. *Jahrgang* (Hamburg: 1855), p.469.
[54]Putnam, *Moderate Man*, p. 305.
[55]Kamen, pp. 123-4.

Egmont and Horn were the most prominent victims of Spanish repression in the Netherlands, but thousands of nameless others had been driven from their homes into exile, arrested, tortured, or killed. In this poisoned atmosphere of mistrust and fear, no one felt safe as respectable citizens with unblemished records ended up on the scaffold, denounced by personal enemies. The leader of Antwerp's opposition, Antoon van Stralen, had been detained during the first wave of arrests in the fall of 1567 and, like the "rebel counts," was also decapitated. His colleague and friend Jan Rubens narrowly escaped detention, but was not slow to read the runes.

Rubens had frequently defended members of the reformed religions and mediated between William and the city magistrate. Although officially Catholic, there were rumors that he was a closet Calvinist who had been blacklisted by the Spanish. In May 1568, when he failed to be re-elected to his judgeship, Jan decided that the time had come to move himself and his family out of the country. "They accuse me of having an evil heart," he wrote, referring to particular group of Catholic clerics, "because they lost a trial which I had presided over as commissioner." With a dossier full of recommendations, accreditations, and testimonials, Jan Rubens joined the vast stream of displaced Netherlanders surging towards the Rhine metropolis of Cologne in western Germany.[56] As another victim of sectarian strife and the Habsburg-Orange feud, Rubens needed to re-start his career to feed his family. It was Anna who would play no small part in his resurgence.

*****

Of the leading Dutch dissidents only William now remained. Tall, dark-haired, with a small mustache, and a short, peaked beard, the thirty-five-year-old Prince of Orange-Nassau found himself catapulted into the unenviable and improbable role of defender of his country.[57] For one, he was facing an alarming shortage of revenues. Voluntary contributions had fallen off precipitously and many former supporters begged William to "sit still." Indeed, the Nassaus were in such desperate financial straits that Orange begged the Saxon elector for a good horse, "because of extreme need."[58] He also spent the early summer dashing off petitions to various noble houses, including the emperor, the Elector Palatine, and Queen Elizabeth I of England. Polemical pamphlets which warned the Dutch of "eternal slavery" left Dillenburg by the thousands. They were probably hidden in barrels, transported up the Rhine River by ship, and disseminated by Orange's agents in the Low Countries.[59]

Most of the prince's entreaties were not answered, but he eventually gained some traction with the French Huguenots and issued a joint proclamation of Protestant unity with the Admiral of France, Gaspard de Coligny. He even found a sympathizer within Philip's entourage. One of the king's private secretaries, a Monsieur Vandenesse, sent Orange copies of crucial memoranda from Madrid.[60]

---

[56]de Dijn, pp. 37-8.
[57]Kamen, p. 123.
[58]Kruse, "Wilhelm von Oranien," p. 171. On May 9, 1568, Orange begged the elector for a good horse. "Die ernste, hohe Not" ("serious, dire want") forced him to seek help.
[59]Cellarius, "Propagandatätigkeit,"p. 129, p. 134.
[60]Cellarius, "Propagandatätigkeit," p. 144

But William also thought it necessary to personally step into the breach by leading an army of about 30,000 men into Flanders. Brought together by a Herculean monetary effort on his and Count John's part, troops gathered at the Ginsberger Meadow near Siegen and departed at the end of August, much to Anna's chagrin. Local boys excitedly shouted the slightly humorous Nassau battle cry *"Riewekooche"* ("Reibekuchen" - a type of potato bread and one of the region's culinary specialties), not knowing that few of them would live to see home again.[61]

This motley crew of untrained farm hands, adventurers, and down-on-their-luck mercenaries made up Orange's threadbare defense force. Even before their departure, there was widespread doubt that such a tattered band could take on Alba's special units. In September, Spanish spies reported William's soldiers camping north of Bonn on the Rhine River with banners fluttering in the wind, displaying the prince's motto "pro rege, pro lege, pro grege" ["for the king, the law, and the people"]. The rebels were stopping all north-west bound vessels carrying cargo for the Alba administration. That in turn put the mayoralty of nearby Cologne on highest alert. Some of William's irregulars had entered the city and become embroiled in criminal mischief, an ominous sign that the prince and his officers were not in control of their ragtag army. Cowed by Alba's posturing, town officials also denied William a much needed loan of money.[62]

Fifteen miles west of Cologne, at Kerpen, a Spanish vanguard gave short shrift to several of Orange's battalions, while the few rebel bands that managed to make it into the Low Countries were slowly ground up by disease and surprise skirmishes. An experienced battle tactician, the duke held the exasperated invaders in constant suspense by never facing them directly. He had sails and stones removed from the famous Dutch windmills to deprive the enemy of provisions and destroyed houses, even entire hamlets, which could have afforded the intruders shelter. Alba's agents also breached vital intelligence. A high-ranking rebel officer, Jean de Villiers, revealed the prince's plans in Spanish captivity; a recruiter of Orange's was caught at St. Omer and talked.[63]

Eventually, William and some scattered stalwarts staggered across the border into the French city of Strasbourg. The prince's fortunes were so impaired, messengers reported, that he was unlikely to ever recover from this stunning military blow, and Orange himself wrote resignedly, "We are left high and dry by the entire world."[64] At the end of September 1568 Nassau's counselor Dr. Jacob Schwartz reported to the Elector Palatine that the prince "was living in great melancholy."[65] Meanwhile, Alba triumphantly gloated to King Philip, "The majority of Orange's army is broken, starved, and cut to pieces."[66] Others were equally skeptical of William's chances of recovery. "The prince is no warrior," opined Duke Christian of Wurttemberg, and the English minister William Cecil thought William a lost cause. He wrote, "Things are bad in the Low Countries, because the Prince of Orange lacks money."[67]

In order to raise funds yet again, the prince and his brothers started selling their remaining gold and silver as well as the much cherished *Piscaria* wall hang-

[61]Irle, p. 250.
[62]Ennen, Leonard. *Geschichte der Stadt Köln* (Köln und Neuss: Verlag der L. Schwann'schen Verlagsbuchhandlung, 1875), pp. 842-3.
[63]Cellarius, "Propagandatätigkeit,"p. 143.
[64]Cellarius, "Wilhelm," p. 75
[65]Cellarius, "Propagandatätigkeit," p. 121.
[66]Putnam, *The Life of William the Silent*, p. 124.
[67]Cellarius, "Wilhelm," p.78. See also Cellarius, "Propagandatätigkeit," p.145.

ing. In the end, only the jewelry of their mother Juliana remained untouched.[68] Count John also dismissed the castle's artisans, and it was not until 1594 that Nassau account books would list a court painter again. That same year, John also bought back the *Piscaria* from the Bishop of Strasbourg.[69]

Messengers hurried back to Dillenburg to keep Anna abreast of the terrible events. Even under the best of circumstances, the emotionally fragile princess was unequipped to handle adversity. Now she crumbled completely. Her trusted companions depression and irritability returned with a vengeance, putting William's family on edge. Again, Anna detected slights where there were none and felt patronized by household regulations recently instituted by her brother-in-law. Novel directives admonished all of the castle's denizens to carefully guard their behavior down to table manners or face punishment. For those in doubt, written reminders were posted on walls in plain sight.[70] Perhaps even worse in Anna's opinion was the reduction of domestics. Due to the Nassau's precarious finances, a great number of staff was let go, with only sixty-one court and state servants remaining.[71]

Lost without William and languishing in her self-imposed quarantine, the princess drowned her sorrows in alcohol. Count John's wife wrote to her sister-in-law Catherine about Anna's excessive consumption of spirits. "She starts the morning by guzzling almost a liter of wine," Elizabeth sighed, "continues to drink through the afternoon and takes a "sedative" - perhaps wine laced with ginger and cinnamon - before going to bed."[72] On top of it all, the princess was pregnant with her fifth child.

While Elizabeth and Juliana continued annoyed, an extraordinary thought began to germinate in Anna's mind. It would be dreadful to spend her confinement among her husband's dour relations, when she craved entertainments in a livelier place where she could do as she pleased.[73] A return to Breda was impossible, as was Saxony because of the domineering electoral couple. After her uncle, the landgrave of Hessen, declined to house her in one of his numerous manors, Anna resolved to settle in Cologne.[74]

The sprawling city on the Rhine was filled with Dutch émigrés like the Horn and van Culenberg families, and Anna probably hoped to reconnect with these old acquaintances. Once in Cologne, she could even rekindle some of that Burgundian flair as a society hostess. In other words, recover a slice of paradise lost. By residing in a miniature version of Breda palace, she looked forward to welcoming "handsome women, Flemish lords, and the wives of noblemen" into her parlor.[75] Provided Nassau would approve of her scheme, she simply had to establish contact with Cologne-based Nassau agents like Gerhard Koch or Archbishop Salentin of Isenburg, who both supported the Orange cause.[76]

Anna found a convenient pretext for her planned departure in early October 1568. Several members of the castle's kitchen staff had fallen ill, and the

[68]Schuppener, *Hatzfeld*, p. 120.
[69]Becker, "Malerei," pp. 123-4.
[70]Schuppener, *Hatzfeld*, p. 136.
[71]Cellarius, "Propagandatätigkeit," pp. 123-4.
[72]Kruse, "Wilhelm von Oranien," p. 46.
[73]Putnam, *Moderate Man*, pp. 349-51. Count John had been waiting to complain to August and the landgrave about Anna's constant criticisms. Apparently she had haughtily told the Nassaus that since they were no princes and could not provide adequate entertainment, she could do as she pleased ("mache wie man wolle").
[74]Kruse, "Wilhelm von Oranien," p. 46.
[75]de Dijn, p. 55.
[76]Cellarius, "Propagandatätigkeit," p. 133.

princess claimed that the lives of her children and the unborn were in danger on account of the "epidemic." She also argued, quite correctly, that "There is neither an apothecary nor barber nor doctor to dispense the smallest piece of medical advice" in the entire *Westerwald* (Western forest) around Dillenburg.[77]

Irrespective of the health crisis, Anna's intentions were highly irregular. The princess was neither a widow nor without family, and to remove herself from the supervision of her relations was not only scandalous, but also quite unheard of in Renaissance society. Anna's contemporaries had definite opinions about wives who left husbands and kin to be on their own, and usually compared them to harlots. Martin Luther had sharply rebuked an unnamed German princess who had deserted "her lord and spouse out of boldness and moved away from him." "If I had been in his place," the reformer commented sharply, "I would not have looked through my fingers for so long, but would've taken the advice of her brother and all her blood relatives and compelled her with blows." Although this particular woman had supplied Luther with a list of unidentified marital griev-ances, the reformer instructed her to bear her fate "with patience, as a Christian." "Gracious Lady," he wrote in closing, "you will not be able to stop up everyone's mouth and prevent them from speaking ill of you; rather, they will regard you as guilty of adultery. Even if you are honorable, the example you set is similar to adultery."[78]

Nassau entertained concerns of a similar nature. No one could tell what would befall Anna in Cologne if she was left to her own devices, merely accom-panied by a few ladies and serving personnel. There was no denying that the princess possessed a marked penchant for frivolity, and, without proper super-vision, might cause a scandal reminiscent of her infamous trip to Spa. Lastly, her move to Cologne would not only be costly, but also reflect badly on her husband's relations, leaving them open to speculations of mistreatment. William's moth-er Juliana was particularly opposed to Anna leaving the confines of Dillenburg, which contributed to the princess's ever deepening aversion towards the ageing countess.[79]

Despite these concerns, Anna eventually had her way. All of the Nassau brothers were away on campaign, and the princess probably saw no reason to yield to the authority of the castle's appointed regent, the Count of Holstein-Scha-umburg.[80] Besides, patience had long been wearing thin on all sides. By the time Anna departed Dillenburg, Juliana and her ladies looked forward to days without heated scenes and histrionics in the women's wing. As for the twenty-three-year-old Princess of Orange, she could not wait to experience freedom from family fetters for the very first time in her life. In Cologne, she would be the sole mistress of her own little realm, unencumbered by the shackles of marriage and social ob-ligation.

---

[77]Goebel, p. 17. The first official pharmacy in the area was indeed not established until the middle of the nineteenth century. Until then people had to make do with home remedies.
[78]Karant-Nunn and Wiesner-Hanks, p. 155.
[79]Böttcher, pp. 152-3.
[80]Cellarius, "Propagandatätigkeit," pp. 122-3.

Independence

On October 20, 1568 Anna, her maid-of-honor, Emilia van Brederode, and a throng of servants hastily bid William's relations good-bye. She had been given one hundred fifty crowns of hard-gathered travel money, a paltry sum that certainly restricted her possibilities for high living, but apparently did not dim her enthusiastic mood of departure. Like many other aristocrats, the princess was pinning her hopes on kindly creditors.

While Orange was caught up in skirmishes near Linsmeau in Brabant, his wife's carriage clambered down the steep causeway of Dillenburg castle, escorted by Nassau horse guards.[1] In many ways, she appeared unconcerned, her frame of mind one of elated confidence that resembled her invigorating pre-wedding days, now long past. Anna had convinced herself rather effortlessly that everything would sort itself out. After escaping the hated "Westerwälders" ("people of the Westerwald forest") - her new pejorative term for her in-laws - she would at last be able to preside over a small court of her own, without Juliana and Elizabeth's constant interference. She set forth with reckless naïveté.

Beneath leaves turning color, the princess's baggage train slugged along the Dill River towards the hamlet of Irmgarteichen, where the travelers turned west on the ancient Siegen-Cologne road. A popular pilgrimage route, the highway was a busy stretch any time of the year, with groups of pilgrims, merchants, and other folk thronging their way to the Rhine metropolis of Cologne about fifty miles ahead. Past Siegburg, Anna and her entourage could already make out the outlines of the city's many churches. There was St. Martin with its massive towers, the great Romanesque basilica of St. Gereon, the Church of the Apostles in the south, and St. Mary of the Capitol straight ahead.[2]

If the weather cooperated, they might have also espied Cologne's most famous landmark, the cathedral, which was already depicted on countless copper engravings and woodcuts. The incomparable Gothic structure would eventually become the biggest house of worship in Christendom, although during Anna's lifetime it was still a bizarre, half-finished construction nightmare with incomplete towers. Due to exploding costs and the effects of the Reformation, work had come to a temporary halt in 1560.[3]

After the princess had passed through one of the city's south-eastern gates, she decided not to stay at the *Nassauischer Hof* (Nassau Court) - a villa owned by William's family - but at the residence of John Mohren's, her husband's exchequer.[4] There, she met the Dutch merchant Gerhard Koch, a Nassau employee who was to act as her banker and creditor.[5] William had kindly instructed him to "furnish" his wife with adequate means to meet her needs.[6] The life that should have been hers long ago was finally beckoning.

*****

---

[1]Kruse, "Wilhelm von Oranien," p. 46.
[2]Rombach, Otto. *Anna von Oranien* (Munich: Deutscher Taschenbuch Verlag, 1982), p. 107.
[3]de Dijn, p. 40.
[4]Becker, "Malerei," p. 103.
[5]Kruse, "Wilhelm von Oranien," p. 47.
[6]Böttcher, p. 154.

By all accounts, Anna was not a person of small intellect. She possessed linguistic talent and, in addition to her beloved romances, read historical, scientific, and botanical works in several languages. Her adept use of written Bible quotes gives evidence of a thorough, well-grasped knowledge of scripture.[7] And yet her quickness at learning and above-average education could not deflect from the fact that at almost twenty-four, this mother of two with a third on the way was still woefully naïve and inexperienced in matters of the world. Perhaps it was this lack of practical knowledge that prevented Anna from taking honest stock of the realities that awaited her.

Her courageous foray into independence, propelled by thoughtlessness and hatred towards her in-laws, are comprehensible, even impressively brave. They were also rash, ill-considered, and self-centered. She was no longer the rich heiress of independent means, but the unfortunate spouse of a bankrupt prince who was embroiled in a risky political gamble. No secret treasure chest awaited Anna's opening in Cologne, nor was a wealthy Flemish benefactor willing to cover her expenses in the name of Dutch patriotism. There was only the merchant Koch whose promised assistance did not come free. But Anna banished such thoughts. After the "privations" of Dillenburg and the ordeal of expulsion from Flanders, she deserved distractions and amusements.

However sympathetic we might be to her newfound concept of female independence, Anna's contemporaries were not. After seven years of marriage, they expected the princess to have settled into a comfortable domestic routine. She was a mother and wife who had endured the hardships of dispossession and buried two children; a matron and lady of exalted rank whose position in life came with substantial duties and responsibilities. From a sixteenth-century standpoint and perhaps from ours as well, Anna was frightfully selfish.

Unlike many others, she had also weathered Alba's repression reasonably well. Thousands had ended up destitute or lost their lives; the princess received immediate shelter from one of Germany's oldest families. While Anna complained about the pawning of her jewels and lack of comfort, Juliana and her children mourned Adolph's death and feared that William stood to suffer that same fate any day. Instead of being a source of support, the princess nagged the Nassaus about money. Such insensitive behavior was a growing stain on the reputation of her husband's family as well as her own.

*****

Her vision clouded by pursuits of leisure, Anna breathlessly settled into her new surroundings, a fantasyland of bygone glories temporarily recouped. She imagined her new situation as the panacea for everything that ailed her, a pattern of thinking that had emerged shortly before her wedding and would continue for the rest of her life. Rather than facing her demons, Anna ran when trouble arose: from Saxony to the Netherlands, from Breda to Dillenburg, and now to Cologne. Wherever she stayed for an extended period of time, Anna inevitably felt the need to move on to "greener pastures." Her lack of staying power and difficulties in finding her footing were certainly linked to her inability to connect with oth-

[7]Schuppener, "Hochzeitslied," p. 222.

ers. William, who had occasionally succeeded in penetrating Anna's "emotional thicket," was unavailable in the fall of 1568 and the princess allowed no one else to advise her. Access into her confidence and inner self was not something she desired: it could open her up to criticism and other unpleasant personal reflections.

Anna's first days in Cologne were exhilarating, of course. Word on the street was that Her Highness, the *Princesse d'Orange*, had arrived, and merchants, craftsmen, and artisans crammed into her apartments, proffering their wares and services. After a fortnight the money ran out, and Anna hastily dispatched her chamberlain to Dillenburg to procure more funds. He returned with a trifling sixty crowns, painfully pinched by Count John from the Nassau budget. After another disastrous campaign in the Low Countries, William's brother was burdened by almost unmanageable debt and simply unable to pay for his sister-in-law's extravagances.[8] A week later, on November 11, a wholly chastened Anna addressed fawning petitions to her aunt and uncle in Dresden. Suddenly frightened, she begged the electress to send her money and the Moserin (an old governess and trusted servant) to assist her during her upcoming delivery. She also asked for a pair of noble Saxon ladies to keep her company "during these miserable and sad times" and signed the letter "your poor, deserted, obedient daughter."[9]

The electress refused. Although she often "loaned" her best midwives to friends and family members, Anne declined her husband's niece the same favor.[10] As to Anna's request for company, the Danish princess tartly alleged that there was little willingness among "Saxony's young daughters" to conduct themselves "abroad" during these dangerous times of "war and death." And with Alba fighting William, nobody could actually pinpoint the exact location of the Orange court. Besides, Anna had become accustomed to such high living in Burgundy, the electress mocked, that "ill-dressed, clumsy maids" from home would surely not do for her now. Instead, she was to place her trust in the Almighty.[11] Unlike his wife, Elector August did not even bother with a reply.

Suffering from "extreme want," Anna shot off another plea in December, this time requesting a 12,500 thaler loan - money still owed to her from her late mother's bequests. If the elector refused, she clamored, "it will be the death of me." Her uncle, of course, had not the least intention of parting with a small fortune of the kind, and, in the usual manner, decided to have his trusted counselor Eric von Berlepsch evaluate the state of affairs. Berlepsch arrived around New Year's, traditionally a happy time for gift giving and the exchange of a new-fangled item called "New Year's cards." It was a thriving trend that even the purportedly "backward" Nassaus had adopted. Unlike today, the upper half of the card usually contained a woodcut or a copper engraving, beneath which the sender inscribed New Year's wishes in rhyme form. The recipient acknowledged these elaborate greetings with a small return gift.[12] It is not recorded if Anna received either presents or cards, but in her current state, any greeting would have been a comfort.

Berlepsch, a well-travelled lawyer who had attended universities in both Italy and France, immediately tried to get to the bottom of Anna's domestic woes

---

[8] "Graf Johann Wolf", p. 262. See also Putnam, *Moderate Man*, 351. The Nassaus also did not have the money to rebuild the manor house at Diez, which was one Anna's widow's estates, for her.

[9] Kruse, "Wilhelm von Oranien," p. 160. Dresden Archive, Locat. 8510 [b], fol. 250.

[10] Keller, *Kurfürstin*, p. 170.

[11] Wartenberg, p. 80-1.

[12] Pletz-Krehahn. "Das Neujahrsfest," *Heimatjahrbuch für das Land an der Dill*, No. 24 (1981), p. 105.

by carefully observing and documenting the goings-on in the princess's household. He had already served her father Maurice, and was well-acquainted with the princess. She had always warned William against challenging Alba, a distraught Anna told the envoy, but had been rudely put in her place by others who told her to concentrate on her spinning. A pitiable two hundred fifty crowns was all the prince had ever given her since their departure from the Low Countries. But she could not "eat feet and hands" with her children, Anna wailed, or "live by the wind."

Berlepsch concurred that the princess's financial situation was indeed upsetting, but also interjected that her plans of residing in fashionable Cologne had all but foundered. Forty-three household personnel were too many for a person without a regular income and she needed to economize. Upon careful consideration, Berlepsch advised, it would be best for her to return to Dillenburg. She could not survive much longer in such expensive surroundings and might as well cut her losses.

Anna responded violently to this extremely unwelcome suggestion. She would rather die than crawl back to her in-laws, she howled in protest. "It goes wholly against my heart and would cost me my life!" The pious Berlepsch took his leave after four days and, perhaps unbeknownst to Anna, continued on to Dillenburg to pay the Nassaus a visit. To his surprise he found that life in the country was not nearly as primitive as Anna had painted it.

Upon questioning, family members readily apprised the Saxon envoy of the princess's "stiff-necked" and condescending attitude towards their elderly mother, while Count John relayed tales about Anna finding everything "too little and too despicable." They had been deeply offended by the princess's ingratitude and her claims of being left to rot in destitution. After all, they were inundated by debts after contributing the astronomical sum of 170,000 florins towards William's war effort. Despite these difficulties, Count John informed Berlepsch, there was always a place for his brother's wife at his side. If she decided to return to Dillenburg, he would be glad to pay for her upkeep as well as a household of ten to twelve servants.

On January 18, Eric von Berlepsch forwarded a forty page report to Elector August from his home in Salza (Bad Langensalza today) in western Saxony. Everyone, including the children on the street, was familiar with Anna's precarious circumstances, he wrote. And with the Prince of Orange unable to send her regular maintenance payments, his niece's time in Cologne had to come to an end. Otherwise, the emissary concluded gravely, she stood in danger of becoming the talk of the town.

*****

Unfortunately, Anna's move to Cologne coincided with a period of rapidly rising prices for which William was at least partly to blame. The war in the Netherlands disrupted shipping on the Rhine which led to bottlenecks in food distribution as well as inflation. Herman von Weinsberg (1518-1597), a Cologne alderman, wine merchant, and advocate, described the issue of price hikes in his extensive diary. He wrote, "A hat of salt costs thirty-two thalers now, an unheard of increase ... great lords pleaded and begged for solid." All the salt pans in the

Low Countries had been destroyed, and shipments from France and Spain could not make it past the embattled Dutch ports. "Many villagers had slaughtered pigs and believed to be able to get salt quickly in the city, as usual, but then could not get any while their meat was turning bad."

The princess's problems were far greater than an empty salt cellar. While she nervously awaited the elector's reply to her petition, she was forced to pawn some of her jewels to put food on the table. In February 1569, the Cologne merchant Peter Regk recorded the following precious items of Anna's in his inventory: "Seven carats with altogether 106 diamonds, rubies, and emeralds bordered with sixty-one pearls, among them a medallion of a naked Judith, seven pieces made in Spain with altogether 336 golden buttons and 257 diamonds, a choker made out of rubies and 114 pearls, etc." Gradually, a great many of Anna's Saxon and Hessian heirlooms - items that had once belonged to her mother and must have been of considerable sentimental value - ended up in pawnshops or even at the Frankfurt market fair. They had once been valued at 17,000 thalers; Anna pawned them for a measly 4000. Apparently, the price of hard won independence justified the loss of treasured mementos, and was altogether preferable to going back to Dillenburg as the prodigal daughter-in-law.[13]

*****

Against all hopes and expectations, life in the city proved more challenging as Anna had wished. Other Dutch immigrants rebuilt their careers, lived in comfortable new homes, and engaged expensive foreign tutors for their children. The princess, on the other hand, was selling her possessions to keep her straitened household afloat. There was also not enough left to entertain. Although Anna was the highest ranking émigré in Cologne, there is no record of her mingling with the town's one hundred fifty gentlewomen or the Countesses Hoogstraten and Horn from Flanders.

Perhaps she was shunned. The princess's difficult temper, her run-ins with Egmont's wife, and clashes with servants had not raised Anna's social profile, and few might have felt the desire to reconnect with her, even in exile. Conversely, perhaps it was the rank-conscious Anna who rejected company. The fact that she was no longer the wealthy elector's daughter did not need advertising, making her loath to receive anyone of note in her reduced circumstances. Moreover, a somewhat disappointing letter from the elector had just arrived. He could not send her the requested sum, but promised to appeal to the emperor in regards to her widow's estates in the Netherlands. If successful, the princess might obtain a percentage of their yields as an income.[14] Of course, such a petition would take time.

An invitation to a wedding in Mannheim near Heidelberg provided new hope. Anna's maid-of-honor, the sweet-natured Emilia van Brederode, widow of Louis's rebel friend Henry, was getting married. The twenty-nine-year-old had caught the eye of Frederick III, Elector Palatine, who was her senior by twenty-five years. The flat-nosed, wealthy widower had decided to follow his heart in the matter of his second marriage, and Emilia, whose suitor vastly outranked her, gladly agreed.

[13]deDijn, pp. 56-7.
[14]Kruse, "Wilhelm von Oranien," p. 52.

William was to attend the nuptials as well. Frederick III was a devout convert to Calvinism and generously supported the French Huguenots. The Prince of Orange hoped that such largesse might also trickle into his own, glaringly empty purse. While his wife was bartering away family treasures in the name of self-realization, the Prince of Orange humiliated himself by begging the Dukes of Wurttemberg and Baden for additional loans. He already owed more than two million florins to various noble creditors, and his remaining worldly goods lay deposited in Strasbourg pawn shops. Even the altar furnishings of William's private chapel in Dillenburg were gone, and he barely managed to pay his skeletal staff of loyal retainers.

As for the rest of the prince's demoralized, unpaid militia, those that had not been killed or perished from disease plundered and raped their way back home. Emperor Maximilian II exhorted William to check his marauding troops within imperial territory, but the prince could only stand by powerless as his runaway mercenaries pillaged through western Germany. He had reached rock bottom. Alba's henchmen chased him, his own *Landsknechts* wanted his head for defaulting on pay, and the emperor was about to declare him an outlaw for taking up arms against the Habsburgs. Burned-out, beaten, and aged, Charles's former wunderkind furtively crawled back to Dillenburg via Heidelberg, a broken condottiere. Alba gloated, while Granvelle waxed triumphant, "Ladies will not gladly receive those who come to them penniless and ruined" least of all, his own wife.[15]

Anna was largely in the dark about the full extent of the grueling winter campaign of 1568-69 which Francis Junius, one of Orange's army chaplains, described as one of the "unhappiest wars of the century."[16] Hoping to receive some badly needed funds, she had agreed to meet William at Emilia's wedding in March 1569. The princess was eight months pregnant, irritated by the bitter cold and bad roads, but also looked forward to the celebrations. To keep up appearances, Anna made a showing in her most exquisite finery.

The couple's reunion was immediately fraught with tension, especially when Anna pressured her husband to relocate, yet again, to better, nicer places as was her habit. "It is not a question of where we shall go, but who will receive us," Orange exclaimed, exasperated. "You know the perplexity I am in, nor is there anything in the world which can bring greater solace to a man than to have his wife with him for comfort." In an appeal that mixed entreaty with reproach, he told her, "If you have any love or kindness for me, these great affairs of mine should be nearer to your heart than the frivolities with which you fill your heart and head."[17] Anna listened, but remained unmoved.

The couple departed on uneasy terms. Orange, together with Louis and his youngest brother Henry, left for France to meet with the Huguenot leaders Coligny and Condé, while Anna, against William's wishes, returned to Cologne to prepare for her lying-in and to hire a lawyer. Since the prince could no longer be depended upon, the princess decided, she had to take matters into her own hands.

---

[15]Wedgwood, pp. 111-2. Mörke, pp. 145-6.
[16]Cellarius, "Propagandatätigkeit," p. 139. See also Putnam, *Moderate Man*, 324. Elector August's diplomatic agent, Hubert Languet, wrote "The prince is a dead man. He is not merely deserted by his soldiers, but is in actual danger from them, as they threaten to strangle him and lay waste to Nassau."
[17]Wedgwood, p. 113.

Sometime in early 1569, Anna learned that the Countesses Horn and Egmont were receiving stipends and other moneys from the Alba administration. Reimbursements for lost incomes from their Dutch widow's estates, they enabled the women to lead the kind of life that Anna desired. Indeed, Egmont's widow Sabine, who had spent long months destitute after her husband's execution, was living very comfortably now in one of her former palaces on a yearly allowance of ten thousand crowns.[18] What applied to them, Anna surmised with an unerring sense of entitlement, must apply to her as well. She straightaway requested the legal services of Dr. John Betz, a famous jurist from Mecheln, who had also fled the Low Countries. The lawyer was a trusted acquaintance of the Nassau brothers and probably also their agent in Cologne.[19] Anna presumed with a sudden surge of optimism that it was Betz who could salvage some of her Flemish dower lands and restore her former standing in society. Frenetic with anticipation, she directed all her energies towards the upcoming lawsuit.

As so often, the princess's children played no part in this show of single-minded tenacity. On April 10 Anna gave birth to a third daughter, Emilia, who was perhaps named after the mild-mannered Madame Brederode. Shortly after the delivery, Anna had the newborn packed off to Dillenburg where Juliana took the baby under her wings.[20] Her two older children - five-year-old Anna and toddler Maurice - continued with the princess in Cologne, little shadows on the periphery of their mother's consciousness that hardly ever found mention in her copious correspondence.

When not waylaid by melancholy, most of Anna's waking hours were filled with the hatching of plans involving the retrieval of her fortune. Since William could no longer care for her, Anna argued forcefully, she should be allowed to draw money from her jointure in the Low Countries. Dr. Betz was also to demand a regular income from either the Duke of Alba, her Uncle August or the Nassau brothers. The Saxon elector still owed her 35,000 thalers, she calculated, from her late father's legacy.[21] As for William's family, according to her marriage contract she was the mistress of two estates in the small towns of Diez and Hadamar as well as their yields.

His pockets filled with gold (Anna had sold eighty gold buttons and reduced her staff by half), the good doctor Betz soon repaired on missions to Kassel, Vienna, and Dresden to reclaim his noble patron's lost lands.[22] Equipped with three horses and a retinue befitting a royal delegation, Betz was supposed to impress. If necessary, Anna wheedled, he might even have to go to Spain to plead with King Philip in person. Her uncles, she assured him optimistically, would pay for these particular expenses.

At the imperial court in Vienna, Betz spent interminable hours waiting for an audience, and finally left after being put off with vague promises. At the behest of the Saxon Elector and Landgrave William, the emperor had agreed to forward his supplication to the King of Spain and to put in a good word for Anna

[18] Robert van Roosbroeck. "Der Schöffe Jan Rubens," *Siegerland, Band* 53, Heft 3-4 (1976), p. 63. See also Vogt-Lüerssen, p. 68.
[19] Goebel, p. 18.
[20] Wedgwood, p. 113.
[21] Vogt-Lüerssen, p. 67.
[22] Kruse, "Wilhelm von Oranien," p. 171. According to a July 5 household roster, the princess had reduced her staff to twenty-four personnel, a considerable change since Berlepsch's visit in January. The following domestics were now listed in Anna's service: a master of the household, two ladies and a serving maid, two chamber maids, a nanny and two maids for the youngest child, a laundry woman, another household master, a page, kitchen scribe, tailor, cupbearer, cook, lackey, a driver as well as a stable boy and preacher.

with the Duke of Alba.[23] Even so, all participants of this charade were fully aware that failure of their appeals was a foregone conclusion. Philip would not be inclined to show mercy to the rebel leader's wife, while Alba supported Mesdames Egmont and Horn because their husbands' execution still weighed on his conscience. The same could not be said for the arch traitor Orange, the Habsburg's onetime protégé, who was still fomenting war against his sovereign. Besides, the Mrs. Egmont and Horn were widows, in the true sense of the word.

Dr. Betz's negotiations, diplomatic dinners, and socializing lasted several months. All the while Anna fretted back in Cologne, obsessed with the thought of recuperating a piece of land, an annuity, anything. In a misguided surge of impatience and without seeking anyone's opinion, she eventually decided to take matters into her own hands and personally appealed to King Philip and the Duke of Alba by addressing them as a widow in the de facto sense. Because of her husband's refusal to answer the duke's summons, Anna inferred with somewhat circuitous logic, the Prince of Orange had suffered civil death ("civiliter mortuum") which rendered her a widow. Moreover, since the Spanish had confiscated the majority of William's lands, he was no longer able to care for her and the children, which further buttressed her need of a dowager's estate.[24]

Finally, her husband's war in the Netherlands had nothing to do with her, Anna insisted, however noble his intentions. She had advised William to come to terms with the Duke of Alba and the King of Spain, and if he had only listened, they would still be dining in Brussels and Breda. Unfortunately, the prince had let down and abandoned his family, plunging her and the children into penury. She was simply forced to appeal to the mercy of Madrid, since no one else would.

There was little reaction to the princess's adventurous legal forays from Kassel and Dresden. When informed about Anna's petition to the Habsburgs, William of Hessen merely commented that his father, Landgrave Philip, had always warned her about marrying the Nassau prince.[25]

*****

From a legal standpoint, Anna was by no means out of line in demanding the spousal support that her marriage contract - an early modern prenuptial agreement - had always guaranteed her. The Orange household was technically disbanded, and the silver, jewels, and clothes that Anna had taken to Breda almost eight years ago as part of her trousseau still belonged to her. She was also entitled to receive between five and ten percent of the combined worth of her dowry, dower, and other incomes.[26] But since the majority of William's lands had been seized, and the couple had already sold or pawned most of their valuables, the princess's case was complicated.

A few of her relations might have agreed with Anna that the prince had shamefully misused her property for his own purposes and that she was justified in seeking redress. Most of Anna's peers, however, viewed her decision to approach William's enemy as disgraceful, if not treasonous. Husbands and wives

---

[23]Kruse, "Wilhelm von Oranien," p. 56.
[24] Maike Günther. "Schloß Rochlitz als Residenz und Witwensitz," *Witwenschaft in der Frühen Neuzeit* (Leipzig: Leipziger Universitätsverlag, 2003), p. 87. See also Putnam, *The Life of William the Silent*, p. 126.
[25]Fellmann, p. 37.
[26]Spiess, pp. 97-8.

were one, according to the tenor of the times, and if the head of the family sold personal belongings to pay off debts, his obedient wife and helpmeet was to back his decision.[27] A contemporary judicial court in Basel had argued that "The marriage bond obligates both husband and wife, as one flesh, to help one another in times of trial and suffering and bear one another's cross."[28]

Besides, Anna's self-indulgent decision to move to Cologne had triggered her panicky pursuit for money. Had she stayed with her in-laws, the princess's critics charged, she would still live in relative comfort. A woman's place was with her husband and his family, wherever they chose to go; only "stupid women" did otherwise.[29] Even worse and quite unforgivable was Anna's decision to declare herself a widow, although her suffering spouse was still alive. In the early modern era, the female domestic martyr was admired and applauded; the self-serving individualist shunned and maligned.[30] And yet Anna was in no mood for self-sacrifice. She had been in a constant state of inconvenience since leaving Breda and was planning to enjoy life, regardless of society's dictates.

Even if her bold widowhood claims had found acceptance, the nobility still expected Anna to adhere to certain guidelines of behavior. Few sins were more despicable in the eyes of her fellow men than the free-wheeling, wanton dowager who failed to demonstrate proper fidelity to her dead husband's memory. A widow was to perpetually honor her late spouse by leading a pious, simple life, removed from loud company and worldly temptations.[31] Egmont's widow Sabine was a prime example of such perfect devotion. Before her return to the Netherlands, she mourned her late husband in complete seclusion. Upon inquiries made by the Alba administration, the city council of Cologne informed the duke that the countess remained sequestered in a convent with her children. [32]

Nothing could have been further from Anna's mind. Instead of spending her days dressed in plain widow's weeds like her mother-in-law Juliana, she still envisioned herself the mistress of a small, but exquisite residence in Cologne. A portrait of the princess by an anonymous artist dated to 1570 shows Anna grandstanding in costly jewels and finery. Rivaling her earlier Breda likeness, the princess continued to display her status with undimmed pride.[33]

It is certainly possible that the painting was a copy of an earlier work and that Anna never posed for an artist in Cologne. But even if we give her the benefit of the doubt, Anna never indicated that her newly desired "widowed" status implied any kind of curtailment of her leisure activities. Fine foods, clothing, and frippery still mattered greatly to the princess, and with Dr. Betz still abroad, she had to sell additional pieces of her once extensive jewelry collection. Cologne merchants purchased her mother's diamond studded wedding ring worth four thousand thalers, and the choker given to Anna by William on the morning after their wedding (valued at six thousand thalers) for a pittance.[34]

[27]Harris, p. 78.
[28]Ozment, *Fathers*, p. 95.
[29]Karant-Nunn and Wiesner-Hanks, p. 93.
[30]Lilienthal, p. 222. Some might have even accused Anna of *desertio maliosa* (malicious desertion), a loosely defined felony that applied when an individual permanently moved away from his or her partner, usually to foreign, unreachable places.
[31]Ingendahl, Gesa. "Elend und Wollust: Witwenschaft in kulturellen Bildern der Frühen Neuzeit," *Witwenschaft in der Frühen Neuzeit* (Leipzig: Leipziger Universitätsverlag, 2003), pp. 272-4.
[32]Ennen, p.836.
[33]Spies, p. 242.
[34]Vogt-Lüerssen, p. 65.

Perhaps the sold choker was an unconscious expression of Anna's waning affection for her husband. Sometime in the late 1560s, her love for William and the passion that had once pulsated through her body and almost made her lose her head, appeared extinguished. An aggregate collection of frustrations - his neglect in Breda and Brussels, affairs, and the ruinous foreign war - curdled all feelings of fondness. What remained was not merely indifference, but bitterness intertwined with icy disdain. Regardless of the worthiness of the prince's struggle, his failure to adequately provide for his wife and children was an unpardonable offense in Anna's mind, a dishonor to her name and standing. The demotion of the shining gentleman into a mere shadow of his former self, a pauper hounded by his own unpaid troops and Spanish agents, quenched the remainders of any of those ardent emotions that William had once awakened in her.

Two years after their flight from the Low Countries, Anna determined that she no longer owed William any of the respect commonly accorded to husbands by their wives. Orange had clearly abdicated his position as lord and master of a no longer existing household, and any continued connection with the prince poisoned others against her. Neither of her uncles dared to support her financially, she had learned, since the Habsburgs considered such payments war money for the prince's rebel cause.[35] For these reasons, the time had come to distance herself from William, Anna resolved. This had to be done as a protective measure, and to give weight to her widowhood claims.[36]

*****

When an exhausted Orange returned to Dillenburg in the fall of 1569, Anna sharply refused a meeting. The location was not convenient, she claimed, and then suggested Siegburg, outside of Cologne, for talks. However, the small town was swarming with Spanish spies and therefore too dangerous a rendezvous point for the hunted prince. Other alternatives, like Frankfurt, were also rejected by the princess whose ill-concealed contempt for William now cruelly spilled into her letters. "You know full well that all of Germany is complaining, because of the disorder caused by you," she scribbled dismissively. "What that war has done to the people, I know very well, but it is your fault and you may be certain that you have more enemies than you think. Go to England or France where you have many friends." She signed the letter, "your obedient and loyal wife *while I am alive*, Anna of Saxony." She had carefully omitted the appellation "Princess of Orange," [37]therewith implying the severance of marital ties.

After reading his wife's scornful message, William finally dropped some of his unflappable politesse. "My wife, I have seen by your letters and heard from our secretary, the reasons why you have not come to meet me, and I do not find them sufficient, considering the duty and obligations a wife owes her husband in case she bears him the slightest affection," he wrote. "When you say that you promised yourself never again to be found in this land, you ought to consider that you promised before God and his church to abandon everything in the world to cleave to your husband, and I think you should have this more at heart than

[35]Kruse,"Wilhelm von Oranien," p. 60.
[36]Putnam, *Moderate Man*, p. 334. At the time, William kept himself so well hidden that the Dutch statesman Viglius—a partisan of the Habsburgs—spread news of his death. "The head gone, we need not fear the rebels as they are shorn of their strength."
[37]Kruse, p. 61.

all other trifles and frivolities, if you have any idea of your responsibility. These words are not intended to persuade you to come hither. Since you dislike that, I will not press it, but they are to remind you of your obligations, as I am in duty bound to do." He added in a more conciliatory tone, "When a man is immersed in difficulties, there is nothing in the world that can give him greater succor of spirit than to be comforted by his wife, and see her bear her cross with patience, especially when her husband is suffering for his efforts to advance the glory of God, and win the liberty of his country."

There was also a note of warning. Anna's refusal to meet him had already started rumor. Cardinal Granvelle had gossiped maliciously, "If the Princess of Orange is doing what people say she is doing, she is only doing as any woman who wishes to use what God has given her."[38] She should be more guarded in her behavior, William cautioned. "It seems to me that if you felt the slightest friendship for me, you would be governed more by your heart than by frivolous pretexts. I will not lay further stress on the fact that we are giving everyone an opportunity to talk about our private affairs, but will leave you to judge whether such publicity is pleasing to me."

As for Anna's suggestions to move abroad, Orange answered resignedly, "Our affairs are in such a state that it is no longer a question of our deciding upon a place of residence. In both towns and republics I imagine that they will think more than twice before giving me shelter, as would the Queen of England, the Kings of Denmark and Poland, and all the German princes. I do not speak here of your will, but of myself, because I am out of favor with the emperor." He concluded his letter on a conciliatory, but grave note: "It is better for me not to stop in any one place, but be here today, tomorrow there. I would have been glad enough of the relief of seeing you, if only for a few days. I am off tomorrow. Concerning my return, or when I can see you, on my honor I can tell you nothing for certain. Nothing would please me more than to see you contented."[39]

Anna was neither touched by these sentimentalities nor William's hardships. In fact, her replies stand out for their scornful, condescending tenor. In February 1570 she snarled, "I will never again go near any of your friends. If you go on urging me to do so, I shall consider it as proof that you wish my death." Two months later, she categorically dismissed any further suggestions of a meeting in a lethal message that signaled her intention of breaking with the House of Nassau. She was not mincing words. "I have received your letter and note. I cannot believe that you write concerning your desire to see me, for you have not acted at all in accordance with your words. In respect to the place that you wish me to come to, it is not at all convenient for me, and I do not know how to get the means of traveling to join my lord and his relations. You're right that you're unable to send me money, but I have noticed that you do not care much about helping me. As I cannot get what belongs to me from you and your family, I must appeal to my friends. I realize I need not expect any good from you, and I do not wish to be called a disgrace and ruin of the House of Nassau, which I can rightfully call my disgrace and ruin."

[38]Wedgwood, p. 113.
[39]Putnam, *The Life of William the Silent*, pp. 127-8. See also Putnam, *Moderate Man*, 356-8. This was not a carelessly written letter, as a draft in German shows. Unlike his love letters before their marriage which he gave Louis to write, Orange went over this particular message at least twice and did not entrust it to a secretary.

The letter ends with Anna justifying her anger and leaving any chance of a future get-together open to question. "As to your saying that when I come to you I had better leave my anger in Cologne, I have never been angry at you or yours, except with just cause. Our meeting will probably be the cause of increasing my justifiable irritation instead of diminishing it, if you expect to go on in your old way. For my part, I cannot go to the place you have appointed, so I command you to God's protection, and hope He will treat you better that you have me."[40]

*****

In addition to a crumbling marriage, William continued to suffer from unrelenting political and military setbacks. Except for his immediate family, most of his friends and peers had distanced themselves from the pariah prince. For instance, Anna's Uncle August was no longer willing to publicly acknowledge him. Initially, the elector had not been unsympathetic to Orange's plight, but William's repeated military debacles and the unrestrained brutality of his disbanding troops had turned public opinion against him.

The previously genial correspondence between the Wettins and the Nassaus gradually dried up as did their friendship. During Christmas 1569, when a despairing William travelled to Dresden to shore up capital for his troops, the elector had the prince cool his heels in various ante-chambers. After several days of wait, August let Orange know that he would be unable to receive him.[41] Together with the Landgrave of Hessen, the elector was loath to endanger the peace in the Holy Roman Empire by aiding the Dutch rebels, who were Calvinist "heretics" after all.[42]

Deserted by pivotal allies and even his wife, William was a tragedy in the making, a ruined outlaw who could be murdered by anyone at any time. Three Spanish assassins, disguised as Bavarian noblemen, had already followed Orange to Saxony, but were apprehended by authorities.[43] Count John stationed guards around Dillenburg to sound alarm in case of Spanish incursions, and anxiously awaited couriers to arrive with uplifting news. He was usually disappointed. William often requested help with problems that were dire reminders of his mounting hardships. At the beginning of 1570 the prince asked John to "send me two pairs of silk trunk hose. Your tailor has one that Neuenahr gave him to mend; please, have the other pair taken from things I recently used at Dillenburg. Pray forgive me for troubling you with my affairs. I hope to repay you some time."[44] The former grand seigneur with the legendary wardrobe now had to make do with mended shirts.

Later that spring, when misfortune threatened to crush him, William decided that the time had come for plain talk. Although he was no longer in control of his political destiny, he was still capable of reining in his errant wife. After another haughty putdown by the princess, Orange fired off a lengthy, irritated dispatch to her uncles in Hessen and Saxony. The letter was an exercise of catharsis and justification after months and years of marital difficulties as well as a

[40]Putnam, *The Life of William the Silent*, pp. 128-9.
[41]Kruse, "Wilhelm von Oranien,"p. 60, p. 64.
[42]Keller, *Kurfürstin*, pp. 204-5.
[43]Pletz-Krehahn "Neujahrsfest," p. 105.
[44]Putnam, *The Life of William the Silent*, p. 125.

final plea for intervention by her relations. Her complete lack of support for his war of liberation, her refusal to show even an iota of understanding or empathy for his plight saddened him greatly, William wrote, while her cruel abrasiveness increased his misery.

At this point, Orange asserted, he was no longer certain if their marriage had a future. The elector or the landgrave needed to "set her head straight" and teach Anna how to behave as consort to a prince. Otherwise, she would have to suffer the consequences. He had simply run out of patience with a spouse, who, "instead of comforting [me], insults me 100,000 times."[45] "I can simply no longer show as much patience as I have until now, because so much unpleasantness, one after the other, eventually results in the loss of all … respect [for such a person]."[46]

His frank complaint immediately set off alarm bells in Kassel. If William repudiated his niece, the landgrave worried, the House of Hessen might be facing a scandal greater than the shame caused by his wayward sister Barbara a few years ago. Instead of regaling the princess with another piece of pious advice, he invited her to the landgravial court to discuss an annuity. An elated Anna readied for travel, and notified the Nassaus about her departure for Hessen with a new lawyer from Antwerp. Enter Jan Rubens.

---

[45]Kruse, "Wilhelm von Oranien," pp. 66-8.
[46]deDijn, p. 59.

Jan

While William struggled to regain any kind of military foothold in the spring and early summer of 1570, Anna labored to set her life on a firmer course. Despite clear evidence pointing to eventual failure, the princess doggedly continued in her lawsuits against the Spanish Habsburgs as well as her in-laws. Dr. Betz had still not returned from his travels and because of disappointing news from Madrid, Anna hired an additional lawyer to aggressively push her case. In Spain, her astounding claim to "widowhood" had first been noted with bemused disbelief and then rejected. Although she could indeed be considered a widow in the legal sense, the king's jurists argued, she was also an aider and abettor of rebels. The princess had sold her personal effects to finance William's unlawful rebellion, and was therefore an accessory to his "devilish designs." Without merit, her case was now considered ad acta, which is to say, closed.[1]

Anna, of course, was not deterred. She still believed in an eventual understanding with the Duke of Alba, and if that failed, her lawyers were to focus on securing a pension from her German relations. Regrettably, her premier counsel Dr. Betz balked. In view of the princess's dwindling finances, the futility of the lawsuit, and his growing eagerness to return to his regular law practice, the doctor declined any further assignments on his noble client's behalf. Clearly impatient to return to his home in Heidelberg after frittering much of Anna's retainer away, Betz did not even take the time to personally brief his erstwhile client of his findings. In the middle of June the princess received a cowardly letter filled with profuse regrets. Due to his workload and other obligations, Dr. Betz wrote, he could no longer proceed with her case.[2] Anna had sold her eighty gold buttons in vain.

And yet, the princess was by no means disheartened, even by this substantial setback. She had found a new and attractive helper in the "fight for her rights," a distinguished attorney who had promised to pursue her claims with the utmost diligence and energy. Anna was utterly confident that her situation was about to improve.

Sources differ as to when she first hired forty-year-old Jan Rubens, but sometime between the late fall of the preceding year and spring 1570, the former Antwerp lay judge - erudite and well-travelled - appeared in the princess's life. There is even the possibility that he was a familiar face. Jan had met the Prince of Orange during various legal negotiations in the mid-1560s, and perhaps Anna had been present or nearby during one of them. At any rate, she became quickly attached to the eminent jurist. As a fellow refugee, Jan could empathize with the plight of exile, and the two reminisced nostalgically about life in the Netherlands. Rubens's mother-in-law owned land near Breda, and while he evoked past days of glory, the lawyer also charmed a woman who was widely thought of as "uncharmable."

After a relatively short acquaintance, Anna began to lean on Jan in a wide range of matters. The princess and her dependents quit their apartments at John

---

[1]Putnam, *The Life of William the Silent*, p. 126. See also Karl Wolf. "Des Syndikus Dr. Fickard zu Frankfurt a. M. rechtliche Gutachten für den Prinzen Wilhelm von Oranien 1568 und 1570," in *Bijdragen voor Vaderlandsche Geschiednis en Oudheidskunde*, Ed. Dr. N. Japiske, VII Recks Deel IV (1934), pp. 236-40. As for the Nassaus, their Frankfurt lawyer, Monsieur Fickard, had recently rejected all of Anna's demands for additional payments and the requisition of the County of Diez, since Orange was neither dead nor exiled from German lands. In fact, Fickard enjoined Anna to show consideration for Orange's plight.
[2]Kruse, "Wilhelm von Oranien," p. 55.

Mohren's estate after owing him three months' worth of rent, and began to share a house with the Rubens family at the *Rinckenpfuhl* (Rincke's Pool) manor.[3] The estate's owner, the rich merchant Rinck, supported the Dutch opposition against Alba.[4] Anna leased several rooms, while the Rubenses inhabited a separate wing of the handsome mansion in the Cologne parish of St. Mauritius.[5]

Convinced of her new counsel's aptitude in law and business, Anna soon entrusted all her valuables, pertinent documents, and private papers to the advocate cum property manager. Observers noted that the former Antwerp lawyer was also a welcome regular at the princess's dining table and that barely a day went by without Anna sitting entranced in one of Rubens's business consultations. By the time she left Cologne to meet with the landgrave in May of 1570, unfavorable talk had already reached her sister-in-law, Maria of Nassau, Countess Berg. In a postscript to her brother John, Maria remarked, "The lay judge named "Rubens" is with her [Anna]. [This] will come to no good end." The countess did not dare expound on the matter any further, she informed him.[6] And yet her silence spoke volumes.

Why a pedantically rank-conscious person like Anna spent much of her time in the company of a commoner was a riddle that did not remain unsolved for long. Jan was known to be engaging and quick-witted, and although no likeness or description of his person has survived, good looks - which ran in the Rubens family - might have also played a part. Perhaps Anna was equally drawn to his force of character. After many meager months in Germany, she had come to the humbling realization that her fortunes depended on this man's dedication and commitment to her cause. She could no longer afford that liberally displayed attitude of aloof arrogance, especially since her lofty titles no longer corresponded with her scanty financial assets.

Before he was introduced to the Princess of Orange, Rubens already had a flourishing legal practice in Cologne. He enjoyed an excellent reputation as a solicitor, and his affluent clientele paid him small fortunes to litigate against the Spaniards. Although not of aristocratic extraction, Jan's family background was highly respectable. Anna might have told herself that during these tough times, there was nothing wrong in mingling with individuals of a lesser station. Not since her wedding nine years prior, did the princess invest so much effort to please.

From Jan's point of view, his connection with a person of the princess's stature was highly advantageous. While her financial situation left much to be desired, Anna outweighed her relative poverty with her quasi-royal title, a fabulous image enhancer for any ambitious advocate.[7] As Anna's personal attorney, confidant, and manager, he and his family stood to recapture their former place in society. And depending on the outcome of the war, his efforts to reclaim her confiscated holdings might eventually bear rich fruit too.[8]

Good fortune, complemented by hard work and diligence had so far guaranteed Jan Rubens's steep professional ascent, while caring parents of means

[3]Putnam, *Moderate Man*, p. 352.
[4]Goebel, p. 18.
[5]Ennen, p. 855.
[6]de Dijn, p. 59.
[7]de Dijn, p. 50.
[8]Nils Büttner. *Peter Paul Rubens* (Munich: C. H. Beck, 2007), pp. 8-9. After Jan Rubens appealed to the Alba administration for a return of Anna's confiscated lands, the "Council of Troubles" condemned him to eternal exile in absentia.

set the proper conditions. Born in March 1530 to Bartholomew Rubens and his wife, the beautiful Barbara Arents, Jan spent his privileged childhood in Antwerp wanting for nothing. His paternal descendants, affluent fur and leather traders, were mentioned in charters as far back as the fourteenth century. Sometime in the 1400s, the Rubens clan switched to the even more profitable business of medicine and spices. Jan's father Bartholomew specialized in healing herbs and other pharmaceutical paraphernalia and was allowed to carry the title "apothecary," an up-and-coming profession. In 1529 he married Barbara, daughter of a genteel family with expensive tastes.

Financially comfortable, the couple had their portrait painted by the well-known artist Jacob Claesz van Utrecht. The proud sitters are clad in their Sunday best, quietly reflecting the growing confidence of Antwerp's well-to-do patricians. In 1538, their bourgeois idyll was rudely interrupted when Bartholomew suddenly passed away of an unidentified illness. Barbara, still young and attractive, quickly secured another match with a spice trader and drug merchant, the widower Jan de Landmeter. A kind and loving stepfather to Barbara's only child, de Landmeter treated the boy like one of his own children, and bequeathed Jan an equal share of his property in his 1566 testament.

The merchant also encouraged Jan's love of learning, and like Orange's oldest son Philip William, young Rubens read at the prestigious University of Louvain, east of Antwerp. In later years, de Landmeter's wealth allowed the young man to study abroad, an expected requirement for members of the Netherlands' fortunate *jeunesse dorée*.[9] In 1550, after a stint in Pavia, Jan passed the bar exam in Rome. The newly minted doctor - a multi-lingual, well- trained academic - stood poised to dictate his legal trajectory.

*****

Despite their diverging backgrounds and careers, Jan Rubens and William of Orange were influenced by the same intellectual currents of the time. Both men passed their formative years in an environment where the terms "freedom," "open-mindedness" and "toleration" had begun to percolate through the minds of many educated Dutchmen. Sometimes called the "young wild ones," a growing number of Netherlanders belonging to this particular generation reveled in the greater openness of Renaissance humanism, a movement coupled with the rediscovery of the writings of antiquity that had allowed "man" to move into the center of individual consciousness, instead of only God. Humanist philosophers also promoted the burgeoning sciences and an incipient discussion regarding religious pluralism.[10] William considered freedom of worship a fundamental human right, while Catholic-born Jan seems to have dabbled in several different creeds before settling on Calvinism in its least stringent form.[11]

For both men, the 1550s were also a time of carefree hedonism, enjoyment of newfound wealth, and conspicuous consumption. Orange was showered with titles, honors, and moneys by the Habsburg Emperor Charles; Rubens spent most of his twenties travelling through Europe on an extended grand tour, free of family ties, and apparently rarely lacking money. He did not return to Antwerp until

---

[9]de Dijn, pp. 14-5.
[10]de Dijn, p. 17, p. 22.
[11]Wedgwood, p. 61.

1557.

By that time, political unease and religious tensions were already starting to becloud the buoyant atmosphere in the Low Countries. Philip II had acceded to his father's throne and the faraway kingdom of Spain with its Inquisition and unbending faith was portentously moving into the Netherlanders' field of vision. Liberals like Jan and William noticed with growing concern that the budding spirit of Dutch humanism was being stifled by reactionary proponents of the old faith, who championed the supremacy of Catholicism in its most unyielding version.

In 1558 authorities suspected Rubens of membership in a group of Anabaptists, a heavily persecuted religious minority, and only the testimonies of Catholic relatives and friends saved him from arrest.[12] William, on the other hand, played regular host to his stalwartly Lutheran family in Breda, and was slowly moving into the crosshairs of Cardinal Granvelle. Both men looked towards the future with disquiet, and in 1566 their paths crossed in Antwerp during interfaith discussions. They never met again, but their lives became painfully intertwined in a most unexpected manner.

*****

As if to mark the end of his youth and the beginning of more troubled times, Jan chose to settle down four years after his return to the Low Countries. In November 1561, the year of William's Leipzig nuptials, Jan married twenty-three-year-old Maria Pypelinckx, the second child of the tapestry manufacturer Hendrik Pypelinckx and his wife, Clara du Touion. By all accounts, Maria was an excellent parti. Her father, a shrewd business man, owned St. Arnold, an impressive mansion on Antwerp's *Meir* promenade in addition to many other properties. This *maison de maître* [mansion] - already worth a fortune in her parents' lifetime - later secured Maria an annual pension of six hundred gold crowns in rents, and was to stay in the family's possession until 1601.

Jan's bride was also assured of a sizeable inheritance, since her only brother had died early, and merely a sister, Susanna, remained. We do not know if the marriage was arranged or a love match, but relations between Jan and the merchant's daughter, whom he fondly called Maayken (little Marie), appeared quite affectionate. The couple decided to stay put in Antwerp, a center of sophistication and culture like few other places in Europe. The fortunate, the successful, and the courageous were all part of the city on the River Scheldt, and the ambitious Rubenses strove to take their place among them.[13] One dressed in fashionably Spanish black, displayed silver goblets in every room of the house, and employed a black servant among many others.

In May 1562 the city council of Antwerp elected Jan to the position of lay judge, a position that immediately heightened his public status and secured the family's standing in society. At the time, the city magistrate consisted of two mayors and sixteen judges selected from respected patrician families.[14] Jan's professional success was complemented by domestic happiness as Maria gave birth to four children in five years. Concerns about continued economic slowing af-

---

[12]Wedgwood, p. 61.
[13]de Dijn, p. 12, p. 21.
[14]Roosbroeck, "Schöffe," p. 60

ter decades of unstoppable boom gradually marred the family's private contentment. Stricter heresy laws deterred foreign merchants, and Jan and his colleagues
struggled to find creative ways to reconcile Dutch mercantile customs and usages
without offending the rigid Spanish. Like William, Jan Rubens was inexorably
moving towards a confrontation with the Catholic Habsburgs, especially when
the number of condemned heretics began to crowd his courtroom in ever greater
numbers.

At first, Antwerp's judges tried to counter Brussels' heresy directives
with delay tactics. Since a verdict of capital punishment required all judges to be
in session - which was rarely the case - the court conveniently prorogued unpop-
ular rulings. Ultimately, however, these adjournments were merely stopgaps that
failed to adequately address the fundamental reluctance of Dutch jurists to apply
foreign, meaning Spanish, laws in their chambers.

By the mid-1560s, life in the Low Countries had become poisoned by fear
and paranoia. Terrified burghers sent a city alderman to Madrid to renegotiate
the dispatching of a Spanish bishop to Antwerp. The prelate might strengthen
the heresy rulings to an unacceptable degree, they worried, and introduce the
Inquisition. Habsburg officials had already cast a widening net of government
agents across the country, who compiled lists of alleged anti-Catholic elements in
every town and village. A Spanish merchant in the employ of Philip II gathered
information on suspected Calvinists in Antwerp, and Jan was among them. The
report read, "The lay judge Jan Rubens spends a lot of time in the house of Mme.
Inquefort, a rich Calvinist."

There is reason to believe that Jan was at least peripherally involved in
the mounting opposition movement, for unlike the majority of his colleagues,
he was never invited to the regent's court. When the Duke of Alba swept into
Brussels in the late summer of 1567, an anxious Jan and his family started to ponder emigration. Shortly afterwards, Ruben's friend and fellow judge Antoon van
Stralen was arrested after being denounced as a Lutheran, and in May of the following year, after a thorough re-organization of the judiciary, Rubens's name was
not put up for re-election.[15] Rumors also circulated that the Alba administration
was preparing to put him on trial. Jan had either co-authored or signed a protest
declaration against the eradication of time-honored Burgundian privileges and
was subsequently blacklisted.

During that terrible summer of 1568, when van Stralen and the Counts
Egmont and Horn paid for their convictions with their lives, Maria and Jan joined
the long eastbound procession of refugees. Armed with certificates of good conduct issued by faithful associates in Antwerp's city council, they made their way
to Germany, into relative uncertainty.[16]

Like many educated Dutchmen, the Rubens family picked Cologne to
reignite their interrupted lives. A large, prosperous city, about half the size of Antwerp, Cologne generally impressed. Philip II had visited the metropolis in 1550,
and together with his retinue, was dazzled by its beauty and prosperity, "the
splendid countryside along the Rhine," and green cornfields stretching into the
distance. A major pilgrimage site because of the Shrine of the Three Kings (a rel-
iquary claiming to house the bones of the Three Wise Men) the city was teeming

---

[15]Büttner, p. 8.
[16]de Dijn, pp. 36-8; Also see Roosbroeck, "Schöffe," pp. 62-3.

year round with visitors. Clever street vendors sold vast quantities of "genuine" religious relics which were dutifully acquired by the more gullible pilgrims.[17]

For the Calvinist Rubens and his wife Maria, the rebuilding of a successful law practice weighed foremost on their minds as they approached Cologne from the west. With almost a thousand Dutch refugees already more or less settled within city walls, locals often looked askance at the steady stream of additional arrivals. The influx of so many newcomers had resulted in a sharp rise in food prices, and city fathers agonized about being unintentionally drawn into the Flemish conflict.

A staunchly Catholic town by tradition, Cologne's citizenry tolerated Lutherans, but was deeply opposed to the presence of Anabaptists and Calvinists. In 1567, the pious Herman von Weinsberg growled in his diary that "on March 16, a Sunday, a Calvinist minister from Bacharach" had preached openly on a field in the afternoon. The "heretic" had misinterpreted Holy Scripture in the most shocking manner and insulted the Catholic clergy. To Weinsberg's great chagrin, thousands of people had gathered and listened to the seditious sermon. Like many of his colleagues in the municipal assembly, he worried that "It might be here like in Brabant soon," and declared in a public speech that troublemakers should lose their civic rights.[18]

His concerns were not unfounded. Rome took a strong interest in the affairs of the metropolis on the lower Rhine and warned of radical elements seeking to subvert the city's Catholic character. Town gates should be closed to individuals threatening the faith of the populace, Pope Pius IV commanded, and instructed the mayoralty to act like "the good shepherd who protects [his] flock from the wolf." The Duke of Alba was equally emphatic on dangerous, heretical "infection" threatening Cologne. A citywide purge of non-Catholics would be advisable, he cautioned sharply, "if relations [with Brussels] were to remain neighborly and friendly. The King of Spain had noted with severe displeasure that Cologne was harboring enemies of the true faith."

Another issue was Orange's initial selection of Cologne as his operational headquarters and propaganda center until Alba exerted enough pressure on the town council to prevent it. New ordinances barred the prince's troops from entering through any of the city gates and prohibited Orangist purchases of munitions and provisions.[19]

City officials also ordered curfews, conducted house searches, and fined individuals for yelling out pro-Orange slogans like "Vive les Geux!" and "Here like in Brabant!" Informants reported on families who failed to attend mass and confession and refused to have their children baptized according to Roman tradition. Anna's first landlord, John Mohren, only narrowly evaded deportation after he had his brother-in-law buried according to Calvinist rites, outside the city walls. A secret report noted that Mohren had a funeral sermon read that "most shamelessly blasphemed the Catholic church."[20]

By 1570, Cologne's civil administration had come under so much pressure from the Spanish Habsburgs that certain refugees - usually troublemakers

---

[17]Kamen, p. 44.
[18]de Dijn, p. 46.
[19]Ennen, p. 835, p. 843.
[20]Ennen, p. 851, p. 856.

or the poor - were permanently expelled. Jesuits compiled lists of all new arrivals from Flanders as an additional precautionary measure, while city officials instructed landlords to inspect renters' good conduct certificates.[21] The Rubens family entered Cologne with the right kind of papers, including proof of Jan's Catholic faith, and initially took up lodgings across from the Romanesque basilica of St. Martin's. With a number of Flemish aristocrats like the Counts Herrenberg and Culenberg already resident in Cologne, Jan rebuilt his law practice with confidence. Most of his countrymen had left their property and valuables in the Netherlands and needed legal representation to reclaim them. Jan's business flourished accordingly. Within a few months, he made a name for himself as the elegant "Lord von Rubens" whose lodgings included a winter garden and a pretty courtyard.[22]

In May 1570, after almost two years of relative calm, Jan and Maria received official word that the family was no longer welcome in Cologne. The Duke of Alba had issued a decree ordering the deportation of all Netherlanders - Catholics included - and declared that Dutchmen were no longer free to attend foreign colleges, except those in Rome. Cologne University, which heavily depended on the tuition payments of its Flemish student body, feared its ruin.[23] As for Jan, a Jesuit communication accused the lawyer of suspected heresy because of his absence at Sunday mass. Rubens had been subpoenaed by the magistrate once before, but successfully refuted all charges. This time, there was reason for worry. With the governor of the Low Countries threatening to bring Orange's rebels to heel, the town council had already issued an extradition order.

Undaunted, Jan presented Cologne's city council with a carefully crafted address. He had been a prominent citizen in his hometown of Antwerp, a long serving lay judge of its magistrate, and arrived in Germany neither an outcast nor a refugee. He had settled in Cologne solely to set his legal affairs in order. This was not entirely untrue. Rubens had been neither sentenced nor condemned by Alba's "Blood Council." Moreover, Jan added, "Her Most Serene Highness, the Princess of Orange," had recently employed him as her personal counsel, while the princess's children, Anna and Maurice of Orange, were cared for by his wife Maria. Impressed by his lofty connections, Cologne's city fathers amended their previous ruling. The Rubenses were permitted to remain in Cologne as long as the lawyer provided authorities with proof of his Catholic faith by St. Michael's day.[24] Jan and Maria stayed, Anna moved into their home, and fate took its course.

*****

The princess's new abode in Cologne's city center was an estate of great architectural beauty near the market square. Established around 1473 by the Rink clan, a family of rich wholesalers and city officials, the *Rinkenhof* mansion at Rinkenpfuhl 24 consisted of three separate wings. Particularly impressive was the adjacent "Knight's Tower," a slim, octagonal edifice about one hundred feet high whose intricate stone friezes and dainty escutcheons reflected the social standing of the owners who had received a knighthood at the beginning of the sixteenth

---

[21]Roosbroeck, "Schoeffe," p. 63.
[22]de Dijn, p. 50.
[23]Ennen, p. 838.
[24]Roosbroeck, "Schoeffe," p. 63. See also de Dijn, p. 48.

century. The complex was only demolished in 1911, after its buildings had become irreparably run down and dilapidated.[25]

Unlike Dillenburg, Anna voiced no complaints about her reduced situation as tenant to a family of commoners, but settled in quite happily with the Rubenses. Jan vigorously pursued her claims with the Duke of Alba, and two of her uncles' envoys were on their way to Heidelberg to discuss her case with the emperor.[26] With her fortunes so clearly on the upswing, Anna no longer felt it necessary to meet with her battered spouse and answered pleas for a meeting with chilling contempt. In a reply to William's sister Maria, Anna wrote dismissively, "If the prince wants to see me so badly, he might betake himself to a place of my choosing; he knows only too well that he has left me without money and possessions, [and] during the nine years that I lived with him, I had daily cause for complaint. I am not a rented horse that follows the prince wherever he wants me to, and I have no intention of meeting him until I am granted the County of Diez. I know what steps to take in order to receive what is owed to me."[27]

Buoyed by Jan's support, Anna confidently assumed that her persistent appeals to her relations were finally bearing fruit. The elector and Landgrave William had at last agreed to meet her for discussions in Kassel, and Rubens - as her official attorney - was to accompany her. Although she required Jan for genuine legal advice, personal reasons also played a role in her decision. Sometime in March 1570, the princess and the lawyer had begun to exchange meaningful glances and "other signs of natural love." Rubens had kissed her, and while Anna had only given in under much blushing, she responded willingly. The princess later admitted that she reciprocated his advances not out of malice, but because she wished to repay him for his "pure friendship."[28]

---

[25]Goebel, p. 14; Ennen, p. 831.
[26]Kruse, "Wilhelm von Oranien," p. 59.
[27]deDijn, p. 58.
[28]Kruse, "Wilhelm von Oranien," p. 77.

The Secret Garden

Si non caste, tamen caute. [If you can't be chaste, be careful] Eleventh-century proverb

It was looks that started it all. Rubens later admitted that he and Anna began "to shoot glances and signaled each other with signs of love, but without going any farther than simple kisses."[1] The reasons for their attraction were surely complex, and cannot be re-construed without a certain amount of speculation.

For an ambitious individual like Jan, the princess's favor surely fueled his attraction. His family, while affluent, held no titles; Anna, on the other hand, belonged to the royal sphere of demigods. The force of his charm, appearance, and personality had gained him personal access to this almost mystical circle of majesty and when the princess responded to his initial overtures, the apothecary's son was filled with heady pride and exuberant disbelief. Surely, it was the excitement of the forbidden that imbued the incipient affair with additional, piquant frisson.

Vanity often accompanies love, and it probably figured into the attraction Monsieur Rubens felt for a woman who was generally considered unattractive in more respects than one.[2] Arrogance might have also played its part. So far, Jan's life had been pleasingly smooth; a comfortable ride that was only temporarily interrupted by exile and even then, quickly resumed its careerist track with few complications. Within months of his arrival in Cologne, Rubens's law practice was thriving, while a grand house stood at his disposal. Life, he might have figured overconfidently, had not been able to get the better of him.

As for his private affairs, perhaps the Rubenses marriage had grown a little stale after nine years, with both partners occupied with children or the business. The princess's interest, meanwhile, revived dormant feelings of lust and hunger for the new. It was a potent mixture of awed surprise, adventure seeking, and simple conceit that made Jan act against his better judgment.

As for Anna - that wayward, tormented, perpetually misunderstood soul - she found herself entirely smitten with her new savior. After many misguided searches for true companionship, the princess now shared confidences with someone who listened, comforted, and soothed without judgment. Jan offered "pure friendship," and not surprisingly, Anna quickly became a woman lost in amorous feelings. Perhaps an admiration for Rubens's professional successes played a role as well. Unlike her husband, Jan had rebuilt his life in Germany rather quickly and without much effort. An eloquent speaker and fast thinker, he provided handsomely for his wife and children. William, on the other hand, sent pennies and criticized her spending habits. In Anna's opinion, there was no question as to who was the better breadwinner.

That Orange's monumental struggle in the Low Countries hardly compared with the setting up of a barrister's office, apparently did not register in the princess's mind. Mired in her own circular logic, Anna imagined herself the forsaken widow, deeply wronged, and therefore freed from all wifely obligations. In a quiet moment of reflection, Anna must have realized that she was about to embark on a dangerous journey that could spell ruin and societal disgrace. William

---

[1]Kruse, "Rubens," p. 4. See also Putnam, *Moderate Man*, p. 362. In his confession, Rubens said: *"de dire qui fut le premier il faut bien presume que je n'auroie jamais eu la hardiesse d'approcher, si j'eusse eu crainte d'être refuse."* He claims that Anna approached him first, since he would have never possessed the boldness to do so, fearing her refusal.

[2]Martin Levy. *Love and Madness: The Murder of Martha Ray* (New York: Harper Collins, 2004), p.49.

was still alive, she was not officially divorced, and Jan was a married commoner. But there were few, if any of those moments, and Anna proceeded to gamble her life and honor away by giving into her feelings.

*****

The trip to Kassel gave Anna the opportunity to spend even more time with Jan, especially since the good-natured Maria Rubens had offered to look after the Orange children during her absence. Qualms about brazenly entrusting her son and daughter to her lover's unsuspecting wife did not figure into the princess's travel planning.[3] With her pronounced sense of entitlement, Anna probably found ready excuses for such selfishness. Her flirtation with Rubens, which so far had not evolved into a full-blown sexual relationship, was barely worth fussing about, she might have argued, blotting out any bothersome scruples.

On a day in May 1570, Anna and a small retinue, which included Jan, her banker Gerhard Koch, and some servants, set forth on their journey. From Cologne the party travelled east towards the city of Olpe, and then took a highway through the hilly Sauerland region towards Kassel where Landgrave William awaited them. A surviving letter by Rubens sheds some light on the visit. In addition to the landgrave, August of Saxony was also present during talks. He had not seen his niece since her wedding almost nine years earlier, and had just arrived from Dresden with a splendid entourage. It is unclear if the elector and landgrave led most of the negotiations with Jan as a mere observer, or if the attorney played an active part in the talks.

Whatever the case, the princess's long-desired mission proved successful, because she secured the promise of a regular income. Her uncles agreed on "a yearly, friendly allowance until God will turn things in a better direction." On the twenty-fifth of the month, the landgravial chamberlain disbursed an initial one thousand thalers to an exultant Anna. A day later she signed for the sum - a payment intended as a first installment - and quickly departed Kassel before either the landgrave or the elector could change his mind.[4]

Instead of returning to Cologne, the princess's party turned south towards Butzbach, near Frankfurt, where Anna had at last agreed to meet William again. Details of what transpired between the Oranges during their first meeting in two years (save for the Mannheim wedding) are scant. Much of their conversation apparently centered on William's financial situation, which was as dire as ever, as well as personal matters. Despite his wife's unkind letters and lack of support, the prince still hoped for reconciliation. Would she travel back with him to either Dillenburg or Siegen? he asked cautiously. To his surprise, Anna consented. A return to Dillenburg was still out of the question, she declared, but nearby Siegen was a possibility.[5] The prince was unaware that his wife's newfound graciousness was far from selfless, but part of a larger, surreptitious scheme.

After she had left her uncle's court in Kassel, the landgrave and the elector had agreed on a plan for the Oranges' future, which, although generous, inadvertently frustrated certain personal stratagems of Anna's. Her uncles determined that relocation to Erfurt in western Saxony would be in the bankrupt couple's

[3]Kaestner, Horst. "Peter Paul Rubens' Eltern in Köln und Siegen," *Heimatland,* Nr. 7, Jahrgang 2 (1927), p. 98.
[4]Kruse, "Rubens", p.4.
[5]Kruse, "Wilhelm von Oranien," p.72.

best interest. Landgrave William was particularly insistent on his niece leaving Cologne and the County of Nassau. Orange's sister Maria had apprised him of Anna's romantic entanglement with Rubens, and he was anxious to remove her from the lawyer's orbit.

The fallout from his sister Barbara's unfortunate "misstep" with her household manager was still fresh in the landgrave's mind, and although she was now safely married to the childlike Count of Waldeck, the family still smarted from Barbara's betrayal of the family's honor. Apprehensive about another, perhaps even greater scandal, Landgrave William dispatched a courier. He was to present Anna with a summons to Marburg, the residence of his younger brother Louis in western Hessen. She could prepare her final move to Erfurt from there, he instructed, and was not to return to Cologne at all. A second letter sent from Kassel a few weeks later carried the same frantic urgency. The princess must betake herself away from Cologne and nearby Siegen, the landgrave demanded, if the honor of the Houses of Wettin and Hessen was to be salvaged.[6]

Anna, of course, had no intention of transplanting herself to Erfurt, despite her anxious uncle's veiled warnings. Although part of Ernestine Saxony, the city was close to Elector August's domains, and she recoiled at the thought of her uncle's interference in her personal affairs.[7] Most importantly, a move from Cologne would permanently separate her from Jan Rubens, who had recently become her lover in the true sense of the word.

Anna thus continued on to Siegen, where she first ignored her uncle's communications, and finally sent an evasive reply on June 18. Of course she would like to obey him and journey to Marburg, the princess wrote obliquely, but she had no intention of uprooting her family until she received more information on the proposed new home in Erfurt. Especially, since her two children and household goods were still in Cologne with Maria Rubens. Due to a feverish illness that both she and the Prince of Orange had contracted, she was also prevented from travelling anywhere in the coming weeks. Could he be so good and to tell her when she was move to Saxony, and if a house had already been prepared?

The landgrave doubtlessly saw through Anna's feints, because he responded with another roundabout letter of caution. Fortunately she had not travelled to Cologne, he wrote, since that might anger the Saxon Elector and induce him to rescind her hard-won allowance. As to the house in Erfurt, the elector had contacted Count Schwarzburg, who possessed an estate there, "decked out with a garden, beds, and other items in the most convenient manner and so well furnished that it is fit for a prince." He, August, and Count John would cover all expenses for the little residence which was to have a staff of twenty-four personnel. The landgrave closed his missive with some words of pious encouragement. The princess should not take her difficult situation too much to heart and "carry her cross with Christian patience."[8]

But Anna was no longer willing to carry any crosses that, in her opinion, she had already borne well enough and for too long. She would remain in Siegen, ostensibly to keep her husband company while he was trying to shore up support for another Dutch campaign. The landgrave and the elector would simply have to wait for her decision until she gave them further notice.

---

[6]Kruse, "Rubens", p. 4.
[7]Kruse, "Wilhelm von Oranien," p. 73.
[8]Kruse, "Rubens", p. 4.

*****

Unbeknownst to William and the landgrave, Anna's early summer journey from Butzbach to Siegen had been as eventful as it was portentous. While the prince returned straightaway to Dillenburg, Anna and her entourage rode northwards to the city of Marburg, home of Landgrave Louis of Hessen, another maternal uncle of Anna's.[9] There she was to anticipate further instructions about future living arrangements for herself and William. Orange had specifically asked her to patiently stay put while awaiting her uncles' decision regarding a new domicile. But the princess, increasingly intoxicated by her lawyer's presence, refused to honor his wishes. Erfurt was over two hundred miles east of Cologne, and therefore too far removed from Rubens and the *Rinkenhof*. After clamoring for years to leave the detested *Westerwald* region, Anna now wanted nothing but return.

As her carriage inched north, the princess spent nervous hours searching for a credible pretext to leave Marburg. Otherwise, Anna realized with dread, she would have to say her good-byes to Jan, who was readying to return to Cologne. A domestic spat provided Anna with the much needed excuse to depart before her relations could finalize any changes of residence. The princess had quickly apprehended that neither her uncle nor his wife, Hedwig of Wurttemberg, intended to spend any time in her company. The landgrave had instructed his staff to tell Anna that he and his wife were away on business. Chatty maids eventually disclosed that their lordships were promenading in the castle grounds. Embarrassing scenes ensued with Anna exploiting the situation to the fullest. She shot off an indignant message to William, arguing that she was simply forced to leave Marburg. Indeed, she would rather beg or break a leg than stay in a house where she was not welcome. Her uncle's rudeness had provided the princess with the perfect opportunity to select a domicile of her own choosing.[10]

Anna slyly picked Siegen - about sixty miles south-east of Cologne - as her new home of choice. Although still in Nassau County, the city on the Sieg River was situated far enough away from her husband's troublesome family, but not too far for Jan Rubens to visit her.[11] Anna also calculated that her uncles would laud her decision to resume married life with William, and continue to pay her annuity - a tidy sum of five thousand thalers per annum.

Count John, meanwhile, agonized in Dillenburg. Perhaps he had been apprised of Anna's illicit liaison, because on June 3 he wrote to his trusted advisor Dr. Jacob Schwarz, urging him to appoint Hessian and Saxon officials for the Orange's estate in Erfurt and to hire a purveyor for her household goods. He was afraid that the princess might betake herself to Cologne again, and suggested another stay with the landgrave in Kassel until her Saxon manor had been readied.[12]

Anna, of course, paid as little attention to the count's instructions as she had to the landgrave's letters and departed Louis's residence after her cleverly displayed fit of pique. One of the first stops on the princess's journey was the small village of Ewersbach, twenty-six miles west of Marburg, on the border of

---

[9]The late Landgrave Philip's testament stipulated that the landgraviate was to be split among his four sons; Hessen, therefore, had four landgraves in 1570.
[10]Kruse, "Rubens", p. 4.
[11]Kruse, "Wilhelm von Oranien," pp. 70-3.
[12]Kruse, "Wilhelm von Oranien," p. 172. Marburg Archive: Nassau-Oranien, Kasseler Akten 1570/71, p. 764.

Nassau County and the Landgraviate of Hessen. Situated on the old Marburg-Cologne highway, the hamlet served as an overnight stop for pilgrims who, after worshipping at the shrine of St. Elizabeth's in Marburg, continued on to the Three Kings in Cologne.[13]

Anna's party arrived on the eve of June 15 after having negotiated narrow mountain paths and valley roads for much of the day. While the princess and her attendants were to spend the night in the *Amtshaus* (district manor) belonging to Count John, Jan planned to continue home on his own. However, the lovers decided that they could not part from each other just yet. Jan later confessed that in the sylvan loneliness of Ewersbach, amidst the rolling foothills of the Rothaargebirge Mountains, his feelings for Anna overwhelmed him. During this short spring night, in the romantic setting of deep forests, the unlikely twosome gave themselves to one another.[14] Rubens later recounted that "the dangerous fire of illicit affection had already been ignited ... and had, for the first time, at Ewersbach unfortunately turned into a highly punishable offense."[15]

Trembling with arousal and anticipation, "we approached each other and she said "be careful that you don't mess up the bed," Jan later acknowledged.[16] Apparently, Anna was still clear-headed enough to take some precautionary measures. She knew that her servants were hovering about, even in this isolated remoteness. Chambermaids and ladies-in-waiting usually slept close to their mistress, and would have noticed unusually disheveled bed sheets in the morning. Perhaps Jan tiptoed into her chamber after he assumed the household asleep after their long day of travel.

At the time, a lady's boudoir consisted of a grand bed with curtains and was connected to the adjoining presence or living room through a door that could be locked. Anna perhaps feigned illness and shooed her women away from her bedroom, citing the need for quiet and privacy. In Renaissance romance literature, the venue for a secretive tryst was oftentimes called "the secret garden," an enchanted spot, surrounded by a wall and filled with fragrant, blooming flowers reminiscent of the Garden of Eden.[17] During this momentous June night Anna and Jan, driven by an assortment of emotions, succumbed to each other in their own private Arcadia.

By no later than the next morning, the lovers came to realize that sex had carried their affair to another level not only in a personal, but also a legal sense. If their secret intrigue came to light, they would be branded and shamed as adulterers. Weeks and months of social ostracism and scandal could be followed by a possible death sentence. The jurist in Jan was doubtlessly aware that adultery was a capital offense in Nassau County as it was in many other states at the time. What had started out as mutual affection had taken on a hazardous dimension; an aspect that seemed to electrify the unlikely pair, despite the potentially dreadful consequences.

Boosted by sexual excitement, the delirium of genuine love or perhaps a combination of both, the adulterous duo decided that their star-crossed encoun-

---

[13]Kruse, p. 172. In 1552 William's father had escorted Anna's grandfather Philip to the Hessian border after his release from captivity in the Netherlands and said his good-byes to the landgrave in Ewersbach (also noted in Nebe, 'Chronik von Ebersbach,' *GesammelteZeitungsaufsätze*, Stadtarchiv Siegen).
[14]Kruse, "Wilhelm von Oranien,"p. 72.
[15]Böttcher, p. 247.
[16]Otto Riedel. "Die Rubens Affäre," *Heimatjahrbuch für das Land an der Dill*, No. 24 (1981), p. 183.
[17]Bastl, p. 415.

ter in Ewersbach was not to be the end of their affair. In the following months, Jan and Anna repeatedly met for additional, furtive assignations. Although their most intimate thoughts have gone unrecorded, we can construe possible sentimental impulses from the princess's behavior and later statements.

It seems that Anna had at last found some solace with Jan Rubens. The eccentric connected with the learned doctor who appeared to have her best interests in mind and put her first in his thoughts. Indeed, he even endangered his own life to please her. Such selflessness was a first in Anna's experience, making her revel in Jan's attentions.

The altogether loved-starved princess, who had been devouring romances since her teens, might have been influenced by a developing genre of prose that promoted desire and marriage between individuals of differing social ranks. The popular Alsatian writer Jörg Wickram (~1505–approx. 1558) was the most well-known advocate of love beyond class barriers. Seemingly hopeless amours ended in marital bliss, such as the story of the shepherd's son who conquered the heart of a countess and then went on to win the consent of her father. The noble lady's blood, that signifier of incomparable perfection, was neutralized by a suitor of equal virtue.

Like Anna, many of Wickram's characters were without parents, giving children greater control of their personal lives, unbound by familial obligations. Love simply struck at random as protagonists were hit by "Cupid's arrow" and therefore powerless to resist each other, despite opposition from friends, relatives, and petty courtiers. Interestingly, the novelist awarded women considerable room for action. Since they outranked their lovers, Wickram's ladies took the initiative in declaring their feelings first, and did so courageously, regardless of prevailing etiquette and even in the face of death.

It is obvious that this sort of storyline would have suited the impulsive Anna. She had not shied away from advertising her attraction for William nine years earlier, and now succumbed to her feelings for Rubens whom she regarded as her equivalent in love. Incidentally, the Almighty, via Wickram, regularly disposed of inconvenient husbands in order to bring struggling couples together.[18] In her current, infatuated mindset, Anna already imagined herself a widow who was no longer encumbered by the obligations of marriage or pangs of conscience.

If forgetting William came easy to Anna, Rubens's charm and personality might have kept her besotted. One of his children, the world-renowned painter Peter Paul Rubens, was noted for his spellbinding charisma, a veritable magic that drew people to the attractive man with the regular features, arresting eyes, and noble expression.[19] Like most people, the princess was receptive to attentions from a handsome individual, especially since her looks had always been described as lacking.

Rubens's motives in the affair remain largely obscure. He was intelligent enough to realize that meddling with Orange's wife was a foolhardy, if not suicidal caprice. Moreover, as the married father of four, wedlock with the exalted Anna was an absolute impossibility. At the age of forty Rubens was no longer a spirited young buck, but a mature professional who should have thought twice

---

[18]Jan-Dirk Müller. "Jörg Wickram zu Liebe und Ehre," *Wandel der Geschlechterbeziehungen zu Beginn der Neuzeit* (Frankfurt: Suhrkamp, 1991), pp. 27–36.
[19]Pletz-Krehahn, "Krankheit," p. 209.

about forfeiting his life and the well-being of his family for a sexual escapade. Anna's relations would violently defend their sullied honor if this affair came to light. Landgrave Philip had once declared that he wanted his daughter Barbara's married lover "taken by the head"and worse.[20]

Some histories describe Jan as a screwball character and adventurer, and perhaps there was a hidden, reckless side to his personality that the proper attorney could not always contain.[21] At the start of their acquaintance, Rubens's diligent assistance to Anna was purely professional, since helping his client would ultimately translate into a higher retainer and further his legal reputation. But why sleep with his noble patron? As mentioned before, Anna's aristocratic status may have magnetized Jan. Psychological studies have shown that men become more sexually active after receiving a promotion. Their potency is literally ignited by the increase in status and power.[22] Rubens, whose reputation soared among Cologne's upper crust after being hired as Anna's personal privy counselor, might have derived a similar sense of empowerment. As he wined and dined at the princess's table and began to share her bed, Jan lost sight of reality.

While he basked in his improbable role of lover to a royal, there seems to have been at least a sliver of unaffected feeling that pulled Jan inexorably towards Anna. He was not known as a ladies' man, and his marriage to Maria was generally considered happy. Still, he did not rein himself in after exchanging a few kisses, but took their affair a serious step further. Rubens deepened his growing bond with Anna in Ewersbach, because of his fondness for her.

*****

Displaying a new kind of wifely devotion in Siegen, an agreeable Anna passed the summer months with William in relative concord. For the first time in years, neither Saxon nor Hessen officials received angry letters nor damaging reports about the princess - a change for which Jan deserves credit. Anna was exhilarated by her secret intrigue which lifted her long-flagging spirits and kept her unpleasant side in check. Relief from financial worries also had a calming effect, and when payments started to arrive on a regular basis neither Rubens nor Anna saw the need for further appeals to the Spanish crown. In August 1570, when Anna of Austria - Philip of Spain's fourth wife - spent several days in Cologne on her way to Madrid, Jan did not approach her with a petition like so many others.[23]

Her mind no longer occupied with money and lawsuits, Anna's spent several weeks in Cologne in late summer, allegedly to settle her affairs and pay her staff that had gone unpaid for months. Afterwards, as she shepherded her children to Siegen, the princess tried to devise novel ways of rendezvousing with Rubens. For the time being, William and his relations appeared properly deceived by her farcical display of conjugal harmony. In fact, Count John was so pleasantly surprised by his sister-in-law's newfound serenity that he helped her settle in Siegen palace by providing furniture.[24] During the early fall of 1570, goodwill prevailed between Anna and the Nassaus, for the first and last time.

---

[20]Löwenstein, p. 423.
[21]*Kleine Geschichte*, p. 11.
[22]Annette Lawson. *Adultery* (New York: Basic Books, 1988), p. 303.
[23]Ennen, p. 838.
[24]Kruse, "Wilhelm von Oranien," pp. 74-5.

In September Anna sent off an insincere letter to William, Landgrave of Hessen. She no longer had any intention of moving to Erfurt, the princess wrote dishonestly, because life with her children and new household in Siegen was most satisfactory. Count John had applauded her decision to return from Cologne, and now she only requested that her allowance be sent to Dillenburg instead of Marburg or Erfurt.[25] Although small-town Siegen could not compete with Breda or Cologne and her new domicile was far from grand, Anna accepted her reduced circumstances with an astonishing, newfound equanimity.

Perched on the Siegberg, at an elevation of about one thousand feet, Siegen Castle looks out on seven hills lining the horizon. Other stately homes dotted the nearby uplands, but the Nassau stronghold dominated the area. Built in the early thirteenth century, the Counts of Nassau had once shared the castle with the archbishops of Cologne, but eventually moved their court and administration to Dillenburg, a day's ride to the southeast. After the death of her husband, William's mother Juliana often spent time in Siegen as the palace formed part of her widow's estate. At the time of Anna's arrival, however, the countess had become a fixture in Dillenburg as caretaker of her children and grandchildren.

Unfortunately, not much is known about the palace's Renaissance interior. A fire had destroyed large parts of the compound in 1503, and after extensive renovations, a staircase, a "Gothic Hall" as well as a great hall named *Oraniersaal* (Hall of Orange) were added. The castle had sixty-six rooms, each named after an animal.[26] By the early 1570s, the chambers were already quite threadbare with few pieces of furniture and no paintings or other ornaments remaining; ten years later not a single precious object was still in the possession of the family. Except for some incidentals, Count John had sold all of his valuables to assist his older brother's campaign in the Low Countries. Although tapestries still adorned the walls here and there, inventories mostly list basic bed and house wares. The linen closet boasted sixty tablecloths, but only a paltry twenty-three "good and bad" bed sheets.[27]

In addition to these economies, which could not have pleased Anna in the least, there were other aspects of her new living arrangements that must have irked the princess. Siegen's climate is similar to Dillenburg's, with plenty of overcast skies and rain, but little sunshine. In addition to dreary weather, Anna now inhabited a secluded castle which had been set apart from town by design. Connected to the city walls, but separated from the municipality by a belt-like grove, the estate's detachment served as a visual and physical reminder of the existing divide between the Lords of Nassau and their subjects. Until the late Middle Ages, even the local nobility was prohibited from residing within these hallowed grounds. Of course, the fortress housed gatekeepers, custodians, porters, stable boys, maids, and valets, but few other high ranking personnel who could have kept Anna company.

Geography also detached the princess from the goings-on in town.[28] If she wanted to venture into the city, Anna had to cross a small forest where the count's gamekeepers regularly caught rabbits and wildfowl for the princely table.

---

[25] Kruse, "Wilhelm von Oranien," p.74.
[26] Gerhard Scholl. "Von Burgen und Schlössern im Siegerland," *Siegerland zwischen gestern und morgen* (Landkreis Siegen: Kreisverwaltung Siegen, 1965), p. 29.
[27] *Kleine Geschichte*, pp. 11-4.
[28] *Kleine Geschichte*, p. 6, p. 11.

On her return, she had to clamber up a precipitous incline. Even today the ascent is quite steep, making one wonder how carters managed as they hauled Anna's heavily laden wagons into the courtyard.

With a population of about 2,200 souls, Siegen possessed nothing of Cologne's cosmopolitan infrastructure. Although Nassau County's most populous town boasted the urban requisites of walls, towers, and cobbled streets, there was no rich city life, and even the better-off patricians had to keep careful watch on their expenses. Bombastic displays of splendor in the form of gigantic churches, representative fountains, and luxurious burghers' residences were altogether unknown before the eighteenth and nineteenth centuries. Such miracles could only be seen in Cologne or Frankfurt.[29]

Like in Dillenburg, the local populace was generally poor and wary of outsiders. Malicious tongues claimed to know that "in the Sauerland (further north), the wall of the house exposed to weather is slated; here, in the Siegerland, the entire house is slated."[30] Nevertheless, Siegen's city fathers did their best to accommodate their exalted resident. By law, the town was obligated to cover certain expenses that the ruling family incurred such as meals and wine.[31] Anna, who was slowly falling back into her habit of heavy drinking, may have been the center of heated budget discussions among worried city council members.

Free wine or not, as the days were growing shorter, a bored Anna grew fed up with her new situation. She could not tolerate the hilly, verdant seclusion, and resented her inability to meet Rubens in private. Frustrated and skittish, her foul moods returned and she started to lash out at William and the help in the old manner. After an acrimonious exchange concerning the prince's Dutch war, Orange had enough. He withdrew to Dillenburg and did not return until Christmas. Left to her own devices, Anna briskly announced that she and her children would also travel - to more agreeable locales.

And indeed, the princess spent a fairly busy autumn running up bills and taking trips to various places such as Cologne, Frankfurt, Bad Ems, and Siegburg with Rubens as her shadow. It was not until the end of November that the itinerant Anna returned to Nassau County. According to Rubens's later testimony, he had spent much time with the princess, and the couple had engaged in sexual relations on various occasions. At the same time, William and Count John were no longer unaware of the princess's romantic entanglements.

According to a memorandum dating to March 1572, the lovers were far from discreet. One report read that "She carried out those conscious deeds in such an open manner that servants and several noble persons took notice."[32] Orange was informed, but decided to bide his time. He had Anna carefully observed; her correspondence read. If he wanted to obtain a divorce from his burdensome wife, the prince calculated astutely, he had to act with circumspection. Anna still had formidable connections in Saxony and Hessen, and any overhasty reaction could quickly derail plans that promised final release from his marital tortures. To soften the elector's anger and despite his precarious financial situation, William sent August - a hunting enthusiast - a pair of bloodhounds, three greyhounds, and a famous gamekeeper from England.[33]

[29]Bingener and Fouquet, p. 103.
[30]de Dijn, p. 75.
[31]*Kleine Geschichte*, p. 9.
[32]Kruse, "Wilhelm von Oranien," p. 94.
[33]Kruse, p. 171. Dresden Archive, Locat. 8510 (b) fol. 240, 246, 254.

Apparently, neither Anna nor Rubens noticed any of the Nassaus' informants lurking about, since their liaison continued quite unguarded. The pair was at least prudent enough to keep their correspondence limited to business matters. There was only one letter that Rubens signed with the innocuous "I kiss your hand."[34]

By Christmas, the princess sensed that something was afoot. Although William had come to Siegen for the holidays, he refused to visit her quarters or spend any time with her.[35] Outwardly, Anna feigned indignation at Orange's failure to pay his respects; inwardly, she trembled with fright, racking her brain what may or may not be known to her husband. She was not aware that in late December 1570, William was already laying plans for a separation and collecting information on property rights in case of divorce.

In the middle of January, the princess must have seen the proverbial writing on the wall, for she suddenly offered to renounce her dower in case of her husband's death. The Nassaus had taken care of her family for the last four years, despite their grave financial burdens, and she no longer wanted to encumber them with additional demands for assistance. Past demands for payments - 12,500 thalers annually - were no longer necessary.[36] As a sign of her sincerity and good will, Anna turned necessity into a virtue. For New Year's, she visited Dillenburg.[37]

*****

It was a long, hard winter in many respects. "From Christmas until January 20 and a few days after that it snowed. There was lots of snow like I've never seen it before in all my life, up to the knees and even the belt, but I was not that cold," the Cologne wine merchant and alderman Hermann von Weinsberg noted in his diary. In the countryside near Siegen, wolves struck terror into people's hearts. But there were more ominous portents presaging disaster. "On January 26 people saw three suns and a rainbow in Cologne and after that it snowed again for another three days," Weinsberg wrote anxiously. When the snow finally melted, the dikes broke and the entire countryside was under water.[38]

For Anna, who had grown up in a world where spirits and witches easily intersected with the sober tenets of Lutheranism, such omens foretold trouble. She was in a financial bind again after spending most of her uncles' allowance, and the next installment was not due until late spring. Her shortage of funds had forced her to task Rubens with the sale of some of her remaining diamond jewelry. Rubens had immediately established contact with the Antwerp merchant Caspar Kropf, but was still awaiting an offer.[39] Money, however, was a relatively minor worry, compared to the true catastrophe that Anna would unavoidably face. After the birth of five children, the princess certainly recognized the signs of pregnancy. Soon she would no longer be able to hide the fact that she was carrying Jan Ruben's child.

Anna's "condition" could not have remained unnoticed in the Siegen

[34]Kruse, "Wilhelm von Oranien," p. 78.
[35]Hans Kruse. "*Christine von Diez, die natürliche Tochter des Jan Rubens und der Prinzessin Anna von Sachsen, der Gemahlin Wilhelms I. von Oranien, und ihre Nachkömmlinge,*" Siegerland, Band 19, Heft 4 (1937), p. 135.
[36]Kirstin Bromberg. "Anna von Sachsen," *Auf den Spuren der Siegerinnen*, Band I (Siegen: Frauenrat der Universität-Gesamthochschule Siegen, 1996), p. 16.
[37]Kruse, "Wilhelm von Oranien," pp. 75-6.
[38]de Dijn, p. 50.
[39]de Dijn, p. 61.

women's quarters for long. Within households, mothers, maids, and daughters kept a sharp eye on each other's bodies. Prying servants were often the first witnesses to acts of infidelity and other improprieties, and watched carefully for any physical evidence indicating immodesty on their mistress's person.[40] A more affable employer might have inspired loyalty and discretion among the help, but Anna, puffed-up and rude, could not count on any favors from her staff.

It was a well-known fact that domestics were the perennial hindrance in one's almost futile quest for privacy, and no one, even royalty, managed to put a stop to menial snooping. Around 1618, a British lady of rank caustically recounted in her memoirs that "[Servants] will seek to know all that their master knows and observe all that he does and will harken diligently unto every word he speaks ... They will ponder thereupon and make what use they can, as it best pleases them, being furnished thereby to take what part they will with or against their master as may make most of it for their own advantage." Knowing that maids could be privy to intimate details, some ladies tried to minimize servile intrusion by speaking to friends and confidants in a foreign language.[41]

A pregnancy, unfortunately, was much harder to conceal. Sharp eyes around Anna took gleeful note of possible morning sickness, missed periods, and a thickening waistline. Besides, the Nassau brothers had been paying Anna's staff to provide them with compromising information since the fall. Hawk-eyed informers, who had infiltrated the errant princess's entourage, clandestinely recorded dates of furtive rendezvous, locations of trysts as well as tantalizing tales on the state of Anna's bed - a relatively easy task since the couple had settled into a thoughtless routine.

In such cases, devastating testimony by attendants usually told of disordered and discarded clothing, washerwomen noticed rumpled and stained sheets, and bribable valets overheard sounds of lovemaking - evidence that had undone many an unfaithful spouse.[42] With Anna's star so clearly on the descent, even her more high-minded courtiers concluded that allegiance to the princess no longer paid any dividends. By March 1571 the sum of their carelessness was closing in on Anna and Jan, reported by a cadre of spies that the princess had once called her help.

*****

On March 3 Rubens sent Anna a note about the imminent sale of her diamonds. The princess responded two days later with several letters, urging him to come to Siegen to discuss "business" in person. Jan took his leave of Maria, had his horse saddled, and ordered a manservant to accompany him. Unbeknownst to both, Rubens was not the only one who had read the princess's message. Upon crossing into Nassau County northwest of Siegen, the lawyer and his attendant were intercepted by a group of strangers who pulled Jan from his horse. Their leader, the local sheriff named John Braunfels, snarled, "You knave, you are the princess's lover, let yourself be arrested or you will die!" He then shouted at Jan's hapless escort, "And you are the pimp!"

---

[40]Gowing, p. 69.
[41]Linda Pollock. "Living on the Stage of the World: The Concept of Privacy among the Elite of early modern England," *Rethinking Social History* (Manchester: Manchester University Press, 1993), pp. 86-7.
[42]Jo Manning. *My Lady Scandalous* (New York: Simon & Schuster, 2005), p. 93.

By order of William's brother Count John, the startled men were taken into custody. After marching them along the Haincher Heights road, Braunfels conducted the captives to the isolated hamlet of Liebenscheid, a place of little consequence except for its ten fishponds that regularly replenished the count's dinner table.

The location had been carefully chosen. In addition to its remoteness in the Westerwald forest, the village possessed a sturdy hunting lodge where Rubens spent the next few days, locked away in its massive cellar. He was too well known to be detained at Siegen Castle, where news of his arrest would have spread and reached Anna immediately. Count John and William wanted to gauge the princess's reaction when her lover inevitably failed to appear. More importantly, in the event of a confession, it would be easier for Nassau officials to keep the captive's admissions a closely guarded secret away from town. And that in turn would give them a better hold over the princess.[43]

As Jan languished in rustic Liebenscheid, an overwrought, hysterical Anna agonized about her paramour's whereabouts. Tormented by foreboding, she sent several frantic messages to the *Rinkenhof* in Cologne. On March 11 the princess wrote, "I am at a loss, Rubens, since there has been no reply at all to the letters I have sent of which this one is the fourth. I see that my two couriers are still absent. I don't know what to think. I am greatly worried that something untoward has happened to you since there is treachery everywhere in the world." She hoped for her agent to return with "an answer the day after tomorrow." "You don't even have to send a note," she assured him, "since that would only detain the messenger whom I have ordered on his life to return here by Monday. May God keep you in his protection." Anna also included a postscript to Maria. "Mrs. Rubens, in case your husband is not at home, please let me know, your good friend, Anna of Saxony."[44]

In Cologne, Anna's desperate communications alarmed Maria Rubens. Terrified that Jan had been waylaid by bandits or highwaymen, she hurried her own runner to investigate her husband's whereabouts. Maria also posted an express to the princess, listing her concerns. Anna was to immediately apprise her of the latest news, she begged fearfully. On March 15 she had two additional couriers on the lookout for her missing spouse. Three anxious days later Mrs. Rubens received a devastating dispatch, informing her of Jan's imprisonment by Nassau authorities at a classified location.[45]

While his wife and lover spent days full of anguish, the miserable object of the women's mutual affections was "sharply" interrogated. Rubens twice confessed to protocol that "He had been in demand as the princess's private counsel on an almost daily basis, and had also traveled with her to Kassel," due to his professional duties. He explained further, "[I] did feel that she had taken a liking to me and have to concede that I was not opposed to it." "Matters evolved due to these daily interactions, while the cunning seduction of the devil unfortunately caused both of us to forget ourselves completely which brought God's current punishment on us." Rubens also admitted to having engaged in sexual relations with the princess about twelve to fourteen times.[46]

[43]Hans-Jürgen Pletz-Krehahn. *"Rubenskerker und Rubenszelle in Dillenburg,"* Heimatjahrbuch für das Land an der Dill, No. 24 (1981), pp. 187-8.
[44]Pletz-Krehahn, *Rubenskerker*, p. 186.
[45]Pletz-Krehahn, *Rubenskerker*, p. 186.
[46]Kruse, "Wilhelm von Oranien," p. 77.

As a jurist, Jan continued, he was keenly aware of adultery being a capital offense. He himself had presided over many such decisions and followed the letter of the law to the "t." Mercy could not take the place of justice. The roles were reversed now, Jan acknowledged, because he no longer judged, but was judged. Remorse had overtaken him and he was ready to atone for his and Anna's sins by offering up his life. He only asked to be granted one request: he did not want to be hung on the gallows like a common criminal, but executed by the sword in order to spare his "poor children eternal shame and disgrace."[47]

---

[47]Fellmann, pp. 39-40.

Downfall

What is left when honor is lost? - Publilius Syrus, Maxims, Roman mimographer (circa First century BC)

On March 19, Anna's master of the household announced the arrival of a visitor. Against all hope it wasn't Rubens or the long awaited messenger, but Dillenburg's dour superintendent and court preacher, Dr. Maximilian Mörlin. Responsible for the city's clerical administration, Dr. Mörlin had arrived in Dillenburg only the previous year, but had already gained a reputation for righteous combativeness. He had been raised in an academic, but impoverished family and actually apprenticed with a tailor before his parents' slowly improving financial situation allowed him to pursue theological studies. At the University of Wittenberg, Mörlin quickly became a particular favorite of Martin Luther's and served at several courts in Saxony before a falling-out with the Duke of Saxe-Weimar led him to Nassau County.[1]

Practically inclined, but religiously rigid, the severe theologian had been hand-picked by William and Count John to make Anna confess. In Mörlin's mind, the princess had most shamefully sullied the name of her husband and family and, as a Saxon princess, dishonored her native Lutheranism with sordid escapades. There were no excuses, mitigating circumstances or Christian mercy to be applied in such an abominable case, and Anna had most certainly forfeited the respect customarily owed to members of the Houses of Wettin or Nassau.

Mörlin's mentor, Dr. Luther, and the majority of Anna's contemporaries would have applauded the doctor's ceremonious belligerence. Adultery, especially by a female, was considered one of the gravest violations of God's law - a wife's ultimate betrayal of her spouse. St. Paul had considered illicit sex as grave a sin as murder and medieval theologians classified adultery the second most serious offense after heresy.

On Sundays, churchgoers were regularly treated to homilies recounting biblical chastisements of adulterers that resulted in the flood and the Egyptian plagues alongside various gruesome punishments meted out against sexual offenders in ancient Greece, Rome, and Egypt.[2] Civil authorities in the Renaissance were no less lenient. Penalties for unfaithfulness included heavy monetary fines, whipping, exile, and, in the worst case, the death penalty.[3] Public humiliation was also common. In some parts of France adulterers were led around town by their genitals.[4]

Although canon law proscribed the slaying of treacherous wives, Orange's master, Philip of Spain, had just issued an edict permitting injured husbands to dispose of their unfaithful consorts as they saw fit. Spanish law decreed that "If a married woman commits adultery, she and her adulterer shall both be at the mercy of the husband, and he may do with them as he wishes."[5] In Reformation Germany honor killings were not as common as in Spain, but views of unchaste women had certainly not softened since the Middle Ages. The Protestant

---

[1] Julius August Wagenmann. "Mörlin, Maximilian," *Allgemeine Deutsche Biographie,* Band 22 (Leipzig: Duncker & Humblot, 1885), p. 325.
[2] David M. Turner. *Fashioning Adultery* (Cambridge: Cambridge University Press, 2002), p. 57.
[3] Brundage, p. 60, p. 72, p. 520.
[4] Camille, p. 89.
[5] Georgina Dopico Black. *Perfect Wives, Other Women* (Durham, NC: Duke University Press, 2001), p. 114.

Reformation was known for its strong "moral character," especially in matters of marriage. Holy wedlock, according to Luther, was God's intended state for mankind and inseparably connected with reputation and social position. Adulterers like Rubens and Anna destroyed this sacred family bond and "aroused God's anger."[6] Many legal codes, including the criminal law of the Holy Roman Empire of 1532, the *Carolina Constitutio Criminalis*, defined adultery as a capital offense, although it was seldom enacted.

On a personal level, a woman's infidelity was the ultimate betrayal; in the greater community, men were warned, it sent society tottering towards dissolution. Martin Luther's language towards adulteresses was extremely harsh, irrespective of rank. He called a cheating wife a man's greatest sorrow, and when Mrs. Luther once asked him if a shoemaker had been justified in partially cutting off the nose of his wife's lover, the reformer responded, "I'm afraid I would've stabbed her."[7]

Luther would have censured Anna in a similar manner. She had destroyed her family and household with her illicit liaison, defiled her body and soul. Her honesty had been lost by sleeping with Rubens, while her other virtues congealed into "beautiful rottenness."[8] In popular lore, this "rottenness" of sexual unchastity left visible marks on a woman's body like scratches or other blemishes.[9] In Anna's case, it had left a rapidly swelling belly.

Despite being presented with evidence to the contrary, Anna decided to retreat into that kind of stubbornness that is often the refuge of the weak.[10] Pretending to be mortally offended by Dr. Mörlin's brusque manner, the princess fired off a seven-page justification to William, venting about the superintendent's presumptuousness while denying all charges against her. "Don't you know how the saying goes that a mean bird is one who shits in his own nest?" she railed. Mörlin was unfairly turning an honest woman into a whore and the prince into a cuckold.[11] Of course Rubens had perjured himself, she exclaimed. "If you fell into the hands of the Duke of Alba, which God forbid you do, you would confess that white were black. He cannot be blamed for what he said nor should my honor be tarnished, because unfair questions receive false answers."

Anna also refuted the testimonials of her servants who had by now been deposed by the superintendent. "You assert that you have witnesses of my faults in my servants. God in heaven! What falsehood it is to testify about something I never thought of! Anyone can see its falsity, for if I had so far forgotten myself, which God forbid, I think I would hardly have called in witnesses. Sometimes one admits into one's house beasts worse than dragons or lions," she added. "I would like to know the names of such witnesses. I could easily answer them. I have examined my conscience closely and find myself innocent of the sort of dishonor you accuse me of. My children should suffer no contempt on my account."[12]

Indeed, William better take care not to make this matter public. After all, her reputation and that of the House of Nassau were at stake. Also, it was surely unnecessary to have all knives taken from her. However great her desperation,

---

[6] Lyndal Roper. "'Wille und Ehre,'"*Wandel der Geschlechterbeziehungen zu Beginn der Neuzeit* (Frankfurt: Suhrkamp, 1991), pp. 182-3.
[7] Karant-Nunn and Wiesner-Hanks, p. 226.
[8] Fletcher, p. 109.
[9] Gowing, p. 31.
[10] Fraser, *Marie,* p. 88.
[11] Kruse, "Wilhelm von Oranien,"p. 78.
[12] Putnam, *The Life of William the Silent,* p. 129.

Anna promised, she would not lay hands on herself. She ended the letter with customary pathos. "I trust in God to release me [from my suffering] as he has done with the sainted Susanna and Daniel in the lion's den."[13]

Anna's protestations evaporated a short while later, despite heartfelt appeals to the Almighty and select saints. When Count John visited her in her chambers, a letter from Jan in hand, her resolve crumbled. In an admirable display of character and integrity, Rubens had explained the reasons for his confession in writing and urged his lover to do the same. He was ready to shoulder all responsibility for the affair and was willing to make amends by giving up his life. She was not to blame, he wrote generously, being so young and frail. He only asked of her to write him once more before his execution.

Desperately shaken, Anna replied and confessed.[14] "I was afraid that you would not own up to our missteps out of concern for me. Now I do not have to worry about your eternal soul. I also plan to beg my husband's forgiveness whom I have gravely insulted." She hoped that William, who by her own admission possessed an inborn goodness, would show mercy by letting Rubens return home to his wife and children.

The following day, on March 22, Anna addressed a letter to the prince. Unlike her previous epistolary attacks, this one was an exercise in contrition. "Although I am not worthy of joining your presence, I plead for your forgiveness and beg you not to let the children feel my great crime, but to always remain a good father to them." As promised, she also asked Orange to issue a pardon for the "poor prisoner" Rubens.

The princess concluded her entreaty with a peculiar request, a request that betrays a mind locked in trenchant bitterness as well as abject fear. "My greatest worry is that you will inform the elector and the electress of my faux pas." The Electress Anne was her "greatest adversary" and she did not want to grant her this triumph. Upon further reflection, Anna continued, she also realized that her relatives, particularly August, were the ones to blame for her misfortunes. After all, they had "miserably deserted her" when she had been marooned in Cologne. Anna's resentment towards her former Saxon guardians temporarily blotted out her concerns for her children, her spouse, and even her captive lover.

After assuaging her own guilt, Anna continued with a frantic appeal: "As to the elector, if he is to be told, I am lost. And I shall then ask no further grace than that I shall not have more trouble in this world as I hope soon to be in another. I implore you as earnestly as I can that this affair may not be brought to the elector's attention."[15] Regarding Rubens, whom she remembered towards the end of her plea, he was not to blame. "Men can't help themselves when one wants to do them a "favor", she asserted. In retrospect, she knew that she should have been more constant. If she could only take her "miserable body" out of this world, all problems would be solved.[16]

Long days and endless nights followed as Anna agonized under house arrest at Siegen Castle. In her waking hours, she oscillated between bitter regrets and impotent fury, a bundle of nerves. Knowing herself cornered, she wailed at

---

[13]Kruse, "Wilhelm von Oranien," p. 78..

[14]Putnam, *Moderate Man*, p. 362. According to Ruth Putnam, Anna's admission of guilt to Rubens fell into the wrong hands and was subsequently made known to William and his family.

[15]Putnam, *The Life of William the Silent*, p. 131.

[16]Kruse, "Wilhelm von Oranien," p. 79.

one point, "Ah, ah, Rubens, how could your liberal tongue have publicized our shame? I wouldn't have thought you capable of doing so. Perhaps it is all God's will." Holding others - that is, the Almighty or the Saxon uncle - responsible for her ill-starred liaison was of course easier than admitting any fault of hers, especially after Rubens's wife, Maria Pypelinckx, arrived in Siegen after finally hearing of her husband's arrest. Maria had looked so careworn that even the self-absorbed Anna felt ashamed at the distress of Rubens's "hausfrau."

In the meantime, a terrified Maria had left Cologne to plead with Count John for Jan's life, thinking that his execution was imminent.[17] The count, however, was in no mood to receive the wife of the man who had just turned his beloved older brother into a cuckold, impregnated his wretched sister-in-law, and stained the reputation of the House of Nassau. He curtly ordered her to return home until William had ruled on Jan's fate.[18] Maria Rubens dutifully departed Siegen, still in the dark about her husband's whereabouts.

After several days in Liebenscheid, Rubens was transferred to Dillenburg.[19] He either spent his first weeks in the notorious *Kappeskeller* (cabbage cellar), a cavernous well-cum-storage room where the Nassaus' cooks stocked vegetables and herbs, or in the fortress's official prison, the *Stockhaus*. Hewn into rock, the *Kappeskeller* was at the bottom of a funnel-shaped vault, accessible solely by ladder and twenty-eight feet below ground. If at all, Jan could have endured there for only a limited time; the insalubrious temperature and moisture levels spelled certain death for any long time detainee, and Rubens could not have composed the numerous defense petitions and elaborate letters of appeal under such tough conditions.[20] It is more likely that he was held in the *Stockhaus*, a small building within the palace grounds near the *Scharfe Eck* (sharp corner). Named for the stocks that encased the feet of delinquents, it is the only structure of the old castle complex that is still standing today.[21]

With the family's primary breadwinner in prison, Maria Rubens faced an uncertain future. Although she received an annuity from her parents' properties, it was apparently not enough to cover debts, rent, and household expenses of the well-appointed *Rinkenhof* mansion. Since Alba's regime of terror continued unabated, she was also barred from returning to Antwerp. Maria eventually appealed to her parents, but received a disappointing response. The Habsburg administration had confiscated most of their real estate, forcing the formerly affluent Pypelinckxes to leave Antwerp for the nearby town of Lier where they eked out a modest living. They were inconsolable about her situation, they replied apologetically, but could not send their daughter any money.

Maria must have informed Jan of her financial predicament, because in July 1571 he told her to sell their valuables. She should trade in the family's silver, he wrote, as well as the tapestries together with his legal, Greek, and theological books. The children were to live decently, he explained; they were still young and did not necessarily have to go to university. But Maria, perhaps uncomfortable with selling family heirlooms and still guardedly optimistic about the possibil-

[17] Kruse, "Wilhelm von Oranien,"p. 79.

[18] Kaestner, p. 99.

[19] Kruse, p. 172. On 26 April 1571 Rubens wrote Anna a quick note in French from Dillenburg prison. "Vostre Ex'cescait, qu'estant appellée par ses lettres datés du 5. Mars à Siegen, j'ayesté aresté sur le chemin et conduit icy prisonnier." If she received this message is unknown. Cited from the Royal Archives, Den Haag, O. p. 255.

[20] Kruse, "Wilhelm von Oranien," p. 172.

[21] Rubenskerker Pletz-Krehahn, pp. 197-9. *The Stockhaus* served as a youth hostel in the second half of the twentieth century.

ity of her husband's release, decided to keep the family's prized possessions.[22] Interestingly it was Anna, who might have saved the Rubenses from destitution during Jan's incarceration. Despite the delicate nature of the situation, Jan's wife and his lover remained in contact and exchanged messages throughout 1571. The princess even paid the couple's mortgage of 200 guilders.[23]

Although Rubens was not allowed visitors, he could write and accept letters from his wife. Together, the couple sought comfort in prayer. Jan found solace in Luther's sermons and interpretations of the Gospel of John, chapters 14 to 17; Maria was consoled by Psalm 130 *de profundis*.[24] While the Rubenses tried to rally their spirits through contemplation, Count John labored to contain the spreading of the scandal. He had just received a fervent letter from William, begging him to cover up his wife's shameful affair.[25] It was a futile effort. In Dillenburg as well as in Siegen Anna's liaison with a commoner had become the talk of the town; "It was no longer spoken of in secret, but openly at court."[26]

Tales of the shocking mesalliance also spread to neighboring principalities whose denizens felt it only right and necessary to weigh in with unsolicited advice. The Nassau brothers' younger sister Magdalena, Countess Hohenlohe, wondered smugly why John was helping the "knave [Rubens]." After all, John had never favored "such people." Like most of her family, the countess thought little of Anna and commented sharply, "I wish I could send her to her friend, the von Waldeck; that would be a just punishment. There's not going to be a good end to this, since she will not curb her maliciousness. Anna's villainous deeds are well known."[27]

Magdalena's "von Waldeck" allusion could have referred to Anna's aunt, Barbara, who, after giving birth to two illegitimate children had been forced into a marriage with the third son of the von Waldecks, the simple-minded Daniel. By this time, however, Barbara had recovered some of her lost status through prudent estate management and sober living. In all likelihood Magdalena was alluding to Anna-Maria von Schwarzburg-Blankenburg (1538-1583), wife of Count Samuel of Waldeck and Barbara's sister-in-law.

Like Anna and Barbara, Anna-Maria was a known troublemaker. Her indulgent husband had chosen to overlook various unidentified youthful hijinks, but after his relatively early death in January 1570, his family was no longer willing to countenance Anna-Maria's "unhealthy lifestyle." Letters in her possession pointed toward an adulterous love affair with a commoner, even before the count's passing. Magister Göbert Raben, strangely nicknamed "calf's head," had been the late count's personal secretary, and Anna-Maria's alleged paramour.

In the fall of that same year the unlikely couple secretly married which provoked a firestorm of outrage. In addition to the Waldecks, Anna's uncle Landgrave William immediately moved to nullify the match. He violently opposed the unequal union that tarnished the memory of Anna-Maria's first spouse, and, as the Waldeck's overlord, summoned Magister Raben to Kassel for "serious questioning." As in Rubens's case, the former secretary was thrown into prison. He spent twenty-eight months in confinement and was subsequently banned from

[22]de Dijn, p. 67.
[23]Böttcher, p. 206, p. 218.
[24]de Dijn, p. 67.
[25]Putnam, *Moderate Man*, p. 363.
[26]Kruse, "Christine", p. 135.
[27]Kruse, "Wilhelm von Oranien," pp. 78-9.

the Landgraviate of Hessen. His life ended tragically when a student stabbed him to death.

An even crueler fate awaited his highborn bride, for unlike Göbert, she was never set free. After years of house arrest in the Castle of Altenwildungen, her relatives had Anna-Maria transferred to the former convent of Höhenscheid where she was interned until her death in August 1583. Her two children were raised by relatives.[28] Incarceration and permanent separation from family - such was the fate that Anna's sister-in-law Magdalena had in mind for the Princess of Orange.

While her relations debated various forms of punishment, Anna implored Count John to bring about her lover's release. "The misstep caused by me" should not cost him his life, she begged in a slew of beseeching letters and requests for an interview.[29] She also sent apologetic notes to William, who was spending the year in Dillenburg. Like his brother, he also declined a visit. Orange was following political developments in France with cautious optimism and had no desire to deal with Anna whose betrayal had brought him such humiliation.

In recent months, William's younger brother Louis had established important connections at the Valois court in Paris with the help of Jeanne, Queen of Navarre. Jeanne, the headstrong teenager who many years ago had tried to defy her uncle by refusing to marry Willam of Cleves, had long grown into an even more headstrong woman and zealous Calvinist. Nominal ruler of the kingdom of Navarre, a small territory north of the Pyrenees, the queen was the acknowledged spiritual and political leader of the French Huguenot movement.[30] She had first met the Nassau brothers in 1568, during talks about the formation of an international Protestant coalition, and the intelligent, passionate Louis quickly became one of her closest confidants.[31] In a letter to a friend she enthused that "Count Louis de Nassau is the only one here of my party who supports me altogether; he sees as I do."[32]

Jeanne had eventually paved the way for Louis at the French court and the count carefully pleaded his case with King Charles IX, a Catholic with Huguenot sympathies. Wary of Spain's seemingly unstoppable rise to a Renaissance world power, Charles gave Louis a warm welcome in Paris and expressed his support of the Dutch struggle for liberation.[33] This was good news for William. He was hopeful that his brother's budding relations in France would ultimately translate into tangible military assistance, and tried to rally additional support from sympathetic backers in Germany and England.

With the prospect of valuable allies lending money and men to his cause, the breaking of the Rubens scandal could not have come at a more inopportune time for Orange. The sordid affair impugned his position, honor, and credibility as a gentleman. "Honor is not in the hand of who is honored, but in the hearts and opinions of other men," contemporary wisdom dictated, and William's inability to control Anna's passions imperiled his standing in society. Manhood required the domination of one's wife, and if the prince could not govern his womenfolk,

[28]Johann Adolph Theodor Ludwig Varnhagen, . *Grundlage der Waldeckischen Landes-und Regentengeschichte* (Arolsen: Verlag der Speyer'schen Buchhandlung, 1853), pp. 76-7.
[29]de Dijn, p. 68.
[30]Strage, *Women of Power* (San Diego: Harcourt Brace Jovanovich, 1976), p. 148.
[31]Roelker, p. 308, p. 351.
[32]Martha Walker Freer. *The Life of Jeanne d'Albret, Queen of Navarre* (London: Hurst and Blackett, 1855), p. 377.
[33]Roelker, p. 344.

he could hardly be trusted to lead and rule over others.[34]

Honor and reputation could only be saved if the Nassaus could quickly snuff out public embarrassment and idle rumors. This meant, in practical terms, that Anna and her lover had to be dealt with in a private action and without the involvement of regular courts. With dishonor removed from open view, the prince's good name could be restored, leaving his public facade relatively unblemished.[35] The whitewash also required the Nassaus to privately inform friendly houses about Anna's transgressions before wild tales could take on lives of their own. That, of course, included the Saxon court, despite Anna's fervent pleadings to keep her indiscretions a secret.

Informing Dresden was not something that came easy to William. Although he had wished to relay the details of the "calamity" in person, Orange wrote wearily on 5 June, he was aware that such a visit might not meet with the elector's approval, given his outlaw status. Therefore, he was sending his brother-in-law, Count Hohenlohe, as his personal emissary. As of late, Anna had become involved with a married Dutchman from Antwerp, repeatedly broken her marriage vows, and carried on her "criminal mischief" in such a free and open manner that not only her domestics, but "many strangers" were talking about it openly. Out of consideration for the princess's children and to spare the elector pain, he had kept the matter to himself. The whole affair, however, remained extremely delicate. No one had wanted to serve as his messenger, and even Hohenlohe showed hesitation.[36]

He was aware that August, "who had raised Anna like a daughter," would be distressed by the news, William continued apologetically. And yet the princess was acting so strangely and leading such an unchristian life that he no longer entertained any hopes for improvement. He added, "As a Christian, I have decided to forgive her." Although God had given him a heavy domestic cross to bear, "he was not looking for revenge." That being said, he simply could not consider reconciling with a woman who had committed the ultimate wifely sin of expecting another man's child. In regards to her upkeep, William concluded, he no longer considered himself responsible. He was, in any case, without money, but his brother John had kindly agreed to contribute to Anna's household expenses.[37] As to the poor children that had sprung from this marriage, they would not in the least be affected by the scandal.

*****

With William and John refusing to see her, Anna talked to few people as her pregnancy progressed. She was a pariah now, a fallen woman and egregious sinner who had violated God's law and shamed her family. As summer neared, the princess tried to make provisions for her lying-in; unlike previous births, this one was an occasion of sorrow, guilt, and humiliation. In mid-August, Anna appealed to her brother-in-law for money. She had been unable to properly prepare for the delivery and the baby's needs due to financial worries, she wrote. Lastly,

[34]Fletcher, p. 270.
[35] Arlette Farge. "The Honor and Secrecy of Families," *A History of Private Life, III: Passions of the Renaissance* (Cambridge, MA: Belknap Press, 1989), p. 590.
[36]Kruse, "Wilhelm von Oranien," pp. 96-7.
[37]Kruse, "Wilhelm von Oranien," p. 87, pp. 96-7.

she'd be greatly indebted to John if he could also send a female relation to see her through this extremely trying birth.

According to her pastor, Bernhard Bernhardi, Anna's requests remained unanswered. None of her Dillenburg in-laws, including the still sprightly Juliana, visited the princess in Siegen, and an anxious and restless Anna battled worries about Rubens as well as flagging spirits. If he could only be released before the Frankfurt fall fair, she fretted. Many Dutch merchants were scheduled to attend and request his services. With naïve concern, but still oblivious to the gravity of her situation, she wrote, "It would be horrible if he missed such an opportunity."[38]

On 22 August Anna prematurely delivered a healthy, but unwanted baby girl. Several days earlier, Rubens's conditions of imprisonment had been tightened (perhaps he was sent to the *Kappeskeller*) which had so upset the princess that she went into early labor. The agony of childbirth provided Anna with a much-needed outlet to vent her frustrations. She screamed, cursed, and accused, sometimes in the vilest manner. Bernhardi, who was present or nearby, did not dare tell the Nassaus what the princess had howled during those long, desperate hours. The child was christened without ceremony, and named Christine after Anna's maternal grandmother. She also received the surname "von Diez," the title of Anna's widow's estate.

Naturally, the birth has sparked endless questions and speculations about Christine's paternity that continued for decades, if not centuries. Years later, Anna's uncle Landgrave William challenged the child's fatherhood by spreading the rumor that no child of Orange's resembled him as much as Christine did. He also alleged that William had incriminated his troublesome wife in order to obtain a divorce, while Rubens was cowed into admitting an offense he never committed.

And yet the Rubenses' correspondence belies such arguments. On more than one occasion, Jan begged his wife's forgiveness for a severe wrongdoing which Mrs. Rubens readily granted. Besides, still extant sources allow the re-creation of a timeline. In May 1570 Orange met the princess in Butzbach and the couple shared quarters for the summer. The baby, then again, was not born until the following August. Since Anna spent most of the fall travelling, she could have only seen William during Christmas in Siegen, a time when the prince had her shadowed and was avoiding her company. And even if the Oranges had come together one final time in late December, an eight-month-old infant would hardly have survived the birth, given the lack of proper medical care at the time. Christine was most likely conceived in early November, perhaps during a furtive assignation with Rubens in Siegburg. Unfortunately, there are no definite portraits of Christine, and the two surviving likenesses can hardly serve as pictorial evidence affirming either William's or Rubens's paternity.[39] It is rather the Nassaus' treatment of Anna's youngest child in later years that further corroborates the charge of Jan being indeed the girl's father.

Anna, who had never shown much interest in her legitimate offspring, displayed even less willingness to pay attention to her baby daughter, the shameful product of her sin. According to witnesses, she never talked about Christine, and it is only because of testimony by the child's nurse and Anna's lady-in-wait-

---

[38]Kruse, "Wilhelm von Oranien," p. 82.
[39]Kruse, "Christine", p. 137.

ing, Dorothea Burgmann, that we know that the baby had been allowed to remain with her mother. While Dorothea bathed and cared for the newborn, a much-weakened Anna passed her days in fitful spasms of despair allowing her neither sleep nor rest. Unsettled to the point of derangement, she worried over Rubens's fate and if William would ever readmit her into his good graces.

Writing steadied her frayed nerves somewhat, and in the early fall Anna dispatched a number of rambling letters to Dillenburg whose tone alternated between deep remorse and harsh accusations. Orange had led such a free life in the Netherlands, she charged, it was no wonder she had also become infected with Dutch licentiousness. God knew there had been few happy days in her ten-year marriage. On the other hand, she knew herself to be a miserable creature, and was now appealing to his inborn kindness. In spite of everything, Anna added meekly, she had borne William beautiful children whose lives were hanging in the balance now.[40]

But it was the amiable Count John who remained the center of Anna's epistolary therapeutics. "I beg you, brother, that you will give me answers to all this, because I sit here so miserably between hope and fear," she clamored towards the end of the year. "I am in a more desperate state than the fear of hell." At the end of one particularly distraught message, she flattered him, writing "you are my only savior in this world." In her more rational hours, the princess appeared to acknowledge the count's honest decency, only to spew barrages of abuse during recurring episodes of blind anger.

When John maintained a persistent silence, Anna shifted her focus to Dr. Jacob Schwarz. A well-educated jurist, Schwarz had some influence over Count John and, unlike Dr. Mörlin, understood human frailty. Anna resolved to make him her new confidant and sounding board. In addition to a constant stream of "urgent messages," the princess pried the legal expert with gifts of pastries and exotic fruit from the Netherlands, expensive items that she somehow obtained from Cologne or Dutch merchants. In November 1571 she fawned, "I sent you three pomegranates and some apples and quinces."

Apparently, Anna recommended this alimentary approach to Rubens's despairing wife as well. Dr. Schwarz subsequently thanked Maria for a basket of "refreshments" that had helped him get over a recent bout with illness. Flooded with pleas, letters, and presents from two brokenhearted women, Schwarz spent a good deal of 1571 searching for a solution to this wretched affair—a solution that would gratify all parties and keep public embarrassment for the House of Nassau to a minimum.[41]

Although Dr. Schwarz assured Maria that he was assiduously working on her husband's behalf, Mrs. Rubens also personally rallied to her spouse's defense. Until now she had merely been known as the lawyer's wife, a housewife, and appendage of the eminent Cologne attorney. But when faced with Jan's arrest, Maria tapped into unknown personal reserves, transforming herself into a plucky individual undaunted by the glare of the public eye. Instead of wallowing in self-pity or lashing out with bitter rebukes, the saintly Maria stepped in the breach for a man whose lover was carrying his child, fully aware that he was almost certainly facing death. Adultery was a capital offense in Nassau County

[40]Kruse, "Wilhelm von Oranien," p. 82.
[41]Kruse, "Wilhelm von Oranien," p. 82.

and enforced in extreme cases. Court records show that two adulterers were beheaded in the village of Beilstein, south of Dillenburg, in 1593.[42] The Rubenses
had already lost their home once. Maria was hopeful that they would not lose it a
second time, and that there would still be a life for them, after the affair.[43]

The first task Maria set herself was to soothe frantic, depressed Jan with
words of encouragement and compassion. "Dear and beloved husband," she
wrote right after the scandal had broken, "the messenger we had sent returned
with a letter from you which gave me joy, because I see from it that you are satisfied with my forgiveness. I never thought you would have believed that there
would be any difficulty about that from me ... How could I have the heart to be
angry with you when you are facing such peril, when ... I would give my life to
save you? Be assured then that I have forgiven you completely. Let it please God
that this may suffice to set you free. We should soon have reason to rejoice."

In the second part of her missive, Maria rebuked Jan for his pessimism. "I
find nothing in your letter to console me, and it has broken my heart ... [that] you
have lost courage and speak as if you were on the point of death. One would think
that I desired your death since you ask me to accept it as penance. Alas, how you
hurt me by saying that. In truth, it passes my endurance. If there is no more pity,
where shall I find a refuge? Where must I seek it? I will ask it of heaven with tears
and cries." Towards the end of her communication she added humbly, "How
could I not forgive your misstep against me, since I sin so much myself and have
to pray daily? I would be much like the evil creditor in the Bible who was in such
need of forgiveness, but forced his brothers to pay him back to the last penny. Say
no more "your unworthy husband" because all is forgiven."[44]

Maria's uplifting words carried Rubens through the long winter of 1571-
72; the favorable prison conditions preserved his health. Except for a few painful
days in the draughty, subterranean *Kappeskeller*, Jan's detention had not been an
unbearable ordeal in a windowless dungeon. His cell only measured 8 x 11 feet
with a 7-foot ceiling, but in September Rubens informed his wife that he was doing well physically, and continued to hold up admirably through the winter. He
spent hours standing at the windows of the *Stockhaus*, looking down at the city
of Dillenburg and the Protestant church which lay below. Whoever designed the
small penitentiary had unintentionally provided inmates with a wonderful bird's
eye view of the town, but also cut them off from the castle's inhabitants since
none of the windows faced the courtyard. The lords of Nassau did not want kitch-
en boys and scullery maids ogling and chatting with their captives. Set directly
above the defensive wall of the outer part of the fortress, Rubens was conveniently disconnected from most human contact.

Books, writing, and contemplation were Jan's other diversions. From
time to time, he asked Count John for more candles so that "I may have a light in
the evening after supper for two or three hours in order to read and pray." His
request was granted. There is evidence that he might have also passed the overflowing hours painting. Recent renovations in the *Stockhaus* have unearthed walls
covered with animals, flowers, and Bible inscriptions that have been dated to
around 1575. It is impossible to prove if Jan was indeed the amateur sketcher who

---

[42]*Beilstein*, (Heimat und Verkehrsverein Beilstein, 1978), p. 52.
[43]de Dijn, p. 63.
[44]Christopher White. *Peter Paul Rubens* (New Haven, CT: Yale University Press, 1987), p. 2. See also Kaestner, p. 99.

colored the inner building in this rather primitive fashion, but it is conceivable. Maria once mentioned in a letter that her husband was not only an experienced lawyer, but was also well versed in the arts.

Occasionally, Rubens's days were brightened by the sight of his wife. Ninety-eight feet below his window ran a footpath from the church to the outer walls. In one of his entreaties to Count John, Jan begged permission for Maria to "come beyond the walls so that I can see her through the window" during her visits to Dillenburg.[45]

While she might have been allowed a glimpse of her husband, Count John continued to ignore Maria's pleas for Jan's release. In desperation, Madame Rubens approached William's mother, Juliana, who comforted her, but was also unable to make any headway with her son. As the months wore on without change, Maria's letters take on a twinge of anxiety. The Almighty was not answering her prayers and the children were missing their father. She groaned, "I hope that God will hear me, that they will spare us, that they will take pity on us; otherwise it is certain, that they will kill me together with you; I will die of a broken heart, because I could not bear to listen to the news of your death; no, my life would come to an immediate end."

"But the words of Her Grace [probably Juliana] that I have sent to you in another letter still give me some hope. My soul is united and tied to yours in such a manner that you cannot suffer without me suffering in the same manner." If all else failed, Maria told Jan, she would go against his wishes and confront Count John with copious fits of crying. "Oh, we don't demand justice, we only beg for mercy, mercy, and when we do not receive this, what else can we do?" she argued. "Oh heavenly and merciful Father, help us now! You do not want the death of the sinner, on the contrary, you want him to live and change his life. Pour clemency into the souls of these good lords whom we have offended so greatly that we will soon be released from these horrors; we have been suffering for such a long time!"[46]

While Jan and Maria hoped for some kind of speedy judicial resolution, Anna's relatives readied for talks about the princess's fate. She was still under virtual house arrest at Siegen Castle, and, according to her ladies, deteriorating mentally. Dr. Schwarz complained about Anna's interminable messages asking for Jan's release. Monsieur Rubens had a faithful wife and children to return to, she cried, and if he were to be executed, his entire family could call her a murderess. Of course, she was not to blame, but the Electress of Saxony, who bore the responsibility for her calamity. Luckily, she had a solution for her problems in mind.

In a long-winded and labored proposal addressed to the landgrave, the princess explained her newest schemes. Since she could no longer reside in her husband's lands, she had decided to move to Duisburg, forty-five miles north of Cologne. It was a "supposedly pleasant and healthy place" and she would be in no one's way there. In reality, it was not salubrious living that was on Anna's mind, but the fact that Duisburg was close to the Netherlands and had once been mentioned by Jan. Her suggestions were, as usual, accompanied by requests for money. She was aware that the Nassaus had no resources to spare, and there-

[45]Pletz-Krehahn, *Rubenskerker*, p. 199-200.
[46]Hermann Knackfuss. *Künstler-Monographien II: Rubens* (Leipzig: Verlag von Velhagen & Klasing, 1898), pp. 4-6.

fore wondered if the landgrave could appeal to one of her Saxon cousins about a certain sum still owed to her mother. The good-natured Dr. Schwarz eventually forwarded Anna's outlandish bids while visiting Kassel in December 1571.[47]

Anna's proposals raised eyebrows among the landgrave and the Saxon envoy von Berlepsch, who had just arrived from Dresden. "Although I am your good friend and relative," the landgrave responded gravely, "your moral lapse has greatly wounded my feelings." He supported the release of her lover, but was strongly opposed to the princess moving to Duisburg. With Anna's history of irresponsible behavior, this could hardly have come as a surprise. If she had only betaken herself to Erfurt as originally planned, he added, the "subsequent filth" would never have happened.

But there was another option if she really wanted to leave Siegen. He could recommend the charming village of Beilstein in the Westerwald forest as a possible future residence. Anna could settle there with friendly, reliable servants (no Dutch under any circumstances) selected by her husband. He and the elector would cover her expenses. In any case, the landgrave advised, "The good Lord is the best and most loyal helper." "And please," he directed in closing, "exercise patience and cease those unending cries for your lover's discharge. Such demands might give people the wrong impression."[48]

In conversations with others, the landgrave often wavered in his attitude towards Anna and occasionally defended his niece and the family honor by blaming William. "Instead of giving her good Christian books, which he considered depressing, the prince gave her the *Amadis de Gaule* and other reading matters about love. He also encouraged her to dance a gaillard instead of sewing and knitting and other such things which he claimed were expressions of courtoisie in the Netherlands." He pontificated further, "The prince only has himself to blame, because he turned a virtuous young lady, who was young and like other people made out of flesh and blood, into a dissolute wife."[49]

Written excuses of the kind were also conveniently put forward by August of Saxony. He had heard of his niece's "serious crime" (he prudently crossed out the word "adultery"), but did not feel in the least accountable.[50] William should remind himself that Anna had been raised in a God-fearing Dresden household and diligently trained in all female virtues. Orange had married "a well-bred maid" in Leipzig. The electress had admonished him to direct the princess along similar lines of Christian living as a married woman, but if that really happened was doubtful. Never in his life could he have foreseen that his niece would set such an "abominable example." After washing his hands of all responsibility, the elector promised to consult with the landgrave about what was to be done with his wayward former ward.[51]

Despite such professed nonchalance towards Orange, August was livid with rage. Internationally, Saxony had gained fame as the cradle of the Protestant Reformation, and under his own leadership the electorate was blossoming into the most powerful state within the Holy Roman Empire. August's authority was compounded by his position as the head of the Lutheran church in Saxon

[47]Kruse, "Wilhelm von Oranien," p. 81, pp. 85-6.
[48]Kruse, "Wilhelm von Oranien ,"pp. 85-6.
[49]Kaestner, p. 98.
[50]Kruse, p. 173. August of Saxony was already girding himself for an adultery charge against his niece which threatened to prevent him from reclaiming her dowry in case of divorce.
[51]Kruse, "Wilhelm von Oranien," p. 98.

lands, which meant that he and his relations - especially his womenfolk - were to live moral, Christian lives.[52] Anna's behavior threatened to embarrass the Wettins in no small measure, and the pious electress, whose father had introduced the new faith to Denmark, was mortified. Anna had brought shame on the house and desecrated the name of her late father, the great Elector Maurice, by bringing spurious bastard issue into the world. Besides smearing the reputation of her faith and kin, the degenerate princess had also offended her ancestors and the entire nobility.[53]

But even now she would not remain quiet. August had received disturbing reports about Anna's increasingly strange conduct in recent months. Although she had come to an agreement with Count John and Dr. Schwarz to keep herself "discreet and secluded" in exchange for maintenance payments, the princess had already reverted to her old "stubbornness."[54]

In March 1572 George von Scholley, an envoy of the landgrave's, visited Anna in Siegen. The princess's behavior was turning progressively erratic, the court in Kassel had been told, and Scholley was to investigate in person. The head of the kitchen, her personal cupbearer Jacques Charlier, as well as a trusted female servant named Margaret had plenty to say about their mistress: when she did not write letters to various relatives, she hectored and tormented her staff, respectful valets and maids, who had already fled in a panic to their lordships in Dillenburg.

On one occasion, they recounted, a silver spoon had gone missing and Anna accused a group of domestics of theft. She threatened them with beatings and the gallows, apparently a preferred bullying tactic. Other petty incidents sent soup bowls and pieces of firewood flying, leaving Anna's ladies ducking for cover. There was also her escalating alcohol consumption. Completely inebriated, the princess would have fallen into the fire on a recent evening, if her women had not pulled her back in time. Anna was so drunk that she could no longer stand on her feet, but had to be carried to bed by her menservants.

According to Jacques Charlier, the princess's increasingly wild imagination often got the better of her. For example, she claimed that Count John had an attempt made on her life. During military exercises outside the city walls, she had screamed that one of the count's men had taken potshots at her window. That evening the drunken princess had allegedly hidden a sharp letter opener in her sleeve in order to stab Count John in the neck during one of his visits.[55] Anna was also penniless, but brazenly insisted on a sizeable household. A person in such a quandary, Dr. Schwarz told Scholley, should live humbly and quietly, but instead the princess grows "more insensible and wild by the day. There is no fear of God and wine is used all the more. Would God improve her lot."

Yet the worst episode involved the above-mentioned Dutch cupbearer Jacques - a sad and outrageous incident that dissolved any remaining sympathies for Anna. Ready to serve his mistress either lunch or dinner, Jacques entered her chambers, two piping hot bowls in both hands and therefore unable to perform the customary obeisance of a deep bow. The ever imaginative Anna immediately interpreted this omission of Burgundian *courteoisie* as a slight to her noble person

---

[52] Frank-Lothar Kroll. "Vorwort," *Die Herrscher Sachsens* (Munich: Beck'sche Reihe, 2007), p. 8.
[53] Fletcher, p. 110; Bastl, p. 529. Being noble went hand in hand with virtuous behavior which included gratitude, a strong sense of family, loyalty, as well as consciousness of duty and responsibility – character traits that Anna generally lacked.
[54] Bromberg, p. 16.
[55] Böttcher, p. 224.

and went berserk. "Jacques, who am I," she yelled, "that you brazenly pass me by with the food, without paying your respects?" His explanation and apology no longer registered as Anna turned incandescent with rage. While stupefied ladies and footmen looked on in shock, the princess attacked her hapless attendant. She smacked Jacques so hard in the face that his nose and mouth started to bleed; then she ripped his smock apart, and threw bowls, knives, salt cellar, and bread at him. "I am going to kill your wife, that fat whore Johanna," she shouted, "and both of your children too."[56] Fearing for their safety, the Charliers, who had faithfully served the princess since December 1568, immediately left Siegen. Dr. Schwarz's brother Meffert, who related some of these shocking scenes, predicted that things "cannot end well" here and turned in his resignation. Anna was "driving with the devil," and was beyond help.[57]

If this litany of complaints was not enough for the elector to stomach, there was more aggravation. Anna continued to insult Count John, especially during her frenzied bouts of intoxication. William's brother had suborned Rubens into giving false testimony about Christine's paternity, Anna spluttered. The child's real father was the Prince of Orange, but he too had conspired against her. Such talk was exacerbated by gossip about the princess mixing with unsuitable company again. Her pastor Bernhard Bernhardi had become Anna's drinking companion and was allegedly lingering in her rooms past midnight.

Bernhardi was indeed a somewhat suspect individual.[58] Born in 1528, the son of a prominent preacher showed such intellectual promise as a young man that Orange's father paid for his higher education. William the Elder had awarded scholarships to more than twenty talented scholars from Nassau County who left home to study Lutheran theology at Wittenberg University in Saxony.[59] After the completion of his training and a stint at his father's Latin school in Siegen, Bernhardi was appointed superintendent and court preacher by Count William and moved to Dillenburg in the spring of 1555. According to some, however, there was a darker side to the studious, young cleric. Unlike his austere, puritanical brethren, Bernhardi was repeatedly accused of professional "irregularities" and drunkenness, conduct that he seemed unwilling or unable to control. His spectacular rise in church ranks thus came to a halt in 1569, when an exasperated Count John demoted him to the position of head pastor in Siegen.[60] Dr. Maximilian Mörlin, Anna's reviled interrogator, subsequently took over as the Nassaus' spiritual counsel.

Even after this public rebuke, Bernhardi continued to run into trouble. Described as confrontational and overly litigious, he ran afoul with a number of Siegen burghers who accused him of running an illegal wine and horse racket. Slanderous remarks about the princely family, carelessly hurled about, finally led to the minister's complete disgrace and eventual expulsion from Siegen in the mid-1570s. During Anna's house arrest, he was still lurking about, keeping the

---

[56] Hans-Jürgen Pletz-Krehahn. "Das Schicksal der Anna von Sachsen," *Heimatjahrbuch für das Land an der Dill*, No. 24 (1981), p.189.
[57] Kruse, "Wilhelm von Oranien," pp. 89-90, p. 92.
[58] Bernhard Bernhardi (1528-90/91) was the son of the Protestant theologian Johannes Bernhard(i)(around 1500-51) and Katharina Kraut, daughter of a Frankfurt fustian weaver. An early adherent of Martin Luther's, Johannes helped introduce the Reformation to Frankfurt. He was a radical defender of the new faith, and instigated the destruction of relics and altar pieces at Frankfurt Cathedral, compelling Luther to intervene. In 1544, Johannes found employment with Orange's father, William the Rich, who tasked him with the establishment of a Latin school which his son Bernhard attended.
[59] Becker, "Beiträge," p. 140.
[60] Schuppener, "Hatzfeld", p. 133.

shunned princess wine-fueled company.[61]

*****

After the surfacing of these detrimental reports in the summer of 1572, August of Saxony reached his, admittedly low, limits of toleration. He addressed a stern missive to the Landgrave of Hessen, commanding that Anna be "put away silently and without notice" and placed under the supervision of a select number of people. To punish her adulterous deeds and prevent future misbehavior, he also recommended lifelong incarceration. If need be, the elector continued, he was willing to house her at a convenient and secure location somewhere in Saxony.

The lily-livered landgrave responded about a week later. Anna deserved severe chastisement, he conceded, but her husband was to blame as well. Orange had spoken such careless words about dancing and the *Amadis de Gaule* during their wedding, instead of encouraging his wife to read Holy Scripture. "Your Grace has to take into consideration that gambling is allowed in the monastery when the abbot carries dice with him." The primary fault thus lay with the prince. He had persuaded Anna to adopt the loose mores and customs of the Netherlands and introduced her to the "vices of the flesh." Furthermore, it was a well-known fact that a "courtly" woman was preferred to an honest one in the Low Countries, and those who rejected these fast fashions were disparaged and called country bumpkins.[62]

Besides, her parents' blessed memory forbade any excessive punishment, Landgrave William continued. Anna was a person of noble rank and neither he nor the elector possessed the legal authority to detain her without imperial permission. Other electors and princes had treaded very lightly in such cases, and if the scandal reached the emperor's ears, their humiliation would be complete. With word spreading throughout the empire, Anna's children stood to partake in their mother's disgrace. One should not give up hope for betterment, he wrote insincerely, "From the bottom of my heart ... I want to help her, if not for her father's sake."[63]

An inconvenient woman could, in regular circumstances, indeed not be locked away for life without proper justification. Sixteenth-century German law regarded women as minors, but females were free to appeal to local authorities or even the imperial court — the empire's equivalent of a supreme court — for a hearing. Founded in 1495 by German princes and other dignitaries, the imperial court was itinerant for the first thirty-five years of its existence, sitting in no fewer than ten cities before finally becoming more or less stationary in Augsburg around 1530. In civil cases, the court held jurisdiction over complaints against governing persons; that is, Anna could litigate against Count John. It also possessed appellate authority over the rulings of territorial courts, like the Nassaus' in Siegen.[64]

Even a morally compromised individual like Anna was permitted to seek redress from perceived injustices. A few decades before the Orange scandal erupted, a plucky and resourceful mayor's daughter from the southern German city of

[61]Manfred Fay. *Anna von Sachsen-Kurzgeschichte* (Elsterwerda), pp. 1-2.
[62]Kruse, "Wilhelm von Oranien", p. 98
[63]Kruse, "Wilhelm von Oranien", p. 99.
[64]Ozment, *Daughter*, p. 109.

Schwäbisch Hall had sued her relatives for embezzlement and wrongful imprisonment in a lengthy legal battle. Miss Anna Büschler charged that her father had unlawfully chained her to a kitchen table for six months, while her siblings cheated her out of her rightful inheritance. In addition, she accused Schwäbisch Hall's town council for illegal arrest and detention without due cause.

Like the Princess of Orange, the feisty Miss Büschler was no docile maiden. In her youth, she conducted simultaneous affairs with a local nobleman and a soldier, and stole alcohol from her father's wine cellar - misdeeds that led to the kitchen table restraint. Yet despite her reputation as the town's enfant terrible, Anna Büschler received an impartial judicial hearing when she appealed to Germany's highest court. Imperial authorities subsequently ruled that Miss Büschler had suffered an unrequited wrong at her father's hands and also acknowledged that the local city council had unlawfully imprisoned her in 1544. Schwäbisch Hall was not a legal island, the emperor's judges painfully reminded the municipal assembly, but an entity subject to the overriding powers of imperial statutes. The ruling validated the female plaintiff's pursuit of justice, and although her inheritance issues were never satisfactorily resolved, nobody ever dared to lay hands on Schwäbisch Hall's female malcontent again.[65]

Litigation was of course an option that the Princess of Orange also carefully considered. Anna's Aunt Sidonia had recently approached the imperial courts and Emperor Maximilian II for help, with the express approval of her brother, Elector August. The duchess had been languishing under house arrest since 1565, when Duke Eric refused her demands for a divorce. While Sidonia's family - particularly the image-conscious August - had initially opposed her legal forays, the elector finally stopped wavering after Sidonia's detention was still not relaxed after four years of virtual imprisonment. His sister was to petition the emperor for a resolution, August instructed, while he would personally contact his friend Maximilian.

As in Anna Büschler's lawsuit, Sidonia's complaints were duly noted. Emperor Maximilian shot off a thunderous reprimand to Duke Eric, chiding the neglectful treatment of his wife, the sale of her valuables, and his consorting with "suspicious women in a vicious, bothersome, indecent manner ... that has already spawned illegitimate fruit." Unless the duke wanted to risk his severest displeasure, the emperor warned, Eric better return to his long-suffering spouse or at least grant her the use of an estate.[66]

In 1572, after the duke accused Sidonia and some of her ladies of witchcraft yet again, Maximilian subpoenaed Eric, together with the unfortunate women, to Vienna.[67] A princess like Sidonia, the emperor argued, was simply above a poisoning attempt due to her noble birth, while the witchery claim was preposterous. Malfeasance of that sort was limited to commoners, specifically members of the lowest orders. The duchess knew she could breathe easier again.

*****

August of Saxony had used his lofty connections to help his hard-pressed sister; he could also do the reverse. It had taken him years to finally bestir himself

[65]Ozment, *Daughter*, p. 169, p. 187.
[66]Lilienthal, p. 224, pp. 226-8.
[67]Lilienthal, pp. 233-5.

into action on Sidonia's behalf, and only because she was married to a ruffian who had crossed certain bounds of acceptable behavior. Not only that, the duchess had led a blameless married life, devoid of even a hint of amorous scandal. The same could certainly not be said of his wayward niece, and August intended to intercede on the Wettin's behalf if Anna ever managed to attract the attention of the imperial court. The emperor had a penchant for weakening its jurisdiction by overruling verdicts on behalf of favored clients. In other words, if Anna managed to obtain a judgment that contravened the elector's wishes, Maximilian was sure to overturn it.[68]

The princess, meanwhile, refused to stay quiet. William had broken his marriage vows long before she did, neglected her for years, and pursued ruinous adventures in the Netherlands, much like Duke Eric. After being informed of her uncles' plans to move her to a new location, the princess confidently sounded off about approaching the empire's judges who were currently residing in Speyer near Heidelberg. "There," she asserted, "learned people will pursue justice on my behalf."[69] It is unclear how much Anna knew about the latest developments in Sidonia's case, but she was surely aware of her aunt's earlier, successful appeal to Vienna which had become a cause celebre before the Princess of Orange had lost her good name.

*****

In July 1572 August brushed off any of the landgrave's suggestions for leniency in a letter written from Güstrow, near the Baltic Sea. Anna was guilty of a "great wrongdoing" and deserved harsh punishment, especially since there was no hope for improvement. Everyone knew that "she would hardly leave other vices alone." As for requesting the emperor's permission to detain her, that was certainly unnecessary. His Imperial Highness usually gave free rein to his electors and princes as far as their efforts of "good housekeeping" were concerned. "Old German honor" must be upheld, August postulated gravely. As he had twice suggested before, the princess should be shut away somewhere secret, preferably with a preacher as sole company. Perhaps then, he argued, she would realize the enormity of her sins and display proper contrition. If the landgrave failed to see eye to eye with him, August threatened, he would cut all ties with Hessen, and no longer concern himself with any business pertaining to his niece.

Landgrave William promptly caved, intimidated by his powerful cousin and neighbor. By all means, the elector should choose the stricter route, since Anna hailed from Saxony. He did, however, feel very sorry for his poor relation, William added in a timid, but two-faced side note.[70] Only a few weeks earlier, in June, the landgrave had dashed off a few patronizing lines to Dr. Schwarz in response to the Nassaus' suggestion to put up Anna somewhere near Kassel. Pious incantations notwithstanding, the Hessian prince had coldly declared, "As to the princess, that we should invite her to live with us in our land and our court, that does not sit well with me. Talk someone else into this design with your sharp

[68]Ozment, *Daughter*, p. 109.
[69]Kruse, "Wilhelm von Oranien," p. 114.
[70]Kruse, "Wilhelm von Oranien," p. 100. On 9 July 1572, Elector August to the Landgrave of Hessen. Dresden Archive: Locat. 9942 (b), fol. 21-24.

wittedness, but not me!"[71]

*****

If incarceration for bad judgment and moral lapses seems cruel and un-usual to us - particularly as there was no true crime to speak of in our understand-ing - it was a commonly applied punishment in the Renaissance. Families general-ly intervened to silence or neutralize wrongdoers who threatened the honor of the house by willful disobedience. Honor had long been considered a vital good that was almost as essential as life itself, and defended by all means available. "A loss of property or patrimony is always repairable in one way or another, but never a loss of honor in life," a contemporary saying went.[72] In seventeenth-century France, a young adult who engaged in behavior detrimental to family interest could be imprisoned for a cautionary period under a so-called *lettre de cachet*. It was hoped that during detention, he - or sometimes she - would return to their senses.[73]

A number of noble houses had family members held in remand for much smaller infractions than Anna's. At the time, the mere questioning of the parental choice of marriage partner or religious vocation sufficed to warrant internment, and some surviving prison records make for heartbreaking reading. One young gentleman said he would consent to the marriage his father desired; another agreed to become a monk as his family wished. Despite the authorities' willing-ness to release them, their relations ultimately refused to take them back, even though both young men were prepared to submit to any decision made on their behalf. Their honor could again be compromised by future escapades, their fam-ilies claimed, making it preferable to let their offspring languish behind bars. In view of the abundance of such records, the degree to which families accepted the detention of one of their members as a means of preserving honor and secrecy, and compensated for any challenge to their authority, is truly remarkable.[74]

Leaving our modern sensibilities aside, however, societal pressures and entrenched concepts of honor virtually forced dynasties like the Wettins to re-pudiate a troublemaker like the Princess of Orange. The enormity of the scandal caused by her adulterous liaison and subsequent pregnancy cannot be overstated, and Anna threatened to do additional damage to the reputations of all concerned parties by tumultuous judicial action.[75] Instead of a public hearing, which could have exposed her relations to ridicule and embarrassment, the elector decided on a family tribunal consisting of the landgrave, the Nassaus, and himself. The ruling on Anna's preventive custody was to take place in strictest privacy.[76]

Anna's relations were certainly familiar with such proceedings, since the internment of a disobedient brother, uncle or wife in the name of honor was hardly unprecedented. Duke William III of Saxony (1425-1482) banished his consort, the Habsburg princess Anna, to the isolated Eckartsburg castle near the Thuringian border after an embarrassing public quarrel concerning dowry payments. Rem-

---

[71]Kruse, "Rubens", p. 4.
[72]Farge, p. 579.
[73]Hufton, p. 102.
[74]Farge, p. 593.
[75]In the Middle Ages and Renaissance, ladies of Anna's rank rarely committed adultery resulting in pregnancy due to the egregious social stigma attached to female infidelity.
[76]Farge, p. 590, pp. 592-3, pp. 603-4.

iniscent of Duke Eric's treatment of his wife Sidonia, he then permanently installed his mistress, the comely widow Catherine von Brandenstein, at his court.
Anna made one last effort to reconcile with her estranged husband by appearing
unannounced at his doorstep, only to have a shoe thrown in her face. She died a
few years later under house arrest, only thirty years old.[77]

Compared to the Austrian princess's "mouthiness," Anna of Saxony's
adultery was a far more serious matter, and therefore less likely to be pardoned
by her husband and family. William, for one, also wanted his errant wife discarded, because his political fortunes appeared on the upswing. After a two-year wait
in Germany, the situation in the Netherlands had progressed to such an extent
that he was preparing for another summer invasion. On 1 April 1572, a group
of England-based Calvinist exiles known as the *Gueux de Mer* (Sea Beggars) had
seized the Flemish port of Den Briel, thus creating a strategic base for William's
followers inside enemy territory.[78] Although the Duke of Alba felt confident in
another quick victory over the rebels, his attempts to collect a new tax—the so-
called 10th penny—aroused such fierce opposition that many Dutch towns decided to collaborate with the Orangists. In May, Mons opened its gates to a small
army led by Louis of Nassau, while additional contingents, aided by French Huguenots, invaded other provinces.[79] To retain his rising momentum, the prince
could not be hampered by domestic scandal.

As a man faced with the living evidence of his wife's infidelity, William
found his honor challenged to the extreme. Anna had put the so-called "cuckold's
horns" on him, an indignity that threatened to destroy his standing in society.[80]
The common image of the cuckolded husband was one of humiliation and degra-
dation, and satirical literature stigmatized him as an incomplete male who could
not adequately service his wife in the bedroom, in one instance "eight times less
than another man." Townsfolk regularly made sport of "horned husbands" by
affixing animal horns or antlers to their front doors, while plays and ballads likened cuckolds to "passive beasts, either complacent or stupidly unaware of their
spouses' infidelities." In other words, unless William took swift and determined
action to restore his good name, he risked becoming the butt of tavern jokes.[81]
Painfully aware of the scandal's ramifications, Orange did just that by agreeing to
the elector's proposed detention of his wife.

*****

With William wrapping himself in silence, Anna began to crumble under
the weight of depression and fear about her lover's fate. In February 1572 she

---

[77] Joseph Chmel and Karl Friedrich Wilhelm Lanz. *Monumenta habsburgica*, Vol. 1 (Vienna: Kaiserliche Hof und Staatsdruckerei, 1854), p. 80.
[78] The Sea Beggars were led by William II de la Marck, Lord of Lumey, and his two captains Willem Bloys van Treslong and Lenaert Jansz de Graeff. After their expulsion from England by Elizabeth I, de la Marck's 25 ships searched for shelter and found the Den Briel garrison undefended since the Spaniards were dealing with unrest in Utrecht. The event sparked the famous rhyme, "Op 1 april verloorAlva zijn bril" (on April 1st Alba lost his glasses), a pun alluding to the fact that 'Briel' sounds like 'bril' which is Dutch for 'glasses.'
[79] Kamen, p. 140. See also Putnam, *Moderate Man*, pp. 296-7. Louis was the heart and soul of the war of liberation according to contemporary chroniclers like the Frenchman Brantôme. He adopted the motto, "Nunc aut nunquam, recuperare aut mori" (Now or never, reclaim or die").
[80] Manning, p. 63. This highly insulting term is derived from the Middle English *cukeweld* or *cokewold*, which was in turn adapted from the old French *cucuault* and has been in use for some eight hundred years. The word in modern French, *cocu*, is also the name of the European cuckoo, a bird that lays its eggs in the nests of other birds for them to raise. It implied that men unknowingly brought up children like Christine, the spurious result of an adulterous, wifely liaison. A cuckold is often depicted as wearing horns, and giving a man "the horns"—pointing at him with all the fingers of the hand turned in except for the little and the index digits—is widely recognized in European culture as referring to the sexual conquest of his spouse and the impugning of his potency.
[81] Turner, p. 85, pp. 87-8, p. 94.

wrote, "I don't think the Turk or the Tartar torment a poor woman in the way I have been harassed here." She was willing to forgo a lengthy trial, which would have attracted publicity but also exposed William's infidelities, if only Jan was released. Maria and Rubens's brother Philip had already sworn off open legal proceedings in order to spare the Nassaus further humiliation.

In May, Anna made three additional attempts to contact William, hoping against all odds that reconciliation was still a possibility. If he refused to take her back, she asked, could she then move to either Cologne, Duisburg, or Wesel—or any other city close to the Netherlands from where she could keep track of Orange's political affairs? And could he please visit? She was feeling somewhat feebleminded of late. When an answer failed to materialize, Anna shot off a wrathful, final goodbye to her once beloved spouse.

"My death will surely be miserable, but all the happier, because I will be released from that tyrannical husband and relative of mine. I'd rather my body be buried under the gallows, and outside this land full of enemies." She also reserved vengeful last words for her Saxon uncle. "Alas, alas, I will have to complain into eternity that I followed the advice of the elector and wed myself to your Lordship, because that is the reason that I have lost my body, soul, honor, and possessions." Her future, she announced, would be spent fighting for her release from Siegen as well as Rubens's discharge from jail. Besides, she could no longer fill her mind with Christian thoughts. Even the flowers in the fields of this accursed land had turned against her and betrayed her.[82]

As spring turned into early summer, Anna's despondency and "feeblemindedness" did not vanish with the June sun. Her maid-of-honor, Madame Risor, quit her services and the princess was overcome by such fits of anger that she lashed out at the one person still kindly disposed towards her: Dr. Schwarz.[83] Frazzled and confused, she called him "a traitor, villain, and a rogue" in a conversation with his brother Meffert and accused him of embezzlement. The upstanding doctor angrily denied the charge which, in any case, no one took seriously.

Then the last of her ladies, the loyal Dorothea Burgmann from Saxony, considered resigning. The agitated princess, Madame Burgmann wrote to Count John, had recently threatened to jump out of the window and wanted to cut her own head off. With her mind ever more clouded, her mistress also accused the servants of "wanting to suck her blood and [claimed] that Your Grace and Landgrave William thirsted for her blood as well." No longer willing to endure such harassment, Dorothea asked the Nassaus to look for a replacement.[84]

*****

At the end of summer, Anna's Hessian and Saxon uncles finally discussed her future after interminable weeks of high-minded moralizing. Both recoiled at the thought of hosting Anna in their respective domains for reasons of prestige, and instead proposed to deposit the princess in Beilstein, a small hamlet on the southeastern corner of the formidable *Westerwald* forest.[85] The Nassaus owned

---

[82]Kruse, "Wilhelm von Oranien," p. 94.
[83]Kruse,"Wilhelm von Oranien,"p. 173. Madame Risor might have been the wife of one of Orange's Dutch commanders, Charles van der Noot, Seigneur de Risor.
[84]Kruse, "Wilhelm von Oranien," p. 93.
[85]Knöfel, *Heiratspolitik*, p. 137.

a small castle there, half a mile from a lonely highway, and isolated enough to thwart any escape attempts. Dr. Schwarz posited, perhaps somewhat unconvincingly, that it was a healthy place with plenty of fresh air; the elector opined that his niece would enjoy safe, but "princely custody."[86] The landgrave, who had long laid his conscience and other concerns to rest, was in full agreement. Anna's actions had been her own undoing, since she had "forgotten God and followed the devil."

"We ... advised her to show due respect to her husband who was not forced upon her, but whom she took voluntarily. We warned her of light, foreign customs ... and to hold on fast to praiseworthy German manners, and ... to be very chary of strangers in her own apartments," the landgrave wrote. "Had she followed these counsels, she would not be under so heavy a cloud now."[87] Together with the Nassaus, he and the elector had agreed that Anna was to leave for Beilstein before the onset of winter. Cold weather arrived earlier in the *Westerwald* than in other parts of Germany, and the roads had to be passable for her baggage train. At her new abode, with a stern preacher by her side, William's disgraced wife would have plenty of time to reflect on her egregious moral failings.[88]

At first, the news of her impending resettlement seemed to please Anna. In September 1572 she politely thanked envoys from Kassel and Dillenburg for finally moving her to a better place and quickly gathered her personal belongings. Life in Siegen had been hellish of late, the princess claimed, and if she was not permitted to go to Duisburg as requested, perhaps Beilstein would herald fresh beginnings. She sorely needed to start anew, especially after signing a document by which she had consented to a separation from William. Afterwards, she took mournful stock of her marriage and distilled her life's tribulations to one essential element, "There I was, the daughter of the greatest lord that was in Germany ... and now I find myself poor and miserable. Yes, my suffering is so great that I can hope for nothing else but the beggar's staff."[89]

Her days and nights had been filled with torrents of tears and entreaties to Dr. Schwarz, Anna informed her uncle's emissaries. She doubted that her friends had the right to treat her in this fashion, and William's refusal to pay for her upkeep and his plans for divorce weighed particularly heavy on her. It was all quite unfair. Indeed, the prince should remind himself of the times when he cavorted with "a maiden in a white skirt during a banquet ... and other such actions," actions that she could recount before a court of law if necessary. Yes, Orange resembled the unjust moneylender in the Bible who had been released from a considerable debt, but would not do the same for his employee who owed only a small amount, Anna indignantly told Dr. Schwarz, while shaking with rage about "this great disappointment."[90]

*****

Anna's logical questioning of the accepted double standard addressed an issue debated by a small number of Renaissance moralists, while ignored by the

[86]Ulbricht, p. 160.
[87]Putnam, *The Life of William the Silent,* pp. 131-2.
[88]Kruse, "Wilhelm von Oranien," p. 96, pp. 101-2.
[89]de Dijn, p. 71.
[90]Kruse, "Wilhelm von Oranien," p. 88.

majority of thinkers, clergy, and the nobility for its simple, but uncomfortable obviousness. Baldassare Castiglione, author of the aforementioned advice manual *The Book of the Courtier*, had opened up a philosophical discussion on the subject that echoed Anna's sentiments. "We ourselves, as men, have made it a rule that a dissolute way of life is not to be thought of as evil or blameworthy or disgraceful, whereas in women it leads to such complete opprobrium and shame that once a woman is spoken ill of, whether the accusation be true or false, she's utterly disgraced forever," he wrote. "If you wish to be truthful, you must recognize that we [men] have granted ourselves the license by which we want the same sins that are trivial and sometimes even praiseworthy when committed by men to be so damnable in women that they cannot be punished enough, save by a shameful death or at least everlasting infamy."[91]

The Italian writer asked his fellow men, "Is her lapse so grave that the poor creature doesn't at least deserve the mercy that is often shown even to murderers, thieves, assassins and traitors?"[92] The German humanist Albrecht von Eyb (1420-1475) and the Hungarian Matthew Corvinus (1443-1490) posed similar queries. "If your wife becomes unchaste and breaks faith with you, consider whether you have also been unfaithful to her; those husbands are completely unfair judges who demand that their wives be chaste, while they are not, and excuse their own promiscuity with fine words, while severely damaging and punishing that of their wives, as if it were right for them to have every freedom and their wives no faults at all," von Eyb criticized. Nor did Corvinus mince words in his moral instructions to Saxon noblemen: "The Bible teaches that a man should leave father and mother and cleave to his wife; it does not say that he should cleave to other men's wives, but only to his own."[93]

Such theoretical musings between smatterings of thinkers unfortunately remained just that, and naturally failed to influence ingrained sexual patterns. Promiscuity among male elites had been an unalienable prerogative since time immemorial, and even the Protestant Reformation with its emphasis on "family values" was not going to change that. Sexual dalliances with women of all classes, especially servant girls, were part of aristocratic gallantry and often regarded as a measure of true manhood.

For women, of course, adultery remained the gravest of sins for centuries to come, and Anna's affair served as a cautionary example why this was so. If not for William's vigilance, his wife could have passed off her illegitimate issue as Orange's progeny, leading to a dilution and pollution of the Nassaus' noble bloodline. In order to prevent further scandals of the kind, Anna had to be permanently removed from society - for her own good as well as that of her family.

*****

With the departure date for Beilstein fast approaching, the princess found herself beset by doubts as to the suitability of her new home. She had trouble sleeping and fussed the nights away with worry. The thirty-mile journey would endanger her life as she was feeling very weak of late, Anna informed Count

---

[91]Castiglione, p. 195, p. 142.
[92]Castiglione, pp. 254-5.
[93]Ozment, *Fathers*, pp. 55-6.

John's privy counselors. Instead of Beilstein, she would prefer to live with friends, and even a pigsty would do for a house. When she was mockingly told that the pigsty was indeed a possibility, the princess fell quiet.

One late September night Anna beckoned Dorothea for help. The loyal Madame Burgmann had decided to continue in her mistress's service, despite grave misgivings. "I need some simple clothes," Anna begged, explaining that she was about to escape to Cologne. Disguised as a commoner, she would make her way on foot to Cologne, with the help of a local courier named Neunfinger, whom she intended to pay 500 thalers. When her frightened attendant warned her of the consequences, the princess stated correctly that the Elector of Saxony held no jurisdiction in the imperial city. Dorothea, however, demurred, clearly loath to take part in this risky enterprise and not at all willing to offend Count John. Anna then promised Dorothea and her husband 3500 thalers if the latter would spirit her away to Cologne. When the servant refused again, listing concerns about the Nassaus, Anna screamed, "I do not care about the count," and then beat the lady maid and her husband, Monsieur Burgmann, with fists and a piece of wood. Indeed, she cared as much for Count John, "that little man" ("*dat menchin*") as she snidely called him, as "for a fart" ("*ob ein furtzs*").[94]

The following days were unbearable for everyone, especially the Burgmanns. The couple had carefully kept Anna's promissory note, surely to profit from it in the future, and when the princess demanded the document's return, more ugly scenes ensued. In the event, the city of Siegen now controlled all persons entering or leaving through its gates in order to prevent a possible escape attempt of Anna's.[95]

According to Dorothea, the princess spent most of her time reading unsuitable French books and prattled on about imaginary love affairs which she expected her lady-in-waiting to arrange. Dorothea, naturally, declined. Bored and despondent, Anna also indulged in late night binge drinking, resulting in hangovers and oversleeping. "Sometimes she gets up at four o'clock in the afternoon," Madame Burgmann sighed, "other times at two or at noon." The princess had also tried to make good on throwing herself out of the window, but was stopped at the last minute. Another disagreement erupted between the princess and Dorothea when Mr. Burgmann refused to forward a letter of Anna's to the Duke of Alba. She was ill-kept and imprisoned, Anna rambled in a non sequitur of that missive, and Alba needed to send her money and an envoy.[96]

---

[94]Pletz-Krehahn, "Schicksal,"p. 190. See also Kruse, "Wilhelm von Oranien," pp. 104-5.
[95]Böttcher, p. 238.
[96]Kruse, "Wilhelm von Oranien," pp. 105-6.

A Teenage and Possible Adult Portrait of Christine von Diez

Beilstein

J'ai un ciel de desir, un monde de tristesse. (I have a heaven of desire, a world of sadness)
Marguerite de Valois (1553 - 1615)

From 27 September 1572 until the end of the month, a penal court in Nassau County debated Anna's culpability and fate. Six men ultimately declared her guilty of adultery in a closed session and without the accused present. There was no room for negotiation, Anna was curtly told. On the last day of September, Count John's officials ordered the princess to gather her incidentals, since her carriage was to depart in the first hours of the following morning. Fall was coming quickly; temperatures had already dropped precipitously in the preceding weeks and soon the roads into the uplands would be difficult to negotiate. Discussions about Anna's relocation took up 70 folio pages and were signed by Count John and the Saxon counselors von Berlepsch, Schenck, and von Kram.[1]

In regards to provisions, the princess was not to worry. There was enough fodder for the horses, and Count John was supplying Beilstein manor with "two cart loads of good table wine, eight cart loads of beer, wheat and grain, four hundred chicken, over two hundred pounds of fish, 188 cart loads of fire wood, dishes, tableware, bedding, and linens." The estate also possessed hunting grounds for rabbits, a fishpond, and a garden, in case Anna required additional sustenance. As befit her station, her personal needs would be seen to by a pastor, a master of the household and his wife, a lady-in-waiting, a nanny for baby Christine, maidservants, doormen, kitchen scribes, a cook, a kitchen boy, a gatekeeper, and a woodcutter. John of Nassau — despite his precarious finances — had shown himself generous and paid for a third of the costs.[2]

On 1 October, three carters arrived at Siegen Castle to pull the possessions of the repudiated princess past Dillenburg towards the *Westerwald* forest. Anna traveled in a coach provided by her sister-in-law, Elizabeth of Leuchtenberg, while Count John, together with a group of Saxon and Hessian dignitaries, accompanied her on horseback. New household personnel, picked out and hired by her Uncle William, had arrived from Kassel a few days prior. They journeyed in a larger conveyance, supplied by the landgrave.

The heavily laden wagons and pack horses foundered when the princely party left the main highway near Herborn and turned into a derelict country road. Beyond the village of Driedorf, a winding path forged through sloping terraces as Anna and company lumbered past innumerable greyish basalt columns that dotted the landscape. They reached their destination, Beilstein Castle, after about eight to ten hours of arduous travel with Anna completely exhausted and in the lowest of spirits.

The princess's new home was a sparsely populated hamlet amid bleak surroundings. Twenty-nine miserable houses, thatched with straw and steep gables, huddled below the fortified manor, one of the most insignificant and remote Nassau outposts perched on a rock outcrop next to the Ulmbach stream. William's ancestors had used the twelfth century castle as a defensive station and gradually expanded it. During Anna's time in residence, the fortification was a

[1]Böttcher, p. 249.
[2]de Dijn, p. 73.

sprawling, if charmless complex of grey towers and stone buildings.

An anonymous author once claimed that Beilstein was located in "a valley between jolly mountains," but Anna found the desolate countryside deeply
depressing. At an elevation of almost twelve hundred feet, the settlement was
exposed to the rough climate of the *High Westerwald* forest and only occasionally
received mild air from the nearby Lahn valley.[3] Incensed that a daughter of Saxony should be subjected to such undignified living, Anna gave her escort a proper
earful. She was an innocent woman unfairly banished, the princess shot off in a
verbal fusillade that soon deteriorated into vulgarities about her relations.

Count John and his advisers remained unfazed. If she failed to pull herself together, they threatened, the Nassaus would inform the elector about her
recent flight attempt and foolish letter to the Duke of Alba. Such senseless fuss
"would only wake the sleeping dog" (August) and she knew what that meant.
She had better behave or face permanent immurement as the elector proposed.
Besides, Rubens had confessed his sins and was now awaiting his fate with Christian resignation and patience. Anna replied with a laugh. Jan had lied like a traitorous villain, and "Since his neck was itching [for the noose], she wished that he
be cured of that itch right soon."[4]

After Anna had sufficiently collected herself, Beilstein's major domo acquainted her with the manor. She was given use of half of the castle; the other
being taken up by military equipment. The interior of the princess's wing boasted a number of tapestries depicting scenes from history and mythology. There
was also a small library with roughly one hundred books, among them a volume
about tournaments as well as the *Sachsenspiegel* (The Saxon Mirror), one of the
most famous German law codes. The great hall had been refurbished not too long
ago and sported various coats of arms amid painted rose garlands, while the in-
house chapel was ornamented with tiling showing biblical scenes. Of less interest
to Anna was the armory. Some of its artillery pieces had just been removed for
William's use in the Netherlands.[5]

After touring the various buildings and garden, there was nothing left
to do. The Nassaus had confiscated Anna's "worldly" book collection, among
them two editions of the now "infamous" *Amadis de Gaule,* a French adaptation
of the romance of *Tristan,* and the first three volumes of the erotic tales of Matteo
Bandello, commonly known under the title *Histoires Tragiques.* It is possible that
these books had been part of an amatory section in the Breda court library which
William once collected with the intention of "educating" his wife at the beginning
of their marriage.[6]

Grinding boredom soon set in and was compounded by the bitter realization that Anna was Beilstein's mistress in nothing but name. Servants shadowed her every move to thwart escape attempts, while daytime turns in the castle
grounds called for at least two minders. Per Count John's orders, Anna could only
receive noble ladies as visitors, and even they had to be chaperoned by her staff.

The installment of physical barriers further imbued Beilstein with a pris-
on-like air. Before Anna's arrival, workers had latticed all windows with bars and

[3]Beilstein, pp. 4-5, pp. 20-1, p. 37, p. 47.
[4]Kruse,"Wilhelm von Oranien," pp. 109-110
[5]Beilstein, pp. 26-7.
[6]Verwey, p. 97, p. 123.

bricked up every door and gate, except for the main entrance.[7] The Nassaus had also instructed Beilstein's master of the household to keep an eye on his mistress's letters and finances. Deemed a flight risk, Anna was not to send private messages to unknown recipients who could help her abscond from her remote reformatory.[8]

As the world closed in on her, the princess fired off an angry reproach to the landgrave. She sat miserably in a wretched jail and needed to be transferred to another location, Anna wrote. Otherwise, she would be devoid of her senses come winter. If he let her live in Hessen, she would "be his humble servant for the rest of [her] life." Furthermore, she needed a good tailor to make her shirts and other things.[9] There was no reply to Anna's demands.

As the days wore on, Anna struggled to adjust to her new surroundings. Her three children with William - Anna, Maurice, and Emilia - had been taken away to be raised by Count John and his wife Elizabeth, and only the illegitimate Christine remained in her mother's company. Although the princess mentioned her youngest daughter only a single time in writing, it is possible that the toddler enlivened her desperate mother's dreary existence. If Anna pined for her other children is unclear. She had been criticized in the past for her pronounced disinterest in the children's welfare. During her months in Cologne, for example, the princess foisted her eldest daughter and Maurice on Maria Rubens, while baby Emilia was delivered to Dillenburg. After her arrest, Anna's letters mention her son and daughters only sporadically, in a cursory fashion.

*****

With winter at her doorstep, Anna needed distractions. The last sunny fall days were quickly waning; fog and morning mists had already started to descend upon the valley.[10] Although Beilstein was charmingly situated between tree covered hills, its isolation from the rest of the world weighed heavily on Anna. Within weeks, she was nursing a fear and disgust of the "menacing" *Westerwald* forest that bordered on the pathological. The woodlands were ghoulish phantoms that invaded her dreams and many of her waking hours, because she had always been a restless urbanite, unable to find peace in a quiet moment. Resting her eyes on the area's great natural beauty - its mountains, picturesque rock formations, and romantic valleys - held no charms for the princess. In her mind, there was nothing but dreary sky, mud puddles, and rocks.

Admittedly, winters in Beilstein were harsh and dismal, the climate differing markedly from Siegen and Cologne. In fact, the higher *Westerwald* elevations are so forbidding that they later became known as the Siberia of Nassau County, with winter lasting a full six months. By the time November arrived, stabbing winds tormented the few brave souls who still dared to venture outside from every direction.[11] Inside her chambers, Anna tried to keep warm. She also sought to contain the seething rage that threatened to bubble over at any given time.

[7]Bromberg, p. 18.
[8]Fellmann, p. 43
[9]Kruse, "Wilhelm von Oranien,"p. 115.
[10]"Die Landschaft des Westerwaldes," *Heimatjahrbuch für das Land an der Dill*, No. 24 (1981), p. 145.
[11]Gustav Georg Lange. "Der Westerwald," *Heimatjahrbuch für das Land an der Dill*, No. 24 (1981), p. 176, p. 178.

The princess was particularly frustrated with her master of the household, Magnus von Rosenfelt, called Heyer. A former manservant of the landgrave's wife, Heyer had been given an impossible task: he was to transform his wayward mistress - the "careless criminal" - into a vision of repentance and princely godliness. As long as Anna followed Heyer's instructions, Landgrave William had argued, she stood to save her soul and perhaps even reclaim some of her honor, much like his own sister Barbara. The landgravial rehabilitation program included the study of edifying devotional materials and the curbing of drink.

Heyer, as the princess's overseer, was to assist Anna in achieving these goals, but had also been invested with considerable powers over her person. By orders of William of Hessen, he was authorized to lock the princess in her chamber which she was not privy to leave unless he had given permission. Heyer was even allowed to restrain her, in case Anna reprimanded the help too severely or beat them as she had in Siegen. In effect, the major domo did not have to carry out any of the princess's orders unless they corresponded with his Hessian patron's express directives.

At night, Anna's new maid-of-honor, Madame Heyer, and a small group of maidservants slept with their mistress in order to quench any nocturnal shenanigans. Even the smallest deviation to this well-structured routine had to be reported to Anna's relations, who expected regular and precise updates concerning the behavioral improvement of their ward.

Judging from the style of his exasperated letters, Anna's major domo was not a particularly educated man. Like many of his contemporaries, Heyer viewed foreigners with suspicion, and soon complained about the non-Hessian domestics' dishonest ways. Particular thorns in his side were Anna's faithful Dutch cupbearer, Jacques Charlier, and his wife Johanna, who, despite the notorious "hot bowl incident" in Siegen, had apparently agreed to return to the princess's service. By the time winter set in and Anna and her small troupe of attendants spent long hours indoors, the fishbowl of Beilstein castle began to simmer with tension. Petty squabbles, excruciating dullness, and constantly rising tempers poisoned the atmosphere, while the princess's ever darkening moods stretched already taut nerves. She had come to perceive life as a never ending struggle and, according to one of Count John's privy counselors, found her situation a "tough nut to crack."[12]

Despite its miniature size and remoteness, Beilstein castle was not exempted from the traditional household regulations of greater residences. Monsieur's Heyer's particular instructions have not survived, but domestic ordinances issued at a small estate near Driedorf, barely three miles north of Beilstein, allow for a glimpse into a tightly supervised noble microcosm. The so-called *Young Lady's Ordinances* were composed in rhyme form some time during the sixteenth century, and listed infractions against decency, order, and virtue along with their corresponding punishments. An iron fisted maid-of-honor was in charge of both men and women, and dispensed heavy-handed justice. Almost every noble household in the area employed such a taskmistress, and as far back as the fourteenth century, gentlemen like the valiant Reinhard von Westerburg, knight errant, bewailed the fact that he could expect no mercy from the harsh rule of his estate's disciplinarian.

---

[12]Kruse, "Wilhelm von Oranien," pp. 116-7.

Violations included taking God and the sacraments' name in vain, care-less swearing, missing mass, tardiness, and inappropriate table manners. Indeli-cate behavior and filthy talk, uncleanliness, waste of food and drink, gambling as well as slandering the headmistress resulted in monetary fines or whippings. A contemporary poem warned, "Ich bin ein Jungfraw tugendsam, den Lastern bin ich feind und gram." ("I am a virtuous woman, sworn enemy and foe of vice").[13] The same regiment certainly applied to Beilstein, and if Anna had entertained any notions of somehow gaining the upper hand in the wilderness of the *Westerwald*, she was sadly mistaken. Monsieur Heyer and his motivated wife were resolute in the quelling of all forms of misconduct.

*****

Melancholy darkness descended upon Beilstein in mid-winter as the weather steadily worsened and sunlight grew sparse. Whirlwinds ripped the roofs off some of the more modest village dwellings and inundated the ham-let with vast amounts of snow. During some weeks, the snow, swirled about by gusty winds, piled up on houses, virtually burying its dwellers alive. In such cases, it could take days of shoveling through the thick white mass for residents to reach one another. The biting cold further aggravated already harsh living con-ditions. Basalt is a bad heat conductor, and until the advent of refrigeration, the wealthy had ice stored year round in the rocky crags of the nearby forest.[14]

While the wind howled and the peasantry shivered, Anna put her myr-iad of grievances into writing. In a message jotted down in December, she com-plained of ill-prepared food that was, in any case, insufficient for her needs: meals were served half raw and she was unable to fall asleep at night because of hunger pangs. If the landgrave could dispatch one of her former cooks from Cologne, she would be much obliged. Indeed, Anna claimed, she was subsisting on cheese and apples.[15] Unlike the steely elector, who refused any kind of contact with his niece, the more soft-hearted landgrave responded to Anna's doleful message. He promptly hurried one of his own chefs with two barrels of expensive "preserved red and black game" to the Westerwald, and also asked Count John to deliver fresh venison to the princess on his behalf.

In the beginning of 1573, the landgrave and Anna's brother-in-law re-mained the sole individuals with an active interest in the princess's well-being, but were limiting their contact to the sending of an occasional food cart along with a reminder of God's mercy. She was living in comfortable rooms and had loyal people around her, they wrote cheerily after Anna had beseeched them for the umpteenth time to be released from the hated *Westerwald*. Her stay should not be regarded as a kind of imprisonment, they soothed. Rather, their decision to put her up in Beilstein had sprung from "fatherly, well-intentioned concern." The princess, naturally, was not persuaded by these vapid sentiments, growing more aware by the day that only escape or death could end her current trials.[16]

With little news of the outside world and no entertainments to speak of, Anna probably spent a good many hours wondering how William was faring

---

[13]Lange, p. 62.
[14]"Die Landschaft des Westerwaldes," p. 178.
[15]Böttcher, p. 257.
[16]Kruse, "Wilhelm von Oranien," pp. 117-9.

and if Jan was still alive. Louis of Nassau's little army and his Huguenot allies had been crushed by Spanish troops in the early summer. In July 1572, William had come to his brother's aid with 20,000 men, only to be routed by Alba's forces who quickly recouped the rebel towns. Three months later, a Spanish observer confidently remarked to King Philip that "Before long they will all be back in the obedience of Your Majesty."[17] William, on the other hand, groaned to a confidant that he had lost all hope in mankind.[18]

And yet the prince had not slunk back to Germany where, in any case, only creditors and unpaid bills awaited him. Instead, he carved out a new and secure power base in the northern Netherlands and consolidated his residual rebel holdings. Change was in the air, and William had correctly assessed the mood of the Dutch whose patience with the Spanish had finally run out. A group of distinguished intellectuals - a Renaissance version of today's "spin doctors" - fashioned William into the official leader of the liberation movement, the anointed savior destined to free his people from Alba's yoke. With letters, fiery speeches, and thousands of printed pamphlets, they portrayed Orange as the *"hooft en beschermer"* ("head and protector") of the fatherland who vowed "to protect and preserve the country from foreign tyrants and oppressors."[19]

This powerfully evocative image of *"Vader des Vaderlands"* ("Father of the Fatherland") received an additional boost when an impatient Alba allowed his soldiers to sack entire cities to engineer a general capitulation. When almost every man, woman, and child was massacred in the small town of Naarden at the duke's behest, a tidal wave of outrage seized the Low Countries.[20] After a multitude of setbacks, William's time had come at last. The Dutch estates appointed him *stadholder* of the breakaway provinces of Holland, Zeeland, and Utrecht, and asked him to lead his people out of servitude as Moses had once the Israelites.

While William's political fortunes were on the upswing, Maria Rubens prayed for her own changes in luck. Until recently, the Prince of Orange had firmly opposed Jan's release, forewarned by various "noble people" that his prized reputation would suffer if his wife's lover was let go.[21] With the propaganda war in the Netherlands in full swing, Orange could not have his name compromised by the Spanish spreading tales about his cuckoldom.

Now, however, with Anna safely hidden away at Beilstein, the Nassaus allowed a review of Rubens's case. Although Jan had forfeited his life after admitting to the capital crime of adultery, fear of unwanted attention and Dr. Schwarz's counsel let Count John err on the side of leniency.[22] Moreover, Maria had approached the impecunious Nassau brothers with a tempting proposal: in exchange for her husband's freedom, she offered Orange a six thousand thaler loan with only an annual interest payment in return. Count John counter-offered. If Rubens gave another notarized confession in front of witnesses that contradicted Anna's assertions of innocence, he would agree to his release under certain conditions.[23]

---

[17]Kamen, p. 142.
[18]Cellarius, "Wilhelm," p. 75
[19]Mörke, p. 158.
[20]Jardine, p. 37, p. 39.
[21]Kruse, "Wilhelm von Oranien," pp. 106-7.
[22]Knackfuss, p. 3.
[23]de Dijn, p. 74. It is unclear how Maria Rubens came into such a sizable sum of money. Perhaps Jan's half-brother Philip Rubens had forwarded the funds, perhaps overdue rents had finally arrived from the Netherlands.

Jan jumped at the chance. Chastened by long months in the *Stockhaus*, he claimed that his conscience compelled him to confess his crime a second time. He also wanted to thank the Almighty for revealing the awful magnitude of his offense. Any concession by the Nassaus showed great magnanimity on their part, Rubens gratefully assured them, since he deserved death a hundred times over. In fact, his shame was so great that he still cried every day. Satan had led him astray, although he had never committed a wicked act of this sort before. Before consorting with the princess, Jan avowed, he had lived in perfect wedlock with his "dear housewife."

Everything had started with a Dutch physician in Cologne, Rubens recounted before a select panel of witnesses. The doctor had known Her Serene Highness and had introduced him. He started to call on the princess, met some of her ladies, and discussed the latest news. Anna was impressed with his erudition and position as a lay judge in Antwerp. Matters eventually progressed beyond the professional stage when the princess developed an attraction for him that he reciprocated. Because of the devil's cunning, they eventually forgot themselves. Out of shame and for reasons of propriety, Jan asked to remain silent on the carnal aspects of the affair.[24]

Count John was satisfied. The lawyer's frank honesty, his desire to avoid additional publicity as well as his own, innate tendency to render forgiveness to a repentant sinner probably all contributed to John's clemency ruling. Rubens was free to leave the *Stockhaus*, he announced, but had to remain under Nassau supervision until further notice. After swearing a solemn oath of obedience, the lawyer was to betake himself and his family to Siegen where he would live under house arrest. Only Mrs. Rubens and the children could leave the city at their leisure, while Rubens was to report to Dillenburg whenever so ordered. On the first day of Pentecost 1573, prison doors opened for Jan Rubens after twenty-six months behind bars.[25] Unlike his lover, he had been granted a new, if limited, start in life, together with his paragon of a wife and their children.

During that same spring of 1573, while the Rubenses celebrated the return of their beloved husband and father into the family fold, Anna continued to languish alone. Flowers were already blooming in the lower elevations, but winter stubbornly retained its hold on Beilstein.[26] Weeks passed with Anna still feeling hungry and irritated, much to the distress of her harried servants.

Due to Heyer's aversion to outside help and the restrictive rules on Anna's movements, the princess's contact with the villagers must have been minimal. Perhaps she sometimes watched from the castle's windows as farmers' wives labored, their traditional red and blue scarves bobbing up and down fields in a rich bouquet. On feast days, local women donned colorful aprons and light blue stockings with red decorations, while men wore dark blue linen shirts and pants with round hats.[27]

Apparently, they were a deeply superstitious lot. Until the nineteenth century, belief in dwarves and other small forest folk was widespread in the *Westerwald* as were curious healing methods. Instead of applying a poultice when a pig broke its leg, one bandaged the foot of a chair and left the chair untouched

---

[24]Kruse, "Wilhelm von Oranien," pp. 111-3.
[25]Kaestner, pp. 99-100.
[26]"Die Landschaft des Westerwaldes,"p. 145.
[27]"Die Landschaft des Westerwaldes," p. 147.

until the pig had recovered.[28] As for diversions, except for the usual weddings and baptisms, there was only the much anticipated annual country fair. Count John stopped at the fair from time to time, but if he ever visited during Anna's tedious stay at Beilstein Castle is unknown.[29]

Small stacks of desperation mail left the estate on an almost daily basis; few letters arrived for Anna in return due to Monsieur Heyer's constant vigilance. Over time, the princess tried to skirt the mail embargo by bribing various servants, artifice that did not remain unnoticed. Heyer promptly reported that he had caught his mistress with one of the kitchen maids inside her chambers, trying to have the girl smuggle a message to Cologne. Lately, there were frequent missives arriving from the Rhine metropolis, he informed the landgrave warily, including one from the mayor.

Furthermore, Anna was severely depressed and mistreated her staff. A few chamber and kitchen maids had already run away, irrespective of the consequences.[30] He had enough of a hard time keeping his menagerie in check, Heyer moaned, especially since many of the princess's servants, like the accursed cupbearer Jacques, were untrustworthy and failed to heed his orders. Even worse, Anna violently scolded him when he refused to do her bidding. As a result, he and his wife were thinking of resigning from their respective positions.

The landgrave took the chamberlain's concerns very seriously. "The Dutchman and his spouse have to be dismissed immediately," he ordered in a stern address to the princess. As to Anna's correspondence, she was only to write to himself, the elector, and Count John, and was not permitted to receive any letters from persons other than her guardians. If she failed to obey, he added harshly, he would have her loaded onto a cart and driven to Dresden. There, she would be locked in a cell and given food through a small window.

The effect of the landgrave's threat was immediate. In an express reply to his lordship, Anna implored him to take mercy on her. Life in Beilstein was simply unbearable and she was desperate to leave the Westerwald. "There is no good food available in this godforsaken place," the princess wrote, and she was by no means a picky person. In fact, she was lying awake at night due to "great, bitter hunger."[31]

Landgrave William properly noted Anna's complaints, and invited the Saxon envoy von Berlepsch and Count John to Kassel for a reassessment of her case. The count concurred that the princess's economic situation was indeed dire, but also declared that he could no longer cover the household expenses for Anna and her four children. Peace in the Netherlands was still not in sight, and the only way to make ends meet was to draw from her dower. In response, August of Saxony promised to pay for the princess's upkeep, but only if Landgrave William housed her somewhere in Hessen. He was not open to other suggestions, he dictated firmly, and added that she was not to come to Dresden under any circumstances.[32]

With neither the landgrave nor the elector willing to host their burdensome niece, Anna remained in draughty Beilstein. She was almost twenty-nine

[28]Westerwald, p. 180
[29] Leonhard Hörpel. "In der Beilsteiner Rüstkammer," *Heimatblätter zur Pflege und Förderung des Heimatgedankens*, 8. Jahrgang, Nr. 7 (1935).
[30]Fellmann, p. 43.
[31]Kruse, "Wilhelm von Oranien," pp. 118-9.
[32]Kruse, "Wilhelm von Oranien,"p. 119.

years old, and had squandered her life and happiness away. The woman who had once sat for a portrait decked out in inestimable jewelry had vanished, never to return; a realization expressed in her missives, which she had long reverted to signing with her maiden name "Anna of Saxony" instead of "Princess of Orange." The days dragged on, and life was mind-crushingly dismal. Three times a week a pastor from nearby Herborn named Eobanus Noviomagus stopped by to deliver sermons on sin and redemption which the princess did not care to hear.[33] Anna eventually declined his services, and did the same with the few ladies, who had occasionally visited to gawk at the curiosity of a fallen princess.[34]

We do not know if thoughts of Jan Rubens - regret, longing or both - haunted Anna throughout these endless months. It is quite likely. She probably remained unaware of her lover's release, as such information would have been considered unsuitable for the princess's ears. Perhaps Anna was not even apprised of the auspicious turn of events in Calenberg, where Duke Eric had finally yielded to his wife's demands in a stunning marital defeat.

Between 1571 and 1572, the protracted quarreling between Anna's aunt and the Brunswick duke had culminated in the arrest and indictment of some of the duchess's ladies on the grave charge of witchcraft. Sidonia subsequently fled to Vienna, where Emperor Maximilian II not only sided with the sister of his friend and ally August, but also chastised Duke Eric. He pronounced the witch trials illegal and commanded the duke to pay his wife long overdue restitution in both money and lands.[35] The browbeaten Eric duly acquiesced to his wife's financial terms and eventual release of the suspected witches. Sidonia, riding high on a wave of victory, exulted, "I, one of the most forsaken princesses, [have recaptured] my honor and good name which is the most precious gem in this world."[36]

Her triumph over her loathsome husband was sweetened by the arrival of congratulatory letters from all over Germany, complimenting the duchess on her acquittal and restoration of her good name. The Bishop of Halberstadt, for example, wrote that he had received the verdict with "particular joy." With public opinion so firmly behind her, Sidonia found herself in a rather unique position for a noble female: she could chart her own destiny. After deliberating with her brother and Electress Anne, she turned her back on Calenberg and relocated to Castle Weissenfels in her homeland of Saxony.[37]

While Sidonia and Jan - both loved ones of Anna's - had been granted new chances in life, no such luck lay in store for the former Princess of Orange. In her aunt's words, she had irretrievably lost that "most precious gem in world," her honor, which was difficult if not impossible to recoup. Anna's adultery clung like an invisible, yet self-evident stain to her person, alerting those around about her disgrace. A new addition to the small Beilstein household pointedly reminded the princess of just that, in the cruelest manner.

Sometime in 1574 Godfrey of Nassau (†1582) - illegitimate son of Count William the Rich and half-brother of William of Orange—arrived in the Wester-

---

[33] Böttcher, p. 245.
[34] de Dijn, p. 86
[35] Lilienthal, p. 235. In May 1573, the captive women were handed over to Duke Julius of Brunswick-Wolfenbüttel and later released
[36] Lilienthal, p. 236. The truth about the 1564 poisoning affair has never been established. It is certain, however, that Eric was personally present during the interrogations of Sidonia's friends and servants. He badgered the suspects into implicating his wife, the reason why he balked at facing the emperor in Vienna. And yet, for all his vicious deeds and the resulting scandal, Eric emerged from the affair by no means a ruined man. Philip of Spain inducted the duke—one of his most experienced battle commanders—into the Order of the Golden Fleece, a highly exclusive chivalric organization that elevated the chastened Eric to a person of consequence.
[37] Lilienthal, pp. 237-8.

wald after fighting Alba's forces in the Netherlands. As a former commandant of Beilstein Castle, he had been appointed the estate's chief administrator by Count John and tasked with the defense of the small outpost.

Apparently, there was no love lost between Anna and Godfrey. The haughty princess had probably run afoul with this lower-ranking relative of her husband's during her stay at Dillenburg Castle, where Godfrey served as major domo in 1567.[38] At the time, Anna had rudely insisted on her rights of precedence and William's half-brother had not forgotten those slights. Recently informed about the princess's reversals of fortune, he decided to exploit his newfound authority to the fullest.

An uncouth, loutish man of low character, Godfrey paid Anna back in kind by viciously degrading her. According to the princess's testimony, he and his maid servants shouted, "Princess, you are a whore, yea, yea!" every time she peered out a window. On certain occasions, he even went so far as to insult her in the presence of her staff, emphasizing that he, and not the elector's daughter, stood in charge of the small court.[39]

During one particularly testy exchange of words, Godfrey called Anna a harlot in front of the entire household. When the princess retorted that she would tell her friends, "the bastard" hollered, "What friends? Who still cares for you? You don't have any friends." To which Anna shrieked, "If the elector knew [about this], he would not like it." "Yes, by God," Godfrey mocked brutally, "you can rely on the elector; he really does care for you. Sixteen years ago the elector wanted you below ground, and even now there couldn't be happier news for him and the landgrave if they were told of your death. I tell you, you loose nag, your friends have ordered you to be taken by the neck and dragged to Dillenburg where you will be put in a hole reserved for hussies. After all, you are locked up for whoring."[40]

Trembling with indignation and hurt, Anna rushed a letter to Count John. His half-brother's venomous abuse was unheard of, she wrote. In addition to calling her a harlot, he had slandered her son and daughters, libeling them "three whore children brought up at Dillenburg," although no one knew "which devil had made them."[41] At the beginning of 1575, she also questioned the landgrave by post. Was it fitting for a person of her standing to endure such mistreatment? If this was the case, Anna posited, he might as well send the executioner to chop her head off, which she preferred a thousand times to living among the faithless Nassaus. Lastly, she wanted to apologize for using such "ugly writing paper." She had been forced to cut pages from a book after running out of stationary. It was bad enough to be kept under lock and key, but one did not have to add insult to injury.

Anna's uncle received her plea, but refused a personal response. Instead, one of his secretaries answered that the landgrave had been distressed by other

[38]Kruse, "Wilhelm von Oranien," p. 174. Godfrey had already served as commandant of Beilstein from 1561 until 1564. He was married three times and had several children. On this topic, see also Wagner, Jacob. *Die Regentenfamilie von Nassau-Hadamar*, Band 1 (Vienna: Mechitharisten-Congregations-Buchhandlung, 1863), p. 154. Wagner describes Godfrey as the son of Count William I and an anonymous mistress. He was acknowledged by his father and allowed to carry the name "von Nassau." His coat-of-arms contained the lion of Nassau, although most likely with the baton sinister. In 1547 Godfrey's father and half-brothers awarded him the lands of the extinct Nassau-Löhnberg line as well as the fief of Camberg, north of Wiesbaden. In 1636 Godfrey's male line became extinct with his grandson Hans Wilhelm.
[39]Pletz-Krehan, "Schicksal," p. 190.
[40]Kruse, "Wilhelm von Oranien," p. 120.
[41]Pletz-Krehan, "Schicksal," pp. 190-1.

messages. His Grace had just received word about the princess's despicable behavior towards the Madams. Heyer and Seidensticker, and cautioned that the use
of harsh words towards her staff was unusual and unacceptable.[42] If Anna could
not live in peace with the Nassaus and her servants, she would be walled up
"never to see sun and moon again" as the elector had previously proposed (this
is the sixth mention of this horrific type of punishment by either the landgrave
or August of Saxony). Her brother-in-law, the generous Count John, had recently
suggested a return of hers to Dillenburg to cut household expenses. It was an
offer worth considering. She would be among company there, and if she showed
herself to people, her misdeeds would be all the sooner forgotten.

Strangely enough, despite the isolation and tedium at Beilstein, Anna
recoiled at John of Nassau's surprisingly open-minded proposal, which would
have also meant a reunion with her legitimate children.[43] The landgrave could
not possibly expect her to live among William's malevolent relations, the princess replied, for she had suffered enough at their hands. Furthermore, as his sister's daughter, he owed her assistance. There was no reply from Kassel this time
around as the landgrave claimed to be occupied with affairs of his own. An enthusiastic stargazer, he was looking forward to hosting the Danish nobleman and
famous astronomer Tycho Brahe at his court. Count John, on the other hand, had
just changed his mind about letting Anna return to Dillenburg. Strange news had
recently arrived from the Low Countries: the Prince of Orange had decided to
remarry.[44] Godfrey's insults about Anna being friendless, powerless, and alone
had been savagely accurate.

During those testy exchanges between Anna, the landgrave, and Count
John, the Elector of Saxony remained remarkably quiet. His envoys kept him
abreast of the Westerwald turmoil for much of 1574, but he refused any kind of
intervention, claiming that his niece was solely the Nassaus' concern now.[45] There
were other reasons as well. After his sister Sidonia's marital odyssey had finally
come to a satisfactory conclusion, the elector and his Dresden court had plunged
into the festive carnival season. Saxon miners put in a much talked of appearance
along with August, who had played Mercury, "the God of all metals," in a won-
drous costume.[46] Then, in an elaborately staged tournament, a giant fire spitting
dragon had roared through the tiltyard, while a walking procession of courtiers
acted out a world turned upside down in which animals were hunting the hunters.[47]

Soon after, the electress, who until then had enjoyed the rudest of health,
fell seriously ill. Anne later recounted that the unidentified ailment had been so
severe that she felt herself on the brink of death. Her symptoms might have been
of a psychological nature. The electress was gravely concerned about her oldest
daughter Elizabeth's dysfunctional marriage, and had written that she had taken
sick "worn out by lengthy troubles and sorrows."[48]

After weathering his wife's brush with death, the elector was shocked to
learn of a heretical conspiracy that had sprouted within his privy council and was

[42]Keller, *Kurfürstin*, p. 210.
[43]Böttcher, p. 271.
[44]Kruse, "Wilhelm von Oranien," pp. 120-1.
[45]Kruse, "Wilhelm von Oranien," p. 117.
[46]Watanabe, p. 121.
[47]Keller,*Kurfürstin*, p. 60.
[48]Keller, *Kurfürstin*, p. 175.

aimed at him and Anne. Unfortunately, sources on the 1574 plot are scant because of a loss of documentation, rendering an exact recreation of events impossible. It is certain, however, that the electoral couple severely punished a specific number of suspects because of a sense of personal betrayal.[49]

Among the victims were August's most trusted adviser, Dr. George Craco, and his personal physician, Caspar Peucer, as well as the electoral chaplain, Christian Schütz. The three men had apparently spread the tenets of Calvinism — Protestant teachings that the Lutheran elector and his wife abhorred and had prohibited at court.[50] August felt greatly deceived by their actions and, egged on by his wife, initiated a purge of these so-called "crypto Calvinists" whom he also suspected of political plotting.

Caspar Peucer - godfather to August's son Adolph - was thrown into prison together with Schütz and Craco. Craco died under torture which August personally attended, while Peucer languished in solitary confinement for twelve years.[51] Evidently and true to the times, neither the elector nor his spouse considered forgiveness one of the essential elements of the Christian faith. August imagined himself the stern moral authority of Lutheranism in the empire; Anne was its premier patroness, who lived her personal motto, "Fear of the Almighty is the beginning of wisdom," to the very fullest.[52]

In addition to heresy, embezzlement, and murder, the electress thought adultery a particularly grievous offense in her calendar of sins, a transgression so great that it equaled the crime of political dissent.[53] It was with therefore with good reason that the fallen Anna trembled each time the landgrave threatened to banish her to Dresden. If the electoral couple lashed out at former friends and confidants with intemperate cruelty, their miscreant niece could not expect much leniency. In 1575, August and his wife took careful note after hearing that Anna was throwing food at her servants and issuing death threats.[54]

---

[49]Bruning, p. 122.
[50]Bruning, p. 121. This rather abrupt change in confessional politics has partially been attributed to August of Saxony's reaction to the horrors of the French St. Bartholomew's Day massacre on 23 August 1572.
[51]Fellmann, p. 27
[52]Keller, *Kurfürstin*, p. 121, p. 125.
[53]Keller, "Landesmutter", p. 270.
[54]Kruse, "Rubens", p. 7.

At the Brambach's

During her third winter in Beilstein, Anna found herself in increasing mental and physical disarray. The isolation and crushing monotony, combined with Godfrey's brutishness, were slowly robbing her of her senses, and she spent most of her days swilling tankards of wine, wretched and insufferable in her alcohol-induced haze. Eventually, the princess sank into a deep psychosis. Disorientation gave way to feelings of elation at times, only to be followed by glummest melancholy. By now, Anna's letters were a jumble of deep piousness, rejection of faith, and sexually explicit slurs. On certain occasions, the princess was so violent that she had to be subdued by a strongman.

Servants decided that her small daughter, three-and-a-half-year-old Christine, had to be removed from her foul-mouthed, unstable mother. Whether the princess spurned Christine, a daily reminder of her downfall, or had become attached to the little girl has not been recorded. In any case, Anna's behavior had become unreasonable enough for her staff to intervene. They probably feared that Anna could harm her daughter in a fit of drunkenness or expose her to indecent outbursts of temper. Naturally, the princess was outraged to have her child taken away. At the end of January 1575, she dispatched an irate letter to her uncle, Landgrave William, protesting that the cook had taken Christine under her wings.[1]

Despite her young age, Christine was probably aware that something was amiss at the place she called home. Her mother's hysterical sobs often alternated with shrill laughter, and she had just been told to spend most of her time in the castle's kitchen. Perhaps the girl found something of a father figure in Heyer, never having laid eyes on her other parent, Jan Rubens. In fact, the unwanted Christine existed in a strange limbo of quasi "orphandom," unclaimed by either father or mother and with an uncertain future ahead of her. Anna was clearly an unfit parent, and Jan, while trying to rebuild a life for himself and his family, was still under house arrest.

In the spring of 1573 Maria Rubens had thanked Count John profusely for letting her husband settle in Siegen, but also appealed to him for help. Finding a rental house would be problematic for a man of Jan's notoriety, she wrote. The city was already playing host to more immigrants from the Netherlands than it could afford, and the locals were generally distrustful towards the foreigner who had impregnated Prince William's wife.[2]

"In order to inquire about a house for rent," Maria begged, "could Your Grace have some of your people give me addresses and assist me so that such a home will not be denied to me? My husband will stay in Dillenburg until I have secured lodgings and everything that we need has arrived. And when we are there, he [Jan] will keep himself as quiet and invisible as it is possible."[3]

Her docile appeal paid dividends. Count John asked one of his administrators, William von Brambach, to lease the Rubenses a room on his city estate. The Brambachs were prominent landowners in the adjacent County of Diez on the Lahn River, and had loyally served the Nassaus for generations. Currently,

[1]Kruse, "Christine", p. 136.
[2]Goebel, p. 20.
[3]de Dijn, p. 78.

none of the family was residing in town, leaving the manor empty and available for the Dutch ex-convict and his kin.[4] On May 10, Jan arrived in Siegen on horseback and finally joined his children and Maria in their new, single chamber abode.[5] A happier, but no less daunting chapter in the Rubenses' lives was about to begin.

Today, only the cellar remains of the old Brambach domain which in later centuries was acquired by the Catholic Church and finally served as a secondary school and parsonage. It was finally torn down in 1911, around the same time the infamous *Rinkenhof* in Cologne made way for new construction.[6] In close vicinity to Siegen Castle, where Anna had spent nerve wrecking months in preventive custody, the Brambach mansion was part of a series of old halls owned by the local gentry. Although depictions have not survived, we can assume that the residence offered a certain standard of living. Dwellings of the type usually consisted of three floors, were spacious, half timbered, and kept in good condition. The Brambach residence should have been no different, since the family was well-off and could afford quality amenities. And while the Rubenses certainly lived in cramped quarters, they probably enjoyed at least a modicum of domestic comfort.[7]

Notwithstanding these newfound family joys, Jan Rubens could still not call himself a free man. Except for occasional, chaperoned walks in the neighborhood, Anna's erstwhile lover was prohibited from leaving the confines of the estate which was permanently guarded by armed sentries. Sometimes, the tutor of the count's children, Adrian Damman, accompanied him on an outing. One or the other Nassau official, such as Pastor Wigelius, also called sporadically. As for the rest of Siegen's populace, they assumed a hostile stance towards the infamous jurist and even his family.[8]

Lack of money posed another problem for the Rubenses. The count's terms of release apparently included an occupational ban, for there are no records of Jan resuming legal work in Siegen. Guards screened the comings and goings at the Brambach estate and kept visitor traffic to a minimum. The lawyer's family, which included four growing children, had to subsist on Maria's leftover savings, the interest of the six thousand thaler loan (which amounted to three hundred thalers annually), and the proceeds from her gardening. The unflagging Mrs. Rubens had leased a vegetable patch close to the city walls which she cultivated with imported seedlings from the Low Countries.[9] A merchant's daughter at heart, she then sold her produce at market. For additional income, Maria also rented a barn together with another piece of land from a neighbor, Mr. Fuchs, whose house in the *Webergasse* (Weaver's Alley) adjoined the Brambach mansion.

Despite her efforts, making ends meet was a continual challenge. The debt-ridden Count John paid the promised interest only in irregular intervals, and then mostly in kind. Maria sold these wares - bushels of wheat, wine, an ox or a pig - at the Siegen fair.[10] Jan's half-brother, Philip de Landmeter, sometimes

[4] Gustav Siebel. "Rubens' Geburtshaus." *Siegerland, Band* 57, Heft 1 (1980),p. 22.
[5] Goebel, p. 20.
[6] de Dijn, p. 85.
[7] Siebel, p. 22.
[8] Kruse, *"Rubens,"p. 8.*
[9] Goebel, p. 20.
[10] de Dijn, pp. 78-9.

sent money, but apparently not enough.[11] It must have been a definite blow to Jan's already shrunken ego that the well-being of his family rested squarely on Maria's shoulders, and that he, despite of his learning, could contribute so little to the household budget.

In January 1574, less than a year after his discharge from the *Stockhaus*, a restless and frustrated Rubens composed an elegant petition to Peter Dathenus, Calvinist theologian and official in the employ of the Prince of Orange. The Latin plea, crammed with paradigms taken from antiquity, the bible, and Luther's writings, was a sort of *Apologia*, a defense mixed with admissions of his wrongdoings. Maria signed as well, and together the couples hoped for an easing of Jan's house arrest.[12] The prince did not answer.

A year later, the Rubenses continued to struggle, still ostracized by a hostile public. At times, resentment towards the lawyer's family ran so high that Nassau officials bought food for them; local shopkeepers were refusing Maria service. There was even an incident of false and malicious denunciation. An anonymous agitator charged that Jan was freely walking about Siegen, slandering the House of Nassau. Since Rubens was still on probation and could be re-arrested for any form of untoward behavior, this was a serious accusation. It was also a bitter reminder that the wretched adultery affair was still very much part of his life. Luckily, Count John shrugged off the allegation as a spiteful prank, and no action was taken.[13]

There were bright spots as well. Somehow the family scratched enough money together to rent additional rooms on the Brambach estate. It was much needed space, since Maria had recently given birth to the couple's fifth child, a son named Philip who, as an adult, would make his mother proud by becoming a respected legal scholar. As to the Rubenses' marital relations, the kind-hearted Maria had long forgiven her husband for his disastrous folly. Given her affectionate nature and Jan's relief at having eluded the hangman, it is entirely possible that the pair re-established a warm, if not loving, rapport.

In addition to her mercantile activities, Maria also grew into her role of family negotiator and business manager. Jan remained confined to the Brambach mansion, and had given his wife full control over his Dutch properties. In May 1576, in the presence of the theologian Peter Ximenius of Cologne and Meffert Schwarz, the lawyer signed the following declaration of debt, "I, Jan Rubens, herewith affirm that I owe my wife, Maria Pypelinckx, eight thousand thalers which she paid to bring about my release from prison. I promise to reimburse her as soon as possible. I sign over all my other goods - furniture, rights of inheritance, interest, stocks, household items, silver, books, clothes, etc. - to her. Moreover, everything that I will inherit once my parents have passed, I also cede to my wife. She can sell, charge, or retain these items according to her own discretion; even if the said sum exceeds eight thousand thalers. I trust she will do as is fitting for herself and the children. The six thousand thalers that Count John of Nassau has promised to return after my death - a sum that might also be repaid should I return to prison - should be given to my children after my passing."

---

[11]Fellmann, p. 40; Kruse, "Wilhelm von Oranien," p. 129. In 1575 the Nassau agent Tobias Scheffer mentioned another relative of Rubens, an apothecary, who also resided in Cologne. However, there are no records of this individual ever helping the family.

[12]Kruse, "Rubens", p. 9.

[13]Goebel, p. 21.

These were the grateful words of a chastened husband to his faithful spouse who had stood by him during his darkest hours. Apparently, Maria was both touched and embarrassed by this gesture of appreciation, a gesture which she might have regarded as unbecomingly humbling for a man. Only a few days later she virtually revoked Jan's bequest and insisted that he remain the undisputed household head. What was hers was his as it always had been, and as it should be in the future. And in case of her pre-deceasing Jan, her own will determined that he was to receive the entirety of the family's possessions. Notwithstanding these arrangements, Maria continued as the administrator of the Rubenses' estate out of pure necessity. Jan remained domestically fettered by the terms of his release, and lingered on at the Brambachs, a virtual bondservant of Nassaus.[14]

As Maria toiled, news arrived from the Netherlands that Rubens's step-father had passed away. Monsieur de Landmeter had loved Jan like a son and bequeathed him a sizeable sum of money as well as tracts of land. Hoping to take advantage of this much desired financial break Maria immediately appealed to her own father in the Low Countries. He was to forward Jan's power of attorney to de Landmeter's lawyers, she explained, and intervene on her husband's behalf.

Unfortunately, the power of attorney generated in Siegen was not accepted in Antwerp. Flanders jurists refused to recognize the seal of the rather obscure Nassau town and demanded further proof. Papers dating to August 1576 show that a payment to Jan Rubens was temporarily halted, possibly because of a lack of required documentation. There were additional obstacles. According to his stepfather's testament, Rubens had to pay a one thousand florin initial retainer fee in order to inherit a large amount of money that was not immediately available. Substantial rents, farms, and fields in Antwerp thus lay in Jan's reach, but were infuriatingly unattainable.[15] In desperation, the couple deliberated about sending Maria to Antwerp. She was pregnant again, and the political situation in the Netherlands was still volatile. Was money worth risking the life of the family's primary breadwinner? they pondered tensely.

Before they could reach a decision, terrifying news arrived from home. On 4 November 1576, Spanish troops - angered at having gone without pay for months - swept through Antwerp, looting, maiming, and killing at will. The event, which later became known as the *Spaanse Furie* (The Spanish Fury) or the Sack of Antwerp, reduced the Low Countries' glorious port city to ruins. Its principal buildings, along with the world famous cloth market and town hall, were laid to waste during three days of carnage, while over seven thousand people lost their lives.

Despite the age's notoriety for deliberate brutality and wholesale slaughter of innocent civilians in times of war, the atrocities sent shock waves through Europe. Spain's already declining reputation and that of its king plunged even further, while delicate peace negotiations between Madrid and the Netherlanders stalled. Together, Dutch Catholics and Protestants stood in disbelief at the remnants of their once mighty city. The Estates of Brabant wrote to King Philip in the aftermath of the bloodbath, "It is notorious that Antwerp was but yesterday one of the chief ornaments of Europe, the harborage of all the nations of the world, the nurse of art and industry ... the protector of the Catholic religion, she was

---

[14]de Dijn, pp. 79-80.
[15]de Dijn, p. 80.

ever faithful and obedient to her sovereign prince. Now the city is changed to a gloomy cavern, filled with robbers and murderers, enemies of God, the king, and his loyal subjects."[16]

The universal condemnation of the Antwerp massacre further strengthened the resolve of Dutch parliamentarians to make their own peace with the Prince of Orange, *stadholder* of the dissenting provinces of Holland and Zeeland. They also approached Madrid with demands which were finally heard. Together with rebel representatives, Philip's new Dutch governor and half-brother, Don Juan of Austria, signed an agreement which became known as the Pacification of Ghent four days after the destruction. The king, who had recently declared bankruptcy and was worn out from the incessant troubles in Flanders, instructed Don Juan that all possible concessions should be made to his arch nemesis Orange in the name of peace. One of the most significant aspects of the treaty was the immediate withdrawal of all Spanish troops from the Netherlands. The following spring, astounded, but relieved Dutchmen watched groups of soldiers making their way towards Spain's possessions in Italy. In effect, Philip's new governor was left without authority and armed forces.[17]

This latest turn of events infused the Rubens household with new hope. The much needed inheritance was finally within their grasp, prompting an elated Jan to burst with joy. "Now that peace has come, I can receive my legacy," he jubilated, and begged Count John for permission to travel to Cologne. There, he could attain the required power of attorney for his father-in-law. Of course, he would return to Siegen immediately after the signing, Jan promised, and pledged his wife and children as collateral. Authorization was granted, and Maria, already heavily pregnant, packed for her first trip home in almost ten years.

In May 1577, with the necessary legal documents in hand, Mrs. Rubens traveled down the Rhine to Antwerp. In addition to Jan's bequest, she also intended to collect back rents and interest from her own holdings that had not been forwarded to Germany since 1575.[18] There was even news that the new governor of the Netherlands, Don Juan, was restoring formerly confiscated property to returning refugees in a magnanimous gesture of reconciliation.[19]

Such luck, however, was not with Maria and Jan. Perhaps the de Landmeter houses had been smashed by marauding Spanish troops or vital ownership records destroyed, because there are no accounts of a triumphant Maria returning to Siegen with pockets full of gold. There are also no indications of an improvement in the Rubenses' living standard. We must therefore conclude that Maria received nothing or only a small percentage of the much hoped for monetary windfall. At the end of June, exhausted and worn out from her exertions, Madame Rubens gave birth to her sixth and final child, Peter Paul, in Siegen. The baby was an additional mouth to feed and perhaps there was little rejoicing. But it was this son, born during tough times, who would elevate the family name to unprecedented fame and brilliance.

Demoralized by the Dutch holdup and Jan's continued dead-end existence, the lawyer and his spouse started grasping at straws. At their wits' end, they enlisted the help of Maria's aging mother, Clara du Touion. Count John had

[16]Putnam, *The Life of William the Silent*, pp. 211-2.
[17]Kamen, pp. 160-1.
[18]de Dijn, p. 83.
[19]Goebel, p. 22.

shut his ears to all their entreaties, they wrote, but perhaps the sight an elderly lady would soften his heart. Clara consented. She would undertake the arduous trip to Dillenburg and plead for her son-in-law, despite her advanced years and frail health. Meanwhile, Maria dispatched additional petitions to the Nassaus. "Would they allow Jan to relocate to Lier, outside of Antwerp, to be close to his in-laws?" she asked. "He would not venture beyond her parents' street," she promised, "and the count, who still owed them 176 thalers in interest payments, would finally be rid of them."[20] But John declined, yet again.[21]

As a final resort, the Rubenses also addressed a petition to William of Orange. Perhaps the prince, still flush with euphoria after his recent successes in Flanders, would be more favorably disposed to their appeals than his brother.[22] Written in Maria's hand, but devised by Jan, the letter listed of the lawyer's merits at great length. Monsieur le docteur was an individual of exceptional erudition, well versed in art and the legal sciences, the scion of a respectable family. As an Antwerp lay judge he had received "praise and honor," and, like the prince, been forced to flee the Low Countries for his beliefs. Now, he was longing to return to his homeland. Jean Taffin, an old friend of Jan's and Orange's current court chaplain, presented the supplication to the prince.[23]

Softened by his latest triumphs, William relented. After a series of protracted deliberations with his brother John, the prince gave the Rubens family permission to settle in the Netherlands. He also lifted Jan's occupational ban. As can be expected, these goodwill gestures came at a price. Maria not only paid 1400 thalers in bribes to various court officials, but also waived Count John's repayment of half her loan which amounted to three thousand thalers.[24] William also specified that Rubens could not settle in any of his lands nor approach his person at any time.[25] And whenever ordered to do so, Jan was to report to either Dillenburg or Siegen.[26]

In order to avoid any future confrontations with the House of Nassau, the Rubenses settled in Cologne. In case of a subpoena, Jan could easily travel the short distance to Dillenburg, and there was little chance of offending the Flanders-based Orange from their new home on the Rhine. Apparently, the couple had kept in contact with Cologne's large immigrant community, and was given a warm welcome when they arrived in the summer of 1578. In November of that same year, Rubens was already called as a witness at the Calvinist baptism of little Hans de Koninck. Calvinists themselves, Jan and Maria started to live under the familiar cloud of religious suspicion again, suspicion that had already complicated their lives in the early 1570s until Anna had "saved" them. Cologne's city police still raided clandestine prayer meetings and services, and punished repeat offenders with exile.[27]

Nevertheless, life was improving. No longer prisoner within his own four walls, Jan resumed his legal career to provide for his wife and children, although the family continued in straightened circumstances. The shadow of the Nassaus still loomed, but its nightmarish proportions had decreased to a bear-

[20]Goebel, p. 21.
[21]de Dijn, p. 83
[22]Goebel, p. 21.
[23]Roosbroeck, "Schöffe," p. 64.
[24]Kruse, "Rubens", p. 9.
[25]Roosbroeck, "Schöffe," p. 64.
[26]deDijn, p. 84.
[27]Roosbroeck, "Schöffe," p. 64.

able level.

At least occasionally, Jan's thoughts must have wandered off and lingered on his other daughter, Christine, and her mother Anna. By the late 1570s, Rubens had probably been apprised of his lover's horrible fate, but since he was not allowed near either of them, it is likely that he pushed this most painful chapter of his existence out of his mind. He and Maria were working day and night to keep the family fed. The older children needed education and dowries, and the youngest, one-year-old Peter Paul, was growing fast. It was better to break with the past.

Charlotte

Je Maintiendrai, (I will maintain), William of Orange Motto later adopted by the Houses of Nassau and Orange

Like Jan Rubens, William of Orange also tried to banish the ghosts of bygone indignities. While Anna was wasting away in Beilstein, his fortunes had seen a slow, but steady upturn. Habsburg forces had made continuous incursions into the rebel-controlled provinces of Holland, Zeeland, and Utrecht, but Orange held his ground. He never gained renown as a field commander, but his persistence, diplomatic agility, and personal charisma eventually marked him for success.[1] William also forged close ties with powerful rebel Calvinists by attending their church services and inspired the common man to persevere in the fight against the Spanish. Harbor taverns and military encampments reverberated with political songs and ditties hailing Orange's achievements. Some of them, it was rumored, had even been composed by the man himself.[2]

By the mid-1570s William had become the unchallenged cynosure of the revolt against the Spanish Habsburgs, and exploited the power of print to the fullest. The prince proved, for the first time in history, that pamphlets could be more destructive than weapons. In fact, his broadsheets were so devastatingly effective that the Spanish, who stood helpless at the onslaught of rebel propaganda, finally tired of responding.[3] Unlike Flanders, the printing industry on the Iberian Peninsula was a primitive affair. King Philip had to have his own books printed in the Low Countries or Italy, and the few Spanish book presses were no match for Orange's efficient public relations machinery which Cardinal Granvelle's secretary compared to *"une grande armee."*[4]

Madrid was facing additional difficulties as the conflict in Flanders ate up both government revenue and American silver. In 1573, Philip's expenditures in the Low Countries were roughly four times of what he had spent seven years prior, and two years later the king declared the third "bankruptcy" of his reign. "I am trembling with fear at what the next post from Flanders will bring," Philip was said to have uttered, ready to turn his back on the now discredited policies of wholesale slaughter and violent repression.

In December of that same year the monarch accepted the resignation of his old war horse, the hated Duke of Alba, whose stratagems had brought so much suffering and destruction to the Netherlands. Gentler tones advising appeasement could suddenly be heard from rather unlikely quarters. Cardinal Granvelle, now Viceroy of Naples, sounded off, "If they do not win the goodwill of the people there [in the Netherlands], even sending 20,000 Spaniards will achieve nothing." Three years later he commented, "For the last ten years, I have always written that the policy adopted was very mistaken."[5]

With the Spanish slowly retreating and William no longer on the run, the prince began to contemplate the idea of a private life again. In addition to the forfeiture of his fortune and long years of physical hardship, Orange had suffered horrific personal losses in the past seven years. In 1568, his brother Adolph had

---

[1]Vetter, p. 142.
[2]Cellarius, "Propagandatätigkeit," p. 142.
[3]Verwey, pp. 106-7.
[4]Kamen, pp. 179-241; Cellarius, p. 120.
[5]Kamen, pp. 179-241; Cellarius, "Propagandatätigkeit," p. 120.

given his life at the Battle of Heiligerlee, and when one military failure followed the next, his wife Anna had turned her back on him and made him a laughing-stock by giving birth to another man's child.

Other relatives had betrayed William as well. His brothers-in-law - the Counts Berg and Schwarzburg - defected to the Spanish side, with Schwarzburg even working as one of Alba's advisers. And in April 1574, he lost his best friend, confidant, and favorite sibling, the fearless Louis, along with his younger brother Henry at the Battle of Mookerheyde.[6] At forty-two, William was emotionally and physically drained, but still hopeful. He had survived the ordeal of war, and there was someone with whom he wished to spend his remaining years. To everyone's disbelief, Orange decided on a dynastically inconvenient, but personally reward-ing love match.

Orange must have anticipated the censure and ire that rained upon him when word reached Anna's relations of his engagement. For one, an official di-vorce from the Saxon princess had never taken place, since William had decided against a public trial for fear of unwanted publicity.[7] Besides, Lutheran courts in Germany were generally reluctant to invalidate a marriage.[8] The prince there-fore looked for an official ruling elsewhere. Calvinism allowed divorce in cases of adultery, and in 1575 the prince received a pronouncement of dissolution of wedlock from a panel of reformed Dutch theologians. His union to Anna was indeed disbanded, yet only from a Calvinist standpoint.[9] Still, William considered himself a free man, since reconciliation with the mentally unbalanced Anna was clearly out of the question. When her relatives offered to take charge of her, he readily agreed.[10]

Anna's uncles, of course, protested William's divorce and plans for re-marriage. Their niece's name would be dragged through the mud once Orange remarried, they clamored, and his Calvinist annulment was not accepted in most German principalities. Even more important, the prince's prospective union opened up the issue of a financial settlement. Since Anna had never declared her guilt in front of a judge, they would mandate the return of her dowry and all other payments given to her upon her wedding - a vast fortune lost during the Dutch war of liberation. Moreover, they objected to William's notorious choice of bride for the next Princess of Orange. She would bring shame and embarrassment to all parties concerned, the landgrave and elector huffed in concert.[11] Anna had caused scandal during her marriage, but William's intended, the Frenchwoman Charlotte of Bourbon, got everyone wonderfully excited even before the nuptials. For Charlotte was a renegade nun.

William probably made Charlotte's acquaintance in the spring of 1572, while visiting his ally Frederick III, Elector Palatine, in Heidelberg. At the time, Anna was already under guard in Siegen Castle and the prince sought financial help from the elector for his second invasion of the Low Countries. Orange could hardly have been in a romantic mindset. His pregnant wife had just confessed to an illicit relationship with her Antwerp lawyer, and military progress against

[6]Dupuy,Trevor N., Curt Johnson, and David Bongard. *The Harper Encyclopedia of Military Biography* (New York: Castle Books, 1995), p. 539. Louis was shot in the arm, but carried on fighting. After losing copious amounts of blood, he was brought to a hut to rest. Louis was never seen again, neither alive nor dead.
[7]Wartenberg, p. 85.
[8]Ozment, *Fathers*, p. 57.
[9]Mörke, p. 201.
[10]Putnam, *The Life of William the Silent*, p. 185.
[11]Bromberg, p. 18.

Alba's forces appeared unlikely. Perhaps the warm-hearted, intelligent Charlotte soothed the battered prince with some words of comfort.

She certainly made an impression. Despite the brevity of their encounter, William remained in contact with the French princess who was described as rather plain. Three years later he sent his close friend and envoy, Philip Marnix, Lord of St. Aldegonde, to the electoral court to ask for her hand in marriage.

*****

William's resolution to marry the Bourbon princess was one of only a handful of decisions that did not spring from political calculation, but was motivated by a deep desire for personal happiness. It could be argued that the match furthered William's alliance with the Calvinist Elector Frederick and strengthened his ties with the Dutch Reformed Church, but the disadvantages of the union clearly outweighed its benefits.[12] In addition to Anna's uncles' enraged outcries, Orange's friends and family voiced serious reservations. The French princess had no dowry, they correctly argued, and William still owed large amounts to his troops and numerous creditors. His intended also had few Protestant connections, while the prince was in desperate need of additional allies. Lastly, the Bourbon princess's shocking convent background rendered her fair game for the vilest sort of carnal speculations.[13] But Orange brushed off all advice. After his marital melees with Anna, he was thirsting for domestic contentment, regardless of public opinion.

William was one of several notable Protestants who selected former religious women as partners. Martin Luther - himself a onetime Augustinian monk and priest - married a runaway Cistercian nun, Katharina von Bora, after she fled her convent in a covered fish wagon on Easter Eve 1523.[14] The theologian Martin Bucer (1491-1551) wedded the erstwhile nun Elisabeth Silbereisen with whom he had thirteen children, while in neighboring Switzerland, the reformer Heinrich Bullinger married Anna Adlischwyler, once a nun in a Zurich monastery, who bore him eleven sons and daughters.[15]

Unfortunately, these high-profile marriages could not gloss over the fact that even the most ardent Protestants regarded recreant churchmen and women with a certain amount of skepticism, if not outright disdain. Unlike today, a sacred vow once taken was considered everlasting, and for a nun like Charlotte to renounce holy orders in favor of a secular life was nothing short of shocking. True, William had not spirited his bride away from her cell in a nocturnal cloak-and-dagger operation, but her controversial decision to discard the veil made many wonder. Such bold initiative showed a disquieting amount of "unfeminine" defiance - the kind of defiance that was usually the mark of a wanton woman.

Charlotte of Bourbon was the fourth daughter of Louis II of Bourbon, Duke of Montpensier, and his wife, Jacqueline de Longwy, Countess of Bar-sur-Seine. Extended relations of the French royal family, Louis and Jacqueline were regular attendees at important court functions. In 1559, the couple had taken part in the magnificent coronation ceremony of King Francis II and his beautiful wife

---

[12]Mörke, p. 199.
[13]Wedgwood, p. 154.
[14]Bainton, Roland H. *Here I Stand: A Life of Martin Luther* (New York: Penguin, 1995), p. 223.
[15]Ozment, Steven. *The Age of Reform 1250-1550* (New Haven, CT: Yale University Press, 1980), pp. 386-7.

Mary, Queen of Scots.

In their younger days, both of Charlotte's parents had shown interest in Protestant teachings, proclivities that evidently did not lessen their standing with the staunchly Catholic Valois kings. Jacqueline in particular appears to have been a favorite in Paris, much beloved and influential with all court factions. In fact, as a lady-in-waiting and close friend of Catherine de Medici, she had often interceded with the dowager queen on behalf of the Huguenots. That, however, did not prevent Jacqueline from placing her daughter Charlotte in the Benedictine convent of Paraclet at Jouarre when she was only two weeks old.[16]

Although disconcerting for our modern sensibilities, little Charlotte's abbey transfer was not an unusual practice at the time. Duke Louis was deeply indebted like most of his noble peers and lacked the funds for another daughter's dowry. Economic considerations thus easily outweighed any crises of conscience when Charlotte, like her older sister Jeanne, vanished behind convent walls. In their parents' mind, the monastic profession not only assured their daughters' well-being and physical comfort in an uncertain age, but also guaranteed splendid clerical careers for the girls. Louise de Longwy, Jacqueline's sister, was Jouarre's abbess, and had already agreed to bequeath the dignities and emoluments of that rich convent to her niece.

In 1559, Louise fell fatally ill and the Montpensiers pressured twelve-year-old Charlotte to take the veil. The rich revenues of the convent's lands could only remain in the family if Charlotte acquiesced to becoming a nun, and she was to renounce her inheritance in favor of her only brother. Duke Louis concluded that this was an excellent arrangement for all concerned parties.

There was no mistaking, however, that the young woman opposed her parents' dictates. Quick thinking and mature, the reluctant nun-to-be made a formal declaration to several sworn witnesses. She was about to take her vows under compulsion and at the command of her elders whose displeasure she feared. Apparently, Charlotte's mother had tried to cow her daughter with some particularly intimidating letters.[17] The princess's written testimony stated that the document was "to serve in such time and place as I may require" and was undersigned by notaries.[18] Afterwards, she submitted to a ceremony that was far from tranquil. Observers later remembered that Charlotte wept and protested, and continued to do so even after all the guests had assembled in the chapel.[19]

Six years passed and like her sisters Jeanne and Louise - both encloistered at neighboring convents - Charlotte received her final training as a future abbess. Her disinclination towards the religious vocation had, however, remained, and those around her agreed that the princess had become extremely wary of her permanent seclusion.[20] In 1569, thoughts of alternatives were flitting through Charlotte's mind as she made another formal deposition before a notary, describing the irregular circumstances of her reception into the order. Incidentally, as she was nursing these grievances, a provincial synod of reformed French churches was held nearby. This gathering of Huguenots just outside the Jouarre gates may have further swayed the young abbess in her growing resolution to quit holy

[16]Roelker, p. 417.
[17]Freer, p. 394.
[18]Putnam, *The Life of William the Silent*, pp. 185-7.
[19]Putnam, *The Life of William the Silent*, p. 187
[20]Freer, pp. 393-4.

orders. If the new faith was about to receive official recognition in France, she determined, she could take steps to arrange herself with the anti-Catholic party.

There were examples of such procedures within Charlotte's family. Although her father had renounced his Protestant proclivities in favor of militant Catholicism, the elder branch of the Bourbons boasted several eminent Huguenots. Louis, Prince de Condé, championed the new teachings with fervor, while Jeanne, Queen of Navarre, was widely acknowledged as the noble leader of the French reform movement.[21] Soon after, an anxious Charlotte approached the Navarrese queen, a distant cousin.[22]

The redoubtable Jeanne - onetime wife of William of Cleves - had lost none of her edges at age sixty. An unyielding, bigoted devotee of the Huguenot cause, she had declared Calvinism the official religion in her small kingdom of Navarre. Priests and nuns were banished; Catholic churches destroyed. Warmly attached to Charlotte, the queen evinced an active interest in the young woman's religious uncertainty and advised her on the legal effects of a possible renunciation of her profession.[23]

Perhaps Charlotte reminded Jeanne of her own, ultimately futile struggles against parental commands, and therefore embraced her kinswoman's cause with particular interest. But the queen was also a clever tactician. Charlotte's worth as a royal "poster child" for Protestantism was immense. In 1570, the princess's widowed father had married eighteen-year-old Catherine of Lorraine, sister of the Duke of Guise. The alliance strengthened the duke's ties to the ultra-Catholic Guise party and undoubtedly played a role in Jeanne's keen interest in the abbess of Jouarre. If Charlotte openly converted, the queen calculated, she could be an invaluable boon for *la cause*.[24] Her father, of course, would be mortified.

By the summer of 1571 Charlotte had gathered the courage to defy her family, the church, and society in order to assert her independence. She left Jouarre on horseback—accompanied by two nuns and her brother Francois as well as a small escort of abbey soldiers - on the pretext of visiting a neighboring monastery.[25] At some point during the excursion, Charlotte managed to escape to the baffled fury of her brother, a devout Catholic.

As can be expected, the French court was instantly agog with this juiciest of scandals, leaving the princess's father baffled, overwhelmed, and furious. While he fielded a barrage of questions from inquisitive courtiers, messengers spread the incredulous news around the kingdom that the Abbess of Paraclet had fled her convent in disguise and was travelling east towards the city of Sedan.

Sedan had become a safe haven for Protestant refugees during the Wars of Religion, and was governed by the husband of Charlotte's eldest sister Francoise, Henri-Robert de la Marck, Duke of Bouillon. Due to its position in the northeastern corner of France, close to the borders of the Netherlands, the Palatinate, and Lorraine, the small principality offered ideal shelter for the escapee. Although the dukedom belonged to France, the de la Marcks behaved like sovereign princes and readily offered Charlotte asylum.[26]

---

[21]Putnam, *The Life of William the Silent*, p. 186
[22]Freer, p. 394.
[23]Putnam, *The Life of William the Silent*, p. 186.
[24]Putnam, *The Life of William the Silent*, pp. 187-8.
[25]Putnam, *The Life of William the Silent*, p. 188.
[26]Verwey, p. 108.; Roelker, p. 417.

Henri-Robert and his wife had once been the vanguard of the Huguenot movement and were highly sympathetic to the defector's decision. In 1562,
the duke had already announced that "in a brief time," he and his like-minded
spouse would "eradicate the mass and priests from their lands [which] should not
be prevented because it depended upon God and himself alone."[27] Henri-Robert
was also an ally of William's brother Louis of Nassau, and had openly voiced his
support for an invasion of the Habsburg-controlled Netherlands. He purchased
a printing press which produced Dutch and French religious tracts for his beleaguered co-religionists in the Low Countries.[28] Unfortunately, even the de la
Marck's could not shield Charlotte from her father's boundless wrath, which
eventually forced the princess to flee across the border to the court of the Elector
Palatine, an acknowledged protector of Calvinists. She arrived there in February
1572, and met her future husband, William, a few weeks later.

In France, Charlotte's father Louis mulled his options. His daughter had
to be returned to the Catholic fold, he announced, while engaging in truth-twist-
ing subterfuge concerning the irregularities of Charlotte's ordination. "If she had
only told me herself of her distaste for the convent, I would've looked about for
honest means to take her out and placed her with the least scandal in a position
she preferred," he feigned in apparent surprise. "But who could have dreamed
that she disliked her office after she had lived in her abbey thirteen or fourteen
years, invested with the quality and title of abbess, giving the habit to and receiving the vows from many in my presence and out of it, fulfilling all the duties of
her charge?"

As to his daughter's motives, others were clearly to blame for her ill-conceived escapade. "I cannot agree with you," he wrote to the Elector Palatine, "that
she was moved to take this step by zeal for God's service. It was rather the intrigues of others that tempted her to a liberty devoid of sanctity, and tainted by
the world and the flesh, as is shown by the fact that her sole escort consisted of
two or three companions, vicious and bad people, notorious for their scandalous
lives."

Egged on by his fanatical young wife, Louis roundly expressed his sentiments. "I've never heard that God's glory was advanced by violating an oath
offered voluntarily and frankly, nor that kings, queens, princes, and princesses
of this crown acquired the name of "most Christian" by such extraordinary and
damnable methods," he fulminated. "She is the first of her race to desert the holy
faith of her ancestors, the first who was willing to wear religious garb for eighteen
or more years, live under vows, enjoying the title of abbess … and then, all of a
sudden, without confiding in her father, brother, sister, or kinsfolk, to abandon
everything, king and fatherland, to flee to Germany. The alleged [claim of] compulsion is nothing but a masque to cover her duplicity."

The duke closed his angry missive with complaints about Charlotte's ingratitude, the shameful flow of gossip that was circulating through the realm,
and the impossibility of her receiving any of the property she once renounced in
her brother's favor. He then ordered the Palatine elector to send the princess back
to France, still utterly perplexed that his daughter dared to put personal choice

---

[27]Putnam, *The Life of William the Silent*, p. 187. See also Putnam, *Moderate Man*, p. 158. De la Marck often went to masquerades dressed as
a cardinal or a Franciscan to mock the old religion.
[28]Verwey, p. 108.

before family duty. "Return her to me dead or alive," he bellowed.[29]

Seeking blame elsewhere, Duke Louis also dispatched a commission to Jouarre to investigate why "[T]he lady discarded her habit worn for thirteen or fourteen years without a murmur and [to establish] an inquiry into what had suborned her to such action." His face-saving measures were only partially successful. While all witnesses concurred that Charlotte had fallen under the wicked spell of the "pretend reformed religion," they also testified that the princess had protested her ordination at an uncanonical age before succumbing to maternal pressures.

These blatant irregularities notwithstanding, few of the duke's friends would have raised an eyebrow to such consecratory "inconsistencies." "Forced vocations" were an accepted evil in aristocratic houses with an abundance of daughters but a scarcity of dowry funds. Even if girls showed no proclivity for the strict religious regimen of the cloister, parents expected daughters to submit for the greater good of the family. Tens of thousands did exactly as they were bid, but often smarted in these "dumping grounds for unmarried women." The Italian nun Arcangela Tarabotti (1604-1652), a bitter victim of compulsory monastic enclosure, wrote chillingly that young women like Charlotte were witnesses to their own "funerals" as they received the nun's habit.[30]

Louis of Bourbon, despite his protestations of being caught unawares by his daughter's discontent, had almost certainly been cognizant of Charlotte's religious doubts. When questioned about the princess's state of mind before her elopement, a certain Catherine de Perthuis alluded to a recent breach between the duke and his daughter. Louis had allegedly visited Paraclet to force "the baptism of several Huguenot children." "My lady declared that since her father had played that trick on her, she would play him another and prove that she had no vocation for the convent, but had been forced into her profession."[31] Rather than remaining sorrowfully immured behind the walls Arcangela Tarabotti called "*l'inferno monacale*" ("the monastic hell"), Charlotte bolted.

If her newfound freedom brought personal fulfillment, permanent estrangement from her family weighed heavily on Charlotte. In late March 1572, the princess appealed to Jeanne of Navarre to intercede with her relations. The queen - the highest ranking Protestant in France — replied about a fortnight later that her petition to her father had been in vain. "I perceive how Monsieur de Montpensier views your circumstances; it is true that he continues very irritated." She continued soothingly, "[B]ut I shall never weary of doing what a mother should do for you."[32] It appears that Jeanne withheld much of the duke's latest tirades from her friend. Charlotte was to return to the convent right away, Louis had roared, however not as its honored abbess, but as a humble penitent; that very depth of her humiliation might perhaps earn her the pardon of heaven. A few weeks later, in May, Queen Jeanne was able to send the princess some words of encouragement. "You have many sympathizers, but few dare say anything on account of the bitterness felt by M. de Montpensier."[33]

---

[29]Putnam, *The Life of William the Silent*, pp. 189-90. In past years, Charlotte's father had fought the Huguenots with such ferociousness that even his own captains had turned away from him in disgust.

[30]Laven, Mary. *Virgins of Venice: Broken Vows and Cloistered Lives in the Renaissance Convent* (New York: Viking, 2002), p. 23, p. 27.

[31]Putnam, *The Life of William the Silent*, pp. 190-1.

[32]Roelker, p. 417.; Freer, pp. 394-5.

[33]Putnam, *The Life of William the Silent*, p. 192.

William I, Prince of Orange by Adriaen Thomasz. Rijksmuseum, Amsterdam. Circa 1579

As spring turned into summer, the duke's fury gradually subsided. After the Jouarre commission reported its findings, confirming that Charlotte's statements had been upheld by several nuns at the Paraclet convent, he petitioned the Holy See for a cancelation of his daughter's profession, provided that she renounce her heretical faith. In good time, Louis coaxed, he might even find her a suitable husband. Charlotte, however, respectfully declined her father's overtures. She was content in her new surroundings, she wrote, and devoted to the reformed religion.[34]

Charlotte remained at the Elector Frederick's court in Heidelberg, where her benefactor and his kindly wife Emilia - the former widow Brederode of Anna's Cologne days - treated their guest with affectionate consideration. Along with other French Protestants, Charlotte attended services at the castle chapel that were specifically geared towards her countrymen. The elector prided himself on taking on the role of an ersatz father to the former nun, and also inquired about a suitable husband for his "aging" ward. Yet despite talk of an eligible parti, the only serious contender was William. At the beginning of 1575, his envoy Philip Marnix made a definite offer to the princess who by then was almost thirty years old.[35] The erstwhile abbess gladly accepted the proposal of a man who no longer had much to give in material terms, but perhaps all the more as a spouse and partner.

After years of the most pressing financial worries, William was only just beginning to bring his affairs in order. Towards the end of April, the prince dispatched his brother-in-law Count Hohenlohe with an open letter to his fiancée which spelled out his shaky economic situation in plain language. His explanations left Charlotte with no illusions about the prince's financial state of affairs, and extinguished any notions of a princely life of comfort - if she had ever entertained them. Most of Orange's legendary household goods had been pawned or sold years ago, while unpaid troops and bankers still hounded him for money.[36]

William also pointed out that "Nearly all my property must fall to my older children, so that I am currently unable to assign to Mademoiselle [Charlotte] any dower. But I mean to do the best I can in that respect, according to the means it may please God to give me in the future. The house I have bought at Middelburg and the one I am building at Geertruidenberg are nothing to boast of, but if you will accept them as a beginning, and as a testimony of my goodwill, there will be no difficulty. You must bear in mind, moreover, that we are in the midst of a war whose outcome is uncertain, and that I am deeply in debt for this cause, to princes and other gentlemen, captains, and men-at-arms."[37]

The prince also added an honest note of personal concern: he was no longer the shining young swain of yesteryear. Grueling years of physical deprivation, occasional illness, and mental stress had prematurely aged him, and he was anxious to forestall any disappointment on his bride's part. Hohenlohe was to remind the princess that he "was beginning to grow old, being forty-two years of age."[38]

---

[34]Freer, pp. 394-5.
[35]Putnam, *The Life of William the Silent*, p. 189, p. 193.
[36]Wedgwood, p. 155.
[37]Putnam, *The Life of William the Silent*, p. 196.
[38]Wedgwood, p. 155.

Sober, chastened, and much matured, the prince approached his third marriage with careful consideration. Whereas Anna had received a variety of misleading promises that left her disappointed and hurt, Charlotte was given plain talk. The times of equivocation were long over, William decided. He would speak candidly to his fiancée, an excellent and undemanding woman whom he greatly admired.

She did not disappoint him. Concerning her dowry, Charlotte wrote, she was asking nothing better than "to share with your Excellency what God may please to send our joint lot." Perhaps William could be relied upon to make some suitable property arrangements for her, possibly a house in Burgundy or Orange, she continued, "but only if these estates are not already pledged to your children."[39]

On 12 June 1575, in the small town of Den Briel in southern Holland, the runaway abbess and the rebel prince became man and wife in a simple ceremony. The bride was formally received by deputies of the cities of Dordrecht, Alkmaar, Flushing, and Den Briel, and presented with a gift of six thousand pounds. The previous evening, five Dutch Calvinist divines had reviewed William's request for divorce from Anna of Saxony on the grounds of adultery, and concluded that "Monseigneur the Prince is free according to human and divine law to marry and that she whom he espouses will be, before God and man, his lawful wife."[40] The ruling was, of course, legally contestable. Anna's guilt had never been pronounced by an imperial court, therewith nullifying Orange's argument for a valid divorce in Germany. In fact, William's opponents were already discussing the leveling of bigamy charges against the prince.

Hopefully, Charlotte and her new husband banished any gloomy thoughts as they made a quiet entry into Den Briel's *Grote Kerk*. Jean Taffin, Orange's trusted court chaplain, officiated. In the barebones Calvinist church, gilded statues of angels and saints no longer stared down upon the faithful; instead, somberly clad figures demurely hearkened to the pastor's earnest words. This time around there was no ostentatious display of multi-shaded silk hoses and Venetian brocade capes. Perky bright colors offended God, the austere reformers argued, and anyone who wore them was nothing "but a blown bladder, painted over with so many colors, stuffed full of pride and envy."[41]

After the solemn service, the newlyweds travelled to nearby Dordrecht for a small celebration.[42] Thirteen years and ten months had passed since the bombastic Leipzig nuptials when, among wagon loads of gifts, William had received that dubious prize of a glitteringly arrayed Anna. Charlotte's reception was nothing like it. Armed hostilities in the Netherlands were still ongoing, and it would have been in bad taste to waste much needed funds on costly, ostentatious trinkets. Besides, the prince did not want to provoke the already piqued Elector of Saxony with opulent festivities. We do not know what presents were exchanged, except for a crystal looking glass — a thoughtful gift sent by Catherine de Medici.[43]

Dordrecht's amateur poet association then presented the pair with their written creations. After the horrific loss of life suffered by the Dutch, the prince

[39]Putnam, *The Life of William the Silent*, p. 195.
[40]Putnam, *The Life of William the Silent*, pp. 199-200.
[41]Jenkins, p. 16.
[42]Mörke, p. 202.
[43]Wedgwood, pp. 155-6.

and his new wife made a point of sharing their joy with a select number of ordinary burghers. The couple's conversion to Calvinism also put an end to William's days of raucous dancing. On express orders of the local church council, such gamboling was strictly prohibited.[44]

While the Orange-Bourbon wedding was abstemious and sedate, the ensuing firestorm of outrage was anything but. William's agent in France, Gaspar Schomberg, reported that the union had elicited vicious talk in certain quarters.[45] The Prince of Orange takes a new wife, it was said, as if it wasn't known that his last one had already been too much for him. But then this one was a renegade nun, gossip mongers continued, alluding to the purported sexual insatiability of such women. She had been the mistress of his brother Louis as well as John Casimir's of the Palatine, and Admiral Coligny's "in full measure." Within two months of the nuptials, town chatter confidently reported that *la nonnain* was to be divorced. Her betrayed husband had been informed of her previous dalliance with his late brother.[46]

Charlotte immediately conceived after the wedding, exposing her to additional smears. The Elector of Saxony was particularly prolific in spreading specious rumors after hearing of Orange's third nuptials. By marrying the ex-abbess, he clamored in his correspondence, William had publicly repudiated his niece. This was an open affront to the dignity of the Wettins which would not go unpunished. For all he knew, the Bourbon princess might have been a prostitute before her wedding. After all, she was known to be of the basest character. She had lied and stolen in her youth, and was eventually put in a convent by her helpless parents. After fleeing to Heidelberg, she quickly consorted with that chief of knaves, William of Orange. Was Charlotte already pregnant when she met him? he wondered.

In fact, August pounced, the grown-up whore (Charlotte) was presenting her faithless husband with a little whore. William was getting two harlots for the price of one. He ended his poisonous letters, which he addressed not only to personal friends, but also to a number of imperial princesses, with a smattering of dirty jokes.[47] Orange, whose former wife Anna had already given birth to an illegitimate child, might have cringed at such hateful spite.

Eager to add to the Saxon invective, the Landgrave of Hessen continued the mudslinging. He told Count John that tales about Orange's "beautiful wife" had recently been spread during a diet of princes in Regensburg. Charlotte had allegedly "lain with many others and multiplied," putting William's paternity in doubt.[48]

Although Anna's uncles took obvious pleasure in maligning an innocent woman, the real issue at hand was the return of Anna's fantastic dowry. The electress had requested Luther and Melanchthon's collected opinions on adulterous husbands from Wittenberg University right after the Rubens scandal had broken, hopeful for a return of Anna's riches into Saxon treasure chambers.[49] In May 1575, the Saxon envoy von Berlepsch arrived in Kassel to consult with Landgrave

---

[44]Mörke, p. 202.
[45]Putnam, *The Life of William the Silent*, p. 201.
[46]Wedgwood, p. 156.
[47]Kruse, "Wilhelm von Oranien," p. 143.
[48]Kruse, "Wilhelm von Oranien," p. 127.
[49]Keller, *Kurfürstin*, p. 126, p. 232. The university's findings have gone unrecorded, but at the time, the Wettins clearly expected a divorce to take place, accompanied by dowry repayments.

William and Count John on the matter. The Nassaus had to realize, the elector stressed via Berlepsch, that the Prince of Orange had triggered Anna's moral lapse. He had not only exposed the princess to sin, but led her directly into it. For that reason it was only right and proper that he return her legendary wedding portion.

August and the landgrave indulged in moral outrage for much of the remaining summer months, both assuming a moral high ground that was not theirs to claim. The elector had previously lectured his sister Sidonia on bearing her husband's blatant infidelities in the most cavalier manner, markedly unconcerned about Duke Eric's "sinful" lifestyle. In contrast, August's very personal quarrel with William was fueled by lingering embarrassment over his niece's failed marriage, spite, and simple greed. A prudent householder with a talent for finance, the elector had already amassed unprecedented wealth, and was hardly in need of funds from the impecunious Orange.[50]

As for William of Hessen, his pique stemmed from worries about another blow to his family's prestige. He was, of course, acutely aware that bigamy charges could wreak havoc with the prince's reputation, and prodded Orange with some rather unpleasant insinuations about the effects of a public trial. William pointedly ignored these barbs. Perhaps he looked back on those dreadful Christmas days in 1569, when he had camped out in the ante-rooms of Dresden palace, pleading for an audience which the elector never granted. Assistance from either Saxony or Hessen had dried up long ago, and the prince was no longer afraid to cut ties with allies that had rarely stood by him. After the Den Briel wedding, William composed a polite epistle to the elector, informing him that after his many sufferings, he had tired of life as a quasi-widower and desired to enjoy the comforts of marriage. He neither mentioned his ex-wife nor the refunding of her dowry.[51]

William's Nassau relations soon joined the Saxon and Hessian choruses of rebuke, albeit for different reasons. A few weeks before the wedding his usually deferential younger brother, Count John, had gathered the family in Dillenburg to discuss Orange's upcoming nuptials. As the head of the impoverished German branch of the family, John could ill afford to alienate his neighbor, the influential landgrave, or the even more powerful August of Saxony.

The count had been quite ill and had trouble writing, but rushed off an anxious note to William's confidant Philip Marnix, Lord of St. Aldegonde. "Dear Aldegonde, if you have any love for the prince … and if you do not want to run into danger yourself, let this thing be delayed for a time; at least until we can be sure of the foundation of other friendships. It is a shame to put all friendships in jeopardy. The matter is surely worthy of consideration. But of what use is endless writing? I and other good hearts must look on sadly and let it go as it will, because it cannot be otherwise, but I cannot help telling you, that if this matter be pushed on so roughly, you will not be seen in Germany."

He also shared his apprehensions with the resourceful Dr. Schwarz. He could simply not fathom that his brother was in earnest, John groaned. After all, no divorce had been officially granted, and if Orange persisted in this course,

---

Anna's position might be altered. Imperial judges would reach a verdict of mutual delinquency and demand compensation which the Nassaus did not have.[52] Feverish with worry, the count felt it necessary to apologize to the landgrave. The marriage was not his fault, he wrote, for he had tried everything in his power to change his brother's mind.

William of Hessen's reply was magnanimous. He could well believe that such a union did not meet with the Nassaus' approval, or with any person of sound mind for that matter. Orange must be distracted by his political troubles to even dream of such mad, insensate action. He commented, "I cannot understand what the prince is thinking of, let alone that wiseacre Aldegonde, or whoever else has helped in the affair."

Giving his thoughts free reign on paper, he continued, "The Bourbon princess could not have been any less suitable. You must remember that she is French, and a nun, a runaway nun at that, about whom all kinds of stories are told of the way she kept her cloister vows before the prince wanted to put himself out of the mud into the sea. ... If it is beauty he's after, you could hardly believe he was charmed by that, since, undoubtedly, no one can look at the bride without being frightened rather than pleased." He concluded with a cautionary postscript, "They had better look to it that it does not go as it did with the admiral at the Paris wedding, for gentlemen do not pardon such injuries without mercury and sublimated arsenic."[53]

The landgrave was alluding to the so-called "Blood Wedding" of August 1572, one of the darkest episodes in French history. A massacre had taken place during the nuptials of Henry of Navarre and Marguerite of Valois when all of France's great leaders—Protestant and Catholic—had gathered in Paris for the festivities. It was generally hoped that the union between the Huguenot prince and the Catholic princess would ease faith relations and put a halt to the ongoing religious wars. The mother of the groom, Jeanne of Navarre, had entertained particularly high expectations for "la cause."

On August 22, however, Paris slid into tense disquiet when the leader of the French Protestants, Admiral Gaspar de Coligny, survived an assassination attempt. Two days later, on St. Bartholomew's Eve - the feast day of William and Anna's Leipzig wedding - Coligny was brutally murdered. His death unleashed a spiral of bloodshed which resulted in the extermination of some three thousand Huguenots in Paris and a further 25,000 or more in various parts of the country.[54] Along with members of the royal family, Charlotte's father, the Duke of Montpensier, had approved the carnage.

As a convert to Calvinism with a heretical wife, the landgrave insinuated, William stood in danger of meeting an equally sudden end through the more subtle means of poison. It was, though, not the French who wanted him dead. With Charlotte established outside the kingdom, an agent informed William in March 1575, "The king does not wish to mix himself up in this affair, and the Queen Mother [Catherine de Medici] is of the same opinion. In short, they will not take an ill part what Mademoiselle does by the advice of Count Palatine, provided it is not against the service of the king."[55] This position was confirmed at

---

[52]Putnam, *The Life of William the Silent*, pp. 197-9.
[53]Putnam, *The Life of William the Silent*, pp. 199-200.
[54]Kamen, p. 141.
[55]Putnam, *The Life of William the Silent*, p. 195.

the wedding, when Catherine de Medici sent the newlyweds a valuable mirror. It was rather the Elector of Saxony who, ruffled by William's repudiation of his niece, might resort to aggressive measures. The purge of Caspar Peucer and the "crypto-Calvinists" a year earlier had laid bare August's violent personality. It was well-known by now that the elector knew no bounds if he felt his honor and reputation compromised.

Somehow William remained unfazed by the ongoing uproar. He was convinced of the merits of his impending marriage, possibly even in love, and therefore willing to flout the wishes of family members and peers. He had converted faiths several times, married twice for the good of the house, and reached a point in his life when the opinions of others mattered less to him. With engaging frankness, Orange reiterated to his brother John what he had already told Anna's uncle. He was simply tired "of the state of widowhood in which, to my great regret, I had to remain for so long."[56]

William also addressed some of his brother's legal worries in regards to Anna. All documents pertaining to her adulterous affair should be put in safekeeping with the Elector Palatine, he instructed. "I would be obliged, if you made the culprit [Rubens] confess his misdeeds again before some gentlemen and people of quality, so that you and I should be more at ease, and be sure of him for our greater security if anyone should hereafter malign us, and accuse us of illegal imprisonment."[57] At the time, Rubens was still living at the Brambach estate in Siegen. It is possible that Count John summoned him for another interview of which records, unfortunately, have not survived.

Still, John was unable to shake his sense of discomfort. At the beginning of June he appealed to his brother for a final time, begging William to halt the upcoming ceremonies. "Honored Prince," he wrote respectfully, "although it does not become me to prescribe measures to Your Highness, I must confess that the unseemly haste in this important matter shocks me, and I certainly cannot further your public affairs. The "other party's" relatives [in Saxony] will be furious," he worried, and "her dowry [Anna's] will be demanded, which will be very inconvenient to pay back, as it amounts to 12,500 thalers a year."[58]

Orange did not reply until several weeks after the wedding. "My method has always been ... not to trouble myself about objections to anything I could conscientiously do without wronging my neighbors," he explained nonchalantly. "If I had heeded the objections of princes and others, would I ever have embarked on the enterprise [the war of liberation] I have undertaken? As soon as I was convinced that neither prayers nor exhortations would have any effect, I saw that active resistance was the sole course open. It is the same thing now with my marriage. It is something I do with a clear conscience before God and without just cause for reproach from men. Concerning the difficulties you raise, of dowry and provisions for children who may be born to me, pray consider that no delay until the next diet, or the next century, so to say, would have solved them. I firmly believe that I have taken the right course, not only for myself, but for the public good."[59]

[56]Wedgwood, p. 154.
[57]Putnam,*The Life of William the Silent*, p. 199.
[58]Putnam, *The Life of William the Silent*, p. 199.
[59]Putnam, *The Life of William the Silent*, p. 201

The storm eventually subsided. Most of the Nassaus and Bourbons, bar Count John and the Duke of Montpensier, progressively swallowed their dismay. At the end of June the newly-minted Princess of Orange addressed a dutiful note to her mother-in-law Juliana, evidently hoping to be received into the family. The countess was happy to oblige. Among Charlotte's own relations, her younger sister Louise, abbess of the convent of Farmoutiers, was the first to extend the olive branch to her disobedient sibling. She dispatched a warm note to William in August 1575, offering congratulations on his recent marriage. "I count her very happy to be sought by a prince as virtuous and sage as your reputation makes you." The victim of a forced vocation like Charlotte, Louise may have empathized with her sister's motives for leaving the religious life.

And even Francois, the princess's stalwartly Catholic brother, did not repulse his sister's feelers and entered into a lasting correspondence with the Oranges that same summer. In turn, William pleaded with the French prince to use his "singular courtesy and honesty" in persuading his father "to take back my wife into his good graces, and to recognize her as one who has the honor to be his daughter."

Unfortunately, the Duke of Montpensier was less forbearing than his children. The shame and disgrace connected with Charlotte's shirking of family duty had so contravened the Lord's commandment of filial piety that he could not bring himself to forgive her. The Elector of Saxony proved equally unrelenting. Enraged that Anna's wedding portion could never be recouped, August engineered a campaign of intimidation against William's supporters. In the fall of 1575 the Elector Palatine, Charlotte's fatherly Calvinist mentor, suddenly distanced himself from the newlyweds. Pressured by Saxony, he publicly declared that the controversial union had not been his doing.[60]

---

[60]Putnam, *The Life of William the Silent*, p. 201.

Charlotte of Bourbon (1546.47-1582), William's third wife, attributed to Daniël van den Queborn (fl. 1577–1602)

Unhinged

If Anna was kept in the dark about William's Dutch wedding is uncertain, but it was during that early summer of 1575 that she unraveled physically and mentally. In addition to her ex-husband's Bourbon marriage, the death of her aunt may have further shaken her fragile equilibrium and contributed to her gradual descent into madness. Sidonia had been preparing for another journey to Vienna to sue Eric for non-payment of certain obligations, when she passed away at the beginning of the year.[1] Her funeral sermon suggests a stroke as cause of death, since the duchess had been complaining of faintness and loss of speech. It is entirely possible, however, that Eric finally managed to have his wife assassinated by means of poison.[2]

Except for the landgrave and the electoral couple, relations who hardly had her best interest at heart, Anna was virtually friendless now. Still sequestered in Beilstein, she spent many days in a haze of paranoia and depression, nonetheless aware that something in her head was not working quite right. To find relief, Anna doused herself with vast quantities of olive oil, most likely following the advice of a popular medical manual that she kept by her bedside. She also asked to see a "doctor from an imperial city," instead of "a *Westerwald* quack."[3] In October she requested a physician from Marburg and apothecary from Cologne to attend to her in Beilstein. Since the latter turned out to be Dutch and a relation of Jan Rubens, Count John appealed to the landgrave for permission, who promptly denied it.[4]

As before, Anna complained about inadequate meals, despite her kitchen staff's best efforts to serve her fish and meat, and was drinking heavily. It can safely be said that the princess was an alcoholic by now, an unusual and rarely mentioned addiction for a sixteenth-century noblewoman.[5] On November 30 Count John informed the landgrave that according to her servants, the erstwhile Princess of Orange was no longer in command of her senses. In addition to uncontrollable tremors in her hands, she was foaming at the mouth and suffered from exhaustion, leaving her barely mobile.[6]

This was grave news. Madness was a frightening thing; a horrifying affliction that upended respected families, wreaked havoc among ancient dynasties, and stigmatized the affected. Worse, in the absence of competent physicians or medicines, there were few, if any, effective cures. According to historian Adrian Tinniswood, the responsibility for those suffering from disorders of the mind largely lay with relatives. Adequate facilities for mental patients were still in the far off future, and options for care extremely limited. There were no state-run institutions at a time when the concept of a nation state was only just emerging, and city and county officials did not get involved in what was considered a private family affair. Individuals deemed harmless, such as the proverbial "village idiot," freely prowled around town, their upkeep usually paid for by parish funds if there were no kinfolk.[7]

---

[1]Lilienthal, p. 238.
[2]Knöfel, *Dynastie*, p. 125.
[3]Midelfort, pp. 59-60.
[4]Böttcher, p. 268.
[5]Keller, *Kurfürstin*, p. 210
[6]Kruse, "Wilhelm von Oranien," p. 129.
[7]Tinniswood, p. 380.

The first privately funded madhouses on record appeared in the Netherlands in Den Bosch and Utrecht in the first half of the fifteenth century.[8] In England, by comparison, the first insane asylums only sprung up about two hundred years later, and then only in large metropolitan areas. For example, in the northeast corner of London stood the vast and decaying Bethlehem Hospital - commonly known as the "Bedlam" - a frightening place that was a lock-up rather than a therapeutic center. It catered to paupers who were a danger to themselves and to others. "Patients" were chained and on view to anyone who cared to wander into the hospital, usually kept for a year, and then discharged. Contemporaries made no secret that madhouses were prisons, just like the institutions where beggars and thieves were confined, and inmates often spent their days in chains.[9]

Only a few of these institutions were run by actual physicians, while many boasted of the fact that they were actually not run by medical professionals. It was considered inappropriate for those who stood to benefit from a patient's protracted state of illness to be in charge of the treatment.[10]

The day to day care of the suffering was thus left to untrained wardens who often abused their helpless charges, depriving them of what little dignity they had managed to retain. In addition, madness often served a source of amusement for the sane, who visited lunatic asylums to tease and mock the unfortunate internees.[11] For these reasons, public establishments were clearly not an alternative for the wealthy. Mental troubles were a source of shame and anxiety and required extremely delicate handling. Disagreeable "occurrences" were usually hushed up; the unstable locked away in secrecy.[12]

Among royalty, trusted officials and minders were experienced in covering up the embarrassing paroxysms of their betters. Mental illness was a common predicament as centuries of inbreeding steadily took their toll. Until the mid-sixteenth century, "imbeciles and lunatics" were summarily dealt with since no ruling dynasty could afford to let the personal disaster of insanity threaten the stability of the house. While well-meaning families sometimes hired patient gentlewomen servants and nurses to care for mentally sick, others disposed of their ill with startling brutality. Children stashed parents away in remote wings of their castles and vice versa, often under miserable conditions.

Those who were not incarcerated encountered rejection and ridicule, if not hostility, due to widespread ignorance about mental disease. Unfeeling relations told persons experiencing depression and other symptoms of mental disturbance to simply pull themselves together. A seventeenth-century English aristocrat said about his unhappy daughter-in-law, "I doubt all the physic in the world will cure her, unless she strives against her melancholy and in a good measure prove her own doctor." The fault as well as the solution thus lay with the patient.[13]

---

[8]Spierenburg, p. 184. The first Dutch madhouse was founded at Den Bosch in 1442, financed by a bequest from Reinier van Arkel. Twenty years later Utrecht got the second madhouse, given by the nobleman Willem Arntsz. The charter admitted six "poor, miserable, mad, and raging people who are in need of being kept constrained or under lock." In the northern Netherlands the word *dolhuis* was to become customary (*Tollhaus* in German).

[9]Spierenburg, pp. 185-6. In a 1603 document, the cells in Utrecht madhouses are called jails. In the absence of drugs, madhouses like one in Bruges also used handcuffs, strait jackets, and masks to subdue unruly patients.

[10]Tinniswood, p. 381, p. 383, p. 394.

[11]Spierenburg, p. 186. In 1657, crowds visiting Bedlam had become so huge that administrators decided to close on Sundays. In the Netherlands, visits to the insane were more regulated. At Den Bosch the staff treated patients to warm pies on the day preceding Shrove Tuesday which many people found worth watching. Utrecht had its own "madhouse fair" on Easter Monday and the Tuesday after.

[12]Farge, p. 607.

[13]Tinniswood, p. 359, p. 374.

By the second half of the 1500s, attitudes towards princely madness were gradually changing in Germany. A new generation of physicians attempted to label the gamut of the different psychological disorders and treated patients with a range of rudimentary healing efforts. As a rule, families no longer immured their ill without an echo of therapy, but hired groups of healers who tried, with varying rates of success, to restore the master to health.[14]

Nonetheless, cures for mental disease were still in their earliest infancy, and while the prescribed potions and suppositories were usually non-toxic, they rarely mended an unstable mind. For example, when Duke Albrecht Frederick of Prussia (1553-1618) refused to change his shirt, because "Turks and Muscovites were about to overwhelm Germany," his physicians discussed a hair-raising regimen of "remedies." Changes in diet, bleeding, and the administering of purges and emetics were standard responses, but a myriad of outlandish creations that seem to defy any logic also found regular prescription. The application of the entrails of a freshly killed snow white dog to the duke's head might do the trick, they deliberated, or the similar utilization of a black hen, also freshly slaughtered. Or perhaps His Highness would regain his senses after ingesting a restorative of powdered pearls or a roasted concoction of bean straw and vermouth.[15] Every doctor had his own particular recipes, from pimpernel juice taken through the nostrils to suppositories of Castilian soap. Another cure for depression hints at magic in its insistence on using a virgin ram.[16]

While doctors commonly agreed that madness was a medical condition that could and should be treated, Renaissance remedies offered few curative options for the insane. The ancient Greco-Roman system of health with its four humors of black bile, yellow bile, phlegm, and blood was still the predominant theory on the workings of the body and mind. Any imbalance between these interconnected fluid substances from either excess or deficit could produce or increase mental instability, such as excessive anger and hilarity or fear and sadness. Culprits ranged from disproportionate exposure to heat or smoke to music and sexual excitement, all of which could throw the body off balance. If such a disturbance continued too long, or if one lived immoderately, like Anna, one of the natural humors might become overheated and degenerate into an unnatural sludge called "melancholy adust" or "burned black bile." This in turn could induce severe mania, a raving melancholy combined with visual and aural hallucinations, uncontrollable weeping, and a general madness that was increasingly difficult to treat.[17]

The Saxon princess, who was experiencing all of the above, would have been diagnosed with such an unfortunate "imbalance," had she been granted access to a physician. Improvement, however, could not realistically be expected, since the theories of humoralism were not questioned until a hundred years later, and effective drugs to treat illnesses such as bi-polar disorders and schizophrenia were still hundreds of years away[18]. Moreover, while changing attitudes in regards to treatment methods for the mentally unstable were progressing in some

---

[14]Midelfort, pp. 15-6, p. 45.
[15]Midelfort, p. 77
[16]Tinniswood, p. 361. See also Spierenburg, 182. In the Netherlands in the sixteenth and seventeenth centuries, so-called stonecutters were active. They profited from the popular notion that insanity might be caused by a stone in one's head. Apparently, the cutter pretended to make an incision in the forehead and then presented a stone to the credulous client.
[17]Midelfort, p. 10, p. 14.
[18]Tinniswood, p. 361.

parts of the empire, harsh handling of the afflicted was still common, even in the highest circles of society.

A strict regimen of discipline was the preferred response to madness, an attempt to impose behavioral norms on those whose most obvious symptom was a refusal to abide by them. "Therapies" ranged from sedation and stern words to more violent attempts at a cure. For rowdy women like Anna, one such "management" was the medieval practice of ducking in water. And yet, even the most enthusiastic advocates of this particular form of shock therapy admitted that it was a good idea to clear things with the local magistrate beforehand, "since some through fear, or because they are not strong enough to stand out this method, may miscarry and die."[19]

Disturbed men were just as cruelly manhandled, though by different techniques. Don Carlos, son and heir of William's enemy, the King of Spain, is a case in point. A genetic victim of intermarriage - he only had four great-grand-parents instead of the usual eight - the Prince of the Asturias was born deformed and frail in 1545. At age fourteen, tales of his peculiar character already made the rounds in Madrid. Ambassadors recounted blood-curdling stories of animal abuse and sexual harassment of servants. Portraits at the time also hint at misshapen legs and a twisted face.

In 1561, the prince fell down some stairs while chasing a maid, incurring a severe head injury. At first, doctors despaired for his life, but when upon the Duke of Alba's suggestion, Don Carlos touched the mummy of a local saint, the Franciscan Diego de Alcala, he recovered. Unfortunately, his health remained poor and his character difficult. Three years later, the imperial ambassador commented on Carlos's violent nature, intemperate speech, and gluttony. To his father's chagrin, he also developed a bizarre attachment to the queen, his stepmother, which took the form of buying her expensive jewelry. Much more serious, of course, was the deranged infante's inability to handle affairs of state. Philip was well aware that his inept heir could never be entrusted with the governing of unruly Flanders.[20] The problem was that the prince fully expected to do so.

When the Duke of Alba took his leave from the king as newly appointed governor of the Netherlands in April 1567, Don Carlos went berserk during the farewell ceremony. "It is I, not Alba, who should be going to Brussels," the prince screamed, and according to one version, then attempted to kill the duke. After his father cancelled a promised later sailing to the Low Countries, the infante threatened to murder Philip. "If God does not send a remedy," the French ambassador sighed, "some great mischance may happen."

After his humiliating public tantrum had blown over, Carlos retreated into plotting. He spent much of his days hatching a coup d'état and fired off numerous letters to the grandees of Spain, asking for their support. The prince also chased phantoms of escape such as taking a ship to Italy with the king's half-brother, Don Juan. On Christmas Day, a crestfallen, but not unsurprised King of Spain received the news that his successor was intriguing against him and immediately consulted with his advisers.[21] The infante's behavior had become untenable, they decided. He had to be stopped.

---

[19]Tinniswood, p. 362.
[20]Kamen, pp.120-1.
[21]Kamen, p. 121.

On 18 January 1568, Philip asked his valet for his armor and helmet. Together with his aides and members of the council of state, the steel-clad monarch proceeded to his son's bedchamber just before midnight. They entered the room stealthily and seized all weapons and documents. Don Carlos, roused from sleep, asked drowsily, "Who is it" before catching sight of his beweaponed father. "Has Your Majesty come to kill me?" he asked. After some words of reassurance, Philip informed Carlos that despite their affinity, he would not treat him as a father ought to, but as a king should. He then commanded officials to remove all heavy objects and nail up the windows. Afterwards they withdrew. Don Carlos, confused and frightened, remained shut up in a tower of the Alcazar palace, watched over by a permanent guard of two.[22]

With his attempt at filial rebellion an utter failure, the infante's disordered psyche went into a tailspin. He refused food for several weeks and ultimately swallowed one of his rings, believing that diamonds were toxic. As summer approached, Don Carlos subjected himself to extreme changes of temperature by covering his bed with ice. His health already battered, he fell ill and died in the early hours of July 24, only twenty-three years old. The court went into mourning for a year. An observer later claimed that the king "wept three days for his son." If he wept, it was probably not from mere sorrow, for Philip had never felt close to his heir.[23] He mourned for Spain and the loss of the child who should one day have ruled the vast Spanish possessions in Europe and the Americas. But he also knew that Carlos could not have fulfilled the tasks that were expected of him. Philip once told the pope that the crown prince had been, quite simply, "completely lacking in the capacity needed for ruling over states."[24]

Like Don Carlos of Spain, Anna was never given the benefit of a medical diagnosis by a physician, but merely shut away. Disturbed women unsettled society even more than men, since their bodies and minds were still a mystery to the medical establishment. There was something inherently grotesque and secretive about the female anatomy, medical experts argued, and no one, even women themselves dared to talk or speculate about its workings in the interest of chastity.[25] Explanations for womanly abnormalities of the brain such as anxiety, choking sensations, and symptoms of hysteria had long been thought to be caused by the uterus moving up through a woman's body until, in extreme cases, it blocked her throat. The theory of "uterine displacement" was persistent and taught until the late nineteenth century.[26]

Confinement without treatment was therefore a preferred option, especially for someone like Anna whose moral compass was dangerously misaligned. Her list of unbalanced behavior included the mistreatment of servants, depression, violence, sexual wantonness, and alcohol addiction. Since she had been given plenty of chances for improvement, but failed miserably at redeeming herself, Anna deserved no therapy in the eyes of her relations, only the strictest discipline.[27]

*****

[22]Kamen, p. 121.
[23]Kamen, p. 122.
[24]Kamen, p. 121.
[25]Gowing, p. 10, p. 30.
[26]Tinniswood, p. 361
[27]Midelfort, p. 154.

Sadly, no one at the time could have known that much of the princess's disorderly behavior probably stemmed from an unrecognized medical condition that can be treated today. Although a retrogressive diagnosis is certainly problematic, a team of German doctors considered contemporary accounts by relatives, officials, and servants sufficient for a partial analysis. While Anna had been known for erratic behavior and an eccentric streak even in her teens and early twenties, other symptoms joined her youthful idiosyncrasies around the time of her house arrest in Siegen, and worsened after her punitive transfer to Beilstein. There, the princess's irritability, "hard head,"and depression were compounded by extreme fears and unpredictable spurts of anger.[28] After months of house arrest in the *Westerwald*, observers commented on her ever worsening agitation, gradual mental disassociation, confusion, and hallucinations. Yet she was never catatonic, and there were no signs of schizophrenic behavior.

Other clusters of symptoms point to a specific disease pattern: the princess complained of a rapid heartbeat, tremors, and muscle weakness that sometimes confined her to her bed for weeks on end as well as menstrual difficulties. Her household staff stated that Anna's face often appeared flushed and that bursts of feverish, almost manic activity rapidly alternated with drastic slumps in stamina. Together with her moodiness, exaggerated sensitivity, and an inclination to self-pity and rages, the puzzle of the princess's mystery illness has ultimately been identified as Graves' disease, a relatively severe thyroid disorder.[29]

Even before Anna's symptoms clearly manifested themselves, there were possible indications of the disorder, which is known as Basedow's Syndrome in Europe. In addition to prickly fretfulness, sufferers of this condition sometimes develop bulging eyes. The 1561 portrait by Le Bouq, sketched shortly after the Leipzig nuptials, shows Anna with protruding eyes - a trait that neither of her parents exhibited. In fact, images of her father Maurice depict him with smallish, slightly slanted eyes.

Graves can also provide an explanation for the princess's immoderate wine consumption. Individuals with the disease sweat up to five liters per day, leaving them perpetually dehydrated. While there is no doubt that Anna used alcohol as an anti-depressant, her unquenchable thirst can also be ascribed to her defective thyroid gland. A similar explanation has been found for the princess's constant hunger pangs in Beilstein. Although she was by no means denied food - Count John allotted her a monthly average of thirty-three chicken and eighty-three pounds of fish - the princess cried about falling asleep with a grumbling stomach.

Regrettably, Anna's lifestyle inadvertently aggravated her steadily deteriorating autoimmune complaint. Doctors usually advise patients with the disease to limit their alcohol and meat intake. Yet besides spirits, the princess devoured enormous meat portions as was custom at the time. A perennial culinary favorite in the Renaissance, meat was a popular aphrodisiac and therefore prohibited during Lent. The contemporary Flemish advice book *The Regimen of Health* encouraged its readers to forgo fruits and vegetables for a "more wholesome diet"

---

[28]Keller,*Kurfürstin*, p. 211.
[29]Pletz-Krehahn, "Krankheit,"p. 207.

of pork and beef.[30] In December 1572 Anna's well-meaning Uncle William even had two barrels of game delivered to Beilstein; veritable poison for the ailing princess.[31]

A number of other factors also contributed to Anna's tragic decline. The emotional traumas of her unhappy youth in Dresden, the unsuccessful transplant to the Netherlands, and repeated pregnancies further weakened a brittle psyche that had already been damaged by her parents' deaths. Of course, immaturity played a part as well, as evidenced in the princess's flightiness and lack of interest in her children. Overall, Anna was a woman overwhelmed by the demands of her station, perhaps even life in general, and that, combined with the effects of her failing health, set her on a troubled path.

Anna often stated the need to be protected. A healthy lifestyle, select diet, but most importantly, persons willing to devote an enormous amount of patience and forbearance to her problems could have eased her plight. Instead, relatives and clerics showered her with cautionary warnings and threats that were mostly counterproductive.[32] As Godfrey of Nassau taunted and the walls of her Beilstein quarters stifled, the "evil forest" was inevitably closing in on her. In severe cases, untreated Graves' disease can lead to a symptomatic psychosis, which may have been the case during Anna's final months in the *Westerwald* forest.

On top of her thyroid disorder, the princess was also burdened with a genetic heritage of insanity and inbreeding. All of Anna's paternal forebears, except for her father's parents, were also included in her mother's genealogy, and several of her ancestors had exhibited peculiar, if not downright deranged behavior. Her Hessian great-grandfather, William II, was called an "impure satyr"and died in 1508 after three years of "melancholy insanity" which was largely attributed to syphilis.[33] But his older brother, also named William, had to relinquish the rule of the landgraviate due to mental infirmity. Contemporaries called him "weak," "sick," and possessed by "the devil."[34]

On her father's side, both grandparents were noted for strange conduct. Chroniclers described Catherine of Mecklenburg as mean and violent-tempered, with a strong penchant for vanity and profligacy. If angered, she sometimes refused to talk to her immediate family for weeks on end, and her fierce reaction to Maurice marrying Agnes certainly raised eyebrows.[35] In a reversal of the traditional gender roles, Anna's grandfather Henry once admitted that "[H]e was not man enough for his Käthe (Catherine)."[36] Before his death, the duke became so apathetic and feeble-minded that he left the running of his lands to his wife and heir.

Anna's father, the subsequent duke and elector of Saxony, had inherited his mother's intelligence, but also her volatile personality. He was known by friends and foes alike for his passionate, fearsome nature as well as his extreme willfulness and emotional instability. His unfortunate daughter might have been the ostensible heiress of her father's unhappy disposition.[37]

[30]de Dijn, p. 178.
[31]Pletz-Krehan, "Krankheit,"pp. 210-1.
[32]Pletz-Krehan, "Krankheit,"p. 208.
[33]Kruse, "Wilhelm von Oranien," p. 149, citing the Zimmerische Chronik.
[34]Midelfort, pp. 41-2.
[35]Ulbricht, p. 107.
[36]Kruse, "Wilhelm von Oranien," p. 147.
[37]Pletz-Krehan, "Krankheit,"p. 210.

*****

By the time Count John apprised the elector of Anna's violent delusions, the latter's shallow reservoir of patience had long dried up. Throughout the ages the wealthy are generally permitted to act out more of their whims and obsessions than ordinary folk, but there was a limit to what was considered acceptable behavior, and Anna had crossed that limit long ago.[38] The "lawyer's whore" had to be sequestered behind thick walls in Saxony, August decided, as he had suggested many times since the scandal broke. Even her erstwhile husband had finally agreed to this necessary measure. In a letter to Dresden, William of Orange had plainly stated that he no longer objected to the elector's plan of incarceration and even consented to letting a report of Anna's death go abroad. He only stipulated that her Saxon family bear the full onus for such a "procedure."[39]

Clearly, August harbored no reservations about said "procedure." The elector wanted family honor restored and had long tired of Nassau stratagems that prevented him from dealing with his intractable niece. Only recently, the dawdling landgrave had declined his suggestion of keeping the princess in one of his Kassel manors, citing a litany of excuses (the hunting lodges were occupied, his wife was ready to give birth, the plague was in the land, etc.) and instead proposed to have Anna extradited to Saxony. On 15 November 1575, the irritated elector instructed one of his officials, Captain Wolf Bosen, to bring the wayward princess home. [40]

After one uncle washed his hands of Anna's fate, the other set a diabolical plan in motion. Besides silencing the mad adulteress of Beilstein, August wanted her former paramour neutralized. Captain Bosen was riding toward the *Westerwald* with a retinue of armed guards, when August's right-hand-man, Eric von Berlepsch, travelled west to find Jan Rubens. The lawyer remained a dangerous witness, the elector determined, able to divulge inconvenient truths to a jury on the Nassaus' behest, namely admitting under oath that he had carnally known his niece. Such testimony threatened to undermine the Wettins' case for the return of her dowry, a matter August would not let die. To that end, Rubens had to be waylaid unnoticed, the elector told von Berlepsch, and brought to "a secret end." This should be an easy task, he assured the envoy, since Rubens was no longer behind lock and key, but under house arrest at the Brambach's.[41]

For unknown reasons, the elector's directives were not carried out. Perhaps August rescinded his orders, or the armed guards patrolling the estate scared any would-be assassins away, because Rubens spent the next few years in Siegen, unmolested. Anna, on the other hand, did not escape the elector's wrath and was removed from Beilstein by carriage. In legal terms, such a procedure was commonly known as a "mandate for surreptitious capture." Usually pronounced by an imperial court ruling, it was a special order that permitted a parent or guardian to take a willful relative into paternal custody, for example "a woman who had behaved in a bad and dishonorable way, contrary to maidenly disci-

---

[38] Midelfort, p. 155.

[39] Putnam, *The Life of William the Silent*, p. 185.

[40] Kruse, "Wilhelm von Oranien," p. 130.

[41] Kruse, "Wilhelm von Oranien," p. 130, p. 174. At the time, heated negotiations were still taking place between Nassau and Saxony concerning Anna's upkeep. 'Schickung an Graf Johann zu Nassau betr. des Prinzen Neue Heirat 1575-79," encompasses forty-five folio pages of letters and protocols, written in the illegible hand of Eric von Berlepsch between 30 November and 10 December 1575 concerning this touchy issue.

pline, thereby setting a bad example and giving offense."

The resolution could be carried out by force if necessary. Assisted by clerks, the responsible party would locate and bind the delinquent for transport in an open cart.[42] Naturally, such a journey was a degrading and humiliating affair for the "felon" and a public spectacle for passersby who jeered and mocked the unfortunate passenger. The elector spared Anna such debasement by ordering a closed, curtained conveyance. Yet he probably did not bother with the legalities of the princess's "capture," confident in the knowledge that the emperor was unlikely to overturn his self-directed decision.

As for the Nassaus, the long-suffering Count John - insolvent and saddled with a tribe of thirty-five children and grandchildren - gladly surrendered custody of his troublesome former sister-in-law. He had taken stock of his life of late, and realized that he had been "the stupid one," the chump who was still caring for a woman no longer related to him.[43] After the enormous sacrifices of recent years, all in the name of Dutch liberation, he was simply unable to carry this particular burden any longer.[44]

As could be expected, Anna gave Nassau and the embattled John a farewell that was not soon forgotten. When Bosen's delegation rode into the courtyard at Beilstein, the princess had them wait for an entire day before granting an audience. Subsequent negotiations, painful and protracted, lasted almost a week, although the brusque woman was never in a position to dictate terms. She should appreciate the elector's efforts of selecting a better place for her to live, the emissaries coaxed, for Anna had always hated life in Beilstein. They did, of course, carefully refrain from divulging the location of this supposedly superior destination, knowing full well how much the princess despised her Saxon relations.[45]

And yet the princess continued to stall, still lucid enough to comprehend the enormous ramifications of the proposed move. Only if the envoys showed her an imperial letter of conduct, Anna retorted cleverly, could she follow them in good conscience. When none was produced, she became filled with sinister, but accurate premonitions and panicked. She took a knife and threatened to slit her throat.[46]

After additional rounds of diplomatic palaver, Anna finally consented to relocate to Saxony, only to balk at the mode of travel. She blustered that whatever coach had been provided so far was not befitting her station. Count John, inconvenienced for one final time, provided her with a Brabantian carriage, pulled by eight horses.[47] The sad procession eventually took off, much later than planned, on December 19. Due to the princess's continued dawdling, the party failed to make their first scheduled way station, forcing a furious Anna to spend the night in a run-down farm house in the small village of Eisemroth, eight miles east of Dillenburg. The following day she refused to ride any further, telling Captain Bosen that "Instead of Saxony, I need to betake myself to one of the imperial cities, like Frankfurt, where my case will go to trial." It was only after three days that she could be persuaded to continue her journey.[48]

---

[42]Ozment, *Daughter*, p. 113-5.
[43]Fellmann, p. 44.
[44]Kruse, "Wilhelm von Oranien," p. 131
[45]Fellmann, pp. 44-5.
[46]Kruse, "Wilhelm von Oranien,"p. 132
[47]Pletz-Krehan, "Schicksal,"p. 191.
[48]Kruse, "Wilhelm von Oranien," p. 132.

As the coach and its escort rumbled eastwards into Hessen, an exasperated Bosen decided to appeal to the landgrave for help and inquired if the sorry party could remain for several days in Homburg, north of Frankfurt. He wanted nothing to do with the woman nor let her remain in his lands, Landgrave William let Bosen know, but allowed him to use force on his niece if necessary. The captain was taken aback. A decent man, he was afraid to lay hands on the confused princess and could not bear to see her pushed around. In the end Bosen allowed one of his men to "set her straight," but walked away in shame as Anna was being subdued. Afterwards, she did not speak to him for four days.

New trouble arose when the princess was finally informed of the actual endpoint of her journey: Castle Rochlitz in central Saxony. "I will only go to Zeitz or the convent at Weissenfels," Anna screamed, beside herself with horror. In fact, she would rather be torn to pieces, then go to that accursed place.[49] At a complete loss, Bosen asked the elector for guidance. It was against his honor to force the noble lady to Rochlitz, he bravely informed Anna's uncle in Dresden. In his opinion, only judges and jurors could order such compulsory measures. On the other hand, the princess was truly out of control and directed "evil words" at him. Indeed, when she "has her head altogether, she storms about like a broken ship."

August's snappish response left his subordinate in no doubt that Anna, despite her rank, was not to be indulged. Apparently, the good captain had let himself be influenced by a wimp like the Landgrave of Hessen, the elector boomed on 12 January 1576. It was his duty to deliver the princess to Rochlitz or suffer his most serious displeasure. Also, for an underling to talk about courts and judges verged on insubordination.

The sympathetic Bosen found himself in an unfortunate bind. He felt at odds with the formidable elector's directives, but was understandably afraid of defying him. In desperation, he appealed to his uncle, August's envoy von Berlepsch, for help. Anna refused to continue as ordered, he recounted wearily. She was pleading and begging while he and his wife tried to change her mind. The princess was afraid, deathly afraid of the appointed destination and would not budge.[50] What was he to do?

About a day's ride from Leipzig, Rochlitz is nestled on the scenic Mulde River in the so-called "Valley of Palaces." Known for its unique red porphyry quarries, the small market town experienced something of a flowering in the fifteenth century, but by Anna's time had already lost what little significance it had gained in previous decades. Its castle, however, with its jutting towers, is and was the most prominent structure in the area, picturesquely enthroned on a rocky promontory. It had been the widow's estate of the late Elizabeth of Rochlitz, Philip of Hessen's self-assured sister. Members of Saxony's ruling family regularly overnighted at the residence on their way westwards or on return to Dresden, since Elizabeth had equipped the estate with the latest conveniences. The main, three-story building dated back to the fourteenth century and sported a 130 foot long, completely refurbished great hall. Other "well-built, pretty chambers" even boasted in-floor heating. The jewel of the castle is the "Red Room" with its ornate coffered ceilings that visitors can still admire today.[51]

[49]Kruse, "Wilhelm von Oranien,"p. 133.
[50]Kruse, "Wilhelm von Oranien,"p. 133.
[51]Thieme, Andre. "Burg, Herrschaft und Amt Rochlitz im Mittelalter," *Witwenschaft in der Frühen Neuzeit* (Leipzig: Leipziger Universi

And yet for Anna, the castle was not a place of cozy comforts, but a terrifying habitat that filled her with unspeakable foreboding. Elizabeth had died there in 1557, and had to the last been so connected with the fortress and surrounding lands that the moniker "Duchess of Rochlitz" clung to her even after death. A frightening adversary of Anna's mother Agnes, Elizabeth's name carried equally disturbing connotations for her daughter who was pathologically afraid of the dead woman's specter. With her overactive imagination playing tricks on her, Anna fell on her knees, begging Captain Bosen not to make her live in a place of such horror. She pleaded, "The ghost of the late Duchess of Rochlitz frightens me too much."[52]

The princess might have also known the castle, despite its charming gazebos and spacious halls, as a notorious place of detention for unruly family members and political detainees. About a hundred years earlier Duke Sigismund of Saxony (1416-1471) had spent twenty-seven years under house arrest in one if its wings, after being accused of inappropriate relations with a nun and conspiratorial activities against his brothers.[53] The unhappy Dr. Peucer, prisoner of conscience and one of the main targets of August's Calvinist purge, had only just been moved from Rochlitz to another location of imprisonment.[54] He had to make room for Anna who, according to the elector, was to be just as strictly held.

On 18 January 1576 Anna wrote what was perhaps her final letter to the elector. "Most Serene, Highborn Prince," she started, "I have been told that I am to move to Rochlitz, but I would like to apprise Your Highness of the fact that I do not intend to do so … I do not intend to carry the name of the person that has lived there, but the name my pious lord father gave me at my birth."[55] Apparently, the princess recoiled at being called "the new Duchess of Rochlitz," an appellation that resurrected nightmarish memories of the reviled Elizabeth.

Surprisingly, August relented. Anna was allowed to settle in the former cathedral chapter of Zeitz, about twenty-five miles south-west of Leipzig. The small town in the charming "White Magpie Valley" had been ruled by a series of prince-bishops until the Reformation when the Wettins dissolved the diocese in 1564. The princess was to live in the former bishop's palace whose partial use as a place of confinement is attested. During Anna's negotiations with her uncle concerning Rochlitz Castle, Dr. Peucer sat incarcerated at Zeitz.

It is safe to say that few expectations were shattered when Anna failed to conform to the routine mapped out for her at Zeitz Castle. She had moved into Dr. Peucer's former quarters, and just like in Beilstein, faced exits that had mostly been walled shut. Bosen allowed her only two maids and a kitchen boy for company, and Anna soon complained, as so often, about the unreliability her staff. At least her dietary needs were adequately met. Still extant weekly menus mention roast veal, salmon, cake, and fruit among other dishes only found at the tables of the very wealthy.[56]

In her golden cage of isolation, Anna's mental and bodily decline continued with frightening rapidity, driven by the hopelessness of her situation and lack of proper medication for her autoimmune disorder. Moments of clarity only

tätsverlag, 2003), p. 35, p. 46, p. 49.
[52]Günther, pp. 78-9.
[53]Günther, pp. 78-9.
[54]Fellmann, p. 45.
[55]Kruse, "Wilhelm von Oranien,"p. 164.
[56]Kruse, "Wilhelm von Oranien," p. 174. Menu list from 27 February to 12 March 1576.

served as cruel reminders that the rest of her life would most likely be spent at various estates under house arrest, gagged and patronized, without the company of a husband or her children. As winter was turning into spring, Anna let herself go completely. The loyal Bosen wrote to Dresden in desperation, "Her Highness guzzles wine all day long, and if she does not receive as much as she demands, she turns into a raging fury and spouts off such vicious, mean, and peevish words that my heart is aching. When I come to talk some sense into her, she runs into her chamber, locks herself in, and starts barking behind the door like a ferocious watchdog."[57]

By March the captain was sufficiently fed up with Anna's canine performances, her drinking, and insults that he contemplated quitting his position. After mentioning the elector, Bosen recounted in disbelief, Anna replied with a gesture that in the name of decency could not be committed to paper. "The devil will fetch me," she had told him, "and then I will stab you as well as your wife and children to death."

It was all too unfortunate, Bosen testified. Although Anna had been volatile during their journey to Saxony, she had also enjoyed some phases of relative well-being. Now, she was so mean-spirited that his poor wife fled into the attic while he was away on errands. Much like her final months in Beilstein and Siegen, Anna posed a danger to herself and those around her. The other day, the exasperated captain continued, the princess had accosted him with a knife and stabbed him in the arm. He had struck her in return and then carried her into her chamber. All the while Anna cursed to the high heavens, threatening him and his family with her everlasting wrath. "We have a heavy cross to bear," Bosen's wife groaned during those terrible months at Zeitz manor.[58]

[57] de Dijn, p. 89.
[58] Kruse, "Wilhelm von Oranien," p. 134.

Full Circle

Three days before Christmas and at the start of the ominous "rough nights," a heavily curtained carriage pulled into the courtyard of the Dresden residence shortly before midnight. Christof Zaun, an electoral gatekeeper, stood shivering in the cold, awaiting further instructions from August's master of the household. An errand boy would inform him of the arrival of a carriage that was to pass any gate controls without delay and continue on to Dresden's palace.[1] The coach's mysterious occupant was to be spirited away to a distant wing of the castle without any further ado the major domo had barked earlier. The gatekeeper might have felt uneasy. Not about the clandestine assignment, for such work was routine at the court of a disciplinarian like the elector, but because of the lateness of the hour and the dangers of the season. This was the most frightening time of year, with the days fast approaching when the earth unleashed hordes of angry spirits that were part of the terrifying "Wild Hunt." These nocturnal demons were known to slither through chimneys, bringing bad luck and causing mischief.[2]

The being that eventually emerged from the dimness of the carriage - a disheveled, unkempt, and rundown alcoholic - might have been almost as frightening. Older members of the staff, who had known Anna in her youth, probably stood aghast at the princess's shocking transformation. The daughter of the late Elector Maurice was barely recognizable.[3]

Three weeks earlier August and his wife had decided to bring Anna back to Dresden after yet another unsettling report from Zeitz reached their ears. Captain Bosen had complained that the princess attacked him with knives and was "raging foolish as if she were possessed." Instead of sending for a doctor or an exorcist, the electoral couple placed the princess under their direct controls.[4] It would be easier to manage her in situ, they determined, without having to go through a weak-willed intermediary like Bosen, a man who obviously possessed neither the skills nor the mental toughness to deal with a disobedient strumpet like the princess.

In regards to Anna's transport, the elector had given precise instructions. Only a handful of individuals were let in on the night-time action which was carried out in the strictest secrecy. The princess remained uninformed about the destination of her journey and was not even permitted to gaze at passing towns. Accompanied by Bosen, she traveled in a closed carriage during hours of wintry darkness. August saw no need to publicize the Wettin's shame.[5]

The princess's homecoming to the city of her birth a day before her thirty-second birthday was nothing short of tragic. Almost twenty years ago Anna had arrived from Weimar after her mother's death, a scared, unhappy girl raw with grief. After her spectacular wedding, she had vowed never to return, only to be forced back as a fallen woman, deflated under a heavy cloud of infamy and

[1]Böttcher, p. 277.
[2]Schönfeldt, p. 344.
[3]de Dijn, p. 88.
[4]Midelfort, p. 59.
[5]Kruse, "Wilhelm von Oranien," p. 135. The elector meticulously planned Anna's transfer to Dresden. He instructed Bosen to send a boy ahead of their arrival so that Zaun, the gatekeeper, could keep one of the heavy portals open. They were to pass through Dresden's western gate (named *Willisches Tor*), past the *Zwinger* (outer ramparts), directly into the electoral residence. During the journey, Bosen was to sit next to Anna and keep her secure. During way stops at Nossen and Kolditz, Saxon officials were to provide the party with food and fodder for the horses, unaware of Anna's identity.

dishonor. If she was still coherent enough to take in the silent wall of contempt exuded by her new staff is uncertain; perhaps her gorgon of an aunt "welcomed" Anna with some choice Bible greetings. Under the circumstances, it was perhaps this brief reunion that smarted the most. Anna had left Saxony many years ago, overjoyed to be free of the electress's charge, and confident in new beginnings. Now she was fetched back in the most degrading fashion by her "bitterest enemy."

Paul Burgel and Alexander Pistorius, Anna's newly appointed guards, ushered the princess to a secluded area of the palace, along with a group of elderly maids.[6] They were to keep a watch on the princess by standing in front of the so-called "old hall."[7] Within a few days, however, Anna had turned so violent that August's long advocated proposal of solitary confinement was at last being put into place. The former Princess of Orange was moved to an even remoter part of Dresden's *Residenz*, and deposited in an apartment consisting of an antechamber and bedroom whose every opening had been walled up with bricks, except for a single entrance. A grated window — cut into the thick, iron-enforced wooden door — possibly served as the sole light source in the entire room.[8]

Servants passed Anna's meals through the small aperture, and, one would hope, received her full chamber pot. Except for occasional visits by a pair of pastors, tasked by the elector to sermonize through the iron-grilled window, the princess was cut off from all human contact and courtly society.[9] Domestics might have cut off her hair as was often done to the insane, since lice and other vermin quickly congregated in cramped, squalid spaces that Anna was now forced to inhabit.

Perhaps she screamed for mercy until her voice was hoarse. It would have been in vain. Her uncle, the Saxon elector, remained unmoved, his treatment of Anna smacking of anger, revenge, and the deepest disdain. At this point, his physicians were still debating whether the princess was sinful or sick; a mute discussion since August would not release her from detention irrespective of their findings.[10] Even if Anna was suffering from a dangerous disease of the brain as some believed, the elector had long determined that the wild, untamable creature had forfeited all rights accorded to upstanding women when she bestowed her favors so generously on the Dutch lawyer. In short, the enormity and flagrancy of Anna's corruption made medical care irrelevant, since her crimes demanded proper atonement.[11] Instead, Anna received a steady stream of sermons. Since she had sinned egregiously and incurred God's wrath, she was chastised by the Almighty with an affliction of the mind. Any proper therapy, the elector determined, should start with God.[12] It was hard to defy such logic.

These expectations, surely never very high, were soon frustrated. As in Beilstein, Anna had little patience for pious pontificating and religious instruction. Besides, her health was starting to fail her completely. She spent a good many days in bed, suffering from "a female disease" that rendered her feeble and apathetic. The princess's excessive consumption of meat and alcohol in pre-

[6]Fellmann, p. 45.
[7]Kruse, pp. 135-6.
[8]Pletz-Krehan, "Schicksal,"p. 191.
[9]Kruse, "Wilhelm von Oranien," p.132, pp.135-6.
[10]Midelfort, p. 108.
[11]Midelfort, p.154.
[12]Midelfort, p. 86.

vious years had aggravated her thyroid condition, and she now complained of debilitating general weakness. She could no longer receive her meals through the opening in the door, but asked servants to place bread and beer on a box next to her bed.[13] In May 1577 Anna started to bleed vaginally which continued unabated for months. Hormonal changes might have caused this frightening side effect of her ailment, and not cancer, as assumed by the earlier historians. Graves' disease can lead to ovarian tumors which in turn could have caused the constant blood flow.[14]

The harsh conditions of her detention naturally exacerbated Anna's mental deterioration and she began to suffer from occasional blackouts. Records do not attest if she was ever permitted to leave her chamber for a bath or a walk, while the squalor and stench, together with the lack of vital sunlight, would have defied the wherewithal of much hardier natures. At the time, it was not unusual to board up the housing quarters of deranged individuals for reasons of propriety and decorum. One simply wanted to keep the insane under wraps. Nothing was more embarrassing than a Saxon duchess or a crown prince of Spain shouting vulgarities while presenting a gawking crowd with a pair of naked buttocks.

No inventories have survived about the amount of candles allotted to Anna, but in view of the elector's penchant for miserliness and spite, it is entirely possible that she was forced to spend long hours in almost total darkness. The sensory deprivation without a sufficient light source must have been devastating, especially for someone as unwell as the princess. Among many studies, a 2008 BBC documentary has pointed out the harmful effects of solitary confinement in the dark. Six volunteers in excellent physical condition were subjected to a similar kind of experience like Anna's, albeit for only a few days. Shut up in a lightless nuclear bunker, all participants reported spending long hours sleeping, only to wake up completely disoriented. One individual recounted the need to "squeeze my face and my chest, thinking to myself, am I still alive?"

Within a few days, the group expressed difficulties in forming sentences. "It's really hard to stimulate your brain with no light. It's blanking me. I can feel my brain just not wanting to do anything," another test subject recalled. The same participant, a self-admitted extrovert, started hallucinating about seeing "a pile of oyster shells." Another common reaction was restless pacing up and down the cell. In longer studies of this kind, most participants dropped out after seventy-two hours, with only a few managing to stay for more than four or five days, overpowered by the experiment's boredom and oppression. A volunteer commented that "The nothingness ... was extremely hard. Because the question in your head is how am I going to get through the next ten minutes? Is there enough left in my head?"[15]

Unfortunately, Anna was not part of a carefully monitored control group, but the victim of ruthless relatives who regarded her plight as just retribution. Unaware of the change of seasons, she withered and wilted in a miasma of sweat, excrement, and desperation, her thinking becoming more and more disordered.

In July, her two Protestant ministers, Daniel Creyser and Peter Glaser, informed the elector of their latest visit to Anna. As in Beilstein, she was regularly

---

[13]Böttcher, p. 280.
[14]Pletz-Krehan,"Krankheit," p. 212.
[15]Jones, Huw. "Alone in the Dark," *BBC News*, 21 Jan 2008.

reminded of her serious transgressions and as in Beilstein she cared not to hear about it. The princess remained defiant and told the pastors that despite being a grave sinner, she did not consider herself guilty of the sin she was accused of by her detractors. Yes, she had erred by letting herself be talked into a marriage with that "sodomite rogue" as she now called William of Orange, but her name had been unjustly blackened by false allegations.

Even more worrisome, according to the preachers, was her refusal to take the sacrament. Anna regretted that despite her best efforts, she could not bring herself to pardon her enemies (possibly her aunt and uncle) whose offenses were beyond human forgiveness. In fact, the wrongdoings of her adversaries were a thousand times greater than her own. And as for the visiting vicars, she snarled, they were loose, lying hypocrites.

As she vegetated in the unaired hole of her father's residence months after months, the princess started to talk nonsense. "There are four men in the room," Anna fantasized. On other occasions, August was told, she made disgusting, repulsive allegations. One of her daughters had become the mistress of one of the emperor's son's, she babbled, and that same daughter had killed her own sister as well as the other children and was now conspiring against her mother. The girl had even meddled with her father William, Anna maintained, foaming with fury. Despite the obscene talk and continued intransigence, Creyser and Glaser felt sorry for the wretched captive who had begged for some bread and beer. Her overall care should be addressed, they pleaded with the elector, and perhaps His Grace could be persuaded to have an old family servant keep her company.[16]

August did no such thing, since his conscience was clear. He and his wife had agreed that even the harshest of confinements could not disabuse his niece of her abominable willfulness. More than six months into her imprisonment, Anna still possessed the audacity to blame him and his consort for letting her marry the "sodomite rogue." She was a lost cause, the elector concluded, a useless woman whose death would benefit all, including herself.

Such cold-bloodedness was common at a time when patience with non-conformists of any kind was notoriously low. A case in point is Mary Abell (1641-1715), wife of the British nobleman Edmund Verney, who suffered from symptoms somewhat similar to Anna's. Mary had trouble adjusting to her husband's household as a newlywed and soon became aggressive. Upset at Edmund's philandering, she shouted and raged, and acted in an altogether hysterical manner. Over time, family members grew irritated and edgy while despairing of a cure. One loyal retainer expressed what everyone was thinking, but did not dare say when she wrote to Mary's father-in-law, "Nothing but death can free her from that disease which will be a blessing to her, and to us all." When doctors were unable to produce relief for the raging Madame Verney, the same servant prayed loudly for her swift death. No one protested. The awful reality for Mary and Anna was that nobody actually wanted them cured. Their relations either wished them chained and removed from their sight or dead.[17]

The cruel-edged electress was just as blunt in her wishes for Anna. In the fall of 1577 she was recovering from severe dental problems, the pain of which might have put her into a more ferocious mindset than usual. When her aunt and

[16]Kruse,"Wilhelm von Oranien,"pp. 136-7.
[17]Tinniswood, p. 378, p. 389, p. 395.

closest confidante, Elizabeth of Mecklenburg-Güstrow, inquired if the princess was still alive, Anne answered, "We do not know which princess you mean, but if you are referring to the Elector Maurice's daughter, him of blessed memory, unfortunately she still lives, although it would be preferable if she had already breathed her last." Even to Elizabeth, the electress did not divulge the location of the prisoner.[18]

As the days grew shorter, a "horrible comet" appeared in the sky portending calamities and the electress contracted a mild case of smallpox.[19] Anna, meanwhile, became increasingly moribund as her own chimerical existence and that of the outside world drifted farther and farther apart. In December, five individuals were admitted to the princess's cell: a pair of pastors and three Saxon officials.[20] By now Anna was claiming to have killed her own children, leading her jailers to conclude that she was *non compos mentis*, a condition induced by malice. During her tirades, they reported, the princess talked uninhibitedly about things that any honorable woman would keep to herself and involved her son and daughters as well as his Imperial Majesty. At the same time, August's physicians remained undecided about the exact nature of her ailments. They hoped to determine whether Anna suffered from melancholy or mania, and if medication rather than castigation would relieve her travails.

The clerical delegation agreed to wait for a few days until a trusted doctor could pronounce a final diagnosis which would then be presented to the elector. At this point, August had apparently accepted the princess's need for some form of medical attention, although his preachers still tried to extract an admission of guilt and repentance from Anna. Her "stubborn, petrified malice," they announced, would hopefully soon be broken.[21]

"Once Your Grace has recovered, God willing, you should beg the elector and his wife for forgiveness and promise reform," the pastors coaxed. If Anna refused, however, and remained dogged in her "deliberately obstinate maliciousness," "sharp measures" might be taken to relieve His Grace from "this irksome hardship." Her uncle was inclined to move her to Radeberg, east of Dresden. There, only few people knew about her whereabouts and she would be sorely forsaken. At first, the princess's response was disobliging as always, but then changed in a sadly involuntary manner. As the electress had wished, Anna of Saxony, the most obnoxious, female troublemaker in living memory, suddenly passed away on 18 December 1577, five days before her thirty-third birthday.[22]

Officially, the House of Wettin issued no details on the cause of her death, but after nine months of almost continuous bleeding, the anemic Anna most likely died of an internal hemorrhage. There is of course the possibility that the elector sped things along - especially after the princess's outrageous remarks in the week preceding her demise - although this is pure conjecture. And while her final hours remain shrouded in mystery, we can be certain that she expired in the most miserable circumstances.[23] Perhaps the princess clutched the lead bullet, that long-kept memento of her father's death, in her final moments.

[18]Keller, *Kurfürstin*, p. 175, p. 209.

[19]Schuppener, "Hatzfeld", p. 127; Ulbricht, p. 179.

[20]Kruse, "Wilhelm von Oranien,"p. 137. On December 11 the electoral privy counselors Hans von Bernstein, Tam von Sibottendorf, David Pfeifer, and Hartmann Pistorius put together a report based on the testimony of George Listhenius, Johannes Trüller, Superintendent Daniel Creyser and Minister Peter Glaser.

[21]Midelfort, p. 58.

[22]Kruse, "Wilhelm von Oranien," p. 137.

[23]Pletz-Krehan, "Krankheit,"p. 211.

Anna's burial was a muted affair. Unlike her father Maurice's interment, which had been the grandest of state occasions, the luckless princess could claim few such honors.[24] Her funeral, or lack thereof, was an echo of her multitude of failures: as a woman, as a member of the House of Wettin, as a wife. Nowhere did the body of a princess offer a clearer object of contemplation and reflection than during her memorial service. If Anna had fulfilled her family's expectations, her corpse would have been laid out in state for several days, with hundreds or even thousands of people filing past the open casket. Valets would have handed out expensive funeral pamphlets expressly printed for the occasion to the higher ranking guests. And a few not so noble mourners would have eagerly snatched up copies of these much sought after texts, to solemnly study the life of Her Serene Highness, the late Princess Anna.[25]

Instead, the second wife of William of Orange was buried with much less fanfare, noble honors or even the attendance of a single family member than usually accorded a Saxon princess. Although bells announced her passing and an honor guard kept vigil over her simple coffin for a night, Anna was also deemed unworthy to find her ultimate resting place next to her immediate relations.[26] She was alternatively interred in an unmarked grave near the old Wettin crypt of princes in Meissen Cathedral. She still rests there, next to a flying buttress, at the foot of the tomb of her great-grandmother, the virtuous Sidonia of Bohemia (1449-1510), another Duchess of Saxony.[27]

A clergyman intoned a hastily put-together service, while pallbearers lowered the coffin into the stone vault amid few spectators and the ringing of church bells. What would Maurice and Agnes have said about their daughter's tragic end? Would they have welcomed their lost girl home, attended her funeral? In dying, Anna had returned to Saxony where everything had begun and where everything ended. She had come full circle, and as so often, it had been against her will.

---

[24]Watanabe, p. 10. Maurice's brother August had gone above and beyond in brotherly remembrance by commissioning a magnificent monument to the self-styled "savior of Protestantism" at Freiberg Cathedral. Eight bronze griffons exalt the heroic deeds of the first Albertine elector in perpetuity, while the great man himself kneels in front of the cross in a pose of eternal adoration, a true soldier of Christ.

[25]Bepler, Jill. "Die Fürstin im Spiegel der protestantischen Funeralwerke der Frühen Neuzeit," *Der Körper der Königin* (Frankfurt: Campus Verlag, 2002), pp. 135-7.

[26]Böttcher, p. 282-3.

[27]de Dijn, p.89, p.91.

Legacies

One does not need hope to act; one does not need success to persevere. - William of Orange

Except for her children, Anna did not leave much of a legacy. Art historians have remarked on the conspicuously few surviving images of the princess, mostly companion pieces in royal portrait galleries. It is exceedingly likely that after her downfall, the Houses of Saxony, Nassau, and Hessen engaged in a systematic *damnatio memoriae* which involved the obliteration of her memory through the destruction of her likenesses. Not a single image of Anna's can be found in the collections of the three dynasties, and the few, still extant pieces were discovered in the possession of unrelated noble families.

The princess's case of erased remembrance parallels that of Anne Boleyn's (1507-1536), second wife of King Henry VIII of England, who was also accused of adultery, and ultimately beheaded with her alleged lovers. Anne's official state portraits were altogether smashed after her execution and still existing images of the disgraced queen are exceptionally rare.[1]

Anna's relations discussed similar measures in regards to the hundreds of letters, memoranda, and diplomatic notes pertaining to her dishonorable way of life. In a letter of condolence written in January 1578, Landgrave William asked the elector if confidential records pertaining to their niece were to remain in both chancelleries or should be "commanded to the fire." Apparently, the Nassaus were none too keen on retaining evidence that might diminish William's growing historical legacy. In a fortunate coup for posterity, the elector decided to keep the incendiary papers in his archives.[2]

Other aspects of Anna's life could not be as easily wrapped up and stored away. The electress, for one, was strangely discomfited about coming face to face with the residual horrors of the princess's "dying chamber," and did not have Anna's prison cell unlocked until July 1579, a full year and a half after her demise. Her trusted secretary, Hans Jenitz, opened the thick wooden door with a notary, and was hit by an unspeakable stench of noxious decay. The room had been left unaired since that fateful December day, and much of the late captive's "pitiful estate" was in an advanced state of rot. Anna's clothes still lay strewn about, half eaten up by moths and other vermin. Disgusted, Jenitz had the iron-banded door with its tiny window removed and replaced. He sighed, "I hope to God that He will protect us in his mercy from similar guests that have to be kept secure in princely houses."

Soon after bucket-carrying maids scoured the floors, while valets unboarded the windows. Despite the putrescence pervading the room, Jenitz established a meticulous inventory of every item at the behest of Anna's aunt. Ever the thrifty household manager, the Danish princess saw no reason to throw even a scrap of salvageable material away. There was only one item not worth keeping, the secretary reported: a petticoat so soiled that all cleaning efforts had been for naught.[3] The dirty piece of clothing was one of several chilling reminders of the indignities and neglect Anna had suffered while languishing in filth for endless

[1]Spies, pp. 237-8.
[2]de Dijn, p.91.
[3]Kruse, pp. 139-40.

months. In addition to the decomposing skirt, workers were also unable to restore the urine-soaked floorboards to their former condition and Jenitz had new ones installed.[4]

Surprisingly, there were a few items which the electress still deemed in good enough condition to forward to Anna's children. Stowed away in sturdy wooden boxes, they had remained unaffected by the damp and stench of her dungeon. A notary signed the register while servants loaded Anna's flotsam on a cart bound for Hessen. Attached to it was a note from Electress Anne to the landgrave, requesting him to forward the tiny inheritance to the princess's children "who should not be left without their mother's estate." The remnants of Anna's worldly goods were paltry, the importance attached to them by their late owner already unknown: a colorful smattering of clothes, some knickknacks, souvenirs, and toys, toiletries as well as cooking and beauty recipes.[5]

There were also some religious and secular books: a German tome on herbs and household management as well as compendia of recipes in French and Dutch. More valuable were a splendid series of five French folio volumes from the time of Henri II, two translations of classical historical works by Diodorus Siculus and Flavius Josephus, and the first French Pliny in two volumes. The fifth folio volume was a French Bible, bound in costly morocco. Finally, there was a booklet that had escaped the censor's attention in 1572: a comedy by Marguerite of Navarre, containing frivolous subject matter which Anna's jailers would have certainly considered unsuitable.[6] The landgrave immediately sent the crate on to Dillenburg. Like Anna's Saxon relatives, he recoiled at anyreminders of his ill-starred niece.[7]

One wonders how Anna, Maurice, and Emilia — Anna's legitimate children — reacted when their mother's belongings arrived in Dillenburg. Count John was away on business in the Netherlands, leaving it to his wife Elizabeth to inform them of Anna's death.[8] The siblings had not seen their mother since 1571, and Maurice and Emilia could have only had the dimmest, if any, recollection of their late parent.

Since William's political obligations prevented him from spending much time with his son and daughters, John and Elizabeth had long ago taken on the role of surrogate caregivers for Orange's small brood. At the time of Anna's passing, the children considered Dillenburg, and not Breda or Brussels, their home. In 1577, when William and his new wife Charlotte deemed conditions in the Netherlands stable enough to return to Antwerp, Orange's children initially continued in Germany, but eventually returned piecemeal to the Low Countries.[9] Anna of Saxony's oldest daughter and namesake married her childhood sweetheart and cousin, Count John's heir William Louis, in November 1587. The couple lived in the Dutch province of Friesland where William Louis was *stadholder*. Unfortunately, the union lasted less than a year, because the younger Anna died while pregnant in the summer of 1588, leaving a heartbroken husband behind who never remarried.

[4]Fellmann, "Wilhelm von Oranien,"pp. 139-40.
[5]Kruse, "Wilhelm von Oranien,"p. 141.
[6]Verwey, pp. 98-9
[7]Fellmann, p. 46.
[8]Kruse, "Wilhelm von Oranien," p. 138.
[9]Putnam, *The Life of William the Silent*, p. 204.

Anna's only son Maurice left Dillenburg in the early 1580s to study in Heidelberg and later joined his father in the Netherlands where he embarked on a glorious political and military career. The most eminent general of his time and talented mathematician, his name was recounted in awe throughout Europe. Unlike William, whose battle tactics had always been lacking, Maurice managed a Trojan coup in 1590 when he took Breda from the Spanish by smuggling seventy soldiers into the city.[10] The prince also turned Orange's haphazard uprising against the Spanish crown into a tightly organized, successful revolt. Described as extremely ambitious, vengeful, and brusque, Maurice might have inherited some of his mother and grandfather's Saxon tempers.[11] He also never married, despite a slew of mistresses. Perhaps early childhood experiences proved unconducive to healthy adult relationships.

While the older children lived up to the expectations of their elders, it was Anna's youngest daughter, Cologne-born Emilia, who became embroiled in scandal. An uncanny character replica of her tempestuous mother, the passionate princess had an unquenchable thirst for life. After years in Dillenburg, Emilia eventually joined her father and Charlotte of Bourbon in the Low Countries, and later acted as hostess at her brother Maurice's court. Contemporaries speciously described her as a woman with nymphomaniac tendencies, but there is no doubt that Emilia, much like Anna, was strong-willed and determined when in love. In the 1590s she developed an obsession for the Portuguese pretender to the throne, the "bastard" Don Emmanuel, who was a Catholic and therefore considered unsuitable as a husband. By then Maurice had become the head of the family and categorically opposed the match.

Like her mother, however, Emilia cared little for family duty and confessional differences. On one occasion she tried to force her brother's approval of the romance by personally traveling to one of his military field encampments, begging him to relent. The prince refused. As the head of Europe's foremost Calvinist house, Maurice could hardly give his sister to a "heretic" in marriage. Emilia followed her personal inclinations nonetheless, counting on her family's eventual forgiveness. She eloped and secretly wed Emmanuel in a Catholic ceremony in Den Haag in November 1597.

Fearing his brother-in-law's wrath, the groom fled to Wesel near Düsseldorf; Emilia was taken into custody. Her conversion to Catholicism was a considerable embarrassment to the Dutch States General and her siblings, especially since the war with Spain was still ongoing. Scenes reminiscent of her mother's detention followed: for several weeks Emilia cried and screamed from morning till night, complained of total exhaustion, and refused to eat to get her way.[12] After a suicide attempt and hunger strike, Maurice had her released.[13]

Brother and sister remained estranged for another decade, resulting in substantial financial hardship for Emilia and her partner of choice. Although she carried the lofty title "Titular Queen Consort of Portugal," the princess and her husband never acceded to the throne and Emmanuel was ultimately forced to seek employment with his brother-in-law. Shunned by Maurice's staunchly Calvinist entourage, the Catholic prince then engaged in secret negotiations with the

[10]Schuppener, "Breda," p. 126.
[11]Kruse, "Wilhelm von Oranien," p. 152.
[12]Kruse, "Wilhelm von Oranien,"p. 152.
[13]de Dijn, p. 92.

Spanish Habsburgs, specifically, King Philip's daughter Isabella. The archduchess had offered Emmanuel a considerable raise in apanage if he joined her inner
circle. This put him at odds with Emilia, who had never forgiven the Habsburgs
for engineering her father's death. She left her consort and moved with her five
daughters to Calvinist Geneva where she settled at Castle Prangins. A sufferer
of depression like her mother, she died there in 1629.[14] Her eldest daughter, Maria Belgica, inherited her own as well as her Grandmother Anna's independent
streak. Instead of marrying a Margrave of Baden, Maria Belgica absconded with
one of the groom's officers, a Colonel Theodor Croll.

While Emilia's life was filled with emotional high and lows, her father William's
conjugal odyssey came to a happy conclusion with his marriage to Charlotte of
Bourbon. Although the couple did not "ride into the sunset" - the struggle against
the Spanish continued and money was always a worry - they enjoyed private
joys that fulfilled both to a heretofore unknown extent. Perhaps her years at the
convent had taught Charlotte to endure material privations without expectation
of improvement, because she soldiered on bravely at her nomadic husband's side.
Political setbacks, his frequent absences, and constant moves could not dampen
the princess's affection for William.

In the summer of 1576, while Orange was seeking additional supporters
in various Dutch provinces, and exerted himself so strenuously that he hardly
had time to "breathe from morning to night," Charlotte stayed behind at their
modest manor in Delft. She was busy caring for the pair's first child, Louisa Juliana, born on March 31.[15] A year later, the Oranges relocated to Antwerp where
the couple revived something of the court life that William had enjoyed in his
adolescence. Although they had to economize over time, the Antwerp residence
boasted 182 souls for several years. It included the households of William's heir
Maurice and "Monsieur de Nassau" (Orange's illegitimate son Justin) as well as
seventeen ladies-in-waiting. The glittering palace in Brussels that had once boasted tablecloth made of sugar was unfortunately forever lost to the prince. It had
long been taken over by the Habsburgs.[16]

The family's frequent changes of residence and Charlotte's abundant fertility made for busy years. From 1576 until 1581, the new Princess of Orange gave
birth to six girls. Besides mothering her growing brood, Charlotte also mastered
the duties of prudent household management - tasks that the unfortunate Anna
had never quite grasped. Through letters we can catch glimpses of the princess
nursing William through a heavy cold, worrying about his diet, and writing letters
to family for which he could not find time. In later years she received diplomatic
deputations and presided over festive occasions while Orange was otherwise engaged. Little by little Charlotte also established a home for the scattered offspring
of her wifely predecessors, who arrived intermittently in the Low Countries.[17]

The disapproval of William's family, so unexpectedly insistent at the beginning of the marriage, gradually dissolved in view of Charlotte's quiet steadi-
ness and humility. Mindful of her background, she claimed no place for herself
in the Nassau family orbit, or the world, except "such as might be given to [me]."
She wrote to the old Countess of Nassau, "I hope you may grant me some little

[14]Putnam, *Moderate Man*, p. 350.
[15]Putnam, *The Life of William the Silent*, p. 219.
[16]Verwey, p. 104.
[17]Wedgwood, p. 156.

part in your good graces." Although Charlotte would never meet her mother-in-law in person, she built up an affectionate correspondence with Juliana over the years, and together the two worried about Orange's well-being. "I implore My Lord (William) not to allow himself to be persuaded to go to dangerous places for the world is full of craft," Juliana wrote from Siegen in April 1577, to which Charlotte replied that her husband's life was indeed always threatened by deceit and trickery.[18] Before her death in 1580, the countess made special mention of a treasured bracelet that was to be given to Charlotte after her passing.

But the highest praise for the former abbess came from the formerly standoffish Count John who, over time, completely revised his opinion of his sister-in-law. William had found a wife "so distinguished by her virtue, her piety, her great intelligence, in sum as perfect as he could desire her," he commented approvingly.[19] In 1580 John wrote to a friend, "He loves her tenderly," and added that his brother had only been able to muster new courage against the Spanish because of his wife's unstinting backing.[20]

Not only the Nassaus accepted the pairing of William and Charlotte. In the late 1570s, shortly before his death, the princess's belligerent father, the Duke of Montpensier, readmitted his grateful daughter into his heart. Small gifts sent by his granddaughter and namesake Louise Juliana had softened the old man's stance and he responded with an affectionate note of thanks to the six-year-old girl. "My grandchild, you have achieved no slight thing in learning to knit at your tender age as I can see a belt of pretty violet silk bordered with silver lace which you have sent me," he wrote, clearly touched by the child's gesture. "Nothing could have pleased me more than to have your first knitting work dedicated to me. You could not have given it to anyone who would have prized it more, or liked it better than I."[21]

Such kind words healed past breaches with William's French relations to the point that the Oranges' fourth daughter, Charlotte Flandrina, was dispatched to France to be reared at her grandfather's court. When the duke died a year later, in 1582, the girl came under the tutelage of her mother's cousin, Jeanne de Chabot, abbess of the Princess of Orange's former convent. Suffering from hearing loss which might have lessened her chances in marriage and evidently taken with the faith of her maternal forbears, Charlotte Flandrina converted to Catholicism and became a nun in an ironic twist of fate. In 1605 she was appointed abbess of the Benedictine monastery of Saint-Croix near Poitiers, despite the vocal protests of her siblings who attempted time and again to make her abjure her adopted creed.[22] Neither William nor Charlotte was still alive when their daughter decided to enter the religious profession.

At the beginning of the 1580s this particular family scandal was still in the far off future as the Dutch entered another somber decade. After William's glorious entrée into Brussels and the Pacification of Ghent three years earlier it looked, at first, as though the rebels' ideals of freedom and toleration were about to become reality. These hopes were soon dashed. The Dutch standing united as a single alliance against the King of Spain was still nothing but a pipe dream as

---

[18]Putnam, *The Life of William the Silent*, p. 222.
[19]Wedgwood, p. 157.
[20]Mörke, p. 204; Kruse, "Wilhelm von Oranien," p. 122.
[21]Putnam, *The Life of William the Silent*, p. 262.
[22]Roelker, p. 417.

internal discord frayed the disjointed provinces. The country ultimately split into a Catholic, Habsburg-dominated south, and a Calvinist north led by Orange.

Besides, King Philip was thirsting for revenge. When the seven northern provinces prepared to formally declare their independence from Spain and form a republic with the prince as their *stadholder*, the Spanish monarch issued a so-called ban. In March 1580 he pronounced William "the chief disturber of the state of Christendom" and an "enemy of the human race" for continually challenging Habsburg rule and for having married a consecrated nun and abbess. In the name of His Majesty, Orange's already reduced lands and possessions could be seized by anybody with sufficient military force. Even worse, the edict was an explicit invitation to murder, calling on anyone "to hurt and kill him [William] as a public plague." The person "so noble of courage" who succeeded in liquidating the disobedient prince would be most handsomely rewarded: lands, a noble title, 25,000 gold crowns as well as a general pardon of all previously committed crimes beckoned any would-be assassin.[23]

Like most rulers of his time, the Spanish monarch considered murder a legitimate weapon of state. The idea of slaying William had been tossed around within the king's inner circle for at least eight years when it was initially approved by the Alba administration. There had been reports of such plans even before that, when Spanish assassins dressed as Bavarians loitered near Dillenburg around 1570. So far, Orange had managed to outfox the king's henchmen, including an assassination attempt in 1579 during a Habsburg-sponsored "peace conference" in Cologne. A Flemish priest had been paid to do away with "the world's worst traitor" but failed. Afterwards, William's old tormentor Cardinal Granvelle suggested an idea to his master which led to a carefully thought-out, near lethal plan.[24] The cardinal had long ago announced, "If you don't have him (Orange), you have nothing."[25]

*****

The Oranges tried to bear these adversities with Christian fortitude, but the strain put a cloud over their final years. William, the once free-wheeling, exuberant grand seigneur had long given way to the buffeted "father of the fatherland." Portraits cut of William and Charlotte by Hendrik Goltzius in 1581 show two prematurely aged individuals, the cares and sorrows of long periods of turmoil etched in their faces. At the time, the prince was forty-seven, Charlotte thirty-five years old, but time had left visible marks of "fatigue and decrepitude." Despite striking a battle-ready pose in sumptuous armor, the prince looks exhausted, with heavy bags under his eyes, his hair thinning. His wife, depicted in an ornate, dark dress with a white ruff, gives the impression of a self-possessed, but careworn matron. She was much given to sober contemplation and, unlike the late Anna, uninterested in the brilliantly gilded and brightly colored romances that had once filled Orange's library. In the Goltzius woodcut Charlotte stands behind her constant support and refuge: the Geneva New Testament.[26]

[23]Jardine, p. 139, p. 142.
[24]Kamen, pp. 254-5
[25]Ennen, p. 830.
[26]Verwey, p. 81, p. 99, p. 101.

While the Princess of Orange entrusted her sorrows to the Almighty, plotting against William continued in Spain. The king had tasked one of his agents, a certain Jean de Yzunca from Lisbon, to find an Antwerp-based Spaniard to murder Orange. Yzunca approached Gaspar de Anastro, a businessman, who had recently fallen on hard times. The merchant was on the verge of bankruptcy after three of his ships had been raided by pirates and two others sank on their way to Laredo. Although Anastro was unwilling to carry out the king's design, he convinced one of his junior clerks, Jean Jauregay, to assassinate the rebel prince. In addition to acting "for the love of his master and honor of his name," Jauregay was lured by the promise of "eighty thousand silver ducats, or property to the same value, and the Order of St. James." As Anastro slipped away to avoid capture, Jauregay sought out a Jesuit priest to receive advance absolution for the murder he planned to commit.[27]

On Sunday March 18, 1582 William agreed to receive a petitioner after a festive luncheon. Seated in an alcove, the prince was approached by a short, badly dressed eighteen year-old with a thin black moustache and a melancholy demeanor. Instead of presenting him with a document, the lugubrious youth pulled out a pistol and fired point blank at the prince. The bullet shot through William's neck just below the jaw - somehow without damaging either tongue or teeth - and exited through the cheek. In stunned disbelief, Orange later recounted that he thought the house had collapsed on his head. Courtiers as well as the prince's son, fourteen-year-old Maurice, immediately cut down Jauregay, stabbing him multiple times.[28]

For several days Orange hovered between life and death, attended by a team of renowned surgeons and his devoted wife. The hole in his neck was about the size of a dollar coin, but had ironically been cauterized by the explosion which apparently prevented infection. To stop the copious bleeding, doctors stuffed pads of lint cloth into the wound. One of these swabs was "mislaid" somewhere in the cavity and could not be found for twelve days. Despite such mishaps and against all odds, the prince made a complete recovery.[29] Cardinal Granvelle commented sourly, "I wish he was dead, he should've died twenty years ago."[30]

In the end, the real victim of the plot was Charlotte. On May 5, a day after William had attended a public service to give thanks for his recovery, the princess died. Overwrought after spending week after week at his bedside, she allegedly caught a chill which turned into "double pleurisy." Some feared that Orange would falter after this terrible blow and quickly follow his spouse in death. At the end of the month he wrote to John, complaining of general weakness which he attributed not only to the failed attempt on his life, but "sorrow about the death of the highborn princess, our much loved Madame Charlotte of Bourbon."[31] An English observer noted that, despite William remaining outwardly composed, "the separation of lovers secretly gnaws at the heart."[32]

Comforted by his children, William carried on. A year later he even took a new wife: twenty-eight year-old Louise de Coligny, a widow and daughter of

[27]Jardine, pp. 69-71.
[28]Jardine, pp. 64-5; Mörke, p. 239. The Jesuit priest was subsequently caught and arrested along with three additional individuals who had acted as accessories to the plot. They were executed on March 28 in front of the Antwerp town hall, but granted an "easy death." William had asked his friend Philip Marnix to spare them the customary torture and let the delinquents die "une courte mort."
[29]Jardine, pp. 72-4.
[30]Cellarius, "Wilhelm," p. 78.
[31]Mörke, p. 240.
[32]Wedgwood, p. 235.

the late Huguenot leader Gaspar who had been slain during the infamous St. Bartholomew's Massacre. During that fateful night, Louise's then-husband, Charles de Teligny, was murdered as well. In January 1584, Louise gave birth to a son, Frederick Henry, but her second marriage was also cut short by murder.

After Jauregay's botched assassination effort, William's security foiled three additional attempts on his life, but in July 1584, after enjoying a meal with his immediate family at his Delft residence, Orange's luck ran out.[33] As he left the dining room, he encountered a twenty-five-year-old Frenchman, Balthasar Gerard, on the stairs. An agent recently recruited by William to provide intelligence on the activities of Spanish troops, Gerard stepped forward from the assembled company.

He pointed a pistol at William's chest and fired, unloading his single barrel handgun containing three bullets. Two passed through the victim and struck the staircase wall; the third lodged in the prince's body "beneath his breast." Orange collapsed, mortally wounded. He was carried to a couch in one of the adjoining rooms, where his sister Catherine and distraught wife tried to stanch the wounds in vain. He passed away a few minutes later, his dying words spreading like wildfire. The prince had allegedly breathed, "Dear Lord, dear Lord, take pity on me and your poor people [the Dutch]."[34]

During the ensuing pandemonium the assassin dropped his weapon and fled, pursued by a throng of courtiers. He was apprehended just before reaching the ramparts behind the royal lodgings. Cross examined on the spot, Gerard "very obstinately answered that he had done that thing which he would willingly do again." Asked who had ordered the attack, he only divulged that he had done it for king and country.[35]

One of eleven children of a well-to-do, devoutly Catholic family of Habsburg supporters from Burgundy, Monsieur Gerard had come to regard the "heretical" Prince of Orange as the embodiment of evil. With the help of accomplices, he devised an elaborate sequence of ruses that gained him access to William's entourage. For example, he posed as the son of a Huguenot who had been burned at the stake and presented the prince's security detail with forged testimonials.[36] Like Jauregay, the Frenchman was also enticed by the large reward. If he martyred himself in the name of the true faith, Gerard determined, his family would enjoy undreamed-of riches and honors.

He died after undergoing horrific tortures with remarkable composure, defiant and convinced of his divine mission to the last. According to an eyewitness account sent to the English government, Gerard stretched out his hands during the public torment and then pointed at his body, exclaiming "Ecce homo" [Pilate's words identifying Christ]. Afterwards, as they declared their dead son a hero, his parents received the immense reward of cash, lands, and titles as recompense for his suffering.[37]

In the meantime, the Orange-Nassaus tried to rearrange themselves after the head of the family had perished so suddenly. Orange's eldest son with Anne van Buren—the boy who had been abducted many years ago at the behest of

---

[33]Mörke, p. 246.
[34]Mörke, p. 247. William's last words were in French, "Mon Dieu, mon Dieu, ayez pitié de moi et de ton pauvre peuple."
[35]Jardine, pp.50-1.
[36]Mörke, p. 246.
[37]Jardine, p. 55, pp. 59-60.

Cardinal Granvelle - was still in Spain and would not return to the Low Countries until 1596. As a Catholic and loyal servant of the Spanish crown, he was naturally ill-suited to continue his father's Calvinist legacy in northern Flanders. Instead, Anna's sixteen-year-old son Maurice gradually assumed the role of governor of Holland, Zeeland, and Utrecht. Louise de Coligny took William's other children under her wing. A dedicated caregiver like her predecessor Charlotte, the princess ensured that all of Orange's daughters - save Charlotte Flandrina and Emilia - found suitable partners.

While the Oranges continued as best as they could, the rebel provinces struggled without their leader. The assassin's bullet had cut down the one man capable of sustaining the fragile alliance among the fractious Protestant factions, but without the prince that accord crumbled and the Spanish regained a firm foothold in the north.[38] To make matters worse, Philip of Spain was on sound financial footing again and poured money into new armies stationed in the Habsburg-controlled southern Netherlands. Ypres, Bruges, and Ghent surrendered in 1584, Brussels in March of the following year.

Five months later, Philip's commanders forced the capitulation of Antwerp. Granvelle was present to witness the king's enormous joy when informed of this latest Spanish victory. "Not for the battle of St. Quentin nor for Lepanto nor for the conquest of Portugal nor for Terceira nor for any other past success, has His Majesty shown such contentment as for this of Antwerp," the prelate gloated, his triumph only lessened by the fact that Orange was no longer alive to witness this latest setback. The cardinal did not know that Elizabeth of England had already committed herself by the secret Treaty of Nonsuch to intervene militarily in the affairs of the Netherlands. In December 1585 the Earl of Leicester arrived at Vlissingen to take charge of an English volunteer force of eight thousand men.[39]

And so the conflict dragged on for decades. It later became known as the Eighty Years' War, led by Anna's son Maurice, and after his death in 1625, by his half-brother Frederick Henry, son of Louise de Coligny. In 1648, after an inestimable loss of life, Spain conceded defeat in the northern Netherlands and recognized the Dutch Republic. The occasion was marked by extravagant festivities; its "birth" solemnly promulgated on June 5. It was the 80th anniversary of the execution of William's old friends and comrades-in-arms, the Counts Egmont and Horn.

By this time, William's apotheosis into the pantheon of Dutch luminaries and great statesmen was firmly assured. Although he had been unable to effect the liberation of the Low Countries in his own lifetime, his enormous sacrifices earned him the lasting honorific "Father of the Fatherland" or "pater patriae," the Latin inscription on his sumptuous tomb in the *Nieuwe Kerk* (New Church) in Delft. It also reads, "To the honor of Almighty God and to the eternal memory of William of Nassau, Prince of Orange, who considered the well-being of the Netherlands a higher calling than his own." His loyal followers christened him "our good Moses," a hero sent "from Nassau who released us from fetters that have tormented us until now."[40]

---

[38]Jardine, p. 53.
[39]Kamen, pp. 255-6.
[40]Cellarius, "Wilhelm," p. 79, p. 138.

Anna's uncle William had once disdainfully told Orange that "It is a losing game you're playing, give it up while you have anything to save."[41] But the prince, the former dandy and bon vivant, persevered while sticking to his motto "tranquillus saevis in undis" ("tranquil in raging waves"), despite enormous personal costs to himself and his family. Regrettably, he also did not live to see that his struggle opened new doors of human consciousness, not only for the Netherlands, but Europe as a whole. William's ideals led the way to the emerging concepts of individual freedoms, tolerance, and human dignity and gave birth to the "miracle" of the Dutch republic.[42]

In subsequent centuries, William's proud legacy did not sink into obscurity. In fact, the name and colors of the little principality of Orange in southern France have become integral to the Netherlanders' national identity. The Dutch football team wears an orange strip, while its fans sport the prince's colors in everything from scarves, wigs to face paints. But the onetime son of a count received an even greater posthumous honor when the Dutch chose "*Het Wilhelmus*" ("The William") as their national anthem in 1932. It celebrates the courage of a "Prince undaunted of Orange," prepared to resist the tyranny of the King of Spain and his occupying forces, and is perhaps only second to the French Marseillaise in its patriotic fervor.[43] Its first verse proudly reads, "William of Nassau, scion of a Dutch and ancient line, I dedicate undying faith to this land of mine. A prince I am, undaunted, of Orange, ever free, to the King of Spain I've pledged a lifelong loyalty." Four centuries later, the Spanish crown acknowledged his pledge in a gesture of reconciliation. In 1980, King Juan Carlos placed a beribboned laurel wreath on William's Delft tomb.[44]

Amidst these lasting accolades, William's marriage to Anna remains a dark spot on his otherwise brilliant legacy. Even during Orange's lifetime, his brother John feared that the princess's dramatic end might reflect badly on his accomplishments, especially with her German relatives seeking to blacken the prince's name. But William remained unruffled. In the spring of 1576 he wrote to John, "You mentioned that there is the prospect that the Elector of Saxony and the landgrave may try to make trouble about the obligations assumed by you in regard to "her of Saxony." I'm not afraid of this, because they really have no foundation for the accusations, and I cannot believe they will take any steps."[45] He was correct.

The Hessian landgrave had seen enough scandal during his father Phillip's bigamous marriage, while Dresden's reputation suffered on account of Anna's suspicious death. Eventually, all sides decided to let the matter rest by adopting the convenient face-saving fiction that all was well within the empire.[46] Even the vindictive August relented, much taken up with Saxon affairs. Throughout the first half of the 1580s he turned his princedom into a model of financial stability, and in the process transformed himself into his own version of "pater patriae." The elector and his practically minded wife strengthened their patrimony's agriculture, dairy, and mining industries with considerable success.

[41]Putnam, *The Life of William the Silent*, p. 155.
[42]Cellarius, "Wilhelm," p. 87, p. 90.
[43]Jardine, p. 15. The lyrics of the Dutch national anthem date back to the late sixteenth century and may have been written by William's close friend Philip Marnix, Lord of St. Aldegonde.
[44]Cellarius, "Wilhelm," p. 87.
[45]Putnam, *The Life of William the Silent*, p. 220.
[46]Kruse, "Wilhelm von Oranien," p. 142.

Working side-by-side for the good of the country, the pair became affectionately known as "Father August" and "Mother Anna." They epitomized the Lutheran ideal of master and mistress of the house, and by extension, that of parents of the electorate - not unlike William of Orange in the Netherlands. Together, the couple entered Saxony's national imagination, and the mystique of the "good old days" - when "Father August" and "Mother Anna" still toiled amidst "the people" - persisted for hundreds of years.[47]

Much like his late brother Maurice, the elector attained a position of unequaled power among German princes. A skillful mediator between Catholics and Lutherans, he has been credited with sparing Germany the fate of neighboring France where religious strife tore the kingdom apart. His subjects gratefully called him "imperii cor, manus ac oculus" ["the heart, hand, and eye of the empire"] as well as "conciliator, arbiter, and steerer" of the realms.[48]

As with his niece, August was less successful in steering his own children towards happiness. The marriage of his eldest daughter Elizabeth to John Casimir, son of the Elector Palatine, was troubled from its very onset, and proved more detrimental to princely relations than it was helpful.[49] A withdrawn woman who had trouble adjusting to her husband's Calvinist court, Elizabeth was stuck in a loveless union for many torturous years. Her consort relentlessly pressured her to convert to Calvinism, and when Elizabeth refused - egged on by her Lutheran mother - John Casimir's frustrations eventually turned vicious.

Over time, Elizabeth came to resent the never-ending haggling about her eternal soul and blamed her parents for marrying her to a cruel man. Not surprisingly, the electress countered her daughter's reproaches with indignation. She wrote, "Your Grace should neither be ashamed [of the match] nor complain. Your Grace has [seen] many examples of other ladies of the same rank married into vastly more unpleasant places."[50] Although Anne was surely aware that this particular union had been a mistake - despite her protestations to the contrary - she could not acknowledge her failing, neither to her unhappy child nor herself.[51]

After the death of her parents, Elizabeth's domestic situation turned into a terrifying nightmare. Her alcoholic husband abused and imprisoned the princess and, reminiscent of Sidonia's trials, brought charges of adultery and attempted murder against her. His allegations remain unsubstantiated to this day, but with no relations to plead her case, the princess - much like her cousin Anna - was at the mercy of her detractors. In April 1590 she perished in detention, thirty-eight years old, after a hunger strike and self-imposed sleep deprivation. Surviving notes left in her prayer book give testimony that Elizabeth died in deepest desperation.[52]

Elizabeth's younger sister Anne completes the sad troika of female Saxon misery. Compared to her older sibling, she endured an even worse fate, one which eerily resembles that of her cousin, the late Princess of Orange. Carefree and pleasure-loving, the younger Anne had married Duke John Casimir of Saxe-Coburg in 1586 after she had just turned eighteen. The groom was only three years older than his bride, but spent most of his time hunting. Like Anna, the princess possi-

---

[47]Rankin, pp. 30-1.
[48]Bruning, p. 123.
[49]Keller, *Kurfürstin*, p. 189.
[50]Keller, *Kurfürstin*, pp. 20-1.
[51] Keller, *Kurfürstin*, p. 192.
[52]Keller, pp. 192-3, p. 195.

bly suffered from scoliosis, which may have accounted for the duke's distance.[53] Alone, bored, and neglected in Franconia, Anne found the small town of Coburg achingly dull, its court a pale replica of her father's sparkling Dresden residence.[54]

Failure to conceive and her husband's indifference eventually made Anne the target of malicious court intrigues. The duchess was leaving the castle in disguise, one story went. Another, particularly spiteful rumor accused her of adultery. With her parents already dead, Anne's brother Christian and his wife Sophia were apprised of the scandalous tales. The latter issued a severe reprimand to her sister-in-law, but the princess vehemently denied any wrongdoing and even John Casimir took her side.[55]

When Anne found herself childless after six years of marriage, she started grasping at straws. A wife's overriding duty was to be fruitful and failure in this respect was a matter of apology. Many women internalized Protestant teachings that they were created for maternity and that a life devoted to the endurance of multiple pregnancies and child care represented the best way of serving the Lord. At this point, Anne's level of desperation probably equaled that of an English lady who professed to her husband that she would gladly lay down her life to procure him a son.[56]

An Italian alchemist from Piacenza, Jerome Scotus, promised ready relief. The foreigner was newly arrived at the Coburg court and had been hired to discover the secret formula for gold. Anne's husband had also given him license to address the princess's fertility problems. Anxious and depressed, the duchess did not resist when the charlatan first demanded expensive jewelry as compensation, and then asked for sexual favors to cure her barrenness.

When the unlikely couple was about to be discovered, and to deflect attention from his own offense, Scotus passed Anne to Ulrich von Lichtenstein, a squire and vice marshal in John Casimir's services. As in the Rubens affair, the lovers had been unable to keep their liaison a secret after a lady-in-waiting divulged incriminating confidences in October 1593. Livid with humiliation, John Casimir had Ulrich and Anne arrested and charged with fourteen felonies. Scotus, meanwhile, fled town and remained untraceable despite all search efforts. Upon facing her husband's unrestrained anger, the duchess admitted to everything and implored him "not to have a deserted, poor orphan spend her youth in prison. I am ready to be your humble maidservant."[57]

Her pleas went unheard, for the cuckolded prince refused to show his wife or her paramour any leniency. He immediately obtained a divorce, and a Coburg consistory court granted John Casimir the entirety of his ex-wife's dowry. Anne, meanwhile, was remanded at various estates and convents, completely sealed off from the outside world. As in her cousin Anna's case, only a pastor and a maid were allowed access to the elector's daughter. At least her windows were not boarded up, and witnesses reported that the princess spent most of her time reading religious conduct books and embroidering.

[53]Keller, *Kurfürstin*, p. 196.

[54]Schultes, J. A. von. *Sachsen-Koburg-Saalfeldische Landesgeschichte* (Koburg, 1818), p. 105. Perhaps John Casimir, an Ernestine, also held a personal grudge against his wife's family. He was the oldest son of John Frederick II of Saxony, Agnes of Hessen's second husband and archenemy of Maurice and August. John Frederick II spent almost thirty years in captivity while his lands were divided among his sons which greatly weakened the family's position in the empire.

[55]Keller, *Kurfürstin*, p. 196.

[56]Fletcher, pp. 181-2.

[57]Schultes, p. 105; Keller, *Kurfürstin*, p. 197.

In 1599 John Casimir married Margaret of Brunswick-Lüneburg, and further humiliated Anne by issuing a silver medal known as the "Coburg Kiss Thaler." One side depicts a couple necking while locked in an intimate embrace with the circumscription "How nicely those two (Margaret and John) are kissing." On the obverse is a depiction of the disgraced ex-duchess in a nun's habit exclaiming "Who will kiss me now, poor little nun?"[58]

In May 1603 the princess was forcibly returned to the fortress of Coburg, because of recurring rumors of a clandestine rescue which never materialized and was, in any case, highly unlikely. Anne's sole brother Christian was already dead and his successor, her nephew Christian II, a simpleton. The divorcee remained locked away in Franconia, and as the years went by, she became morbidly disheartened. In the end, Anne refused food like her sister Elizabeth, and died of general weakness after twenty years of uninterrupted confinement. She was buried without ceremony in the cemetery of a local church. The Wettins had long ago refused her interment in the Freiberg Cathedral family crypt.[59]

The Duke of Saxe-Coburg was just as merciless in the treatment of Anne's cavalier. Initially calling for Ulrich and his wife's execution, their sentences were commuted to lifelong imprisonment after the emperor intervened on the squire's behalf. The latter went on to spend most of his captivity in a tower inside the city wall which later became known as the *Lichtensteintower*.[60] He died at age seventy, three days after the duke's successor, John Ernest, had issued a pardon. Because of the turmoil of the Thirty Year War, the message of his acquittal did not reach Ulrich in time.[61] He had spent forty endless years behind bars.

When the Coburg scandal erupted in 1593, both of Anne's parents - Elector August and Electress Anne - were already dead. It is one of those ironies of fate that not only one, but two of the moralist couple's daughters were accused and confined for infidelity. The question whether the Saxon sovereign and his wife would have shown mercy to Elizabeth and Anne had they still been among the living can unfortunately never be answered. In view of the electress's frigid advice to Elizabeth concerning her marital troubles and August's unremitting punishment of his former counselors, it is rather unlikely. And without willing protectors to assist her in her difficult predicament, Anne of Coburg was as lost and forsaken as her deceased cousin, Anna of Orange, had been two decades earlier.

If Elizabeth and Anne were sources of shame to the House of Wettin, August's son Christian was perhaps the greatest disappointment. The eighth child, but only surviving heir of the elector, the prince turned out quite differently as his parents had wished. Influenced by a tutor with Calvinist leanings during his youth, the prince continuously rebelled against the Lutheran orthodoxy of his elders. An unquiet character, he was described as talented, but extremely volatile.[62]

It did not help matters that the electress was as meddlesome in her son's affairs as she had once been with her niece Anna and her daughter Elizabeth. When the twenty-one-year-old prince traveled to Berlin to celebrate his engage-

[58]The coin read in German: "*Wie küssen sich die zwey so fein,*" and "*Wer küsst mich, armes Nunnelein.*"

[59]Knöfel, Anne-Simone. "Anna von Sachsen," *Sächsische Biografie. Online Ausgabe:* http://www.isgv.de/saebi/ (accessed 18.11.2009); Keller, *Kurfürstin,* p. 199.

[60]Keller, p. 199.

[61]Göpfert. Ulrich. "Eine peinliche Familientragödie am Hofe von Herzog Casimir in Coburg," Online Edition: http://www.ulrich-goepfert.de.

[62]Nicklas, pp. 126-7.

ment to Sophie of Brandenburg, his mother pestered him about the guest list which was said to include some hard-drinking invitees. She not only sent "friendly reminders" to her son, instructing him to watch his alcohol intake, but also ordered his personal physician not to let Christian eat anything from the bride's kitchen. The good doctor took the liberty to ignore such a tactless request.[63]

Constrained and perhaps patronized, Christian turned to drink, started to gamble, and made the hunt his greatest hobby. Inherently lonely at his father's bustling court, the prince's sole friend was Nicholas Krell, son of a well-heeled privy counselor who sometimes covered Christian's gaming debts. But neither this friendship nor the death of his imperious father could halt the new elector's inexorable decline. The center of every raucous party, Christian spent most his days in a drunken haze and at the card tables, leaving matters of state to his ministers. He died in October 1591, barely thirty-one years old, most likely of stomach and intestinal complaints exacerbated by his debauched lifestyle. As so often, rumors also circulated that poison had cut his life short.[64] The elector's eight-year-old son Christian II, simple-minded and morbidly obese, became Saxony's new sovereign.[65]

It was a mercy, perhaps undeserved, that August, the coolly calculating tactician, and his hard-nosed wife were spared the knowledge of their offspring's disgrace. But even during their lifetimes it might not have escaped them that their son and heir was as maladjusted and given to drink as his ostracized cousin Anna. We are too far removed in time to make a judgment about the reasons for the misadventures of August's three children, but it might not be mere coincidence that their lives, whether by genetics or upbringing, mirrored Anna's in so many ways.

*****

In the fall of 1585 Electress Anne fell ill with a disease that could not be cured by any of her potions, concoctions, or aqua vitae. Physicians, and perhaps Anne herself, diagnosed the plague which ultimately proved fatal. She died alone. Eleven of her fifteen children had already preceded her in death and her husband of thirty-seven years carefully stayed out of town, claiming fear of infection. Contemporaries were unsure about how to interpret August's refusal to come to his wife's deathbed.[66]

She had been ailing for many months. Two years earlier, Anne had told one of her daughters that she was praying to God to release her from her sufferings. Racked by abdominal pains, she was often too weak to receive messengers and could barely take a turn in her chambers. Her husband, meanwhile, kept his distance. At the end of August 1585, while August was out hunting and the electress bedridden, her preacher George Listhenius acted as a go-between, delivering messages back and forth. In one of these letters, Anne promised to follow her consort's wishes in all things and requested a visit so that she might "enjoy the old constancy in grace." "But since this had not happened and His Serene Highness has stayed away," she concluded mournfully, "she was prone to think that she was left alone and that there was no forgiveness."

[63]Fellmann, p. 15
[64]Ulbricht, p. 201.
[65]Nicklas, Thomas. "Christian I 1586-1591 und Christian II 1591-1611," *Die Herrscher Sachsens* (Munich: Beck'sche Reihe, 2007), pp. 126-7.
[66]Fellmann, pp. 28-9.

Anne was evidently worried about having forfeited her husband's good-will, and was desperately hoping for a reconciliation. We do not know what cast a shadow over the last weeks of her life, but it is tragically ironic that the woman who had preached wifely obedience to one and all died estranged from her lord and master.[67]

The elector's anger did not cease with her death. He neither attended Anne's lying-in-state nor her funeral. He also did not accompany the body to Freiberg, but left this particular task to his son Christian. Even if it was not customary for a prince to show himself at his wife's official burial, August left Dresden in an almost indecent hurry to partake in a wild boar hunt with the Elector of Brandenburg. As his wife's cortege ambled past the city gates, courtiers sent out invitations to two young sisters whom August considered ideal bridal candidates - for himself.[68]

Eight weeks later August remarried. To everyone's surprise, his choice fell on Agnes Hedwig of Anhalt-Dessau, the thirteen-year-old child of a minor Saxon royal. Prince Joachim-Ernest had presented his two daughters to the elector on November 7, and August, an "impatient, pressing suitor," asked for the hand of the younger one the following day. Cheerful and flirtatious, the "winter wooer" soon engaged in sentimental banter with his teenage fiancée about a hand sewn cap. He cooed at the end of the month, "I am waiting for your night cap with great longing, and since Your Grace will fashion it from your own hands, I will cherish it all the more, and have it sleeping with me every night until the seamstress herself will come." A week later, he travelled to Dessau with five sumptuously prepared ships and stayed there until the wedding on 3 January.[69]

Until she caught the eye of her sixty-year-old admirer, Agnes had been abbess of one of the few Protestant convents in Germany, the imperial abbey of St. Cyriakus in Gernrode in western Saxony. She had lived there since the age of eight, but her impecunious father, Joachim-Ernest, saw no reason to let a monastic vow come in the way of a brilliant offer of marriage, and happily presented his daughter to her sexagenarian suitor. In view of August's crude splutterings about the ex-abbess Charlotte of Bourbon in the 1570s, the strangeness of his choice could have hardly been lost on the man himself.

Not much is known about this short union which certainly bewildered the elector's friends and family. Someone even issued a mocking medal depicting Adam and Eve. Eve, meaning Agnes, is not only reaching for the proverbial apple, but also for the Saxon coat of arms. More disconcerting for many, however, was the speed with which August led his bride to the altar. Princes only remarried in such "unseemly haste" if the succession was in danger or a large number of young children needed a mother figure. Neither was the case here. Agnes's father was an unimportant princeling and the resulting alliance promised few political advantages for the elector. It therefore appears that the aging Wettin prince contracted the union for purely personal reasons. After long years with his ailing, but resolute spouse and perfect fidelity, he wished to spend the winter of his life

[67]Keller, *Kurfürstin*, p. 176-7, p. 185.
[68]Keller, *Kurfürstin*, p. 183, p. 213. If not her husband, there were plenty of others who were shaken by Anne's death. The Viennese burgher Wolfgang Wagner wrote in his 1585 chronicle that even simple folk in far-flung parts of the Holy Roman Empire were aware of her passing which they viewed as "something important, something remarkable." The influential Saxon counselor Andreas Paull commented, quite correctly, "This death will bring great changes to the court and to the entire electorate."
[69]Knöfel, *Dynastie*, pp. 131-2; Ulbricht, p. 180. Ten days later, 400 noblemen and princes, all clad in black velvet robes and hats with yellow and black feathers, welcomed the newlyweds to Dresden. Ten cannon shots were fired upon the couple's entry into the electoral palace, and celebrations included sleigh rides and ring races.

with a nubile nymph who knew her place.[70]

It was a short winter. Adolescent Agnes gained the distinction of enjoy-ing the shortest reign of any Saxon electress, because her husband died of a stroke on 11 February 1586, barely six weeks after the grand nuptials. The young dowa-ger first moved to her widow's estate, and then married another widower, Duke John of Holstein-Sonderborg, the youngest brother of the late Electress Anne, with whom she had nine children.[71] As for August, he was buried next to his first wife and left behind "the wealthiest and most technically progressive princedom in Germany, perhaps even central Europe" as well as an incompetent heir and two very unhappy daughters.[72]

*****

With the death of Anna's chief tormentor, the only surviving protagonists of the Orange-Wettin melodrama were the Rubens family and Jan's illegitimate daughter Christine. After his release from house arrest in Siegen, Jan labored to regain his footing in Cologne's legal community, but enjoyed only modest suc-cess. The many Dutch Catholics settling in Cologne in the early 1580s hardly de-manded the services of a Calvinist lawyer, and the city's cost of living was still exorbitant. Moreover, Count John paid the interest still owed to Maria only spo-radically, forcing the latter to appeal to his wife, Elizabeth of Leuchtenberg. She received no answer.

In the fall of 1581 the Rubenses economic woes brightened temporarily when Maria's mother, Clara du Touion, signed over lands and two manors to her bedraggled daughter. Clara's husband had recently passed away and she wanted Maria to come into her inheritance as quickly as possible. A notary forwarded the bequest to Germany. Unfortunately, the thrill of anticipation was cut short when Landgrave William's privy councilor Andreas Christiani arrived at the Rubenses' doorstep. He presented Jan with an official writ, commanding the lawyer to re-port to Siegen in November of the following year.[73]

The landgrave had always spoken out against the release of his niece's paramour, and now wanted Rubens detained while meetings were taking place regarding Christine's inheritance. Jan immediately suspected that the summons could lead to lifelong imprisonment or that Count John, egged on by Anna's vin-dictive relations, would finally do away with him. Together with Maria, he im-plored the count to rescind or delay the summons.[74] William's brother remained firm, however, forcing Mrs. Rubens to pen another frantic letter of appeal "for the sake of our Lord Jesus Christ."

"We are so poor and have to carry a heavy burden; due to this situation we work day and night. We have found several well-to-do widows, who have lent us money for interest," she explained. If her husband was arrested again, "our children will perish ... yes indeed we will all perish ... All this frightful want at the end of our days, while the children are still growing up."

[70]Keller, *Kurfürstin,* p. 183, p. 29.
[71]Ulbricht, p. 182.
[72]Vogt-Lüerssen, p. 97
[73]de Dijn, p. 102. Jan Rubens established a correspondence with Colonel Charles de Croÿ, son of the Duke of Aarschot, but continued to be plagued by financial troubles.
[74]Goebel, pp. 23-4.

Perceiving the subpoena as grossly unfair, an infuriated Mrs. Rubens continued angrily in the second part of her missive. "Since you have decided to ruin us, I cannot hold back but reproach you in my name and that of my seven children. [I] beg you to realize how important it is for us whether we have to follow your orders or not. If word spreads that my husband is to be incarcerated again, the creditors will want to see their money and we will lose our credit, and from this will follow that we have to give up our business and declare bankruptcy. At the same time I will have to say goodbye to our boarders; my husband will lose his practice; everyone will talk about this affair, we will be condemned and, pining away crying and sighing, I will not be able to hide our misfortune."

Deftly appealing to Count John's sense of justice, she continued, "Dr. Schwarz assured me [in 1572] on your behalf that [Jan's] life would be spared and promised that he should be free, and that the other lords and relatives of the lady would never take action against him."[75] Furthermore, if her husband was to go to prison again, then the six thousand thalers of bail money would have be returned, Maria argued slyly, fully aware that the Nassaus did not possess such a sum. Her petition concluded with a well-placed reminder about unwanted publicity. "For the honor and well-being of the princely children, it would not be good to give people reason for talk once more."[76]

The count duly folded, his intentions bludgeoned by feisty Maria's not-so-subtle entreaty. In early 1583, the kindly Dr. Schwarz arranged a final understanding between the Rubenses and the House of Nassau: except for a one thousand thalers, Mrs. Rubens waived re-payment of the debt still owed to her in exchange for a guarantee of true liberty for Jan. Count John in turn rescinded the dreaded summons, allowing the Rubenses to stay on in Cologne, unmolested by Hessian or other henchmen.

The lawyer's family remained in Cologne until 1587. Money remained tight since apparently none of the Dutch bequests ever made it to Germany, and a dishonest estate manager was embezzling rental income from Maria's Antwerpian properties. A friend eventually lent Mrs. Rubens sufficient funds to set up a small shop. In a letter written to the Antwerp city council in 1584, she signed as an independent tradeswoman. Her husband had already joined her line of work, perhaps unable to make a proper living with his floundering legal services. The couple was listed in Cologne's official roster of merchants as persons dealing in "wholesale, foodstuff, and manufacture."[77]

But even that source of income only covered basic expenses, and Maria took in boarders to supplement the family's meager earnings. Their lodgings were modest, and at least one tenant complained about the lack of proper maid service, prompting his departure for more upscale accommodations.[78] More than ten years after Jan's Saxon misadventure, his family was still paying dearly for his thoughtless indiscretion.

Yet life was not all hardship. At least in the reminiscences of the Rubenses' youngest son Peter Paul, who later recalled his Cologne years with fondness. Perhaps his was the perspective of childhood nostalgia, coupled with an unawareness of his parents' momentous struggles. For his father, however, the city

[75]Roosbroeck, "Schöffe," pp. 66-7.
[76]Roosbroeck, "Schöffe," p. 68.
[77]Kruse, "Rubens", p. 9.
[78]Roosbroeck, "Schöffe," pp. 65-6.

on the Rhine - which had once been intended as a temporary stopping point in an otherwise glorious legal career - became his final resting place. Jan died there on 1 March 1587, shortly before his fifty-seventh birthday, in many ways a ruined expatriate who never saw his homeland again. Why he never returned to Antwerp remains a mystery. The new governor of the southern Netherlands, Alexander Farnese, had issued a general pardon for former "heretics" and Maria still owned her family's mansion Sint Arnoldus in the most affluent part of town.[79]

Anna's onetime lover was buried in St. Peter's cemetery in Cologne. His faithful consort had a plaque affixed to his grave which commemorated Rubens's vast amount of knowledge and good character. Naturally, the inscription made no mention of the couple's marital troubles, but declared that the deceased had co-habited with his wife "for twenty-six years, in concord and without any quarrels."[80]

Much has been made of Rubens's interment in St. Peter's, since his church burial points to a possible re-conversion to Catholicism. Or, Maria decided on Catholic funeral rites for appearance's sake. At the time of her husband's death, Calvinists could not be officially laid to rest as their faith was still considered heretical. They were usually buried outside the city walls in the Dutch cemetery of the Weyertal valley in the dead of night. With few savings, Rubens's widow could ill-afford to endanger her little trade with an illegal funeral.[81]

The lure of home and a yearning for things Dutch eventually prompted Maria to return to Antwerp. At the end of the 1580s she was almost fifty years old and wanted to spend her final years among people and places she had known as a child and young wife, and which reminded her of times that were probably her happiest. Accompanied by three of her children, Madame Rubens settled in her late parents' mansion on the upscale *Meir Boulevard*. How she paid for its upkeep is unknown, but she possibly shared expenses with her sister Susanna, the house's co-owner.[82]

But even with Susanna's help, it was not easy to reconnect and rebuild after an absence of almost two decades. More than fifteen years had passed since the eruption of one of the sixteenth century's most talked about scandals, but a mark of disgrace continued to cling to the Rubens's family name. With the future of her children foremost in her mind, Maria applied for a so-called certificate of rehabilitation. She also rejoined the Catholic faith.[83]

In the mid-1580s, Antwerp had reverted to Catholic control and the Spanish-run administration only promoted the interests of merchants with flawless character references. To that effect, Maria sought out three eminent patricians willing to vouch for her person in front of a civic tribunal. In November 1589 Mrs. Rubens received her good conduct credentials. They would serve as a safeguard against slander and an affirmation of her steadfast religious devotion.[84]

As with Jan's burial, there have been debates if Maria truly converted to the old religion. According to Frans Baudoin, curator of the *Rubenshuis* (Rubens House) in Antwerp, Madame Rubens might have remained a Calvinist at heart,

---

[79] de Dijn, p. 112.
[80] de Dijn, p. 106.
[81] Roosbroeck, "Schöffe," p. 65.
[82] de Dijn, p. 124, p.127.
[83] Büttner, p. 9-10. Before leaving Cologne, the city magistrate issued a good conduct certificate for Maria Rubens which certified that she had continually resided in Cologne since 1569.
[84] de Dijn, p.131.

yet with her hometown still firmly in Spanish hands, Maria decided that an out-ward switch in belief was not only more practical, but necessary.[85]

The Widow Rubens spent the following years furthering her children's educational and marital opportunities. Much ground had to be made up after the lean years in Germany, but Maria was a woman of astounding spirit and energy. She sold lands, collected rents, and conducted complex business transaction. Her hard work quickly paid dividends and enhanced the family standing.

In August 1590, on the occasion of her daughter Blandina's wedding to the nobleman Simeon du Parcq, Mrs. Rubens was able to endow the bride with a substantial marriage portion as well as a cash gift to the groom totaling 2600 florins.[86] With Blandina's future assured, Maria put the remainder of her funds towards the education of her boys.[87] Philip became a well-known lawyer like his father, but the youngest, Peter Paul, would do even better. He eclipsed all of his forebears in professional success, and experienced a stratospheric rise to fame and fortune which his long-suffering mother partially lived to witness.

The living embodiment of a Renaissance man, Peter Paul gained renown as a humanist scholar, courtier, and diplomat, although these accomplishments pale in view of his artistic genius. Already recognized for his creative virtuosity during his own lifetime, Peter Paul became a fixture at Europe's most imposing residences. He painted masterpieces for the Queen Mother of France, Marie de Medici, and Charles I, King of England. His popularity has never waned and a newly discovered work entitled "The Massacre of the Innocents" was acquired by Kenneth, Lord Thomson for $76.2 million at a Sotheby's auction in the summer of 2002.

Maria celebrated her son's early successes, but did not live to see the apogee of his stardom. Nearing seventy, her health started to decline due to worsening asthma attacks. Peter Paul was working in Rome at the time, and although messengers had been dispatched to bring him home, he did not reach Antwerp soon enough. His mother, who had bounced back from all of the adversities which fate had thrown in her path, died in October 1608. It had been a "wild ride" in today's parlance: poverty, exile, religious upheavals, marital drama, and harrowing fear were the features of her life's panoply. And yet she passed on with the comfort of knowing that her children were well taken care of and that her youngest was on his way to glory. She had finally been granted a reprieve.[88]

Unlike his parents', Peter Paul's personal life was not nearly as tumultuous. He married twice and had eight children. Although he was born several years after Jan's release from jail, there are indicators that the younger Rubens wanted to atone for his father's misdeeds by creating a number of works for the House of Nassau. A fire gravely damaged Siegen Castle in 1695, but surviving records list nine Rubens originals in the palace's inventory, including a life-size portrait of the Prince of Orange.

Perhaps Frederick Henry, youngest son of William and Louise de Coligny, had commissioned the likenesses, since he was personally acquainted with the artist. There was also John Maurice of Nassau-Siegen, second son of Count John and a great promoter of the arts, who might have approached Peter Paul

---

[85]de Dijn, p. 117, p. 141.
[86]Büttner, p. 11. At the time, du Parcq was Lord of Aubechies, Baudimont, and Bois d'Arquennes.
[87]de Dijn, p. 133.
[88]de Dijn, pp. 141-3.

with the assignments. One painting survived the blaze and can be found in London's National Gallery. It is the "Apotheosis of William of Orange," produced by the grateful artist who owed his life to William's lenience.[89] Peter Paul understood that his father had been lucky. If Jan had fallen into the hands of August of Saxony, the older Rubens would have died. And, by extension, the world would have been deprived of his painter son's genius.

[89]Kruse, "Rubens", p. 10.

Possible likeness of Maria Rubens in old age by her son, Peter Paul Rubens. Munich: Alte Pinakothek

Christine

During his long, illustrious career, Peter Paul Rubens became a regular fixture at the pleasure palaces and hunting lodges of the rich. Towards the end of his life he even owned his own chateau outside of Antwerp called *Het Steen* ("The Stone"). Yet he never met his aristocratic half-sister Christine, his father's daughter with Anna of Saxony. Unlike the cosmopolitan Peter Paul who spent years travelling and playfully signed his name Pietro Paolo Rubens after extended stays in Italy, his sibling led a carefully monitored existence for most of her early adulthood.

Surnamed "von Diez" after Anna's widow's estate, Christine was raised in Count John's household after her debilitated mother could no longer care for her in Beilstein. When Anna was forcibly returned to Saxony, four-year-old Christine joined the Nassaus in Dillenburg and retained few memories of those confusing early years. Of a more balanced mind than her mother, she easily adjusted to people who, unbeknownst to her, were of no relation.

Although notoriety had surrounded Christine from the day of her birth, Count John and his court somehow managed to keep the very open secret of her controversial parentage quiet. The girl probably thought herself the offspring of a deceased relation, because she remained unaware of her true origins until much later. Together with John's daughters Juliana, Marie, and Anna Sibylla, she enjoyed a relatively carefree childhood, while the elderly Countess Juliana and her lady-in-waiting, Magdalena Kreutzer, looked after her needs.[1]

Whereas Christine thrived in happy ignorance, her guardians agonized about her future. In 1578 the loyal Dr. Schwarz brought up the awkward topic when he visited Count John—now *stadholder* of the Dutch province of Gelderland—in the Low Countries, but the latter shrank from mentioning the matter to William, blaming political turmoil. The good doctor made another attempt a year later, and again the count responded with a variety of excuses. When the Landgrave of Hessen initiated inquiries about Christine, John first tasked Dr. Schwarz and then his successor, Dr. Christianus, to handle the sensitive subject, hoping that the troubling issue would somehow resolve itself without his direct involvement.[2]

After Christine turned ten, the Nassaus enrolled her at the cathedral chapter school of Keppel in the small town of Hilchenbach near Siegen. Count John's wife, Elizabeth of Leuchtenberg, had recently died in childbirth; Madame Kreutzer shortly afterwards. Countess Juliana's health was failing as well, leading to the dissolution of the women's wing at Dillenburg castle.[3] While the count's daughters found husbands or served at other courts as ladies-in-waiting, Christine was sent to the *Collegium Virginum Nobilium* (College of Noble Virgins). The institution was housed in a former Premonstratensian convent that William's father, Count William, had turned into a Protestant seminary of genteel learning.

In addition to a thorough grounding in religion, the college's young ladies acquired a smattering of reading, writing, and math as well as instruction in spinning, sewing, knitting, and lace making. Household management, along

---

[1]Kruse, "Christine", p. 136.
[2]Wolf, K. "Christine von Diez," *Siegerland*, 20. Band, Heft 4, Oktober-Dezember (1938), p. 104.
[3]Wolf, "Christine," p. 105.

with gardening, cattle cultivation, and cheese and butter churning also filled the curriculum. The intent was to raise industrious gentlewomen, who would not shy away from getting their hands dirty while running a small manor.[4]

Dr. Schwarz had initially hoped to place Christine at Louis of Hessen's court in Marburg, together with one of Count John's daughters. His design was quickly rebuffed by Lord Louis and Her Ladyship, Hedwig of Wurttemberg. Hedwig, in particular, made it abundantly clear that she had no intention of hosting the love child of her husband's niece. Count John was none too disappointed. He had recently become a fervent adherent of Calvinism and had already objected to exposing his own daughter to the Lutheran teachings in neighboring Hessen. The fact that Christine would not have to forego the "true, pure teachings" of the reformed faith pleased him greatly.[5]

By 1582 the Dillenburg Nassaus had still not mustered the courage to talk to William about his ex-wife's misbegotten daughter. Their reticence reveals the sensitivity of the subject as even Orange's beloved mother, Juliana, refused to broach the issue before her death two years prior. When Dr. Schwarz also declined, Christine's former governess, Madame Kreutzer, suggested William's oldest daughter and favorite, Maria, as an intercessory. But Maria was equally reluctant and informed Count John that "[I]n reference to Christine, I have not talked about it to my Lord, the Prince. There is not much time here to deal with this strange affair and besides, it is not seemly that I take up this topic, since he does not like to hear about it. I have the impression that there is no intention here to look after her." "It is better not to talk about it," she advised meekly, but added that "I will do my best so that she will receive one hundred florins annually or whatever … for her expenses. It suits me well that she is at Keppel [and] I think my Lord would agree with that."[6]

William was shot to death before his family had another chance to discuss Christine's situation with him. The responsibility of her maintenance now rested squarely with Count John and the Hessians, since Christine's maternal blood relations, the Wettins, refused any involvement. In December 1586 Landgrave William wrote to Hans Jenitz, the Saxon secretary who had drawn up the inventory of Anna's odds and ends after her death. "Could the elector do something for the dowry of "the child"?" he asked, carefully omitting Christine's name. In remembrance of the good Elector Maurice, "as well as our own honor and reputation," he felt obliged not to forsake the poor creature. The young woman in question was of the House of Saxony and Jenitz was to tell the elector to give Christine a dowry of about six thousand thalers. The landgrave also wanted to know if His Grace would consent to her marrying a Frenchman. William's widow, Louise de Coligny, had reportedly found someone suitable.

The answer from Dresden was speedy and curt as Saxony's new elector, Christian, had no interest in the affairs of the House of Orange. He had been under the impression that the child had died in infancy, August's son claimed, and the landgrave's request came as a complete surprise. In reality, it was a case of complete disinterest.[7] Christian was squandering his father's legendary wealth on his gambling addiction and other forms of dissipation, prompting a contem-

[4]Kruse, "Christine," p. 136.
[5]Wolf, "Christine," p. 105.
[6]Wolf, "Chrsitine,"pp. 104-5.
[7]Kruse, "Christine", pp. 136-7.

porary to remark that in regards to magnificent living "no other German prince could hold a candle to him."[8] Giving away money to his dead cousin's spurious offspring made little sense to the elector. As to the French match, Christian continued, he was all against it. There could be trouble for Saxony and Hessen if the couple had children, he argued evasively. In any case, he would gladly leave all of these decisions to the landgrave.[9] Lastly, he also objected to John's suggestion to legitimize Christine, although such kindness would have notably raised her chances for a good marriage.

Shortly after Christian shirked a responsibility that should have been his, Count John posted an urgent petition to Kassel. He had already appealed to the Orange branch of the family about Christine's future, he wrote, but in view of the complicated political situation in the Netherlands had not received an answer. The headmistress of the college at Keppel had informed him that she could not keep the young woman much longer, since the girl had almost completed her studies which worried him greatly. Keppel was close to the Cologne-Westphalian border, and Christine might leave Nassau County if a husband or other living could not be found. Perhaps she could be dispatched to the Netherlands or France and educated at a small court. But she needed suitable clothing befitting her rank, John continued, if she was to be sent away. Unfortunately, he was already in arrears with her tuition payments. As for the young lady, she had grown into a "fine person."[10]

As so often, there was no reply to the count's petition. After the Wettins had relinquished all responsibility for Christine, Landgrave William followed suit and did not even grace the Nassaus with a reply.[11] John, however, refused to give up. The following June he composed another request. "Could the landgrave appeal to the Saxon elector to pay him at least a fraction of those thirty-thousand thalers of dowry money owed to Christine's mother Anna?" he asked. He wanted to spend the capital on Anna's legitimate children as well as Christine who was still in Keppel. Over the course of many years, he had sacrificed over twenty-thousand thalers annually for the Dutch cause, while having to feed his own flock of children and grandchildren. He had reached a financial impasse and required assistance.

Despite continued silence from Hessen, John tried yet again. He was thinking of giving Christine to Count Joachim of Ortenburg in marriage, he informed the landgrave in July 1587.[12] Forty-one years her senior and a widower, Joachim had previously been married to Ursula, Countess Fugger, a member of the powerful banking family. Although of ancient lineage, highly educated, and well-liked, the count was financially insolvent after decades of legal struggles. As one of the few Bavarian Lutherans, he had stubbornly fought for the survival of his tiny Protestant enclave and ruined himself in the process.[13] For Christine, such a union would have meant elevation in status without the requisite resources.

---

[8]Ulbricht, p. 191.
[9]Kruse, "Christine", p. 137.
[10]de Dijn, p. 95.
[11]Kruse, "Christine", p. 137.
[12]Kruse, "Christine", p. 137.
[13]Springer, Markus. "Evangelischer Panther im Staatswappen," *Sonntagblatt: Evangelische Wochenzeitung für Bayern*, Ausgabe 31/2005 (2005).

Other schemes soon replaced plans for wedded life in Bavarian Ortenburg. Perhaps Christine could marry a Swedish aristocrat or someone in faraway
Königsberg? John deliberated with his advisers. Known today as Kaliningrad
on Russia's very Western fringe, Königsberg was home to the Dukes of Prussia
whose star was on the ascendant in the late sixteenth century.

Not many individuals in the remote eastern dukedom would be familiar
with Christine's infamous origins, John surmised, hoping for a speedy resolution
to the lingering matter. He had appealed to the Margrave of Brandenburg-Ansbach, a close family friend and guardian of the mentally deranged Albert Frederick of Prussia, to find a suitable match for Christine.[14] At this point, any minor
Prussian nobleman would do, the Nassaus hoped in vain, although none of the
Eastern or Northern matches ultimately panned out.[15]

And so Christine remained unhappily at Keppel, despite being the oldest
student by far. In 1588 Count John sent her ten florins as a New Year's gift, but
no husband.[16] He felt guilty about his failure to procure an establishment for the
"poor, forsaken orphan," especially "in memory of the Lord Prince's sake." But
the undignified spectacle continued; a sorry repeat of the mid-1570s when nobody could agree on the fate of Christine's mother, Anna. To be sure, the whole
subject remained extremely delicate. In the Nassaus' correspondence to other noble families, Christine's name was never directly mentioned, but always written
in "code."[17] John liked to use the rather unimaginative "Christinus" as a cipher.

In the early 1590s the count finally enlightened his step-niece about her
scandalous background, "her difficult position, and great misfortune."[18] As can
be expected, the pious girl's world crumbled about her. To be the product of an
illicit affair between a prince and a commoner was one thing (Emperor Charles's
"bastards" served in the highest positions of the Habsburg administration), being
the daughter of a "whore" quite another. Although she was not condemned to
complete societal death, Christine would inevitably be scrutinized by her peers
for any signs of inherited "looseness." In other words, she already had a "reputation" without ever giving cause for it. "I can never go anywhere, visit anyone, or
talk to anyone," she cried, "without being severely reprimanded and reminded of
my scandalous origins. My shame will be continually spread."[19]

After the initial shock had subsided, Anna's youngest daughter grew fear-
ful and despondent. She did not know how to thank Count John for his unstinting
kindness, especially since she was of no relation to the Nassaus, and feared that
the count would eventually tire of her and her demands for a husband. Such scruples eventually gave way to despair and she moaned, "I feel deserted by everyone
in this world. Next to God there is no refuge for me and if His Grace [John] were
to pass away, I will be completely abandoned." "Settle something for me," Christine begged him. She no longer enjoyed life behind college walls, because, unlike
her younger companions, she had no friends that came and visited.[20]

---

[14]Midelfort, p. 77. Albert Frederick of Prussia had attempted suicide twice and was known for his unexpected flights into violence. He
was consistently worried about "Turks and Muscovites" overrunning Germany.
[15]Wolf, "Christine," p. 106.
[16]Pletz-Krehan, "Neujahrsfest," p. 105.
[17]Kruse, "Christine", p. 138.
[18]Wolf, "Christine," p. 106.
[19]Kruse, "Christine", p. 138.
[20]Kruse, "Christine", p. 138.

Count John, soft-hearted as ever, sympathized. He wanted Christine removed from melancholy and hardship, he wrote, because she possessed such a good mind and was deeply pious. Against all odds, he sent another envoy to Kassel to sound out the landgrave's willingness to contribute a certain sum towards the girl's dowry. Perhaps Christine could finally be legitimized as Landgrave William had suggested years ago in order to save the honor of all concerned. The landgrave, unfortunately, rejected any assistance for his great-niece yet again.

At his wit's end, the count dispatched his own son and namesake to the Netherlands to negotiate debt relief and the matter of "Christinus." After having paid out one and a half million florins to aid the liberation of the Low Countries, John expected repayments that also covered his expenditures for Anna's lovechild. She could not remain in Keppel much longer, he stressed, but needed to marry. "It needn't be a lord of a great family with extensive lands, but all the same a fine, pious, young fellow" who would make a good husband, John pleaded with William's heir Maurice. In order to arrange such a match, his half-sister required a decent dowry.[21]

When the younger John returned to Dillenburg empty-handed, his father blew up in anger. He was furious with his nieces and nephews in the Low Countries, the grown-up children he had raised and cared for while their father fought the Spanish. Neither the reputation of his late brother nor that of the House of Nassau was of importance to them, he fumed. And despite his unwavering loyalty and personal sacrifices for the Dutch branch of the family, he had still not been recompensed in any way. He exclaimed, "I simply do not have the heart to look at "Christinus" and shrug her off, like [I have] so many times already, with empty promises."

Regrettably, he was alone with his complaints. Even his son showed nothing but embarrassment for the protracted affair, and had clearly not put his best foot forward during his visit to Flanders. In fact, the younger John had asked his older brother William Louis, a close friend of Prince Maurice's, to take charge of the negotiations. If necessary, he announced, Christine would have to retire to one of the Nassau estates an old maid.[22]

By 1594 Christine had reached the end of her patience. The prospect of spinsterhood was too terrifying to contemplate and she addressed several beseeching letters to John, explaining that at the advanced age of twenty-three she was in great danger of ending up "on the shelf." Her concerns were not unfounded. Renaissance society regarded unmarried women as sad, pathetic creatures who were forced to live a life of subservience and humiliation, given their dependence on others. Only wedlock could bestow status on a woman, especially among Protestants. Ape-leader, tabby, and vestal virgin were some of the unkind monikers attached single females who dwelt in the shadows of a society that looked askance at them.[23] One desperately single princess angling for a spouse told her father she'd marry "a baboon" to finally become a wife.[24]

Christine also informed John's consort Johanette that she was in need of clothes. She had been wearing the same petticoat for two years and simply could

[21]Wolf, "Christine," p. 106.
[22]Wolf, "Christine," p. 106-7.
[23]Manning, p. 57.
[24]Baker-Smith, p. 30. Anne of Hanover, Princess Royal, and daughter of George II of England, despaired at age 23 of still being single. She eventually married the hunchbacked William IV, Prince of Orange in 1734. The marriage was said to be extremely happy.

not mend it anymore. Furthermore, the prioress of Keppel requested money for unpaid expense outlays. At the beginning of May 1595, despondent and "melancholy of heart," Anna's daughter did what Count John had always proscribed her to do: she appealed to her half-brother Maurice for help.[25]

Although the Dillenburg Nassaus were livid at Christine's "presumption," her letter achieved the much-desired results. Amid a torrent of apologies Count John hurried his counselor Erasmus Stöwer to Holland to negotiate, and Maurice eventually agreed to award his half-sister an annual stipend of 594 florins. Furthermore, the prince furnished her with a sizeable dowry of 16,000 florins which was disbursed in four installments and for which he pawned the County of Monster near Den Haag. Such munificence came with conditions as the small fortune was also meant as a payoff. From now on, the head of the House of Nassau-Breda stipulated, Anna's illegitimate daughter was to cease all communications with her highborn relations in the Low Countries.[26]

Equipped with the proper prerequisites for matrimony, a suitor was not long in coming. On 10 December 1597, twenty-six-year-old Christine married Captain William of Welschenengst whose family was also known by the name of Bernkott. The groom hailed from ancient *Westerwald* stock, the Squires of Welschen Ennest, who had served the Nassaus since the fourteenth century. William eventually rose to the position of castellan of Dillenburg, and in 1603 was listed as a lieutenant colonel in Count John's defense force.[27]

The marriage was a happy ending to Christine's Cinderella-type existence. Count John naturally forgave his step-niece her boldness, attributing it to youthful "faintheartedness and impatience," and knowing full well that the good woman had never intended to anger him. No records have survived to tell us if the marriage succeeded in the modern sense, but even if Christine did not love her partner romantically, her most pressing concern had been fulfilled. "The bastard" had found her much longed for place in society as Lady Bernkott.

With his wife's capital, William purchased an estate in the village of Langendernbach in the *Westerwald*, the region that Anna had always hated with such passion. The *Hofhaus* manor is still standing and also included a mill, sixty acres of farmland, meadows as well as seven attached villages who paid a tithe to the Bernkotts.[28] Apparently, the couple managed their holdings quite cleverly. They extended the *Hofhaus* by adding a tower, extra rooms, and a moat which allowed access to the residence only by drawbridge. Eventually they leased another mansion, the so-called *Volenhof*, which incidentally had once been owned by the Brambachs, the family that had given Christine's father a place to stay after his release from prison. Between 1624 and 1636, the Bernkotts spent most of their time in a small Renaissance palace north of Siegen near Bruch that was eventually torn down in the nineteenth century.[29]

Anna's youngest daughter had at least three children: John Henry, Anna Elizabeth, and Katherine. John Henry became an officer and served in a Swedish regiment. Anna Elizabeth — probably named after Christine's "two mothers" Anna of Saxony and Elizabeth of Leuchtenberg — married an Alsatian knight and captain in the imperial guards. Her younger sister Catherine became the wife of

[25]Kruse, "Christine", p. 138.
[26]Gesincke, Hellmuth. "Die Bernkott von Welschenengsten," *Nassauische Annalen*, Band 102 (1991), p. 225.
[27]Kruse, "Christine", pp. 138-9.
[28]de Dijn, p. 97.
[29]Gesincke, pp. 234-5.

Arnold von Quernheim, a colonel serving the Swedish crown like his brother-in law, John Henry. Their descendants live to this day.[30]

Although marriage closed the chapter of her scandalous birth, the remainder of Christine's life was not without upheavals. By 1616, her husband had left Nassau County and found employment with the Count of Hanau-Münzenberg; during the vicious Thirty Year War we find the squire listed as a lieutenant colonel in Swedish services. He was subsequently outlawed by the Swedes' opponent, the emperor, and had the entirety of his possessions confiscated, including the castle in Bruch. William died in 1636, with Christine following two years later.[31] The family lands were only restored to their heirs after the end of the war in 1649, after the late couple's children had fought tooth and nail for their return.[32]

Unfortunately, many aspects of Christine's life will forever remain in the shadows. We do not know how much she knew about her biological parents or if she was aware of the existence of her brilliant half-brother, Peter Paul. Jan and Anna's illicit liaison had affected Christine gravely, ruined her adolescence, and plunged her into moments of deepest despair and shame. But she also had a caring guardian in Count John, a man who tirelessly fought for her rights although he was no direct relation. Perhaps such compassionate concern wiped away the bitterness Christine must have felt in regards to her parents' thoughtlessness. The fact that she named her first daughter after her stricken mother might be interpreted as a sign of forgiveness. Or perhaps Christine thought along the lines of the late eighteenth-century poet Goethe, who wrote "To punish or spare, one has to see humans as human."[33]

[30]Kruse, "Christine", pp. 138-9.
[31]It appears that the dispossessed Christine spent her final years with her daughter and son-in-law, Arnold von Quernheim, at his Alsatian estate. Von Quernheim was commandant of the local fortress Benfeld. See HessischeBiografie.
[32]Kruse, "Christine", p. 138; Gesincke, p. 236.
[33]Pletz-Krehan, "Krankheit,"p. 212.

Epilogue

'Mine honor is my life; both grow in one: Take honor from me, and my life is done.' Richard II.

Catastrophe can cement reputation; in Anna's case, it did the opposite.[1] As an aberration of decent womanhood, the story of "this most wretched and unhappy of all princely children," as Landgrave William termed it, was tightly kept under wraps for about two hundred years.[2] Even after the death of the main protagonists of this Renaissance drama, the Nassaus and Wettins remained profoundly affected by the sins of the poor little rich girl who first lost her heart and then her mind.[3] The first, timid effort to recreate her life was not made until 1776, and then only in the most cursory fashion.

By all accounts, Anna is not a sympathetic character. Her histrionics, penchant for quarrels, and constant grasping for attention brand her as an uninhibited solipsist who put her personal desires before anyone else's, including her small children. While infidelity is no longer considered a criminal offense - at least in most Western nations - Anna was culpable of being a ruthless home wrecker, seemingly devoid of human sentiment. On the other hand, the princess hardly acted the femme fatale that she was later made out to be. True, she obnoxiously inserted herself into the lives of her birth relations for many years, but not as a black-hearted villainess or guileful schemer who spent her days immersed in venomous plots.

More than four hundred years after her death, too many gaps remain in Anna's story to adequately furnish us with all answers for her occasionally grotesque conduct, but mitigating circumstances can certainly be found to explain the princess's transformation from a truculent, amorous young girl into a quarrelsome, degenerate madwoman.[4] The seeds for her tragedy were surely laid in her youth, when, after her parents' death, Anna received none of the care and empathy often available to traumatized children today. Her mental and physical health issues, which were aggravated by an unhealthy diet and the unfamiliar milieu of the Netherlands, further contributed to her inexorable descent into mental illness. William's neglect, his affairs with other women, and her relatives' indifference to her troubles also accelerated Anna's spiral into self-destruction. Although she very much tried to make others love, respect, and honor her, the princess never cracked the vital code of interpersonal relationships, and through this very failure continued on her bumpy road of unsubtle maneuverings and personal frustrations to the last. To what extent were her willfulness, cruelty, and emotional volatility a result of her debilitating thyroid disorder? Was Anna imbued with unpleasant, inborn character traits like her father or was she the mere victim of a number of unfortunate situations beyond her control? We will never know, because the princess is "like a Rorschach test, leaving others to form their impressions of her."[5]

And yet for all her faults and shortcomings, Anna also possessed a considerable amount of boldness and courage. She demonstrated a savvy ability to

---

[1]Schiff, Stacy. *Cleopatra* (New York: Little Brown and Company, 2010), p. 1.
[2]Pletz-Krehan.Anna "Schicksal", p. 191.
[3]Tinniswood, p. 395.
[4]Ozment. *Daughter*, p. 192.
[5]Smith, Sally Bedell. "The Wisdom of Queens," *TIME* Magazine Online, 16 January, 2012.

strategize, rebel, and assert herself in the face of constant opposition, and energetically promoted her economic interests. Although the princess was hardly an early feminist - such terminology was, in any case, unknown at the time - she insisted on being regarded as an individual with inherent rights, unrelated to her gender. In this, she stands out among her contemporaries, especially in view of her stubborn, perhaps admirable persistence to claim such privileges. Whereas the great majority of men and women fully accepted the notion that sexual continence was the foremost duty of any female and that a husband exercised exclusive control over his wife's body, Anna did not. She would have opposed Mr. Modern in Henry Fielding's "The Modern Husband" (1732) who famously told his spouse, "Your person is mine: I bought it lawfully in church."[6] With a sexual freedom rare among her peers, Anna defied the prevailing double standard and daringly satisfied her most personal desires with Jan Rubens.

Although her forays into independence faltered miserably - after all she had never been equipped with the necessary tools to lead a life independently of others - Anna gathered the courage to move to Cologne in a desperate effort to chart her personal destiny. Like her aunts Sidonia and Barbara, the princess thirsted for a space of her own, freed from male fetters and uncaring relations. Her efforts, much like anyone else's, who overstepped crucial boundaries of socially acceptable conduct in the sixteenth century, were thwarted with draconian swiftness. They also failed, because Anna sabotaged her own interests with unfortunate choices.

In the end, Anna of Saxony stands out for her unbridled rebelliousness against a life that she found undecodable and in which she was often her own worst enemy. To the last, this life was a decades' long spectacle of self-destructive defiance, even in its final, suffocating darkness. The princess died with fury in her heart, fury at a wasted existence that had been controlled, manipulated, and dominated by others, and that concluded in a chamber of horrors without ever seeing "sun and moon again." To the last, Anna angrily protested a fate that had forced her into reduced circumstances, but also against her manifold insecurities as a woman who was handicapped not only by bad health, but by societal definitions of female gender. Was there any consolation? This we will also never know.

Perhaps one can say that the princess had suffered injuries that could never be healed, because for broken souls like hers, "it makes little difference whether one curses the darkness or lights a candle, for what has been shattered cannot and will not be fixed this side of eternity."[7] The only saving grace in these situations is "the injured party's own refusal to go quietly," a right that Anna robustly exercised for most of her short life and which assures her legacy as a person of consequence. Had she obediently acquiesced to the role of docile femininity, Anna would have faded from memory long ago. We would find her name as merely a footnote, the appendage of a great man hardly worth mentioning. Her defiance - the subject of so many exasperated letters and conversations - ironically "ennobled" Anna's destruction and "distinguishes it from abject defeat." It was perhaps through such irrepressible resolve that the Saxon princess "redressed her own injury and departed the world with a fleeting sense of her own worth, hopefully in the knowledge that her life had been neither a pity nor in vain."[8]

[6]Stone, p. 315.
[7]Ozment, *Daughter*, p. 194.
[8]Ozment. *Daughter*, p. 194.

William at the beginning of the 1580s by Hendrik Goltzius

Charlotte of Bourbon at the beginning of the 1580s by Hendrik Goltzius

Bibliography

Primary Sources

Algemeen Rijksarchief van België. Audiëntie 85, f. 181 r-183 r.
Staatsarchiv Basel-Landschaft, 0936 Urkunde
Because Dr. Hans Kruse has furnished the most complete edition of Anna's corre-
spondence so far, I would like to supply an itemization of his primary source ma-
terials, taken from his 1934 article "Wilhelm von Oranien und Anna von Sachsen."
Haupt-Staatsarchiv Dresden:
Locat. 9941 (a) Acta die Unterhaltung, Ausstattung und Mitgift Kurf. Moritzens
Tochter Fräulein Annen
Locat. 9941 (b) Der Prinzessin von Uranien Reise nach Cöln und derselbes Ver-
sorgung daselbst 1567-69
Locat. 9941 (c) Abschriften von Frau Annen geb. Herzogin von Sachsen Sch-
reibens ..., 1577
Locat. 9942 (a) Des Printzens zu Uranien etc. und Fräulein Annen zu Saxen Bey-
lager 1561
Locat. 9942 (b) Der Frau Prinzessin zu Uranien vorgeßliche handlung belangend,
Anno 1572
Locat. 9942 (c) Wie Sachsen und Hessen des Prinzens von Uranien neue Heyrath
zu hintertreiben gesucht haben. 1575
Locat. 9942 (d) Volum. II. Schickung an Joh. Graf zu Nassau betr. des Prinzens
Neue Heyrath 1573-79 und früher
Locat. 9942 (e) Schickung an Johann Graff tzu Nassau belangende des Prinzen
Neue Heyrath. Item Abholung der Prinzessin und Verordnung gegen Zeits und
totlichem abgang 1575-79
Locat. 8032   Inventarium über Frau Annen Prinzessin zu Uranien vorlassen-
schafft beneben etzlichen Andren Schrieften Ihro F. G. Leibesschwachheit und
andere sachen, 1577
Locat. 8510 (a) Landgraf Philip zu Hessen an Churfürst August zu Sachsen abge-
lassenen Schreiben (1561)
Locat. 8510 (b) Schreiben so an Churfürst August zu Sachsen samt etzlichen l. chr.
Gn. darauf gegebene Antworten, 1562-1570
Locat. 8512   Landgraff Philips und Wilhelms zu Hessen item des Printzen von
Uranien Schreiben an Churfürst Augustum zu Sachsen. Anno 1565.
Staatsarchiv Marburg (Politisches Archiv 2353)
1.   Briefe der Anna von Sachsen, 1561 und 1562.
2.   Landgraf Wilhelms IV. Nassau-Niederlande III, Akten Landgraf Wilhelms und Anna von Oranien, 1561-66.
3.   Zeitungskorrespondenz mit Graf Ludwig von Nassau.
Kasseler politische Akten, Abt. Nassau-Oranien 1572/78.
1.   Landgraf Wilhelm IV. betr. Prinzessin Anna von Oranien 1572, 1573/4,
1575, 1578.
Kasseler politische Akten, Abt. Nassau-Oranien 1575-1612.
1.   Landgraf Wilhelm IV. betr. Prinzessin Anna von Oranien 1578/79.
2.   Ermordung des Prinzen Wilhelm I. von Oranien 1584.
3.   Landgraf Wilhelm IV. betr. Versorgung der Christine Dietz, der von Wilhelm von Oranien nicht anerkannte Tochter seiner Gemahlin Anna 1586/87.

Politische Akten, Abt. Nassau-Oranien
1.   Kasseler Akten 1570/71. 1570 Juni, Schreiben des Grafen Johann von Nassau.
2.   Marburger Akten 1569-1575. 1570 Mai-Juni, Aufnahme der Prinzessin Anna von Oranien in Marburg.
Politische Akten, Abt. Sachsen
1.   Sachsen, Albertin. Linie II, 27. 1570 Mai, Memorial für Johann von Herlinghausen.
Staatsarchiv Wiesbaden
1.   Dillenburger Korrespondenzen von 1570. Abt. 170 Nr. 6877.
2.   Dillenburger Korrespondenzen von 1573. Abt. 170 Nr. 6880.
3.   Akten betr. Korrespondenzen des Grafen Wilhelm über die beabsichtigte Zusammenkunft mit der Kurfürstin Mutter von Sachsen zu Frankfurt. Abt 170 Nr. 6820.
4.   Akten der deutschen Kanzlei des Prinzen Wilhelm von Oranien betr. Korrespondenz mit Kursachsen resp. dessen Abgesandten 1560-1566. Abt. 170, 6723.
5.   Dillenburger Kellereirechnungen 1571. Abt. 190.
Koninklijk Huisarchief Den Haag
2122-2125 Huwelijk met Anna van Saxen
2124 Stukken betr. de nalatenschap van Anna van Saxen, waarbij inventaris der goederen enz: 1577
2238 IIIA, Correspondenzen.
2241 I A, Correspondenzen.
2278 Stukken brief wisselingen enz: betr. Anna van Saxen als:
a)   Verzameling brieven van en aan Johan de Oude van Anna v. Saxen. Willem I., Kuervorst van Saxen en Landgraaf van Hessen 1569/75.
b)   Verzameling van brieven en Stukken allen Anna van Saxen betr. 1565/1572.
c)   Stukken betr. den onderstand te geven aan Anna v. Saxen 1570/1.
d)   Protocool betr. de handelingen van Anna van Saxen gemaakt te Beilstein 1572, en idem geschreven door Jean Rubens, waaronder verklaring van dien person, Siegen 1577.
e)   Stukken betr. de zwakheid van Anna van Saxen en Hare wegvoering van Beilstein 1575.
f)   Briefwisseling tuschen Johan de Oude en Jan Rubens en diens vrouw Maria 1571-1573.

Secondary Sources

Allgemeine Deutsche *Biographie, herausgegeben von der Historischen Kommission bei der Bayerischen Akademie der Wissenschaften,* Band 11 (1880), 601 ff, Digitale Volltext-Ausgabe in Wikisource

Aram, Bethany. *Juana the Mad.* Baltimore: Johns Hopkins University Press, 2005.

Artikel "Johann Casimir (Pfalzgraf bei Rhein)"in *Allgemeine Deutsche Biographie,* Ed. Historische Kommission bei der Bayerischen Akademie der Wissenschaften, Band 14 (1881), page 307, Digitale Volltext-Ausgabe in Wikisource, URL: http://

de.wikisource.org/w/index.php?title=ADB:Johann_Casimir_(Pfalzgraf_bei_ Rhein)&oldid=802649 (Version vom 9. Dezember 2009, 00:18 Uhr UTC).

Aumüller, Gerhard and Krähwinkel, Esther. "Landgraf Philipp der Großmütige und seine Krankheiten," pages 27-44, in *Landgraf Philipp der Großmütige von Hessen und seine Residenz Kassel* . Eds. Heide Wunder, Christina Vanja, and Berthold Hinz. Marburg: N. G. Elwert Verlag, 2004.

Bainton, Roland H., *Here I Stand: A Life of Martin Luther.* New York: Penguin, 1995.

Baker-Smith, Veronica P. M. *A Life of Anne of Hanover, Princess Royal.* New York: E. J. Brill, 1995.

Bastl, Beatrice. *Tugend, Liebe, Ehre: Die adelige Frau in der Frühen Neuzeit.* Vienna: BöhlauVerlag, 2000.

Bates, Claire. "Dying to look good: French king's mistress killed by drinking gold elixir of youth," in *Daily Mail UK*, Online Version. 22 December 2009.

Beck, Lorenz Friedrich. "Residenzbildung und Ausbau des frühzeitlichen Territorialstaates im albertinischen Kursachsen im Lichte der archivalischen Überlieferung," pages 41-56, in *Hof und Hofkultur unter Moritz von Sachsen (1521-1553).* Eds. Andre Thieme and Jochen Vötsch. Dresden: Sax-Verlag, 2004.

Becker, Emil. "Beiträge zur Geschichte Graf Wilhelms des Reichen von Nassau-Dillenburg (1487-1559)," in *Nassauische Annalen*, Band 66, pages 133-159, 1955.

Becker, Emil. 'Die Malerei am Nassau-Dillenburger Grafenhofe im 15. bis 18. Jahrhundert,' in *Nassauische Annalen*, Band 69, pages 94-134, 1958.

Beilstein: *Eine Ortsgeschichte.* Ed. Heimat und Verkehrsverein Beilstein, e.V. Beilstein, 1978.

Bepler, Jill. 'Die Fürstin im Spiegel der protestantischen Funeralwerke der Frühen Neuzeit,' pages 135-161, in *Der Körper der Königin*. Ed. Regina Schulte. Frankfurt: Campus Verlag, 2002.

Bestenreiner, Erika. *Luise von Toscana.* Munich: Serie Piper, 2000.

Betcherman, Lita-Rose.*Court Lady and Country Wife: Two Noble Sisters in Seventeenth –Century England.* New York: Harper Collins, 2005.

Bingener, Andreas and Fouquet, Gerhard. "Die Stadt Siegen im Spätmittelalter-Verfassung, Bevölkerung, Wirtschaft," in *Nassauische Annalen*, Band 105, pages 103-117, 1994.

Black, Georgina Dopico. *Perfect Wives, Other Women: Adultery and Inquisition in Early Modern Spain.* Durham, NC: Duke University Press, 2001.

Blaschke, Karlheinz. "Die Markgrafen von Meissen im 12. und 13. Jahrhundert 1089-1291," pages 13-24, in *Die Herrscher Sachsens: Markgrafen, Kurfürsten, Könige. 1089-1918.* Ed. Frank-Lothar Kroll. München: Becksche Reihe, 2007.

Blaschke, Karlheinz. *Moritz von Sachsen: Ein Reformationsfürst der zweiten Generation.* Göttingen: Muster-Schmidt Verlag, 1983.

Blockmans, Wim and Prevenier, Walter.*The Promised Lands: The Low Countries Under Burgundian Rule, 1369-1530.* Ed. Edward Peters. Philadelphia: University of Pennsylvania Press, 1999.

Bojcov, Michail A. '"Das Frauenzimmer" oder "die Frau bei Hofe"?' pages 327-337, in *Das Frauenzimmer: Die Frau bei Hofe in Spätmittelalter und früher Neuzeit.* Eds. Jan Hirschbiegel and Werner Paravicini. Stuttgart: Jan Thorbecke, 2000.

Böttcher, Hans-Joachim. *Anna Prinzessin von Sachsen.* Dresden: Dresdner Buchverlag, 2013.

Braun, Karl. ,Wurde die Kurfürstin ermordet?,' in *Thüringische Landeszeitung,* page 2, 28 April 2009.

Briefe der Liselotte von der Pfalz. Ed. Helmut Kiesel. Frankfurt: Insel Verlag, 1981.

Bromberg, Kirstin. ,Anna von Sachsen,' in *Auf den Spuren der Siegerinnen: Materialien zu einem Stadtrundgang 'Frauen in der Geschichte Siegens'.* Band I: Frauen im Siegerland. Eds. Kirstin Bromberg, Kornelia Heisener und Monika Rothe. Siegen: Frauenrat der Universität-Gesamthochschule Siegen, 1996.

Brundage, James A. *Law, Sex, and Christian Society in Medieval Europe.* Chicago: University of Chicago Press, 1987.

Bruning, Jens. ,August 1553-1586,' in *Die Herrscher Sachsens: Markgrafen, Kurfürsten, Könige. 1089-1918.* Ed. Frank-Lothar Kroll. München: Becksche Reihe, 2007.

Buchholz, Stephan. "Rechtsgeschichte und Literatur: Die Doppelehe Philipps des Großmütigen," pages 57-73, in *Landgraf Philipp der Großmütige von Hessen und seine Residenz Kassel.* Eds. Heide Wunder, Christina Vanja, and Berthold Hinz. Marburg: N. G. Elwert Verlag, 2004.

Bünz, Enno. "Die Kurfürsten von Sachsen bis zur Leipziger Teilung 1423-1485," pages 39-54, in *Die Herrscher Sachsens: Markgrafen, Kurfürsten, Könige. 1089-1918.* Ed. Frank-Lothar Kroll. München: Becksche Reihe, 2007.

Bünz, Enno and Volkmar, Christoph. "Die albertinischen Herzöge bis zur Übernahme der Kurwürde," pages 76-89, in *Die Herrscher Sachsens: Markgrafen, Kurfürsten, Könige. 1089-1918.* Ed. Frank-Lothar Kroll.München: BecksheReihe, 2007.

Bull, George. "Introduction," pages 9-19, in *The Book of the Courtier by Baldesar Castiglione.* New York: Penguin, 1987.

Büttner, Nils. *Peter Paul Rubens.* Munich: C. H. Beck, 2007.

Camille, Michael. *The Medieval Art of Love.* New York: Harry N. Abrams, 1998.

Cartellieri, Otto. *The Court of Burgundy.*London: Kegan Paul, Trench, Trubner 1929.

Castiglione, Baldesar. *The Book of the Courtier.*Introduction by George Bull. New York: Penguin, 1987.

Cellarius, Helmut. "Die Propagandatätigkeit Wilhelms von Oranien in Dillenburg 1568 im Dienste des niederländischen Aufstandes," in *Nassauische Annalen,* Band 79, pages 120-148, 1968.

Cellarius, Helmut. "Wilhelm von Oranien im Urteil seiner Zeit und der Nachwelt," in *Nassauische Annalen,* Band 96, pages 75-90, 1985.

Cerasano, S. P. and Marion Wynne-Davies. 'From Myself, My Other Self I Turned': An Introduction,' pages 1-24, in *Gloriana's Face: Women, Public and Private, in the English Renaissance.* Ed. S. P. Cerasano and Marion Wynne-Davies. Detroit: Wayne

State University Press, 1992.

Chmel, Joseph and Lanz, Karl Friedrich Wilhelm. *Monumenta habsburgica: Sammlung von Actenstücken und Briefen zur Geschichte des Hauses Habsburg in dem Zeitraum von 1473-1576*, Vol. 1. Vienna: Kaiserliche Hof und Staatsdruckerei, 1854.

Coban-Hensel, Margitta. 'Kurfürst Moritz von Sachsen und seine Schloßausstattungen,' pages 113-136, in *Hof und Hofkultur unter Moritz von Sachsen (1521-1553)*. Eds. Andre Thieme and JochenVötsch. Dresden: Sax-Verlag, 2004.

Cressy, David. *Birth, Marriage and Death: Ritual, Religion, and the Life-Cycle in Tudor and Stuart England*. Oxford: Oxford University Press, 1999.

Cruysse, Dirk van der. 'Madame sein ist ein ellendes Handwerck.' Munich: Serie Piper, 1995.

Die Fernstraße Marburg-Siegen-Köln. http://www.jakobus-info.de

"Die Landschaft des Westerwaldes," excerpt from 'Lesebuch für die oberen Klassen der Elementarschulen des Herzogthums Nassau,' Bd. 1, Wiesbaden, 1841, pages 145-149, in *Heimatjahrbuch für das Land an der Dill*. Ed. Hans-Jürgen Pletz-Krehahn. No. 24, 1981.

"Diez, Christine von", in Hessische Biografie. See http://www.lagishessen.de/de/subjects/idrec/sn/bio/id/6191> (Stand: 24.4.2010)

Dijn, Rosine de. *Liebe, Last und Leidenschaft: Frauen im Leben von Rubens*. Stuttgart: Deutsche Verlags-Anstalt, 2002.

Donath, Matthias. ‚Grohmann (Gromann), Nikolaus (Nickel),' in *Sächsische Biografie*. Ed. by Martina Schattkowsky, Institut für Sächsische Geschichte und Volkskunde. Online-Ausgabe: http://www.isgv.de/saebi/ (22.5.2011)

Dunn, Jane. *Elizabeth and Mary: Cousins, Rivals, Queens*. New York: Alfred A. Knopf, 2004.

Dupuy, Trevor N, Johnson, Curt, and Bongard, David.*The Harper Encyclopedia of Military Biography*. New York: Castle Books, 1995.

Dutton, Ralph. *English Court Life: From Henry VII to George II*. London: B. T. Batsford, 1963.

Ennen, Leonard. *Geschichte der Stadt Köln*. Köln und Neuss: Verlag der L. Schwann'schen Verlagshandlung, 1875.

Fabre, Daniel. "Families: Privacy versus Custom," pages 531-569, in *A History of Private Life, III: Passions of the Renaissance*. Ed. Roger Chartier. Cambridge, MA: Belknap Press of Harvard U Press, 1989.

Farge, Arlette. "The Honor and Secrecy of Families," pages 571-607, in *A History of Private Life, III: Passions of the Renaissance*. Ed. Roger Chartier. Cambridge, MA: Belknap Press of Harvard U Press, 1989.

Fay, Manfred. *Anna von Sachsen -Kurzgeschichte*. Elsterwerda, 2004.

Fellmann, Walter. *Prinzessinnen: Glanz, Einsamkeit und Skandale am sächsischen Hof*. Leipzig: LKG, 1996.

Fletcher, Anthony. *Gender, Sex & Subordination in England 1500-1800*. New Haven: Yale University Press, 1995.

Foreman, Amanda. *Georgiana Duchess of Devonshire*. New York: Modern Library, 2001.

Fraser, Antonia. *Marie Antoinette: The Journey*. New York: Anchor Books, 2002.

Fraser, Antonia. *Love and Louis XIV: The Women in the Life of the Sun King*. New York: Anchor Books, 2006.

Freer, Martha Walker.*The Life of Jeanne d'Albret, Queen of Navarre*. London: Hurst and Blackett, 1855.

Frieda, Leonie. *Catherine de Medici*. New York: Harper Collins, 2003.

Gachard, M. *Correspondance de Guillaume Le Taciturne, Prince d'Orange, Publieé pour la premièrfois.Tome premièr*. Brussels: C. Muquardt, 1850.

Garrison, Janine. *Königin Margot: Das bewegte Leben der Marguerite de Valois*. Düsseldorf: Benziger, 1995.

Gesincke, Hellmuth. 'Die Bernkott von Welschenengsten,' in *Nassauische Annalen*, Band 102, pages 225-236, 1991.

Gleeson, Janet. *The Arcanum*. New York: Bantam Books, 1999.

Goebel, W. "Jehan Ruebens in Köln und in Siegen" in *Siegerland: Zeitschrift des Vereins für Heimatkunde und Heimatschutze im Siegerland samt Nachbargebieten*, 2. Band, 1. Heft, pages 14-25, 1913.

Göpfert, Ulrich. "Eine peinliche Familientragödie am Hofe von Herzog Casimir in Coburg." http://www.ulrich-goepfert.de

Gowing, Laura. *Common Bodies: Women, Touch and Power in Seventeenth-Century England*. New Haven: Yale University Press, 2003.

Gristwood, Sarah. *Arbella: England's Lost Queen*. New York: Houghton Mifflin, 2003.

Groos, Helmut. "Über die Wohnverhältnisse im südlichen Dillkreis um 1830," pages 150-154, in *Heimatjahrbuch für das Land an der Dill*. Ed. Hans-Jürgen Pletz-Krehahn. No. 24, 1981.

Größing, Sigrid-Maria. *Karl V: Der Herrscher zwischen den Zeiten und seine europäische Familie*. Vienna: Amalthea, 1999.

Günther, Maike. 'Schloß Rochlitz als Residenz und Witwensitz,' pages 65-83, in *Witwenschaft in der Frühen Neuzeit*. Ed. Martina Schattkowsky. Leipzig: LeipzigerUniversitätsverlag, 2003.

Guy, John. *Queen of Scots: The True Life of Mary Stuart*. New York: Houghton Mifflin, 2004.

Hale, J. R. *Renaissance Europe: Individual and Society, 1480-1520*. New York: Harper & Row, 1972.

Hamburger Literarische und kritische Blätter, Ed. F. Riebour. 31. Jahrgang: Januar, Februar, März. Hamburg, 1855.

Harris, Barbara J. *English Aristocratic Women 1450-1550*. Oxford: Oxford University Press, 2002.

Heiler, Karl. "Von der Frühzeit der Reformation am Hofe und in der Grafschaft Wilhelms des Reichen Grafen von Nassau-Dillenburg," in *Nassauische Annalen*,

Band 58, pages 69-86, 1938.

Heinig, Paul-Joachim. "Umb merer zucht und ordnung willen: Ein Ordnungsentwurf für das Frauenzimmer des Innsbrucker Hofs aus den ersten Tagen Kaiser Karls V (1519)," pages 311-323, in *Das Frauenzimmer: Die Frau bei Hofe in Spätmittelalter und früher Neuzeit*. Eds. Jan Hirschbiegel and Werner Paravicini. Stuttgart: Jan Thorbecke, 2000.

Herman, Eleanor. *Sex with Kings*. New York: Harper Collins, 2004.

Hoppe, Stephan. "Bauliche Gestalt und Lage von Frauenwohnräumen in deutschen Residenzschlössern des späten 15. und 16. Jahrhunderts," pages 151-174, in *Das Frauenzimmer: Die Frau bei Hofe in Spätmittelalter und früher Neuzeit*. Eds. Jan Hirschbiegel and Werner Paravicini. Stuttgart: Jan Thorbecke, 2000.

Hörpel, Leonhard. ‚In der Beilsteiner Rüstkammer,' in *Heimatblätter zur Pflege und Förderung des Heimatgedankens*, 8. Jg., 1935, Nr. 7.

Hufton, Olwen. *The Prospect Before Her: A History of Women in Western Europe 1500-1800*. New York: Alfred A. Knopf, 1996.

Hyams, Paul. "What Did Henry III of England Think in Bed and in French about Kingship and Anger?" pages 92-124, in *Anger's Past*.Ed. Barbara H. Rosenwein. Ithaca, NY: Cornell University Press, 1998.

Ingendahl, Gesa. "Elend und Wollust: Witwenschaft in kulturellen Bildern der Frühen Neuzeit," pages 265-279, in *Witwenschaft in der Frühen Neuzeit*. Ed. Martina Schattkowsky. Leipzig: Leipziger Universitätsverlag, 2003.

Irle, Lothar. "Der Siegerländer Mensch," pages 249-257, in *Siegerland zwischen gestern und morgen*. Landkreis Siegen: Kreisverwaltung, 1965.

Ives, Eric. *The Life and Death of Anne Boleyn*. Oxford: Blackwell Publishing, 2005.

Jansen, Sharon L. *The Monstrous Regiment of Women: Female Rulers in Early Modern Europe*. New York: Palgrave Macmillian, 2002.

Jardine, Lisa. *The Awful End of Prince William the Silent*. New York: Harper Collins, 2005.

Jenkins, Jessica Kerwin. *Encyclopedia of the Exquisite*. New York: Nan A. Talese/ Doubleday, 2010.

Jones, Ann Rosalind, and Stallybrass, Peter. *Renaissance Clothing and the Materials of Memory*. Cambridge: Cambridge University Press, 2000.

Jones, Huw. 'Alone in the Dark,' BBC News, 21 Jan 2008.

Kaestner, Horst. "Peter Paul Rubens' Eltern in Köln und Siegen," in *Heimatland, Beilage zur Siegener Zeitung*, Nr. 7, Jahrgang 2, pages 97-100, 1927.

Kamen, Henry. *Philip of Spain*. New Haven: Yale University Press, 1997.

Kappel, Jutta and Claudia Brink. *Mit Fortuna übers Meer: Sachsen und Dänemark, Ehen und Allianzen im Spiegel der Kunst (1548-1709)*. Katalog zur Ausstellung Dänemark und Sachsen in Dresden vom 22. August bis 4. Januar 2010 (Gebundene Ausgabe). Munich: Deutscher Kunstverlag, 2009.

Karant-Nunn, Susan C. and Wiesner-Hanks, Merry E. *Luther on Women: A Sourcebook*. Cambridge: Cambridge University Press, 2003.

Keller, Katrin. *Kurfürstin Anna von Sachsen (1532-1585)*. Regensburg: Verlag Friedrich Pustet, 2010.

Keller, Katrin. 'Kurfürstin Anna von Sachsen (1532-1585): Von Möglichkeiten und Grenzen einer „Landesmutter,"' pages 263-285, in *Das Frauenzimmer: Die Frau bei Hofe in Spätmittelalter und früher Neuzeit*. Eds. Jan Hirschbiegel and Werner Paravicini. Stuttgart: Jan Thorbecke, 2000.

Kent, Michael Princess of. *The Serpent and the Moon*. New York: Touchstone, 2004.

Kircher-Kannemann, Anja. "Organisation der Frauenzimer im Vergleich zu männlichen Höfen," pages 235-246, in *Das Frauenzimmer: Die Frau bei Hofe in Spätmittelalter und früher Neuzeit*. Eds. Jan Hirschbiegel and Werner Paravicini. Stuttgart: Jan Thorbecke, 2000.

Klein, Thomas. 'Johann Friedrich II,' in *Neue Deutsche Biographie*, Band 10, p. 530. Berlin: Duncker & Humblot, 1974.

Kleine Geschichte des Oberen Schlosses in Siegen. Siegerlandmuseum im Oberen Schloss. Ed. Ursula Blanchebarbe. Siegen: Druckerei Vorländer, 2005.

Kleinman, Ruth. *Anne of Austria: Queen of France*. Columbus: Ohio State University Press, 1985.

Knackfuss, Hermann. *Künstler-Monographien II: Rubens*. Leipzig: Verlag von Velhagen & Klasing, 1898.

Knöfel, Anne-Simone. "Anna von Sachsen" in *Sächsische Biografie*. Ed. Martina Schattkowsky, Institut für Sächsische Geschichte und Volkskunde e.V. Online-Ausgabe: http://www.isgv.de/saebi/ (18.11.2009)

Knöfel, Anne-Simone. *Dynastie und Prestige: Die Heiratspolitik der Wettiner*. Köln: Böhlau Verlag, 2009.

Kroll, Frank-Lothar. "Vorwort," pages 7-11, in *Die Herrscher Sachsens: Markgrafen, Kurfürsten, Könige. 1089-1918*. Ed. Frank-Lothar Kroll.München: BeckscheReihe, 2007.

Kroll, Maria. *Sophie Electress of Hanover*. London: Victor Gollancz, 1973.

Kruse, Hans. "Christine von Diez, die natürliche Tochter des Jan Rubens und der Prinzessin Anna von Sachsen, der Gemahlin Wilhelms I. von Oranien, und ihre Nachkömmlinge," in *Siegerland, Blätter des Vereins für Heimatkunde und Heimatschutz im Siegerland samt Nachbargebieten*, Bd. 19, Heft 4, pages 135-140, 1937.

Kruse, Hans. "Wilhelm von Oranien und Anna von Sachsen: Eine fürstliche Ehetragödie des 16. Jahrhunderts," in *Nassauische Annalen*, Band 54, pages 1-185, 1934.

Kruse, Hans. "Um Peter Paul Rubens Geburt," in *Siegerland, Blätter des Vereins für Heimatkunde und Heimatschutz im Siegerlande und Nachbargebieten*, Bd. 22, pages 2-10, 1940.

Lambert, Angela. *1939: The Last Season of Peace*. New York: Weidenfeld & Nicholson, 1989.

Lange, Gustav Georg. "Der Westerwald," excerpt from "Das Herzogthum Nassau in malerischen Originalansichten,1862," pages 176-181, in *Heimatjahrbuch für das Land an der Dill*. Ed. Hans-Jürgen Pletz-Krehahn. No. 24, 1981.

Laucht, Lydia. ,Margarethe von der Saale (1522-1566): Die zweite Frau von Landgraf Philipp,' page 13, in *Blickkontakt: Gemeindebrief-Service der Evangelischen Kirche von Kurhessen-Waldeck*. 02/2008.

Laven, Mary. *Virgins of Venice: Broken Vows and Cloistered Lives in the Renaissance Convent*. New York: Viking, 2002.

Lawson, Annette. *Adultery: An Analysis of Love and Betrayal*. New York: Basic Books, 1988.

Laynesmith, J. L. *The Last Medieval Queens: English Queenship 1445-1503*. Oxford: Oxford University Press, 2004.

Lemberg, Margret. "Alltag und Feste in den Residenzen Kassel und Marburg," pages 89-108, in *Landgraf Philipp der Großmütige von Hessen und seine Residenz Kassel*. Eds. Heide Wunder, Christina Vanja, and Berthold Hinz. Marburg: N. G. Elwert Verlag, 2004.

Levy, Martin. *Love & Madness: The Murder of Martha Ray, Mistress of the Fourth Earl of Sandwich*. New York: Harper Collins, 2004.

Lilienthal, Andrea. *Die Fürstin und die Macht: Welfische Herzoginnen im 16. Jahrhundert: Elisabeth, Sidonia, Sophia*. Hannover: Verlag Hahnsche Buchhandlung, 2007.

Loades, David. *Mary Tudor: A Life*. Oxford: Basil Blackwell, 1989.

Loomis, Stanley. *The Fatal Friendship*. New York: Doubleday, 1972.

Löwenstein, Uta. "Mera Melancholia und übermäßig großer Zorn: Barbara Gräfin von Württemberg-Mömpelgard, geborene Landgräfin von Hessen (1536-1597)," pages 403-425, in *Witwenschaft in der Frühen Neuzeit*. Ed. Martina Schattkowsky. Leipzig: LeipzigerUniversitätsverlag, 2003.

Manning, Jo. *My Lady Scandalous: The Amazing Life and Outrageous Times of Grace Dalrymple Elliott, Royal Courtesan*. New York: Simon & Schuster, 2005.

Mansel, Philip. *Prince of Europe: The Life of Charles-Joseph de Ligne 1735-1814*. London: Phoenix, 2005.

Mariejol, Jean H. *A Daughter of the Medicis*. New York: Harper & Brothers, 1929.

McGowan, Margaret M. *Dance in the Renaissance: European Fashion, French Obsession*. New Haven: Yale University Press, 2008.

Midelfort, H. C. Erik. *Mad Princes of Renaissance Germany*. Charlottesville, VA: University Press of Virginia, 1994.

Militzer, Stefan. *Umwelt - Klima- Mensch (1500-1800)*. Studien und Quellen zur Bedeutung von Klima und Witterung in der vorindustriellen Gesellschaft. Vol.I. Leipzig, 1998.

Moraw, Peter. 'Der Harem des Kurfürsten Albrecht Achilles von Brandenburg-Ansbach (d. 1486),' pages 439-448,in *Das Frauenzimmer: Die Frau bei Hofe in Spätmittelalter und früher Neuzeit*. Eds. Jan Hirschbiegel and Werner Paravicini. Stuttgart: Jan Thorbecke, 2000.

Mossiker, Frances. *Madame de Sevigne: A Life and Letters*. New York: Knopf, 1983.

Mörke, Olaf. *Wilhelm von Oranien (1533-1584): Fürst und „Vater" der Republik*. Stuttgart: W. Kohlhammer, 2007.

Müller, Jan-Dirk. 'Jörg Wickram zu Liebe und Ehre,' pages 27-42, in *Wandel der*

Geschlechterbeziehungen zu Beginn der Neuzeit, Eds. Heide Wunder and Christina Vanja. Frankfurt: Suhrkamp, 1991.

Münster, Anna-Manis. "Funktionen der dames et damoiselles d'honneur im Gefolge französischer Königinnen und Herzoginnen (14.-15. Jahrhundert)," pages 339-354, in *Das Frauenzimmer: Die Frau bei Hofe in Spätmittelalter und früher Neuzeit.* Eds. Jan Hirschbiegel and Werner Paravicini. Stuttgart: Jan Thorbecke, 2000.

Nicklas, Thomas. 'Christian I 1586-1591 und Christian II 1591-1611,' pages 126-136, in *Die Herrscher Sachsens: Markgrafen, Kurfürsten, Könige. 1089-1918.* Ed. Frank-Lothar Kroll. München: Becksche Reihe, 2007.

Nolte, Cordula. "Christine von Sachsen: Fürstliche Familienbeziehungen im Zeitalter der Reformation," pages 75-88, in *Landgraf Philipp der Großmütige von Hessen und seine Residenz Kassel.* Eds. Heide Wunder, Christina Vanja, and Berthold Hinz. Marburg: N. G. Elwert Verlag, 2004.

Ozment, Steven. *The Age of Reform 1250-1550.* New Haven: Yale University Press, 1980.

Ozment, Steven. *When Fathers Ruled: Family Life in Reformation Europe.* Cambridge, Massachusetts: Harvard University Press, 1983.

Ozment, Steven. *Magdalena and Balthasar: An Intimate Portrait of Life in 16th-Century Europe Revealed in the Letters of a Nuremberg Husband and Wife.* New York: Simon and Schuster, 1986.

Ozment, Steven. *The Bürgermeister's Daughter: Scandal in a Sixteenth-Century German Town.* New York: St. Martin's Press, 1996.

Perry, Maria. *The Sisters of Henry VIII.* New York: St. Martin's Press, 1998.

Peyroux, Catherine. "Gertrude's furor: Reading Anger in an Early Medieval Saint's Life," pages 36-55, in *Anger's Past.* Ed. Barbara H. Rosenwein.Ithaca, NY: Cornell University Press, 1998.

Piret, Etienne. *Marie de Hongrie.* Jourdan Editeur, 2005.

Pleticha, Heinrich. *Das klassische Weimar- Texte und Zeugnisse.* Munich: Komet, 1983.

Pletz-Krehan, Hans-Jürgen. ‚Das Neujahrsfest,' pages 104-107, in *Heimatjahrbuch für das Land an der Dill.* Ed. Hans-Jürgen Pletz-Krehahn. No. 24, 1981.

Pletz-Krehahn, Hans-Jürgen. 'Das Schicksal der Anna von Sachsen,' pages 188-191, in *Heimatjahrbuch für das Land an der Dill.* Ed. Hans-Jürgen Pletz-Krehahn. No. 24, 1981.

Pletz-Krehahn, Hans-Jürgen. 'Die bislang unbekannte Krankheit der Anna von Sachsen,' pages 207-212, in *Heimatjahrbuch für das Land an der Dill.* Ed. Hans-Jürgen Pletz-Krehahn. No. 24, 1981.

Pletz-Krehan, Hans-Jürgen. 'Die Gefangennahme des Dr. Jan Rubens,' pages 186-188, in*Heimatjahrbuch für das Land an der Dill.* Ed. Hans-Jürgen Pletz-Krehahn. No. 24, 1981.

Pletz-Krehan, Hans-Jürgen. ‚Rubenskerker und Rubenszelle in Dillenburg: Wo hat Dr. Jan Rubens tatsächlich gefangen gesessen?' pages 197-201, in *Heimatjahrbuch für das Land an der Dill.* Ed. Hans-Jürgen Pletz-Krehahn. No. 24, 1981.

Pollock, Linda A. "Living on the stage of the world: the concept of privacy among the elite of early modern England," pages 78-96, in *Rethinking Social History: English society 1570-1920 and its Interpretation*, Ed. Adrian Wilson. Manchester: Manchester University Press, 1993.

Putnam, Ruth. *The Life of William the Silent, Prince of Orange 1533-1584*. Revised Edition by J.P. de Boulogny. London: Lulu Enterprises, 2008 [1911].

Putnam, Ruth. *William the Silent, Prince of Orange: The Moderate Man of the Sixteenth Century. The Story of His Life as Told from His Own Letters, from those of His Friends and Enemies and Official Documents.*Volume I. New York: G.P. Putnam's Sons, 1895.

Rankin, Alisha. 'Becoming an Expert Practitioner: Court Experimentalism and the Medical Skills of Anna of Saxony (1532-1585),' in *Isis*, 98:23-53. The History of Science Society, 2007.

Ranum, Orest. 'The Refuges of Intimacy,' pages 207-263, in *A History of Private Life, III: Passions of the Renaissance*. Ed. Roger Chartier. Cambridge, MA: Belknap Press of Harvard University Press, 1989.

Ribbeck, Walter. ,Wilhelm IV., Landgraf von Hessen' in *Allgemeine Deutsche Biographie. Ed. Historische Kommission bei der Bayerischen Akademie der Wissenschaften*, Band 43 (1898), pages 32–39, Digitale Volltext-Ausgabe in Wikisource, URL: http://de.wikisource.org/w/index.php?title=ADB:Wilhelm_IV._(Landgraf_von_Hessen-Kassel)&oldid=1415070 (Version vom 26. Januar 2011, 12:33 Uhr UTC)

Riedel, Otto. ,Die Rubens Affäre,' pages 182-186, in *Heimatjahrbuch für das Land an der Dill*. Ed. Hans-Jürgen Pletz-Krehahn. No. 24, 1981.

Riley, M. Beresford. *Queens of the Renaissance*. Williamstown, MA: Corner House, 1982.

Roelker, Nancy Lyman. *Queen of Navarre Jeanne d'Albret 1528-1572*. Cambridge, Massachusetts: Belknap Press of Harvard University Press, 1968.

Rombach, Otto. *Anna von Oranien*. Munich: Deutscher Taschenbuch Verlag, 1982.

Roosbroeck, Robert van. "Der Schöffe Jan Rubens" in *Sonderheft zum Thema* "Peter Paul Rubens" der Zeitschrift "Siegerland – Blätter" des Siegerländer Heimatvereins e.V., Bd. 53, Heft 3-4, pages 60-68, 1976.

Roosbroeck, *Robert van. Wilhelm von Oranien: Der Rebell*. Göttingen: Musterschmidt Verlag, 1959.

Roper, Lyndal. '"Wille" und "Ehre": Sexualität, Sprache und Macht in Augsburger Kriminalprozessen,' pages 180-197, in *Wandel der Geschlechterbeziehungen zu Beginn der Neuzeit*, Eds. Heide Wunder and Christina Vanja. Frankfurt: Suhrkamp, 1991.

Rudersdorf, Manfred. 'Moritz 1541/47-1553,' pages 90-109, in *Die Herrscher Sachsens: Markgrafen, Kurfürsten, Könige. 1089-1918*. Ed. Frank-Lothar Kroll. München: Becksche Reihe, 2007.

Rückert, Ulrike. 'Erstes Reich der Reformation,' in *GEO Epoche: Martin Luther und die Reformation – Europa im Zeitalter der Glaubensspaltung 1517-1618*, Nr 39, pages 88-89. Hamburg: Gruner + Jahr, 2009.

Sävert, Thomas. *Tornadoliste Deutschland.* http://www.tornadoliste.de/tornado-liste1600.htm

Scaer, David P. "Did Luther and Melanchthon Agree on the Real Presence,"pages 141-7, in *Concordia Theological Quarterly,* Volume 44, Numbers 2-3, July 1980.

Schiff, Stacy. *Cleopatra: A Life.* New York: Little, Brown and Company, 2010.

Schirmer, Uwe. ‚Die ernestinischen Kurfürsten bis zum Verlust der Kurwürde 1485-1547,' pages 55-75, in *Die Herrscher Sachsens: Markgrafen, Kurfürsten, Könige. 1089-1918.* Ed. Frank-Lothar Kroll. München: Becksche Reihe, 2007.

Scholl, Gerhard. ‚Von Burgen und Schlössern im Siegerland,' pages 25-30, in *Siegerland zwischen gestern und morgen.* Landkreis Siegen: Kreisverwaltung, 1965.

Schönfeldt, Sybil Gräfin. *Das große Ravensburger Buch der Feste und Bräuche.* Ravensburg: Otto Maier, 1987.

Schultes, J.A. von. *Sachsen-Koburg-Saalfeldische Landesgeschichte,* 4°. Abth. 1. Koburg, 1818.

Schuppener, Ulrich. "Die Nassau-Oranische Residenzstadt Breda," in *Nassauische Annalen,* Band 120, pages 83-130, 2009.

Schuppener, Ulrich. "Das Hochzeitslied zur Trauung Wilhelms von Oranien mit Anna von Sachsen und seine Vorgeschichte," in *Nassauische Annalen,* Band 118, pages 209-275, 2007.

Schuppener, Ulrich. "Der Dillenburger Rentmeister Gottfried Hatzfeld, Chronist der Grafen Wilhelm und Johann VI. Von Nassau," in *Nassauische Annalen,* Band 103, pages 113-139, 1992.

Seward, Desmond. *The First Bourbon.* Boston: Gambit, 1971.

Siebel, Gustav. 'Rubens' Geburtshaus,' in *Siegerland, Blätter des Siegerländer Heimatvereins e. V.,* Band 57, Heft 1, pages 22- 23, 1980.

Smith, Sally Bedell. ‚The Wisdom of Queens,' in *Time Magazine,* Online Edition, January 16, 2012.

Somerset, Anne. *Ladies in Waiting.* London: Phoenix Press, 2002.

Sommerfeldt, Rene. *Der großmütige Hesse: Philip von Hessen (1504-1567).* Marburg: Tectum Verlag, 2007.

Spierenburg, Pieter. *The Broken Spell: A Cultural and Anthropological History of Preindustrial Europe.* New Brunswick: Rutgers University Press, 1991.

Spies, Martin. 'Die Bildnisse Annas von Sachsen,' in *Nassauische Annalen,* Band 116, pages 237-248, 2005.

Spiess, Karl-Heinz. "Witwenversorgung im Hochadel," pages 89-114, in *Witwenschaft in der Frühen Neuzeit.* Ed. Martina Schattkowsky. Leipzig: Leipziger Universitätsverlag, 2003.

Springer, Markus. "Evangelischer Panther im Staatswappen: Die ehemalige Reichsgrafschaft Ortenburg war die einzige evangelische Enklave in Altbayern," in *Sonntagblatt: Evangelische Wochenzeitung für Bayern.* Ausgabe 31/2005 vom 31.7.2005.

Starkey, David. *Six Wives: The Queens of Henry VIII.* New York: Harper Collins,

2003.

Stone, Lawrence. *The Family, Sex and Marriage in England 1500-1800*. New York: Harper Torchbooks, 1977.

Strage, Mark. *Women of Power*. San Diego: Harcourt Brace Jovanovich, 1976.

Streich, Brigitte. 'Anna von Nassau und ihre 'Schwestern': Politische Gestaltungsmöglichkeiten fürstlicher Witwen in der Frühen Neuzeit,' pages 163-189, in *Witwenschaft in der Frühen Neuzeit*. Ed. Martina Schattkowsky. Leipzig: LeipzigerUniversitätsverlag, 2003.

Tabri, Edward A. *Political Culture in the Early Northern Renaissance – The Court of Charles the Bold, Duke of Burgundy (1467-1477)*. Lewiston, New York: Edwin Mellen Press, 2004.

The Age of Magnificence: The Memoirs of the Duc de Saint-Simon. Ed. Sanche de Gramont. New York: Capricorn Books, 1963.

Thieme, Andre. "Burg, Herrschaft und Amt Rochlitz im Mittelalter," pages 35-63, in *Witwenschaft in der Frühen Neuzeit*. Ed. Martina Schattkowsky. Leipzig: Leipziger Universitätsverlag, 2003.

Tierney, Tom. *Renaissance Fashions*. Dover Publications: 2000.

Tillyard, Stella. *Aristocrats*. New York: Noonday Press, 1994

Tinniswood, Adrian. *The Verneys: A True Story of Love, War, and Madness in Seventeenth-Century England*. New York: Riverhead Books, 2007.

Tuchman, Barbara W. *A Distant Mirror*. New York: Ballantine, 1978.

Turner, David M. *Fashioning Adultery: Gender, Sex and Civility in England, 1660-1740*. Cambridge: Cambridge University Press, 2002.

Ulbricht, Sabine. *Fürstinnen in der sächsischen Geschichte, 1382-1622*. Beucha: Sax Verlag, 2010.

Varnhagen, Johann Adolph Theodor Ludwig. *Grundlage der Waldeckischen Landes- und Regentengeschichte*. Arolsen: Verlag der Speyer'schen Buchhandlung, 1853.

Verwey, Herman de la Fontaine. 'The Bookbindings of William of Orange,' 81-143, in *Quaerendo*, Vol XIV, Number 2, pages 81-143, 1984.

Vetter, Klaus. *Am Hofe Wilhelms von Oranien*. Stuttgart: Deutsche Verlags-Anstalt, 1991.

Vickery, Amanda. *The Gentleman's Daughter*. New Haven: Yale University Press, 1998.

Vogt-Lüerssen, Maike. *Anna von Sachsen*. Norderstedt: Books on Demand, 2003.

Vötsch, Jochen. ,Geschenke in Gold und Silber: Beobachtungen zur höfischen Praxis beit Moritz von Sachsen,' pages 87-98, in *Hof und Hofkultur unter Moritz von Sachsen (1521-1553)*. Eds. Andre Thieme and Jochen Vötsch. Dresden: Sax-Verlag, 2004.

Wagenmann, Julius August. "Mörlin, Maximilian," in *Allgemeine Deutsche Biographie* (ADB). Band 22. Leipzig: Duncker & Humblot, 1885.

Wagner, Jacob. *Die Regentenfamilie von Nassau-Hadamar: Geschichte des Fürstenthums Hadamar*. Band 1. Vienna: Mechitharisten-Congregations-Buchhandlung,

1863.

Wartenberg, Günther. 'Eine Ehe im Dienste kursächsischer Aussenpolitik–zur unglücklichen Ehe der Anna von Sachsen mit Wilhelm von Oranien,' pages 79-86, in *Die Wettiner: Chancen und Realitäten*. Ed. Reiner Groß. Dresden: Kulturakademie, 1990.

Watanabe-O'Kelly, Helen. *Court Culture in Dresden*. New York: Palgrave, 2002.

Weber, Karl von. *Anna Churfürstin zu Sachsen*. Leipzig: Bernhard Tauchnitz, 1865.

Wedgwood, C. V. *William the Silent*. New York: Jonathan Cape, 1967.

Welle, Florian. "Ein Sieg der Toleranz," in *GEO Epoche: Martin Luther und die Reformation – Europa im Zeitalter der Glaubensspaltung 1517-1618*, Nr 39, pages 124-125. Hamburg: Gruner + Jahr, 2009.

Whitaker, Katie. *Mad Madge: The Extraordinary Life of Margaret Cavendish, Duchess of Newcastle, the First Woman to Live by her Pen*. New York: Basic Books, 2002.

White, Christopher, *Peter Paul Rubens*. New Haven: Yale University Press, 1987.

Wilde, Manfred. ,Kursachsen – Hexenverfolgungen,' in *Lexikon zur Geschichte der Hexenverfolgung*. Eds: Gudrun Gersmann, Katrin Moeller, and Jürgen-Michael Schmidt, in: historicum.net, URL: http://www.historicum.net/no_cache/persistent/artikel/1639/ (29.6.2011)

Wilson, Derek. *All the King's Women*. London: Pimlico, 2004.

Winter, Sascha. "Die Residenz und Festung Kassel um 1547," pages 109-127, in *Landgraf Philipp der Großmütige von Hessen und seine Residenz Kassel*. Eds. Heide Wunder, Christina Vanja, and Berthold Hinz. Marburg: N. G. Elwert Verlag, 2004.

Wolf, K. 'Christine von Diez,' in *Siegerland*, 20. Band, Heft 4, Oktober-Dezember, pages 104-107, 1938.

Wolf, Karl. "Ein Urteil des Grafen Johann des Älteren von Nassau-Dillenburg über die Regierungszeit seines Vaters, des Grafen Wilhelm des Reichen," in *Nassauische Annalen*, Band 67, pages 258-264. 1956.

Wolf, Karl. "Des Syndikus Dr. Fickard zu Frankfurt a. M. rechtliche Gutachten für den Prinzen Wilhelm von Oranien 1568 und 1570," in *Bijdragen voor Vaderlandsche Geschiednis en Oudheidskunde*, Ed. Dr. N. Japiske, VII Recks Deel IV, pages 236-40, 1934.

Wolff, Markus. "Der Fürst des Geldes: Jakob Fugger, 1459-1525, in *GEO Epoche: Martin Luther und die Reformation – Europa im Zeitalter der Glaubensspaltung 1517-1618*," Nr 39, pages 44-55. Hamburg: Gruner + Jahr, 2009.

INDEX

Christine of Diez, 179-180, 184, 195, 204, 249, 259
  children, 258
  marriage, 258-259
    on her illegitimacy, 257
    portraits, 193
  struggle to find a husband, 256-258
  upbringing, 254-255, 258
Christine of Hessen, Duchess of Holstein-Gottorp, 35, 128
Christine of Saxony, Landgravine of Hessen, 58-62, 77-78, 94
Clough, Richard, 79
Coligny, Gaspar de, 138, 141, 149, 218, 220
Coligny, Louise de, Princess of Orange, 242-243, 244, 252, 255
Cologne, 141, 143, 145, 160
Columbus, Christopher, 13
Conrad, Count of Solms-Braunfels, 139
Corvinus, Matthew, 191
Council of Blood/Troubles, 136-137, 161
Coverdale, Miles, 84, 88
Craco, George, 203
Cranach, Lucas the Younger, 24, 38
Croll, Theodor, 239
Cropf, Caspar, 171
Damman, Adrian, 205
Daniel, Count Waldeck, 128, 164
Dathenus, Peter, 205
Diane de Poitiers, 37
Dillenburg and Dillenburg Castle, 64-66, 130, 132-134, 138, 143, 176
Dorothea of Brandenburg, Queen of Denmark, 89
Dorothea of Saxony, 29, 31
Dresden Residenz (palace), 7-8, 31
Edward VI, King of England, 126
Eleanor of Austria, Queen of Portugal, Queen of France, 91
Elincx, Eva, 41
Elizabeth of Hessen, Electress Palatine, 52, 80, 115
Elizabeth of Hessen ("Rochlitz"), Hereditary Duchess of Saxony, 10, 12, 59, 60, 230
  personality, 10, 23

Elizabeth of Leuchtenberg, Countess of Nassau-Dillenburg, 134, 142-143, 145, 249, 254, 258
  raising of Anna's children, 195, 238
Elizabeth I, Queen of England, 11, 32, 35, 53, 126, 138, 141, 243
Elizabeth of Brandenburg, Duchess of Brunswick-Calenberg-Göttingen, 111
Elizabeth of Denmark, Duchess of Mecklenburg-Güstrow, 235
Elizabeth of Saxony, Countess Palatine of Simmern, 29, 203, 245, 247
Elizabeth Stafford, Duchess of Norfolk, 91
Elizabeth of Valois, Queen of Spain, 72
Elizabeth of York, Queen of England, 91
Elizabeth Charlotte ("Lieselotte"), Princess of the Palatine and Duchess of Orléans, 95, 120
Emilia, Countess of Nassau, Princess of Portugal (disputed), 150, 195-196, 238-239, 243
Emmanuel, Hereditary Prince of Portugal, 239
Engelbert I of Nassau, 64
Eric II, Duke of Brunswick-Calenberg-Göttingen, 186, 200, 219, 223
  broken marriage, 110-1, 115, 201
  witch hunt, 116, 186-187, 200-201
Eric XIV, King of Sweden, 35
Ernest, Elector of Saxony, 7
Fernando Alvarez de Toledo, 3rd Duke of Alba, 113, 123, 129-130, 136, 138-139, 140, 141-142, 147, 150-151, 156, 159, 160, 161, 189, 192, 195, 198, 210, 225, 241
Ewersbach, 166
Eyb, Albrecht von, 191
Fielding, Henry, 260
Flok, Erasmus, 83
Florin, Baron Montigny, 83, 107
Francois, Duke of Montpensier, 213, 221
Francoise of Bourbon, Duchess of Bouillon, 214
Francis, I, Duke of Lorraine, 41
Francis I, King of France, 35, 53, 83, 85,

Look for more books from Winged Hussar Publishing, LLC - E-books, paperbacks and Limited Edition hardcovers. The best in history, science fiction and fantasy at:

https://www. wingedhussarpublishing.com

or follow us on Facebook at:

Winged Hussar Publishing LLC

Or on twitter at:

WingHusPubLLC

For information and upcoming publications

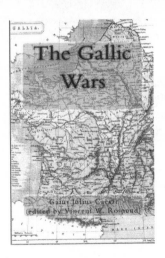

About the Author

Ingrun Mann was born in Germany and lives in the United States. After receiving a master's degree in history from the University of Arizona, she worked as a political analyst for seven years. She is currently an adjunct lecturer of history and political science.

Illustrations